THE MIDDLE EAST

Temple of Janus

THE MIDDLE EAST
Temple of Janus

By DESMOND STEWART

1971
DOUBLEDAY & COMPANY, INC.
Garden City, New York

To Carl D. Brandt

Preface

IF I were to name all those who have contributed insights or information to this book, I should have to compile an almanac whose diacritical signs (since most of the names would be Arabic) would give a printer apoplexy. It would probably begin with Dr. Saleh al-'Ali, who, in the Oxford summer of 1948, wrote me a painstaking account of what I should find as a lecturer in the then nascent University of Baghdad; it might well end with the young Israeli contractor who, on board the SS *Apollonia* in 1969, told me that some of his best friends were Arabs. The almanac would include some of those who appear as actors in this history: President Anwar al-Sadat and the late President Nasser as well as M. Camille Chamoun, former President of Lebanon. It would include among those who have signed their beliefs with their blood my private student Abdul Karim Kassem, "Unique Leader" of Iraq, and Adnan Saoud, bank employee in Beirut who died exploding a tank loyal to President Chamoun. But the list would be a skeleton if it failed to include writers such as Fathi Ghanem and Abdul Rahman al-Sharqawi, who allowed me to translate their novels; poets from left and right who read me their poems; directors who discussed their films; businessmen such as the late Émile Bustani, who spoke of ideas underlying the accumulation of profits; and singers such as Um Kalthum and Fairouz, who discussed the inspiration of their songs. I should remember heroic drivers, such as Ali Murad, who drove me through mud-seas to Kurdistan, or Sayid Hassan, who drove me through rivers in southern Turkey; and this would lead me to devoted physicians such as Khalid Najji or Zuhair Farid who made me better after such ordeals. Patient students taught me more about the East than I could teach them about the West; innumerable friends taught me the greatest lesson of all, what the ordinary people feel about their recent annals. The people I would not name would be those givers of particular insights, my enemies, or those confiders of information whom dictatorial regimes might suspect. I should have, in fact, to write an autobiography, and not a preface.

But I cannot allow this book to appear without mentioning and thanking those whose contributions to it were direct, through reading what I had written, in suggesting sources of information or in allowing me to quote from their works. I list them in no particular alphabetic or political order: Mr. Ian Gilmour, M.P.; Mrs. Renee Winegarten; Dr. Yusif Sayigh; Mr.

Vincent Sheean; Dr. Zaki Saleh; Mr. Jon Kimche; Mr. Meric Dobson; Sayid Adnan al-Himairi; Dr. Walid al-Khalidi; Miss Jean Sulzberger; Sayid Ali-Haidar al-Rikabi; Mr. John Haylock; Dr. Doreen Warriner; Mr. Alan Neame; Sayid Ahmed Baha al-Din; Sayid Michel Abou Jaoudé; Dr. Ezzat Abdul Karim; the staff of the London Library and of the Library of the Geographical Society of Cairo.

Contents

BOOK ONE

Ismail the Magnificent
and the Reunion of Two Seas

*Egypt is no longer in Africa;
it is part of Europe.*
KHEDIVE ISMAIL

Chapter 1

IN November 1869 a Europe responsible for the fortunes and fashions of the world focused its attention on the eastern Mediterranean. Here, on a sand bar between the sea and a stagnant marsh, a shantytown of workmens' huts had become within a decade a city of ten thousand, a whispered rival to Alexandria. Off this new city of Port Said, by this low-lying coast, the ships of nine European nations had assembled with those of Egypt for an exploit worthy of the century: a ceremonial voyage from "the White Middle Sea," as the Arabs call the Mediterranean, to the Red Sea through a man-made trench. The trench, a maritime canal, reunited seas divided since prehistory; it put the North Atlantic, as well as the Mediterranean, in communication with the Indian Ocean; it rejoined an East and West divided since the fall of Rome and the rise of Islam.

On September 28, the man whose perseverance created this new waterway—what a British magazine described without exaggeration as "the most costly and magnificent enterprise of modern times"—had cabled his sponsors in Paris:

> *Having left Port-Said this morning we reached Suez this evening*
> *after a direct and uninterrupted passage by steam in fifteen hours.*
> FERDINAND DE LESSEPS

The Canal had taken fifteen years from concession to completion. More than once shortage of money or international complications had threatened to keep the Isthmus of Suez a lock, not a door. Now that the Canal's sponsors could at last expect a return on their money, a spectacular opening was required.

A Europe of entrepreneurs was inspired, rather than ruled, by emperors and empresses, by kings and queens. In such fairyland figures, in their uniforms and jewels, the masses toiling in satanic mills, as much as politicians in whiskers and frock coats, saw their own transfiguration. Eugénie, Empress of the French, Franz Josef, Emperor of Austria, the Crown Prince of Prussia, the Prince and Princess of Holland, would, by their simultaneous presence on Egyptian soil, christen the new Canal in the radiance of myth.

We can look at this occasion, the occasion on which nineteenth-century Europe was most self-confidently itself, through bifocal lenses. One lens, a commemorative album, has the grand title: *Inauguration du Canal*

de Suez: Voyage des Souverains; its text is by G. Nicole, its watercolors
and portraits by Riou, painter to His Highness the Khedive. "For a whole
month," the album reports, "thanks to the lavish hospitality of the Khedive,
Egypt has submitted to a peaceful invasion by scholars, writers and representatives of industry and commerce." Ibsen has come from Norway;
Germany has sent her Egyptologists Lepsius and Dumichen; Britain has
sent Mr. Grave, the Mayor of Manchester, and Messrs. Lloyd and Ramsay,
presidents of the Birmingham and Glasgow Chambers of Commerce. The
largest contingent comes from France and includes, besides Riou and
Gérôme, Eugène Fromentin, a painter who keeps a journal. His account,
and that of others, corrects the official view.

We look first at the man who invites to the magic feast, who pays the
bills for more than 900 guests, who has swept more than a hundred of them
on a tour of Upper Egypt and who has arrived to welcome his guests to
Port Said: the Khedive Ismail.

Riou's portrait shows a calm potentate of thirty-nine (middle age dressed
older then than it does today) whose soft red fez with backward-hanging
tassel surmounts a full, not unkindly face. A close-cut beard strengthens
the lack of bone. Riou's pencil hardly hints the doom that distinguishes
the males of Ismail's clan: premature corpulence. The Khedive's chest
blazes with decorations large as cakes, then, at the waist, blurs. The hands
are not shown. No portrait could evoke their deadness: his right hand
feels to those who shake it like a glove stuffed with horsehair. Nor can a
portrait show the characteristic movement of the eyes, shadowed as they
are by shaggy brows, half hidden by heavy lids. A facial tic swivels them as
they stare. It is extraordinary that his charm—"his words, when he sought
to please," the American consul at Alexandria reports, "were usually accompanied by a smile of ingratiating charm"—survives such eyes. For in
audience the left blinks hard while the right, probing for weakness, roams
the visitor's person. Ismail knows this. Teased that he speaks with one eye
and listens with the other, he rejoins: "And you might add: I think with
both."

On Ismail's perspicacity the album agrees with Ismail. The completion
of the Canal, begun under his uncle Said, for whom the new port is named,
"is due to the personal influence of the Khedive, to the sympathy inspired
in Europe by this enlightened and generous Prince who pursues with a
perseverance nothing can disconcert the arduous task he has assumed: that
of regenerating a people. Among the means of this regeneration the
Khedive's practical spirit has put works of public utility first. All that can
knit together the diverse regions of his realm, all that can facilitate the
peaceful accession to Egypt of the men and things of Europe, all that can
contribute to the swift development of agriculture, industry and commerce,
comprise his constant care. Thus each year sees the digging of new har-
bours, the opening of new canals, the rising of new dikes and dams, while

the whole country is covered with a network of rail. Finally at a sign from the Khedive, his capital, in several months, has been made new, airy and beautiful."

His latest project has been an expensive palace, on Gezira, the main island in the Nile, for his most valued guest, Eugénie de Montijo, cousin of De Lesseps and wife of Napoleon III. Her palace is oriental Victorian, of wrought iron and sentimental vision all compact. Marble statues—a virgin writhes in drapes which slip south over her pert and bared behind—surprise in an Islamic city which, in a thousand years, has produced much but never this. Pompous satin-covered chairs with sprawling seats are not unfunctional: the buttocks of aristocratic Albanians and Turks need more space than those of their Western counterparts. In a hungry East obesity signifies the benison of God.

Some sneer at the khedivial taste: an Englishman describes his reception room at Abdin Palace as "a monument of the meretricious style which rejoices in gold and crimson and pier-glasses." The same critic decries the Khedive's readiness to aerate his capital by driving boulevards through medieval mosques, by "pulling down the old houses of the oriental style, and leaving local builders to set up whatever they choose in their place." A Dutchman speaks of the *Haussmannisation* of the ancient city. It will take another century to appreciate that vulnerable though Ismail's taste may be, a taste it is. Its fragments, as one by one they vanish in a century of impersonal concrete and glass boxes, will acquire a savor: flimsy, so much wooden lacework, so much intrigue of metal; yet human, even delicate, beside its impersonal successors.

Ismail, then, is the Aladdin in the uniform of a headwaiter who has summoned a thousand guests, who has decided to pay (or borrow) another million sterling—the equivalent of five million dollars—to see Egypt physically severed from Asia and joined in spirit to the Europe he admires.

His guests have now returned from Upper Egypt. In Cairo they have attended the opening of the new Opera. On the Khedive's suggestion to Mariette, the Egyptologist, Giuseppe Verdi was commissioned to write an opera with a pharaonic theme. But *Aïda* has taken longer to complete than the lath and plaster Opera House; so *Rigoletto* was performed instead. On another night Eugénie saw the pyramids lit by magnesium flares. Now the time has come to open the Canal.

The Khedive has journeyed to Port Said on his yacht the *Mahroussa*. With him are the Minister of the Interior, Sherif Pasha, a Turk, and the Prime Minister, Nubar Pasha, as an Armenian, the first practicing Christian to be raised to the Pashadom. Punctual arrivals are the Prince and Princess of Holland on the *Valk*. A storm is raging at Jaffa, up the coast in Palestine, part of Egypt's empire in Ismail's boyhood but regained for the Ottoman Sultan since 1841. Angry seas threaten to delay the second most important guest, the Emperor Franz Josef of Austria, who has been on a brief side trip to Christendom's holiest shrines. But to delighted cheers the *Greif* defies the storm and the Austrian emperor (the same age as the Khedive) arrives in time to welcome the Empress of the French.

It is now the sixteenth. First gunfire heralds the Crown Prince of Prussia, son-in-law of Queen Victoria of England. He arrives only just in time. The French imperial yacht, the *Aigle,* has been waiting for some hours outside Port Said; it has conveyed the Empress from Alexandria, to which she had traveled by train from Cairo the previous morning. The first to salute her are five British ironclads: Sir. A. Milne's flagship *Lord Warden,* then *Royal Oak, Prince Consort, Caledonia* and *Bellerophon.* Other nationalities take up the greeting. The mutual cannonading lasts an hour.

The *Aigle* is the summit of marine elegance: a paddle-wheel steamer with three raking masts, her tall funnel slim and black between the foremast and the main, her jaunty lines unmarred by the great paddles which give her power. A saloon and awning rise on the quarter-deck between mainmast and mizzen. There the Empress stands. Married for sixteen years to a voluptuary who trusts her judgment, preserving her Spanish beauty into her early forties, Eugénie is overwhelmed by the hurrahing crews. She will record her arrival in a telegram to Paris, where the ailing Emperor is facing the most critical twelve months of his life: a situation so menacing that she had hesitated whether it were safe for her to leave. "I have just arrived at Port Said in good health. Magical reception. I have never seen anything like it in my life."

The sailors cheer her in nine tongues. In Arabic: for the host squadron, the Egyptian, comprises six ships. In French: from a similar flotilla: France's pre-eminence is marked by her Empress, not by numbers. English is shouted by the crews of twice as many ships as those of anyone else. (England, who has fought the Canal, knows that she will use the Canal the most.) The crews of eight ships speak German: but the eight ships are hardly friends. Five belong to the North German Federation, three to the Austria she defeated in a seven-week war, three years before. Dutch, Spanish, Swedish (or Norwegian, since Norway is not yet independent), and Russian are spoken on two ships each. Danish, the language of an earlier victim of the Prussian state, is heard from one ship only. The open vowels of Italian should have been loud. But the Italian squadron, anchored at Alexandria since September, has had to return to Italy because of the illness of Victor Emmanuel, a king worn out by a successful but protracted struggle to unify his country. Portuguese would also have been heard had their squadron not been late. Alongside the navies shout the pursers, stewards and cabin boys of commercial steamers: French, Austrian, Italian and British.

The day is dingy; for eight hours there is rain. But rain in the East is a heavenly gift, an excellent omen.

The Opening of the Canal is to be sanctified with religious rites. The European princes, the Egyptian Khedive, are associated with varied forms of a monotheism which in the Middle East, and in particular in the Egypt of Akhnaton and Moses, had found its cradle. The varied sects of this monotheistic cult have frequently fought: Protestants with Catholics, Orthodox with Copts. Here in the Levant the Latin Christians of Western Europe had long ago clashed with Islam. French Crusaders from Palestine had surged into the Egyptian delta, reaching Cairo. Now all will invoke God's blessing on a canal destined to change God's world for all His creatures. Such is the Khedive's ecumenical plan. The ceremony takes place this Tuesday afternoon at 3 P.M. on the Port Said beach.

The participants must walk along wooden planks: first comes the Princess of Holland on the arm of young Prince Towfik, the Khedive's heir. Then the Empress of the French. She is plainly robed in a lavender silk walking dress. A black hat, not too high, with a black plume, covers her hair; a black spotted veil half hides her lovely face. She wears none of her famous jewelry, only a simple locket at her throat. She walks on the arm of the Austrian Emperor, whose white tunic, scarlet trousers and cocked hat cannot rival Ismail's finery: a blue uniform with gold lace and broad green ribbon; a scimitar whose hilt flashes with gems. To all this poetry the drab clothes of five English MPs and sundry men of commerce are the prose.

The dignitaries sit in the most imposing of three pavilions; it faces towards the sea. Their gilt chairs are arranged beneath a baldaquin hung with red and gold; in its wings, under the flags of many nations, Coptic and Orthodox clerics wear their distinctive hats. To the left and right, two other pavillions are set aside for the Muslim and Roman Catholic clergy. The crescent of Islam, the symbol against which the Crusaders fought, decorates the corners of both pavilions. In the Islamic pavilion sit the Chief Cadi, the religious judge appointed from Constantinople, the Grand Mufti and the Ulema, or learned men. All wear turbans. The cleric who, standing, intones a passage from the Koran and then invokes God's blessing on the Canal, is the Sheikh of the Water-Sellers. Ill paid though they are, Egypt's water-sellers have long formed a guild with a quasi-religious prestige. "From water all that lives," says the Koran, and without the *saqis* and their muscles the cities would die from thirst or perish from fire; without their assistance no pilgrim caravan could advance through the waterless wastes. Modern engineering will reduce the importance of this caste; pipes made in English foundries will bring water to houses in old Cairo as a pipeline already brings Nile water to Port Said. So the Sheikh welcoming the future in a sense dismisses the past.

Since this is a Muslim country, the Catholic priests perform second. Their brilliant vestments contrast with the austere robes of the majority faith. After Mass said by Monsignor Curcia, bishop of Alexandria, the

Empress's confessor, Monsignor Bauer, eulogizes Ferdinand de Lesseps, saluting him as a new Columbus.

This comparison seems far-fetched to no one. De Lesseps, with his waxed mustache, black suit and piercing eyes, has in his lifetime become a myth. His maxims are of the kind to endear him to the Victorian age. "Opponents," he once said, "are tutors you need not pay." He has had many such tutors: the British Government, the Ottoman Sultan, at times the Khedive, the shareholders in France, to say nothing of humanitarian consciences shocked at his use of forced labor for digging the Canal. Go-getting visionary, De Lesseps has seen further, harder roads than other men, and pushed where he has seen. "It's not a question of putting the Nile in communication with the Red Sea"—that feat had been accomplished by the Pharaohs and maintained by the Roman emperors and early Caliphs—"but of driving, in a straight line, a vast trench from the Mediterranean to the Red Sea, of creating, in a word, a veritable Bosphorus." There is more to De Lesseps than engineering and push, as there was more to the *saqi* than his merchandise. Like many great men De Lesseps is superstitious. In a letter to a woman friend he has described the omen which encouraged him to ask Said Pasha, Ismail's uncle, not only for the right to dig a canal, but other perquisites as well.

"The camp was about to awake. A freshness showed that shortly the sun would rise. To my right the east was splendid; to my left the west was sombre, cloudy. Suddenly I beheld a rainbow of most vivid colours; its extremities stretched from furthest west to east. My heart beat violently. I had to calm my imagination since, in this sign of alliance referred to by Scripture, it already greeted the completion of my dream, the moment when west and east would be conjoined."

That same afternoon—15 November 1854—Said Pasha, touched at the way in which the Frenchman had hastened to Egypt to congratulate him on his recent inheritance, embraced De Lesseps and his vision. "You have convinced me, De Lesseps. I accept your scheme. You can count on me."

The practical visionary had no intention of doing anything else. He had nursed his friendship with Said since the time when he had been French consul in Cairo and the future ruler had been an overweight schoolboy. Muhammad Ali, as tyrannical a father as ruler, had forced his son Said to climb masts, to run, to eat salads only. De Lesseps had welcomed the boy to his house and secretly indulged his craving for pasta. Once this spaghetti friendship began to pay off, De Lesseps had no intention of lightening the bill. Back in Cairo at the head of an army of ten thousand, the euphoric Said announced at a Citadel levee that he was resolved to sponsor a canal through the Isthmus of Suez and had commissioned his friend De Lesseps to form "a company of capitalists from all nations," which could have the concession to execute the project. The economic advantages of such a canal could equal its glory. "The two hundred millions of Europeans who send their manufactured products to the East, and the seven hundred millions of Orientals who consume these products, and send in exchange their raw materials to the West, will be brought into closer, less costly and more intimate relations." But De Lesseps saw that the Canal would only appeal to ordinary investors if the Egyptian rulers threw in certain perquisites. The first was an ample supply of unpaid labor: the extension to the Canal of the existing principle that villagers could be conscribed in times of flood to mend broken dams. De Lesseps also obtained the cession to his company of large tracts of desert land between the delta and the future waterway. Irrigated by the fresh-water canal which would be a necessary adjunct to the maritime canal, this land would soar in value. It might become the nucleus of a French colony between Africa and Asia; in any event it would be an asset.

The rainbow of good omen reappeared on the evening of November 16. To the Catholic clergy massed in Port Said it symbolized something nobler than a commercial triumph.

The Roman Church had known a century of despair flecked with hope. In France the Revolution had enthroned a harlot of Reason in Notre Dame; the Catholic view of human origins had been bruised by the theories of Darwin in much the same way as Catholic cosmology by the earlier discoveries of Galileo; the communist dictum that religion was the people's opium promised an anti-clericalism sharper than in the past. Against these defeats were auguries of resistance and triumph. If the Pope was to lose Rome, he was, as prisoner, to be declared infallible by the Vatican Council meeting this very year. At Lourdes, only eleven years before, the Virgin had appeared to a peasant girl, Bernadette Soubirous; water from the cave of the Virgin's apparitions had cured the Prince Imperial, Eugénie's only son, of sunstroke. Eugénie's influence over Napoleon III favored the Church. The Mass now said on Muslim soil in her presence symbolized expanding vistas. French gunfire or French influence was reopening North Africa, a territory long lost to the Church, to Catholics. Algiers had been French since 1830; into Egypt, Europeans, most of them Catholics, had been migrating in large numbers under the francophile rule of Ismail; no less than 80,000 had landed at Alexandria in one year (1865) alone. To triumphalists dreaming of a Church powerful and united upon earth the alliance of gunfire and religion seemed fecund of good.

Gunfire marks the dawn of the seventeenth. At breakfast time, around eight o'clock, the flotilla begins to file south. (Just in time a last obstruction has been discovered underwater and blasted away.) Screws or paddles impel the ships one by one into the great trench which De Lesseps has planned, for which French and Egyptian investors have put up the cash and which Arabic-speaking conscripts have largely dug.

The *Aigle* leads. At the Empress's side, in the place of honor, stands Ferdinand de Lesseps. The sixty-four-year-old Frenchman has planned a celebration of his own: his second marriage, in a few days' time to Helène de Bragard, forty-three years younger than himself. She will bear him eleven children in addition to the brood he already has.

After France comes Austria on the *Greif*. Then sinister Prussia on the *Grille*. Then, in the person of her ambassador to Constantinople, Britain on the *Rapid,* a corvette. The *Archontia* brings another ambassador, General Ignatieff of Imperial Russia. Next the Emir Abdul Kader on the *Elisabetta.* And then a medley of warships and private yachts, of English ships carrying to Suez the Indian telegraph and passenger ships and cargo ships linking the world.

The Khedive was not present at the start. With his habitual courtesy, our album suggests, he has gone ahead; he will greet his guests where the Canal, having made its most difficult passage through the Menzala swamps, admits the Mediterranean into a halfway lake. Lake Timsa was a marshy depression teeming till recently with wildfowl, tempting sportsmen; its Arabic name suggests that it once had crocodiles. Now it has become a lake to tempt a yachtsman; its clear blue water washes the quays of Ismailia, the brand-new city where Ismail has arranged the chief festivities for the Canal.

Yet in an East which mixes wealth with chaos nothing is so plain. The courteous Khedive has first-night nerves. Eugène Fromentin, the French artist, can take us behind the scenes. Fromentin had not bothered with Port Said. Instead, he had taken the train—the *chemin de fer de la Basse Egypte* —from Alexandria across the delta to Ismailia. He had traveled with a hurly-burly of international pilgrims. His painter's eye noted slanting-eyed Tartars in fur pelisses and pale-skinned Turks; sheikhs whose green turbans proclaimed their descent from the Prophet; women who carried children, young men who carried old; and with the healthy and the blind, the noisy and the paralytic, their equipment: mattresses and blankets, cooking implements and coffeepots. Exhausted, Fromentin reached an Ismailia in chaos: Europeans had mislaid their baggage or their friends; some had been tossed at sea for three nights, others been dumped miles from anywhere on the sand. From Khedive down to fellah everyone trembled lest something might now go wrong.

That something was going wrong seemed certain. The *Latif,* as ill luck would have it, an Egyptian brig, had grounded near Kantara and blocked the Canal. The credulous East believes in plots. The *Latif*'s captain was not Egyptian. He was British, and the British had proved the Canal's persistent foes. Conclusions were not difficult to draw.

De Lesseps and Nubar Pasha were doing what they could; while officials wrung their hands, the Khedive threatened to reintroduce impaling, an anal-sadistic punishment to make the bravest cower, for the guilty officers. A cohort of Egyptians—the people who had dug the Canal—were now heaving at the *Latif*.

Can the *Aigle* get through? That will be the test. If she does, the Canal is open; if she does not, a catastrophe, attended, since Europe is watching, by undying shame.

Fromentin is carried away by excitement; he will check for himself. He rides to a declivity [what the French call *le seuil*], where the Canal is a brief canyon before it enters the lake. No point in the isthmus is more than sixty feet above sea level, but the *seuil* offers a point of vantage. "Huge crowd. Batteries of artillery, regiments of Egyptian lancers in battle order on the shore. It is 4 P.M. From the Suez end three big steamers hung with flags enter the lake and anchor. Hurrah! The Suez end is free. At five-thirty a puff of smoke, then the tip of a mast, project above the sandy banks of the Canal. The ship itself cannot be seen but from its mast flutters the imperial standard of France. The *Aigle*! Slowly she passes at our feet; her wheels barely turn. This prudence, these precautions, underline the gravity of the moment. At last she issues into the lake. Salvos of gunfire: the batteries salute, the concourse cheers. It is truly magnificent. The Empress on her high deck waves her handkerchief. M. de Lesseps is beside her, but, faced with this vast public, come from every point of Europe, she is so overcome by emotion that she forgets to shake his hand."

The city where Ismail waits is eight summers old. It stands almost halfway down the Canal, forty-eight miles south of Port Said and sixty-five miles north of Suez. A tabula rasa place, it is as typical of the nineteenth century as St. Petersburg had been of the eighteenth. St. Petersburg had represented Russia's intrusion into the world of power; for Egypt this inland port represents its reconnection with the trade between Europe and the East. Its first name, Timsa, was dropped by De Lesseps the day he showed a former governor-general of British India the guidelines of the projected town. In a rhetorical flourish De Lesseps exclaimed:

"Port-Said already commemorates the Viceroy under whose patronage the Canal was begun. Let us place this new city under the protection of the Khedive who will preside over its completion. Ships will thus proclaim to the peoples of Indus and Ganges that they owe to the dynasty of Muhammad Ali the benefits of civilisation and the fulfilment of a millennial dream. More, it will signify our affectionate gratitude to his people, the Arabs, called as they are to make fertile the barren lands of the Isthmus, reminding them of the founder of their race, Ishmael, Abraham's son by Hagar."

So named, the city has enjoyed the particular attention of Ismail.

Ismailia could not exist without the fresh-water canal, the open ditch that brings the Nile to the barren isthmus. Only when this was well advanced had the workmen leveled the unpromising dunes. The first stone was laid on 17 April 1862. The beanstalk city was planned in the European style. Volney, a French visitor to Egypt just before the French Revolution, had complained that Cairo lacked "those public or private buildings, those regular squares, those aligned roads, which enable architecture to display its beauties." This lack was made good in Ismailia's geometry. A rectangle some 2,400 yards long by 450 wide was divided into five blocks, each separated from the next by four great avenues named after the Empress of France, Queen Victoria of England, Isabella of Castile and Cleopatra of Egypt. (By race Cleopatra was no more Egyptian than her royal sisters; her family, the Ptolemies, had derived from much the same area of the Balkans as the Khedive's.) Five piazzas —each the focus of a block—carried male names: Monge, Leibnitz, St. Francis de Sales, Champollion and Ibrahim. St. Francis was soon to yield to Paleocapa, a member of the international commission that approved the plan of the Canal, and the mathematician Monge to Towfik, Ismail's heir.

The desert-born city was green with the verdure Europeans loved. Exotic trees and shrubs, imported from all over the world, flourished on the watered sand. A straight quay was laid beside Lake Timsa and named in honor of Ismail's grandfather, the founder of his dynasty, Muhammad Ali. Here the Khedive had built a palace and De Lesseps a Swiss cottage. The humanity of De Lesseps, shown in his maxim that "men, like horses, are bad only when they fear," is displayed in his attitude to his Canalside property. A child thief was found climbing his fence and disturbing his flowers. De Lesseps ordered that, in future, doors and gates should be left unlocked, so that entrants would have no need to break his fences or trample his flowers.

In this city of gardens and small villas, girdled by the fresh-water canal and facing the lake, the chief buildings were a waterworks for pumping the fresh water north to Port Said, a church, a mosque and a railway station. The European settlers already numbered between five and six thousands. The bulk of them were males; one piazza was known as the Bachelors' Square. Although most of the bachelors derived from southern European slums, Ismailia had a different atmosphere from Alexandria, which more numerous migrants had turned into a paradise for confidence tricksters and thieves, for pimps and whores. The settlers in Ismailia, working under the Company's control, had innocent diversions. After work, in the late afternoon, they could go for rides into the desert. A favorite goal for such excursions was the retreat which the Khedive had built amid dunes overlooking the Canal. The desert charmed Ismail in much the same way as the countryside charmed European kings. The air was fresher than in Cairo; he could escape his cares. Ismail's Saint-Cloud was a chalet of red brick and fretted wood. Perched on a stone platform, dormer-roofed and steepled, it bravely defied the sand that encompassed it and from which an imposing staircase led to a verandah with a lacelike balustrade; from this verandah great arched doorways gave access to French-furnished rooms within. Officials of the Company reining their horses outside the chalet would sometimes find themselves welcomed in by the Khedive as guests at an impromptu dinner or ball. On more humdrum occasions they could return to some innocent entertainment in Ismailia.

Bachelors untempted by musical evenings need not despair. They had at hand a cornucopia of darker pleasures. Just beyond the squared blocks of European Ismailia sprawled a second and less orderly town. Strips of matting draped haphazard over posts formed little huts; in these simple abodes lived the camel-drivers, sailors, porters and other manual laborers, all of the Eastern races, whom the new city and port employed. Here, as in the native quarters of Port Said or Suez, dwelt men whose exotic appearance proved irresistible to the pencils of generalizing white men: "The broad-faced Ethiopian with his wavy hair and prominent nose; the Chinaman with rounded cheeks, squashed nose and eyes stretching up towards his temples; the glistening black Indian with hair smoothed flat; the fuzzy Negro with bulbous lips; the Japanese with his parchment skin; the Arab with haughty mien, noble gestures and slow step; the restless Syrian; the ponderous Turk; the Greek natty in his rags; the disdainful Bedouin, the docile fellah." This second city pullulated with places that provided Eastern joys. Old men told stories from the Arabian Nights; plaintive singers sang of love; and more to the taste of young Europeans out on the tiles, belly dancers displayed their lascivious charms in a whirl of sequins.

This double city was now preparing to welcome the ships of Europe: windows were hung with flags, streets lined with Venetian masts. Between the European town and the fresh-water canal an encampment had sprung up for the Khedive's guests. In a huge outhouse, tables were loaded with food from dawn to latest night.

On the other side of the town, near the lake, a second encampment mustered a human zoo. Here, as Ismail had commanded, foreigners could savor the races subject to the Egyptian throne. They could accept invitations to drink traditional desert coffee, a bitter but refreshing brew, in the shade of tent flaps; they could watch the cavorting of horsemen with copper skins or the daily bustle of veiled women and their half-naked brats.

Ismailia's great day—18 November 1869—starts early as the Empress, who has slept aboard, is rowed ashore. She mounts a horse and rides as elegantly as she is clad. With outriders she reaches the *seuil,* Fromentin's point of vantage, then visits the Khedive's chalet and next the cottage of her kinsman De Lesseps. Like many tourists since, she returns on a camel. Hardly time to repair her toilet at the Khedive's town palace—its thirty-five windows shuttered against the sun—when it is time to greet the other guests. Austria prudently wears a sun-helmet with blue veil.

The afternoon is marked by a Promenade. Phaetons and open carriages, camels and horses, surge onto the yellow sand. Eugénie sits beside Franz Josef in an open carriage, its hood back, drawn by four horses; Prussia and Holland follow in similar style. Prince Joachim Murat drives himself; at a little distance the Khedive does likewise; solemn in his fez he guides his gray horses to the admiration of all. Grooms looking like jockeys in red jackets and gold epaulettes, their boots polished to defy the dust, lead the cortege. The khedivial cavalry try to hedge the notables from horsemen and cameleers, barefoot boys and excited young men. This great running crowd fans the sand into a local storm; the six flagpoles on the palace can hardly be seen.

Fromentin, who stayed up late last night, has not finished shaving. He peeps from his tent flaps. He will be fifty next year; his view is jaundiced. The spectacle seems mediocre. There's insufficient room for real display. The horses gallop badly, since they cannot grip the moving sand. The horsemen, badly armed, poorly mounted, do not, with the exception of one youth on a black horse, catch his attention. The fantasia cannot compare with those he has seen in France's Algerian colony; the *gallabya* is ignoble compared with the burnous. Instead of wearing boots with spurs, the Egyptians push yellow sandals into stirrups so ridiculously large they resemble skates.

The hectic day gives place to solemn night. The dust settles. The stars shine vast in the dry empyrean. Europeans, used to moister skies, utter oohs! and aahs!

Fireworks explode. The two camps, European and oriental, are *en fête.*

Now comes, as climax, the great ball offered to all Ismail's guests. People arrive for it as they can: on horseback or donkey back, drawn by splendid English steeds or surly jades. They press towards the focus of the night: the hall decked with drapes, foliage and plants which awaits *les augustes convives.*

How translate into our century the album's resounding phrase? On Olympus Juno sat as "august table companion" to her consort Jove. Thus these monarchs must seem even if they are not: removed by magic from the world where mortals suffer from Gippy Tummy or bad breath.

The ball is not like those the Empress gives in France. Here will be music but no dancing. How could there be both? Absent from the throng are the ladies of the khedivial house. In the Eastern tradition Ismail is allowed a harem of four wives (all easily divorced) and as many concubines as he can afford. The harem live separately from the men; traditional houses are so contrived that the women, themselves unseen, can watch the men through *meshrebiyehs,* or intricate cedar grilles. The absence of viceregal women leaves the guests three functions only: to be seen, to converse and to dine.

The Empress, who is usually modestly, even plainly, dressed, is now superb. Her robe of cherry-colored satin has an overskirt of finest lace, its train held back by diamond clasps. On her brow glitters a diadem which trails a filmy veil so long it is lost in her dress's folds. The men's sober garb enhances her splendor. Austria wears *tenue de ville:* black coat, gray trousers; his only splash of color—the ribbon of the highest order of the Ottoman Empire. The Khedive has put by bright colors, but he keeps his fez.

The conversation is in French. The Empress had been born in Málaga of a partly Scottish mother, and a Spanish father who admired Napoleon no less than Muhammad Ali or the novelist Stendhal. French is the court language of the other sovereigns; Ismail's own adolescence was spent in France. (At home his family speak Ottoman, a composite tongue in which the Turkish bedrock is submerged in loan words from Arabic and Persian. Though the Khedive is familiar with ritual phrases from the Arabic Koran, he does not speak his subjects' tongue.) The talk is small. The day has fatigued even these *"augustes convives."*

After platitudes, food.

The Empress sits at table between Austria and Prussia; the Khedive sits opposite her between the two halves of Holland. Away at other tables writers and painters, the men of science and archaeology, mayors and businessmen, enjoy similar fare. Still further off, in tents and by the sea, thousands of the poor eat, too: the disparate races of the realm. Unlike the Europeans, they drink no wine.

The buffet served to the sovereigns is described in French; though Constantinople is one of the world's sources of distinctive food, there is no *imam beyildi,* no kebab or stuffed vine leaves.

There are six *Grandes Pièces.*

The fish, *à la Réunion des Deux Mers,* commemorates the day. There is, as second dish, a tactful roast beef *à l'Anglaise.* Then *sur socle,* or on stands, *Galantine de Périgueux, Grand pain de gibier en bastion,* galantine of pheasant *à la volière* and decorated ham. (The Islamic taboo on pork is forgotten. So is the prohibition on wine. *Grands vins* flow freely.)

Then come the *Entrées,* five in all: game pâtés *à la Dorsay;* ox tongue *à l'Anglaise; aspics de Nérac;* galantine of quails *en Belle-Vue; fillets à l'Impériale.*

The salads follow: Suez prawns in cress; truffles in champagne; Russian salad; Italian asparagus *à l'huile vierge.*

The banquet has only begun. Now come the roasts: haunches of venison *à la Saint-Hubert;* truffled young turkeys; pheasants served in cress; capons garnished with quails.

Sated appetites crave something sweet. They have a choice: *Macedoines au Kirschwasser;* Diplomat pudding with pineapple; decorated Savoy biscuits; and, last of all, a Naples ice.

Outside the desert night is cold. So as not to crowd the cloakrooms, guests had been asked to come without coats. Many regret having complied. For on Lake Timsa one last spectacle would have been fun to watch: the anchored flotilla with its rigging lit by lamps.

Eugène Fromentin, with the tender stomach of middle age, alert to the chill, disliking crowds, has cut the ball. A brief turn in the cool night air, a glimpse at the people squatting on the sand—he has had his fill of natives —and in his tent he will enjoy what Pythagoras considered the noblest role—that of the observer. He will sum up what he has observed in Egypt.

The hospitality is without example in modern times or imaginable equivalent in Europe. Seven to eight thousand people fed in the open desert! What magic provides the service or the food? "We are in the Arabian Nights: in the midst of sands, mats on the sand, sand stretching right to one's tent, to one's bed. Admixture of extravagant luxury with incredible deprivation."

He tries to define this blend of planning with chaos, of generosity with indifference. It is a confusion that will puzzle other men from the West. It is good to find it described by so exact a pen.

"It would be difficult to find a more striking example of the juxtaposed elements which comprise Egyptian pomp: the useless, the grandiose, the destitute and the excessive. Or of that collision of chance and magic which has looked after us for forty days and which has contrived the drollest surprises. This is the real point to seize on from this astonishing journey which is as near to a dream as one drop of water to its twin.

"We are in the midst of the impossible, and yet all turns out right. Plans are made—only to go astray. People give up, wait, exclaim: 'Who knows? Inshallah!' Yet we are the living proof that one does pull through, badly or well: and sometimes very well indeed."

Tomorrow the circus moves on: to Suez. But at what time? Fromentin has consulted Nubar Pasha, the Prime Minister, then De Lesseps, the entrepreneur. Neither knows. It is the land of improvisation and the man who improvises is Ismail. Under his direction the expensive charade goes on. As the ships pass the derelict shantytown on the east bank where the canal workers lived before the founding of Ismailia, a display of workmen filling their panniers will instruct the visitors how muscle power has made this trench. The flotilla will then anchor in the Great Bitter Lakes, the original head of the Suez Gulf and now the Marmara of this inland waterway. A reception will be given on board the *Aigle* for the more distinguished. The night—"*calme, douce et claire, as only in the East*"—will be admired. Then, next morning, to renewed salvos, renewed cheers, the *Aigle* will lead sixty-nine ships into the Red Sea. Her log will commemorate the historic event:

Anchored in the roads of Suez (the Red Sea) the
20th November 1869 at 11.30 in the morning:
Signed:

> EUGÉNIE
> FERDINAND DE LESSEPS
> PRINCE JOACHIM MURAT
> J. DE SURVILLE, *Commander.*

That afternoon the Khedive and the Emperor of Austria will travel on to Cairo by train. There will be a ball for Franz Josef at the Palace of Kasr el-Nil: then a little later another one for the Crown Prince of Prussia, who, good Teuton that he is, has slipped off to Upper Egypt to inspect the antiquities. As for Eugénie, after inspecting the Fountains of Moses near Suez, she will return through the Canal on her way back to France. She will not be in time to join her husband when on the twenty-ninth he opens the chambers of Imperial Democracy:

"If today the Empress cannot attend the opening of these Chambers it is because I wished that her presence in a country where our arms distinguished themselves in former times should bear witness to the sympathy of France for a work due to the perseverance and genius of a Frenchman."

The French Emperor mentions neither the Khedive nor the Egyptians. Neither does Lord Clarendon, the British Foreign Secretary. In his congratulatory cable to the Universal Company of the Suez Canal he links the French Government, not the Egyptian, with the grandiose feat.

The Egyptians do not care. To Easterners, the host is more blessed than the guest. But what does the Khedive think, this expressionless sphinx, as the bills come in, as he assesses his autumn triumph? The pomp has cost him a million sterling. Was it worthwhile?

Chapter 2

ISMAIL, frock-coated autocrat and parvenu sovereign, was conscious of standing between two seas: to his front, the sea of Europe in full flood, and at his back, the sea of Islam in apparent ebb. Sea serpents from either direction threatened to make him a nineteenth-century Laocoon.

To understand why he lavished such spectacular hospitality on his guests of November 1869, we must probe to the man hidden behind the blazing chest and jeweled scimitar. Ismail the Magnificent, as he was hailed by Western flatterers eager for his money, had been shaped, like other men, by family circumstances. But in Ismail's case, these circumstances, combining ancient East with newest West, had no antecedents and no successors.

Until the age of fourteen Ismail's life was molded by an East whose assumptions still seemed pyramid-strong.

His birthplace—a Cairo mansion with stone blocks hewn from the same quarries as had served the Pharaohs—is one of the few impressive buildings to survive from the Egyptian eighteenth-century. A poem in classical Arabic carved on a lintel breathes a compliment and a prayer:

> *This, in Egypt, most paradisal of halls:*
> *From envy, and time passing, God protect it!*

The prayer has been granted at the price of museum dust. A caretaker in plastic sandals guides the visitor of today through vast rooms emptied of furniture and life. But in 1830, the year of Ismail's birth, the mansion was the hub of a self-contained kingdom, bustling with retainers and servants, coachmen and horses; a hooded buffalo turned a slow, creaking wheel to grind corn and barley for the household's use. The lord of the house was Ibrahim Pasha, eldest son of the ruler of Egypt. The women of the house watched the masculine bustle from behind floriate grilles. They could eavesdrop as turbaned warriors discussed the prospects of a coming war: an invasion of Palestine and Syria. For besides being his father's heir, Ibrahim commanded armies which were about to extend Egyptian influence from the fringes of the Sudan in the south to the Anatolian plateau in the north.

At the beginning of 1830—or 1245 in the Muslim calendar—two of Ibrahim's wives were expecting babies. The first child to be born, on January 12, was Ismail; he beat a half brother, Mustafa Fazil, by three weeks. Ismail's ambitious mother had some reason to rejoice. True, Ibrahim already had an older son named Ahmed; and even Ahmed would not necessarily succeed Ibrahim, for the Ottoman law relating to succession differed from that obtaining in Europe, where it was customary for the eldest son to succeed his father. Since the seventeenth century, an Ottoman ruler was succeeded by his oldest male relation, who could often be a brother or a cousin. This practice was followed in Egypt. The oldest male after Ibrahim was Abbas, the son of a brother who had been roasted alive on a campaign in the Sudan. But even so, accidents or illnesses could happen and Ismail might one day inherit. If he did, and if the Ottoman system continued, his heir would be, not his son, but Mustafa Fazil. The system encouraged rivalry and envy more than brotherly love.

For by 1830 there was beginning to be much for the ruler of Egypt to inherit, with promise of more to come. Ibrahim's mansion, once the property of an Egyptian merchant, had been seized, with the whole of Egypt, by Ibrahim's father, Muhammad Ali, who ruled from the Citadel, which dominated Cairo. The boy Ismail, with his kindly disposition, was the beneficiary of one of the most ruthless and successful massacres in history. Kept for his first seven years in the harem, then circumcised and taught the Koran, he was raised on a dynastic myth in which his grandfather (who died when he was nineteen) played an overpowering role. In this myth the treacherous slaughter of nearly five hundred guests was presented as a creative purgation of Egyptian life and the start of a new, more hopeful era.

The myth involved Egypt and the Middle East as a whole, not only Ismail; it was as close to the generation which watched the opening of the Canal as two world wars to the generation which has watched man reach the moon.

The basic background to the myth, or story, was the Ottoman Empire, the last great Islamic state. At its apogee, in the sixteenth century, it was more ably administered, more dynamic in its thrust and more tolerant of minorities than any European monarchy of the time. Its Janissaries, soldiers recruited from a boy-levy on Christian families in the Ottoman Balkans, were the best shock troops in the world. To such cities as Salonika and Smyrna, as well as to Constantinople, the capital, flocked refugees from the various intolerances of Christian Europe: Jews, Protestants and dissenters of many kinds.

But since the seventeenth century the empire had been in accelerating decline, its technological and commercial backwardness laying it open to constant erosion of territory and prestige.

One spectacular assault on its dominions had been made in 1798, when the young Napoleon, not yet thirty, landed an army near Alexandria, then a mere fishing town, and advanced on Cairo. Egypt at this time was only a nominal province of the Ottoman Empire. Its real rulers were a caste of white slaves, or Mamelukes, whose numbers were constantly replenished from the slave markets of the Caucasus. The young slaves, transported to Egypt, became part of a swashbuckling and quarrelsome elite who exploited the patient fellahin, or farmers, of the delta and valley. But disobedient and dissident though these feudal barons were, they were as much Muslims as the Sultan, while Egypt formed part of his hereditary estate. After Napoleon had crushed the Mameluke cavalry in a battle fought within sight of the pyramids, the Sultan sent a force of 7,000 volunteers to do what they could against the French; the Ottoman expedition was assisted by British naval power (for Britain knew that Napoleon's objective in invading Egypt was to cut her communications with the East) and had as its second in command Muhammad Ali, a young Macedonian Muslim of the same age as Napoleon; Muhammad Ali's father farmed tobacco near Kavalla. The Ottoman force seized the small peninsula of Aboukir, to the east of Alexandria; but Napoleon's army, which had the advantage of cavalry, soon overpowered them. Muhammad Ali managed to swim from the debacle; British tars pulled him into the gig of an admiral, Sir Sidney Smith, who had accompanied the Turks on their ill-fated expedition.

Muhammad Ali's military activities had done nothing to weaken the French invaders, who went on to invade Palestine and Syria as well. When the French left Egypt in 1801, it was as a result of British naval supremacy, enforced by Nelson's earlier destruction of the French armada anchored in Aboukir Bay. This supremacy made it impossible for the French to maintain indefinitely an expeditionary force in the Middle East. Napoleon himself had slipped back to the power struggle in Paris soon after his defeat of the Ottoman volunteers. Taking with him pharaonic motifs which would influence furniture of the Empire style, he was to look back on his Egyptian adventure as "the most beautiful in my life because it was the most ideal." It may also have been the most fruitful. Whereas his achievements in Europe were largely ephemeral, his picturesque victory over the Mamelukes was the first boulder in an avalanche of change; contact with French ideas forced the people of the Middle East back into the arena where in the distant past they had played important roles.

Like many other young Europeans of what we may call the Stendhalian generation, Muhammad Ali had been captivated by the French leader and the aspirations he seemed to incarnate. With respect to Egypt, the young Macedonian shared something of Napoleon's vision of how this country could be transformed by fifty years of prosperity and good government. "One's imagination delights," Napoleon dictated on St. Helena, "in the enchanting vistas. A thousand irrigation sluices would tame and distribute the overflow of the Nile over every part of the territory. The eight to ten billion cubic yards of water now lost every year to the sea would be channelled to the lower parts of the desert . . . all the way to the oases and even farther west."

When the French were safely out of Egypt, the Sultan sent Muhammad Ali back to Egypt for the second time. The Mamelukes had rallied from their defeat, many returning from the Sudan, to which they had fled; an unpopular Ottoman governor had been installed. Preferred by popular acclaim, Muhammad Ali was confirmed as the new governor of Egypt by the Sultan in 1805. But Muhammad Ali was determined not to be a puppet of the Mamelukes, as his umpteen predecessors had been: in his own interest, not the Sultan's. He would first complete Napoleon's destruction of the Mameluke caste and then accomplish his personal interpretation of the Napoleonic vision. Napoleon had linked the renovation of Egypt with good government as well as good engineering; he had thought to enlist the Ulema, the native-born men of religion, in the huge effort which would be required if Egypt were to be reborn. Muhammad Ali, a product of the Ottoman Balkans, not of rationalist France, conceived of renovation based on tyranny: his own.

The destruction of the Mamelukes was accomplished on 1 March 1811. Muhammad Ali chose his occasion well. His young sovereign, Sultan Mahmud II, had authorized an Egyptian campaign against a puritan sect, the Wahhabis, who then controlled Central Arabia and were fighting against what they saw as the decadence of Islam: in particular the cult of holy places and saints. Mahmud's motives in authorizing the war were probably as much to involve his strong-willed subject in an exhausting war as to defeat the Wahhabis. Muhammad Ali's second son—who five years later would perish in the Sudan—was to lead the campaign with the title of Pasha of Jedda. The "dignity of a two-tailed pashalik" would be conferred on him by the Sultan's envoy at a ceremony in the Cairo Citadel. To this ceremony the leading Mamelukes were all invited, only one choosing not to attend. In the manner of the East, the Pasha's guests were offered coffee. What happened next obeyed no canon of hospitality, whether of the East or West. As the turbaned aristocrats defiled on horseback through a passage in the naked rock, the gates at each end were closed. Mounting the rocky sides of this improvised trap, the Pasha's riflemen, out of range themselves, butchered the horsemen below. Four hundred and seventy Mamelukes perished in the slaughter and its aftermath; their property was looted.

Now that Muhammad Ali had secured control of Egypt, he could proceed with its renovation. He took no account of revolutionary abstractions such as liberty, equality and fraternity, but saw progress largely in military terms. He first needed to secure a power base for himself: an efficient army under his secure control. Here a problem at once presented itself: where could he recruit his soldiers? The Mamelukes had been part of a hierarchical system. Inside this system, native Egyptians cultivated the land and practiced their religion; the minorities, Jews, Syrian Christians or Copts, collected the taxes; while the Mamelukes themselves did the fighting and ruling. Muhammad Ali could no longer use imported white slaves as officers. For one thing, he distrusted the surviving Mamelukes as much as they distrusted him; for another, the supply of such human robots was drying up now that Czarist Russia in the Caucasus and Central Asia and movements for independence in the Balkans were taking over areas which the slave merchants had once found productive. Muhammad Ali decided on a bold and novel solution to the problem: Egyptian conscripts could be whipped into military shape by Turks and Albanians; later some fellahin might be promoted to be corporals or even sergeants.

Muhammad Ali's militarist ambitions had valuable, if indirect, results. Schools were started to train officers and military technicians; a medical service with the first modern hospitals was organized to safeguard the soldiers' health; factories, the first in Africa, were founded to produce military equipment. Europeans, and in particular Frenchmen, served as experts in advising or directing these useful schemes. Such innovations cost money and Muhammad Ali proved as enterprising in producing new funds as new soldiers. Egypt's chief potential wealth was agricultural. Under the Mamelukes, the country had been divided into large, ill-managed estates. Muhammad Ali consolidated the entire irrigable land in his own ownership; the fellahin became serfs on one huge state farm. On this farm the Pasha grew, with great success, a new crop: Sea Island cotton, introduced from South Carolina. This long-staple variety quickly replaced the short-staple plants which were as old as the Pharaohs. Muhammad Ali commanded that one ninth of Egypt's arable acreage should be devoted to Sea Island cotton. The export of cotton soared dramatically from 650 pounds weight in 1820, the first year of its introduction, to eighteen million pounds only three years later. Like many innovations commanded in the East, Muhammad Ali's cotton did not maintain its first momentum; the low morale of the fellahin, who were driven to work by the lash and whose sons were drafted for military service in distant lands, contributed to setbacks; the Pasha's dream of exporting a million kantars a year was only to be a third fulfilled in his lifetime. Even so, cotton was established as Egypt's chief source of revenue for the century to come. Once again hard facts inspired the Pasha to further innovations. Crops of the scale he envisaged required better irrigation and transport. He started, but did not live to complete, a huge barrage across the neck of the delta just north of Cairo; this would make perennial irrigation a possibility. After crushing the pirates that endangered traffic on the Nile, he constructed a canal, named the Mahmudia in honor of Sultan Mahmud II, which reconnected Alexandria with the Nile. The crops produced by controlled irrigation could now be shipped through an expanding new port to the markets in Europe; Alexandria itself would rapidly regain its lost importance.

The innovating energy of Muhammad Ali—here summarized all too briefly—had made him richer and stronger than his sovereign, the Sultan. He had become a virtually independent ruler: but not quite. He lived and died, to his detriment, as the nominal vassal of Constantinople. For thirty-one years of Muhammad Ali's long reign, the role of Sultan, "Commander of the Faithful" and Caliph was played by Mahmud II, his pupil and frustrating rival. For Mahmud was first to imitate, then resent and oppose, his vigorous vassal.

Mahmud had succeeded to the Ottoman throne in 1808, after the deposition of his cousin by the Janissaries. The Janissaries had degenerated over the centuries in morale and professional skill; by the beginning of the nineteenth century they had become a sprawling, hereditary caste opposed to any radical renovation of the empire; they had as adverse an effect on Ottoman society as the Mamelukes on Egypt. Mahmud set out to destroy the Janissaries as Muhammad Ali had destroyed the Mamelukes. He first created an independent corps of artillery devoted to himself: his pretext was a good one—the need for a modern force capable of resisting the Europeans, whose support for the Greeks in their fight for independence had undermined Ottoman authority throughout the Balkans. At the height of the Greek struggle, in 1826, the Janissaries upset their heavy iron soup kettles: a gesture customarily made at the start of one of their periodic riots. Normally such disturbances won them what they wanted, either more pay, or the head of some official of whom they disapproved. This day they were in for a bitter surprise. The guns of the new artillery corps were focused on their barracks. As the turbulent Janissaries assembled, the guns opened fire, massacring thousands.

So far Mahmud had imitated Muhammad Ali. He was now in a position to build up a stronger Army and to centralize a bureaucracy under his personal control. He hoped with these two instruments of power to reknit the tattered fabric of an empire in which local war lords controlled most of the provinces, including valleys in mountainous Anatolia.

In this context Muhammad Ali no longer appeared as tutor; he was, rather, the most defiant enemy of centralized Ottoman power.

In the conflict between a sultan trying to strengthen his empire and a vassal trying to increase his independence, Muhammad Ali had had the advantage. His destruction of the Mamelukes had taken place fifteen years earlier than Mahmud's destruction of the Janissaries and he had used this start to good effect; he had also exploited Mahmud's difficulties in Greece, culminating in the destruction of the Ottoman fleet at Navarino in 1827. Egyptian armies occupied Palestine, Syria and a portion of southern Anatolia from 1831 to 1841. The rule of Ibrahim Pasha, who deputized for his father, was in many respects beneficial. He allowed missionaries to implant Western ideas in the parts of the Levant under his control. French Jesuits and American Protestants founded, with Egyptian encouragement, schools and colleges; local presses printed, for the first time, works in Arabic, French and English, whose effect on the Middle East was to be of permanent importance.

Ibrahim's military triumphs, which at one moment threatened Constantinople, made it a serious possibility that Cairo might become the capital of a new empire rapidly modernizing the whole Middle East. This possibility was thwarted, not by Sultan Mahmud, but by the West which Muhammad Ali and his son so greatly admired. A divided Europe of feuding nation-states was united in a puzzled concern for the dying Ottoman Empire. Such concern involved nothing as clear-cut as a wish to destroy the empire, or renovate it. In the sixteenth century, when the Crescent had conquered Rhodes and threatened Vienna, an Ottoman collapse would have seemed a godsend. Things were now more complex. The Crescent threatened nobody while the Cross played little part in the politics of Europe. The greedy were tempted by detachable Ottoman provinces while the conservative were alarmed lest the indulgence of such appetites upset the balance between Slavs and Germans. To Great Britain, after her defeat of Napoleon the leading conservative Power, the preservation of the ramshackle empire astride her imperial communications seemed less dangerous than its disintegration. But renovation was just as perilous as destruction. An independent Power, firmly established at the junction of Asia and Africa, would have policies of its own; these could threaten the interests of Britain; the strong French influence at the court of Muhammad Ali increased this danger.

Britain decided to cut Muhammad Ali down to size. But how? Lord Palmerston, the architect of British nineteenth-century policy, now regretted that Palestine, the very hinge of the new Egyptian empire, contained no suitable minority whose protection Britain could undertake as a pretext for evicting the Egyptians. (Similar pretexts were to be used by other Powers in other provinces of the Ottoman Empire. France, for example, was to exploit a traditional relationship with the Maronite Christians who lived on Mount Lebanon.) But the overwhelming majority of the Palestinians were, like the Turks and like the Egyptians, Sunni Muslims; their identification with the Muslim world had been clearly shown during Napoleon's invasion of their country. Since there was no protectable minority in Palestine, Palmerston wondered if it might not be possible to inject one. Could Jewish nostalgia for the Holy Land perhaps be used in Britain's interest? Having ascertained from the British vice-consul that there were already ten thousand Jews living in Palestine, Palmerston next wrote to the British ambassador in Constantinople:

> It would be of manifest importance for the Sultan to encourage the Jews to return to, and settle in Palestine; because the wealth which they would bring with them would increase the resources of the Sultan's dominions; and the Jewish people, if returning under the sanction and protection and at the invitation of the Sultan, would be a check upon any future evil designs of Muhammad Ali or his successors.

But the Sultan, as upholder of the Sharia, or Holy Law of Islam, could hardly have countenanced such a chimerical scheme; Jerusalem was one of the three holiest Islamic cities, and Jews, while allowed to practice their religion and run their own sectarian affairs, were regarded, along with Christians, as practicing a less perfect form of monotheism than that of the Muslim majority living in Palestine.

England contrived instead two defeats of a different order for the ambitious Pasha. Both depended on British influence at Constantinople. The first blow was economic. The Ottoman Government authorized a Commercial Convention, signed in 1838 and put into effect in 1842, which gave England a double freedom: the freedom to buy raw materials or finished goods throughout the Ottoman Empire and the freedom to sell her own goods inside the same large market; the British would pay a 12 per cent tax on Ottoman goods they bought and a 5 per cent tax on their own goods that they took in and sold. Since Egypt formed part of the Ottoman Empire, Muhammad Ali's policy of running agriculture and industry as monopolies under his own control collapsed. Far more serious, British manufactured goods, freely imported into Egypt, would outsell, for quality and cheapness, the first, unripe fruits of the Egyptian industrial revolution.

In theory the Commercial Convention vindicated the liberal principle of Free Trade. In practice it dealt a lethal blow to the Egyptian economy. Other new industrial systems—the North American, for example, or German—only survived their infancy by erecting tariff barriers against those who had started earlier. The Sultan's acceptance of Free Trade—the Convention was soon extended to other European countries, such as Austria—made it illegal for Muhammad Ali, as his vassal, to erect such windbreaks; without them his industrial plants withered; Egypt did not become, what she might have become, the workshop of Africa. For a country 97 per cent of whose surface was desert unfit for agriculture and whose population would double and redouble, the inability to industrialize was a calamity.

A second, political blow would make this economic blow effective. In 1839 Mahmud II died and was succeeded by his son Abdul Mejid, who read French newspapers and approved, more gently than his autocratic father, of reform. The new Sultan's ministers issued, in November, the "Noble Rescript of the Rose Chamber." This charter promised to abolish the abuses which disfigured Ottoman society; in particular it promised that for the first time all citizens, regardless of creed, would be treated equally. This liberal proclamation, whether it could be put into practice or not, stole Ibrahim's reformist thunder. Armed with it, and mindful of the late Sultan's Commercial Convention, England now used military force against Muhammad Ali. A British and Austrian fleet helped the Ottomans to regain control of the Levant, including Lebanon. Muhammad Ali had to recall his army to Egypt and disband most of it; his expensive fleet rotted in harbor.

It was not, however, British policy to reimpose Ottoman control over Egypt, since such a strengthening of the Sultan might be dangerous; nor was it desirable that the Pasha, provoked too far, should break free from Constantinople altogether. The new Sultan was therefore advised to placate him with a consolation prize: the guarantee, expressed in an official firman, that the governorship of Egypt would be hereditary in Muhammad Ali's family. The system of succession would duplicate that of the Sultanate. This made Ibrahim the heir to Muhammad Ali; followed by Abbas. After

Abbas, Muhammad Ali's next surviving son Said; and on his death, Ibrahim's son Ahmed, or if he were no longer living, Ismail himself.

Against this background of family triumphs and frustrations, Ismail had grown up. He was destined, he knew, to take part in a pawn-despising game in which the family rook, Muhammad Ali, had overwhelmed bishops and knights: but on a board where the Ottoman Sultan remained nominal King while Europe was the vizir—as the Eastern chessplayer knows the Queen—able to strike fast in any direction.

From his earliest boyhood Ismail was conscious of the Ottoman Sultan as a sovereign who fettered pashaly independence and as a spiritual authority in whose name Egyptian mosques echoed in prayer. But as he grew older, he became equally conscious of Europe, a furnace of energy and a source of peril.

Ismail first set foot in Western Europe when he was fourteen. He spent the summer of 1844 having his eyes treated in Vienna. Instead of going back to Cairo, he traveled the following spring to Paris. His education was to be completed in the European manner at the Egyptian Military School newly created by Muhammad Ali and attached to an Egyptian Mission established in France since 1826. Like many Eastern potentates, Muhammad Ali had sired uncountable children, most of whom died young. The school was intended for two of his younger sons and two of his grandchildren, Ismail and his older brother Ahmed. To create a proper environment for four princely scholars eighty youngsters from the Egyptian upper class (which in effect meant those of Albanian or Turkish extraction) had been recruited for the school. A headmaster and teaching staff were appointed by the French Minister of War. Then in 1848 Louis Philippe (whose friendship for Muhammad Ali was symbolized by the clock tower he presented to the old man's Citadel mosque) was overthrown. Muhammad Ali happened to be visiting Naples. He dreamed of one last chimerical exploit: he would lead an Egyptian army into Europe and restore his deposed friend! His alarmed advisers rushed him back to Egypt, where he was confined, obviously senile, to his palace. Ibrahim Pasha was made Regent. But Muhammad Ali's physical stamina outlasted his son's; Ibrahim died after a brief reign and Muhammad Ali lingered into 1849 under the tutelage of his grandson Abbas, now the oldest male in the family.

The Egyptian school closed with the overthrow of Louis Philippe. Ismail was transferred for a last year at Saint-Cyr. In 1849 he returned to Egypt, his formal education finished. He had obtained good marks at both the Egyptian school and Saint-Cyr, though his progress had been hindered by the weakness of his eyes.

An English proconsul destined in a sense to be his successor would later claim that "Ismail and his brother Mustafa, when they were in Paris, used to buy whatever they saw; they were like children, nothing was fine enough for them; they bought carriages and horses like those of Queen Victoria or the Emperor, and let them spoil for want of shelter or cleaning." The critic, Sir Evelyn Baring, later Lord Cromer, was to have his reasons for belittling Ismail.

To bolster the impression that the Khedive had been untouched by French culture Baring quoted an English coachman in Ismail's later employ: "I have known him sometimes try to read a French novel, but he would be two hours getting through a page. Once or twice I saw him attempt to write. His letters were half an inch high, like those of a child's copybook. I don't think he ever finished a sentence." The same quotable coachman served to cast doubts on the company Ismail by preference kept. "The people he liked best to talk to were his servants, the lads who brought him his pipes and stood before him with their arms crossed. He sometimes sat on his sofa and smoked and talked to them for hours, all about women and such things."

The proconsul and the coachman he used as evidence missed two vital points about Ismail's formation: the way in which he remained of the East and the way in which he was affected by the West.

He was not uprooted by his French experience; he did not return to Cairo as an internal exile, a man alienated from the East in which he had been born. In this East autocratic rule could still go with democratic manners. A Muslim despot could discuss "women and such things" with his servants on a man-to-man basis impossible to a Victorian gentleman. Such informality made him respected; not the reverse.

Ismail's experiences in France had at the same time modified the way he looked on life; Muhammad Ali had been a francophile without knowing France or French. Ismail knew both. It is true that he appreciated neither Balzac nor Baudelaire. But study of French novelists and poets could hardly help in renovating Egypt. It is also true that the French influences which Ismail accepted were often of the surface. While his mother, living in her oriental palace by the Nile, would continue to dress in the Eastern style, with "a beautiful Persian shawl wound round her body," his wives and daughters would be dressed in the style of Europe, and would live where "large lustres hung from the ceiling, and girandoles from the walls." For his children Ismail would seek a Western education. In 1868, for example, he sent two of his sons, Hussein Kamil and Hassan, respectively to Paris and London. "The household of Hussein Pasha," he wrote personally, in French, to his Prime Minister, "should be proportioned to his rank; he should have a town-house, rented, if it is possible, for four years, a steward, a sufficiency of domestic servants, three carriages (Victoria, coupé and landau), seven horses, including saddle horses and that for his tutor; I don't want exaggerated luxury, nothing that might approach extravagance; a sum of between 150 and 200 thousand francs will be allotted to Hussein for all his annual expenses." For his daughter Princess Zeyneb he imported an English governess, Miss Ellen Chennels, who would find her little charge "magnificently dressed in black velvet, made in the last Parisian fashion. The trimming was of white ostrich feathers; a diamond brooch, which, with the pendants attached to it, was as large in circumference as an orange, sparkled on her chest. She wore diamond earrings, a clasp of the same precious stones at the waist, black velvet boots with diamond buckles, and a velvet hat with the same feather trimming as on the dress."

The acceptance of Western modes was neither easy nor total. Eating habits would, for instance, sway between two worlds. "At Abdin his Highness ate with them always *en famille*," Miss Chennels reports with much governess French. "The table was served *à la franque,* but during Ramadan that of course ceased, and afterwards, when the regular meals began, the slaves, disliking the extra trouble which a dinner *à la franque* gave them, and having received no fresh orders on the subject, gave us everything *à la turque*. This service is extremely simple: a round table, on which a large circular tray is put; the dish is in the middle, and is frequently changed; and a small plate and spoon are put for each guest, with a large piece of bread; the spoon is to be used if the dish contains any liquid food, but if it is meat or anything solid, the fingers are applied." Ismail deserves sympathy. It was not easy to adapt Western manners to a society in which female slaves in Paris costumes might suddenly, for not averting their gaze on the approach of men, be bent over and whipped by irate eunuchs.

But the moral aspects of French civilization, itself the epitome of what Europe then had to offer, impressed Ismail as well as its furbelows. He acquired something of European detachment, a legacy at second hand of the *philosophes* whose spirit had educated the France which had educated him. This detachment helped him survive the fourteen years between the death of Muhammad Ali in 1849 and his own accession in 1863. They were years of pendulum, dangerous years in which Ismail prudently cultivated his many gardens.

Abbas Pasha reverted to the modes of eighteenth-century Turkey, modes which Lady Mary Wortley Montagu, wife of the British ambassador in Constantinople, had described to such friends as Alexander Pope: inertia and jealousy in slumberous palaces. In what resembles an Oedipus complex misplaced towards a grandfather, Abbas opposed in every detail the course charted by Muhammad Ali. His grandfather had steered by a new Western star; Abbas wanted to harbor in a known and familiar East. Muhammad Ali had trusted Frenchmen and Italians and employed them on his schemes; a distrustful Abbas expelled them. Muhammad Ali had fought the English, who had frustrated his chief ambitions; Abbas preferred them to the French. Closing schools, hospitals and factories, reducing the army to a shadow, he espoused the Western innovation particularly associated with the British: the railway. Opposing the notion of a maritime canal (which Napoleon had pondered till informed, erroneously, that the Red Sea level stood ten meters higher than the Mediterranean), he agreed with the British that a railway link from Alexandria to Suez by way of Cairo would be safe and profitable. In arguing thus he was no fool. A rail link would enhance a route which had become increasingly used in the 1840s. Steamers from Europe brought travelers to Alexandria, whence they traveled on barges drawn by steam tugs up the Mahmudia Canal to near Cairo; large-wheeled carriages then took them to Suez, where the Indian steamer was waiting. This method of travel by way of the Egyptian delta had cut the journey from England to India from four months, by way of the Cape, to forty days; a rail link would make it still more comfortable and quick. Such a rail link, traversing the populated delta, would be under surer control than a canal through desert which could be detached from Egypt; a railway would bring business to Cairo, the capital. Thus in 1851 Abbas put George Stephenson, whose father had invented the "Rocket," under contract to build a railway from Alexandria; this line, planned by Muhammad Ali but never started, was completed by 1856 and was the first in Africa and the East; by 1857 the line from Cairo to Suez was added. For the convenience of travelers Abbas authorized a Mr. Samuel Shepheard to open a hotel.

In his instinctive distrust of the sub-Europeans who thronged his grandfather's Eldorado, Abbas may well have been wiser than the rest of his tribe. But to the sons and grandsons of Muhammad Ali their kinsman seemed a dour and dangerous reactionary, fearing, like the Turk he felt himself to be, a brother, or cousin, near the throne. In a country where opposition was as yet unthinkable, Ismail became the leader of a "party of princes" who maintained the francophile attitude of Muhammad Ali during this period of reaction. Political action was impossible; the princes (collectively self-indulgent and out for their own interests) were hardly the stuff of which martyrs are made; they turned their surplus energies towards improving their estates; Western technology, in the form of steam pumps and ginning machines for cotton, made its appearance.

Ismail's survival probably owed less to his concentration on agriculture than to Abbas' premature and typically Eastern death. Like many Ottomans, the Pasha enjoyed the embraces of young men. Two handsome mamelukes, bought in the still flourishing Cairo slave market, were planted in his service, either by envious relations or guardsmen with a grievance; in either case Abbas dug his pit when he appointed the two youths to his bedroom rota. On a dark night at Benha Palace the hirelings murdered their employer and then escaped from his bedroom to Constantinople, where no charge was brought against them. Abbas left an adored but adolescent son, al-Hami, whom the Ottoman law prevented from succeeding. A member of Abbas' entourage tried to set aside the law. Propping the

cadaver of Abbas in his carriage, so that he seemed dozing, not permanently dead, the official drove him to the Citadel and there tried to proclaim
al-Hami. The envoys of the Powers aborted this plan and Muhammad
Ali's fourth son, Muhammad Said, was quickly installed as Pasha.

Said's pudgy, well-shod foot kicked the pendulum back towards France
and Frenchmen. A monogamous *bon vivant* who employed a French chef
and prided himself on his taste in wines, he was kindly and easily influenced. Within weeks of his accession he had given De Lesseps his concession to dig the Canal. (For this to be fully legal it still required Ottoman
authorization, too.) Though the surviving princes were as francophile as
Said, this did not necessarily make them safe, particularly as the new
Pasha's temper changed with ill health. Ismail, second in succession to the
throne, became first through an "accident" (the suspicions East always
hangs quotation marks round this word) which might have killed him as it
killed his elder brother, Ahmed. In 1859 Said, on holiday, invited the
young princes of his family to visit him by the sea in Alexandria. He laid
on what was still a novelty of speed and comfort: a special train to take his
guests back and forth across the delta. At Kafr al-Zayat a British-made
swing bridge carried the permanent way across a major branch of the Nile.
On the return journey, as the train pounded towards the bridge the driver
saw, too late, that it was open. Prince Halim, one of Muhammad Ali's surviving sons, saved himself by diving into the Nile. Ahmed, the heir, too
portly, or perhaps too befuddled, to follow his example, was drowned.
Ismail, indisposed, had stayed in Cairo.

Relations between Said and his new heir were outwardly good. Ismail
acted as Regent when Said went abroad; Said sent him on missions to the
Pope, Napoleon III and the Sultan. In 1861 Ismail distinguished himself
in action by quelling an insurrection in the Sudan, an unstable Egyptian
dependency. Even so, Ismail tactfully kept agriculture as his chief concern.
An appetite for land and more land went with a meticulous attention to its
upkeep; this won him the reputation of being a tight-fisted landowner with
the best cotton in Egypt. "His lands," the Austrian consul-general wrote in
a report of April 1862, "are the best administered in Egypt; his crops are
the best on the market and fetch the highest price. Economy is his strong
point. Provided you are straight with him, you can deal with him frankly
and in complete confidence and get the best results. As to faults, I know of
only one: he's stingy. However, from the point of view of administering
Egypt, this fault may make him the most capable member of his family."

Ismail's success as a cotton grower (unsurprising when we remember
that his ancestors had grown tobacco in Macedonia) came at a convenient
time.

The American Civil War initiated an economic crisis which was to
straddle Said's last years (he died in 1863) and Ismail's accession. The
North's blockade of southern harbors cut Europe off from its traditional

source of supply. The effects were not felt at once, since European factories had overstocked. But as the Civil War continued beyond its first year, so the worst economic famine of the century developed. The price of cotton soared as the commodity became almost unobtainable, as cotton importers looked frantically for new sources of supply.

The price of Egyptian cotton quadrupled in the five years following 1860. In the same period the production soared from half a million kantars to over two million. As Lancashire workers lined up at soup kitchens, Egyptians dipped into generous stew pots. Exports increased in value from just under 3.5 million Egyptian pounds in 1861 to almost 14.5 million pounds in 1864. Ismail now entered that dangerous middle state between *hybris* and *nemesis* which the Greeks called *atê:* a state of culpable blindness where the protagonist ceases to recognize his true situation.

Ismail forgot that Egypt was still a poor and undeveloped country; he failed to foresee that the cotton boom would end with the American Civil War. The impatience of his dreams, the extravagance of his folly, both had their roots in an Eastern attitude to money which was small help in dealing with the nineteenth century.

The Islamic world as a whole, from Morocco in the West to Indonesia in the East, had inherited, quite apart from its Koran and Prophet, legacies from Bedouin Arabia. One was an attitude to wealth characteristic of nomads whose property consisted of what their camels could carry. In a world of dearth where freak storms brought sudden greenery or harsh winds devastating droughts, the traveler depended on the hospitality of the tents he came to; without it he would die. Desert steppes withered husbandry, undermined economy. The Arabian ideal of generosity carried to the point of insanity was expressed in the story of a generous youth who slaughtered all his father's camels for some passing guests. This Bedouin ideal, which canonized a spendthrift and gave God himself the epithet "The Generous," was transmitted to the races converted to Islam. The dour Turks were no exception; Mogul maharajahs and Ottoman sultans flaunted their wealth while despising the labor which created it as much as the mechanism which kept its accounts. Since Islam prohibited the practice of usury, no indigenous banking system had developed; the Eastern *seraf* was simply a man who changed one currency to another; there was no native system for providing development capital.

Ismail had won his reputation as a sober, even stingy, manager when he was still fresh from a France whose peasant stock is the least extravagant in Europe. He had frowned when his uncle Said had made himself the first Egyptian ruler to incur a debt to Western moneylenders. (Said was, in fact, to bequeath Ismail a debt, from all sources, of over sixteen million pounds.) But as yellow gold tumbled into Alexandria in return for the white gold of cotton, Ismail's divided head was turned. One part harbored dreams from the West; the other, atavistic responses from the East. "He wanted by a stroke of the pen," wrote a contemporary, "to turn the most conservative people on earth into a living embodiment of a progressive and enlightened civilisation. He had no patience for the slow conversion of a nation almost as stolid and immovable as their own Pyramids. Their whole system was to be changed in an instance by a *coup de théâtre,* with trap-doors, stage-thunder, and a shower of fireworks." To place Egypt on a level with Europe, to have roads and railways, harbors and post offices, lighthouses and schools, he needed money. And in order to maintain his own credit, so that he could ask for more and more without blushing, so that a huge new loan could pay for the one before and still leave something over for new schemes, he labored to embellish his capital city. European, or mock European, a gaslit Cairo would glisten to creditors like a lamp to moths. "In the evening, if we like, we can hear a French opera bouffe and see a French ballet in a theatre exactly resembling those we left behind in London. If we call upon our Minister, we shall find him in a Gallican villa surrounded by a hundred similar villas, which might belong to any Mediterranean city but for a vision of negro footmen and bronzed guards. Wherever we go we find palaces of the Khedive or members of his family. Abdin and Ismailiya are the chief palaces in Cairo itself, though there are others, and beyond the limits of the metropolis the names of these gorgeous mansions are legend. At Kasr el-Nil and all along the neighbouring banks of the Nile, on the islands of Rôda and Gezira, at Gîza, Abbasiya, Shubra—everywhere, rise the unsightly and ill-built palaces in which viceregal extravagance and ostentation have found an outlet."

This extravagant dreamer, this ostentatious spender, was the man who had opened the Canal. An Easterner in love with the West, an Ottoman educated in Paris, he nursed political ambitions which were both shrewd and desperate: he would make Egypt as free of the Sultan as he could, and then, through a balance of alliances and influence, as safe as any well-established European state.

He had not foreseen that the year appointed for inaugurating his canal would be a year when the balance in Europe itself was about to tilt, with incalculable effects on all his guests. Still less did he understand the impersonal forces which controlled his century and which were now moving to destroy him.

Chapter 3

AFTER ordinary parties the host weighs the guests who did come against those who did not: wonders if he did right to ask this one, or wrong to exclude that. After the extraordinary party of November 1869 Ismail will have done the same.

Eugénie, Empress of the French, had been his prize catch. In her honor the Khedive had named a boulevard in Ismailia, as well as a beach in Port Said; the palace he had built for her brief use was to outlast her long life (she died in 1920, aged 95), known as the Palais Lutfallah from the rich Coptic family who bought it, until, in the nationalizing 1960s, it would be prepared for a new life as the Omar Khayyam Hotel.

Eugénie's most recent biographer gives her trip to Egypt half a page out of 400; Mr. Harold Kurtz comments that "what made her particularly happy was to see that [Franz Josef] never left her side." For Eugénie the expedition had a political interest which owed nothing to Egypt: the hope of winning Austria to the side of France. Otherwise she was being polite to the ruler of the country which Napoleon I had called, for its strategic position, "the most important" in the world. She was also repaying a debt. Eighteen days before he died, Ismail's uncle, Said Pasha, had sent 450 black troops to Mexico to help Eugénie's husband, Napoleon III, in the most madcap scheme of his reign, the attempt to create a European empire in the Americas headed by Maximilian, Franz Josef's brother. This scheme had foundered on American opposition, Mexican nationalism and the new emperor's ineffectual character. Egypt nevertheless deserved French thanks. That Napoleon III remembered Egypt's black troops and little else had been shown in October 1868, when Ismail's two sons had had a twenty-minute interview in Paris. "How many negro troops do you have?" the sickly Emperor had inquired. "Two regiments," one of the Princes answered. "Why not more? Then you would not need to rely on fellah troops." The Prince replied that black troops did not support the climate and the interview was over.

From her Suez jaunt Eugénie returned to a wintry Paris, where far more was foundering than a Mexican daydream. Against popular discontent and his own failing health, against an all too evident threat from Prussia, Napoleon III was transforming Caesarism into what he called "Imperial Democracy." Eugénie showed little sympathy for such efforts to strengthen the internal front. Her hopes of detaching the Austrians from the North Germans, vain as they proved, were part of an obsessive interest in politics; pale compensation for a marriage blighted early by Napoleon's overt infidelities. If he still respected her mind and depended considerably on her advice, for her part she loved the Emperor, while despairing of the man. She expressed this love by high-handed and finally disastrous interference in public affairs. Within a year of the opening of the Canal she would play her part in pushing France into its greatest disaster since Waterloo. In supporting the war party, Eugénie was unwittingly supporting Bismarck, who could afford to let France declare a war she must inevitably lose. The pretext: a pretended Hohenzollern succession to the Spanish throne which Bismarck had already discarded as a boring toy. Napoleon III did not perish leading his troops as Eugénie half hoped. After a period of tolerable incarceration he was to join her for a few years of middle-class exile in the English Home Counties, then to die, in great pain, of the bladder disease which had tortured his last years. The Second Empire would be succeeded, not by the restored empire of which Eugénie dreamed, but a Third Republic. A new empire was indeed proclaimed in France—but it was German. To this new German empire France had to cede her two provinces of Alsace and Lorraine. (The change of nationality introduced crises of conscience in the annexed lands: an M. Dreyfus, who owned a textile factory at Mulhouse, opted for French nationality and left, with his son Alfred, for Paris; Alfred joined the French army while his brother, Jacques, who had opted to be a German, looked after the family business in Elsass, as the province was renamed.) A France thus humiliated would compensate itself with colonial victories in North Africa and Arab provinces. But the Masonic, anti-clerical republic would lack the power to impose French control on Egypt or to defend Egyptian independence if France's most ancient rival should seek to suppress it.

In terms of influence, Eugénie's presence at the inauguration had been no more potent than the patronage of an outgoing American President in his last weeks of power.

Ismail's second most important guest was the Emperor Franz Josef. If Eugénie's reign was nearing its end, his was only beginning; but as a possible ally for Ismail he was no more effective. Whereas France had interests in the Middle East and could have been a powerful ally, the dual monarchy of Austria and Hungary, combining Czechs, Slovaks, Croats and Bosnians in an uneasy empire, was preoccupied with the Balkans and Central Europe. Franz Josef's polyglot empire would swell, but not with health; by ingesting indigestible provinces detached from the Ottoman Empire it would catch its victim's illness. Its military weakness had been shown in its swift collapse before the power of Prussia; its political weakness was to be a cause of the First World War, in which Franz Josef would die and the empire perish.

The third important guest was the Crown Prince of Prussia; at Versailles in January 1871, Bismarck would proclaim his father, Wilhelm I, as first German Emperor.

In 1888, ten years too late to assist Ismail, if he had wanted to do so, and already dying from cancer, the Crown Prince would occupy the imperial throne for a three-month reign. History remembers him, not for himself, but as the husband of Queen Victoria's eldest daughter and as the father of Kaiser Wilhelm II. His country, always a continental Power, was to show more interest in the railway linking Berlin with Baghdad and the Persian Gulf than in Egypt and its Khedive. Nevertheless Germany would play a small, unhelpful, role in the final stages of Ismail's reign.

Two invited guests who could not come were King Victor Emmanuel II of Italy and General Grant, President of the United States of America. Victor Emmanuel had received Ismail in Florence, the then Italian capital, and had promised to send the Duke of Aosta as his representative; in the event Victor Emmanuel's illness had forced the Italian fleet and its ducal leader to leave Egypt before the inauguration. General Grant could not leave an America still recovering from the Civil War; besides, the eastern Mediterranean seemed an area remote from American interests. The President's absence was no more an intended slight than the revival of the American cotton trade was a deliberate attempt to deflate the Egyptian boom. There was a U.S. consulate at Port Said, but no American ships took part in the festivities. Americans had an achievement of their own with which to mark 1869: the completion of the first transcontinental railroad. Now facing two oceans, not two seas, America's chief interest in the Canal was the evidence it provided that such an enterprise was possible; this would encourage Americans to complete their own Panama Canal some years later; it would first inspire De Lesseps to a failure as great as his present success, when, old and pigheaded, he would vainly attempt, in very different geographical circumstances, to make the Panama Canal a lockless trench like the Suez waterway.

The guest who would not come was the hoped-for member of the British Royal Family. Though fruitful as any polygamous serail, Windsor Castle proffered no princeling to stand beside the British ambassador to Constantinople on the corvette *Rapid*.

This was not for want of trying by Ismail.

The Egyptian Viceroy (as he was generally known outside Egypt) had journeyed to Europe personally to round up his guests. In June he had visited London as guest of the Prince and Princess of Wales. A crowded program involved him in technological marvels (he enjoyed a ride on the new underground railway) and British society (he visited the widowed Queen at Windsor). The Prince and Princess of Wales had recently inspected the work on the Canal and had slept at his chalet; they returned his hospitality by taking him to the Caledonian Ball as well as a fete attended by 30,000 people, embellished with sphinxes, at the Crystal Palace. "On Wednesday morning," wrote the *Illustrated London News,* "the Viceroy, accompanied by the Prince of Wales and the Duke of Sutherland, inspected the Fire Brigade in the gardens of Buckingham Palace. Eighteen of the largest steam fire-engines, one manual engine, two fire-escapes, and nearly a hundred firemen in full uniform were on the ground. The engines and the fire-escapes were tested in every way, to the entire satisfaction of the Viceroy, who complimented Captain Shaw very highly on the excellence of all his arrangements and the efficiency of his men. Later in the day His Highness visited the Archbishop of Canterbury, the Turkish Ambassador, the French Ambassador, the Speaker of the House of Commons, the Duke of Argyll, and Earl Granville, and dined with Frances Countess Waldegrave and the Right Hon. Chichester Fortescue at Strawberry Hill."

Yet despite his cordial welcome, Ismail could not contrive that British royalty should grace the inauguration. The Canal had been fought too stubbornly by the British for its completion to be an event they could publicly patronize.

British opposition to the Canal had been rooted in suspicion of France, the island kingdom's traditional rival. If a French-built and a French-owned canal opened the Mediterranean to the Indian Ocean, and if the canal zone were populated by a colony of French managers, France would not only have effectively divorced Egypt from the Ottoman Empire; she would be within sight of imposing a protectorate over the whole country. Such a strategic position for France, halfway to the Indian empire which had replaced the colonies lost in North America, would be a major threat to Britain. It was true that France had been allied to Britain since the Crimean War, when Napoleon III had seen fit to support the Ottoman Sultan against the Czar. But there was no more certainty that this would continue to be Napoleon's policy than there was that Napoleon would continue in power. New French governments might revert to earlier policies of opposing British interests wherever met.

When Said Pasha gave De Lesseps his concession it must have seemed to Palmerston a renewal of "the evil designs" which he had prophesied when toying with the notion of a Jewish colony in Palestine. His first reaction was to pooh-pooh the projected Canal as too expensive to be profitable; but then added the caution that were it built, "it would be injurious to England because, in any quarrel between England and France, France, being so much nearer to the canal, would have the start of us in sending ships and troops to the Indian seas."

Britain had then exerted her considerable influence at Constantinople to abort the project. The British ambassador, Lord Stratford de Redcliffe, brought pressure on the Ottoman Government and the British Government brought pressure on the French. Four years elapsed unused between the rainbow moment when De Lesseps obtained his concession and the day in 1858 when he could put on offer shares in the Universal Company of the Suez Canal. Neither the British Government or any other took up these shares; the bulk of the money subscribed came from small French investors.[1] For the company to be legally established, De Lesseps had to ask his friend, Said Pasha, to buy the rest. The Pasha's concession was still unsupported by an Ottoman firman, but in stealth De Lesseps shoveled the first bucket for his canal. Even so, British pressure was to seem at one moment victorious. The Ottoman Grand Vizir at the instigation of a new British ambassador, Sir Henry Bulwer, commanded the Viceroy to stop a work which the British characterized as "a political and private piece of swindling." The vacillating Said might have yielded had not De Lesseps played his trump: his relationship with Eugénie. The Empress persuaded her husband that the interests of twenty thousand French investors were worth a clash with Britain. Having lost in the battle of intrigue, Britain now attacked the Canal on purer grounds than imperial inconvenience. The use of Egyptian forced labor (despite De Lesseps' claim that he fed his workers well and tended their health) outraged the humane; Said's concession to the Company of the land irrigated by the fresh-water canal aroused the suspicions of Ottoman and Egyptians as much as those of the British, though for different reasons. Ismail saw the possibility of taking the Canal away from De Lesseps. Backed by the Sultan's denunciation of forced labor and the land grants, Ismail schemed to buy Suez Canal shares secretly in Paris so that he, and not De Lesseps, could have control. But De Lesseps outwitted Ismail as he had outwitted previous opponents. Ismail, expecting Napoleon's sympathy, agreed that the question of forced labor and the company's lands should be submitted to the arbitration of the Emperor. The result was a rebuff to Ismail's pocket and British interests. Ismail was allowed to withdraw forced labor and the ceded land; in return he had to pay monetary compensation amounting in value to almost as much as his holding in Suez Canal shares. This suited De Lesseps, who at this stage needed money more than labor. The one stage where no existing machinery could have substituted for naked labor had been the first and most difficult: in making a trench through the northern swamps. The squelchy mud had to be pulled out and piled by bare hands in dikes which solidified only thanks to the ferocious sun. Machinery was more suitable for the later stages, when the trench had to be hewn from dry, impacted sand. The Emperor's award gave De Lesseps the money he needed and saved the Canal for France. Its completion, Britain's biggest diplomatic setback in the nineteenth century, was also, as perceptive Englishmen soon recognized, a benefit to their interests. De Lesseps was to receive next year a hero's wel-

---

[1] A hundred friends of De Lesseps had put up 5,000 francs each. By the 1890s these shares would have multiplied in value 280 times.

come in, of all places, London; British shipping was quickly to account for an overwhelming share of the traffic through the Canal. But the opening of the Canal was not an occasion which Britain, for all her reputed sangfroid, could honor with a prince.

Eugénie had described her reception at Port Said as "magical." At magic christenings the host bewares of the guests he overlooked; the slighted fairy casts the perilous spell.

Ismail had deliberately omitted three still independent Muslim rulers from his list: the Sherif of Morocco, the Bey of Tunis and the Shah of Iran. They were too remote, too insecure or too ineffectual to be worth inviting. Besides, the Khedive complained, he had no more than seven palaces fit for housing royal guests.

It is doubtful if Sherif, Bey or Shah were unduly distressed. The Sherif, a descendant of the Prophet, may have snorted at a Macedonian upstart; the Shah of Iran may have muttered at tobacco-merchant taste; the Bey of Tunis was preoccupied with mountainous debts. The interests of none of them was affected by the Canal. But even if they cast no spells, Egyptian relations with these three countries were not, in the coming century, to be particularly warm.[2]

The baleful absentee was the one Muslim ruler who mattered: Ismail's liege-lord, the Ottoman Sultan-Caliph.

Since 1861, when Abdul Mejid had died, the Sultan had been his younger brother, Abdul Aziz. Abdul Aziz's nature, hot-headed, irascible, extravagant, capricious, was streaked with lunacy. Even so, Ismail had maintained cordial relations with his sovereign during the first years of his reign. In 1863 he had traveled to Constantinople for his traditional investiture; it had had an unprecedented sequel. For the first time since Selim's conquest in 1517, an Ottoman Sultan had visited Egypt. This was a great compliment to Ismail. From Alexandria the Sultan had chuffed across a delta as April-green as Flanders; his first ride on a railway train (an Ottoman line would be opened three years later) impressed him as much as Egypt's bustling Western-style cities. As well as bestowing a saber of honor on Ismail, he conferred the Grand Cordon of the Osmanli Order on his mother, and the Pashadom on Nubar. These gestures, made so conspicuously to a woman and an Armenian Christian, hinted that Abdul Aziz might imitate Ismail as his father Mahmud II had imitated Muhammad Ali.

Abdul Aziz understood Ismail's desire to add prestige to wealth; having plenty of prestige, the Sultan could do with some of Ismail's apparently limitless cash. Ismail's particular desire was to change the law of succession, so that on his death he would be succeeded, not by his half brother or one

[2] The one dynastic alliance was to be between Ismail's granddaughter, Fowzia, and the Shah Reza Pahlevi in 1941; this marriage was not to last and the Shah, of a new dynasty from the one reigning in 1869, was to become a political enemy of an Egypt also with a new regime in the 1960s.

of Muhammad Ali's surviving sons, but by his eldest son, Towfik. Abdul Aziz would have liked to do the same in favor of his own son, but knew this to be impossible against the weight of Ottoman tradition. But in 1866 a firman decreed that in Egypt the European system should be followed and Ismail's son, Towfik, proclaimed as heir. In return for this firman, and the cession to Egypt of two Red Sea ports, Suakin and Massawa, Ismail agreed to increase the annual tribute from eighty thousand to one hundred and fifty thousand purses. The next year Abdul Aziz upgraded the Pasha-dom itself. A new style more grandiloquent than Pasha, less suggestive of vassaldom, was bestowed on the Egyptian ruler. The search for a title which, stopping short of sovereignty, would yet hint an autonomous dig-nity, was exhaustive. Neither Sultan nor Padishah would do, being already titles of the Ottoman sovereign; king, or its Arabic equivalent, "malik," sounded incongruous in Eastern ears; a Sherif must by definition be de-scended from the Prophet. The term hit upon—Khedive, or in Arabic, *Khedeewi*—derived from an Iranian noun for god; the charm of the title was its lack of definition; it held more awe than Pasha and less precision than Viceroy; the best rendering in a European tongue was the Latin *Princeps* long ago favored by Augustus for its pleasing vagueness and used by Ismail's grandson in an inscription over the entrance to the Cairo Museum.

Ottoman opposition to the Canal had not envenomed the relations be-tween Khedive and Sultan. As an adoptive Egyptian, Ismail had had his own reservations about the projected waterway. "No one is more 'canaliste' than myself," he had said; "but I want the Canal to belong to Egypt, not Egypt to the Canal." Because he recognized the threat of a French colony in the Isthmus of Suez, he had bought back the land his uncle had given De Lesseps. He was also aware, as was the Sultan, that neither of them was entirely free; they lived in a world where certain na-tions were Powers, and others weren't. Besides, the Sultan's opposition to the Canal had ceased. A firman of March 1868 authorized the Egyptian ruler to construct a Canal through the Isthmus of Suez. Since by this time De Lesseps had almost finished his canal, the firman was a face-saving ges-ture which neither party misunderstood.

The quarrel between Ismail and Abdul Aziz was over prestige: the pres-tige which Ismail had secured, but could lose, and the prestige which the Sultan felt menaced by Ismail's actions. Motives of jealousy and fear influ-enced Eastern statesmen more openly than their Western counterparts. Neither the Sultan nor the Khedive was entirely self-assured; both had reasons to fear plots in their family circles; to both prestige made up for what they lacked in power. Ismail had shown the importance he attached to prestige by the bribes he had expended on having his title upgraded. Abdul Aziz compensated for the erosion of his territories by claiming (what earlier Sultans had hardly bothered to do) that the Sultan who had conquered Egypt in 1517 had assumed, on behalf of all succeeding Ottoman rulers, the aura of Caliph. This move had a curious equivalent in the contemporary papacy. As the Pope's physical domains diminished, as Pius IX became the virtual prisoner of the Vatican, he laid claims to the spiritual aura of Infallibility.

The catalyst of this dispute over prestige was Ismail's half brother, Mustafa Fazil. Until the firman of 1866, Mustafa Fazil had been Ismail's heir. Fearing his brother, Mustafa had left Egypt on Ismail's accession and settled in Constantinople. He was as convinced a modernizer as Ismail, and lacking his brother's responsibilities, patronized projects of constitutional reform rather than railways and canals. For his estates in Egypt he received from Ismail a loan of two million pounds. He used his wealth, enormous compared with the resources of upper-class Ottomans, to make himself the leader of advanced opinion in Constantinople. He may have envisaged becoming both Khedive (if Ismail died or was deposed) and first constitutional Prime Minister of the empire. Such ambitions irked a naturally suspicious Abdul Aziz. Now fearing his Sultan, Mustafa Fazil moved to Paris; his house became the focus of exiled Ottoman reformers.

In 1863 the revolutionary Prince had written, in French, a long letter of admonition to the Sultan, urging that the empire be reformed on constitutional lines. Translated into Turkish, this letter was widely distributed inside the empire. In a correspondence arising out of it, Mustafa threw off the term *"jeunes Turcs"* to describe his young supporters. The casual phrase Young Turks would gain currency far beyond its original significance.

So long as Mustafa Fazil was distrusted by Abdul Aziz for his radical opinions, Ismail's relations with the Sultan had been excellent. Distrust of Mustafa Fazil had been one motive prompting the Sultan to issue the disinheriting firman. But in the summer of 1867 the situation suddenly changed. Abdul Aziz visited France. Greeting his sovereign as "a faithful slave," Mustafa Fazil abdicated as a revolutionary leader and joined the Sultan's court.

This reconciliation between his disinherited half brother and the Sultan menaced Ismail. He once more had cause to fear his male relations. Mustafa Fazil was the most dangerous; but Ismail could not afford to ignore Prince Halim, the son of Muhammad Ali who had so bravely jumped into the Nile. Fortunately, both potential rivals spent money like water and this gave Ismail a useful weapon. By advancing them sums against their Egyptian estates (which they feared to visit in person), he could both buy them off and help them plunge deeper into financial ruin.

But this weapon was his only while he retained the throne of Egypt. If the Sultan deposed him, the roles would be reversed and Ismail would be the beggar.

The way Ismail planned his European tour of 1869 was tactless in the extreme. It gave Mustafa Fazil the chance of hoping for the highest rewards: not only the recovery of his estates in Egypt, but Egypt itself.

If Ismail had started his journey from Constantinople, he could have issued his invitations in the Sultan's name as well as his own. Rashly, he put the Ottoman capital at the bottom of his list, planning to visit it only when he had visited the chief capitals of Europe, including St. Petersburg, and after completing a "cure." He had compounded his blunder by making Corfu his first port of call; on that delectable island he met King George of Greece, the Sultan's persistent enemy. As Ismail swanned north through Europe, his semi-royal welcome roused the Ottoman ambassadors to a fury which was communicated to the Sultan; his various hosts, pestered by Ottoman complaints, gave him broad hints that he was behaving unwisely. He had chosen, as it happened, an unwise moment for unwisdom. A Vizir well disposed to himself had just died; his replacement, the stern Ali Pasha, resented the Khedive's flaunting of borrowed gold. In Constantinople a French-language magazine echoed the Vizir's views; Ismail, then in London, was a felon, who should be indicted for high treason. Ismail had been lodged at Buckingham Palace, not the hotel where he had stayed on a previous visit; the British Foreign Office were forced to argue, defensively, that Ismail's reception was simple politeness and in no way implied his recognition as an independent sovereign. Two Turkish pashas who had been in Ismail's employ chose this summer to abandon him; on July 12, Mustafa Fazil arrived in Constantinople to be appointed minister without portfolio. The Sultan, rumor said, was about to depose Ismail and enthrone his brother in his place.

Ismail was so alarmed that he canceled his visit to Russia, as well as his cure, and rushed back to Cairo. From Egypt he wrote to the Sultan defending his behavior.

"During my journey in Europe," he wrote, "I accepted gratefully the invitations with which some of the sovereigns had honored me; and if, when meeting them, I invited these sovereigns or some members of their august families to assist at the inauguration of the Canal, it was only in virtue of the high position which I occupy under the auspices of his Majesty. If these sovereigns by their reception have shown me any proofs of esteem and consideration, I owe it solely to the honourable position of being dependent upon his Majesty, and it is one of the happy results of the gracious favors with which he had loaded me. I may add that it is publicly known that in these circumstances no act whatever has been committed which could be construed as running counter to the sacred rights of the Sovereign—rights which I place above all else, and of which I know how to appreciate the value and importance." The Sultan had complained that in his junketing the Khedive had avoided only his own ambassadors. This was untrue, Ismail protested: in Paris he had invited Jamil Pasha and Daoud Pasha to a family dinner at his son's house.

But the Sultan was not appeased. Neither himself, his Vizir nor any minor functionary of the Ottoman Government had smiled on the opening of the Canal. Turkish crews, as much as American, had been conspicuously absent from the man-made trench.

The party over, Ismail did not have to wait long for a baleful result.

On December 9, Eugénie was back in France; the Khedive sat in his Abdin Palace study weighing the glamour of her presence against the expense. There was a knock at the door. News had arrived which could not wait. On November 29, in Constantinople, Abdul Aziz had signed a firman. After the usual grandiloquent terms of greeting and five long-winded paragraphs came a stinging sentence: "My Will is that in future no loans shall be raised until their absolute necessity has been established and unless my previous authorization has been secured."

Abdul Aziz, as extravagant as his vassal, and as doomed, had known when, and where, to strike. The desk at Abdin Palace was loaded with bills.

Chapter 4

THE quarrel between Ismail and Abdul Aziz was, on one level, a row between insecure and jealous individuals. Their duel over prestige was typical of an East where power had always been seen in personal terms; aggravated by relations and expressed through palace officials, it could, as such, be easily patched up. Brothers and uncles could be kissed and paid off; palace officials bribed. Ismail's charm and Abdul Aziz's quasi-religious awe could mix and make peace.

On a deeper level, however, this was a schism between the only two Muslim potentates who mattered in the world. The mistrust which it symbolized would outlast the persons of Abdul Aziz and Ismail. It would weaken Islamic resistance to two impersonal forces from industrial Europe—loan capitalism and colonialism—which neither Sultanate nor Khediviate was equipped to understand, let alone repulse.

The quarrel was played out, on both levels, against a shift in the European balance of power.

Ismail may not have noticed the war clouds over Europe as he scrutinized the bills, not only for the festivities and the palaces (forty-three in all) which had been built or restored since 1861, but also for the schools, hospitals, lighthouses, roads and railways he was busy building. In May 1870 he defied the Sultan's orders and raised, on the surety of his personal estates, a loan through Messrs. Bischoffsheim and Goldschmidt, the Brussels bankers; it was the fifth major loan of Ismail's reign; from a nominal seven millions sterling he received only five. The Sultan was angry. Was the imperial firman of November 1869 to be so lightly dismissed—or was it not time for the Sultan to dismiss the Khedive? Ismail's argument that the loan being raised on his own pawned land did not come under the Sultan's ban, made a point; but, for the point to convince those who needed convincing, Ismail must take himself (not forgetting his borrowed gold) to the imperial capital. This was no hardship for the Khedive; he owned a charming estate a few miles up the Bosphorus from the Golden Horn. Like the Egyptian upper class in general, Ismail disliked spending the summer in Cairo, since the rising Nile added humidity to heat. He had the means of reaching the Bosphorus in comfort. He could accompany his harem and children on the *Mahroussa,* or, preferably, send them on ahead. "The Mahroussa went well," his daughter's English governess reported; "we made fourteen knots an hour (though I believe that it is not her greatest speed). She is 44 feet long, has four engines, each of 800-horse power, and is 3550 tons burthen. A great drawback to us, however, was that two tremendous chimneys were near the centre of the vessel, so that the deck on which we passed our time lay between them. The heat was intense and the only way of escaping in some degree from it was to remain in one of the kiosks, which did not suit the young ladies at all." As the yacht passed Constantinople, the women must retreat inside, since the males in the bobbing ships and along the quays had less progressive views than the Khedive; the regulations bound even the governess, who took refuge in the chief saloon. "The windows were large, and I was enjoying the beautiful view on both sides, when, just as we were passing St. Sophia, the outer shutters slowly descended, and we were left in darkness! It was like a pall thrown over me! There was no help for it, I must pass the next hour, while going through the loveliest scenery in the world . . . as one who has lost the blessing of sight." The blessing was restored to the governess and her charges when the *Mahroussa* moored at Emirghian. Here, where the shores of the Bosphorus rose steeply from the water—running cold even in summer—the Khedive had laid out grounds in the English manner, half park, half garden. "They were on the slope of the hill—clumps of trees, open grassy swards, and flower-beds, broad gravel-paths, winding about so as to make the ascent easy, and a large piece of ornamental water, with a rockery behind. Every path commanded a beautiful view, which constantly widened as each walk rose terrace-like above the last. At the foot of the hill was the Bosphorus, which like a broad river extends for about twenty miles, connecting the Black Sea with the Sea of Marmara." The noblest view was to the southwest, where Ulu Dag, the Anatolian Olympus, was snow-capped even in summer.

On July 6 the Khedive reached Emirghian; he was in good spirits after presenting his respects to Abdul Aziz at his Dolmabahçe Palace. Topkapı at the point of old Stamboul was now the "palace of tears" in which the concubines of previous sultans lived out damp and boring lives; Dolmabahçe testified to the modernizing tastes of Mahmud II's sons, being built in a style described in contemporary guidebooks as "Bastard Corinthian"; Queen Victoria's gift, the largest chandelier in the world, hung over a carpet equally gigantic. The Khedive's gifts, in particular of money, had been well received. In return, the ambassadors were informed that the Khedive had not, after all, exceeded his rights. The occasion was improved by a reconciliation between Ismail and his brother Mustafa Fazil. Also included in the expensive kissing was Prince Abdul Halim.

But the sun glinting through the cypresses for which Emirghian was famed—so different from the dusty palms, the gloomy Bengal figs of Cairo—was suddenly darkened. The Paris telegraph announced that, since July 19, France was at war with the North Germans. By the end of August the battle of Sedan had been lost; by the first week in September Napoleon III was a prisoner and by the last the Empress, apparent fixed star in Ismail's firmament, had shifted, in astrologer's parlance, to an occluded house: a villa at Chislehurst. Paris, ringed by a Prussian army, held by Communard insurgents, would not in this year, or the next, be a stable star.

In the Middle East, repercussions from the French defeat were swift. The Czar, who had assisted Bismarck by staying neutral, felt free to plan a reversal of the Crimean defeat. The prospect of a Russian advance, involving an Ottoman collapse, alarmed Great Britain. If the empire were to collapse, if pieces were to be grabbed by Russia or Austria, then a frightened England might grab the most delectable piece of all: the Egypt of the opened Canal.

In this crisis the interests of Sultan and Khedive might have seemed to coincide; each would be weakened by the debility of the other; each could be assisted by the other's strength. But in a climate of ancient distrust neither was ready for co-operation. Ismail saw two choices for himself: either to welcome English domination, or to push forward to greater independence. Either choice would involve defiance of Constantinople.

In this predicament Ismail toyed, in secret, with an alliance calculated to outrage the Ottomans. He was in regular correspondence with the Russian ambassador in Constantinople, the same General Ignatieff who had represented the Czar at the opening of the Canal. Ignatieff strove to convince Ismail that Egypt's interests were the same as Russia's.

In the event, the next challenge to the Sultan came, not in the Balkans, where the Russians were nursing insurrections, but in Assir, the northern province of Yemen, at the southern extremity of the Ottoman domains.

(The Ottomans had never controlled the Yemeni highlands.) The Sultan sent a fleet and an armed force through the Suez Canal and south into the Red Sea. Ismail took this as a potential threat to himself and contemplated fortifying Suez. "Arm yourself!" was Ignatieff's urgent counsel. "Take all steps to prepare yourself for a lengthy war. Sign treaties of alliance with Greece, Serbia and Rumania (in this we should certainly assist you) and meanwhile resist the claims of the Sultan step by step." The Russians had long dreamed of controlling the straits between Europe and Asia; the dream would be gloriously enhanced if it included influence over the strait between Asia and Africa as well.

But the Russian ambassador deluded himself if he thought there was any grand design to Ismail's quarrel with his sovereign. What obsessed Ismail was his right to raise money where he wished, when he wished. In this he was obstructed by the reforming Vizir, Ali Pasha, whose enmity was made more formidable by his incorruptibility. To Ali Pasha, now old and sick, Ismail's openness to foreigners, his defiance of the Sultan, his corrupt use of money, symbolized the Empire's sickness.

In September 1871 this obstructive Vizir died, and with him Ismail's motives for a Russian alliance. Mahmud Pasha, soothingly venal, was the new Vizir. Once more Constantinople opened its doors to Ismail's money. But months of dedicated corruption were required before the price was fixed for Ismail's greatest coup. The price—a golden dinner service inset with gems for Abdul Aziz, fifty thousand rifles for his army, around a million sterling in cash—was but the top of an iceberg whose secret douceurs are mostly unrecorded. But their scale is indicated by the reception which Ismail offered on the anniversary of the Sultan's accession, in particular honor of his mother, the Sultana Validé. One hundred thousand lamps lit the paths of the garden at Emirghian. "They were small globular glasses, half full of water, with oil at the top, and the wick floating in it. It was the business of five hundred men to attend to these lamps. They commenced putting in the oil two days before, and there was such a dropping along the walks, as almost to overpower the scent of the roses, and remind one of an Italian warehouse. The three fine steam-yachts that lay moored without the palace were also to be illuminated." To Ismail such expenditure seemed abundantly worthwhile. In two firmans, of September 10 and 25, 1872, the Sultan gave him what he required: a financial go-ahead. "Thus henceforth," Abdul Aziz decreed, "whenever, for the wellbeing of the country, the need to raise loans shall arise, I renew and confirm the authorization for you to borrow such sums in the name of the Egyptian Government, and this without need for further consultation with myself."

In giving Ismail this authorization, Abdul Aziz acted like one alcoholic presenting a crate of whiskey to another. "From first to last," a great historian of Turkey's emergence to modern nationhood was to write, "finance was the Slough of Despond of the Turkish reformers, in which their brightest hopes were bemired, their cleverest plans befouled and engulfed." Abdul Aziz and Ismail, public reformers but personal spendthrifts, were to enter financial traps that would guillotine their reigns.

Loan capitalism, the impersonal force with bases in Brussels, Paris, Frankfurt and London, seemed to the Middle East self-assured and bountiful as some pagan god. To itself it was still newborn, feeling a cautious way in its first century of power. Finance was the affair of tight-knit clans. These clans derived for the most part from three minorities. The first in power and importance were the Jews, a group forbidden by the Mosaic Law to practice usury except to Gentiles and forced by Gentile pressure to practice little else. Such famous names as Rothschild, Oppenhiem and Bischoffsheim were balanced by names from a second group, the Huguenots, or Calvinists, of France. André and Marcuard were in turn balanced by Zafiropoulo and Vlasto, seeds of a Greek diaspora.

Since the Renaissance, European bankers had stored money, lent it on interest or assisted travelers with letters of credit drawn on their foreign branches. The new thing about nineteenth-century loan capitalism was its provision of credit for long-term development. It would be erroneous to picture its pioneers as corsairs of Mammon: they were Mammon's stewards, both prudent and staid. Their ethos, which regarded defaulting on loans as the sin against the golden calf, was shared by the vast majority of their European contemporaries, who saw thrift as a virtue and waste as a sin. With reluctance and apprehension the loan capitalists had provided financial backing for the chief work of the 1840s: the building of railways. The triumph of this enterprise increased their self-confidence. At the same time the conditions of international trade turned their attention from America and Europe to the Middle and Far East. Great Britain took the lead in this shift of interest. For in the late 1850s British exports to the United States shrank by almost a third while her exports to India increased from twelve thousand pounds sterling in 1857 to twenty-one thousand two years later. The Civil War accentuated this trend; British imports from the United States fell from forty-nine million pounds sterling in 1861 to eighteen million in 1864. Simultaneously the East became of the utmost importance. Indian exports to Britain soared from twenty-two to fifty-two million pounds sterling in the same short period. Compared with India, Egypt was small and underpopulated. Yet by 1865 she came third to France and India as a source of British imports.

This newly important trading area, whose rulers thought of luxury and whose peasants produced commodities without which English workshops would have to close—was wide open to Western penetration. There were risky fortunes for the picking. The area lacked a modern banking system. Instead, moneylenders charged between 12 to 20 per cent on the safest ventures; it was quite usual to demand between 3 and 4 per cent a month;

while the peasants, who had to borrow each year on their hoped-for harvest, were charged anything up to 6 per cent a month.

In this situation the stewards of a better organized Mammon could serve their own interests and the peoples of the East at the same time. Or so they assured themselves.

Abdul Aziz, the first ruler to be snared, presided over a rickety financial structure. Throughout the nineteenth century the Ottoman currency steadily lost value in terms of the pound sterling. From 1816 to 1839, in the reign of Abdul Aziz's father, the rate for the Ottoman piaster had slumped from twenty-three to 104 to the pound sterling. Under Abdul Aziz, and particularly after the death of Ali Pasha, borrowing and spending gained locomotive speed. By the autumn of 1875 the Ottoman debt to foreign creditors had reached the figure, astronomical for those days, of two hundred million gold liras. The interest on this debt was fourteen million a year. In addition there was a floating debt of between twelve and twenty millions. Not all this borrowed money had been frivolously spent. Famines in Anatolia had demanded relief; soldiers engaged in war needed supplies.

Things reached a climax in 1875. On October 5 Mahmud Pasha admitted, through a haze of reassuring promises, the virtual bankruptcy of the Ottoman state. Its creditors were in effect compelled to grant a new long-term loan of dubious reliability. Under Mahmud's terms creditors would receive half their interest in gold for the next five years, and half in paper with 5 per cent interest. As surety for these promised payments the Imperial Ottoman Bank would hold in trust the revenues accruing from indirect taxation, the Egyptian tribute, whose annual £650,000 was paid through the Bank of England, and what was needed to make up the rest from the Sheep Tax.

The pledge angered creditors under the earlier Ottoman loans, since the Egyptian tribute had already been set aside for them. The measure as a whole ruined Ottoman credit. When, in the following spring, the government needed urgently to raise three million liras, no one would lend at less than 24 per cent interest.

Financial circles were not only shocked at the Ottoman collapse; they sent financial physicians to advise on the disease—and take advantage of it. A Herr Schenck, acting for Messrs. Hirsch of Frankfurt, offered to buy the railroad already built in the Ottoman Balkans and to put up the necessary capital to complete the Vienna–Constantinople link. Schenck suggested a significant compensation: the Sultan would be asked to cede a belt of land several miles wide on both sides of the railway line. This would be set aside for "colonization."

The Schenck plan (it left unclear who would do the colonizing) was unacceptable to the Sultan, who, however bankrupt, remained a sovereign; nor did it suit the interests of Russia. It was rejected.

English financiers, first a Mr. Hammond, then the firm of Palmer, Rose and Taniforth, proposed what they hoped would be more acceptable. A "Caisse Hypothecaire," with a capital of four millions, would make itself responsible for debt collecting. But this plan, too, violated Ottoman interests. It introduced a "separate and alien administration" into the country, as grave an infringement on Ottoman sovereignty as the Schenck proposal. It also threatened to revive the discredited practice of tax farming.

The financial drama was accompanied by gloomy happenings in the Balkans. During the centuries of Ottoman rule a considerable proportion of the Balkan peoples had, for one reason or another, embraced Islam; though referred to as "Turks," these Balkan Muslims were for the most part Bulgars, Macedonians or Slavs who identified themselves with the Ottoman state; their Christian fellow countrymen had become increasingly restless under Ottoman rule; in turn their restlessness made Ottoman rule more oppressive and unrest then turned to revolt. A series of nationalist risings, successors to the Greek revolt of the 1820s, gained sympathy abroad.

On May 5, 1876 a Bulgarian girl arrived in Salonika on a purpose which in earlier times would have been normal, and if resented, resented silently. She had decided to turn Muslim and to formalize her conversion by declaring, "I testify there is no god but God and Muhammad is the Prophet of God," before the Islamic authorities. The Salonika Christians got wind of the intended apostasy and seized the girl; a mob of Muslims tried to get her back. In the sectarian confusion the French and German consuls, suspected of being party to an anti-Muslim plot, were murdered.

The outrage shocked a Europe already convinced of Ottoman bad faith in money matters. Warships anchored off Salonika while French and German soldiers patrolled the streets. The consuls were buried with Christian pomp and several Muslims executed after a trial.

The Ottomans were far from being the self-confident brutes imagined in Western Europe. Admittedly ineffectual as reformers, they were sincerely horrified by the murder of the consuls; they were genuinely perplexed about what to do in their rebellious provinces. They, no less than the Europeans, were smarting from the steady devaluation of the Ottoman currency. On Wednesday, May 30, an incredulous Abdul Aziz, hiding in the harem at Dolmabahçe Palace, was forced by a group of patriotic notables to abdicate. He was at once transferred, with boatloads of his women, to the "palace of tears" at Topkapı. His replacement, Murad V, was a neurotic youth terrified by his new role as Sultan. Murad readily agreed to his uncle's request for pleasanter quarters; that same night Abdul Aziz was shuffled up-Bosphorus to the palace of Cheragan, between Dolmabahçe and Emirghian. This, too, displeased him and he obtained permission for a further transfer to the palace on the Asian side where he had lodged Eugénie the summer of her Egyptian visit. Too late! On Sunday morning, only five days after his deposition, Abdul Aziz was found dead in his Cheragan apartments.

The new government—its chief figure was Midhat Pasha, the greatest Ottoman reformer of the nineteenth century—was rightly alarmed. Whether innocent or guilty of the Sultan's death, the reformers knew that at some time they might be blamed for it. Nineteen physicians, including European doctors attached to embassies, were hastily conveyed to the room where the dead Sultan lay. Afterwards all nineteen signed a document affirming that the dead man was indeed Abdul Aziz and putting on record what they had seen. "We found a body lying on a mattress, which was placed on the floor; this body was covered with a new sheet . . . There were limpid streaks of blood upon the arms and legs . . . We were shown a pair of scissors, ten centimeters in length, very sharp, and of which one of the blades had a small lateral knob near the extremity. These scissors were stained with blood, and we were told that it was with the aid of this instrument that the late Sultan Abdul Aziz had inflicted upon himself the wounds above described . . . We are unanimously of the opinion, first, that the death of the ex-Sultan Abdul Aziz was occasioned by the haemorrhage of the vessels of the bends of the arms; secondly, that the instrument which was shown to us might precisely produce those wounds; thirdly, the direction and nature of the wounds, as well as the instrument which was said to have produced them, caused us to come to the conclusion that the case is one of suicide."

Although the examination was cursory—the clerics praying over the royal corpse had prevented a close examination—the introduction of specialist witnesses was something new in a country where the inconvenient were traditionally bundled into sacks and dropped in the Bosphorus; but neither the doctors' statement nor the rectitude of Midhat Pasha dispelled all doubts. Suicide is extremely rare among Muslims, who are schooled from early years to accept what fate, or God, decrees; the suicide of a Caliph had no precedent. The examination was less than ideal: the Sultan's body had been lifted from his mother's arms, in which he had died, on to the mattress described. The wounds, though consistent with a frenzied suicide, could have been inflicted by assassins.

The counting-house collapse, the palace violence, were echoed in the subsidence of Ottoman authority in the Balkans. Officials of the sinking empire burned villages, took hostages, shot spies, tortured suspects, used, in brief, the methods that rising empires would employ in the coming century. But at this moment of Ottoman disgrace Europe could afford the ringing tones of moral indignation. A self-righteous typhoon swept from Gladstone's England, boding as ill for Egyptians as for Turks. In a pamphlet, dedicated to the British ambassador who had fought the Suez Canal, Gladstone expressed what seems, ninety years later, exaggerated humbug, but which then carried force:

"Let the Turks now carry away their abuses in the only possible manner —namely, by carrying off themselves. Their *Zaptiehs* and their *Mudirs,* their *Bimbashis* and their *Yuzbachis,* their *Kaimakams* and their *Pashas,* one and all, bag and baggage, shall, I hope, clear out from the province they have desolated and profaned . . . There is not a criminal in a European gaol, there is not a cannibal in the South Sea islands, whose indignation would not rise and overboil at the recital of that which has been done . . . We may ransack the annals of the world, but I know not what research can furnish us with so portentous an example of the fiendish misuse of the powers established by God 'for the punishment of evildoers and for the encouragement of them to do well.' No Government has ever so sinned; none has so proved itself incorrigible to sin, or, which is the same, so impotent for reformation."[1]

Murad V, tender-conscienced as Gladstone but less articulate, was unhinged by the manner of his uncle's death; after a three-months reign he was deposed on the grounds of insanity and replaced by his younger, and abler, brother, Abdul Hamid II.

No Sultan, however able, could prevent further erosion of Ottoman territory; but Ottoman sovereignty, skillfully defended by Abdul Hamid, could prevent the imposition of direct control over its financial and political affairs. Egypt's lack of such sovereignty, the humiliation that nagged Ismail as it nagged his grandfather Muhammad Ali, gave Europe the opportunity to apply an amalgam of Schenck's plans and Hammond's to the finances and then the destiny of a dependent country.

For the discredit attaching to the Sultan had spilt over on to his vassal. Egyptian securities, though not intrinsically vulnerable, fluctuated wildly. Within weeks of the Ottoman crisis Ismail was confronted with a crisis of his own. The merchant bankers, previously so generous with loans, refused to advance any more.

Desperate, Ismail looked round for something to pawn; he lighted on the one asset he should have held on to for dear life. Raphael Borg, a Maltese working in Cairo as "legal vice-consul" for the British, learnt that the Khedive had in mind to raise money on his founder's shares in the Suez Canal Company. Borg pestered the British consul and the latter finally cabled the news to London, where it fell under Disraeli's eye. The Prime Minister contacted the Rothschilds, who offered to buy the shares outright on behalf of the British Government. Despite Gladstone's opposition, the deal went through. Ismail received four million pounds.

---

[1] Gladstone might have produced worse examples if he had consulted, even casually, his considerable library; he would have needed gifts of prophecy to foresee twentieth-century examples. A great rhetor, he used strange-sounding names, here italicized, to make sinister what were, in fact, the normal adjutants of empire: governors, district commissioners and colonels.

For a short-term profit of half a million (on his original price) Ismail had lost his country.

If he did not sense it, others did. The Russians, for example, in a December issue of the Moscow *Gazette:* "The strange mystery which has so long enveloped the actions of the British Cabinet in connection with the Eastern Question has given way at last to perfect candour. England, who has so long and so jealously guarded the sick man, suddenly goes off on the opposite tack and buries him alive. England, who has so long kept watch and ward on the property of the Sultan,[2] all at once adopts a different course and pockets her coveted share of the spoil." The Russian editorialist was particularly struck by the legal innovation involved. "There is no precedent of a Government acquiring a share in a joint-stock enterprise on foreign soil, and thereby virtually extending its own territory." It was a question whether the Khedive even had the right to sell a portion of his sovereign's property.

In getting involved in financial transactions with a European government, and not with individual Jews, Calvinists or Greeks, Ismail had taken the step beyond recall.

A transfusion of money could not solve his problems; the new four millions drained into a marsh so trackless, so squelchy, that guesses varied as to whether Ismail's debts amounted to eighty or a hundred millions. On April 8, 1876, the Khedive announced suspension of payment on his treasury bills. A khedivial decree of May 2 instituted a Commission of the Public Debt. A further decree, five days later, consolidated the debt at £91 million.

Ismail was seemingly unaware of his peril. The Sultanate, if not the Sultan, had scraped home. Why shouldn't he?

Long blind to Egypt's essential poverty, he was now deaf to clamant voices in a changing Europe. For generations Europe had been convinced that it offered the world the best in everything, including constitutions; increasingly industrialized, with surplus wealth and surplus labor, it was collectively convinced that it must use its surplus labor and wealth to assume the burden of more backward societies. The new nations, Germany and Italy, as much as Britain and France, saw the test of nationhood in the acquisition of colonies overseas. Russia acquired hers at the expense of contiguous peoples in the Crimea, the Caucasus and Central and East Asia.

To taste this forgotten mood we may nibble not at the large but the little; following the advice of Maxim Gorki that the moon is best described if shown reflected in a broken bottle on a muddy river bank.

In 1876 Rome had only just become the capital of a united Italy. The new Italians, no longer Neapolitans, Piedmontese or Sicilians, saw them-

[2] The "Porte" in the original.

selves as heirs of a glorious past which could be proved by contemporary expansion. More caustic observers, such as Germany's Bismarck, saw them as carrion-fed vultures, haunting battlefields for leftovers.

One such idealistic vulture was a Neapolitan architect, Francesco de Lorenzo, who in October 1876, two years after Disraeli's purchase of the Canal shares, published a pamphlet at his own expense: *A Memorial on the Present Position of the Italian Colony in Egypt.* De Lorenzo saw the Italians as being pushed aside by the British, the French and even the Americans. (A large number of exiled southern gentlemen were employed by Ismail.) A first-class diplomat was needed to defend, in Egypt, Italian interests. With economic prescience De Lorenzo argued: "On the coasts of the Red Sea, but still within the Khedive's boundaries, there is petrol; long ago our people should have secured the concession." From the Red Sea, Italian settlers could edge into Abyssinia and gradually take it over. An Italian agricultural colony had already been established, with the Negus's permission, inside Abyssinia in the "Schiotel" area. This colony, thirty leagues square, had failed through lack of support and the unsuccessful colonists had slunk back to Italy by way of Cairo. If only there had been a worthy ambassador accredited to the Khedive, these colonists could have settled in Egypt. Ismail would surely welcome Italians as a counterweight to *"una certa potenza"* (De Lorenzo alludes to the formidable British as "a certain Power"), so threatening to his interests.

De Lorenzo's hope was an Italian geographical expedition then in Africa. If this joined forces with the Italian bishop (who was already respected by the local ruler), a new Italian concession might be forthcoming. But a geographer and a bishop were not enough: they must be matched by the dispatch of Italian warships to the Red Sea and the appointment of an energetic ambassador in Cairo. (One can surmise who De Lorenzo had in mind.) The British and others would object: but without result. Italy would have proved "that the homeland of Machiavelli is still that of the Italians." Backed by the moral authority of the state, a capitalist company based in Naples, "would extend its nets from Egypt to the utmost limits of Abyssinia, thus obtaining a monopoly of the trade in Khartoum, Kordofan and Darfur." De Lorenzo's schemes were neatly designed for profit and Italian *amour propre*. Italy must think big: "An eagle does not hunt flies!" The role of the Italians in the new areas is spelt out: "The East has workers; what it lacks is intelligence, that is: the trained artisan, the professional man, the capitalist: we possess such specialised personnel in plenty; with their help we could win for Italy supremacy and money." De Lorenzo had no use for humanitarian scruples: a tiresome instance had been the recent Geographic Congress in Brussels, when speaker after speaker seemed preoccupied with native peoples and their picturesque folkways. Abyssinia produced, beyond the daily needs of its inhabitants, the raw materials most required abroad. Its fertile land had dozed through the centuries; now, thanks to the Canal, it had been opened to Italy.

De Lorenzo's pamphlet ends with a tiny pinch of incense to nineteenth-century ideals:

"If only our compatriots could implant a colony in the Nile valley, particularly in Abyssinia, where former concessions would ease its way, what new lustre would not return to our fatherland? What new impulse would not be given to the extension of civilisation to these remote and all but barbaric lands?"

Ismail was too busy conferring with a succession of financial physicians from England and France to read this pamphlet. If he had read it, he would not have discerned its underlying assumptions. Its surface assumptions would have been to his taste. For Ismail had been dabbling on colonialism on his own account, recognizing it as part and parcel of the modernity he loved. In 1869 he had entrusted a British general in his employ, Sir Valentine Baker, with an invasion in depth of Central Africa. In 1875, the very winter of financial discontent, he authorized two Massawa-based invasions of Abyssinia, the second under his third son, Prince Hassan. Both were ignominious failures. In launching them, as in his dreams of rule over Uganda and Zanzibar, Ismail revealed an atavistic conception of wealth. He had no realization of how little immediate profit could be gained from De Lorenzo's "remote and all but barbaric lands." Commodities such as elephant tusks and Negro slaves were either too rare or too discredited to seal the broken dike of Egypt's credit.

What sealed the dike (and Ismail's fate) was European preparedness to intervene on behalf of his creditors. Faced with this challenge Ismail was limited by his upbringing. He might, if he had acted in time, have united his country around him to fight off the foreigners. He, if anyone, could have done it. He was genuinely popular; even his tyranny, his extortion, were forgiven since they were part of an authoritarian splendor such as the East has always loved. But to have achieved this transformation of his power he would have had to consider the Egyptians as people, and not as serfs. He was to try this last card, but when it was too late to play it well.

For two years he played instead with the foreigners, sagely nodding at their suggestions. He got rid of his worst encumbrance, Sadeek Pasha, his Minister of Finance. This one-time fellah had been Ibrahim Pasha's steward before becoming Ismail's chief tax collector. Sadeek was a master of the ungentle art of squeezing, with whip and menace, their last piasters from his fellow countrymen. In the process he had amassed an ostentatious fortune; his palace and harem rivaled his master's. Sadeek's least reputable scheme for raising money had been a tax known as the Moukabala, introduced in 1871. Under it, landlords were promised that if only they would pay double their scheduled land tax for the next twelve critical years, their tax liability thereafter would be halved. This scheme was dishonest: no one could bind future governments to honoring Sadeek's expedient. It was also unpractical: few fellahin had the reserves of cash which would let them take advantage of the promise, if they believed it. Instead of a hoped-for thirty million, only eight million pounds were raised. Now in 1876 Ismail sacrificed Sadeek. He invited his powerful minister to join him for an afternoon ride. The carriage drove up, when the ride was over, at the palace where Eugénie had been lodged in 1869, and Sadeek was placed under arrest. If, as is possible, he was murdered there and then, the Khedive's agents covered up his death ingeniously. Reports were made to reach Cairo from a distant prison, first of the ex-minister's failing health, then of his mortal illness, and at last of his demise.

But the disappearance of a minister could not save Ismail. Everything went badly. The Nile was low in 1877 and by 1878 there was famine in Upper Egypt. "It is not possible," wrote a British observer, "to state how many died from actual starvation, for in no instance does the death-register show a death by starvation, but I am satisfied that the excessive mortality during the period of scarcity was caused by dysentery and other diseases brought on by insufficient and unwholesome food. The poor were in some instances reduced to such extremities of hunger that they were driven to satisfy their cravings with the refuse and garbage of the streets."

By the end of 1878 Ismail was forced to accept the findings of foreign commissioners and submit to rule by bailiffs. His own vast estates were placed in final pawn; members of his family offered the income on their estates; and a government headed by Nubar Pasha but dominated by two European ministers was installed. The British minister was Sir Rivers Wilson; the French, a M. de Blignières. To the former, Ismail made a last pathetic gesture of collaboration. "Egypt is no longer in Africa," he said. "It is part of Europe. It is proper, therefore, to abandon old ways and to adopt a new system, more in accordance with our social progress." But behind its facade of good intentions the new system had one overriding purpose: to squeeze Egypt in the interests of the foreign bondholders. Petitions and protests from the Muslim clergy as well as from delegates to a rudimentary parliament (its functions consultative only) reminded Ismail of his forgotten card: popular support. The backbone of this support was provided by the native-born army officers, who resented the rule of foreigners and their dependence on ministers like Nubar, an Armenian, and Riaz, a Turk of reputedly Jewish origin. Such Egyptian officers expressed their resentment with some violence on February 18, when they dragged Nubar Pasha and Sir Rivers Wilson from their carriage and roughed them up; the Khedive's personal intervention saved them from worse. Impressed by this new mood, Ismail dismissed the government which foreign pressure had imposed on him and announced a new one, under his direct control, and with it a scheme of his own for paying his creditors.

But Ismail had underestimated the mood, not in Egypt only, but in Europe. Europe's first retaliatory blow was struck by Bismarck. Germany, the Chancellor announced, would not stand for the Khedive's repudiation of the agreed financial measures and the ministry entrusted with their enforcement. One by one the other Powers wrote similar protests. Only Italy, either impressed by De Lorenzo's arguments, or grateful for Ismail's admiration for things Italian, confined her protest to the spoken word.

In vain Ismail spoke of introducing constitutional rule. In vain he appealed to the Rothschilds to divert existing loans to the payment of his floating debt. (This would have removed the grievances of the European Powers except for England and France, whose ministers had been insulted.) In vain he offered Cleopatra's second needle, the Egyptian obelisk standing at Alexandria, as a gift to the American Government for erection in New York.

His last hope was his sovereign, the new Sultan Abdul Hamid. Only the year before the Sultan had lost Bosnia and Herzegovina to Austria, Cyprus to England. He could read the lesson of those losses in one of two ways. He could either back Ismail, in a gesture of defiance to Europe; or he could prudently ditch him.

Ismail waited.

Towards the end of June the London *Times* correspondent, based in Alexandria, described the atmosphere he had found in Cairo. "Here all kinds of rumours were afloat. Abdication, deposition, and intervention were words in every mouth, and the funds were going up, point after point, on the chance of any change. At Cairo, to my surprise, I found everybody still more excited, in spite of the heat. The inside of the houses was like an oven and the outside like a furnace, and the whole European world was grumbling at the sun save one little knot of Englishmen, whose task is to keep the Egyptian world straight and who think they cannot do their duty save under the daily stimulus of a violent game of lawn-tennis."

The *Times* assessed the situation with knowledgeable caution. Ismail deserved respect for his achievements and also pity as "victim of circumstances and a vicious surrounding." But he was responsible in the eyes of the world for a failure: "and diplomacy, which has no heart, listens to no extenuating circumstances." What would come next? "Towfik Pasha, who is now talked of as a successor to his father, is described as an amiable young man and a good landowner, with a taste for economy and a liking for schools . . . But Ismail Pasha, the present ruler, before he came to the throne, fully merited the same praise." The Powers were faced with a greater challenge than a mere change of rule. "Egypt as she is now would be a fatal gift to any man. The two Powers must either not advance at all or they must advance very far." If England were unwilling to assume the total burden, "she had better be content with an open water-way from Port Said to Suez, and let the French bankers and the rest of the bond-holders get out of their financial scrape in the way people do when they have made an unfortunate speculation."

But the Powers had made their decision. On June 19 the British and French consuls-general in Cairo called on Ismail and advised him to abdicate. If he refused, they could not guarantee a pension for himself and the throne for his sons. Rumors weighted their threats. Prince Abdul Halim had powerful supporters. If the Sultan revoked the firman of 1866 he, as Muhammad Ali's son, would replace Towfik in the line of succession.

Ismail asked for forty-eight hours in which to ponder his reply. In hoping for a last-minute miracle from Constantinople, he hoped in vain. Abdul Hamid was pleased to get rid of Ismail. He hoped by doing so to restore Egypt to a more dependent position. His only fear was that he might seem to be acting under foreign pressure.

As soon as the Sultan's telegram deposing Ismail and promoting Towfik reached Abdin Palace, Ismail packed his bags; his harem, or as much of it as he wanted, was prepared for foreign parts.

As the khedivial curtain fell, Europe's eyes were elsewhere. The *Illustrated London News* had published pages on the ceremonies at Port Said; its engravers now had a theme from the other end of Africa. On June 20 news reached England of the death, almost three weeks before, of the exiled Eugénie's only son, the twenty-three-year-old Prince Imperial. The Prince, in the uniform of a British officer, had been killed by Zulu assegais in a minor colonial clash. Engravings filled page after page: The Last Bivouac; At Bay (with the Prince fighting off ugly black men); the "Chapelle Morte" on the *SS Orontes;* the arrival of the coffin at Woolwich Arsenal; the Soldiers' Last Homage to the Dead.

Ismail's departure on June 30 got cold gray print instead of the illustration it deserved.

In the East it was customary for the incoming ruler to receive the applause, the outgoing, oblivion. This rule was reversed for Ismail. There was no enthusiasm for Towfik, though 101 guns saluted his accession. The throngs were for his father. The road to the station was lined with those weeping farewell to a myth as much as to a man. The station square filled as carriage after carriage brought the veiled ladies of the harem. The only person who kept his calm was the Khedive. To avoid the crowds at Alexandria, he was smuggled to the docks by way of obscure back streets. Foreign warships saluted as the *Mahroussa,* laden with his possessions, got up steam. Ismail had been offered a choice of Bursa, the first Ottoman capital, or Smyrna, the rich Aegean city, for his place of exile. He had chosen Smyrna. At the last minute his plans were altered. Ismail was abruptly told that he was unwelcome in the Sultan's domains. He would have to go to Italy instead. Accommodation at the Royal Hotel, Naples, was engaged by cable.

What did Ismail leave behind him as Alexandria faded in the African dusk? A pyramid of debts: this was the answer of a generation whose tone would not recapture the objectivity of *The Times*. "His greatest title to remembrance in history," so Hugh Chisholm concluded his essay in the Encyclopaedia Britannica of thirty years later, "must be that he made European intervention in Egypt compulsory." Chisholm wrote when the *Titanic* was still abuilding and when the Pax Britannica ruled a quarter of the globe. Ismail's extravagance was stressed and his achievements belittled. His expenditure of sixteen millions on the Canal was approved: but nothing else. Not the twelve million spent on irrigation canals; not the six million spent on his sixty-four sugar mills, all equipped with the latest machinery. The British ignored, while they used, a rail network extended by Ismail from 250 to 1,200 miles, a telegraph network covering 3,000 miles in Egypt and over a thousand in the Sudan, and a handful of harbors modernized at the Khedive's command. They raised eyebrows at his schools (including the first for women in the Islamic East), deploring their curricula, their creation of newspaper-readers.

Half a century after Chisholm's verdict, by the 1960s, the European empires would have gone: except for the Portuguese, as late for decolonization as for the inauguration of the Canal. Britain would sigh resignedly when she owed in a month what Ismail had taken sixteen years to squander. Colonialism would have become a dirty word and living beyond one's means would be commended.

What did Ismail take with him? An English proconsul: "eight million pounds." Certainly his exile was not penurious. After some time the Sultan allowed him to live, albeit under surveillance, at Emirghian. His charm, his magical money, his intrigues, would frighten his successors till, safely dead in 1895, he could be given an Egyptian funeral. He was buried near his mother in the Rifai Mosque, two minutes' walk from the house where he was born. From his marble tomb his shadow would reach halfway across the twentieth century. In 1952 his grandson, Farouk, the last of his family to rule, would be deposed. A porphyry pedestal for his gigantic statute dominates Cairo's largest square, untenanted still.

Ismail took with him a sadder burden than eight million pounds or the proof that Europe had to intervene in Egyptian affairs. Ismail had dreamed of reconciling, not merely joining, two different seas: in his vision, European Christians would meet Middle Eastern Muslims as equals; the Mass and the Koran could praise the same God in different terms. In the coming century Ismail's dream would seem crushed by his fate. The European states had acted as bailiffs for bankers who had foreclosed on their loans; they had taken over province after province of the Ottoman Empire; only

Turkish-speaking Anatolia and a fragment of Thrace would survive the ruin of the First World War by becoming a nation-state with European laws, letters and hats, but without a sultan or a caliph. Of the empire's Arabic-speaking provinces only backward Yemen and desert Arabia would retain their independence. Egypt and the Levant, Libya, Tunisia and Iraq would join Algeria in subject status. Palestine would be awarded as a national home to the long dispersed Jews. Muslims would still be impressed, as Ismail had been, by the manners and morals of the West—though the West would expand to include America, not only England and France. Where he built an opera and wore a frock coat, they would build cinemas and sport the changing fashions of Paris and New York. But on the political level the people of the Middle East would sense a brutal challenge: they must either give in, or they must resist.

BOOK TWO

The Occupation of Egypt

From the very beginning our empire was founded upon fraud.
AUSTEN HENRY LAYARD, *discoverer of Nineveh,*
The Observer, *30 August 1857*

*Do not attempt to do us any more good. Your good has done us
too much harm already.*
SHEIKH MUHAMMAD ABDUH, *Egyptian reformer,*
in London, 1884

*It is neither East, nor West, nor any one quarter of the world,
but the lust of adventure and the love of enterprise that are calling to the men of our race. Every undeveloped people, every un-
explored country is calling. Athens and Rome, long centuries ago,
heard that call, and followed it. We are treading, not unworthily
let us hope, where free and fearless men of old have trod before
us. Wherever there are to be found great areas peopled by
strange tribes, wherever mighty rivers roll from sources little visited by man, wherever seemingly illimitable forests bar the way
to human intercourse, wherever the mystery and the fascination
of the unknown or the unfamiliar are felt—all such lands are calling to adventurous spirits among us, for whom there is little room
in the crowded field at home, or who prefer to the well-worn
paths of the old world the hazards and the freedom of a world
which is to them new. A century ago it was—as it still is—India;
today Nigeria, East Africa, Rhodesia, the Egyptian Sudan are
calling.*

SIR AUCKLAND COLVIN, K.C.S.J., K.C.M.G., C.J.E.
*Late Lieutenant-Governor of the North-West
Frontier and Oudh;
Formerly Financial Member of the Council of
the Viceroy of India;
British Comptroller-General
in India; and Financial Adviser to H. H. the
Khedive—in* The Making of Modern Egypt (*1906*).

Chapter 1

THE first target of resistance proved to be Ismail's son, the new Khedive Towfik. In an unparalleled assertion of independence, an Egyptian of fellah origin challenged the Khedive and the arbitrary power he represented. The collision between Towfik, sixth member of his dynasty to rule from Cairo, and Ahmed Orabi, first fellah colonel, was to have as rich, if more delayed results, as the blending of the Red Sea with the Mediterranean.

In September 1881, Orabi seemed, at forty-one, a typical burly, slow-moving delta peasant, in his demeanor and manners more like a village cleric than a military man; his skin had a swarthy darkness which Egyptians compare to the color of wheat; during the monotonous centuries in which his forebears had bent over the rich delta soil, the only admixture to his family's blood had come from the Arabs, who migrated into Egypt after the country's conversion to Islam in the seventh century; this reputed Arab blood gave him a politically helpful claim to be a *Sayid,* a man with arguable descent from the family of the Prophet. Orabi's early experience had been entirely Egyptian: boyhood in the township of Horiya (not far from the place where the Israelites had labored to make bricks without straw), where his father was a village notable and small-scale landlord; study at al-Azhar in Cairo, the nine-hundred-years-old Islamic university whose turbaned sheikhs taught the world's best Arabic and subtly expounded the Koran. Though he had never toiled in the fields, Orabi would—however long he lived, however far he progressed—be known to the country's rulers as a "fellah." This term, from an Arabic verb meaning to cultivate, carried with it a caste society's limitations: These had excluded the fellah from military service at least since Roman times, when the two most famous Egyptian soldiers had been saints: Mena, a legionary officer, was martyred after conversion to Christianity and consequent refusal to bear arms; Pachomius, a retired centurion, initiated a rigorous, barracklike form of the monastic life. After the Arab conquest, military service was the privilege of the Arabian tribesmen who brought the new religion, and later of slaves imported from the Caucasus or the Sudan. The fellahin, armed only with staves, had been spectators at the drama of Egyptian history. They played no active role in such climacteric events as the Ottoman conquest in the early sixteenth century or the Napoleonic invasion at the end of the eighteenth. On both occasions they had contented themselves with chanting prayers, first against the Turks and then against the French.

This situation had changed, as we have seen, when Muhammad Ali allowed the fellahin (though "forced" might be a better verb) to become the cannon fodder of his aggressive armies. This was further changed by his overweight son Said, who, besides opening the Isthmus of Suez to De Lesseps, opened the officer corps to Egyptians. To command the second generation of the new model army, Said appointed some officers, like Ahmed Orabi, of fellah stock; they did not replace the Turks and Albanians (with a sprinkling of Europeans converted to Islam) on whom Muhammad Ali had relied, but worked alongside them in uneasy partnership.

Orabi had been a tall, well-grown lad of fourteen when summoned to the colors from his studies at al-Azhar. (These left him with a command of classical Arabic, which he was to use, on a people uniquely sensitive to the power of words, with considerable effect.) Thanks to the Pasha's personal interest, the young man's rise had been meteoric: lieutenant at seventeen, captain at eighteen, lieutenant-colonel (or *caimakam,* in Turkish) at twenty. Orabi had been privileged to accompany his portly master as aide-de-camp when Said had visited the Prophet's tomb in Medina.

Said Pasha's sudden death blighted Orabi's career. Ismail, shrewder than his uncle, sensed that it was unwise to have his state protected by the fellahin whom it exploited. He reverted to the policy of appointing officers from the same alien stock as himself. Only on one occasion late in his reign had Ismail favored the fellah colonel. For arranging the demonstration against Nubar and Rivers Wilson in 1878, Orabi was rewarded with a bride from Ismail's well-stocked harem.

There is no reason to attribute even a touch of military genius to Orabi. In the words of an Englishman who knew him well, and who admired him for his defiance of Towfik: "He was absolutely without military education of a modern type, or experience beyond that of the common barrack-room routine, and he would, I imagine, have been quite unable to manoeuvre a division had he been called upon to do so even on parade." His experience of war was limited to a support role in the ill-fated Abyssinian campaign conducted by Ismail's son Prince Hassan.

Yet Orabi's mastery of words and dogged moral courage put him in the forefront of a campaign, not against enemies on the frontier, but against officers in the Egyptian army who used their non-Egyptian blood as a magic ichor providing privilege and rank. (It will be convenient to call these officers "Circassian," though this term properly belongs to Muslims from the Caucasus, while many of the caste were Turks, Albanians or Kurds.) The Circassians resented their Egyptian brother-officers, whom they saw as parvenus pushing in where they had no hereditary right to be. In return, the Egyptians—or fellahin, as they were sneeringly called—resented the privileges granted to arrogant aliens.

Tension between the two factions existed from the beginning: a Circassian would not think of allowing his daughter to marry a fellah, even if he were his equal in military rank. The tension sharpened when financial retrenchment, ordained from Europe, blasted Ismail's schemes for an African empire based on expanded military force. Orabi emerged as spokesman for the large number of Egyptian officers who were put on half pay.

Orabi's opponent, the Khedive Towfik, differed from him in everything except religion. Towfik had the pallor of the palace-born; the corpulence that cursed his family already promised to blur his features to a mask only distinguishable by its short, overall beard, to turn his body into a formless sack. While Orabi spoke two varieties of Arabic—the humorous colloquial of coffeeshop and house, the liturgical sonority of the mosque—Towfik's mother tongue was the Ottoman Turkish of the harem, a tongue suited for intrigue, for serpentine thoughts lurking amidst the honeyed clichés of the East.

Yet if Orabi had known contempt from brother-officers, Towfik had known something of the same in the harem. Almost as much as a fellah, he had reasons for self-doubt, for what the coming century would call an inferiority complex. This was because his mother, a Turkish concubine, was only raised to the status of wife when she bore Ismail his first son. The Khedive's three existing wives did not recognize her ennoblement. The woman was snubbed and her offspring belittled. Unlike his half brothers, Hussein Kamil, Hassan and Fuad, Towfik was not sent abroad for his education; he was never at ease in foreign cities and with foreign ways as his brothers were. In probable reaction against the harem, where he had been so unhappy, he only married one wife, the granddaughter of Abbas. When he took over from Ismail, he hastened to disband what was left of his father's harem by marrying off its members to those he wished to honor; with uncharacteristic extravagance he paid for the wedding parties of innumerable khedivial women. He wrongly assumed that these brides bought loyalty to himself.

The time and place for the collision between Khedive and Colonel Orabi was chosen by the colonel. Towfik was spending the summer at Ras el-Tin in Alexandria; the palace overlooking the harbor was cooled by the dominant north wind. He resented being summoned back to the capital, where the flooding Nile had filled the ancient canal which still bisected the city and whose evaporating waters gave off a noisome stench. But trouble in the army was too serious to be ignored. The colonel had informed his sovereign that he would present him with a petition outside his palace of Abdin. This further annoyed Towfik. Abdin was one of the many palaces his father had left him: a large, sprawling edifice on the edge of old Cairo. Towfik preferred, as residence, Kasrel-Nil, the cool palace wing of a barracks complex by the Nile, safely in the heart of the modern city. Abdin was now reserved for official functions alone. But Orabi had chosen his site with deliberation. If he was the first fellah to defy a Khedive, he was not the first fellah to serve one; the fate of Sadeek, the inspector of finances whom Ismail had disposed of, cautioned prudence. He would come to the rendezvous well attended; the square outside Abdin could accommodate a considerable military force. It also stood on the edge of the old city, where Orabi felt at home: the Cairo of mosques and narrow, crowded streets stretching in an intimate tangle to the Citadel of Muhammad Ali. Abdin Square was as much the demarcation point between two worlds as the Suez Isthmus between two seas. As the spokesman of native Egypt, Orabi preferred to meet the Khedive here rather than at Kasrel-Nil. There was one other reason, or pretext, which he advanced: if he had gone to the Khedive's residence, he and his soldiers might have disturbed the ladies of Towfik's household. To Orabi a man's household was set apart: or taboo, as harem originally meant.

Orabi reached the square first. Ready in his hand was the petition: one of its terms was the dismissal of the Cabinet, dominated as it was by men of the Circassian and Turkish ruling class; another was an increase in the size and pay of the Egyptian army.

The heat in the square was fierce; clouds of moist heat hung over bleached brickwork and dust. But Orabi had the physique and ancestry for waiting in the sun. In their daily life his forebears had bent over the irrigated fields or labored to jerk water from the river by means of the weighted shadoof; the fellahin were inured to waiting on their alien lords.

Towfik was in no hurry to meet the colonel. He was a frightened man. During his brief reign he had already had trouble from Orabi. For leading a conspiracy of Egyptian officers against the more reliable Circassians, Orabi had been court-martialed in the military wing of Kasrel-Nil. The president of the court was Stone Pasha, an American Southerner in khedivial pay. When all was going well, when Stone Pasha was on the point of passing sentence, soldiers from Orabi's regiment had stormed into the room and dissolved the court-martial. After this escape from justice, Orabi had become intolerably impudent. In any case Towfik had no use for fellah officers. They were defying the age-old custom that Egyptians should be ruled by foreigners; they represented as grave a peril as the Mamelukes destroyed by Muhammad Ali. What was needed was some similar decisive gesture; perhaps a massacre. But Towfik lacked his great ancestor's ruthless spirit. He had set himself a different pattern of kingship: he would, like Queen Victoria, visit hospitals and act as a model of domestic virtue. He was incapable of an effective deed of force. If Muhammad Ali had been decision incarnate, Towfik was hesitation. Hesitantly he sought advice from three advisers: first Riaz Pasha, an outwardly unimpressive but wily Ottoman who lived in the old city; then Stone Pasha, the American; and most decisive and influential, Sir Auckland Colvin. Born in Calcutta, where his father was an East India Company official, Colvin had served in India before taking the post of Comptroller-General, in the British interest but with a French colleague to assist him, of Egypt's finances.

In dealing with enemies Towfik's instincts were Ottoman and therefore devious. But from his advisers, and in particular Colvin, he got direct, insistent counsel: Orabi must not be allowed to get away with mutinous behavior.

"I advised him to take the initiative," so Colvin summarized his advice to the trembling Khedive. "Two regiments in Cairo were said by Riaz Pasha to be faithful. I advised him to summon them to the Abdin Square, with all the military police available, to put himself at their head, and when Orabi Bey arrived, personally to arrest him. He replied that Orabi had with him the artillery and cavalry, and they might fire. I said that they would not dare to, and if he had the courage to take the initiative, and to expose himself personally, he might succeed in overcoming the mutineers. Otherwise he was lost."

Stone Pasha was joined by Sir Charles Cookson, acting British consul-general, in supporting this advice. Its acceptance and a consequent series of carriage rides kept Orabi and two thousand soldiers sweating in the square.

Hours before the rendezvous Towfik had trundled to Abdin. The commander of the khedivial guard was Ali Fehmy, one of the officers who had been honored with a bride from Ismail's harem. Towfik, trusting him fully, told him to position his soldiers behind the curtains and shutters in the upstairs rooms of the palace; riflemen posted in such excellent and secret cover could command the square. If fate played fairly, they could pick off Orabi and his fifty or so supporting officers; his men would then disperse in panic. Or if things went badly, if Orabi threatened the Khedive, the hidden marksmen could intervene to save him.

After preparing this Eastern ruse, Towfik felt better. His carriage now led a procession of others to the Citadel by way of Boulevard Muhammad Ali, a thoroughfare hacked by Ismail through the ancient city. Colvin, Stone Pasha, the Circassian ministers and half a dozen reliable officers filled the other carriages.

The news at the Citadel was fittingly good. This rocky fortress was the symbol of Muhammad Ali's power. His ornate, Stamboul-style mosque and "Bijou" palace rose proudly on the spur of the Mokattam Hills, which, in the Middle Ages, Saladin had used as lynchpin for fortifications that linked the palace-city of the Fatimids and the earlier Muslim cities in a defensible whole. The regiment now guarding this dynastic strongpoint affirmed their loyalty to the Khedive. In better spirits, Towfik and his friends drove down from the Citadel to the City of the Dead, a vast dusty necropolis where medieval sultans slept under delicate domes. A little-used road skirted inhabited Cairo and took the khedivial party to the northernmost suburb of Abbasia. Named after the grandfather of Towfik's wife, Abbasia commanded the sallow desert stretching to Suez. In its military cantonment the horses of the cavalry were stabled and the artillery's guns kept under guard: elements it was vital to neutralize.

But here the news was bad. It was now after 3 P.M. and all Towfik found was an empty drill ground. The artillery and cavalry had gone with Orabi to Abdin.

Only his foreign advisers persuaded Towfik to return to a city now throbbing with danger. A tedious route enabled him to avoid the populated areas where he might be seen and reach the garden door at the back of Abdin Palace, near the Canal. The palace itself stood silent and gloomy. The silence was welcome, since it must conceal soldiers holding their breath as they crouched near the upstairs windows; welcome, too, was the gloom, being the nearest thing to air conditioning in nineteenth century Cairo.

But again, bad news: Ali Fehmy, whom he had trusted, had joined Orabi. His soldiers had all disappeared. Except for his portly Circassians and pink-faced advisers from the West, Towfik was alone. From the palace windows he had thought to use for a massacre, he could glimpse the square. It was solidly under the colonel's control. Guns and horsemen were drawn up in impudent neatness and behind the rows of foot soldiers seethed the declamatory people. They were shouting for the burly Egyptian on his horse, not for the Khedive skulking in the italianate palace.

Once again Colvin steeled Towfik. He must leave the shelter of the palace and confront the mutineers.

Stepping gingerly, the Khedive did so. Colvin walked with him and at some distance behind followed Stone Pasha and a small group of his Circassian and European officers. The Khedive advanced steadily to where Orabi waited on horseback, a group of his officers behind.

"When Orabi presents himself," Colvin whispered, "command him to give you his sword. Then tell him to give his men the order to disperse. You go round the square and order each regiment to disperse."

Colonal Orabi obeyed the first of the Khedive's commands, which was to dismount. But as he did so, as, sword in hand, he strode forward to present his petition, about fifty of his officers, suspicious of a trick, followed him closely.

"Now is your moment!"

"But we are between four fires. . . ."

"Have courage."

The Khedive did not share the Englishman's confidence. All round the square the Egyptian soldiers were drawn up; Towfik was foreign, but less so than the Englishman. He turned to a Circassian officer, then back to Colvin. "What can I do? We are between four fires. We are all going to be killed."

But Orabi obeyed his next command, which was to put up his sword.

He then handed the Khedive his petition, at the same time explaining its three main points: that the present ministry of foreigners and Circassians should be dismissed; that a parliament could be convened; and that the army, which had been so much reduced, should be enlarged to the complement of 18,000 authorized by the Sultan's firman.

Colvin whispered his urgent advice: it was unseemly for the Sultan's Viceroy to discuss issues of this kind with colonels.

"I am the Khedive of this country," Towfik mustered his courage, "and shall do as I wish."

"We are no more slaves," Orabi answered, "and from this day forth shall not be inherited."

This was the key exchange of the hot afternoon. The Khedive's sentence expressed the Eastern commonplace of fifty centuries. Orabi's sentence, the expression of a commonplace in the world shaped by Hellas and Magna Carta, was a defiance to shake the shadoofs and make tremble the palm groves.

But this memorable exchange was not a climax. The Islamic East was a culture averse to climaxes; its music was repeated involution, its poems were necklaces of single lines, each admirable in itself: its distinctive decorative form was the arabesque, the swirl of shapes that curl back upon themselves. The East had no drama, the principle of debate being as unknown as that of a loyal opposition.

The afternoon curled back upon itself. Having steeled himself to his affirmation, having heard his subject's defiance, Towfik turned to Colvin: "You hear what he says?"

Colvin was pale with anger, not only at the impudence of Orabi but at the Khedive's lack of spine.

"Leave me to palaver with the colonels. It is unfitting for you, as Khedive, to engage in such debate. Go back into your palace."

Towfik obeyed and went back among the oil paintings of his father's wives, the girandoles, the clocks, the European tables and chairs.

For a whole hour Colvin waited. The man to give advice was Sir Charles Cookson, and he had been summoned. As the sun relented towards the pyramids on the Giza ridge, color flooded back to the bleached square: smears of red brickwork showed through crumbling stucco; a gaudy quilt hung from a balcony; palm trees lost their gun-metal glare and dust. Cookson arrived at a trot with an interpreter.

He wasted no politeness on Orabi.

"You, a soldier, ask for a parliament. Why?"

"Because it will put an end to arbitrary rule."

"But you are a military man."

Orabi pointed to the turbaned heads beyond the now slouching soldiers, the citizens of Cairo.

"They are with us."

"If your mutiny goes on, we shall bring a British army."

"You cannot do that. We are subjects of the Sultan-Caliph."

On these lines the afternoon turned to evening and for five, even six, times, there was a trotting into the palace, and out of it. Negotiation had taken over from declamation. Orabi insisted that Riaz Pasha, spokesman of the aliens, must resign. He would accept Sherif Pasha, another card in the royal pack, but known to him personally, and liked.

Orabi was summoned to Kasrel-Nil and went. The Khedive had agreed in principle to all of the Egyptian's demands. Orabi had the tendency, not only to forgive, but to accept that others could experience lightning transformations of mood or mind; this tendency was a feature of the Arabs and reflected something volatile inside themselves. Now having won, Orabi was ready to forgive. Having forced his point of view upon Towfik, he was ready to believe that Towfik's heart was changed, that he had become a ruler an Egyptian might gladly serve. As Towfik gave in on each point—a new ministry, a new parliament, a renewal of the commissions of those officers who had been dismissed when the army was reduced—Orabi tried to thank him.

Only now did Towfik show the Turk behind the beard and the fez.

"That is enough," he said coldly, without expression. "Go now and occupy Abdin. But let there be no music in the streets."

Orabi granted his request. The Egyptian victory would not appear the Khedive's defeat.

Chapter 2

IF Orabi had voiced the grievances of the army only, his impact on history would have been as trivial as that of Towfik. But Orabi and Towfik were more than individuals. Like the two seas, they represented and involved far more than themselves. Orabi was the first Egyptian fellah to stand up to a ruler for two, perhaps five, thousand years. Towfik was more than a weakling in a respectable palace; he represented the instrument of an industrialized Europe that would prove a graver challenge to the Middle East than the agrarian Christendom which had sponsored the Crusades. The backers of the two men deserve analysis, for it is they which give them their true significance.

The Egypt which, after initial distrust, had rallied to Orabi had been remolded by its experiences in the nineteenth century. It was a nation recognizable to the most casual visitor. Dressed in nightgown-like *gallabyas,* woollen scull-caps and floppy slippers, its members dwelt in the mudbrick villages which sprawled on the higher land in the Nile valley or which in the delta rose like hillocks above the emerald fields only to become, in flood time, like scattered Aegean islands. (Outwardly Egypt had not changed since Herodotus made this comparison more than four hundred years before Christ.) As its numbers increased in the limited area where men could plow, it sent waves of immigrants to crowd the untidy lanes of the towns and cities. In Cairo they worshiped in the sumptuous mosques bequeathed by the Mameluke sultans, who, for all their egoism, had believed in the same god as the fellahin. Though lacking any constitutional machinery through which to express, let alone impress, its will, this Egyptian nation possessed one formidable institution. This was the university-mosque of al-Azhar, at which Orabi had studied. Since its foundation, al-Azhar's history had been linked to that of Egypt.

Al-Azhar had been founded in the tenth century A.D. as a propaganda pulpit for a series of rulers, the Fatimid Caliphs, who were regarded as heretical by the more generally accepted Caliphs of Baghdad. For the Fatimids espoused the minority "party" (or in Arabic, *Shia*) of Ali, cousin and son-in-law of the Prophet Muhammad. The Shiites taught that only the direct blood-descendants of Muhammad, through his daughter Fatima, who married Ali, could infallibly guide Islam. After two Fatimid centuries (in which the Shia signally failed to persuade the Egyptians), Saladin had united Egypt and Syria in one Sunnite (the majority party) realm and turned al-Azhar into what it was to remain, the fountainhead of orthodox Islamic teaching. Al-Azhar might be called the Oxford of Islam, but it was an Oxford which had not discarded its medieval customs and costumes. Its methods of instruction and its aims had little in common with those of a modern university. Rooted in religion, it graduated students who automatically filled religious positions in the Muslim lands: not as priests (for there was no priesthood in Islam) but as Ulema, men learned in Muslim doctrine who could instruct the young, lead the prayer in mosques and adjudicate cases according to the Sacred Law. There were no classrooms in al-Azhar. Instead, each lecturer adopted one section of the many-pillared mosque and gathered round him his "seekers," or disciples, who squatted on the carpet. What these young men sought was a detailed understanding of God's final revelation, the Koran, and the classical Arabic in which it had been revealed. Since Islam believed that it possessed absolute truth, there was as little free inquiry at al-Azhar as in the Oxford of the Middle Ages. But bigoted and out of touch with secular thought or foreign science though it was, al-Azhar retained some important assets. Lecturers and disciples were linked by that personal bond which Plato had approved. The university was closely woven into the fabric of Muslim life. An Azharite was not trained to be separate from his community. On the contrary, he articulated what the ordinary Muslim felt. Al-Azhar could claim to incarnate what was, after the Koran and the traditional sayings of the Prophet, a third pillar of faith: the Muslim consensus. It was a broad consensus. Islam had no rigid system of classes, and men of all races and colors met as equals in the mosque. Al-Azhar also flung its net wide: dormitories housed students from as far apart as Java and Morocco.

Nineteenth-century Europe shook al-Azhar in much the same way that Greece and Italy had shaken Renaissance Oxford. Though the French invaders had been resented (their soldiers and their horses had desecrated the mosque), the scholars Napoleon brought with him to Egypt had opened an Institute which had had a profound effect on thoughtful Egyptians. The results of French influence can be seen ricocheting down the century like a chain of crackers or like Hegel's pattern of thesis, antithesis and synthesis.

The thesis was an enthusiastic acceptance of change and was embodied in the career of a man from Upper Egypt called Rifaa al-Tahtawi. Tahtawi was helped by an Azharite Sheikh who had met the French scholars, to become chaplain to one of Muhammad Ali's new regiments. Again as chaplain, he was sent to Paris to look after the spiritual welfare of Egyptian students. Tahtawi was in Paris from 1826 and 1831 and these years sufficed to convert him to the values of the West. His conversion was not uncritical. While supporting a much more liberal attitude to women than prevailed in the East, he complained that French husbands were henpecked by their wives. But in general he devoted his life to popularizing European ideas in Egypt. Besides organizing schools, he presided over a frenzy of translation into Arabic whose only parallel is the translation of Greek texts in sixteenth-century England. The result was an appetizing if indigestible feast of new ideas. While the Khedive adopted European styles of dress and furnishing for his harem, many Egyptians of the 1860s and after adopted, at least in theory, the principles of female emancipation, constitutional democracy, a preference for monogamy, and above all, the conception of territorial patriotism. Before Tahtawi's generation, group feelings in the Middle East were based on religion. A Muslim, in the words of the Prophet, was a brother to every other Muslim; a Muslim living in Cairo felt more in common with a Muslim in Morocco or Java than with a Christian living next-door. The Christian, in turn, felt that his nationality was his *millet,* the Ottoman term for his particular church. Tahtawi, who had become interested in Egyptology while in Paris (and this was the time when Champollion was deciphering the Rosetta Stone) was aware of the greatness of the purely Egyptian past. Patriotism as he preached it meant what it meant to a Frenchman: the love of the territorial unit with its historical past. The Egypt extolled by Tahtawi included Copts and Jews as well as Muslims among its sons.

This enthusiasm for the West—a little glib, a little naïve—coincided with the daydreams of Ismail. Just as the daydreams of Ismail could not last, neither, in its unadulterated form, could Tahtawi's enthusiasm. The assumption that modern European ideas could be easily grafted on the palm tree of Islam was put in doubt as political Europe showed itself increasingly aggressive.

The antithesis to Tahtawi—the doctrine that the West must be resisted —was embodied in the most arresting Islamic thinker of his age: a sane yet burning-eyed visionary from further East. Jamal al-Din al-Afghani (his name means literally "The Beauty of Religion, the Afghan") was more probably of Persian than Afghan origin; he certainly claimed to be a descendant of the Prophet's murdered grandson, Hussein. As such, he was probably a member of the Shia, which besides founding al-Azhar, had founded innumerable secret brotherhoods such as the Order of Assassins. Whatever his origins, al-Afghani set the medieval tradition of itinerant scholar in the context of the nineteenth century. In India he had fallen foul of the British; for the rest of his life he saw the essential problem facing all Muslims as one of spiritual and physical resistance to the West. This West included czarist Russia, then busily extending its Central Asian empire at the expense of the Muslims. But the West's chief furnace of power was Great Britain, the actual ruler of India and the aspirant ruler, as Afghani feared, of Egypt.

Afghani's travels involved both a search and a gift. The search was for an Islamic entity which could resist the West; the gift was to the young men he made his disciples wherever he went. While he died without finding the ruler who could form the nucleus of a reborn Islam, he gave his disciples a new confidence in the potentialities of their inherited faith.

Al-Afghani's suspicion of the West was not linked (as might be the case with the puritan Wahhabis of Central Arabia) to a willful ignorance of Western ways. In India he had studied the mathematical sciences according to the latest European methods. He taught himself French. When he went to Mecca on pilgrimage he made his journey last a year, steeping himself in the customs and problems of the peoples on his route. In Constantinople he became friendly with the Grand Vizir, Ali Pasha. Then from 1871 to 1879 he rented a house in the Jewish Quarter of Cairo. He was not a formal teacher at al-Azhar, though he attended the mosque for the corporate Friday prayers. He had a more effective pulpit: a café behind the Opera, near the Post Office. There he would sit, hour after discursive hour, a slight, olive-skinned man with long black hair who wore trousers under a jibba. He was unmarried, and frugal in his habits, indulging greedily the pleasures permissible to Muslims of tea-drinking and smoking. Any young Egyptian who cared for the things that interested the master was welcome to join him at his café table. None of his listeners knew the outside world as he did; none saw it with his penetration. They would listen entranced to his conversation until, near dawn, the café closed its doors. The seer would return to his lodgings while the young men returned to their villages with their thoughts turned upside down.

His message to his pupils was as shocking as iced water to a people long used to finding arguments why they should do nothing.

"You Egyptians," he would tell them, "have become inured to tyrants; you have grown up in their laps. You have put up with centuries of servitude since the days of the Shepherd Kings. You have patiently endured the whips of injustice and humiliation. They squeezed from you, under the lash, the very substances of your lives, the product of your sweat, and you were patient. If you had blood in your veins, however thin, if your heads had nerves to throb to a sense of honour, you would not have supported this humiliating slavery. After the Shepherd Kings, Greeks and Romans, Persians and then Arabs, Kurds like Saladin, Mamelukes, Frenchmen, Muhammad Ali and his dynasty: all these conquerors ground you down with their greed and you lay as inert as lumps of rock discarded in the desert." Al-Afghani, like other visitors, had inspected the pyramids, where foreigners, not Egyptians, had started to clear the sand from the Sphinx's paws and chest. He had seen the rocks, fragments of long vanished structures, littering the sand. "Look around you!" he exhorted. "Your forebears built the Pyramids and the great temples at Luxor. They prove that your ancestors had intelligence and strength. Wake up! Shake off your weakness, your stupidity. You can live happy and free, like other nations, or die as martyrs and earn God's reward."

This probing, unsettling mind looked on the Islam which he wished to revivify as a total civilization more than a mere system of beliefs. "Religion is the sole source of human happiness." But religion included far more than saying your prayers at the right times, after the right ablutions. Above all, it had political implications. To a generation of young Egyptians already imbued with a veneration for the West (and therefore inclined to belittle their own heritage), al-Afghani had come at a decisive moment. His stay in Cairo precisely corresponded with the years when Ismail's dream of smoothly building a European civilization on African soil had crashed in nightmare. From 1871 to 1879 Egypt's financial mismanagement became an international crisis and the resulting interference by Europeans angered the most docile. Afghani had enjoyed the friendship of Towfik, when he was still only heir to the throne; the young prince had a religious disposition and enjoyed free-ranging ideas. But no sooner was Ismail banished to Europe than the new Khedive banished Afghani from Egypt. He probably did so under British prompting; an Islamic revival could be dangerous if it spread to India. As he left on an odyssey which would take him first to India, then Paris, then Constantinople, where in

1897 he died, Afghani said: "I have to go from Egypt but I leave behind me Sheikh Muhammad Abduh; he is all that Egypt needs."

Sheikh Muhammad Abduh, ten years younger than his teacher Afghani, contrived a vital synthesis between the acceptance of the West and its rejection.

As a man, Abduh was very different from his teacher. Afghani was daring, incisive, extreme; no one who met him doubted that his origins, however mysterious, were aristocratic. Abduh was, like Orabi, a product of the Egyptian delta. Egyptian Muslims (unlike the Christians, the Copts, who only intermarried among themselves) had intermarried over the centuries with the foreigners who came to Egypt for one reason or another. In Abduh's case, the foreign inmixture was Turcoman, deriving from a tribe who had migrated in to the delta; Abduh's house was known in his village as "the Turcoman house." But despite these reputed foreign links, Abduh's father, like Orabi's, was a fellah. There were, however, unusual traditions of revolt in this particular fellah house: Abduh's grandfather and great-uncles had resisted the forcible takeover of their land by Muhammad Ali (who had claimed to own the totality of Egypt's arable soil). Abduh's father had been forced, from the age of fourteen, to wander from province to province as a virtual outcast. He had only returned to his village, to find his property ruined, his house in dereliction, when Said Pasha inherited the throne and allowed the fellahin to regain their land.

Abduh's education began in the conventional way: he learnt his letters at home and then began studying the Muslim scriptures from the village teacher. Within two years the boy knew the whole of the Koran (which is about the length of the New Testament) by heart. His father (who had been enriched by the boom in cotton) took the boy as a pupil to the mosque at Tanta, the capital of the delta. There he was taught first how to recite the Koran with the correct intonation, and then Arabic grammar.

Abduh was to describe his youthful disillusion with the traditional education of a Muslim. "I spent a year and a half trying to learn, but I learnt nothing, thanks to the bad system of teaching. Expressions were used which were completely unintelligible to us and which our teachers did not bother to explain. The method at Tanta was the same as at al-Azhar. Students who understood nothing went on studying until they turned into men with the dreams of children. But they were then ready to assume important posts in which their only function was to make the ignorant more ignorant yet. I felt lost and ran away from my classes, determined to have nothing more to do with education. I married instead." Abduh was eighteen when he made this decision and decided to become a farmer, like his forebears.

But his father was stubborn and insisted that a good brain should not be wasted. Unwillingly, Abduh returned to Tanta. On his way, and entirely by chance, he underwent an experience which changed his life. Calling in on some relatives in a village on the way, he met his great-uncle, an old man called Sheikh Darwish. The Sheikh had lived with members of the Senoussi sect, a Libyan brotherhood which, like the Wahhabis in Arabia, called for a purification of Islam. The Senoussis differed from the Wahhabis, however, in having a mystical approach to their faith. As his uncle explained a book on Sufism, the mystical "Way" of Islam, the young student glimpsed the inner meaning of religion. Terms which had been opaque were suddenly clear; water gushed from arid rock. Abduh now continued his studies, first at Tanta, then at al-Azhar, convinced that behind time-dusted formulae truths existed by which man, individually and collectively, could live.

If his great-uncle was the first influence on his life, al-Afghani was the second and stronger. Abduh had been in his third year at al-Azhar, and aged twenty-one, when al-Afghani had begun diffusing his revolutionary ideas. Abduh already belonged to a group known to the conservatives in al-Azhar as the heretics. By himself he had studied mathematics, logic and philosophy. A young Egyptian, later a famous lawyer and a firm friend to Abduh, described the hostility of the conventionally minded students toward "our great teacher, Jamal al-Din al-Afghani, who was then thirty-two. Afghani expounded theology, literature and philosophy in a manner and spirit entirely alien to al-Azhar of those days. Naturally the students and the Sheikhs ganged up against him. I was only seventeen and I felt a pious hatred for Afghani, which was extended to include Abduh, one of his disciples. My hatred drove me to the point where I falsely accused Abduh to the dean of not making the required ablutions before his evening prayers. Abduh was then aged twenty-two. The dean sent me, with a group of students, to bring Abduh to him. We found him at prayer but dragged him before the dean, who ordered us to punish him. We gave him a good beating."

All his life Abduh was to find himself up against the conservatives of the mosque; they would accuse him of hiding atheism behind a facade of words. But the accumulated force of new ideas was sufficiently strong for him to make significant gains. After graduating in 1878 (one year before the departure from Egypt of Ismail and Afghani) he was determined not to be one of those professors who, "like Gohar's fabled water-wheel, took water from the sea and poured it back in again." (He used this image for the typical Azharite, who, having learnt by rote what the mosque offered, then transmitted it, undeveloped, to a new generation of credulous students.) Although he was connected with al-Azhar throughout his life, he also taught in the new secular schools, which owed their existence to Muhammad Ali and his successors. Refusing to teach grammar and rhetoric, he instead introduced his students to modern European thought, arguing that in their approach to Islam they should differentiate between the essential—belief in God and His revelation, the welfare of society and the use of reason—and the inessential practices which so often obscured it. He made headway early. In 1880, the year before Orabi challenged the Khedive, he was appointed editor of the official Egyptian newspaper. To its rigid format he added a literary section, which was enthusiastically received. Like the English editors of the early eighteenth century, he aimed at a gentle reformation of national life by publishing articles on a wide variety of themes. He was not afraid to deal directly with political issues, attacking in particular a taxation system which forced the peasant into the grips of the moneylender. One result of his articles was the starting, for the first time, of charitable societies, Muslim and Coptic alike, for the relief of the poor.

When Orabi first emerged as a power in Egypt, Abduh feared that he might be a mere adventurer; like most fellahin, he was hostile to the army as an institution. The term *askari* would be used indiscriminately for soldier and policeman deep into the 1960s. Soldiers and policemen were the enemies of the fellahin, whose sons they dragged off to foreign wars and whose piasters they squeezed by use of the *korbag,* or whip.

But Abduh felt a deeper hostility to the dynasty which had first confiscated the land of the fellahin and then had forced them to pay its bills. With the collision in Abdin Square Abduh and his disciples—whose influence on civilian nationalists was immense—ranged themselves firmly behind a man whom they now saw as a national, not merely a military, leader. When Orabi pointed to the turbaned heads behind the soldiers' tarbooshes, he was pointing to a fact: the solidarity with him of an awakening nation.

Chapter 3

IN himself, the Khedive Towfik was the drabbest prince to give his name to a port.[1] Vaguely tricky eyes, a blur of close-cropped beard, a routine fez, a chest emblazoned with absurd medallions, these comprised the son for whom Ismail had, in his own words, "kissed the carpet" and for seventeen years humbled himself before the Sultan, funneling bribes through his own stout hands or those of his Constantinople agent. All this expense in a shameless world to obtain "the much-desired firman of

[1] Port Towfik a suburb of Suez.

direct succession" for a son who in crisis showed, to quote Ismail's French, *"ni tête, ni coeur, ni courage."*

But Towfik possessed what Ismail had lacked: determined backers. Inside Egypt he was supported by most of the Circassian upper class. This mixed bag of dynastic outriders, court favorites or rich adventurers despised the fellahin, or native Egyptians. But their support was not whole-hearted. Some members of the khedivial family as well as many Circassians were partisans of Prince Halim, the last surviving son of the dynasty's founder. This prince had an energetic appeal which Towfik lacked. A typical "Halimiste" was an old gentleman named Osman Pasha Fowzi. Osman was the agent of Shepheard's, for the hotel founded by Samuel Shepheard at this time beonged to a sister of Prince Halim, Princess Zeyneb. Osman had been owned, quite literally, by their father, Muhammad Ali; the ruthless destroyer of the Mameluke caste had retained individual mamelukes for his convenience. The now elderly Osman symbolized the clash of elements possible in an upper-class Egyptian. By race he was, in the correct sense, a Circassian; by sympathy he was an Ottoman Turk; he spoke French with spirit, yet was somewhat of a buffoon (hence his Turkish nickname Deli Osman, or Crazy Osman); proud of having been his great master's slave, he was haughty towards Egyptians. When not busy with hotel affairs, he would ride in his carriage to the Citadel mosque and taking off his buttoned boots approach the ornate structure surrounding Muhammad Ali's grave pit. Grasping its convolutions, he would call on his dead master to send some more worthy descendant to replace Towfik. In the developing struggle between the Khedive and Orabi, his disgust for Towfik placed him in Orabi's camp. But unlike one or two other pro-Orabi Turks, he felt no sympathy for the Egyptians. As a Turk and the son of a Turk, he stated bluntly, "I can have no community of ideas or interests with the Egyptians." But if these despised Egyptians could weaken Towfik, so much the better. The Europeans would be forced out of control and Prince Halim and the Circassians would soon whip the fellahin back into obedience.

During the Abdin incident the Circassians showed hardly more "heart" or "courage" than Towfik. But this did not mean that they lacked "head." Their lack of bravado was backed by logic. They were citizens of the Ottoman Empire. Egypt was a hot and alien land whose corn was worth the reaping (strictly figuratively) while it was easy. If the harvest got difficult, the Circassians could retreat to the Bosphorus. Careers were open to them in the capital, among people of their background and race. Mustafa Fazil, for example, Ismail's brother and their doyen, had been Minister of Finance in Constantinople before his death in 1875.

Towfik's determined backers were European.

This term did not include, in this instance, men like Stone Pasha and the other Confederate officers who had taken refuge at Ismail's court.

There was much in Egypt to remind them of Louisiana. If they shared the Circassian contempt for the dark-skinned Egyptians, they probably despised the Circassians too. But as much as the Circassians, southern gentlemen were a force doomed to eventual diminution. They accepted this fact.

Sir Auckland Colvin and Sir Charles Cookson, on the other hand, represented a force which, far from intending to retreat, intended to advance. God had already given the British Empire boundaries stretching across the planet; these bounds would be wider yet. In so thinking the two Englishmen were in tune with the other leading countries of Europe. Even the Italians, despised by the Germans and by the English patronizingly loved, espoused the same national maxim: "I colonize: therefore I am."

The force behind this maxim has been named, without precision, "colonialism" or "imperialism"; the use of the two words hints the inadequacy of each. The concept needs a cautious approach since it rises in ground entangled with rusty wire and sown with mines.

The terms "colony" and "empire" derive from the period when the Greeks and their Roman inheritors bound the Mediterranean in a common culture.

In Greek times colonialism was no abstract system; the creation of a colony was a response to a social need and took place in an underpopulated world. A city-state with more numbers than it could feed established a hived-off portion somewhere else in the Mediterranean. Thus a "new city," in Greek, *neapolis,* would be established on the site of Naples, Marseilles or Syracuse; it would retain some links with its Greek parent but would also coexist with the surrounding natives. A legend about the foundation of Cyrene attractively illustrates this process. When colonists from the volcano-island of Thera landed on the Libyan coast, the natives kindly told them of a better site for their settlement in the northwest corner of Cyrenaica, where "a hole in the sky" (a poetic term for a freak annual rainfall) made the land green. The result was a Hellenic city which flourished for a thousand years; the Libyans probably never regretted their generous advice.

Only when Greek civilization was in decline did a Macedonian dynasty create a veritable empire. The two features of Alexander's empire were its great extent and short life. No sooner was the Great King dead, than a realm linking Macedonia to India fell apart into kingdoms ruled by his generals. A diffusion of Hellenic culture was matched by an intake of non-Greek manners and ideas. There was no imperial control; Greeks were hardly a privileged caste.

Imperium was the grander Roman innovation. Although the Romans also established colonies such as the settlements of demobilized veterans planted by Augustus in Anatolia, Roman imperialism was essentially the extension of the process whereby, over some centuries, Roman power had consolidated the Italian peninsula, itself a racial microcosm of the Mediterranean. The oligarchy ruling Italy went on to rule an empire embracing the whole Mediterranean. The provinces of this empire were administered in different ways. The more settled were ruled by the Senate and its appointees; others were governed by legates of Caesar; client states, such as the Kingdom of Herod, enjoyed some degree of autonomy; Egypt had a unique status as the emperor's private estate. As the empire developed, it tended to unify its administration and to abolish differences between its free inhabitants. St. Paul's boast—"I am a Roman citizen!" —indicated that in the first century most Jews were still subjects; by the third century the Levantine emperor Caracalla had extended Roman citizenship to all non-slaves.

There were aspects of both the Greek and the Roman system in the way Europeans populated and administered their overseas possessions. Overpopulation at home and the lure of opportunity abroad inspired colonies such as Greeks would have recognized. The Anglo-Saxon settlements on the eastern seaboard of North America were hivings-off from the home country. But a major motive for such settlement was religious bigotry at home, a factor which played an inconsiderable role in Greek history. On the other hand, Latin colonies often embodied an attempt to implant the domestic religion abroad. Religious exclusiveness again had been foreign to the Greeks; when they colonized Egypt they also created a deity, Serapis, who represented a fusion between their own Zeus and the Egyptian Osiris. But culturally the colonization of Spain and Portugal was shaped by the generous Roman ideal envisioning common citizenship for those who accepted common standards. Assimilated Indians in Goa, Chinese in Macao, Africans in Mozambique or Amerindians in Brazil could hope to share the rights of the home-grown Portuguese.

Technological factors, even more than military, helped the modern Europeans to expand. The Portuguese, as the first discoverers, owed their overseas dominions to advances in navigation; they were buttressed by a technology of arms and factory production. As Europeans found themselves controlling more and more of the planet, they looked at themselves in the mirror they knew best—the Greco-Roman classics—and applied a gloss of Latin terminology to something very different: a system designed to secure raw materials for factories in Europe and a market for European manufactured goods.

A better if uglier term for this post-Renaissance form of expansion (in non-contiguous patches all over the planet) might be "expatriate control."

This system of expatriate control had the force of an instinctual drive. Those who promoted it most strongly denied what they were doing. Like all systems it produced men adapted to its needs. These men reflected a society in many ways new: while keeping its records and assessing its daily health, they analyzed it with unequaled zeal. Archivists kept its memory and journalists took its pulse. But its antennae, the quivering nerve ends which gave it the deepest insights into itself, were its writers. Writers portrayed the basic types of expatriate controller with visionary sureness.

Shakespeare wrote his last play, *The Tempest*, halfway through the reign of England's James I, when European empires were young. The play's appropriate setting is a desert island, a setting very different from the classical world, in which so much of his previous fantasy had moved. Shakespeare had read the account by William Strachey, secretary of the Virginia Company, of his shipwreck off Bermuda. On this frail basis he constructed a perceptive myth of the colonial situation. The chief character, Prospero, has often been taken to represent the artist bidding farewell to his craft. But a French anthropologist with experience of colonial rule in Madagascar[2] has discerned in Prospero the archetype of an Olympian colonialist. A prince in his own land, Prospero has taken possession of the island from its previous owner. Caliban, whose name is a near anagram of cannibal, has a degraded and strongly sensual nature. He has been bewitched by the white magician. Like the natives met by many Western explorers, he was originally pleased to co-operate with the newcomers just as the Libyans had been with the Greeks; but with dire results. When Caliban discovers that he has been enslaved, his resentment is bitter:

> *This island's mine, by Sycorax my mother,*
> *Which thou tak'st from me. When thou camest first,*
> *Thou strok'dst me, and made much of me, wouldst give me*
> *Water with berries in't; and teach me how*
> *To name the bigger light, and how the less,*
> *That burn by day and night; and then I lov'd thee,*
> *And show'd thee all the qualities of the isle,*
> *The fresh springs, brine-pits, barren place and fertile.*
> *Cursed be I that did so!*

Miranda, Prospero's daughter, is the symbol of White Womanhood, the fluttering standard of colonizing males. The dusky savage lusts after her and is soundly punished. Having seen the situation so clearly, Shakespeare sees further, to eventual decolonization. Prospero destroys his magic wand, the instrument of his control, the force through which even the genius of Ariel has been corralled; Caliban becomes an autonomous creature with a will of his own, shown, as much as Shylock, as someone who, for all his unattractiveness, has human feelings, and therefore rights.

A century later Daniel Defoe was to create yet another picture card in the expatriate pack. Robinson Crusoe is the European who is thwarted

[2] O. Mannoni, *Caliban and Prospero* (London: 1956).

at home and who finds in a desert island an outlet for pioneering energies
and, in Man Friday, the solace for his celibate existence. In the expatriate
empires the Prosperos in pompous raiment would ordain the lines of policy; they would be exalted as prefects or viceroys or understated as
consuls-general or agents. For the execution of their policies they would
depend on a regiment of Crusoes: district commissioners or commanders
of Beau Geste forts; Balliol graduates devoting decades to jungle villages
or even poets, like Rimbaud, selling alcohol and guns in remote Harrar.

Prospero the King, Miranda the Queen, Crusoe the Jack, or Knave:
these were the picture cards with gentle birth, education or talent behind
them. For these archetypes to become embodied in reality, for the
Governor-General in his plumed hat to wield power, there was a need for
uncourtly, secondary cards: the humble two of clubs or the seven of
spades, the bluff five of hearts or the diamond ten. These were the soldiers
and sergeants, the men who would carry out the rough jobs of empire, the
dying and killing, the guard duties and the execution pickets without which
Prospero's policy or Crusoe's pleasure collapsed in ruins.

The system of expatriate control knew where to recruit its common
cards: from the quick breeding slums of its own rich cities. An Olympian
German, Friedrich Engels, had thrown as cold an eye on the Black Country of England as any English traveler on the country of the Blacks. "He
saw the working people living like rats in the wretched little dens of their
dwellings, whole families, sometimes more than one family, swarming in
a single room, well and diseased, adults and children, close relations sleeping together, sometimes without beds to sleep on, when all the furniture
had been sold for firewood, sometimes in damp underground cellars which
had to be bailed out when the weather was wet, sometimes lying in the
same room with the animals, ill-nourished on flour mixed with gypsum
and cocoa mixed with dirt, poisoned by ptomaine from tainted meat, dop-
ing themselves and their wailing children with laudanum; spending their
lives, without a sewage system, among the pile of excrement and garbage;
spreading epidemics of typhus and cholera which even made inroads into
the well-to-do sections." An infection with its humble roots in human filth
was typhoid, the disease to which Queen Victoria's husband had succumbed.

These pale millions were ready to turn in any direction for escape. Some
were transported to Australia; others, drawn to the Statue of Liberty, sank
or swam in the New York slums; others were caught by the Pied Piper
of Colonialism and bore on their thin shoulders the White Man's Burden.

The Pied Piper's clearest tunes were composed by a middle-class Englishman born in Bombay four years before the opening of the Suez Canal.
Rudyard Kipling, bullied at school, half an alien in England, was the first
major poet to write a considerable body of verse in the spoken English of
the working class. The sentiments his proletarian poetry expressed were

the sentiments of a recruiting sergeant, not of a revolutionary. Expatriate control found its advocate and constructive critic in one who, having suffered in childhood, spent the rest of his life in a masochistic exaltation of the machinery which fostered such pain. Anglo-Saxon expansion, dawn-fresh in the time of Shakespeare and Defoe, had created personal archetypes; in its imperial phase it was to create abstractions. In a poem about an American venture into imperialism in the Philippines,[3] Kipling defined the subjects—or victims—of colonialism in an amalgam of Caliban and Man Friday: "Your new-caught, sullen peoples, half devil and half child." The devil and the child in immature peoples make them resent the civilizing process which draws them—"Ah, slowly!"—towards the light; it makes them reproach their Prosperos and Crusoes with the cry:

> Why brought ye us from bondage,
> Our loved Egyptian night?

Kipling was too careful a writer to have used "Egypt" without deliberation; he included in his "new-caught, sullen peoples," nations with the most ancient cultures in the world.

Because ancient cultures caused a suppressed self-doubt in a recruiting-sergeant poet, one searches in vain through Kipling's canon for any recognition of Hindu metaphysics or Islamic art. But he richly acknowledges qualities that need not embarrass "Gentleman Rankers" or "Er Majesty's Jollies—soldier an' sailor too." The chief such quality is the physical courage later singled out by Ernest Hemingway. In his poems extolling Fuzzy-Wuzzy, the Sudanese, or Gunga Din, the servant of British soldiers, Kipling creates by implication a literary type to set near aristocratic Prospero and middle-class Crusoe: the *Anonymous* British soldier who respects the native provided he cannot read or write. Thus *Anon.* addresses the Fuzzy-Wuzzy:

> You're a pore benighted 'eathen but a first-class
> fightin' man;

or salutes the "regimental bhisti" with the sentimental envoi:

> Though I've belted you and flayed you,
> By the livin' Gawd that made you,
> You're a better man than I am, Gunga Din.

Such lines seem, or are meant to seem, generous: admissions by a trim superior to the qualities hidden behind rags: "the uniform he wore was nothing much before, and rather less than 'arf o' that be 'ind." But the lines are in fact extra shillings for the soldier of the Queen: the assurance that there was someone lower than himself. For how can contempt more shrewdly masquerade than as Kiplingesque respect?

[3] *The White Man's Burden* (1899).

Kipling spoke for the other European nations, or that segment of them engaged in colonization. In the 1870s Wilfrid Scawen Blunt, a lesser poet than Kipling but a more perceptive observer of colonialism in action, had noticed the impact of Europe on the Algerian littoral: "the ignoble squalor of the Frank settlers, with their wineshops and their swine." A Kipling-esque attitude to the unlettered was observable where the French military dealt with the Saharan tribes: "In the Sahara, beyond the Atlas, where military rule prevailed, things were somewhat better, for the French officers for the most part appreciated the nobler qualities of the Arabs and despised the mixed rascaldom of Europe—Spanish, Italian and Maltese as well as their own countrymen—which made up the 'Colonie'." Frenchmen, too, respected the noble fighting man while despising the dregs from the slums they themselves had made.

This colonizing impetus was the force which stood behind Colvin and Cookson as they supported Towfik that hot September afternoon in Abdin Square. These two men were supremely of their time. This does not mean that this colonizing impetus can be limited to the 1880s. Since the age of Vasco da Gama, European states had controlled remote regions of the globe. The Pope himself had blessed the Portuguese and Spanish when they divided South America between them. The Dutch had occupied the Indonesian archipelago with Calvinist approval. The Church of England had seen in the piecemeal acquisition of the Rajahdoms of India a work of God. Even Denmark owned, besides Greenland, a West Indian island. Earlier, other civilizations, including Islam, had blessed and practiced similar expansions. Yet this European movement of the 1880s which had in Colvin and Cookson such fit exponents had links with finance and factory production which were new and distinctive; and though France's conquest of Algeria in the 1830s was its foreshadowing and Italy's conquest of Abyssinia in the 1930s would be its afterglow, the decade of the '80s saw this movement break the shackles of scruple with so strong a drive that liberals, as much as conservatives, became its tools.

The decade had been prepared for by the most romantic of conservatives. Britain's Prime Minister Disraeli, acting in harmony with the most hardheaded of realists, Germany's Chancellor Bismarck, had obtained Cyprus for Britain in 1878 because he envisioned that neglected island, Ottoman since the sixteenth century, as the hub of a great Asiatic empire under the British flag; his novel *Tancred* had explored just such a theme. The Sultan had agreed to cede Cyprus in return for British support in the Arabic-speaking provinces of the threatened empire. Disraeli had obtained another concession: the right to appoint roving British consuls in Anatolia. This second concession was of great importance to Disraeli, who based his visionary empire on Anatolia, not Egypt.

Disraeli's interest in Cyprus was ridiculed by Wilfrid Blunt. "The whole thing was a piece of romantic folly, but Disraeli loved to turn his political jests into realities and to persuade his English followers, whom as a Jew he despised, in all seriousness to the ways of his own folly." Disraeli, it might be truer to say, felt a sentimental attachment to the Levant, from which his Jewish ancestors had derived, akin to the feelings of Queen Victoria for the Scottish Highlands; as members of the Church of England both put British interests first. Wilfrid Blunt felt a similar attachment to the Middle East; in his case it was inspired by a Byronic espousal (his wife, Lady Anne Blunt, happened to be Byron's descendant) of the Muslim cause; Blunt saw in the life of the Bedouin of the Arabian desert (which he had visited in search of horses for his stud) a freedom civilized man had lost.

But sentiments apart, the acquisition of Cyprus had practical results; they involved both further loss to the Sultan and embarrassment to Disraeli. Shortly after concluding the Cyprus deal, Disraeli and his Foreign Minister, Lord Salisbury, met to discuss the "Eastern Problem"—the Ottoman Empire was faced by a total Russian defeat—with the other Powers in Berlin. The two men assured their colleagues they came to the Congress unbound by secret undertakings. The Cyprus deal was then uncovered. The French, neurotic from their defeat, ten years earlier, at the hands of the Prussians, resented imagined, let alone genuine, slights. They were only pacified when Bismarck secured them, in their turn, three concessions at the expense of the Sultan: an equal position with Britain in the control of Egyptian finances; their recognition as protectors of the Latin Christians of the Levant; and more concretely, the right to expand their North African holdings at Tunisian expense; the Bey of Tunis had a position analogous to that of the Egyptian Khedive.

Islamic opinion in general and the Sultan personally were henceforth to have little confidence in England's word. A trail which was to lead to bloodstained cliffs in Gallipoli started in Cyprus.

Disraeli, who had prepared the way for British expansion in the Middle East—first by acquiring a dominant share in the Suez Canal Company and now by controlling Cyprus as a *"place d'armes"*—was not to lead the next move forwards. William Ewart Gladstone, Prime Minister of Britain in the Liberal interest, was to deal with the problem of Egypt.

But it would be wrong to see politicians as the aces in this game of expatriate control.

The majestic yet reticent ace, colorless, able to slip through turnstiles unnoticed, was of course a wielder of money. George Orwell[4] has remarked that Kipling did not seem to realize "any more than the average soldier or colonial administrator, that an empire is primarily a money-making concern." The people who never forgot this supreme truth were the aces. The court cards were played in their interest, not that of their coun-

[4] George Orwell, *Rudyard Kipling; Critical Essays* (London: 1946).

tries. Colvin was not backed because he quoted the Latin classics or held himself with dignity. He was backed because he was comptroller of Egypt's finances. His assistant Cookson was backed because, as acting British consul and judge, he could invoke state power in support of Colvin. Towfik was backed because his fez, medals and title made the whole thing legal—or almost legal, taking into account the complication of Ottoman sovereignty. Towfik had little beneath his fez but memories of harem hurts and notions of bourgeois kingship. This negative nature made him unattractive to his subjects. To the aces it made him usable. He would have all their support in playing his abject role.

Chapter 4

THE Abdin incident left Orabi in a position from which to dominate Egypt. Though never more than War Minister, he was, for a year and two days, virtually all-powerful. Behind him, with him, surged the mass of ordinary Egyptians, stumbling for the first time since the Pharaohs, towards self-rule; their uncertainty the natural product of long swaddled limbs.

In the emergence of a Muslim strong man in North Africa the Sultan, bitter at the loss of Tunis, saw grounds for hope. The hope was tinged with danger. Abdul Hamid as an autocrat was suspicious of popular movements, even when they supported him; as an experienced observer of Europe he saw that the transformation of an army mutiny (as the backers of Towfik described the Abdin incident) into a genuine Egyptian revolution would not be welcome to the colonizing Powers.

Inside Egypt Orabi's popularity was as clamorous as it was sudden. The prayer, "God make you victorious, O Orabi!" rang through the dusty streets of the city wherever his carriage appeared. At Cairo railway station he harangued a crowd with the promise that a united, disciplined army would accomplish a glorious future for Egypt. In the delta, near his birthplace, a thousand people massed under colorful arabesque tenting heard him declare that every level of Egyptian life needed reform; they cheered when he said that Egyptians rather than Europeans should be employed wherever possible. On November 1, more calmly, he outlined his general views to Sir Auckland Colvin, the product of a tradition under which only white men ruled, or argued with rulers.

"He described the Government of the Mamelukes and that of the present dynasty," Colvin reported, "as being equally oppressive to the Arab population. His point was to show that up to the present the Egyptians have had no security for life or property. They were imprisoned, exiled, strangled, thrown into the Nile, starved and robbed according to the will of their masters. A liberated slave was a freer man than a freeborn Arab. The most ignorant Turk was preferred and honoured before the best of the Egyptians." He cited the instance of the one Arab who had risen to power under Ismail: Sadeek, the Minister of Finance whom the Khedive had murdered. "He then went on at great length to explain that men came of one common stock and had equal rights of personal liberty and security. The development of this theme took some considerable time and was curious in his naive treatment" (the Englishman's fidgets puncture his official prose) "but it evidently was the general outcome of the speaker's laboured thoughts, and was the expression, not of rhetorical periods, but of conviction."

Orabi repudiated the xenophobia attributed to him. He had no intention of getting rid of all Europeans, whether as residents or employees. "He spoke of them as the necessary instructors of the people. He himself and the two officers'—pointing to Ali Fehmy and Toulba Bey, his two companions—"had never been to school. Intercourse with Europeans had been their school."

Colvin at this point was impressed by the popular backing for the revolution. He described the political situation to his masters in London as essentially an armistice: "a little breathing-time during which we can take count of the forces that are at work around us, and endeavour to guide or repress them . . . The army is elated by what it has achieved, and its leaders are penetrated with the conviction that its mission is to give Egypt liberty." Orabi had convoked Ismail's rudimentary parliament, the "Chamber of Notables"; he wished to give this tame assembly fuller powers. Colvin had sympathy for constitutional development provided this did not obstruct his own control over Egyptian finances. "I do not think it is at all my duty to oppose myself to the popular movement, but to try rather to guide and to give it definite shape. So long as the financial position of the country, or the influence of the Control, is not likely to be affected by concessions made to the Notables, I believe I should be very foolish to express any hostility to their wishes."

But in England there was less interest in what the Egyptians wanted or did not want. On November 4, 1881, Lord Granville, Gladstone's Foreign Minister, wrote to Sir Edward Malet, the consul-general in Egypt, to whom Cookson was subordinate, outlining the bases of British policy.

In the first place, nominal Ottoman sovereignty must be studiously maintained. Because this was nominal, it could not affect matters; because it existed, it gave Britain a curtain from behind which to act; the curtain could also exclude interference from other Europeans.

But Ottoman sovereignty must under no circumstances become effective: "The British Government desired," Granville stressed, "to maintain Egypt in the enjoyment of the measure of administrative independence which has been secured to her by the Sultan's firmans." This meant, in ruder terms, the enjoyment of foreign control over her finances: something which the sovereign Ottomans had been able to resist in their homeland.

The sting—the sentence which Malet emphasized as he read the British statement to Towfik—came at the end of the third paragraph. After reiterating that Britain's imperial conscience would shrink from any desire to diminish Egyptian liberty "or tamper with the institutions to which it has given birth," Granville concluded: "The only circumstance which would force her Majesty's Government to depart from the course of conduct which he had mentioned *would be the occurrence in Egypt of a state of anarchy.*"

As Malet stressed the last words, their meaning ignited hopes behind Towfik's stolid and despondent face; the Khedive burned to punish the Egyptians.

Watchers from Whitehall, clutching for such anarchy, deplored a new outspokenness in the Egyptian press. "We are the prey of two lions," wrote one newspaper, "who are waiting for the opportune moment to realise their aims." Egypt also showed an objectionable sensitivity to foreign gibes. When a journalist writing in a French-language paper referred to the third Caliph, Othman, as "the fanatical heir of a false prophet," he was asked to leave the country. Again, in Suez the Egyptian troops showed signs of insubordination when one of their comrades was murdered by an Italian. Effervescence; but nothing so far that could be described as chaos.

There were indeed two lions: for after mid-December France was under the rule of Gambetta. The fire-eating Frenchman wrote to Lord Granville that "the enemies of the present system, the adherents of Ismail Pasha and Halim Pasha, and the Egyptians generally, should be made to understand that France and England, by whose influence Towfik has been placed on the throne, would not acquiesce in his being deposed from it." Gambetta proposed the sending of a stern Anglo-French note to the meeting of the Notables.

Britain's advice from Cairo ran counter to such an intervention. Colvin's memorandums argued that the greatest danger for Britain would be to solder the alliance between civilian opinion, represented by the Chamber of Notables, and military force, represented by Orabi and his colonels. No nineteenth-century Prospero wrote more perceptively than Colvin about his particular desert island. "In its origin, the movement is, I think, unquestionably an Egyptian movement against Turkish arbitrary rule." As he wrote his report, Colvin knew that it would be read by the same Gladstone whose ferocious attacks on Turkish rule in the Balkans had rung round Europe. "For the moment it is careful in its attitude towards Europeans because it has need of them in its duel with its immediate opponents, but it cannot look on them with favour, or be animated, *au fond,* by any other desire than of eventually getting rid of them." As Comptroller of Egyptian finances, Colvin sensed a double threat: if the Chamber gained the right to supervise the Egyptian budget, it might defy the Anglo-French control; it might also ease Europeans from the positions of influence in which Europe had placed them. Colvin's assessment of the situation neatly balanced liberal principles with an overall colonial concern. "The liberal movement now going on should, I think, in no wise be discouraged. It has many enemies, no less among Europeans than amongst Turks. But I believe it is essentially the growth of the popular spirit, and is directed to the good of the country, and that it would be most impolitic to thwart it. But precisely because I wish it to succeed, it seems to me essential that it should learn from the start within what limits it must confine itself. Otherwise, expectations may be formed, and hopes raised, the failure of which may lead to its entire discomfiture. In all that is doing or to be done, neither the Government nor the Chamber should be allowed to forget that the Powers have assumed a direct financial control over the country and intend to maintain it." This memorandum reached London on 2 January 1882. The Prime Minister for whom Colvin balanced his truths now acted as delicately as a Highland bull let loose in a khedivial palace. An Anglo-French note was immediately forwarded to Sir Edward Malet and M. Sienkiewicz, his French equivalent, in Cairo. Its key sentence was long-winded but decisive:

"I have accordingly to instruct you to declare to the Khedive that the English and French Governments consider the maintenance of His Highness on the throne, on the terms laid down by the Sultan's Firmans, and officially recognised by two Governments, as alone able to guarantee, for the present and the future, the good order and development of general prosperity in Egypt, in which France and Great Britain are equally interested."

The effect of the joint note was described by John Morley, Gladstone's official biographer, as a bombshell. Only Towfik was delighted: "The Note was taken to mean that the Sultan was to be thrust still farther in the background; that the Khedive was to become more plainly the puppet of England and France; and that Egypt would, sooner or later, in some shape or other, be made to share the disastrous fate of Tunis."

The Ottoman Sultan needed no convincing of the menace to his realms and his caliphal cause represented by Europe. He was well aware that he had struck a sorry bargain when he surrendered Cyprus against a promise of British support in his Arab provinces; to save the Berlin Congress,

Disraeli had authorized the French to occupy Tunis. The fair-skinned Sultan had little sympathy with the desire of dark-skinned Egyptians to rule themselves; but his dominant thought was to preserve the one effective Muslim state on earth, his own. In this devotion to Islam he was sincere; it was this more than autocratic temper which made him oppose the liberals inside his own state and modernize his country technically (by developing railways and telegraphs) while strengthening the central power. In a series of remarkable letters sent secretly to Orabi he outlined the Ottoman attitude to the crisis. It was not ignoble. The first letter, written in the hand of his chaplain, stressed that the prime duty of every Muslim was to safeguard the integrity of the Caliphate. "It is incumbent on every Egyptian to strive earnestly after the consolidation of my power to prevent Egypt from passing out of my hands into the rapacious grasp of foreigners, as the vilayet of Tunis has already passed." As to the Khedive—whose throne the Anglo-French note had proclaimed to be sacrosanct—he was described in scathing terms: "According to the telegrams and news sent by the Khedive Towfik, we see that he is weak and capricious, and also it is to be remarked that one of his telegrams does not corroborate another, but they are all in contradiction." In a second letter, written on the same day, but by the hand of his private secretary, the Sultan spoke yet more bluntly of the dynasty of Muhammad Ali: "It matters nothing who is Khedive of Egypt. The thoughts of the ruler of Egypt, his intentions and his conduct, must be governed with the greatest care, and all his actions must tend to secure the future of Egypt, and to uphold intact the sovereignty of the Caliph, while he must show the most perfect zeal in upholding the faith and the country's rights. This will be required of him. Of the persons who have been on the khedivial throne, Ismail Pasha and his predecessors gave bribes to Ali Pasha, Fuad Pasha, Midhat Pasha and other representatives of the Sublime Porte, traitors! and after shutting the eyes of the officials, dared to overtax and oppress the Egyptians." The Anglo-French note, prating of Towfik as the only hope of Egypt, for the present and the future, had antagonized the Sultan almost as much as the loss of Tunis.

Besides demeaning the Sultan's authority in Egypt, the note undermined the authority of the civilian leaders who might have replaced Orabi. Many Notables distrusted the colonels' arbitrary power; others felt their interests threatened by Egyptian insurgence. Sherif Pasha had been accepted as Prime Minister by Orabi after the Abdin incident. He was, nevertheless, a Circassian by race and temper. His position had now become impossible. On January 10 he called on Sir Edward Malet and protested in the strongest terms at the Anglo-French intervention. The note encouraged the Khedive to oppose reform, while reform alone could obviate revolution; it served to weaken the links between Egypt and the Ottoman state, while such links were the constitutional barrier to violent change; the terms in which the note was phrased showed contempt for a

Chamber which had, in the event, proved moderate and could in the future be another barrier to arbitrary power; worst of all, the note contained a threat of direct intervention, unacceptable to Egyptians of every opinion.

Sherif Pasha if anything understated the Chamber's feelings. A delegation of Notables called on the Khedive to demand a stronger ministry, with Orabi as War Minister. Despite the Anglo-French note, Towfik could only yield. In place of Sherif Pasha he was constrained to appoint as Prime Minister Mahmoud Sami al-Baroudi, a poet as well as a revolutionary. Orabi Pasha, as War Minister, was the dominant member of the new government. Sherif Pasha had rightly discerned that British policy now envisaged direct intervention. A ministry dominated by Orabi was something that Britain could not accept. When constitutional reform was mooted, Colvin commented brusquely: "The house is tumbling about our ears, and the moment is not propitious for debating whether we would like another storey added to it. Until civil authority is reassured and the military despotism destroyed, discussion of the Organic Law seems premature and useless."

But in order to destroy Orabi Britain needed a weighty pretext or undaunted allies. So far she had neither. Gambetta's flamboyant rule was at an end and France, now a timorous partner, proposed the substitution of the more attractive Prince Halim for the discredited Towfik. As for the other Powers—Russia, Austria, Germany and Italy—they had been alienated by their exclusion from the discussions which had preceded the sending of the note. They expressed their resentment of the Anglo-French action by declaring that the situation could only be altered by an understanding between all the Powers and the suzerain authority, the Sultan. If the remote United States felt anything, it was sympathy for the democratic aspirations of the Egyptian movement.

Lacking firm allies, Britain scanned the horizon for a pretext. Anarchy seemed a hair's breadth away when, in May, a group of Circassian officers were accused of plotting against Orabi's life. The East has always been fertile in plots, some genuine, some products of coffeehouse gossip. But it was entirely credible that some Circassians had prepared to act against a leader who threatened their caste; their knowledge of official British feelings would have strengthened their hand. Forty of the alleged conspirators were arrested, including a general, Osman Pasha Rifki. A military court sentenced them to exile in the remote Sudan. Since generals (the Ottoman title was "Pasha") were appointed by the Sultan, Towfik saw a way to serve his Circassian friends: the Sultan should be asked to reprieve Osman. This move did not suit the French: the enhancement of the Sultan's prestige could threaten their position in Tunis. They advised Towfik to assert his own authority in defense of his friends and caste. On May 9 Towfik did so by modifying the court's sentence to simple exile, the place unspecified. The spiritual rift between the Khedive and his nationalist ministers was now total. Towfik had shown that his frequently reiterated concern for Egyptian autonomy meant nothing: to serve his own ends he had been prepared to involve the Sultan. Orabi and the other colonels began thinking in terms of deposing the Khedive, exiling the whole family of Muhammad Ali and appointing a governor-general of their choice.

As the Orabi movement showed an increasing transformation into real revolution, its opponents toyed with one solution after another. Malet, Towfik suggested, might ask the Sultan to authorize the Khedive to invite Anglo-French intervention. The French, hitherto hostile to any Ottoman involvement, began to feel that intervention under an Ottoman banner might be the only alternative to religious or racial fanaticism from the Egyptians.

But Gladstone could not trust an Ottoman Sultan to serve the interests of Western civilization. Instead, he authorized a legal but incendiary move. On May 20 the great western harbor of Alexandria, where the palace of Ras el-Tin confronted across busy water the wharfs and warehouses of the Egyptian Customs, witnessed the arrival of an Anglo-French armada. Among the thousands who watched was Baron de Kusel, a Liverpool-born Englishman employed as Controller-General of the Egyptian Customs.

"The British vessels," De Kusel wrote, "were the ironclads: *Alexandra, Inflexible, Invincible, Temeraire, Superb, Sultan* and *Monarch;* and the gunboats: *Beacon, Bittern, Cyprus, Condor* and *Decoy,* with about three thousand five hundred men, and one hundred and two guns, all under the command of Vice-Admiral Sir Frederick Beauchamp Paget Seymour." The fleet had arrived uninvited. The official British hope, exemplified by the counsel of Malet, was that its presence would steel the Khedive into calling on one of the Circassians—perhaps Sherif Pasha—to seize the initiative and form a new civilian ministry.

The French consul-general, M. Sienkiewicz, was more realistic than Malet. No Circassian, he recognized, would defy Orabi while he controlled the Army. The simplest way to resolve the crisis would be to ease Orabi out. With the backing of the richest financiers in France, Sienkiewicz offered the War Minister a substantial inducement to go into retirement. Informed rumor in London said that "the Rothschilds had offered Orabi £4000 (one hundred thousand francs) a year for life if he would leave Egypt." Orabi himself was to claim, years later, that the French consul-general offered him double his army pay (which would have raised his stipend to £500 a month) if he would accept the same comfortable exile as the Emir Abdul Kader, the Algerian resistance leader. The hope that money, not arms, might deflate the revolutionary balloon did not die quickly. The *Pall Mall Gazette* reported as late as the May 18: "Orabi is said to be thinking of visiting Europe to recruit his health—a commendable intention, and no harm would be done if he were allotted a handsome travelling allowance on condition that he did not return."

Orabi refused such inducements. His own ideals apart, he knew the feelings of the Army. As one of the other colonels remarked, "the officers would hew Orabi in pieces if he deserted them."

If bribery had failed to oust Orabi, the presence of an armada in Alexandria harbor had failed to prompt a palace coup. Nor did the ironclads, in De Kusel's words, "calm the air, in fact, rather the reverse, and the European element began to feel slightly alarmed." The European element were right. The visible menace of ironclads riding in their territorial waters, within pistol shot of their drying laundry, roused the ire of the Alexandrian Egyptians. On May 15, against a background of rumors—that the foreigners were about to exile Orabi, to disband the Egyptian Army and occupy the country—Malet tried direct diplomatic action. As British consul-general he presented an official note to the president of the council of Ministers. Where Rothschild money had vainly asked, the note demanded: Orabi Pasha must be temporarily retired, though with his full rank and pay; Orabi's two associated colonels should be removed to the provinces; the present ministry should resign.

Next morning it seemed as though Malet had won. The ministry tendered its resignation *en bloc,* at the same time addressing a letter to Towfik accusing him "of acquiescing in foreign intervention in contradiction to the terms of the Firmans." Towfik coldly answered that he accepted the resignation of the ministry since "it was the will of the nation."

But satisfaction in London and Paris was short-lived. Malet's *démarche* had aggravated the situation. On the one hand Sherif Pasha refused point-blank to form a new government while the army leaders remained in Egypt; on the other, the army and police officers in Alexandria (the city where the concentration of Europeans was greatest and where any trouble might be expected to start) cabled that they would not permit Orabi to resign and if the Khedive did not change his mind within twelve hours they would not be responsible for public tranquillity. On the twenty-eighth Malet had to cable Lord Granville that the Chiefs of Religion, including the Coptic Patriarch and the Chief Rabbi with the Muslim Ulema, along with all the deputies and other Notables, had waited on the Khedive that afternoon and implored him to reinstate Orabi as Minister of War.

In this impasse Gladstone decided to play one last peaceful, if paradoxical, card. Prompted perhaps by Colvin, he would ask the Sultan "to send a military Commissioner to Egypt, a soldier of the old energetic unscrupulous type, who, by the mere terror of his presence, should frighten the Egyptians out of their attitude of resistance to England, and that as to Orabi, if he could not be lured on ship-board and sent to Constantinople, the Commissioner should invite him to a friendly conference, and there shoot him, if necessary, with his own hand." Gladstone's decision was perhaps the strangest of his career; its inconsistency with his anti-Turkish bias may in part explain why his biographer compressed his Egyptian chapter into a handful of pages. At the time, however, in articles published in his *Pall Mall Gazette,* John Morley seemed delighted when the Sultan agreed to Gladstone's proposal. "The Egyptian crisis has reached its culminating point, and at last it seems that there is a man at Cairo capable of controlling events. There is something very impressive in the calm immovable dignity of Dervish Pasha, who is emphatically the man of the situation. After all the shiftings and twistings of diplomatists and the fitful exhibition of weakness on the part of the leading actors in this Egyptian drama, it is an immense relief to find 'one still strong man' who by the mere force of his personal presence, can make every man bow to his will." Morley's normal distaste for military strong men had vanished in a colonial crisis throbbing like a migraine.

"Dervish Pasha," wrote the Liberal, agnostic journalist, "is at once the more vigorous and unscrupulous of all the Generals of the Ottoman army. Although he is now seventy years old, his age has not weakened his energy or impaired his faculties. His will is still as iron as it was of old, and he is quite as capable of ordering a massacre of the Mamelukes as Muhammad Ali himself." With relish Morley told his readers in the *Pall Mall Gazette* of how Dervish Pasha had shown his mettle in the Balkans when on one occasion he had given his word to a local rebel, an Albanian Voivode, or Bey. "The Turkish engagements were kept by the extermination of the entire family of the Voivode." Morley gave details of the exploit. "The prisoners were marched off to Trebinji and thrown into the dungeon of the fortress, tied back to back, one of each couplet being killed and the survivor not released for a moment from the burden of his dead comrade."

But Liberal hopes that a Turk would accomplish an unspeakable miracle were dashed. In the days of his youth, with an army behind him, Dervish Pasha may have been as ruthless as Morley described him; he was now a rather silly old man. He had no power and his authority was shared. The Sultan had no intention of furthering the interests of those who had taken Tunis and wanted to take Egypt; he therefore sent with the old warrior an Ottoman expert on Arab affairs, Sheikh Ahmed Assad, head of one of the mystical brotherhoods in the Arabian city of Medina. The Sheikh, astute and informed, was instructed to contact Orabi in secret and convey certain messages of continued support from Constantinople as well as a code for direct communication. Orabi was only too ready to co-operate with the Sultan—he was his only potential ally. The Ottoman emissaries were given a tumultuous welcome when they docked at Alexandria. The crowd shouted: "God make the Sultan victorious!" Adding: "But reject the ultimatum!"

Dervish was guided by only one coherent motive—to make his Egyptian visit pay. Hungry for money and gems, he would please anyone with these commodities to offer. He promised the rich Circassians: "We'll get rid of Orabi and send him to Constantinople." He promised the Egyptians: "We shall see that the foreign ships leave Alexandria." The Khedive scraped together £25,000 in cash and the same amount in jewels with which to bind the senile general to his side. In return for Towfik's generosity, the Pasha made one masterful gesture. His first Friday in Cairo he toured the main mosques when they were packed for prayer. He found only four religious leaders adhering to Towfik; the rest shouted for Orabi. Piqued, the old man decorated the four while rebuking the others in peevish terms.

Egypt, thanks to its railways, was a remarkably centralized state and next morning the whole country knew of the old Turk's rudeness. Monster demonstrations supported Orabi, and Dervish Pasha, with no soldiers to back him, quailed. For the first time since his arrival he received the Egyptian Prime Minister and War Minister in audience. He offered them neither coffee nor cigarettes. (This was his nearest approach to Morley's hoped-for ferocity.) But his words were conciliatory. "As sons of one Sultan, we are all brothers. My white beard gives me the right to speak as your father. We have a common goal: resistance to the infidel and the departure of his fleet, since the presence of this fleet threatens the Sultan as much as yourselves. We must all cooperate in zealous service of our Lord. You, Orabi, must cooperate by surrendering your military power to me and going to Constantinople."

Orabi answered firmly: he would resign his commission only when accusations of rebellion and suggestions of misappropriation of funds had been withdrawn, and after the situation in which he bore responsibility had been clarified. When things were calm he would, as a civilian Muslim, be delighted to pay his respects to the Sultan-Caliph.

The Dervish mission reached this impasse at noon on Saturday, June 10. The next day, Sunday the eleventh, produced the anarchy which the British had been predicting with hopeful pessimism since the previous autumn. A row between an Alexandrian donkey boy and a Maltese client swelled into a riot, which, having engulfed the Maltese quarter, spread quickly throughout the port. Since Egyptians and foreigners had long been estranged, since donkey boys played the role of modern taxis and overcharged, since summer made Europeans tetchy, the riot could perhaps have been spontaneous. No observer thought so. Baron de Kusel, the same Englishman who had watched the arrival of the fleet, was convinced that it had been carefully planned; all day long groups of the lower-class Arabs had been seen hanging about, while Bedouin had poured into the city from the country armed with heavy cudgels, or *naboots*. Such a mixed riffraff of urban and desert poor would riot for whoever paid them. De Kusel (writing under the rule of Orabi's victorious opponents) hinted at the people he thought responsible. "It was noticeable that the police and the Municipal Guard did nothing to quell the riot, in some cases being accused of aiding and abetting. In one instance it is reported that some Europeans sought safety at the chief *caracol* (police station). Once inside, the doors were closed, and they were murdered by the guard." The riot, which lasted from lunchtime to teatime, was naturally blamed on Orabi; but no serious witness ever supported this charge. Orabi was responsible for the Army, not the police or Municipal Guard. These came under the control of Omar Pasha Lutfi, the governor of Alexandria. Circassian, courtier and friend of Towfik, Omar Pasha had been suggested as a likely substitute for Orabi if the colonel were ever dismissed.

De Kusel was no more a supporter of Orabi than he was a believer in Egyptian democracy. He saw his prime duty as being to England, not to his Egyptian employers. Yet he was an honest man and described what he saw. He had witnessed the start of the riot, having been on an excursion outside the main town. Rumor of what was occurring sent him hurrying back.

"As we passed through the Rosetta Gate, we found troops drawn up in the empty space inside, the men at ease, with piled arms, the officers seated all along the roadway smoking. As I passed I salaamed to them, and they all returned my salute." The British consulate was one focus of the rioters; Cookson, who had deputized for Malet at the Abdin confrontation, was seriously hurt; his Greek and Italian opposite numbers were injured slightly; two hundred people perished. The confusion near the British consulate ended a few minutes after five, when "the troops appeared on the scene and charged down the streets dispersing the rioters. This gave us a little relief, but as darkness fell, the martial sounds from the streets, the tramp, tramp of the infantry and the deep rumbling of artillery were not conducive to the alleviation of the fugitives' fright; more especially so as we never knew from one moment to the other whether the troops would not join the rioters, and complete the job. Very fortunately for us the officers kept their men well in hand."

Orabi and his officers had reason to keep their men in hand. It was essential for the Egyptians to suppress the riot, since unchecked anarchy would doom the movement for Egyptian freedom. The speed with which the riot was suppressed assisted, temporarily, the Egyptian cause. The European residents, previously hostile to Orabi, now looked on him as their savior. If Orabi could have speedily arraigned the authors of the riot and had them punished, it is possible, Wilfrid Blunt was later to argue, that he might have won the diplomatic game. "Then he would have appealed to Europe and to the Sultan in words of a strong man and they would not have been disregarded; nor would the Government in England, who, after all, were no paladins, have stood against the rest . . . Unfortunately for liberty, Orabi was no such strong man; he was also ignorant of Europe, or of the common arts and crafts of its diplomacy."

For Orabi, and perhaps even for Towfik, the riot was one incident in a monotonous chain; there was a theme but no conclusion; nothing came to a head. The Khedive now moved from Cairo to his palace overlooking

Alexandria harbor; with him moved Dervish Pasha, both of them feeling safer near the British fleet; but neither regarded the move as a final break, since it was the usual habit of the Khedive to move to the sea in summer. Towfik even received Orabi and accepted his word of honor that "come what might he would defend his life like his own"; Blunt was to comment that the Khedive, "who had nothing but treachery in his heart, accepted this promise and abused it to the end." On the sixteenth he appointed a new Prime Minister, Raghab Pasha; but Orabi remained the Khedive's Minister of War.

Orabi himself moved to Cairo. From a capital emptying of foreigners he looked to the far Europe whose ways he so little understood. He had some reasons for hope. In England Blunt organized an influential group of politicians and journalists in support of the Egyptian cause; on a different social level a Workman's Peace Association issued an appeal in late June to the working men of the United Kingdom: "At a moment when angry demands are made that our forces shall attack the Egyptian people, it behoves us to ask the reason why. Among the many complications in which this country became involved by the action of the late Government was what is termed the Egyptian control, which Control consists of an Englishman and a Frenchman who were empowered, with the sanction of their respective Governments, to intercept the revenues of Egypt for the benefit of persons who had floated loans and speculated in shares . . . The Egyptians claim the right to choose their own rulers, and England cannot consistently compel them to accept her nominee who is to act as a puppet in the hands of the European controllers . . . The people of Egypt have risen against their present ruler because his father despoiled Egypt, placed her in the grip of the foreign bondholders' interest. The money lent by foreigners was spent mainly in bribing the Porte, in debauchery, in the building of twenty palaces for the late Khedive, and the maintenance of his 400 wives . . . Up to the present the net result of our threatened intervention has been a riot and loss of life at Alexandria. Nor is this to be wondered at. If a French fleet entered the Mersey and threatened Liverpool, the indignation of the Liverpool people would probably vent itself upon any Frenchman who happened to be residing there. In conclusion we earnestly appeal to you to use your legitimate influence to prevent our Government from making war upon the Egyptians, either in support of the Khedive or in the immediate interest of unprincipled speculators."

If Orabi had some reason to hope for sympathy from England, he had warmer encouragement from Germany; Chancellor Bismarck admitted flatly that Orabi had become a power "with whom it was necessary to count." The other European Powers shared this view while France reiterated her conviction that Towfik should be replaced by Halim, Muhammad Ali's surviving son.

Orabi defined the situation as he saw it in mid-June in language which balanced hope with defiance. "The Khedive has now made peace with me, and in the presence of the Representatives of the six European Powers and of Dervish Pasha, has asked me to take on myself the responsibility for public safety. I have accepted his order, and pledged my word and sworn to defend his life and the lives of those who inhabit Egypt, of every creed and nation; and, as long as I live and my jurisdiction is not interfered with, I will keep my word." But Orabi was aware that despite Gladstone's Commons statement of June 1 that "no troops are to be mobilised in India, and no troops are to be landed in Egypt," British soldiers were being mustered for an invasion; the Cairo British, Malet and Colvin, offered at best a truce. Orabi added more somberly: "We will not be the aggressors, but we will resist all who attempt to attack us. We are a sincere nation, and grateful to those who take us by the hand and help us to reform our country . . . Europeans, and especially England, look upon us as barbarians. They can crush us, they say, in twenty-four hours. Well, if they are willing, let them try it, but they will lose their eighty million of public debt and the twenty million the fellahin privately owe to the bankers. The first shot fired will release us from these engagements; and the nation on this account wishes nothing more than war."

In this statement Orabi again showed himself a son of the East: an East molded by a Prophet who had authorized Muslims to fight in defense of their community, but only when the enemy had struck the first blow. In a clash between land-based forts and ship-based guns whoever struck the first blow was likely also to strike the last.

For what it was worth, the benediction of the Sultan-Caliph protected Orabi. In March he had been raised from the grade of colonel to that of Pasha, or general; in June he received, from the hand of Dervish Pasha, the imperial Order of the Mejedieh. The Ottoman press sang his praises; he was prayed for in mosques as far west as Algiers and Tunis.

But what buoyed Orabi most was the clamorous support of his own people. Wherever he drove through the streets of Cairo, crowds formed to shout: "May God exalt you, O Orabi! May God make you victorious!" It was far from the crowd's thoughts that it might contribute to the longed-for victory. But its cries were encouraging. Louis Sabunji, a Syrian clergyman with Muslim sympathies, was acting as Wilfrid Blunt's agent and reporter in Cairo. He described an evening with Orabi and his friends, Mahmoud Sami al-Baroudi, Muhammad Abduh and others. The hot June hours were passed by the Egyptian leaders in composing impromptu elegies and satires: "Orabi composed a satire, Abduh two, Nadim made four and Sami two. At dinner I sat by Orabi. The courses were about thirty different Arab dishes, besides the European and Eastern cakes, sweetmeats and fruit. After dinner we talked freely about politics, and about different plans and forms of government. The republican form was preferred, and al-Baroudi, who displayed great knowledge and ingenuity, endeavoured to show the advantage of a republican government for Egypt. He said: 'From the beginning of our movement we aimed at turning Egypt into a small republic like Switzerland—and then Syria would have joined; and then Hejaz would have followed. But we found some of the Ulema were not quite prepared for it and were behind our time. Nevertheless we shall endeavour to make Egypt a republic before we die.'"

But Egypt's enemies, wasting no time on writing satires, spent energy and money in ensuring Egypt would remain a puppet kingdom. Having established that the poetizing leaders were barbarians, their people anarchs, the British Government had decided that all it needed for intervention was proof that the Egyptians were dangerous, too. Orabi's actions, or lack of them, admittedly gave little support to such a view. Besides attending prayer meetings, listening to endless recitations of the names of God and receiving delegations ranging from village worthies to nationalist princes and princesses of the khedivial house, the War Minister was doing little to prepare Egypt for the struggle he had half predicted. Only in Alexandria, the point most threatened, did he begin to prepare for a possible attack. Work on the sea forts had indeed started a month earlier, a few days before the riot, but had been stopped on the request of the Sultan, who wanted to give no provocation to the Europeans. On July 3, the British admiral received orders from London to prevent continuance of work on the fortifications. "If not immediately discontinued, he was to destroy the earthworks and silence the batteries if they opened fire."

Two days later a hesitant France dissociated herself from the British ultimatum. The French Government considered that the action envisaged would be an act of offensive hostility against Egypt; the French constitution prohibited the making of war without the consent of the Chamber. The following day Admiral Seymour single-handedly commanded the cessation of fortification and the erection of earthworks. He was informed by the military, now in sole control of Alexandria, that no guns had recently been added, that no military preparations were being made. Dervish Pasha, who as the Sultan's commissioner symbolized Ottoman sovereignty, was on hand to confirm that this was indeed the case. But London was ruled by a Prime Minister who had never been concerned with what Ottomans said or did not say; Gladstone had decided that the British fleet, "lawfully present in the waters of Alexandria, had the right and duty of self-defence." The Egyptian crisis was causing disquiet in the parts of northern England, notably Lancashire, whose factory owners depended on an orderly supply of Egyptian cotton. Gladstone had always had a profound distaste for such military leaders as Cromwell and Napoleon; he had now developed an almost personal loathing for Colonel Orabi.

The British prepared their plans with care. From Alexandria vulnerable foreigners were evacuated to their countries of origin or to the protection of the anchored ships. The well-informed guessed what was coming. De

Kusel was preoccupied with smuggling a large sum of money from the consulate building to the safety of a British man-of-war; this involved him in telling a direct lie to Orabi, who took his word that he was doing no such thing. "Whenever I had a few hours to spare," De Kusel wrote later, "I devoted them to assisting Major Tulloch, of the Intelligence Department, whose headquarters were on board *H.M.S. Invincible* and who rendered great service to Admiral Seymour, by his secret reconnaissance work." Major Tulloch was particularly interested to discover whether Orabi was dug in at Kafr al-Zayat, the obvious line of defense against an attack towards Cairo. De Kusel was so busy that he forgot to transmit a telegram handed to him by a British journalist. An early example of reporter's telegraphese, it preserves the tension of the hours before the storm broke: Meanwhile/Khedive/rests/ashore/in/palace/which/exactly/in/line/of/fire/ he/was/i/believe/almost/first/to/be/informed/Condor/gunboat/placed/ at/disposal/but/refused/in/bravest/possible/manner/his/reply/makes/all/ sad/dervish/i/hear/come/afloat/khedive/will/certainly/be/killed/ashore/ orabi/being/so/enraged/against/him/at/moment.

On the night of July 10 the French fleet steamed out of Alexandria en route for Port Said; the British ships also left the inner harbor for positions assigned to them. At 7 A.M. on the eleventh the British admiral, on board the *Invincible,* signaled for one shell to be fired into the recently armed earthworks termed "the Hospital Battery." This was followed by a general signal to the fleet: "Attack the enemy's batteries." Baron de Kusel had not stayed ashore with his Egyptian subordinates but was safely on board the *Tanjore.*

"To a civilian who had never seen warfare the spectacle was magnificent. We heard the single gun from the *Alexandra,* which was the signal for the attack to commence, and then one by one every ship joined in until the whole fleet was engaged. It was rather terrible and awe-inspiring, and in spite of myself I trembled with excitement. It was not long before all we could see was a mass of white smoke which surrounded the ships. We could hear, though we could see little, and the roar of the broadside, the deep booming of the turret guns, and the quick taptapping of the Nordenfelt, caused most of our hearts, I think, to beat a trifle faster. Occasionally, too, we caught a glimpse of a ship, and many Egyptian shells, which through faulty aim of the gunners, passed right over the English ships, and went skip-skipping along the sea, throwing up clouds of spray before sinking." The Egyptians, though inept, fought bravely. "In spite of the tremendous and deadly fire from the British ships the Egyptian gunners stuck manfully to their posts, maintaining a heavy fire, their shots striking the ships occasionally. They fought very gallantly but they had not the knowledge of their weapons necessary to make their defense successful or even partially so."

The firing lasted till 11 A.M., though some forts continued a desultory resistance a few hours longer.

No sooner had the bombardment ceased than the city of Alexandria began to burn, either ignited by the guns or deliberately set on fire. Orabi himself gave no decisive lead. If he had started the fire as a riposte to the bombardment, he would have been as justified as the Russians when they gave Moscow to flames. Orabi's repeated denials that he had done so testified to a tender conscience rather than a steely will. He did, however, evacuate the Egyptian Army to defensive positions south of the lake that cuts Alexandria from the rest of Egypt. This left a vacuum, since for some reason the British did not at once land troops to control the sprawling port. Nor did the Khedive, who had survived the bombardment, have any power at his disposal. He had escaped execution at the hands of a group of soldiers thanks to a considerable bribe; he had then been smuggled from Ramleh Palace, four miles from the city, to Ras el-Tin, where a force of seven hundred British marines could protect him.

Order was restored to the burnt-out city by a temporary police force under the command of Lord Charles Beresford. It consisted of British marines working with bluejackets and disarmed Egyptians. Its center of operations was the great square of Muhammad Ali, once the sauntering place of the foreign cotton brokers and merchants. A rickety table had been placed amidst the trees in the middle to act as a tribunal for Lord Charles and his first officer, Lieutenant Bradford. The justice they dispensed was summary. American marines, who had been landed to guard the U.S. consulate, shut off the square; De Kusel helped with the interpretation of colloquial Arabic. As those accused of looting or other acts of resistance were condemned, they were tied to the surrounding trees and shot; graves had been dug for them in front of the trees.

"This, although to many it would doubtless appear very terrible, was nevertheless the only and proper way of dealing with the criminals," wrote De Kusel. (Four months later a grateful Khedive was to create him a "Bey.") "There is no folly so great and so conducive to such bad results as sentimentality."

The British showed few signs of this vice.

Gladstone had sacrificed, through the bombardment, the friendship of John Bright, the man who had been nearest to him in ideals. "The British fleet . . ." Gladstone wrote in an effort to convince his colleague, "demanded the discontinuance of attempts made to strengthen the armament of the fortifications . . . Met by fraud and falsehood in its demand, it required surrender with a view to immediate dismantling, and this being refused, it proceeded to destroy. The conflagration which followed, the pillage and any other outrages effected by the released convicts, these are not due to us, but to the seemingly wanton wickedness of Orabi." *The Observer,* a London newspaper then as fervent for colonialism as it would be against it in the coming century, proclaimed that the authority of Great Britain in Egypt had at last been asserted by force of arms. "At last, too, the world has been taught once more that no matter what party may be in power, no matter what principles may direct our national policy, Englishmen cannot be massacred abroad with impunity, and English interests cannot be defied with safety."

Nine days after the bombardment, the British Cabinet decided on the dispatch of an expeditionary force to the Mediterranean, under the command of Sir Garnet Wolseley. Two days later Towfik, under British protection in Alexandria, summoned the courage to dismiss Orabi. For more than a month, however, he did not dare appoint a new government. Orabi, in any case, continued to rule in Cairo and the delta.

But while the British tested the lines south of Lake Mariout (they proved too strong to penetrate) and made plans for opening another route to Cairo by way of the Suez Canal, Orabi showed his character in action: or rather, inaction. He held a daily court at Genjis Osman, to which the personalities of Egypt flocked—the rich merchants, the owners of newspapers and the learned men of al-Azhar. One of his devotees was the beautiful and brilliant Princess Nazli, the daughter of Ismail's brother, Mustafa Fazil. Her zeal for Orabi was partly inspired by hatred for her uncle Ismail, who, by changing the laws of succession, had disinherited her father and made Towfik his heir. She also genuinely admired Orabi. He was, she told Wilfrid Blunt when the affair was over, "the first Egyptian Minister who made the Europeans obey him. In his time at least the Mohammedans held up their heads, and the Greeks and Italians did not dare transgress the law." But she saw Orabi's weakness too. "He was not good enough a soldier, and had too good a heart. These were his faults."

These faults were amply displayed in his last weeks of power. He was charmed by the flattery of the khedivial ladies and the gifts they brought him. He sat, the hero of Egypt, in an enormous tent formerly the property of Said Pasha, and now presented by Said's widow as a national offering to her husband's former aide-de-camp. He was too good-hearted to see that such attentions made some of his officers jealous. If Orabi won, they feared, if he beat the British, he would be all-powerful and they would be nothing. Such tendencies to schism, typical of Arabs, were one factor in the weakness of the Egyptian Army. Another was a skillful use of bribes by the British: the Bedouin on both sides of the Suez Canal were suborned to provide information about the half-hearted dispositions being made by Orabi's Army. But the chief fault lay with Orabi himself. Convinced of his providential role as savior of Egypt, he did little that was practical, preferring to surround himself with holy men. "Much of the time he should have given to the secular duty of organising the defence was wasted with them in chaunts and recitations."

One obvious precaution was to close the Canal. This could easily have been effected between Port Said and Ismailia. But De Lesseps was passionate and convincing.

"Ne faites aucune tentative pour intercepter mon Canal. Je suis là! Ne craignez rien de ce coté. Il ne se débarquera pas un seul soldat anglais sans être accompagné d'un soldat français. Je réponds de tout."

Orabi hesitated before the Frenchman's identification with "his" Canal. By the time he made up his mind to block the waterway, he was too late. Sir Garnet's fleet had sailed, twenty-four hours earlier, through the narrows and into the Great Bitter Lake. (Talking about a proposed Channel Tunnel some years later, Wolseley remarked: "If Orabi had blocked the Canal, as he intended to do, we should still at the present moment be on the high seas blockading Egypt. Twenty-four hours delay saved us.") Sir Garnet had with him an army of thirty thousand. Orabi could muster against him some thirteen thousand men of some caliber; the rest were hastily raised levies good for digging trenches and little else.

The night before the decisive battle Orabi spent in more prayers and recitations with his holy men; he made no inspection of the defenses; if he had done, he would have found that some positions were unmanned, thanks to British bribes.

The next day, September 13, the Egyptian army guarding the eastern approaches to the delta were overwhelmed at Tel el-Kebir. Ahmed Orabi did nothing either desperate or effective, but took the train to Cairo and surrendered his sword to the polite British officers who had taken over Abbasia Barracks. He left behind more than a thousand Egyptian dead. The British lost eleven officers among their fifty-four casualties.

In the euphoria of summer Orabi and his friends had hoped to see a republican form of government before they died. As the poet al-Baroudi expatiated on ideal constitutions, his boots were possibly being blacked by some half-listening child. If that urchin survived the bilharzia endemic in the delta, if his eyes stayed undarkened by trachoma, he may have seen, if he lived into his seventies, the end of the dynasty of Muhammad Ali and the establishment of an Egyptian republic. But Orabi and his friends saw only the reign of Towfik and his son. Behind these unimpressive potentates stood the glittering force of the British Army, installed in the barracks of Kasr el-Nil in the heart of Cairo.

Chapter 5

ORABI's country and person were now at Britain's disposal.

"I am asked," Lord Granville, the Liberal Foreign Secretary, wrote to Lord Salisbury, his Conservative predecessor, a few months later, "to state the exact date of the withdrawal of the troops. I cannot conceive that it would be prudent to make such a statement. We shall not keep our troops in Egypt any longer than is necessary; but it would be an act of treachery to ourselves, to Egypt, and to Europe, if we withdrew them without having a certainty—or, if not a certainty, because we cannot have a certainty in the affairs of this life, until there is a reasonable expectation—of a stable, a permanent, and a beneficial Government being established in Egypt."

An English Prospero, recommended by Sir Edward Malet, was to exercise effective control over Egypt. The baptismal name of this olympian ruler was Evelyn, his surname Baring; he would be known to Egypt and to history as "Cromer," after a Norfolk seaside town from which he took his title; his admiring colleagues knew him simply as "the Lord."

Cromer's direction of Egyptian affairs during the remaining years of the nineteenth century and the first seven years of the twentieth century showed expatriate control in an overt form; Egypt was a veiled protectorate in which Towfik, who died in 1892, had little power and his son, Abbas Hilmi, hardly more. Orabi's personal fate showed a less overt manifestation of British influence.

The Khedive Towfik had lived in unpopular isolation at Ras el-Tin Palace during the interim between the bombardment of Alexandria and Tel el-Kebir. The British victory changed things overnight. The Egyptians for the most part lacked their leader's great virtue of moral courage. "When the news came to Alexandria of Orabi's defeat," wrote De Kusel, "it was really marvellous the rejoicing that took place among the Arabs who crowded to congratulate the Khedive. I suppose it is human nature in Occidentals, as well as Orientals, to fawn on top dogs." Orabi was now delivered by the British, who had treated him well, to the Egyptians, who did not. One lackey of the palace, the Khedive's pipe-filler, organized visits to Orabi's prison so that opportunists could prove their loyalty to the Khedive by spitting on the shackled prisoner. Towfik himself, and his aides, were determined that the man who had frightened them so badly should die, along with his chief supporters. Most vociferous for the death sentence was the Minister of the Interior, Riaz Pasha. Riaz had started life as dancing boy to Towfik's grandfather-in-law Abbas; he was now a shriveled but persistent elder with a nervous, twitching face.

Many influential Englishmen supported Towfik and Riaz in their desire for vengeance. Gladstone, Morley tells us, took "a severe line" when his former colleague John Bright wrote asking for clemency for Orabi. Psychologically Gladstone could hardly do otherwise; if Orabi were not a devil, then Gladstone had been no angel in the cause of peace when he sanctioned the bombardment. "In truth I must say that, having begun with no prejudice against him, and with the strong desire that he should be saved, I am almost driven to the conclusion that he is a bad man, and that it will not be an injustice if he goes the road which thousands of his innocent countrymen through him have trodden." Others spoke more frankly. Sir Julian Goldsmid, who had played an important role in British intelligence, argued: "If we have handed over the leaders of the revolt to the Khedive, it is clear he ought to be allowed to punish them for their offence according to Egyptian law. Consequently we ought not to interfere with the sentence which assuredly would be passed on Orabi and the other principal leaders in any European country as well as in Egypt, viz, the *sentence of death*. In the East," Goldsmid stressed, "clemency is looked on as weakness, and invites others to similar desperate ventures. I therefore urge than no maudlin sentimentality should be allowed to step in and stop the execution of the capital sentence."

Orabi's life was to be saved, and the Khedive's vengeance thwarted, not by the Egyptians, but by an Englishman, Wilfrid Blunt.

During the summer months Blunt had watched what was happening in Egypt with despair. He was alarmed by the ignorance of most of his countrymen, or their malice. He was denounced himself as an "Orabi in a frock coat" when he tried to convince the Liberal leaders that Orabi led a libertarian movement that deserved support. Nevertheless Blunt was not alone: among his allies were Lord Randolph Churchill and the Hon. Algernon Bourke, Blunt's cousin, known familiarly as "Button." In the immediate aftermath of Tel el-Kebir it was possible that Orabi's enemies might use the dust of battle to conceal judicial murder. "Button" was instrumental in a verbal coup: he inserted into *The Times* a short, innocuous statement to the effect that the British Government were determined that Orabi should receive a fair trial. The damage was done. Gladstone could not deny so equable, so liberal a statement, published in so reputable a paper. Having established the principle that the British, to whom Orabi had surrendered, would not countenance lynch law, Blunt next secured the services of a lawyer, A. C. Broadley, who had practiced in Tunis and written a two-volume account of the French occupation, *The Last Punic War*. Broadley traveled from Tunis by way of Europe to Egypt. When he reached Cairo on October 18 he made contact with Sir Charles Wilson, an Englishman controlling Egyptian prisons, whom he described as "firm, intelligent, courteous, just and a hater of all intrigue and oppression." Despite obstacles from the Khedive's government, Wilson sent Orabi's young son to Broadley's lodgings. While the boy Muhammad, blind in one eye and with a cast in the other, was telling a pathetic tale of the treatment he and his mother had suffered, an order came from Riaz Pasha authorizing Orabi's English counsel to see his client. Riaz was obeying instructions from Sir Edward Malet.

Orabi's prison was in the center of Cairo, not far from Shepheard's and the Opera. Orabi's cell was stifling. Its only furnishings consisted of a Shiraz rug, a mosquito curtain, a mattress, some pillows, an embroidered prayer rug, a Koran and some vessels of earthenware and brass. Broadley had awaited his first interview with Orabi (of whom he knew only from the hostile British press) with curiosity. Like other observers, he was first impressed by a forbidding sullenness in Orabi's features when in repose. "But I soon found out that this was the effect of deep and constant thought rather than of moroseness or bad temper. Orabi's habit of perpetually thinking has gained him many enemies amongst those who judge by first appearances. When his countenance lights up with animation, the change wrought in his expression is so wonderful that you would hardly recognise him as the same man. His eyes are full of intelligence, and his smile is peculiarly attractive. His complexion is lighter than that of his son, but his nose is too flat and his lips too thick to allow me to describe him as a handsome man. He is considerably over six feet in height, and broad in proportion. During his imprisonment his appearance was materially changed by the growth of a grey beard. After the manner of the fellahin, an indigo band was tattooed round his wrist, and he rarely, if ever, loosened his grasp on a small black rosary he perpetually ran through his fingers when talking."

Orabi had spent his weeks in captivity pondering his legal position; he was convinced that neither before the bombardment, nor afterwards, could he be rightly described as a rebel. The Khedive had endorsed the Egyptian decision to return the fire of the British ships, and the Sultan-Caliph had constantly expressed his approbation.

But Broadley knew that neither legal quibbles nor rhetorical flourishes would save Orabi. He needed documentation not only of his own legality but of the complicity of others in his enterprise.

The day after the interview with Orabi was the start of the Feast of Sacrifice, the major holiday of the Muslim year. "Everybody put on their holiday best, all Pashadom seemed fairly ablaze with decorations and ribbons, and the streets at an early hour were almost impassable by reason of the crowd of carriages and passengers. All the Cairene world and his wife rushed impetuously to do homage to the rising sun, after the manner of the ordinary Egyptian, and Towfik Pasha was well nigh wearied with flattery and congratulations. Only the British guards marching up and down monotonously outside the palace served to remind him of the cost at which he had propped up his throne, and of the real sentiments of his outraged subjects."

The feast and flattery preoccupied official Cairo. No one noticed two small events of considerable importance for the Middle Eastern scenario, in which Orabi's role was now almost over.

From the Sudan a laconic telegram announced that someone claiming to be the Mahdi had started a revolt against infidel rule. This small news item was to open a new chapter in the story of Middle Eastern resistance. (It was also to provide the British with a new excuse for prolonging their occupation of Egypt.)

From Orabi's ransacked house (it was to be turned into a hospital by the British) came Orabi's half-Negro servant, a youth named Muhammad Ahmad, whom Mr. Broadley was to find more worthy of respect than anyone else he met in Egypt. "He had probably no other property in the world than a blue shirt and a ragged cloth coat to cover it, but neither threats nor bribes could shake his allegiance to his fallen master." With him he brought to Broadley's lodgings a cloth containing a bundle of documents in the Arabic script. This small bundle was to play a major part in saving Orabi from the scaffold. Among the documents were letters from Sultan Abdul Hamid: letters which made it plain that Orabi's actions conformed with Ottoman policy.

The principle of a fair trial having been conceded, and these documents having been secured by the defense, the trial could only end in a compromise. The prosecution could not push for a death sentence without the defendants' counsel producing documents embarrassing not only to the Ottoman Government, whose sovereignty over Egypt was not in dispute, but also to many Egyptian dignitaries now fawning on Towfik. Equally the Khedive could not sanction an acquittal: Orabi and his associates at large and unpunished would be too grave a menace.

Lord Dufferin, an Irishman who had served as British ambassador in Constantinople, arrived on November 7 with full powers to arrange a deal. He defined it briskly:

> *Orabi and his associates will be charged simply with rebellion before the Court Martial. To this charge they will plead guilty. In the event of the Court pronouncing a capital sentence, it will be submitted to the Khedive, who will commute it into perpetual exile.*

In addition the exiles' property (though not that of their wives) would be confiscated; they would lose their military ranks; they would give their paroles that they would go where sent and not return to Egypt, on pain of death.

Blunt, who had paid the considerable legal fees, had saved, with the help of English "fair play," the lives of Orabi and his friends. Instead of mounting the scaffold, they would board ship for Ceylon. Versed in religious lore, Orabi knew that when Adam and Eve had been driven from the Garden of Eden, they had gone separate ways; Adam to Ceylon, Eve to the Hejaz, the holy land of western Arabia. "Nothing could be more just," Orabi now remarked with a quiet smile, when Broadley told him the news. "I am driven out of Egypt, 'the garden of the world'; I go to Ceylon, 'the paradise of Adam.' I hail it as a happy omen."

The last act in Orabi's drama took place at Kasrel-Nil Palace. Three sides of a great square were made up of barracks, lofty buildings with fronts of arched verandahs, piled one above the other. The fourth side comprised the palace proper and the Egyptian War Office. Here Orabi had first been tried by court-martial, then released by his indignant soldiers; from here he had later ruled over Egypt. A line of railway, connected with the main line to the port of departure, Suez, led into the square. "The arcades of the barracks and the more florid architecture of the Palace stood out distinctly in the clear moonlight, which seemed to almost dim the flames of the torches held by some of the soldiers of the Egyptian guard . . . The train was a very long one, almost stretching across the square from one side to the other. In front were the ladies with their children and luggage; behind, the servants, the heavy baggage, and a guard of the King's Royal Rifle Corps (60th regiment) under the command of Major Fraser. Some Egyptian officers and a few soldiers were also there to accompany the exiles to Suez. A first-class carriage in the centre was reserved for Orabi and his companions."

Calculation no less than "fair play" could have prompted the arrangements for this first-class departure. If Orabi and his companions had been killed by the hangman, it would have been sad for their families and friends; but the Egyptian struggle would have had, in such martyrs, a continuing inspiration. In exiling Orabi to an island paradise, from which in due course he could return with a pardon, the British defused him as a danger.

Orabi himself behaved with dignity as he prepared to leave Egypt; he indignantly refused to sign a letter of servile thanks to the Khedive. Muhammad Abduh, who had a shorter sentence of exile, also turned his hardship to good advantage, studying and thinking in Beirut and Europe. But some of the exiled colonels seemed preoccupied with how many servants and eunuchs they and their wives could take with them, or how much baggage. Their bulky impedimenta blurred the issues for which they had struggled. Middle Eastern resistance was to move to two very different arenas: the dusty war tent of the Sudanese Messiah and the cluttered apartments of the last great Sultan.

BOOK THREE

God's Hook-Nosed Shadow

It was necessary that there should be a Sovereign at the head of the State after the Sultan Abdul Aziz, and, in accordance with the law, he was succeeded by the Sultan Murad. He became ill —was deposed—and, still in accordance with the law, the Sultan Abdul Hamid ascended the throne. It has been recognised that he manifested a sincere desire and also the necessary capacity to lead the State into the paths of progress; he showed much esteem for everyone, and his esteem and benevolence for me were prodigious. In the report which the late Mustafa Fazil Pasha laid before the Sultan Abdul Aziz, it is stated that the truth is always the last to gain admittance into the palace of Sovereigns, and indeed this is the case.

MIDHAT PASHA, exiled in Europe, writes to the Grand Master of Ceremonies at the Sultan's palace, 10 December 1877. Six years later Midhat Pasha was murdered in Arabia.

Chapter 1

IN Constantinople, byzantine capital of the Sultan who had deposed Ismail and encouraged Orabi, the argument was not whether to resist the West, but in what manner. Its symbolic climax was another confrontation (this time macabre and private) between ruler and subject.

The private place was a cluttered room in Yildiz Kiosk, the new "Star Pavilion," from which Abdul Hamid II surveyed his threatened empire. Some of his domains the Sultan still ruled: a swath of the Balkans, the Anatolian peninsula, a handful of Greek islands (including Thasos, Crete and Rhodes), Syria (which included Palestine and the area across the Jordan), the once-fertile valley between Euphrates and Tigris known to the ancient Greeks as Mesopotamia and to the Arabs as Iraq, the Hejaz, mountainous fringe of western Arabia made holy by Mecca and Medina, and in North Africa, the Libyan coast. Over other regions the Sultan's rule was tenuous, nominal or non-existent. Yemen and the Arabian interior had never been wholly subdued. Ottoman sovereignty over Egypt and Cyprus was nominal, though both countries paid an annual tribute. Since 1881 the French ruled Tunis.

Abdul Hamid's father, Sultan Abdul Mejid, had bequeathed him the vast rococo palace of Dolmabahçe, its largest room lit by the world's biggest chandelier, its marble steps leading down to the Bosphorus. But neither the extravagance of this palace nor its openness to the world appealed to Abdul Hamid. Instead, he had planted a park on waste land at the edge of Pera, the Westernized portion of Constantinople, and filled it with modest pavilions. The concealing walls of Yildiz, its shady trees, its private theater, its model café, where the solitary Sultan could, like a citizen, clap for a coffee, displayed something simple, even austere, in the ruler's nature; the lack of salons fit for dancing or acts of violence, the narrow corridors where two could barely pass, the many spy holes, the emergency supplies stored squirrel-wise in forgotten cupboards, hinted the caution of a prince brought up near secret enemies and open murder. An atmosphere of secrecy showed the Sultan's determination to surround his power with awe. Yildiz was guarded by two regiments, one Albanian, one Arab, recruited from the extremes of the empire and mutually hostile. The atmosphere at night was particularly haunted. Then, wrote a contemporary, swift death threatened any intruder "in the lonely walks of Yildiz Park, where not a shadow of a mortal was to be seen and where the swift flight of the owls was the only interruption in the dreary calm . . . This awful impression is heightened by the loud and melancholy singing of the Koran-reciters at the gate, whose lugubrious voices fill a great part of the park and penetrate even to the imperial bedroom." Abdul Hamid, as responsive to the super-natural as his people, felt that the sacred verses were the best defense against Satan the Accursed.

To this secluded palace, in August 1883, a messenger from Taif, in the Hejaz, conveyed "a package labeled 'Japanese ivory—an objet d'art for his Majesty.' Abdul Hamid opened it with his own hands, and the severed head was revealed of the man whom in life he had regarded as his most deadly enemy."

This story, taken from Alma Wittlin's, *Abdul Hamid, The Shadow of God*, may be, in its details and date, a harem myth.[1] Abdul Hamid was not only a pious Muslim, to whom decaying flesh was in the highest degree taboo, but a man of temperament so squeamish that he could never bring himself to confirm a death sentence. Midhat had also been murdered in one of the hottest climates in the world. Unless skillfully pickled (and the hospital orderlies at Taif lacked even rudimentary skills), the head would have quickly deteriorated on its camel journey to Jedda and boat journey through the Suez Canal to the cooler August of Yildiz Kiosk.

But the account has mythic truth. The dead man was Midhat Pasha and the live man was Sultan Abdul Hamid II. The contrast between the two illumines Ottoman history in its last tragic phase.

Midhat was twenty years older, and twenty years more optimistic, than the Sultan. Spiritually, he belonged to the same generation as the Khedive Ismail, having been born in Constantinople in 1822; his father had been a religious judge from what was later to become Bulgaria but was then an Ottoman province. Midhat had gravitated to the civil service as naturally as a medieval intellectual to the Church. He soon displayed qualities of energy and integrity which recalled the best days of the empire. While still in his twenties, he successfully accomplished a confidential mission to a Syria in turmoil after a Druze revolt. Winning back more than £200,000 for the imperial Customs, he placed the blame for local discontent on the Ottoman commander-in-chief in Syria. The commander was, as a result, recalled to Constantinople, but not disgraced. When he was made Grand

[1] Ala Wittlin claims to have drawn on the handwritten reports of Austrian and English diplomats: "but more especially on the unpublished testimony of persons who once formed a part of the Sultan's entourage—members of the imperial family, officials, palace-secretaries, sons of members of the Government and women of the Harem." It is significant that Ali Haydar Midhat, the son and biographer of the murderered man, makes no allegation that his father was beheaded after death. He quotes one of Midhat's fellow prisoners for the information that, after being strangled with a well-soaped cord, Midhat and another victim were buried in the military cemetery outside Taif.

Vizir two years later, this same commander chose Midhat to pacify the region administered from Adrianople, the modern Edirne. Giving his young critic this delicate and dangerous task might have been a cunning measure of revenge. That it was rather a recognition of Midhat's outstanding qualities was shown when in 1861 the same Grand Vizir appointed him to the governorship of Nish, the city that administered Serbia.

Midhat had in the interim undergone an experience as formative as the Khedive Ismail's sojourn in Austria and France. In 1858 he spent six memorable months on a study leave in Europe. The impressions he formed in the chief European capitals—Vienna, Paris, Brussels and above all London —strengthened his growing belief in Western methods of constitutional and administrative reform. If the Ottoman provinces in Europe and Asia could follow the lead of Europe, Ottoman nationality, instead of being a burden resented by the many minorities inside the empire, could become a bond between different groups, who would see in co-operation both their honor and their profit. The philosophy of these Westernizing Ottomans was pithily expressed by one of his fellow reformers, who acted as Minister of Education in the early years of Abdul Hamid's reign: "The truth of the matter is that unless Turkey . . . does from now on enter seriously and truthfully into the road of reform and accept the *civilisation* of Europe *in its entirety* —in short, proves herself to be a reformed and civilised state—she will never free herself from the European intervention and tutelage and will lose her prestige, her rights, and even her independence."[2]

Midhat put this Westernizing philosophy into practice as an honest and hard-working administrator: first in the largely Christian Balkans, and then in Muslim but largely Arab Iraq.

The first problem which Midhat encountered in the mountainous Balkans was that of communications. The few existing roads were infected with brigands; they were also a source of exorbitant profit to local contractors. Wooden bridges were built (with the usual addition of bakshish) only to be burnt down again so that the profitable process could be repeated. Because villagers found it impossible to market their produce, the economy was stagnant. To overcome banditry and the problems of distance, Midhat relied on a policy of co-operation with the Balkan peoples, Christian no less than Muslim. A locally raised gendarmerie guarded villages against bandit attacks. At the same time a vigorous scheme of building roads and bridges (with the governor's eye alert for corruption) linked previously isolated regions. The success of improved communications encouraged Midhat, with the support of the two reforming Vizirs Ali Pasha and Fuad Pasha, to create one large province, the vilayet of the Danube. Midhat was put in charge in 1865. His success inside this larger unit was remarkable. Like Ismail in Egypt, he abolished forced labor. Like Ismail,

2 Saffet Pasha; the quotation and the emphasis come from Niyazi Berkes, *The Development of Secularism in Turkey* (McGill: 1964), p. 185.

but without the Khedive's personal extravagance, he spent largely on public amenities. No less than 1,400 bridges and 3,000 kilometres of road, as well as the introduction of steam shipping on the Danube, brought new prosperity. Balkan farmers were encouraged still further when Midhat opened agricultural banks to give them credit. Midhat saw the urgent need for secular education, not the traditional religious schooling based on the separation of Muslims from Christians and Jews; only common schooling could give Ottomans a sense of community. Modern schools for children drawn from all religious groups were Midhat's most cherished ambition and partial achievement.

Midhat's reforms had encouraging financial results: within two years the revenues from the Danube province soared more than tenfold, from 26,000 purses to 300,000.

Midhat's successes were unwelcome in Russia. General Ignatieff, the same Russian ambassador who had exhorted Ismail to defy the Sultan, was the patron of the Pan-Slav nationalists, on whom he urged similar advice. The prosperity brought to the Danube by Midhat's reforms worked against Russian interests. Ottoman neglect had been the chief argument for Slav secession. Ignatieff had considerable influence in corrupt Constantinople. In 1869, the year of the inauguration of the Suez Canal, Midhat was sent to Baghdad as governor of Iraq. In his absence, the incorruptible Midhat, the Slav nationalists could use his bridges and roads, as well as the heightened consciousness of better educated citizens, in their struggle against Ottoman control.

Iraq faced Midhat with an even greater challenge. The cradle of Babylonian civilization and the home province of the greatest Islamic civilization of the Middle Ages had sunk, after Mongol invasions in the thirteenth century, into steadily increasing dereliction. In destroying the network of irrigation canals which had been the foundation of Iraq's agricultural wealth, the Mongols had turned one of the richest countries into one of the poorest. The Ottomans, who had acquired Iraq at the end of their period of imperial expansion, had done little for it since. Nineteenth-century Iraq had known no creative shock such as Napoleon and Muhammad Ali had given Egypt. Not that its strategic and economic possibilities had been unnoticed in the West. As an alternative to the French-sponsored Suez Canal, the British had proposed a railway following the Euphrates Valley south to the Persian Gulf. This had remained a proposal only. But in 1861 a trio of brothers—Henry, Thomas and Stephen Lynch—had established the Euphrates & Tigris Steam Navigation Company with a meager capital of £15,000. But none of these ventures, any more than the discovery of ancient Nineveh by Henry Layard, affected the village-like towns which clustered by the unexploited rivers, their lives at the constant mercy of Bedouin raiders and recurrent floods. The mythical Garden of Eden had turned into a sullen flatland sparkling with salt.

Midhat followed the same policy in Iraq as in the Balkans. His first task was to crush the huge nomadic tribes who traditionally marauded the settled population. For Midhat sensed the hidden potentialities of the desolate landscape once order was imposed. A major problem was land tenure. Midhat's son has recorded his father's assessment of the situation. "The Arab cultivator, for the most part, held his lands from the State on the condition of giving three-fourths of the produce to the State, retaining one-fourth for himself. Such a system naturally discouraged agriculture and rendered all improvements in cultivation impossible. The consequence was that, for the most part, the Arab shunned the soil, preferring predatory to industrial modes of gaining his living. Midhat determined to attach him to the soil by giving him rights of proprietorship, and divided large tracts of land into plots, which were offered for sale on easy and advantageous terms, special provision being made against accumulation of plots into single hands. The success of this policy was remarkable, and whereas the revenues of the State increased, the turbulence of the tribesmen, and the risings which had been chronic, greatly diminished."

The reforms which had given new life to the Danube revived the province between the Tigris and Euphrates. Steamboats flying the Ottoman flag were introduced to the two rivers, whose waters were again exploited for irrigation; a start was made on the task of draining the salted land. In towns fallen into illiteracy, newly built schools reminded Iraqi boys that their ancestors had once been famous for poetry and science. A hospital, an alms house, a newspaper, municipal councils, were other of Midhat's innovations. Youths were called up for service in the Ottoman Army. A tramway seven miles long linked Baghdad with the shrine city of Kadhimain, a compliment to the Shiite Persians, a number of whose imams were buried in such Iraqi shrines. The Shah of Persia returned this compliment by making a pilgrimage to Najaf, the burial place of Ali, in 1870.

Midhat extended Ottoman control beyond the territorial limits of Iraq, so that in the Persian Gulf the empire in fact expanded. A treeless fishing village of no evident value was Kuwait, sixty miles southwest of Basra, Iraq's only port. Kuwait lived by shipping. More than two hundred small vessels sailed from the mud-walled town to monopolize the pearl fishing in the Gulf and penetrate deep into the Indian Ocean. For reasons of convenience, the Kuwaiti dhows had taken to flying the flags of Britain and Holland. Midhat persuaded the Sheikh of Kuwait that his territory should henceforth rank as a sanjak of the vilayet of Baghdad and that the dhows should fly the Ottoman ensign. Ottoman sovereignty was extended even further south along the Gulf's western shores and some distance into the Arabian desert.

Midhat's success in administration and finance briefly appealed to Sultan Abdul Aziz, who made him Grand Vizir for three months in 1871. But proving too independent-minded, he was moved into retirement in Salonika until the financial storm of the middle '70s. In 1876 he played the leading role in the plot which deposed the bankrupt Sultan in favor of his nephew, Murad. Midhat made a poor conspirator. When Abdul Aziz was found dead in his apartments, he had contented himself with publishing a report by a group of foreign physicians to the effect that the deposed Sultan's wounds indicated suicide; the physicians had not been able to conduct a genuine autopsy. Common prudence might have prompted a more meticulous inquiry; it was certain that any irregularities would eventually be used against the reformers. Midhat endangered himself still further when, after three months, he persuaded his colleagues to replace Murad, a neurotic drunkard, with his half brother, Abdul Hamid.

Midhat needed a decent, colorless figurehead behind whom he could reorganize the Ottoman state on Western, constitutional lines. The Sultan's power must be reduced, the empire decentralized. As figurehead, Abdul Hamid seemed an excellent choice. He was known to be sober; he was believed to combine piety with progressive opinions. In physique, the thirty-four-year-old Prince was uncalculated to arouse any dangerous emotions. This slight, unimpressive Prince was rumored to have been begotten by an Armenian intruder into the harem. "His face," to quote Alma Wittlin once more, "differed profoundly from the fresh, powerful, fleshy faces of his ancestors. His big dark eyes were less openly audacious than audaciously cunning. Above all, there was that remarkable nose, starting out from the pale, smoothly curving cheeks like a brand upon him. 'The Armenian nose . . .' Even the least jesting reference to the Sultan's 'Armenian father' was severely punished: but nothing could destroy the rumour or prevent it from rankling in his consciousness."

Yet the large nose needed no adulterous explanation. If Midhat had looked at the portrait of Sultan Muhammad II, by the fifteenth-century painter Sinan Bey, he might have been warned. The Sultan who won Constantinople, Serbia and Greece for the Ottoman Empire, Muhammad the Conqueror, was the startling original of which Abdul Hamid was a diminished copy. Though the Conqueror wore a graceful turban and Abdul Hamid a too large fez, both men had the same hooked nose and the same sensual lips controlled by shrewd strong eyes. A series of degenerate and feeble sultans had made the world forget that the early Ottomans were among the most capable rulers in history and to these Abdul Hamid was a remarkable throwback. From his retired existence as second in succession he knew Midhat's mind more than Midhat Pasha knew his. The Prince had a conception of reform, a notion of resistance, very different from that of the Pasha. And since the empire was in too dire a plight for two physicians with opposing remedies, Abdul Hamid would, with circumspection, destroy the man who had made him Sultan.

Chapter 2

ABDUL HAMID had learnt circumspection in the crowded harem. Losing his odalisque mother when he was a child, he had found a substitute mother in his great-aunt, the mother of Abdul Aziz.

The harem is an institution hard to visualize today. A railway station with only incoming trains, a girls' school of lesbian amours, a hothouse of intrigues, it imprisoned a host of bored, credulous and ignorant women, under the supervision of Nubian eunuchs. While waiting, this multitude of hens, for a capricious and ailing cock, they fed their fantasies on rumor and indulged in gossip whose results could be fatal. One child among many, Abdul Hamid early learnt to conceal his thoughts.

At one phase of Ottoman history, a Koranic saying that death was preferable to dissension justified each new Sultan in putting his surviving brethren to the sword. This caution against brothers had later been subtilized into a system which caged potential heirs in gilded villas. These virtual prisons had changed, like Ottoman costume, with the passage of time. Broad low divans gave way to chairs and couches; Ottoman gentlemen now sat to table instead of tucking their legs beneath them in the Eastern manner; the fez, a North African import, had replaced the turban. But these changes were outward. Life for a caged prince was still a stifling extension of the harem in which he had spent his childhood. A system designed to render a royal brother harmless rendered him aimless. Neither instruction nor pastimes organized or quickened his mind; no travel enlarged his experience of the world. Instead, he learnt what he could from the gossip of women more interested in personalities than issues of state. Once the adolescent prince had been circumcised—this ritual symbolized his entry on manhood—a special category of eunuch known as *Lala* arranged for the satisfaction of his libidinal drive. A prince who neither exerted his muscles in sport nor his pen in study was urged to indulge his sexual desires in whatever direction an idle fancy suggested. Under this system most princes were voluptuaries before they were sultans. Self-indulgence as much as the cage formed part of the Ottoman system of balances and checks. It left the young princes with little surplus energy for political concern.

Abdul Hamid never showed much interest in women; when he made love to them, it was without any deep affection. What he craved was a friend. But he knew that a friend from his own people would be a probable danger and a certain source of corruption. Lacking a trusted wife or friend, he poured his energies into the quiet study of how to rule. His study could not, by the nature of things, be systematic. He learnt French, for example, by sitting in on a sister's lessons with Arminius Vambéry, a Hungarian Jew who became first Muslim, then Protestant, and who coined the memorable maxim: "Traveling in Asia requires neither legs nor money, but a clever tongue." From his beloved great-aunt, the illiterate mother of Sultan Abdul Aziz, he acquired a lifelong obsession with sorcery and magic; he later surrounded himself, by preference, with Arabs from Syria.

Abdul Hamid was less ignorant of the outside world than previous princes. Two years before the inauguration of the Suez Canal he had visited Europe. His trip formed part of a memorable innovation. For the first time in Ottoman history, a sultan, his uncle Abdul Aziz, had agreed to visit Western Europe, the part of the continent which earlier Ottomans knew as "The House of War," since it was the implacable enemy of Islam, "The House of Peace." Formerly a sultan would advance into Europe only as a conqueror, to take possession of a new land and to receive the submission of new subjects. When Napoleon III asked the Sultan to visit the Paris Exhibition of 1867, the invitation posed theological problems. These were ingeniously solved by the Sheikh al-Islam: since, this worthy argued, every piece of ground trodden by a sultan became Ottoman property, the ground was his to redistribute to his vassals. The Sultan's credulous subjects could thus entertain the fancy that, as he journeyed West, he conquered the land his train passed over and gave it back, at the same turn of the wheel, to its existing owners.

The Sultan's two oldest nephews, his companions on this unusual progress, reacted to Europe very differently. Murad, the elder, had responded to the pleasures of Paris like an enthusiastic peasant, his broad, honest face alight as he drank champagne. The abstemious, younger Prince, with the slow, bashful voice, refused to be impressed; he refused, too, to speak the language of the infidel, though by this time he knew French fairly well. But behind a sulky frown his mind was active: he asked not how to copy this glittering Europe, but how to resist its attack. Indifferent to the point of rudeness to the entertainments provided by his hosts, he opened his hooded eyes at the Exhibition itself. What most impressed him were the machines displayed by the German Confederation, so soon to become the German Empire. This great new power in Europe interested him more than France, more than Austria. Germany had been a patchwork of warring kingdoms and duchies, as disunited as the Ottoman Empire. In its disunity it had been repeatedly attacked by France and Russia. Now united and centralized, it had, the previous year, defeated Austria, after Russia, the second enemy of the Ottoman Empire. The day that Abdul Hamid visited the Exhibition, the Crown Prince Frederick of Prussia was there with his five-year-old heir, Wilhelm. A prize exhibit was a fifty-ton cannon of German manufacture.

Germany, whose soldiers had never attacked the Ottomans, whose problems were so similar, but whose answers were so much more effective, could be a model and perhaps an ally. There were precedents for such an alliance with a Christian power. In the sixteenth century, Protestant England had worked with the Ottomans against the Catholic states. By a policy of friendship with Germany, and by playing on the rivalries between the European states, Constantinople might yet withstand its foes.

If Abdul Hamid had distrusted the West in the hopeful days when the Khedive linked Egypt to Europe with a necklace of words, he distrusted it the more as Europeans took over Egypt's finances while the Balkan Christians rewarded Midhat's reforming zeal with renewed and extended revolts. As he matured, Prince Abdul Hamid formed his own notions of what the empire needed. The notions were fully developed when, professing reformist views, he was summoned by Midhat to succeed the insane Murad.

The Ottoman Empire should learn from the German example. Centralization under Prussia, not the devolution of power to the German statelets, had created German strength. Strength was what mattered. When Ottoman infantry and organization had been strong, in the fifteenth and sixteenth centuries, the empire had expanded. The only way to revive Ottoman strength was by introducing railways and telegraphs to knit the European, Asian and African provinces into one coherent Power.

The new Sultan did not share Midhat's belief in a constitution. Western power derived from machines, from railways, from guns, not from constitutions, whether written, as in the United States of America, or unwritten, as in England, or changeable, as in France, or non-existent, as in the Russia of the czars. Naturally, Abdul Hamid had any autocrat's suspicion of measures which would curb his own power. But in assessing the advantages and disadvantages of Midhat's constitution, Abdul Hamid showed the Ottoman flair for statecraft; this had been shaped through the experiences of centuries and practiced as much in the intrigues of the harem as in the deliberate delays of the conference chamber.

A constitution offered some advantages. Like a frock coat, like chairs and tables, it might impress those Europeans who were not indelibly prejudiced against "the unspeakable Turks." The prejudiced were the majority. A sober historian, Edward A. Freeman, had written: "The Turk in Europe, in short, answers to Lord Palmerston's definition of dirt. He is 'matter in the wrong place.' "[1] German historians were no more flattering. "The conscience of the European world," proclaimed Heinrich von Treitschke, "has never recognised the existence of the Turkish realm as a morally justified

---

[1] Edward A. Freeman, *The Ottoman Power in Europe: Its Nature, Its Growth, and Its Decline* (London: 1877).

necessity." Abdul Hamid doubted if an Ottoman constitution would convert many Europeans. For the benefit of the few, as a gesture of public relations, he would adopt a form of words and address a parliament as he already adopted a "Stambouli," or frock coat, when going to pray on Fridays. Like the frock coat, the constitution could be put in a cupboard if that seemed expedient. For the Sultan was convinced that the real struggle was not about words or deeds, but about territory and natural wealth. The European nations were greedy for territory occupying a strategic position or concealing wealth. The Ottomans—disobligingly described by Von Treitschke as "a race of horsemen and consumers of income"—still possessed such territory. It was sinister that England, the greediest and most successful Power, was the warmest advocate of a constitution and that Midhat Pasha (the Sultan's spies informed him) was forever drinking tea with Sir Henry Elliot, the British ambassador.

England had shown repeatedly that her policy was to keep the Ottoman Empire in a halfway house between life and death. When Muhammad Ali of Egypt had threatened to take over the empire and revitalize it, England had intervened on behalf of the Sultan; England had again helped the Sultan in the Crimean War, this time against Russia. Such moves were not intended to strengthen the empire but to prevent other Powers achieving hegemony over the area intermediate between Europe and India. A chaotic, bankrupt Middle East suited England better than an empire revived, or a jackal's share-out. If England now argued for a constitution, it must be because a constitution would keep the empire weak. The vision of a paper document binding, in one secular family, Orthodox Bulgar and Muslim Albanian, Latin Rumanian and Slav Serb, Christian Armenian and Muslim Turk, Semitic Arab and Indo-European Kurd, was the dream of a *hashash*, a man soaked in cannabis fumes. True, in the sixteenth century, the Ottoman Empire had won the loyalty of peoples outside its bounds, peoples of various races and creeds. Hungarian peasants ill used by their feudal lords had begged to be included under the juster roof of Islam; Greek-speaking Cypriot priests had preferred the turban of the tolerant Turk to the tiara of the Pope; Jews expelled with the Moors from reconquered Spain had taken refuge in Ottoman Salonika. But the balance of appeal no longer weighed towards the turban, or its equivalent the fez. Many European countries were secular, making no distinction between religious sects; even reactionary European states were often technically advanced. The Christian minorities inside The House of Peace now had a heady alternative. Like Greece, they could opt out and each build a Chocolate Soldier state. The Rumanians, the Serbs, the Bulgars, the Montenegrins, increasingly demanded secession from a profitless empire whose advantages had gone. In the Asian dominions of the empire the Christians were less bold. But since 1860 the Lebanese minorities enjoyed a form of autonomy in their mountainous sanjak; deep inside Anatolia, on the sensitive frontier with Russia, the Armenians might come to demand a similar concession.

The dilemma was brutal: the Sultan must throw regions of his empire to the wolves or hold on to them by force so brutal that separatist movements would become more violent, waiting their moment to explode in revolt.

Abdul Hamid recognized one last link which could hold together two thirds of his peoples: the religion of Islam.

In so accepting Islam as a political bond the Sultan was not running counter to Muslim tradition. He was reverting to the traditions of his ancestors and the essentials of their faith. Islam had never separated mosque and state; the early caliphs had succeeded Muhammad, not in his unique role as the final Prophet, but as head of the Muslim community. The Ottoman dynasty had risen to authority in the late Middle Ages thanks to the sturdy manner in which it had defended the "Muslim nation" in its struggle with Byzantine Christendom. Converted on their way West through Persia, Turkish nomads of the house of Osman had fought on the borders of Islam with rare dedication. Their sultans had submitted to the privations of fatiguing campaigns; they were Crusaders in reverse and coming from tough, nomadic stock their mettle had taken longer to corrupt than that of the Latin knights. They had shown realism as consistently as courage. They had not bothered with empty words. Their titles for centuries were Sultan (an Arabic word for "power") and Padishah (a Persian word meaning "protecting lord"). They had not pretended to the Caliphate for two good reasons: first, tradition said that the Caliph must derive from the Quraysh, the Meccan tribe to which the Prophet had belonged; second, the Caliphate had become so enfeebled that its last holders, the Abbasids who fled from burning Baghdad to Mameluke Cairo, were shadow popes with puppet courts. The Mamelukes would parade a Caliph on ceremonial occasions as certain regiments parade a mascot goat. When in the early sixteenth century the Ottomans conquered Egypt, they took the last Caliph to Constantinople as prisoner-guest. Only much later, when the Sultans were weak, did they claim that they were Caliphs, too.

To Abdul Hamid, the last great Sultan, this claim was all-important.

For the harem-bred, palace-bound Sultan had arrived at the same conclusion as the widely traveled al-Afghani. (Abdul Hamid was to lend him a luxurious villa adjoining Yildiz for the last five years of his life; like the sixteenth-century Caliph, the incendiary became a virtual prisoner and unkind rumors attributed his fatal cancer of the tongue to the Sultan's coffee.) The sole reality with which to oppose the encroaching West was Islam. The cry of *"Allahu Akbar!"*, or "God is Greatest!" was the one ideal to rally the empire.

The banner of Islam could hardly win Christian hearts, but neither could it alienate them, since they were lost already. The Greeks who had broken away in the 1820s were now agitating to increase their territory. The Bulgars, Rumanians, Serbs and Montenegrins were preparing to follow the same course; since they had European backing, their eventual secession was inevitable. But the cause of Islam could unite the Muslims of the Balkans, of Constantinople itself, of Anatolia, who were loosely described as "Turks," with the Muslims of the Middle East, who were hardly less loosely described as "Arabs." To this advantage of defense was added an advantage of attack. The cause of Islam gave the Ottoman Empire access to hearts and minds outside its boundaries. The Sultan's claim to be Caliph gave him an almost papal appeal to millions of Muslims. Shiite Iran had long been on unfriendly terms with the Sunnite Ottomans. But young Iranians, disgusted by a corrupt monarchy, began to look to Constantinople; for Iran, too, felt the menace of Europe, Russia in the North, and Britain in the South. The appeal was more to sophisticates than to peasants. "The Ottoman empire represented for me the chief Moslem state, heir of the Arab Caliphates and the champion of Islam facing the encroaching European powers." So wrote Hassan Arfa, Iranian soldier and diplomat, as late as 1964. "I dreamed of an alliance between Iran and Turkey and of the subsequent rehabilitation of other Moslem states and burned with the desire to be able to do something myself towards this. I was young, and, in spite of the life I had led in Monte Carlo and Paris, full of idealism, and although I had never been in a Moslem country, knew nothing of Islam and its rites and had been educated by a mother who, though outwardly converted to Islam, had kept her Christian sentiments, I considered myself a member of the Moslem nation, comprising as it did then the three hundred million Moslems of the world." The young Arfa (later a general) enrolled as a cadet at the Ottoman Military College, undergoing brutal discipline for what he saw as the cause of Islam. If Abdul Hamid could thus rally Muslims from independent states, his propaganda could also cross the frontiers of Muslim lands under Christian rule. The greatest Muslim power, in the sense of ruling large numbers of the faithful, was the British Empire. The mutiny against the British in India had been partly caused by the belief among Muslim soldiers that their Christian officers had deliberately outraged their religion by issuing them with cartridges greased with pork fat. To function, these cartridges needed to be bitten, which meant that the sepoys had to taste a food forbidden in the Koran. The Queen of England (created Empress of India by Disraeli in 1877) relied on Muslim soldiers in the border wars against the Muslim tribesmen of the North West Frontier. The Sultan could play a game of tit-for-tat with the British (who often exploited the sentiments of his Christian subjects) by exploiting the sentiments of Indian Muslims. The game could also be played against the Czar: millions of Turkish-speaking Muslims in the Crimea and Central Asia were his involuntary subjects. Nor was that the end of it: North African Arabs under French or British rule looked to

Abdul Hamid with increasing respect now that their own struggles for freedom had collapsed.

Thanks to the emotional appeal of Islam, backed by a growing network
of railways and telegraphs, Abdul Hamid resisted the West for a reign of
more than thirty years. He did not win; the game he played was by its nature unwinnable. But by judicious sacrifice here, by tactical victory there,
by the unending exploitation of his enemies' disunity, the Sultan prevented
any one of them from imposing checkmate. History provides few examples of a player with so few pieces and so vulnerable a position so long
postponing an inevitable defeat.

Chapter 3

DEFEAT had never seemed so close as on the December day in 1876
when the Sultan made his first move.

The violent death of one sultan and the deposition of another, added to
the chaos of Ottoman finance, encouraged the Russians to move in for the
long planned kill; the brutal suppression of Balkan revolts gave them the
pretext. Their armies pushed to within a few miles of Constantinople; Russian control of the Straits, the restoration of Orthodox worship to St.
Sophia, seemed suddenly close. To prevent Russia acquiring such valuable
territory, to win more freedom for Balkan Christians, the Powers convened a conference in Constantinople at which all those concerned with
the "Eastern Question" could debate: with the exception of the Ottomans
themselves, who were not invited.

On the eve of the conference Abdul Hamid played his bishop: Midhat
Pasha, the favorite of the British, was appointed Grand Vizir. The day the
conference opened the Sultan moved his Queen. As the ambassadors of
Europe assembled round green baize in the Admiralty Buildings, man-
made thunder deafened their ears: a hundred cannon were booming from
the Ottoman ships in the Golden Horn outside. The statesmen paled. In
this sinister city noise could signal violence. Sir Henry Elliot, the best-
informed ambassador, reassured the other statesmen. The guns signaled
nothing more lethal than the birth of an Ottoman Constitution. Donning
his ideological top-coat, the Sultan was conceding more rights to all the
peoples of his empire than the ambassadors were planning to demand for
three of them, the Serbs, Bulgars and Montenegrins.

Abdul Hamid's constitution was not the kind he would need to violate, or even repudiate. No constituent assembly had drafted it; instead, a committee had bargained over a draft drawn up by Midhat; they had then submitted a verbose product for the Sultan's revision, or emasculation. The document followed the pattern of the Belgian Constitution of 1831; it also showed the influence of the French Constitutional Charter of 1814 (which had restored the Bourbons) and of the 1871 German Constitution (which had established Bismarck's empire). These three models were in a sense more authoritarian than the traditional Ottoman system existing before Mahmud II: the Ulema, the Janissaries and local lords had then acted as counterweights to the Sultan's power. The European constitutions all sprang from centralized states. Article 13 of the French Charter had proclaimed that the person of the King was "sacred and inviolable." This sentiment Abdul Hamid wholeheartedly echoed. The Ottoman Constitution contained two vital articles safeguarding the Sultan's power. One gave him the right to banish whoever endangered the interests of the state. Midhat fought this article—number 113—hard. Abdul Hamid granted a concession: decrees of banishment must concur with police reports. Such concurrence would not be difficult in the kind of state Abdul Hamid envisaged. A second article proclaimed that Islam was the religion of the Ottoman state.

These two articles made it possible for the Sultan to promulgate the Ottoman Constitution. Article 113 would take care of dangerous individuals such as Midhat; while the special position given to Islam would keep the various minorities in their place. The Islamic masses, the Sultan rightly foresaw, would support him to the end.

The constitution was not a total fraud; it embodied valuable checks on the Sultan's power. A National Assembly was to be elected from all the regions and groups of the empire. Yet even this was limited in scope, since the Sultan had the right to summon or dismiss the Assembly as he saw fit.

The ambassadors, unimpressed by the constitutional frock coat, were indignant that it had been donned just as they convened. Following the advice of Lord Salisbury and General Ignatieff, they continued their deliberations as though nothing had occurred and as though the Ottomans should have no say in their own future. When they broke up, they had conceded to czarist Russia most of its demands.

But the Powers had in a sense assisted the Sultan. He was shown to be right in his thesis that Europe was implacably hostile to Islam. Midhat, on the other hand, was shown to be foolish in his trust in the good intentions of Western Europe. His doom was now set in train.

Invoking Article 113, Abdul Hamid put Midhat on a boat to Europe. Luring him back some years later, the Sultan would make him the star defendant in the reopened case of his deposed uncle, Sultan Aziz. Two of the physicians who had signed the original report now reversed their opinions and proclaimed that the Sultan had been murdered; a wrestler and a gardener confessed to having been hired as assassins. Though conducted in the new Western manner, the trial would strike few Westerners as fair. When the judges (three Muslims and two Christians) sentenced eight of the accused to death, Abdul Hamid commuted the sentence on Midhat to exile at Taif in the remote Hejaz. There he would perish, almost certainly murdered.

But in Midhat's absence, Abdul Hamid had at first respected the constitution. He convened an Assembly and opened it on March 4, 1877 with a practical speech. "I have decided," he announced, "on instituting, at my own expense, a special school for the education of administrative officials. As stated by the published organic regulations of that school, they will be admitted to the highest administrative and political posts. The pupils will be selected without distinction of religion, from all classes of my subjects. Their promotion will be according to the degree of their capacity."

The deputies were enthusiastic as they greeted their fellow citizens from all over the empire. Albanians hobnobbed with Kurds, Armenians with Syrians. Muslim *hojas* chatted with clergymen and rabbis, Arab poets and Hejazi merchants discussed education and trade. The delegates discovered that the empire suffered a similar decay in all its regions. The watching Sultan found their talk as amateurish as their remedies were unpractical. More to his purpose was another brand of mutual discovery. During the ten months that followed the convening of the Assembly the empire was besieged by Russia. As volunteers surged into Constantinople, there was the discovery of the bond of resistance. Outlandish mountaineers and swarthy Arabs from the South joined portly townsmen in the defense of their faith and empire against the Christian invaders. Against the dust of war, the constitution was suspended in the Sultan's cupboard.

Armed solidarity could not win the war; but the reappearance of traditional Ottoman qualities of martial valor revived the empire. For fifty years it had been playing with Westernization. It now discovered in religion a vibrant reality which made defeat endurable.

As the Russian Army swept south through Bulgaria, as the Bulgars rose to join them, Muslim villages were sacked, Muslim women were raped and their children slaughtered. These atrocities assisted Ottoman cohesion; they also increased the empire's self-respect. For decades the Ottomans had been convinced that their rebellious subjects were guilty of atrocities at least as grave as those imputed to themselves. For the first time Western newspapers began to report atrocities committed against Turks by Christians.

Abdul Hamid, still a young man, not yet a total recluse, held the loyalty of his people even when Plevna, the last fortress guarding the road to Constantinople, fell to the Russians in December 1877. The crisis inspired him to use tactics as much Byzantine as Ottoman. Playing on British fears of

Russian expansion, Abdul Hamid invited a British fleet into the Bosphorus. The gray warships anchored off the capital were there ostensibly to protect the Christians in the seething city. In reality they halted the Russian advance and made possible the Congress of Berlin the following year.

The congress was a rescue operation. It did not regain much territory for Abdul Hamid. To win the British to his interest, he had had to concede them Cyprus; the British, caught out over this secret deal, in turn conceded Tunis to the French. In Europe Austria was conceded a protectorate over Bosnia and Herzegovina. Independence was granted *in toto* to Rumania and in part to Bulgaria.

But Russia, the major enemy, was stymied; and stymied, looked elsewhere; and looking elsewhere it ceased to be the major enemy. Russia had conquered Tashkent in 1865; by extending further south, by threatening Afghanistan, she could repay the Britain who had robbed her of Constantinople and the straits.

The rescue operation was hardly lasting and hardly honorable. Only a total transformation of Ottoman society could have achieved a lasting and honorable success. But by his chess-player's skill Abdul Hamid had saved much. Europe, so united when its constituent ambassadors had met at Constantinople, was shown at Berlin to be a gaggle of enemies, each against the other. The Britain who had saved Constantinople became the Sultan's prime opponent, occupying Egypt and supporting every minority against his rule. Abdul Hamid now turned to Germany. Immediately after the British occupation of Egypt a training mission under Colmar von der Golz arrived in Constantinople. Over a period of fifteen years German advisers were to transform the Sultan's Army.

Increasingly Abdul Hamid relied on Germans for the machinery of his empire. By 1888 Berlin and Vienna were directly linked to Constantinople by rail; thereafter German firms were given concessions to build railways piercing deep into Anatolia, and then, to the consternation of the British, through Iraq towards the Gulf. But the project which meant most to the Sultan—also undertaken by the Germans—symbolized the basic force of his empire: the railway linking Damascus (capital of the Omayyad Arab Caliphate) with the two holy cities of the Hejaz. Only partially completed by the end of Abdul Hamid's reign, this would cut the journey from forty days by camel or twelve days by sea through the British-controlled Suez Canal to only five by rail over wholly Ottoman land. The railway was financed in part by voluntary contributions from the Muslims whose duties of pilgrimage would be so much eased by the comfort of the train.

As if to confirm the Sultan's evaluation of Islam as a force, spectacular events had coincided with the occupation of Egypt and the arrival of the German training mission. A revolt in the Sudan was to succeed triumphantly where Orabi's had failed. Naked Islam, lacking modern guns or telegraphs, could be as irresistible a force in the nineteenth century as it had been in the seventh.

The revolt was the result of the coming together of two extraordinary men, as unlike each other as both were unlike the Sultan.

Muhammad Ahmad, son of Sayid Abdullah, had been born near Dongola in Sudanese Nubia about 1844. His father, a humble builder of river craft, had a claim to be a *Sayid,* or descendant of the Prophet. (Prophetic descent was as common a claim in Islam as Mayflower descent in America, and about as checkable.)

Muhammad Ahmad, whatever his descent, was one of those incendiary geniuses which Islam has produced as regularly as Christianity its saints. Leaving three brothers to handle chisel and adze, he devoted himself to the study of the Muslim scriptures. To an ascetic temperament sharpened by fasts and night-long meditations Khartoum under its "Turkish" (or upper-class Egyptian) rulers seemed a travesty of true Islam. To remove himself from such corruption (several schools he had attended had been near Khartoum) he retired to Abba, a wooded island 160 miles further south on the White Nile. Here he lived as a hermit in a cave.

Muslims not only produce incendiaries but respond to them. Rumors of the *baraka,* or blessedness, of this holy man spread fast. Steamers from Fashoda to Khartoum would stop at the island to take on wood; what the sailors really wanted was to pose the biblical question: Is this He who should come, or look we for another?

From early times Muslims, as much as Christians, had taken a keen interest in eschatology, the study of "last things"; this study was keenest when times were worst. What, they would ask, would herald Yom al-Din, the Day of Judgment? Various theories were diffused throughout Islam. The Shia were particularly interested in such problems. The direct descendants of the Prophet (through his daughter) had culminated in the twelfth Imam, a boy who had disappeared in mysterious circumstances in Samarrah, a shrine city in Iraq. Some Shiite theologians believed that this *barakal* youth was in a state of dormition from which he would awaken to lead Islam. Sunnite Islam had its own doctrines of the End. The great Damascus mosque had its Jesus Minaret, on which the Messiah, as the Muslims knew Christ, would alight to herald Doomsday. But the most common belief was that God would send the Mahdi, or Guide. The Mahdi would bear the names of the Prophet himself, as well as being outstanding for his holiness and spiritual power.

The visionary on Abba Island seemed to fulfil such conditions. His first name was the same as the Prophet's; Ahmad, his second name, was a variant on Muhammad; while his father's name Abdullah was the same as the name of the Prophet's father. His message had messianic simplicity. His followers, known as Ansar, or helpers, like the first followers of the

Prophet, should have total trust in God; they should recognize the vanity of this world and value only the happiness granted to believers after death. "This life"—the life of mock-European Khartoum—"is for the infidel." Or in another of his sayings: "This life is only a game; the life to come is the true existence."

The message was like the fulcrum on which a lever can raise the world. The Sudanese had nothing but their manliness and pride. They were poor and pious. They now had a spiritual basis from which to despise rulers whom they saw as debauched and godless.

The religious appeal of the Messenger was doubled by its alliance with a man of action, Abd Allahi ibn al-Sayid Muhammad, who first fought for and then succeeded the Mahdi on his death in 1885, being known to history as the Khalifa, or successor. Once the Mahdi had confided to his Khalifa the truth of who he was, the Mahdist movement spread fast. Alarming rumors reached Raouf Pasha, the governor-general in Khartoum. The government Ulema reassured him by refuting the Mahdi's claims with theological exactitude. But Raouf Pasha knew his Islamic history. Whenever Mahdis had appeared before, their appearance had preceded Jihad, or Holy War. If Muhammad Ahmad was accepted as the Mahdi, the sequel would be violence. On August 12, 1881, the summer of the Abdin incident, the governor sent a steamer loaded with soldiers to apprehend the pretender and bring him to Khartoum. To everyone's astonishment, the soldiers were killed or driven off by the Mahdi's followers. The rebellion had begun.

Within four years the whole Sudan had been wrested from the control of the Egyptians and their new English overlords. Two great colonial servants—Hicks Pasha and General Gordon—had paid with their lives for trying to shoulder the White Man's Burden in this black man's state. The Sudanese were the first to challenge Western power successfully since the Indian Mutiny. Unlike the short-lived successes of the mutineers, the successes of the Mahdi and the Khalifa were to last for a considerable time.

Chapter 4

WHILE the Mahdi's triumph attested the Sultan's shrewdness in recognizing the force of naked Islam, it was beyond Abdul Hamid and his agents to duplicate the impetus of the Mahdi and his Khalifa. The Sultan crouched at the apex of a society which knew itself on the defensive.

The aggressive Sudanese had the strength of simplicity. Their uniform was a simple cotton shirt, or jibba, worn over long cotton drawers. As it got old, the jibba was patched and repatched; the sole luxury permissible to the richer Sudanese, the Mahdi's emirs, was the sewing on of gaudy patches in brilliant designs. The women were denied both ornaments and elaborate hair styles. Tobacco and alcohol were outlawed, as were the merriments of music and the daydreams of hashish. Weddings were austere; the believer's simple burial marked a happy transition from the sun-bleached plains of the Sudan to a paradise of beauty and pleasure.

The Islam of Constantinople was as complex as the Catholicism of the Borgia Popes. While Khartoum marked the featureless intersection of Blue Nile with White, Constantinople held the world's most impressive geographical site, the only city anywhere to straddle two continents at once. The luxuries of Europe arrived by rail from Vienna and by steamer from Venice, Odessa and Marseilles. Narrow cobbled lanes led down to a sea sun-dazzled till December, when cold winds hurled down from Russia and delayed the spring. In all seasons an invisible fog of corruption hung over the half-European, half-Asian city. Poisonous to reformers or idealists, it was ozone to confidence tricksters of every faith and race. Western visitors were astonished at the openness and universality of bribes. Sir Edwin Pears was a pompous English lawyer who spent forty years in Constantinople. He arrived for the first time in the early 1870s and found himself "in a new world with curiously distorted old-world notions, a world which in political matters did not know that any nation or even individuals had ideals or other incentives to action than the meanest form of self-interest. I soon discovered that the Government was honeycombed with corruption. No one seemed to contemplate that any business could be done with it except by bribery, and the open manner in which such form of corruption was spoken of was startling. Every official was regarded as having his price. In every contract that was made, an essential consideration was what amount would have to be paid as 'bakshish'. I found in answer to my re-monstrances on various occasions with reference to these bribes, that na-tives and foreigners usually drew a curious distinction between a present and a bribe. A man would point out that he was not giving a sum of money, be it five or five hundred pounds, to an official as a bribe, because the bar-gain or contract that he was making was perfectly honest and the present was not given until after it was concluded. To my question whether it was expected that the official would consent on behalf of the Government to sign the contract if no present were promised, the answer always indicated the negative. But everybody did it and there was no chance of getting any Government contract unless such presents were promised. I soon learnt that the distinction between present and bribe was without a difference."[1]

European businessmen had to fall in with the system, or fail. They fell in with the system.

To repair the system was beyond the Sultan's power. As he grew older and frailer, he was less and less able to know his subjects, let alone control them. Favorites fostered his fear of violent death. Now he only left Yildiz on religious occasions, for the Friday ceremony of the Salaamlik, when he drove in his carriage to a nearby mosque, or during Ramadan, when he visited the most sacred relics of Islam—some hairs from the Prophet's beard, his battle flag, his cloak, his sword—preserved in the old palace of Topkapı. He had begun to dread these excursions. When he went to Topkapı, he avoided the land route over Galata Bridge; instead he went by water, screened from his subjects like some Caliph's daughter of the Arabian Nights. Ships anchored in the Golden Horn were commanded to keep their distance; telescopes and "kodaks" were forbidden.

Afraid of strangers, distrustful of those who spoke Turkish, Abdul Hamid relied on Albanians and Arabs, who being alien to Constantinople were less likely to form cabals against him. He patronized a motley crowd of foreign agents whose blackmailing pens silenced his opponents or whose glib tongues coaxed loans from bankers.

One such man-about-court was Philip Michael Nevlinski, a middle-aged, upper-class Pole. His family had taken part in an unsuccessful rising against the Russians in 1863. Having forfeited his fortune, Nevlinski discarded the principles while keeping the manners of a grand seigneur. The nineteenth-century equivalent of a public relations graduate, he conned money from the Sultan and the Sultan's enemies alike. His contacts with the pashas, astrologers and charlatans who buzzed round Yildiz like flies on some once splendid haunch of beef, formed his stock in trade. The sums he lavished on wining and dining the potentially useful undermined his health and won him no final friends. In the mid-1890s Abdul Hamid used this battered gentleman in a matter of some importance.

[1] Sir Edwin Pears, *Forty Years in Constantinople* (London, 1916), p. 5.

The Armenians were the latest minority trying to break free; Nevlinski knew their leaders and was party to their plans. The Armenians had managed a thriving state when the Turkish tribes herded livestock on the periphery of China. Armenia could claim indeed to be the first state to have embraced Christianity as its official religion, preceding the Roman Empire by a decade. But the Christianity upheld by the Armenian kings differed in details from the orthodoxy of Byzantium; the quarrel between two orthodoxies made each weaker before the prolonged assaults of Islam, and as a result Armenia and Byzantium had both succumbed to Turkish arms. By the mid-nineteenth century one million Armenians lived under Ottoman rule. Though they were a majority in no single province, they were most numerous in eastern Anatolia, the site of their former kingdom. Elsewhere they were scattered, rather like the Jews, in communities that kept themselves apart. Like the Jews, they excelled at occupations which the Muslims despised. They had a reputation for being both stingy and honest.

For centuries the Armenians, again like the Jews, had seen themselves as a millet, or religious community. The Ottomans knew them as "the faithful millet," according them more trust than any other non-Muslim group. Abdul Hamid's private fortune was administered by an Armenian, Agop Effendi.

But the faithful millet had become inspired by the vision—or infected by the contagion—of nineteenth-century nationalism. American Protestant missionaries, who had encouraged the Lebanese and the Bulgars to seek autonomy, conveyed a similar message to the Armenians. When, however, a delegation tried to convince the Congress of Berlin of the Armenian case, it had failed, for Armenian nationalism promised gain to none of the Powers. Indeed it posed a threat to Russia, the patron of Bulgarian freedom, since a body of Armenians were included in the czarist empire in the Caucasus. A Tiflis newspaper proclaimed in 1872: "Tomorrow we shall be a nation of workers and thinkers." There was a revolutionary tinge to Armenian nationalism which particularly disturbed the Czar. The Armenian Revolutionary Federation, founded in Tiflis in 1890, was under Marxist influence. Its slogan was militant: "The Armenian implores no longer—he now demands with gun in hand."

Abdul Hamid at first met the threat directly. The Kurds, neighbors to the Armenians in eastern Anatolia, had long oppressed them, in particular by quartering themselves on Armenian villages in winter. They were now banded into vigilante regiments named Hamideyeh after the Sultan. The Kurds initiated disturbances which led to massacres; despite their brave words the Armenians were as much an ingested minority as the Negro militants of the USA a century later; their consequent sufferings roused such widespread sympathy in the Europe of the 1890s that there was talk of partitioning the empire, or even making Ferdinand of Bulgaria (a Coburg prince) its king.

Abdul Hamid now turned to the Byzantine methods of intrigue which were his by inheritance and inclination. He would send Nevlinski to Europe, to arrange, if he could, a deal with the Armenian emigrés. Nevlinski was willing to go; though knowing the intransigence of the Armenian leaders, he was sceptical of success.

On his way West, in Vienna, he met the self-appointed spokesman of another minority: a tall, bearded, still youthful journalist and playwright whose most recent publication (which Nevlinski pretended not only to have read but to have shown to the Sultan) was a booklet arguing that the Jews were not so much a religious community as a nation everywhere dispersed in enemy territory: this nation deserved a homeland: where, in the author's pungent words, "we can have hooked noses, black or red beards, and bow legs, without being despised for it. Where we can live at last as free men on our own soil, and where we can die peacefully in our own Fatherland. Where we can expect the award of honour for great deeds. So that the offensive cry of 'Jew!' may become an honourable appellation, like German, Englishman, Frenchman; in brief, like all civilized peoples. So that we may be able to form our state to educate our people for the tasks which at present still lie beyond our vision. For surely God would not have kept us alive so long if there were not assigned to us a specific role in the history of mankind." The booklet was called *Der Judenstaat,* The State of the Jews, and was written in German.

The author, a strange mixture of Moses and Jules Verne, had not insisted that this Promised Land be in any particular area. It would be a *Nachtasyl,* a night-refuge, for a people who had, since the assassination of the liberal Czar Alexander II in 1888, been increasingly tormented in Russia and who, in the France of the Panama scandal and the Dreyfus trial, found themselves at the center of political tempests. But the country which suggested itself and which was indeed demanded by those readers who had taken *Der Judenstaat* as more than science fiction, formed part of Abdul Hamid's domains.

Nevlinski's own lost homeland, Poland, was one of the most bigoted countries in Europe. Whatever of anti-Semitic prejudice remained in him may have welcomed the vision of a mass exodus of Jews from Europe. But long residence in Vienna and Constantinople, as an exile among exiles had forced the Pole to become a cosmopolitan, the nobleman to live off his wits. Nevlinski scented profit, was made to scent profit, thanks to the impetuous yet skillful rhetoric of his new client with the deep brooding eyes and exalted profile. Cloud tills were conjured, vaults heaped with gold. What the visionary called "his people" would offer twenty million pounds to the Sultan in exchange for a home.

Frowning, as though money were no object, Nevlinski calculated fast.

His cut on even half that sum, even a quarter, could be enormous. Nevlinski scrutinized the man more closely. He would normally have dismissed this peddler of Zion with swift politeness: Yildiz was besieged by convinced Flat-Earthers or, searchers for Noah's Ark. But this dreamer had a practical reputation; he worked for the *Neue Freie Presse* of Vienna. He also came at an opportune moment. Nevlinski was prematurely old; his heart threatened trouble. A tired gambler, he longed for one last coup which would enable him to retire in ease. Of course, the man might still be mad, the money might exist in his imagination only. In that case, Nevlinski was going where he could best find out, London, the center of European banking.

The visionary, who was also a banker's son, read his hesitations. Was there something on M. Nevlinski's mind?

Nevlinski admitted there was. There were grave objections to the scheme. The Sultan would as soon part with Anatolia as with the Holy Land. Jerusalem, the site of the Prophet's mysterious night journey to paradise, was particularly sacred. The Sultan cared nothing for money, understood its meaning as little as the Khedive Ismail, who had died in Constantinople the previous year. All that concerned him was his empire, where the Armenians were the current problem. Nevlinski hinted at his mission in Western Europe.

The banker's son, who was also a journalist, smiled with relief. Here, too, the Jews could help. Their influence might promote a settlement; in any case their newspapers could do much to improve the Sultan's reputation.

This was a shrewd touch. Nevlinski himself published a newspaper, *Correspondance de l'Est*. This specialized in information about Balkan and Ottoman affairs of the kind to interest European embassies and the Western press; it could also be used for discreet blackmail. But its circulation and prestige were nothing compared with the prestigious *Neue Freie Presse*.

Nevlinski was candid. "The problem is this: the Armenians—most of their leaders are my personal friends—are planning a blow for July. It's now May. If we can persuade them to hold their hand for a month . . . then perhaps we can get negotiations rolling between them and the Sultan. That would be profitable for me."

The sage, who was also a playwright, understood.

"But the Jewish cause would bring you far greater returns than the Armenian. I personally have nothing to do with finance; but I should certainly recommend you to our men of means."

Nevlinski was heartened. The wealth of the Rothschilds was a legend. Just as the Christian Medicis and Fuggers had financed the Renaissance, the Jewish Rothschilds were financing the industrial revolution. Funds which had bought the Suez Canal might well buy Palestine. Then a moment of panic—the man seemed to think his idea of a Jewish state in Palestine original. It was not. Palmerston had suggested something similar to the British ambassador in Constantinople. As a jest, as an apocalyptic vision, as a means for accelerating the Second Coming, it had cropped up at dinner parties; in Russia and Poland it corresponded to an ancient ghetto dream. What if some diplomat took it up, the official agent of some European Power, now that the empire was on the verge of disintegration? Nevlinski would lose his cut.

"Whatever you do, *mon ami,* don't work through diplomats."

The luminous eyes inquired: why not?

"The Sultan has a suspicious nature," Nevlinski explained. "If a diplomat backs you, he'll frown. Get the diplomats against you, then he'll smile."

The sage was now Nevlinski's pupil. A man of the West, or that part of it which spoke German and ate cream cakes to Offenbach's music, he was awed and puzzled by the specter of Yildiz. He bowed to his new friend's expertise. Bowing in return to the scent of profit, Nevlinski undertook to tell his good friend the Sultan that the Jews had helped his Armenian negotiations; he would say this even if these failed.

The two men would meet again when Nevlinski got back from London. In June they might travel to Constantinople together if all boded well.

The month that Nevlinski was absent was frustrating for the author of *Der Judenstaat.* He had promised Jewish influence, Jewish money. But Jewish friends were indifferent, or hostile, when asked to take up the Armenian cause. Baron Edmond de Rothschild received an emissary in his Paris office, but not his house. In an audience lasting sixty-three minutes the head of the banking house allowed his visitor to speak for ten minutes only. The rest of the time he devoted to castigating the idea of a Jewish state. The Baron had initiated and paid the bills for some agricultural settlements in Palestine. They ran at a loss; they existed sub rosa. The visionary was a firebrand who could only harm the Jews; talk of a Jewish homeland would render suspect their loyalty to France or their other countries of residence. The Sultan would in any case concede nothing; if Jews were to go to Palestine, they must go surreptitiously, attracting no notice.

The news reaching Vienna from the East was no better. A Jewish supporter in Constantinople wrote anxiously: if the promised money proved a mirage, it would be a catastrophe. At the best of times it would have been hard to interest, let alone convince, the Sultan. He was now preoccupied with Crete, whose Greek majority had been rioting against his rule.

Early in June a chastened Nevlinski returned to Vienna. His visit to western Europe had been doubly disappointing. He had settled nothing with the Armenians. His second string had snapped; he had met no one who took the *Judenstaat* seriously; its author was a crank, his vaults were empty; the Jewish money and influence he invoked were not at his disposal.

But when, after avoiding the visionary for a week, Nevlinski met him on June 9, he was cowed by his hypnotic stare; Nevlinski's objections ebbed, his tiredness seemed to go. The dreamer was no beggar. He neither wheedled nor asked a favor. In olympian terms he offered to share the profits of his daydream. If the Sultan gave the Jews their parcel of land, the Jews would set his house in order, would regulate his disordered finances and influence world opinion on his behalf. "We shall devote twenty million Turkish pounds towards the regularisation of Turkish finances—in your absence I have studied them in detail. Of that sum we give two millions in exchange for Palestine, this being based on a capitalisation of its present annual revenue of eighty thousand pounds. With the remaining eighteen millions we shall free Turkey from the European-controlled Commission."

When Nevlinski, fighting a rear-guard action, whispered the impudent word "Utopian," the reply was scathing. Who ever made his fortune from enterprises already successful? The time to go into a business was when it was starting, when onlookers were scoffing. "A year from now and the rabble will be licking my boots."

Conviction convinced. Nevlinski agreed to go to Constantinople. But there was no point in making himself cheap. He would expect the Jews to pay his expenses. A rail ticket was asked for, and promised. Nevlinski pushed further. To show the visionary the world he was entering he added: "I've made a list of things to tempt the court. Get them from Sacher's. I'll board the train at Budapest."

His client was left with an order for delicacies imported from France: strawberries, peaches, grapes and asparagus. To his relief, when he called at the famous hotel, he found that only half the quantity of grapes were to be had, six peaches instead of Nevlinski's two dozen, and one limp bundle of asparagus.

Carrying his basket (it cost him seventy florins) the would-be purchaser of Palestine boarded the Orient Express at Vienna. When the train reached Budapest, the Habsburg Empire's second capital, at 2 A.M., Nevlinski joined him.

The two-day journey to Constantinople, with its solid meals, its smoking sessions, provided an atmosphere fit for pipe dreams. After a bottle of wine Nevlinski put the price up: twenty millions for Palestine was far too little—in view of its special place in Muslim affections. Seeing his patron wince, he threw in hasty counter visions: the Jews might get a monopoly of hydroelectric power in Anatolia.

The journey had two euphoric reinforcements. A number of pashas—as exotic to a Central European as giraffes or hippos—were their fellow travelers. Ziad Pasha had headed the Ottoman delegation to the Czar's coronation. The author described him in his diary: "Ziad is a short, elegant, spruce, Parisianised Turk, who despite his small stature knows how to give himself an air of due importance. There is a bold and serious look in the gaze of his dark eyes; his features are fine and sharp, the nose curved, and the black little beard, like his thick shock of hair, on the verge of turning grey." A younger pasha, Towfik, backed his claim to reading the *Neue Freie Presse* with long quotations from its editorials. The obese Karatheodory spoke brilliant French but ate the unwashed local fruit and drank the suspect water at the wayside stops. In the forty-eight hours they were with the pashas, Nevlinski began his most memorable lesson: how not to be impressed by impressive Orientals.

The most important halt was at Sofia, capital of the new kingdom of Bulgaria. Here an incident gave strength to pipe dreams. A crowd of Jews were drawn up on the platform, first tangible proof of the author's assets. Patriarchs with white beards, women carrying infants, men of all ages, a boy with a bouquet of roses and carnations, had been mustered in honor of the *Judenstaat* and its apostle. Speeches were made in French and German. The more impassioned Jews hailed the first-class passenger as their "Leader," as "The Heart of Israel," to the amused surprise of the watching pashas. Only Ziad and Nevlinski were unimpressed: in Constantinople a rabble of enthusiasts was easy to find. They wanted confirmation of the Leader's money vaults. About the existence of these, and their contents, they still had doubts.

BOOK FOUR

Dreamer of Zion and the Powers of This World

Eretz Israel and the Torah are one and the same thing.
NAHMAN OF BRATZLAV, 1771–1810
Only desperate men make good conquerors.
THEODOR HERZL, *Der Judenstaat*

Chapter 1

THE tall European who strode from the Stamboul station wore a black full beard that recalled the Assyrian kings unearthed, fifty years earlier, at Nimrud. Otherwise little linked Theodor Herzl to the East of 1896. It was his companion, Philip Nevlinski, who called, in Turkish, for a cab.

"We drove," Herzl confided to his diary, "through this astonishingly beautiful and filthy city. Dazzling sunshine, colorful poverty, dilapidated buildings."

They put up at the Royal Hotel. From it the Golden Horn could be seen glittering below, a sickle dividing the mosque-crammed skyline of Stamboul from the new Italianate quarters of Galata and Pera with their waterfront of taverns. The old city was a chaos of rickety wooden houses engulfed by trees, the random foliage erupting like grass through worn-out paving stones: Nature (Herzl thought of it in German, with a capital) triumphing over the corrupt and crumbling city. Twenty years later André Gide was to put Constantinople in his personal hell: "As soon as you admire some bit of architecture, the surface of a mosque, you learn (and you suspected it already) that it is Albanian or Persian. Everything was brought here, as to Venice, even more than to Venice, by sheer force or by money. Nothing sprang from the soil itself; nothing indigenous underlies the thick froth made by the friction and clash of so many races, histories, beliefs and civilisations."

Herzl was not, like Gide, or like Gide's friend, the Oscar Wilde who spent 1896 in Reading Gaol, an aesthete. A playwright without Wilde's wit or scandal, he possessed a cause, the result of three decades of mental turmoil. He was not in Constantinople for the Turkish baths or the St. Sophia mosaics.

Herzl shared one secret experience with the Sultan or the recently dead Ismail. He had grown to manhood between two unequal seas, his ancestral faith and triumphant Europe: in his case the "tideless dolorous midland sea" of the Jewish past and the perilous new ocean navigable to Jews as a result of the French Revolution and their own *Aufklärung*, or secular enlightenment.

He had been born on May 2, 1860, in Pest, the left-bank portion of Budapest, a double metropolis straddling the Danube and forming a Hungarian counterweight to Vienna, the more dominant German partner in the Habsburg monarchy. As the son of Jewish parents Theodor belonged to a minority expanding in numbers and influence; its genuine emancipation, as distinct from the formal emancipation won in 1849, was enforced by Hungarian public opinion, as much as by the 1867 constitution, since the Hungarians were eager to win the Jews (around a fifth of Budapest's population) to the Magyar interest. Hitherto the Jews had found German culture more accessible and more attractive. More accessible, since their own dialect, Yiddish, was akin to German; more attractive, since the Jewish rationalists responsible for the "Enlightenment" had written in German. The boy's first name, Theodor (or Tivadar in its Magyar form) linked him to the culture of a Europe whose intellectual roots went back to Hellas; but like other Jewish boys he was also given a Hebrew name which symbolized the lonely monotheist strand of Judaism: Benyamin Ze-ev. His father and mother were unequal poles. His father worked in the Hungaria Bank; his mother (born Jeanette Diamant), a beautiful bluestocking in love with German literature, was the greatest personal influence on his life. The Herzls' substantial town house was no different in its style and furnishings from the house of any other prosperous middle-class European. Yet a few paces from its front door rose one of the strangest buildings in Budapest, a huge Liberal-Reform synagogue in the neo-Moorish style.

Two seas, then: and two seas of unequal power. The modern, secular, German influences beat more strongly than the traditional, religious Jewish influences. The latter, except on feast days, were repressed; the former were given a daily welcome. The boy Theodor disliked Scripture and was punished for paying little attention to the career of Moses. Only at night in dreams would the old world erupt. Just before puberty he had an experience that shook him. A majestic and transfigured Ancient— surely the Messiah—presented the dreaming boy to the prophet Moses, who declared: "It is for this child I have prayed." The Messiah had then turned to the young Theodor. "Go, declare to the Jews that I shall soon come and perform great wonders and great deeds for my people and the world."

But the daylight Theodor explained his dreams in the terms of science. A book by Aaron Bernstein, a Jewish writer, had suggested that electricity would be the Messiah; this interpretation appealed to the Jules Verne in the young Herzl. Although his aptitudes were literary, he had studied at the Pest Technical School and responded with excitement to nineteenth-century engineering feats. The Messiah was a beautiful myth; steam engines, telegraphs, electric light and canals were the miracles which Scripture foreshadowed.

Though he conformed to the Jewish religious tradition, celebrating his bar mitzvah in 1873 with schoolboy Hebrew adequate for the ancient ritual, he was enthusiastic for the culture whose magnet was Vienna. This magnet drew the Herzl family physically in 1878; Theodor's only sister had died of typhoid and his mother found Budapest unbearably haunted. Although Theodor was determined to make his mark on German literature, above all on the German theater, his parents felt he needed a profession and he joined the law faculty of Vienna University. Fired by Goethe and Schiller, Mozart and Beethoven, he enrolled in the thousand-strong Akademische Lesehalle, whose most famous president, a Jew, had adopted the maxim: In The Temple of Knowledge All Worshipers Are Equal. Herzl conformed now to the mores of Germanic Vienna. He wore the blue pillbox hat of the Albia, a dueling fraternity; besides fighting ritual duels, he drank beer, sang student songs, played cards and chess and did all the other things expected of a German student.

Chapter 2

ALTHOUGH Vienna prided itself on being the Paris of Central Europe, the Habsburg capital had much in common with Constantinople. Admittedly, Vienna far excelled in hygiene, education, medicine and other amenities; its cultural life was richer and its population of around two million bigger. But Franz Josef's metropolis on the Danube shared important traits with the city which was part in Europe and part in Asia. Both capitals ruled empires of rebellious and mutually hostile peoples: Czechs and Croats, Magyars and Slavs, taking in the Austrian case the place of Armenians and Arabs, Bulgars and Greeks. Like Constantinople, Vienna had tasted defeat; after the Prussian victory at Sadowa few Austrians believed in their empire's permanence. In one thing Vienna was yet weaker than Constantinople. The Habsburgs lacked the Ottoman cement. True, Franz Josef was a pious Catholic; but so were the rulers of Bavaria, Portugal, Italy, Belgium and Spain. The Habsburg emperor could not claim to represent Catholicism in the way Abdul Hamid represented Islam. In Christianity the Church was separate from state; the Pope lived, not in Vienna, but in Rome.

Perhaps the most fundamental similarity between the two cities was the manner in which each stood at the margin of its particular world. While the Byzantine walls of Constantinople were within shouting distance of Greeks and Bulgars, Vienna stood at the southeast fringe of German-speaking Europe; beyond its suburbs stretched the lands of Magyars and Slavs. If

Constantinople felt menaced by the West, and by the elements inside the empire with Western affinities, Vienna felt menaced from the East. To outsiders, German-speaking Vienna seemed masterful, indeed domineering; to itself it was an outpost threatened by the same sinister East which had, under the sixteenth-century Ottomans, all but overwhelmed it.

The two cities responded to this sense of menace on different levels. In Constantinople Abdul Hamid based his empire on Islam, a religion which could be generous to minorities until they rebelled. On the popular level, among some Turkish-speakers, a doctrine was being developed as potentially hostile to Arab Muslims as to Christian Greeks. The advocates of "Turkism" argued that the Turks were a separate nation submerged by a heterogeneous mass of non-Turk peoples. In Vienna Franz Josef attempted to maintain a plural society offering civilization to all. But as in Constantinople, there was a belief from below that the ruling people, or race, were both submerged and threatened. Like Turkism, *"Deutschtum"* ultimately implied a belittlement of other races. In Constantinople Turks resented the pampered Arabs and Albanians, the influential Greeks, the prosperous Armenians, in the polyglot empire. In Vienna there was a frightening upsurge of hatred for the Jews. Threadbare Austrians, often migrants from the provinces, envied the wealth and distrusted the influence of the capital's two hundred thousand emancipated Jews. The most devoted enemy of the Jews in modern times had been born to Austrian parents six years before Herzl composed his *Judenstaat*.

Adolf Hitler's Judaeophobia owed everything to Vienna. As a boy, he had lived with his mother in the small provincial town of Linz; his early daydreams were architectural, of rebuilding Linz on glorious and grandiose lines. At the *Realschule* he had met only one Jewish schoolfellow; not until he was an adolescent did he hear the word *Jude* used in political discussion, and then he felt the slight aversion aroused in him by any religious argument. "At that time I had no other feeling about the Jewish question. There were very few Jews in Linz. In the course of centuries the Jews who lived there had become Europeanised in external appearance and were so much like other human beings that I even looked upon them as Germans." The young Hitler explicitly disapproved of anti-Semitism, since it reeked of religious persecution, which he deplored. "Then I came to Vienna." (It should be added that in Vienna the now motherless boy, the aspiring architect, experienced the extremes of poverty.) "Once when passing through the Inner City, I suddenly encountered a phenomenon in a long caftan and wearing black sidelocks. My first thought was: Is this a Jew? They certainly did not have this appearance in Linz. I watched the man stealthily and cautiously; but the longer I gazed at that strange countenance and examined it feature by feature, the more the question shaped itself in my brain: Is this a German? As was always my habit with such experiences, I turned to books for help in removing my doubts."

No less than the Catholic Austrian planning to be an architect, the Jewish Austrian planning to be a writer encountered anti-Semitism in Vienna —though in Herzl's case, as potential victim not potential butcher. Like the young Hitler, the young Herzl turned to the written word for an explanation.

Two books, written from very opposite points of view, helped the student of 1882 to focus on the problem.

Wilhelm Jensen's, *The Jews of Cologne,* gave a sympathetic account of the persecuted Jews of fourteenth-century Europe. This book portrayed what may be called the religious anti-Semitism of the Middle Ages.

Hostility to the Jews, on religious grounds, had existed ever since the Christian Church struggled to independence from its Jewish egg. Jesus of Nazareth had lived and died as an observant Jew: circumcised the eighth day, attending the synagogue on the Sabbath and the Temple at major feasts, Jesus had addressed his message in the first instance to Jews; though this message expanded the concepts of Judaism to a degree which alarmed the rigid and the narrow, the ethical aspect of His teaching was not only consistent with the prophetic Judaism of the past but with the Judaism which would continue into the Christian era. Rabbi Meir, for example, was far from being the dry legalist of legend. "Whosoever labors in the Torah for its own sake," he told the contemporaries of the emperor Hadrian, "the whole world is indebted to him; he is called friend, beloved, a lover of the All-present, a lover of mankind: it clothes him in meekness and reverence; it fits him to become just, pious, upright, and faithful; he becomes modest, long-suffering and forgiving of insult."

The earliest recipients of Christ's message were either Jews by birth or conversion, the "Greeks" so frequently mentioned in the New Testament. The most intellectual and influential of the apostles, the man who presented the new faith to the Mediterranean world in terms it could grasp, was not only a Jew by birth (of the tribe of Benjamin) but a Pharisee by upbringing. In history's most dramatic conversion, he had changed from persecuting the Church as "Saul" to being its chief missionary as "Paul." Paul's indignation at those Jews who refused to join him in accepting the Son of Man as the Son of God and who now persecuted him as he had previously persecuted the Christians, led him, in his earliest letter[1], to denounce the Jews as "the people who put the Lord Jesus to death, and the prophets, too. And now they have been persecuting us, and acting in a way that cannot please God and makes them the enemies of the whole human race."

New movements never break off from old without such acrimony. On the Jewish side animus was equally strong against those whose repudiation of the Mosaic tradition seemed linked to the deification of a man. The exchange of such terms as "deification" and the far more lethal "deicide"

[1] I Thessalonians 2:15.

was typical of ideological brawls between related factions. In his later, and theologically more important Letter to the Romans, Paul wrote in very different, affectionate tones about the Jews; he never doubted that they had been chosen by God for a holy task; he had parted company with the Jewish majority over the way in which they had, or had not, fulfilled this mission. But terms taken from the inter-Jewish disputes of the first century were used in the near barbarous context of the Middle Ages as a pretext for persecution. (In the same way Jesus' own gentle terms about forcing guests to attend a wedding feast were quoted as an excuse for forcible conversion.) As late as 1581 Pope Gregory XIII (the same pontiff who gave his name to the reformed Western calendar) was to argue: "The guilt of the race that rejected and crucified Christ increases generation by generation and condemns every one of its members to everlasting servitude." Servitude was a polite word, first, for the ghetto, then for exclusion, then for massacre. The originally neutral term *borghetto* (or little town) acquired a sinister meaning when it was felt to house the adopted people of the devil. Social intercourse with Jews was forbidden; sexual relations between Christians and Jews (admittedly discouraged by the Jews, also) were punished, from the Christian side, under the laws against bestiality. No wonder if the inhabitants of the ghetto—thought of as black magicians who continued to act out the Passion of Christ on boy victims—became the frequent victims of violent persecution. Crusaders were particularly prone to such barbaric violence. These Christian warriors, on their long trek to butcher Muslims in the Holy Land, would turn aside to sack a ghetto. The fact that rulers often valued and protected the Jews for their ability to lend money did not make them more popular with the ordinary European. And indebted kings would sometimes find a massacre a convenient way to renege on an account.

The emancipation of the Jews, like the abolition of slavery, was the slow maturing fruit of rationalism, owing more to deists than to believers. In Russia and Spain, the countries where rationalism made slowest progress, the emancipation of religious minorities was also tardy. In the France of the Revolution the emancipation had been most complete. But even there, those who opposed the Revolution opposed the new liberties given to Jews and throughout the nineteenth century fought a bitter rear-guard action against those whom they identified with the movement which had destroyed traditional France. If Jensen's book described a world which had been superseded, Herzl's second book showed how old prejudices could jump back in a new costume.

Eugen Dühring, a lecturer in philosophy and economics at Berlin University, typified a generation which substituted for the certainties of religion the certainties of a conquering Europe. He was not alone in posing the related questions: What had made Europe so powerful, and what were the dangers threatening this power?

Dühring's answer—*The Jewish Question as a Question of Race, Morals and Civilisation*—was couched in terms which the Christian Middle Ages would have found unintelligible. Echoing Wilhelm Marr[2] and foreshadowing Houston Stewart Chamberlain,[3] he contrasted two races competing for mastery: the pure Germanic and the impure Jew. The Jew, whatever his beliefs, was irremediably depraved.

It required little reflection to see that this racial anti-Semitism was more dangerous than religious bigotry. The bigot attacked a Jew's religion, which he could change; the racialist attacked his genes, which he could not. Racialism was fed from more complex, envious roots. Men who were little in themselves found a compensation for their own smallness by magnifying the race to which they belonged. In defense of this ennobling race they would go to extremes.

Herzl read Dühring with acute distress. At the same time, with an almost feminine passivity, he tried to acknowledge what validity he could in its generalized hostility.

"The peculiar twist in Jewish morality and the lack of moral seriousness in many—Dühring says in all—spheres of action, are mercilessly exposed and characterised. There is much to be learned therefrom."

Herzl admitted that money lending must deform a man's character, but argued that this odious profession had been forced upon the Jews by Christian society, which had forbidden its own members to lend money on interest while allowing the Jews to do little else.

But Dühring's work was nevertheless a rebuff to nineteenth-century ideals. It was a revival in modish terms of age-old libels. Dühring's allegation that the press was "Judaised" was a metaphorical restatement of medieval charges that Jews poisoned wells.

Yet despite his unease, Herzl's first writings are those of an optimist: prejudices could be ironed away. In a novel written during the same summer that he had read Dühring, he gave a picture of the emergence of a new aristocracy open to the middle class in general and the Jews in particular. He described the presence of Jews at a social reception with ironic but optimistic humor. "Herr Moritz Loewenstein was there too. He came in on the arm of his oldest son, Karl. Symbol of the levelling spirit of the time, Karl's nose in profile was an absolutely straight line. As for the ladies, it was impossible to distinguish between them, they were so alike in dress and bearing and speech. Baroness Loewenstein, who sat next to Countess von Wortegg, was not a bit louder in her dress than the latter, and she spoke as pure a German."

Herzl himself spoke German as well as he wrote it; he possessed a straight and handsome profile.

[2] Wilhelm Marr, *The Victory of Jewry over Germandom* (Bern, 1879).
[3] H. S. Chamberlain, *The Foundations of the Nineteenth Century* (1900). Tr. London, 1911.

His first personal crisis as a Jew came the following March. A German Student Union—explicitly affirming *"Deutschtum"* and its concomitant, anti-Semitism—had recently been founded. Early in 1883 this union used the death of Richard Wagner as a pretext for a nationalist manifestation. Wagner's music was held to embody the ideals of *"Deutschtum";* the unattractive characters in *The Ring,* such as Alberich and Mime, were taken to represent the Jews, while Wagner himself wanted the Nibelungs to speak a kind of Jewish-German and to gesticulate in a manner he held to be characteristically Semitic.[4] At the commemorative manifestation a member of Herzl's fraternity, Albia, applauded "Wagnerian anti-Semitism." This was too much for Herzl. Two days later he wrote a dignified letter of resignation. But even this proud gesture was robbed of its significance. Refusing to accept a Jew's resignation, the angry Teutons expelled him instead.

Herzl's talents won him a considerable reputation during the next decade. As a journalist he specialized in feuilletons, or occasional essays. But his status as a Jew entwined these successes like a convolvulus waiting to erupt with anguished flowers. After a mother-clouded marriage in 1889, he went to Paris in 1891 as correspondent of the *Neue Freie Presse,* the newspaper which besides showing Austria to the world and the world to Austria typified the very best in the Jewish contribution to German culture. Herzl's task was to describe for the educated reading public of Vienna one of the most interesting decades in Europe's most cultivated state.

To most observers the Paris of the '90s was the tolerant and worldly city of Toulouse-Lautrec and Yvette Guilbert, the city which would welcome the released Oscar Wilde to a forgiving if venal bosom. The rational lucidity of France was the opposite pole to the portentous mystagogy of the German mind which (according to Nietzsche, Wagner's sternest critic) dived deeper and came up muddier than any other. While the world of Grimm's fairy tales was haunted and cruel, the world of La Fontaine was ordered and calm. Yet Paris was the new arena for anti-Jewish acrobatics. In 1885 Edouard Drumont's *La France Juive* was the widely publicized culmination of almost a century's attack, sometimes surreptitious, sometimes open, on the liberal attitude of the French Revolution to the Jews. "The Jews of France are not Frenchmen but a guest people, which exploits the expanding economic system for its own benefit and for the achievement of world domination. As the representatives of an international capitalism, with a racial flair for commerce, they have created everywhere the elements of 'big business,' which have destroyed the emergent Christian middle class and concentrated the wealth in the hands of the Jews such as Rothschild." Drumont argued that all the enemies of the Right had been overt or secret Jews. He recommended the withdrawal of emancipa-

---

[4] Robert W. Gutman, *Richard Wagner, The Man, His Mind and His Music,* London, 1968.

tion, the confiscation of Jewish property and its use in expanding the means of production for the exploited poor.

If Drumont gave new arguments to the French Right, similar new arguments had been given to the Left. Karl Marx, the prophet of the Commune, had been baptized as a child; he linked representatives of his ancestral Judaism and his formal Christianity in a conspiratorial view of history. "We find every tyrant backed by a Jew, as is every Pope by a Jesuit. In truth, the cravings of oppressors would be hopeless, and the practicability of war out of the question, if there were not an army of Jesuits to smother thought and a handful of Jews to ransack pockets . . . The fact that 1,855 years ago Christ drove the Jewish money-changers out of the Temple and that the money-changers of our age enlisted on the side of tyranny happen again to be Jewish is perhaps no more than a historic coincidence."

Herzl's few years in Paris coincided with events that showed that emancipation had by no means solved the problems of European Jews. In his first year he reported the trial of a clerical anti-Semite who, accused himself of shady dealings, blamed Jews for the leakage of state secrets. In the Rhineland a Jew was brought to trial on the charge of conducting a ritual murder. This was an ominous throwback to the past. For the alleged martyrdom of a Norwich boy in 1144 had initiated a movement which finally led to the expulsion of the Jews from England under Edward I.

Herzl's convolvulus concern with the Jewish question now began to blossom.

Herzl's first diagnosis was that the Jews were a minority discriminated against for its religion. He would probably have agreed with the philosopher Moses Maimonides writing eight hundred years earlier. "The antagonism of the nations towards us is due to our unique position as a people of faith. That is why their kings oppress us, to visit upon us hatred and hostility." But Maimonides, living in twelfth-century Spain and Egypt, writing in Arabic, had been supported by a religious faith as strong as that of surrounding Islam. He was writing to Yemeni Jews who were under strong pressure to embrace Islam, and whom he urged to stand firm. "The Creator endowed us with confidence, so that whenever persecution or fury against Israel arises, it will surely be endured. The power of the kings presses down upon us and they exercise a hard rule over us; they persecute and torment us with oppressive decrees; but they cannot destroy us or wipe out our name."[5]

Herzl, not living in an age of faith, proposed an opposite cure. Instead of advising the Jews to stand firm, as a peculiar people, he advised them to become as other nations.

How should this be done?

[5] Epistle to the Jews in Yemen, 1172; quoted in *A Jewish Reader*, ed. Nahum N. Glatzer (NY: Schocken, 1961), p. 168.

Herzl's first proposal was formulated in discussions with his Jewish employers of the *Neue Freie Presse* on a visit to Austria in 1893. It was as dramatic and improbable as anything in his later life. The best solution for the Jews was their total assimilation into the gentile world. This would be achieved by embracing the gentile religion. He proposed this solution in the Austrian context. The Catholic hierarchy and the Jewish leadership should jointly approach the Vatican with a bargain: in return for papal assistance against anti-Semitism, the Jewish leaders would organize a great movement amongst the Jews for conversion to Christianity. If Herzl's proposals had been taken seriously, Vienna would have witnessed, one Sunday noon, an extraordinary spectacle: a multitude processing to the great doors of St. Stephen's Cathedral. The procession would be led by adult Jews, men too old to change the attitudes in which they had been raised, but sage enough to plan a calmer future for their children. Respectfully carrying their top hats, the elders would wait outside the cathedral doors while their children approached the fonts. "The entire enterprise should take on a mighty character of integrity. We, the intermediary generation, are to remain where we are; we shall stand by the faith of our fathers, but our children shall pass over to Christianity before their conversion can bear the character either of cowardice or of interested scheming."[6]

This vision showed as little understanding of Judaism as of Christianity. It was rejected out of hand by Herzl's employer, Moritz Benedikt. Religious Jews could never accept Herzl's phrase—"a mighty character of integrity"—as apt for such an act of mass apostasy. Nor would it have been more welcome to Pope Leo XIII. For all its faults in the past, the Church was not so unscrupulous as to want "converts" unconvinced of the theological doctrines which had been obstacles to Jewish conversion throughout eighteen centuries.

This solution through mass baptism was soon discarded by Herzl himself. But it already shows the distinctive Herzlian touch: a boldness commensurate with that of a De Lesseps and, in tune with an age of iron, an indifference to the feelings of men and women on both sides of a confessional divide. These two qualities were to characterize his later and more settled plans. A gigantism of the imagination made him seem larger than other men: at the same time more than human and a little less.

Herzl's next proposal—the proposal for which he was to be remembered—was formulated two years later. It, too, envisaged the Jews becoming as other nations, but in the literal context of the nineteenth-century national state. Herzl formulated it after a traumatic experience: the trial and degradation of Captain Alfred Dreyfus.

L'Affaire Dreyfus had seemed at first a routine case of espionage for money. The German embassy in Paris was discovered to have been buying

---

[6] Alex Bein, *Theodore Herzl, a Biography* (London: East and West Library, 1957), p. 94.

French military secrets through a Major von Schwartzkoppen; his Parisian contact appeared to be the captain of Alsatian origin whose family still owned a factory in what was, since the 1870 defeat, a part of Germany. If prejudice played a part in the original indictment of Dreyfus, the prejudice was probably due more to his German background than his Jewish religion. Herzl himself had noticed "here in Paris how cautiously, shyly and timidly many a German bears himself, hesitating to reveal his identity." Herzl reported the trial of Dreyfus as a human drama. His word picture of Dreyfus is vivid: "He looks ten years older than he really is. It is said that this change came over him in prison. The short hair is tinged with grey, the forehead runs up into a bald patch, the nose is sharply curved, the ears stand away from his head, cheeks and chin are clean-shaven, the thick moustache is close-cropped, the mouth painfully drawn. He wears a pince-nez. Dreyfus's bearing is calm and firm."

The case turned on the evidence of handwriting experts and Dreyfus was found guilty. Herzl described the sequel for the *Neue Freie Presse:* "On this dismal winter's day the degradation of Captain Dreyfus, which was carried out in the grounds of the Military Academy, drew large numbers of the curious to the vicinity. Many officers were present, not a few of them accompanied by ladies. Entry into the grounds of the Ecole Militaire was permitted only to army officers and some journalists. Outside the grounds swarmed the morbid crowds which are always attracted by executions. A considerable number of police were on duty. At nine o'clock the great open court was filled with a detachment of troops in square formation: five thousand men in all. In the centre a general sat on horseback. A few minutes after nine Dreyfus was led forth. He was dressed in his captain's uniform. Four men conducted him before the general. The latter said: 'Alfred Dreyfus, you are unworthy to bear arms. In the name of the French Republic I degrade you from your rank. Let the sentence be carried out.' Here Dreyfus lifted his right arm and called out: 'I declare and solemnly swear that you are degrading an innocent man. Vive la France!' At that instant the drums were beaten. The officer in charge began to tear from the condemned man's uniform the buttons and cords, which had already been loosened. Dreyfus maintained his calm bearing. Within a few minutes this part of the ceremony was over.

"Then began the parade of the condemned before the troops. Dreyfus marched along the sides of the square like a man who knows himself to be innocent. He passed by a group of officers, who cried: 'Judas! Traitor!' Dreyfus cried back: 'I forbid you to insult me!' At twenty minutes past nine the parade was over. Dreyfus was then handcuffed and given into the custody of the gendarmes. From that point on he was considered a civilian prisoner and treated as such. When he had been led away the troops defiled off the grounds. But the crowd surged towards the gates, to watch the condemned man being led away. There were passionate shouts: 'Bring him out here, and we'll tear him to pieces.' "

Herzl's published report made no mention of anti-Semitism. Dreyfus was denounced as a traitor, not as a Jew. But the *Affaire* developed on ominous lines. It was clear that the French military Establishment had, possibly in good faith, made an error which now in bad faith they tried to cover. The anti-Semitic press started to assail Dreyfus as a Jew. To the watching Herzl, Dreyfus began to loom as the symbol of the Jew on trial in gentile society. The symbol was as powerful in Herzl's life as the vision of Christ had been to St. Paul on the Damascus road. It unleashed an outpouring of missionary energy that was to last for his nine remaining years of life.

In Herzl's case there was no period of gestation corresponding to Paul's withdrawal into Arabia. Dreyfus had been degraded on January 5, 1895. By May the same year Herzl was contacting the foremost Jewish philanthropist, the financier-baron Moritz de Hirsch. Four years earlier De Hirsch had founded a "Jewish Colonization Association" with a capital of two million pounds stirling for the purposes of resettling Russian Jews in Argentina. The baron's schemes had failed. More than a quarter of the 3,000 Jews resettled had moved on to the United States: one of Herzl's university friends, Oswald Boxer, had died while investigating the possibility of settling Jewish refugees from Russia in another Latin American country, Brazil. Herzl tried to convince De Hirsch of the need for a political, not a charitable, movement to encourage mass migration to a new Promised Land. The Jews needed to be filled with a grandiose, colonizing spirit. "They must be made strong as for war, filled with the joy of work, penetrated by high virtues." De Hirsch was surprised by these Kiplingesque sentiments from a fellow Jew; he agreed with the need for migration, but was sceptical as Herzl continued: "I will go to the German Kaiser; he will understand me, for he has been educated to the reception of great Ideas . . . I will say to the German Kaiser: 'Let us go forth. We are aliens here; they do not want us to dissolve into the population, and if they let us, we would not to it.' " That evening an overwrought Herzl put his ideas on paper. "I will launch a Jewish national loan. There's always plenty of Jewish money for Chinese loans, for Negro railroad enterprises in Africa, for the most extravagantly adventurous ideas—and will we be unable to find money for the deepest, most immediate, and most tormenting needs of the Jews themselves?" Three letters to De Hirsch, written one after the other, received no answer.

At the Jewish Feast of Pentecost (the last two days of May) Herzl started a secret diary under the title of *The Jewish Question,* which he was to keep up until shortly before his death. In this diary he wrote notes which were to form the first draft of what was finally published as *Der Judenstaat.* The draft took the form of a speech to the family council of the Rothschilds: "The idea which I have developed in this pamphlet is an ancient one: It is the restoration of the Jewish State." To convince the Rothschilds, Herzl argued that their vast fortune could never be secure without the basis of Jewish sovereignty. Neither the idea nor the clarity with which it was expressed was as original as the insight with which he defined the force which would make The Jewish State more than a Utopia. He used a scientific analogy. "Everyone knows how steam is generated by boiling water in a kettle, but such steam only rattles the lid. The current Zionist projects and other associations to check anti-Semitism are teakettle phenomena of this kind. But I say that this force, if properly harnessed, is powerful enough to propel a large engine and to move passengers and goods, let the engine have whatever form it may." Herzl's propellent would be the anti-Semitism which he assumed to be permanent and ineradicable. "The Jewish question persists wherever Jews live in appreciable numbers. Wherever it does not exist, it is brought in together with Jewish immigrants. We are naturally drawn into those places where we are not persecuted, and our appearance there gives rise to persecution. This is the case, and will inevitably be so, everywhere, even in highly civilised countries—see, for instance, France—so long as the Jewish question is not solved on the political level. The unfortunate Jews are now carrying the seeds of anti-Semitism into England; they have already introduced it into America."

This was a profoundly pessimistic diagnosis. Contemporary accounts describe a Herzl who dressed as wildly at this time as Hamlet in his ecstasies. He had become a fanatic and like all fanatics he was terrified of laughter. "One of my fiercest battles will have to be with Jewish mockery. This mockery is the impotent reflex of the prisoner in his effort to appear a free man." Entries in Herzl's diary show the dread seriousness of a man at war with humor. Like the young Hitler who dreamed of rebuilding a grandiose Linz, Herzl also thought in terms of architectural splendor. "We must build something on the order of the Palais Royal or the Square of St. Mark."[7] He envisaged Russian workers setting up huge embarcation barracks on the Dutch or Italian coasts. "Fare and freight contracts with railroads. We must earn a big profit on transportation." The Wonder Rabbi of Sadagura would be installed as a kind of bishop. The constitution would be that of an aristocratic republic, like the Venetian. There would be plenty of *Kultur:* "German theater, international theater, opera, musical comedy, circus, cafe-concert, Café Champs Élysées." There would be pageantry and awe: "The High Priests will wear impressive robes; our cuirassiers, yellow trousers and white tunics; the officers, silver breastplates." Anthony Hope's *The Prisoner of Zenda,* with its imaginary Balkan

---

[7] These quotations come from entries in Herzl's *Diary* made between June 6 and June 12, 1895. The last quotation on this page comes from the *Complete Diaries,* Vol. I, p. 88; entry for June 12, 1895; the others, from Lowenthal, ed.

country, had, significantly, been published the year before. In his diary he could raise the thorniest, most secret problem posed by his dream: what to do with the previous inhabitants of his Ruritania? In his neat hand he roughed out a plan to "spirit the penniless population across the frontier by denying it employment."

Indifference, hostility or ridicule greeted Herzl's Great Idea. The aged Bismarck had no use for a man without either money or battalions and ignored his memorandum; Alfred Rothschild in Vienna ignored his approaches. Some Jews stressed the danger of postulating "a secular Jewish nationality recruited on some loose and obscure principle of race and ethnographic peculiarity"; for this could seem to accept the racial hypothesis of the anti-Semites. Others laughed at the implausibility of detaching an already inhabited province of the Ottoman Empire and stocking it with settlers lacking agricultural or military expertise. Herzl, in no mood for humor, was hurt by the lack of response and was in his turn vindictive. To the danger that De Hirsh might ridicule him by publishing his three letters, he replied: "I should only reply by smashing him—inflaming popular fanaticism against him and demolishing him in print (as I shall apprise him in due course). But I would much prefer to bring him and all the other big Jews under one hat . . . I bring to the Rothschilds and the big Jews their historical mission."

Herzl's most significant Austrian convert was the man who introduced him to the Rothschilds: Moritz Güdemann, the chief rabbi of Vienna. On August 17 Güdemann brought Meyer-Cohen, a businessman, to hear Herzl read his first draft of *Der Judenstaat* in an empty room at the Jochsberger Restaurant. The two men reacted very differently. Güdemann was enthusiastic: "It is as if I beheld Moses in the flesh." Meyer-Cohen (who had interrupted the reading for a business meeting at 4 P.M.) found the scheme utopian. Both thought it inadvisable for Herzl to address his work to the Rothschilds; they were too self-seeking to understand it.

The only Western country where Herzl found instant support was imperial England, at this time ruling a quarter of the world's population and controlling a quarter of its surface.

Herzl went to London with introductions from a fellow Hungarian who had become his closest disciple and was destined to be his successor. Max Nordau's acceptance of Jewish nationalism was more startling than Herzl's. As a polished European, a positivist and enthusiast for science, he had repudiated Judaism by putting it with other religions among *The Conventional Lies of Our Civilization,* the title of his best-known work.[8] "As a literary monument the Bible is of much later origin than the Vedas; as a work of literary value it is surpassed by everything written in the last two thousand years by authors even of the second rank, and to compare

[8] Max Nordau, *The Conventional Lies of Our Civilization* (Chicago: 1895), p. 61.

it seriously with the productions of Homer, Sophocles, Dante, Shake-speare or Goethe would require a fanaticized mind that had entirely lost its power of judgment; its conception of the universe is childish, and its morality revolting, as revealed in the malicious vengeance attributed to God in the Old Testament . . ." Then, like Herzl, Nordau had witnessed the degradation of Dreyfus and abruptly found liberalism shallow and cold. "The emancipation of the Jews," Nordau was to argue later, "was not the result of a conviction that grave injury had been done to a people, that it had been shockingly treated, and that it was time to atone for the injustice of a thousand years; it was solely the result of the geometrical mode of thought of French rationalism of the eighteenth century . . . They formulated a logically correct syllogism: Every man is born with certain rights; the Jews are human beings, consequently the Jews by na-ture possess the rights of man. In this manner, the emancipation of the Jews was proclaimed in France, not out of fraternal feeling for the Jews but because logic demanded it. Popular sentiment indeed rebelled, but the philosophy of the Revolution decreed that principles must be placed above sentiment."

The sole exception to this depressing rule was the island to which he was now sending Herzl. "The English people does not allow its progress to be forced upon it from without; it develops it from its inner self. In England emancipation is a reality."[9]

Nordau was largely right. Since the Protectorate of Oliver Cromwell, the Jews in Britain and its empire had enjoyed increasing public respect. The popular mind was probably more prejudiced against Roman Catho-lics and those Anglicans who used vestments and incense, than against Jews. The last sectarian riots had been against Catholics; the rioters' leader, Lord George Gordon, had embraced Judaism. Responding most warmly to so-called Nordic qualities, an analyst of the British Empire has pointed out, the British also worked closely with Jews. "In South Africa Jewish capitalists and speculators were eager allies of the British in their bid for the Transvaal goldfields, and in India one of the most cele-brated of Anglo-Indian families sprang from the Persian-Jewish clan of the Sassoons, great men in Bombay; in the very heart of the Poona canton-ment, just down the road from the club and the Anglican church, stood the high pinnacled tomb of David Sassoon, its sarcophagus elaborately carved by Samuel of Sydney Street, Mile End Road, with the crest of the Sassoons at its feet, and the Poona synagogue respectfully outside the window. The Jews of other countries remained Jews, observed *The Jewish Chronicle* a propos of the Jubilee celebrations. The Jews of the British Empire be-came true Englishmen."[10]

[9] Speech to the First Zionist Congress, 1897.
[10] James Morris, *Pax Britannica, The Climax of an Empire* (London: Faber, 1968).

But there were nuances to this acceptance.

The British, nurtured on the Bible, admired the Hebrews; those who found it hard to square the Sermon on the Mount with the use of the Maxim gun had identified themselves, at least since the days of Cromwell, with God's warrior people. At the same time upper-class Englishmen had a xenophobia in which Jews were included. Disraeli's colleagues had not suppressed this emotion. Lord Salisbury privately described the Conservative leader he was to serve as Foreign Secretary as "an unprincipled Jew who had no right to be in the House of Commons."[11] The Earl of Derby, Disraeli's first chief, was to be his Foreign Secretary later. Yet Derby wrote of him: "he believes thoroughly in prestige—as all foreigners do."

Neither Derby nor Salisbury was to affect the furtherance of Herzl's ideas. A more interesting example concerns the man, Arthur James Balfour, who was to play, some years later, a major role.

Balfour came of the class which had both created the empire, and made money from it. Balfour's grandfather had worked as an employee of the East India Company until dismissed for accepting the "gift" of an Arab steed. Thanks to this setback he had made his fortune (in modern terms, well over a million pounds stirling) from a contract to supply ships of the British Navy while in Indian waters. Brass improved class. He had married a daughter of the eighth Earl of Lauderdale, bought an estate in East Lothian and then pushed on to membership of the House of Commons. His son, Balfour's father, had showed equal Scots push, working in the then lucrative railways and marrying even better: Blanche Cecil, sister of Robert, the great Lord Salisbury. Lady Balfour brought up her children to be, like the Royal Family, Anglican and Presbyterian at the same time. Arthur was in fact a freethinker, with a romantic feeling for the Old Testament. But he did not have an unadulterated admiration for Jews, as is shown in a letter of 1899:

"To the A. Sassoons, at Brighton. Found there Rosebery, Devonshire and H. Farquar. We discovered to our deep indignation that we had been brought down under false pretenses. The Prince had been opening a hospital in the morning and was staying at the Reuben Sassoons till Monday! We were dragged *both* nights to a long, hot and pompous dinner at the latter—peopled with endless Sassoon girls . . . I believe the Hebrews were in an actual majority—and though I have no prejudices against the race (quite the contrary) I began to understand the point of those who object to alien immigration."

Balfour understood "race" in terms very similar to those of Houston Stewart Chamberlain; he was concerned to preserve what he took to be a superior breed. In this Balfour was a man of his class and day. Certain of his references in a Cambridge lecture to "the alien and barbaric immi-

---

[11] A. L. Kennedy, *Salisbury 1830–1903*, p. 51, quoted by Jon Kimche, *The Unromantics* (London, 1968), pp. 70–71; also for Derby.

grants who became a source of weakness and peril to the Roman Empire" led to a sympathetic correspondence with Theodore Roosevelt. Balfour's sense of race worked in particular against Africans. In a speculative dream on "The Possibility of an Anglo-Saxon Confederation" he was to exclude the dark continent from any place in his imagined future: it could never be the home of the white race and was already occupied by "many millions of an inferior black race with whom white men cannot live and work on equal terms and the climate is not suitable for hard manual labour."

But Balfour was to play a parliamentary part in the struggle against Jewish immigration into England. He was to explain to the House of Commons why he considered that the influx of Jews (escaping from czarist pogroms) must be checked: "A state of things could easily be imagined in which it would not be to the advantage of this country that there should be an immense body of persons who, however patriotic, able and industrious, remained a people apart, and not merely held a religion differing from the vast majority of their fellow-countrymen, but only intermarried among themselves."

This system of nuances worked both ways, as Herzl was to find. Some Jews living in the island equally did not regard England as their homeland.

Herzl's first London call was on Israel Zangwill, who lived in a dingy Kilburn street. Zangwill's contribution to Zionism was to be a slogan: "a land without people for a people without a land." Herzl, never a conscious racialist, was disturbed that Zangwill—whom he described as "of the long-nosed Negro type, with wooly deep-black hair, parted in the middle"— preached what seemed an echo of the racialism of the anti-Semites: "something I can't accept, for I merely have to look at him and at myself. All I say is: we are an historical unit, one nation with anthropological diversities. This also suffices for the Jewish state. No nation has uniformity of race."

But Zangwill was to introduce Herzl to a group of Jewish professional men calling themselves Maccabeans. After a poor dinner Herzl harangued them in a mixture of German, French and English. They gave Herzl a good reception (making him an honorary Maccabee) but raised as a main objection to Zionism that it could conflict with their English patriotism.

More to Herzl's taste was Sir Samuel Montagu, the future Lord Swaythling, with whom he lunched on November 24:

"A house of English elegance, in grand style. At table he presides over his family—which for the rest is unamiable or perhaps merely well-bred —with the air of a good-natured patriarch. Kosher food, served by three liveried footmen. After lunch, in the smoking room, I expounded my case. I gradually roused him. He confessed to me—in confidence—that he felt himself to be more an Israelite than an Englishman. He would be willing to settle with his entire family in Palestine. He has in mind not the old but a larger Palestine. He will hear nothing of Argentina. He is ready to join our Committee as soon as one of the Great Powers takes the matter seriously. I am to send him my pamphlet before its final publication."[12]

Herzl was heartened by this first visit to the country whose Prime Minister had been Disraeli. Sir Samuel Montagu had been elected to Parliament in the Liberal interest; he had not been converted to the Church of England; he had been made a knight, he would be made a peer; but as if to confirm Herzl's thesis that the Jews were everywhere in exile, he felt himself more an Israelite than an Englishman.

This interview with Montagu raised the two principles of the movement to which Herzl was to be more sail than rudder. The whole scheme of a Jewish state would be utopian until it found a Great Power sponsor. On this Herzl and Montagu thought as one. More important, it raised the question of where the Promised Land should be located. Herzl had thought of the state as an abstraction; he was always prepared to consider it as such; its existence more than its geographical position mattered. But Sir Samuel insisted that it must be Palestine, and thought of a Palestine larger than the old one.

Chapter 3

Herzl's first choice for sponsor was, as we have seen, the Ottoman Sultan. He controlled the country which the Zionists wanted; if he gave it to them, there might be no further trouble. Herzl offered the Sultan what he considered an advantageous bargain. In return for Palestine, the Jews would become his allies. As allies they could offer help in three directions. Jewish financiers, such as Sir Samuel Montagu, could help with money. In 1881 the Ottoman debt had been consolidated at the figure of £106 million; its administration was in the hands of a body which represented the creditors and which managed the state monopolies on salt and tobacco. The Jews alone had the resources to free the Sultan from this humiliating position. Then the Jewish press could refurbish the Ottoman reputation (damaged over the Armenian question and the long struggles in the Balkans) in Western countries. And finally, if Jewish settlers loyal

---

[12] Entry of November 24, 1895, Lowenthal, ed.; the uncompressed original is set out in paragraphs.

to the Sultan were established in Palestine, they could help the Ottoman state against possible Arab disaffection.

But hardly had Herzl unpacked in Constantinople than things began to go badly. During the fortnight he spent there he gained an Ottoman decoration, secured for him by the bustling Nevlinski; otherwise, nothing. The Sultan was diplomatically ill and Herzl was not, this time, to meet him. His second day the Grand Vizir's son told him of grave objections to Zionism: Jerusalem must remain unconditionally under the guardianship of Turkey; it was the third holy place of Islam after Mecca and Medina. The next day Nevlinski brought news from Yildiz so bad that he opened a half bottle of the Royal Hotel's champagne to break it: "It's all off! The Great Lord will not hear of it."

Herzl listened stoically as Nevlinski quoted the Sultan: "If Herr Herzl is your friend in the same measure as you are mine, then advise him not to go a single step further in the matter. I cannot sell even a foot of land, for it does not belong to me but to my people. They have won this Empire and fertilised it with their blood. We will cover it once more with our blood, before we allow it to be torn from us. Two of my regiments from Syria and Palestine allowed themselves to be killed to a man at Plevna. Not one of them yielded; one and all remained, dead, upon the field. The Turkish people own the Turkish Empire, not I. I can dispose of no part of it. The Jews may spare their millions. When my Empire is divided, perhaps they will get Palestine for nothing. But only our corpse can be divided. I will never consent to vivisection."

Herzl's stoicism astonished Nevlinski. Herzl himself claims to have been "moved and touched by the truly lofty words of the Sultan. There is a tragic beauty in this fatalism which foresees death and dismemberment, yet fights to the last breath, if only through passive resistance." His good spirits were perhaps explained by his assessment of Ottoman power. It was far weaker than the Jewish determination to get hold of Palestine. Though Herzl was to return to Constantinople, he now envisaged precisely what the Sultan had predicted: the collapse of the empire and through its dismemberment the possession of Palestine.

Though Abdul Hamid referred to Palestine in his message, Palestine corresponded to no administrative division of the Ottoman Empire. (The Sultan had spoken with similar looseness of the "Turkish Empire," using Turkish in its colloquial sense of Muslim, as in the old English phrase for conversion to Islam: to turn Turk.) In referring to "Syria and Palestine" he had in mind the whole region to the south of the Anatolian plateau: a region bounded by the Mediterranean to the west and by the deserts of Sinai, Arabia and Iraq to the south and east. The region was subdivided administratively as follows: the vilayet of Aleppo, based on the northern Syrian city of that name; the vilayet of Syria, ruled from Damascus; the coastal vilayet of Beirut; and two smaller units, the sanjaks of Jerusalem and Lebanon. Most of the inhabitants of this region were Arabic-speaking Muslims, though there were significant minorities, such as the Maronite Christians in the autonomous sanjak of Lebanon and the Druzes divided between the vilayets of Beirut and Syria.

Yet "Palestine"—the word meant originally "the land of the Philistians" —was a region of immense emotive power.

To the Jews of the Diaspora, and in particular to the Jews under harsh czarist rule, Palestine gleamed as *Eretz Israel,* the land of Israel. The more they suffered, the more they clung to the memory of their vanished and brief-lived sovereignty. Rabbis would be laid to rest in marsh towns between Bug and Vistula clutching handfuls of Palestinian earth, brought back by pilgrims. The land was something very different from the Ottoman province; it achieved a mystical, extra-terrene reality as symbol of Jewish, and indeed universal, redemption. In this sense the Ukrainian mystic Nahman of Bratzlav wrote: "All the holiness of Israel clings to Eretz Israel, and every time a man cleanses and purifies his soul, he conquers and liberates a portion of the land." This did not mean that Jews had not returned to Palestine, when they could, throughout the ages, nor that some of them did not dream of a collective return. In Russia, where estrangement from gentile society was sharpest, the "love of Zion" was keenest. An organization of "Lovers of Zion" (*Hovevei Zion*) had, as though fortuitously, prepared the ground for Herzl's Great Idea. One group, the Biluim, had published a manifesto in Constantinople in 1882 which called for a Jewish home in Palestine, to be granted by the Sultan, with complete independence except for foreign affairs.

Palestine was important to Muslims. The holy places of the Jews and the Christians were also sacred to them, since Islam accepted the validity of its monotheistic forerunners. Abraham, or in Arabic Ibrahim, was considered as the first monotheist, the Friend of Allah, and the forefather of the Arabs through his son Ismail. Muslim guardianship of the Jewish and Christian holy places set the seal on Islam as the latest and most perfect statement of the primordial faith. Jerusalem had been the *qiblah,* or focus of Muslim prayer, until the conquest of Mecca, the center of Arabian paganism, for the new faith. Even then Jerusalem remained an important place of pilgrimage since from the rock on the ancient Temple hill the Prophet had been taken up into heaven on his mystical night journey.

The country in which Jesus Christ had spent all but a portion of his short life had always exerted a mesmeric fascination on Christians. Although Jerusalem itself had yielded to Antioch, Alexandria and then Rome as Christian centers, its surrounding country had been favored almost as much as Egypt by the first anchorites and monks. When Constantine was converted to Christianity, Jerusalem became a major Christian shrine, though Julian the Apostate tried to reintroduce both paganism and Judaism as bulwarks against the Christians he despised. The city ceased to be Christian ruled after its conquest by the Caliph Omar in A.D. 638. Under the Caliphate the Christians continued in full enjoyment of their shrines and during the Dark and early Middle Ages Jerusalem was the chief magnet for pilgrims from the West, men who found in visits to the places associated with the life of Christ an escape from the prison of an isolated Europe as well as a religious duty. The supervision of the shrines had been given to the Latin Church at the time of Charlemagne. Only when the self-deifying Fatimid Caliph al-Hakim gave the custody of the shrines to the Orthodox Church did European pilgrimage take a new form: that of armed Crusades. At the height of these a Crusader state ruled most of the Levant from Lebanon to the Egyptian border.

In the nineteenth century Roman Catholics visited new European shrines, such as Lourdes, associated with the continued intervention of the Virgin Mary. Protestants, with their strong biblical attachments, tended to be fascinated by Palestine's association with the history of the Jews—the history that had culminated, to the Christian mind, in the death and resurrection of Jesus.

"The history of the Jews is the most characteristic, the most important and the most sublime, in the world." So wrote in 1842 the Rev. George Croly in the text accompanying two volumes of drawings of the Holy Land by David Roberts. "The history of the Jews establishes, on the most solid grounds, the three truths most important to human knowledge: the Being of a God, a Perpetual Providence, and a Moral Government of the world." On the other hand the ruins of the Temple, now the site of an Islamic mosque, showed that by rejecting Jesus as the Son of God the Jews had brought about the fulfillment of Christ's stern prediction. "In the year 71 of our era Jerusalem was stormed by the legions under Titus, and the Temple was burned; one million one hundred thousand Jews perished by famine and the sword within the walls, and ninety-six thousand were sold into captivity."

Croly, like other Protestants, was fascinated by the question: had the biblical prophecies of a Return been fulfilled with the Return from Babylonian captivity, or would a second Return be the prelude to Christ's Second Coming? Croly's answer was allegorical. "The Jew will be restored, but as the human frame will be restored; he will return from the moral grave, with a nature fitted for a new and higher course of existence."

The drawings of Roberts evoke a landscape of exaggerated rock where idealized Palestinians with swirling turbans contemplate the fountain at Cana or minareted townships. "Fig and olive plantations, in great luxuriance, hung on every part of the hill slopes; and, bathed in warm sunlight, presented a lovely picture." So another pastor, the Reverend G. Fisk, on a visit to Bethlehem, Nazareth, in the North, was no less elegiac. "From the highest point of the mountains, and while traversing a winding path looking westward, a noble landscape opened before us. Immediately below, there stretched out a rich undulating plain, enlivened by villages and olive plantations, through which ran a beautiful glassy river."[1]

Lieutenant W. F. Lynch of the U. S. Navy has left a practical Yankee narrative of the Holy Land in contrast to the biblical, romantic vision of the Reverend Croly and the Reverend Fisk. After the surrender of Santa Cruz, Lynch tells us, he applied on May 8, 1847 for "permission to circumnavigate and thoroughly explore the Lake Asphaltites, or Dead Sea." Lynch picked his crew with a New England eye. "I was very particular in selecting young, muscular, native-born Americans, of sober habits, from each of whom I exacted a pledge to abstain from all intoxicating drinks." The American expedition was armed with one blunderbuss, fourteen carbines with long bayonets, and fourteen pistols, four revolving and ten with bowie knives attached. Each officer carried his sword. Their boats were to be shouldered by porters from the Mediterranean coast, over the mountain ridges of Galilee and Judea, to the Jordan Valley.

Lynch, muscular and sober as his young companions, was impressed by neither the Arab majority nor the Jewish minority inhabiting the Holy Land.

The one virtue he conceded to the Arabs was their abstention from alcohol. In this alone they were superior to "the more taciturn but intemperate hunters of the forest," Lynch's term for Red Indians. "In the American everything proclaims the savage who has not yet arrived at a state of civilisation; in the Arab, everything indicates the civilised man who has returned to the savage state . . . The Arab is yet more lascivious than the Indian; and in no part of the world is the condition of women more abject than it is in the East . . . The Arab will extort money from his guest, and expects a bakshish for the slightest act of hospitality. The Indian, without dreaming of recompense, will share his last morsel, and, with his life, protect the stranger who has sought the shelter of his wigwam."[2]

Lynch was even-handed in his dislike of the natives. He and his party stayed at Tiberias, the township on the Lake of Galilee which had remained, after the destruction of Jerusalem, the last center of coherent Jewish culture in Palestine. It contained two synagogues: one for the Sephardic Jews from Spain and the Arab World, the other for Ashkenazim immigrants from Eastern Europe. The two Jewish communities lived in harmony. Lynch remarked on the absence of "that spirit of trade which is everywhere else their peculiar characteristic. Their sole occupation, we were told, is to pray and to read the Talmud." But otherwise he disapproved. "The house we inhabited was owned by a Jew; and if the king of

[1] Rev. G. Fisk, *A Pastor's Memorial of the Holy Land* (London: 1853).
[2] W. F. Lynch, *Narrative of the United States' Expedition to the River Jordan and the Dead Sea* (Philadelphia: 1856).

fleas holds his court in Tiberias, his throne is surely here. But that the narrow and tortuous lanes of the town (there are no streets, in our acceptation of the word) were crowded with filthy and disgusting objects, I should have given the palm of uncleanness to our host and his family. They were, in person and attire, literally unwashed, uncombed, slouching, shuffling, dirty, and repulsive. Unlike all other places we have seen, the women are not more cleanly than the men; and while the married ones carefully conceal their hair, they all studiously exhibit the formation of their breasts, which renders them anything but attractive. The men have the abject, downtrodden look which seems peculiar to this people in the east. Many of the children are quite handsome; but filth, poverty, avarice, and tyranny, have changed the old into disgusting libels upon humanity. Compared to them, our wild Arabs are paragons of manly cleanliness."

Yet Lynch took a different view of the "Return" from the Reverend Croly. He had no more liking for the ancient Hebrews than for those he met in Tiberias. His résumé of Jewish history is sterner than the Englishman's: "under judges, prophets, and kings, the Israelites were led through wondrous vicissitudes to the trying scene which crowned their perfidy with an act so atrocious that, like the glimmer of an earthly torch before the lurid glare of pandemonium, their previous crimes sank into insignificance; and nature thrilled with horror as she looked upon the deicides, their hands imbued in the blood they should have worshipped." Yet Lynch despised the Moslems just as much; their rule was a political sirocco which withered all before it; writing when Abdul Hamid was six years old, he thought that the time was near when the Ottoman Empire would be dismembered. "It needs but the destruction of that power, which, for so many centuries, has rested like an incubus upon the eastern world, to ensure the restoration of the Jews to Palestine."

Lynch's reasons for wishing to restore the Jews differed from Herzl's. He believed that their restoration would trigger great events and confirm his eschatology. Ezekiel, he observed, had predicted that Egypt should never obey a native scepter: and the history of Egypt down to the time of Muhammad Ali Pasha proved the accuracy of this prediction. It therefore followed that the Jews would be restored and the machinery set in motion whose end would be the Second Coming.

Lieutenant Lynch's views are clearly those of a dogmatic and opinionated young man. They were based on limited experience. He had landed in Beirut in February 1848; by December the same year he was back in the United States.

The men whose decisions were most to affect the Holy Land in the coming century, who were to force upon it a violent destiny in contrast with the idyllic vision of David Roberts and the visiting clergy, were to spend far less time there than Lieutenant Lynch. Some were not to visit it at all. But Theodor Herzl was to spend a total of nine days in Palestine: from October 26 to November 4, 1898.

Chapter 4

WEARING a cork helmet, Herzl disembarked at Jaffa to be met like any other tourist by Thomas Cook's landing boat. Unlike most he jumped ashore prepared to invoke Kaiser Wilhelm in person.

On the journey from Constantinople by way of Greece and Egypt he had written nothing; *impressions du voyage* were left to the pencils of three French writers also on the vessel. Heat did not suit him and this October was particularly humid; at such times the eastern Mediterranean can seem a funnel through which the moistness of the inland sea was sucked towards the mountains of Lebanon and the hills of Palestine.

But Alexandria, rebuilt under British tutelage, did impress him. It showed, he wrote later, "how an intelligent European administration can fashion a habitable, comfortable city in the hottest climate." He was there too short a time to savor the city's dominant north wind, which has made other critics[1] judge its climate to be delectable. His glimpse of the Suez Canal at Port Said impressed him more than the ruined Acropolis in Athens.

From Egypt he chugged up the coast in a small, overcrowded steamship; on the *Russia* he had to share a cabin with four other cork-helmeted Zionists. He feared to be turned back by the Ottoman police at Jaffa and had written out a cable of protest to the Kaiser. He had no need to send it. German officials on the dockside (waiting for the All Highest and his party, including the Kaiserin) helped him through Customs.

Jaffa was more ebulliently Arab than usual. As the Jewish party entered the Hotel Kamenetz, guns roared a welcome to the one European monarch whose policy seemed the preservation, not the destruction, of the Islamic empire. People were excited, curious, awed. Ostensibly the Kaiser had come to dedicate the new Evangelical church in Jerusalem. Arabs had noses sharp for hidden motives even when there were none; they now rightly sensed that the German ruler was among them for political reasons. Having stood by the Sultan in his Cretan difficulties two years

[1] Notably E. M. Forster in his *Alexandria*.

earlier, the Kaiser had come for his reward; he wished to stake out a German claim in the Middle East. An unparalleled welcome in Constantinople had made him euphoric. The Christian Emperor had kissed the wax-pale cheek of a pleased and at the same time astonished Sultan.

Even less than the Kaiser was Herzl in Palestine for tourist reasons. He was not to visit its major monuments nor meet its natives. (These numbered around half a million, or around the population of Cyprus in the 1970s. Most were Arabic-speaking Muslims.) Herzl felt himself a man on an urgent mission.

An early irritant was the lack of carriages at the hotel. He must visit one or two of the existing Jewish settlements; largely as a result of Rothschild philanthropy around 4,500 Jews were settled in eighteen rural colonies. Despite the oppressive heat, Herzl was ready to visit the first agricultural training school at Mikveh Israel as well as Rishon-le-Zion, a settler village, on horseback. Luckily a Russian Zionist, a physician, procured a conveyance.

Bunting in honor of the Kaiser hung over the entrance to Mikveh Israel. Herzl dismissed the scenery (or the small portion he saw) as "Arab-blighted"—one of the few references to the natives in his diary. But the settler village at Rishon-le-Zion seemed equally blighted. The settlement band played its welcome: it was, Herzl confided to his diary, only well intentioned. The faces of the settlers were wan; day laborers, he discovered, slept on plank beds. "Finally I spoke to the physician of the colony, Dr. Mazie. He told me the unvarnished truth: fever! All the colonies suffer from fever; only large-scale drainage operations and the elimination of swamps can make the country habitable. This is also my own view, and intention. It will cost millions but will create millions of new wealth." In a second reference to the indigenous population, he added: "Such Arabs as are immune from fever might be employed to do the work."

Some upstanding young Jews on horseback laid on an Arab-style fantasia. Otherwise Herzl was depressed by the Jews living in Palestine. Nearly all were Sephardim, descendants of the Jews expelled from Spain by the Catholic kings and given refuge by Islam. Though only a few had taken Ottoman nationality, nearly all had merged with the local population. "Whatever their origins, all these Jews," one of their Arab neighbors has recalled, "were Arabic-speaking, ate Arab food (except the meat, as it was not Kosher), enjoyed Arab music, and apart from a few Ashkenazim from Central Europe who had come into the country in the nineteenth century and for the most part wore black caftans and skull-caps with their hair in long ringlets, dressed as the Arabs did."[2] The Jews were accepted by the Arabs, who, coming from a society linked with religion, found it unsurprising that married Jewish women should shave their skulls and wear wigs,

2 Geoffrey Furlonge, *Palestine is my country; the story of Musa Alami* (London: John Murray, 1969), p. 27.

or that Jewish men should wear prayer curls. To progressive Europeans such things were unattractive. A contemporary "Journey to Palestine" (published by the Paris firm of Calmann Lévy) described the Jewish population of Jerusalem as "perhaps one of the most deplorable specimens of humanity; it vegetates in a state of abject ignorance and misery, its ugliness, its depravity inspire a profound disgust; it is not without horror that you pass the sordid quarter where it lives amidst mud, filth, vice and poverty."[3]

Herzl had as little use as the Parisian author for the Holy Land as it was. "When I remember thee in days to come, O Jerusalem," his diary of October 31 records, "it will not be with delight. The musty deposits of two thousand years of inhumanity, intolerance, and foulness live in your reeking alleys. The one man who has been present here all this while, the lovable dreamer of Nazareth, has done nothing but help increase the hate. If Jerusalem is ever ours, and if I were still able to do anything about it, I would begin by cleaning it up. I would clear out everything that is not sacred, set up workers' houses beyond the city, empty and tear down the filthy ratholes, burn all the non-sacred ruins, and put the bazaars elsewhere. Then, retaining as much of the old architectural style as possible, I would build an airy, comfortable, properly sewered, brand new city around the Holy Places."

The Teuton that survived in Herzl had brought him all this way to meet the Teuton Kaiser, on an errand of state. For Zionism had become a political force within months of the publication of *Der Judenstaat*. A first Zionist Congress at Basel in 1897 had institutionalized the movement; a second in 1898 had established a bank, known as the Colonial Trust, and a National Fund for the purchase of land in Palestine. All now depended on finding a Teutonic sponsor.

A German sponsor appealed to Herzl for three reasons. The first was cultural. Herzl, like most of the Western Zionists, had been reared on German culture. As he had remarked the previous month to Philipp zu Eulenburg, the Kaiser's favorite and the German ambassador in Vienna: "The majority of Jews today are part of the German cultural world. I am not saying this because I am sitting in the German Embassy, but because it is true. Proof: German is the official language of the Basel Congresses." The second reason was political. Germany was the European Power most trusted by the Ottomans. If the Sultan were to be convinced, the German Kaiser was the man most likely to do the convincing. The third reason was perhaps the most powerful. Herzl was attracted to the Kaiser as a person. As a dramatist he felt he understood the man behind the showy uniforms and the bombastic speeches. Like a Jew, the Kaiser carried a secret wound; in his case it was the withered left arm, which, if he had been an ordinary

[3] Gabriel Charmes, *Voyage en Palestine, Impressions et Souvenirs* (Paris: Calmann Lévy, 1891), p. 141.

mortal, would have made him ineligible for military service; it made him adopt, by compensation, his masculine and martial gestures. The conflict between innate shyness and a flamboyant public persona had produced, Herzl believed, a man whose genius resembled Herzl's own. Kaiser and Zionist both loved dramatic choices, brilliant slogans and engineering marvels. They were men of the nineteenth century who looked forward to the twentieth. If any potentate could respond to Herzl's vision, it would be Queen Victoria's one brilliant grandson.

Herzl had approached the German authorities the moment the Kaiser's visit to the Holy Land had been proposed. Articles in the Jewish newspaper *Die Welt* advocated the establishment of a Jewish colony in the Middle East under German auspices. Copies of the newspaper, suitably marked, had been sent to the Imperial Civil Office and so to the Kaiser's notice.

Herzl was helped by two German allies. The first was the Grand Duke of Baden. "We need a protector," Herzl had told him, "and German protection would be welcomed more than any other." The second, less stable ally was the already mentioned Eulenburg, whose flamboyant career was later to be quenched in a homosexual scandal. "Our movement exists; I anticipate that one or other of the Great Powers will espouse it. Originally I had thought that this Power would be England. It lay in the nature of things. But I would be even better pleased if it were Germany."

Both men were influential. The Grand Duke was the Kaiser's uncle by marriage, while Eulenburg knew all the officials of Wilhelmine Germany. Happy to ingratiate himself with a prominent journalist and playwright, Eulenburg had arranged, in late September, for Herzl to meet Von Bülow. Herzl was so embarrassed at being received by the Foreign Minister that he felt afterwards he had made more *bons mots* than sense. Herzl had only time to stress, in what was more a chat than a serious discussion, one aspect of Zionism likely to please the conservative Von Bülow: "the anti-Socialist aspect of Zionism was discussed or, more accurately, toyed with longest—on the other hand, little was said about political and colonial matters in the Orient." Herzl had argued with more boldness than truth that the Egypt which had enslaved the Jews had been a socialist state. "Through the Ten Commandments Moses created an individualistic society."

Von Bülow soon received Herzl again, this time in Berlin, and not alone. Also present was the gnarled and bemedaled Chancellor, Prince Hohenlohe. The atmosphere had changed. Herzl recognized that the Chancellor was an anti-Semite from his question: would the rich Jews of Berlin leave their stock exchange for Herzl's piping? The Chancellor probed further. How much of the Sultan's territory was Herzl after? "As far north as Beirut, or even further?"

"We will ask for what we need. The more immigrants, the more land. The rights of private property will, of course, be respected, and the land will be purchased from its present owners."

"Who are these?"

"Arabs, Greeks, the whole mixed multitude of the Orient."

Herzl was evasive when the Chancellor asked him what the Sultan's attitude would be; Von Bülow then refused to confirm that the German ambassador in Constantinople had reported that Ottoman attitudes were favorable. It was agreed that Herzl would submit a memorandum in Constantinople. But Von Bülow's coolness had spoiled the omens.

Tirelessly tired, driving himself against his health, Herzl pushed for and obtained a secret hour with the Kaiser in Constantinople. The Emperor and Empress were staying at Yildiz. Herzl's spirits soared when the Kaiser agreed to receive him in Palestine as head of an official Zionist delegation. He at once bought a ticket on the *Emperor Nicholas II* to Alexandria, the first leg of his journey. The Kaiser must make a public pronouncement in favor of Zionism. Herzl knew what to offer in return: not the financial aid he had dangled before the Sultan, but something to the taste of an emperor neurotically jealous of Great Britain. A nucleus of German-speaking Jews (Herzl did not envisage his settlers reviving Hebrew) would advance German influence in the Middle East; it would also act as a bulwark against the Asiatic hordes which the Kaiser (inventor of the phrase "the yellow peril") so much dreaded.

Now Herzl and the Kaiser were in Palestine.

The Kaiser's route would take him, early in the morning, past Mikveh Israel. Herzl reached the settlement for his second visit soon after sunrise.

Arabs thronged the dusty highway. They wanted to see as well as welcome the strange Christian visitor, the one European who had kissed their Sultan, the one human being for whom their Sultan felt something of that friendship possible only between equals. Ottoman cavalry galloped past, menacing with glares and guns the Eastern crowd. As the Kaiser's party rode up, Herzl, standing close to a symbolic plow, signaled the settlement's children to start the imperial anthem: "Hail to Thee in Victor's Crown!"

The Kaiser recognized his Yildiz visitor and to Herzl's delight reined in his horse and, as the settlers watched, bent from the saddle. But the few words that the two men exchanged were Teutonic, not Zionist, and the Kaiser kept them so.

How had His Majesty found his journey?

Hot! Yet the country had a future.

It was still sick, Dr. Herzl answered, hinting the physician.

It only needed irrigation . . .

But irrigation on a large scale . . . Herzl hinted the physic: the migration of Jews and Jewish capital.

Repeating that the country had a future, the Kaiser galloped off.

Herzl, still thinking his man an iron-willed genius, took the meeting, which had impressed and irritated the Rothschild administrators, as auguring well for his official meeting. This took place on November 2 in the Kaiser's tent. Wilhelm had by this time made his official entry into the Holy City through a gap specially cut in its ancient walls and had proclaimed himself Islam's Protestant champion.

Now wearing a turban with his gray Prussian uniform he was friendly and evasive in equal measure. He gave Herzl his hand but less time than at Yildiz. To Herzl's impassioned plea that Palestine was the land from which the Jews had derived in the past and a land in the present ripe for colonization, the Kaiser replied that it was a land needing water and shade.

"The settlements which I have seen, the German no less than the Jewish, may serve as examples of what can be done with the land. There is room here for all. Only provide the water and shade. For the native population, too, the colonisation will serve as an example of initiative."

The Kaiser had no objections to colonization as such. On the contrary, he smarted under the indignity which gave his young empire colonies of so little value: Togoland and Kamerun, Tanganyika and a part of New Guinea named after himself. When he said, "There is room here for all," he meant, for Germans, for Jews and for natives. Part of his private grand design was to make the Ottoman Empire the German equivalent of British India. Germany's population had increased by eighteen millions since the war with France. A rapidly growing industrial machine needed raw materials.

But to the Kaiser Dr. Herzl was an exotic figure in a landscape where other Jews had disappointed him. He had been disappointed, like most Europeans, by the squalor of the Holy City's Jewish quarter.

But something more practical than distaste made the Kaiser cautious. In Constantinople it had been made clear to him that the Holy Land, won for Islam by Omar, Muhammad's second and perhaps greatest successor, would never be voluntarily surrendered to the Jews. The Jews could live there, pray there; they could not colonize or hope to rule it.

The Kaiser's new coolness to Herzl's proposals was therefore explicable in terms of German interests. Germany had already secured concessions to build important railways in the Ottoman Empire. She could secure further advantages as the patron, not the bully, of the Sultan.

Conceded no public statement of support, Herzl left Palestine on a British freighter shipping out the oranges which Arab farmers had begun to make a sizable export. To the last moment Herzl expected an attempt on his life. Yet the Ottoman police waved him past with indifference. "If the Turkish government were possessed of a grain of political foresight," Herzl wrote in his diary, "it would have finished the job there and then."

Safe and sound in Naples, Herzl read the official communiqué on the imperial visit. After detailing the All Highest's visits to the shrines of Islam, his calls on the clergy of the Greek and Latin rites, his reception of the French consul, it added that the Kaiser had also received "a Jewish deputation, which presented him with an album of pictures of the Jewish colonies in Palestine. In reply to an address by the leader of the deputation, His Majesty remarked that he viewed with benevolent interest all efforts directed towards the improvement of agriculture in Palestine, *so long as these accorded with the welfare of the Turkish Empire, and were conducted in a spirit of complete respect for the sovereignty of the Sultan.*"

The italicized clause represented disappointment. Herzl would have to look for a more forthright, or less scrupulous, sponsor.

Chapter 5

GREAT BRITAIN, Herzl's original choice for sponsor, had the most to gain from a Turkish funeral. It was also the country which had first toyed with Zionist assumptions. Though British control of Egypt made Palmerston's calculations invalid, twentieth-century circumstances might give new impetus to the idea. Palestine guarded the eastern approaches to the Canal which Palmerston had opposed but which had become the artery of the British Empire. A Jewish Palestine dependent on Britain would be a counterweight to the ambitions of France and Russia, who both had clients in the eastern Mediterranean: the Russians patronized the Orthodox while since the days of Louis XIV the French had taken an interest in the Maronites of Mount Lebanon. Britain lacked a client minority, though it had, in Egypt, a client dynasty.

Germany's successful intrusion into the Middle East could prompt Great Britain to a counterthrust. If German influence dominated Constantinople, as it threatened to do, Britain would have a clear interest in killing off the empire she had long kept alive; this was the occasion under which Abdul Hamid had predicted that the Zionists might get Palestine for nothing.

But the Ottoman Empire was dying more slowly than the century: or, for that matter, Herzl.

"I am thinking a great deal about Cyprus," Herzl confided to Gustav Cohen, a Hamburg banker, in the last summer of the century.

Herzl never visited the island birthplace of Aphrodite; nor did he seriously consider Cyprus as a substitute for Palestine. It might, however, serve as a springboard for the invasion of the Holy Land, and perhaps as an auxiliary colony.

Herzl raised the Cyprus question with someone more influential than Gustav Cohen when Joseph Chamberlain, "the famous master-figure of England," received him for an hour in October 1902. Much had happened to Herzl and his friends since the nine days in Palestine. Philip Nevlinski had died of a heart attack in Constantinople. The death of his Polish go-between had troubled Herzl; he reproached himself for sending a sick man on one last Zionist errand; Nevlinski's death also foreshadowed his own probable fate; for Herzl's heart, too, had been troubling him. But Nevlinski had prepared one Pyrrhic victory. The Sultan had finally received Herzl, as a distinguished journalist, though not as a political leader. The interview was practically worthless. The Sultan had offered another decoration; he had expatiated on the potential wealth of his empire—that very day a telegram from Baghdad reported the discovery of oil fields richer than Russia's. The Sultan had also enthused over the electric light he had just installed at Yildiz. Herzl was indignant (not for himself, but for the people whose representative he claimed to be) that the decoration was second-class. He in his turn expatiated on what the Jews could do for the country and for Constantinople—they could even build a bridge over the Bosphorus.

But there was no deal: Palestine was still not for sale.

Herzl worked off his disappointment in his diary. "I can see him before me now, the Sultan of this declining robber empire. Small, shabby, with his badly dyed beard touched up apparently once a week for the *selamlik*, the hooked nose of a Punchinello, the long yellow teeth with a big gap to the right in the upper set, the fez pulled low over his doubtlessly bald head, his stuck-out ears serving, as I say to my friends, as a pants protector—to keep the fez from slipping down below his waist, the feeble hands in their white over-size gloves and the loud-colored cuffs that don't match his suit, the bleating voice, restraint in every word and fear in every glance."[1]

Joseph Chamberlain was a massive contrast to the feeble Sultan. The British Colonial Secretary seemed cast from the same mold as the artifacts of Birmingham, source of the family fortune. The artist in Herzl recoiled before this gigantic Philistine. "Chamberlain did not make any impression of brilliance. Not a man of imagination. A matter-of-fact screw manufacturer, who wants to expand the business. A mind without literary or artistic resources, a businessman, but an absolutely clear, unclouded head."[2] Yet a prejudiced head. Chamberlain disdained Orientals; in this category he included Jews. He once told an Italian statesman: "There is, in fact, only one race I despise—the Jews, Sir. They are physical cowards."

It cost Herzl courageous effort (in uncertain English) to make this anti-Semite smile. He played on Chamberlain's contempt for another brand of

[1] Entry for May 21, 1901.
[2] Entry for October 23, 1902.

Orientals, as he humorously described his negotiations with Abdul Hamid. "You know what Turkish negotiations are. If you want to buy a carpet, first you must drink half a dozen cups of coffee and smoke a hundred cigarettes; then you discuss family stories, and from time to time you speak again a few words about the carpet. Now *I* have time to negotiate, but my people has not."

Chamberlain was amused by Herzl's turn of phrase. He laughed. Herzl at once made clear what carpet he wanted.

"I brought up the territory which I desired to obtain from England: Cyprus, El Arish and the Sinai Peninsula."

Herzl's indifference to the tangle of Middle Eastern legalities astounded Chamberlain. Since Egypt was part of the Ottoman Empire, albeit under British control, El Arish and Sinai were the concern of the Foreign Office. On Cyprus, however, he could speak. Though nominally still part of the Ottoman domains, the third largest island in the Mediterranean was a de facto British colony. Cyprus was inhabited by two religious groups, each backed by outside Powers. The Greek Orthodox majority had the support of Greece and Russia; the Muslims, the support of the Sultan. It was unthinkable that Britain should allow the eviction of these two peoples for the sake of newcomers. If Herzl could think of some other territory without white settlers or native Europeans, things might be different. But Cyprus was out of the question. If it was hinted that the British Government were contemplating any such bargain, there would be a public outcry.

"Not everything in politics," Herzl replied, "is disclosed to the public: but only results, or what can be serviceable in a controversy." He had worked out a plan. A climate of opinion must be created in Cyprus which would favor Jewish immigration. "We must be *invited* to come into the country. I would lay the ground for this through half a dozen emissaries. And when we had founded the Jewish Eastern Company, with five million pounds capital, for settling Sinai and El Arish, the Cypriots would be anxious to divert some of that golden rain to their own island. The Muslims would leave, and the Greeks would gladly sell their lands at a good price and migrate to Athens or Crete."

Chamberlain's smile may now have been ironic. He had considerable sympathy for the armchair machiavel; he took his point about not disclosing to the public all you planned to do. Yet there was a paradox. Dr. Herzl was arguing that his people, the Jews, had been wounded by a millennial deprivation of territory. Yet the same Dr. Herzl assumed that the villagers of Cyprus would barter their territory away for money. Chamberlain's latent dislike for Jews erupted in a way not uncommon in Herzl's experience. No one liked Jews more than he did, the Colonial Secretary protested; at the same time he feared that anti-Semitism, at present nonexistent, would infect the English if too many Jews poured into their island.

His barb hurt. "That was evidently a hint to me, the gypsy chieftain, to warn off my hordes."

In return Herzl would despise him and smile. At the mention of El Arish Chamberlain had been puzzled as to its precise location. "The most extraordinary thing was his ignorance of British possessions which were undoubtedly under his supervision. It was like a big second-hand store whose proprietor didn't know exactly where a particular article might be. I need a gathering place for the Jewish people. He'll look around to see if England happens to have such a place."

There was an atlas lying on a large table. Chamberlain opened it at the page marked "Egypt" and then looked up.

"In Egypt you would have the same trouble as in Cyprus with the native inhabitants."

"No, we won't go to Egypt—we've been there before."

Once more Chamberlain laughed; once more Herzl struck home. While the Englishman was still bent over his map, Herzl explained that he needed an assemblage center for the Jewish people in the neighborhood of Palestine. "In El Arish and Sinai there is empty land. England can give us that. In return she could gain an increase of power and the gratitude of ten million Jews." He came to the point: would Chamberlain agree to the establishment of a Jewish colony in Sinai?

"Yes," was the quick reply, as quickly qualified: "Provided Lord Cromer does not object."

Once again Herzl bought tickets for train and steamship: this time for Cairo.

In the twenty years since Orabi's revolt Egypt had been outwardly tranquil; the veiled protectorate was claimed by its protectors to be the most beneficent in history. Finance, irrigation, justice, education, even Orabi's defeated Army, had been remolded (in some cases cut down) under British guidance. The Egyptian budget now balanced; Egypt was a cotton farm for the mills of Lancashire; there was no higher education, except for al-Azhar, but five years before Herzl's visit Khartoum had been reconquered from its Sudanese Khalifa. Lord Kitchener had pushed a railway south from Wadi Halfa and introduced lofty gunboats whose Maxim guns could enfilade the Nile banks. The Land of the Blacks had been restored to civilized control as an Anglo-Egyptian condominium. Egyptian officials did the menial, unpopular tasks, such as collecting taxes; British overlords took decisions and administered justice.

Egypt was so stable that the elderly Orabi was brought back from his exile in Ceylon; the defeated leader was deferential to the new Khedive, Abbas II, son of his old enemy Towfik; Orabi gave approval to many of the English reforms.

Yet castrated Egypt provided Herzl's bitterest reverse. On his return to Vienna he would write in despair: "I thought the Sinai matter was so certain that I no longer wanted to buy a family vault in the Doblinger cemetery, where my father is provisionally laid to rest. Now I consider the matter so utterly shattered that I have been to the borough court and have acquired vault 28."

The Egyptian reverse would have been foreseen by anyone less sanguine. But Herzl was as credulous to the vague promises of others as he expected others to be to his.

The scheme for an autonomous Jewish colony in Sinai failed for economic and political reasons; as always the reasons owed much to the individuals who advanced them.

The Zionist request for Sinai was considered as a question involving water resources. No mustering ground for the Jewish people within striking distance of Palestine, let alone a Ruritania, could be established in the desert without water. The wells of El Arish were inadequate for an expanding colony. The only solution would have been to divert into Sinai a new sweet-water canal similar to the one which now supported a chain of towns by the banks of the Suez Canal. Being more than 95 per cent arid, Egypt could ill afford such loss of Nile.

But the fatal objections to the scheme involved the old theme of sovereignty and the newer theme of Egyptian nationalism.

Despite the temporary British occupation—looking more permanent with each passing year—Egypt remained in law an Ottoman province. To alienate a portion of this province in favor of the Jews, and a portion so sensitively close to the Ottoman border, was both beyond the legal rights of the Khedive and against his interests. The Sultan would see the danger which Chamberlain himself had referred to in his chat with Herzl: that from Sinai Jewish settlers might stage a raid into Palestine similar to the Jameson Raid into the Boer Republic of the Transvaal.

More important yet, any such alienation of Egyptian territory would outrage a growing spirit of Egyptian nationalism. A generation earlier this group feeling, or a form of it, had been the flame which ignited the Orabi bonfire; and though the British had smothered the flame, they had by no means quenched it. Muhammad Abduh's disciples, as well as young men educated under the secular influence of France, were fusing a nationalism very different from Orabi's instinctive fervor. This new secular nationalism may not have been what Abduh wanted. With his Islamic temper he had intended, as Albert Hourani has put it,[3] to build a wall against secularism; but in fact he had provided an easy bridge by which it could capture one position after another. By 1903 a Nationalist Party was playing an increasingly influential role among Egyptian youth. Its leader was a brilliant, irresponsible and attractive young man named Mustafa Kamil. His good looks and charm had won him friends in France, where he had studied

[3] Albert Hourani, *Arabic Thought in the Liberal Age* (Oxford: 1962), p. 144.

law and where his fiery rhetoric brought Egyptian nationalism to the attention of a country eager to needle Britain. He had a gift for resonant phrases. "In this century the slavery of individuals has been abolished; in its place has been introduced the slavery of peoples." In Cairo this nationalism, with its slogan of "Egypt for the Egyptians," enjoyed the moral and monetary support of the young Khedive. He had persuaded the Sultan to make the middle-class young man a pasha.

For Abbas (whose most persistent quality was avarice) was shrewd enough to see that he could reign as a popular khedive if he showed himself the defender of Egyptian interests. In this way, with a volatile and generous people, he could live down the abject record of his father, Towfik. Early in his reign Abbas had clashed with Kitchener, the insensitive but successful commander of his forces. Though worsted in the clash he had gained stature in the eyes of his people.

Egyptian nationalists tended to transpose into an Egyptian setting the nationalism rampant in Europe. European nationalism often felt itself of age when it acquired a colony, Egyptian nationalists were similarly proud that Muhammad Ali and his heirs had made of Egypt an imitation colonial power. Khedive Ismail was remembered with approval for having established Egyptian border guards in the little ports of the Red Sea and as far south as the great African Lakes. Nationalists would regard the loss of Sinai, a territory linked with Egypt since the dawn of history, as an intolerable insult.

But although Abbas was the Khedive, the authority to accept or reject Herzl's proposals lay with Lord Cromer, the sexagenarian Englishman to whom even Chamberlain deferred.

Evelyn Baring had, in successive ennoblements (baron in 1892, viscount in 1897 and earl in 1901) linked his name with Cromer, a resort with a golf course and high cliffs on the coast of North Norfolk.

In other societies Evelyn Baring might have been an odd man out; in the *fin de siècle* British Empire he was the odd man in. It was an age of nicknames. A streak of cold arrogance, directed more to his English subordinates than to the Egyptians, turned Baring to "OverBaring." It was also an age of doggerel. Baring's Victorian prudery was playful, as is shown by his three-line composition:

"Naughty little cuss words,
Just as much as worse words,
Point the way below."

Baring had reached the way above, thanks to stamina, for his education had been ill directed to his talents. Born to a modest branch of the family whose fortune had been built by the Baring Brothers—financiers descended from eighteenth-century immigrants from Holland—he was flogged through a school at Carshalton which prepared boys for the Royal Military College at Woolwich. Military education contributed little to his intellectual interests, which later ranged from Greek poetry to finance; but it helped to develop an icy self-control. Military service—he was commissioned in the Royal Artillery at the age of seventeen—was still the pursuit of a gentleman and allowed Baring to travel widely. One long trip through the unreformed Balkans made him a lifelong anti-Turk. In the Ionian Islands, then under British control, he supported self-determination for the islanders; he also formed an untypical friendship with Edward Lear, overt humorist and covert lover of young males. Baring's liberalism, which made him a convinced supporter of the North in the American Civil War, slowly evolved into something which few would recognize as liberalism today: the belief, strengthened by sojourns in the two islands of Malta and Jamaica, that imperialism was the best policy both for Britain and the many peoples she made her subjects. At a time when the English mood was on the whole against the acquisition of overseas possessions, Malta taught him the need for a chain of bases to uphold the Pax Britannica in a naughty world. Jamaica, still smarting from an unsuccessful black revolt against white planters, helped him formulate his ideal of ruling darker peoples for their own advantage.

He had, for an aspirant Prospero with financial genius, one great handicap. Though related to some of England's richest bankers, he had little cash in his current account. Attracted by eventual prospects of salary, he joined the Staff College in 1868, and in the year of the opening of the Suez Canal was appointed to the Topographical and Statistical Department at the War Office: the seed from which British Military Intelligence was to grow.

Always near to Intelligence, Baring was possessed of the kind with a small *i* also. Against majority opinion, he predicted the crushing German victory of 1870. He was the first to adapt the system of Prussian "war games" to British needs, publishing an abridged translation of *The Elementary Tactics of the Prussian Infantry*. In his army career Baring was the sober *novus homo,* deliberately standing apart from the extrovert and boastful officers of aristocratic tradition. In co-operation with his kinsman Lord Northbrook, he played a molelike role in undermining the "Purchase System," which had contributed to British losses in the Crimean War. (Lord Cardigan had spent £30,000 in purchasing the retirement of all senior officers, thus securing personal command of the famous Light Brigade.) After the French defeat the system seemed more menacing still.

It was a civil age and Baring's talents were essentially civilian. Good fortune and family connections helped their development. In 1872 Lord Northbrook was appointed Viceroy of India, in succession to the assassinated Lord Mayo. During his now forgotten period of office, Northbrook, an honest, pedestrian man, was the most powerful Eastern potentate on earth, ruling an estimated fifth of the human race. His integrity seemed unflawed when "looking round in search of someone on whose judgment he could rely to take charge of his personal staff, his gaze fell not unnaturally upon the brilliant young officer who had proved so efficient an assistant in his parliamentary battles and who was attached to him by ties not only of sympathy but blood."[4]

In India Baring won, as "vice-Viceroy", a reputation for financial prudence and administrative caution. In March 1877 he was the obvious choice for Britain's representative on the financial board reporting on the Khedive's debts. Baring was drawn by the salary: £3,000 a year. His first bout with Egypt lasted for two frustrating years and ended with his exasperated resignation. "I was interested in the work of Egyptian reform; but I had no wish to remain in Egypt as a mere receiver of money for the bondholders. I was their representative; but my sympathies lay more with the wretched taxpayers of Egypt, who were ground to the earth by excessive fiscal burdens, than with those whose interests it was my legal duty to defend." Baring probably did feel an abstract compassion for the fellahin; but his exasperation sprang more from the despair induced by a situation in which, lacking real power, he had to untangle an arabesque of hopes and promises, to find his way through a snakes and ladders game of promissory notes and reneged-on debts, a maze in which the four million sterling which Ismail had received for his Canal shares had vanished without trace.

Baring returned to Egypt after the British occupation. His new terms of reference gave his autocratic and clear-sighted nature the scope it needed. Nominally British agent and consul-general, having the rank of a minister plenipotentiary in the diplomatic service, he was in fact the civilian re-maker of a society shattered by Ismail's extravagance and Orabi's failure. From 1884 onwards he took all the basic decisions concerning Egypt. With draconian prudence he advised the abandonment of the Sudan when Gordon was its governor; when Egypt was in a position to have a surplus, he sanctioned (without great enthusiasm, for he would have preferred to spend the money on irrigation) its reconquest by Kitchener.

The civilian virtues had a Spartan spine. "Lord Cromer is the nicest person in the world, without a doubt." Thus a bluestocking[5] destined to play her own role in Middle Eastern history. "Nicest" had connotations which were only intelligible in the apogee of empire; they were connotations alien to Central Europe and Theodor Herzl. Cromer's first marriage shows what a cold, controlled niceness it was. He had married Ethel Stanley, daughter of Sir Rowland Stanley Errington, eleventh baronet and Roman Catholic, stipulating that the marriage should be conducted according to Protestant rites and that any children (there were to be two sons) should be raised in their father's, not their mother's, faith. Lady Cromer was one of the loyal, indomitable women without whom the empire would have collapsed and whose aloofness may have hastened its demise. The

[4] Zetland, the Marquess of, *Lord Cromer, being the authorized life of Evelyn Baring, first Earl of Cromer* (London: 1932), p. 50.

[5] Lady Bell, ed., *The Letters of Gertrude Bell* (London: 1947), p. 190.

Cairo climate never suited her. Yet when she was dying in October 1898, in the aftermath of Kitchener's victory, a political crisis made it essential for Cromer to return to Egypt: there was trouble with the French at Fashoda on the Upper Nile. Lady Cromer knew her duty. She insisted on returning with her husband through the same Mediterranean heat that had upset Herzl, and within a few days died, uncomplaining, under turning fans in the sultry Agency as the sun slumped behind the pyramids. In his distress during his wife's last hours Cromer turned to a redoubtable Crusoe: Harry Boyle, his oriental secretary. Boyle has left the following account:

"In the afternoon of that day Lord Cromer went out into the garden with me, about four o'clock, and we sat on the terrace overlooking the Nile. He kept quite silent for a while; then suddenly he leaned over and seized my hand in a grip which I remembered for some days after and said: 'By God, Boyle, it's more than I can bear.' He was, of course, in his wife's room when she died, and in a few minutes he came down into his study, where I found him drafting a long and intricate telegram to the Foreign Office on the much-discussed international question of the Red Sea Lights. It happened that at that moment the band in the neighbouring British Barracks struck up some merry airs. (Lady Cromer's death was, of course, not yet known.) I asked him if I should telephone to have the music stopped, to which he replied: 'No, no, she would have liked it.' "[6]

Boyle filled a contrasting panel in an imperial diptych: the two men represented the British Egypt with which Herzl would have to deal. Like Cromer, Boyle had a small title concealing much power. He was officially employed at the Agency as "vice-consul at Massawa," a Red Sea port he was not to visit until after his retirement. While Cromer inhabited a stately mansion by the Nile, Boyle rubbed along in a house on the corner of the Bulak Road; garrisoned with a company of books and a platoon of pipes, the marble-lined house lacked curtains and carpets. Boyle did not sleep alone. At least five dogs shared his bed, even at the humid height of Cairo summer. There was also a cat who delivered regular litters between the snoring Englishman and his amicable dogs. Like a good Crusoe, Boyle had his Man Friday. For the twenty-seven years of his service in the East, he was looked after by Guiro, a Montenegrin whom, at the age of eighteen, Boyle had recruited as his bodyguard in Constantinople. Guiro was lazy and smiled on the simplicity in which his master lived, since it involved little work. But in the East a servant's prestige is linked to his master's. Proud when Boyle appeared in impeccable togs on public occasions, Guiro was ashamed when he wore his off-duty suits, most of them secondhand reach-me-down garments bought from the native bazaar. The relationship

---

[6] The information to do with Harry Boyle, and the quotations come from Clara Boyle (London: Methuen, 1938); *A Servant of the Empire, a Memoir of Harry Boyle* and her *Boyle of Cairo* (Kendal, England: Titus Wilson, 1965).

between master and servant was informal and Guiro begged Boyle not to recognize him if they met on a Cairo street: Guiro was ashamed of his handiwork as a valet.

In one garb Guiro was used to accompanying his master on secret errands. If Cromer brooded on Olympus, his secretary strolled the streets. "How does our little busy Boyle," to quote the doggerel of a senior official, "delight to blot and gum. He adorns the Chancery all day, at night he loves to slum." On his nocturnal excursions through a city rich in slums, Boyle did not try to pass as an Egyptian; he would have been given away by his accent and a dozen details. Instead, he and Guiro arrayed themselves as Turks and spoke only Turkish. In this way they attracted little attention in the cosmopolitan Islamic crowd. Boyle gained an unrivaled knowledge of what the bazaar, or Turkish bath, was saying.

Boyle's liking for practical jokes was typical of the humor of that vanished day. One involved Sir Thomas Lipton, a rich Englishman who had pestered him on behalf of a nephew wanting a job. One evening Sir Thomas and Boyle were seated at different tables on the verandah of Shepheard's Hotel. Boyle's shabby clothes misled an American tourist into thinking him a pimp. Coming over to Boyle's table the tourist asked for an introduction to "some personable young man," at the same time pressing half a crown (in those days rather more than fifty cents) into his hand. Boyle saw his chance for a double revenge. Pocketing the coin, he whispered that he was presently off duty. "That gentleman over there," he pointed to Sir Thomas, "is taking my place. Address yourself to him." Boyle then took a horse-drawn cab and watched some way off as the outraged Sir Thomas assailed the tourist.

But Boyle was more than an eccentric buffoon. A brilliant linguist, he was almost as influential as "the Lord, with whom he walked always": this biblical quotation won him his nickname—"Enoch." He was entirely satisfied with his life in Cairo, only going to England twice in twenty-seven years. His mother yearned in vain for his return.

Yet Boyle was as fond of his parents, who lived shabbily in London, as they of him. He would send home little sums from his salary—a pound here, or thirty shillings there—to buy them luxuries; his father sternly forbade his mother from telling him how poor they were.

Yet the affections of a Crusoe were as austere as a Prospero's. When, on Christmas Day, 1900, he received a telegram telling of his father's death, "he was busy deciphering a despatch and reading it to Lord Cromer. He glanced at the telegram and without a change in the tone of his voice he went on reading, so that Lord Cromer was not aware that there had been an interruption. It was only later, at dinner, that he told him, and the Lord realized that Harry was worthy of the training in Spartan self-control which he himself had given him by his own example."

Both Cromer and Boyle put Britain first in all decisions. Neither believed that natives were ready for self-rule. Jewish sufferings or ambitions meant little to either. If, as is probable, Cromer was of remote Jewish origin, through the Barings of Groningen, he will have had an added predisposition against a movement stressing links which his forebears had snapped and his family forgotten. Harry Boyle shared the amiable anti-Semitism of his caste and time. A Young Turk leader snubbed him when Boyle spoke to him in Turkish.

"Croyez vous que je puis comprendre cet argot là?" Boyle's immediate reaction, when telling the story, was to exclaim: "The man's father was a Polish Jew." The Turk, for Boyle and his generation, was a gentleman even when his hands were bloodstained; the Jew, however virtuous, was not.

Herzl's visit to the Eygpt of Cromer and Boyle was a total failure. Herzl found Cromer the most disagreeable Englishman he had ever met: "rather too much morgue, a touch of tropical distemper, and a streak of absolute vice-regalism." As for Cromer, he made no reference to Dr. Herzl in *Modern Egypt,* the magisterial, two-volume account of his Egyptian stewardship; the reader equally hunts in vain for a reference to the Jewish leader in Cromer's official biography by the Marquess of Zetland.

Disconsolate, Herzl trekked back to London and Joseph Chamberlain. He found the screw manufacturer radiant with good news.

"I've seen a land for you, Dr. Herzl, on my recent travels, and that's Uganda. It's hot on the coast, but the climate of the interior is excellent for Europeans."

Once again Chamberlain had shown himself a poor geographer. The area he had found—already inhabited, but only by black men—was in fact part of Kenya. But Herzl was in no mood to carp. His Egyptian defeat put him in a mood to snatch at a straw. East Africa could be defended to the Jews as a jumping-off place for Palestine; it would act, in any case, as the equivalent of a Salvation Army shelter.

Herzl's apparent readiness to accept an alternative to Palestine was one of the two actions of his last year of life which involved him in bitter controversy with other Zionists and helped to overload his heart. The second was a journey to Russia to meet an unsavory Minister of the Interior, Vyacheslva Plehve. Both actions were prompted by a bitter reminder of the Jewish plight.

Easter Week, 1903, had seen a vicious pogrom at Kishinev. If Plehve's police had not organized it, they certainly condoned it, passively watching while a rampaging mob destroyed Jewish property and lives. Herzl was to be assailed for calling, in a friendly spirit and with courtly compliments, on the anti-Semite responsible. But Herzl hoped that Russian embarrassment over the Kishinev pogrom—its harrowing details had been cabled round the world—could be exploited. The Russians might bring pressure on the Sultan to give the Jews a home. Herzl argued to Plehve, and to his critics, that the Russian anti-Semites and the Zionists had arrived at a similar conclusion from differing departure points. The Russians, eager to construct a common loyalty to the Christian Czar, found the Jews what the Zionists claimed them to be: an unassimilable element. Both parties would rejoice if the Jews left a territory where they were not wanted for a territory where they wanted to be. For by this time Herzl had seen that Russia with its unhappy millions, not Western Europe with its assimilated hundreds of thousands, was his reservoir of strength.

Intellectuals like his friend Max Nordau had come to Zionism through a particular analysis of the situation confronting Jews; their journey was theoretical, their conclusions were expressed in books, pamphlets or speeches composed in High German. Russian Jews had tramped to the same conclusions earlier and with lemming instinct. Groups such as the "Lovers of Zion" found in the hope of a Jewish return to Palestine—on foot, by ship, through force, by fraud, as gift, as right—an Aladdin's lamp which they secretly polished in the mud of exile.

But if the Jews of the Russian Empire (which included Poland) were the unexpected source of power for the Zionist movement, they were Herzl's equally unexpected foes when the "Uganda Congress" discussed the question of where the Promised Land should be. With destructive effects on Herzl's health and incalculable effects on the Middle Eastern future these Russian Zionists were to insist that a country occupied by Arabs, and not by Negroes, should be their goal.

Chapter 6

AFTER countless journeys by boat and train, Theodor Herzl was still a young man when his exhausted heart stopped beating on Sunday, July 3, 1904.

The following Thursday thousands of Jews escorted his remains to vault 28 in the Doblinger Cemetery. In obedience to his instructions he was interred without flowers or speeches, beside the metal coffin of his father; but his sojourn in Austrian earth was to be temporary only: "until the Jewish people shall transport my remains to Palestine."

Herzl dead became more effective than Herzl living. His critics now forgot, or forgave, what they had previously disliked: a byzantine deference to worldly rank, an obsequiousness to money and power. On one occasion Herzl had insisted that Sir Francis Montefiore, a titled nonentity, not a Russian activist, should be vice-president of the Zionist Congress. Herzl's defense—"Sir Francis opens to me kingly portals"—had seemed to at least one Zionist the pretext of a snob.[1]

The Zionist movement, recruiting its supporters from five million subjects of an anti-Semitic Czar, now canonized the man who, despairing of the powerful and well-born, had finally turned to them. Herzl had admitted what the Russian Zionists knew well, that his idea of restoring the Jewish state was not new. By stating an age-old dream in terms of the nineteenth century—the nation-state with uniforms and flag backed by a Jewish Colonial Fund—he had diverted torrential, wasted longings into a political turbine.

Yet to others beside his admirers Herzl bequeathed a legacy.

Hostile bystanders as well as enthusiasts had watched his funeral pass, had noted the hatted Jews with prayer curls, the spruce financiers, the men of letters. The force of this "King of Israel" encouraged a counterforce—the anti-Semitism to which Herzl had been sensitive as litmus. He had, as in judo, where a man uses his opponent's weight against him, envisaged using anti-Semitism as an explosive charge to get the Zionist engine moving. In his nightmares Herzl cannot have imagined the almost nuclear vigor this irrational odium was to show; in his most Teutonic reveries of self-examination he cannot have allowed himself to foresee how much pain as well as movement this odium might engender.

The year before Herzl died, a St. Petersburg newspaper, *Znamya,* published, over two weeks, the first known draft of what was to become, according to one authority,[2] a best seller second only to the Bible: *The Protocols of the Learned Elders of Zion.* Republished, emended, expanded, annotated, illustrated, translated into countless languages, *The Protocols* were a twentieth-century Donation of Constantine, that is, a pseudo-document with historical impact; they served, Norman Cohn has perceptively pointed out, as a warrant for mass murder.[3] *The Protocols* were not without literary ancestors. The central idea—"the belief that Jews, all Jews everywhere, form a conspiratorial body set on ruining and then dominating the rest of mankind"—had been advanced by three nineteenth-century writers, two of them Jews, one a German. The German, Hermann Goedsche, wrote under the respectable English pseudonym of "Sir John Redcliffe", a novel, *Biarritz,* which in 1868 foretold that by 1968 world Jewish rule would have been established. The two Jewish contributors to

[1] Chaim Weizmann, *Memoirs* (London: 1949), p. 45.

[2] H. Rollin, *L'Apocalypse de notre temps: les dessous de la propaganda allemande d'après des documents inédits* (Paris: 1939).

[3] Norman Cohn, *Warrant for Genocide, the myth of the Jewish world-conspiracy and the Protocols of the Elders of Zion* (London: Eyre & Spottiswoode, 1967).

the myth were, of course, renegades. "Osman-Bey," Ottoman pseudonym for a crook named Millinger, evoked in his *World-Conquest by the Jews*[4] a secret Jewish parliament convening somewhere in Poland to discuss the conquest of the planet for Judaism. Jacob Brafmann, a convert to Russian Orthodoxy and an employee of the czarist police, gave[5] an exaggerated and distorted picture of the Kahal, a Jewish community organization, which he portrayed as an instrument both for taking over gentile businesses and for world conquest.

Such works of fantasy foreshadowed many Protocular ideas. The literary form of the document derives, Norman Cohn discovered after careful detection, from a satire written in 1864 against Napoleon III; its author was Maurice Joly, a brilliant stylist and liberal who killed himself in 1879. To attack the French emperor in a way which might get past the censors, Joly imagined a dialogue in hell between Machiavelli and Montesquieu; Machiavelli's unscrupulous ideas were implied to be those of Napoleon. The author of *The Protocols* lifted many passages from Joly's satire, sometimes in his haste hardly bothering to make the changes needed for coherence. But where Joly's Machiavelli smirked over an existing tyranny, the imaginary Elder of Zion spoke in the future tense. Only the imagined duplicity was the same. Having corrupted the gentile world, having headed all its factions and divided it against itself, the Jews would take it over and rule it for their own designs.

A probable patron of the fantasy was Pyotr Ivanovich Rachkovsky, an employee of the Okhrana, or czarist security police. Rachkovsky was in charge of the Okhrana's overseas activities for the eighteen years from 1884 to 1902. Hiding a genius for intrigue and skulduggery behind a somewhat Pickwickian mask, Rachkovsky planned operations which would divide the enemies of czarist Russia against themselves. He would, for example, have a socialist printing press blown up and at the same time implicate some rival socialist faction in the explosion. An expert in forgery, he organized bitter wrangles in the press (their effect being to discredit Russian exiles) by writing every letter in the correspondence himself. It is known that Rachkovsky hated the Jews and saw in them the prime enemies of the Czar. It is also known that he was allied in a court intrigue with the monk who would, in 1917, edit the most widely circulated version of *The Protocols*, Sergei Nilus.

But the author of *The Protocols* is still undetected. He may have been a Russian who lived in France; he may even, like Osman-Bey and Brafmann, have been a Jew revenging himself on his people or indulging in a dangerous daydream of the oppressed.

But the unknown author, however deranged and however deadly, was no automaton. Like other authors he fed on material at hand. The work

[4] Osman-Bey, *Die Eroberung der Welt durch die Juden* (Wiesbaden: 1875).
[5] *The Book of the Kahal;* Cohn, op. cit., pp. 53–55.

which stoked the flames of anti-Semitic hatred, the work which seemed to Adolf Hitler a revelation and whose genuineness he never seems to have doubted, purports, in most of its editions, to have links with the historical career of Theodor Herzl. "These Protocols," Nilus wrote in his preface to the edition which was to be taken seriously not only by Hitler but also by the editor of the London *Times* and Henry Ford, "are nothing else than a strategic plan for the conquest of the world, putting it under the yoke of Israel, the struggle against God, a plan worked out by the leaders of the Jewish people during the many centuries of dispersion, and finally presented to the Council of Elders, by 'the Prince of the Exile,' Theodor Herzl, at the time of the first Zionist Congress, summoned by him in August 1897."

The suggestion that the delegates to the three-day congress at Basel spent their time listening to these long, turgid chapters is, of course, grotesque. The author pictures the congress as the cemetery gathering of vampires, not the press-attended, German-speaking, telegram-opening rally it was, held in the unromantic premises of the Basel Stadt Casino, a concert and dance hall. The delegates from Russia, Germany, Austria-Hungary, Rumania, Bulgaria, Holland, Belgium, France, Switzerland, Sweden, England, the United States, Algeria and Palestine were far too tired after the day's speeches by Herzl and Nordau, the resolutions, the messages of loyalty to the Sultan, the plans for a colonial bank and a World Zionist Organization, to listen to some learned elder speaking French, a language unintelligible to most of the delegates.

Yet Herzl—whose handsome profile had reminded Israel Zangwill of Tiglath Pileser—had provided the enemies of the Jews with a baleful shadow.

For this Herzl was in part to blame. By his promises, his contradictions, his deference to the Sultan in public, while privately planning to divide his empire, his deliberate evocation of Jewish power, of a Jewish press and a Jewish influence at the disposal of those who helped, at the throats of those who opposed, his readiness to believe in chimeras as well as his skill in building on realities, his indifference to sincerity in his first suggestion for the mass baptism of Austrian Jews, his private unconcern for the indigenous people involved in his colonizing plans, his published[6] protestations about living with them happily—his whole meteoric myth made the Jews of the world seem a monolithic and formidable power, while in fact they were as vulnerable and schismatic as only an often brilliant, sometimes cantankerous and always articulate religious group could be. This myth was useful for Herzl; for millions of Jews it was to prove catastrophic.

Herzl thus left a unifying dream to many Jews and a unifying night-

---

[6] Herzl's novel *Altneuland* pictured a Palestine where Arabs lived gratefully alongside Jewish settlers.

mare to their enemies. The nightmare as much as the dream provided the tragic petrol to propel his engine—in other words, to move Jews from their countries of origin to the Levant; but the nightmare was to incinerate millions who would not or could not move. Herzl's dream would become fact in the upheavals of two world wars and in so doing it would inherit the pains of fact, as well as the triumphs. It would sear Jews and Arabs, colonizers and colonized, in unending strife.

For the Middle East the publication of *Der Judenstaat* was no less a date to remember than Ismail's opening of the Suez Canal.

BOOK FIVE

The Altar

The sword also means treachery and change.

Chapter 1

B Y April 1909 Abdul Hamid had ruled the Ottomans for almost thirty-three years. Only the elderly remembered a time when the hook-nosed little Padishah in the large fez had not driven to Friday prayers, coachman of an empire that like some lurching wooden omnibus still rumbled on its way, patched and hooped together by strips of iron.

Yet in the next ten years, under the guidance of erratic new coachmen, the vehicle was to career down an ever stonier, ever more potholed road, losing as it lurched now a carriage light and now a door, its springs breaking, its wheels flying off, till, grinding to a halt, it fell apart, only its glum passengers losing neither courage nor nerve. Its final ruin coincided with Armageddon.

The "Great War" of 1914–18 seemed to some a struggle for democracy; to others, a war to end war; cranks believed it the coefficient of a turn in the Great Pyramid's prophetic tunnel. Though unexpected, it had been symbolically prefigured by the sinking, on April 16, 1912, of the world's largest ship, the newly launched *Titanic*. For if the Ottoman Empire was an outworn, horse-drawn coach, the Europe of the Powers was a self-confident liner: one moment domineering and proud, the next moment ripped apart by a hidden iceberg. On the unsinkable *Titanic* the crunch of collision had been greeted as a joke; smiling first-class passengers threw snowballs while the ice mountain slid gently past. So the outbreak of war had been cheered by European crowds. Poets saluted a new experience as cleansing as a summer bathe. The mood altered as the war continued and the American poet Ezra Pound gave his final wry summation:

> *There died a myriad,*
> *And of the best, among them,*
> *For an old bitch gone in the teeth,*
> *For a botched civilization . . .*

Few people, fifty years later, can detail the constitutional respects in which Kaiser Wilhelm's Germany was less democratic than the Britain of George V; further wars have made the slogans of 1914 absurd. Yet the protracted conflict which brought down in spasms four European dynasties left, in Europe, two nominal victors: France, though weakened by the loss of two million men, regained Alsace and Lorraine and gained new territories overseas; Britain, too, ended the war ampler in territorial flesh than she began—though time would show how dropsical these compensations for a lost generation were.

But, however weakened, Britain and France were in a position to dissect the Ottoman corpse. Having lost most of its Christian outer limbs, the empire wielding the Turkish sword and the Arabic Koran had become divided against itself. The Turks were weary of ruling, and dying for, discontented minorities; they began to act with collective egoism. The Arabs despaired of finding protection or reasonable comfort in the rickety House of Peace; they followed their indignation, or foreign lures, towards separatism and revolt. Thus divided the last great Muslim empire was to fall under foreign influence or direct control. Whether the empire perished from suicide or assassination was as debatable as in the case of Sultan Abdul Aziz.

The decade of Ottoman collapse began with the euphoria of a celebration. The cause was a revolution against a Sultan who had ruled too long.

Though still wrapped in awe for millions of Muslims, Turk and Arab alike, the old man with the badly dyed beard seemed to his educated subjects a tyrant who used 30,000 spies and misused Islam to bolster his reactionary power. Minor officials proved the chief opponents of Abdul Hamid; they ran the telegraph, postal or railway services with which the Sultan had sought to bind his empire; many had graduated from the military schools, which gave the best secular education of the day. The revolutionaries had imbibed Western values from foreigners living in their midst, from American or French teachers in such cities as Constantinople and Beirut, or from visits abroad. Europeans knew these restless young men as "Young Turks," in the phrase coined in France by an Egyptian prince. "*Jeune turc*" was a phrase familiar in Constantinople, though its pronunciation was so close to "John Turk" that it had become a term of disdain, standing for a Muslim who had renounced his birthright for a mess of foreign ways. The angry young men who met over hookahs to discuss why England and America were so much ahead of the East, who would be trapped by the secret police and would continue the discussion in jail and after it, felt themselves Ottoman patriots. Like Midhat a generation earlier, they were ashamed of the backwardness which blighted their empire; they burned to unite its heterogeneous elements and make of a reorganized Middle East a force for progress. Their outlook was put vividly by Ziya Gökalp, a writer who had graduated from a military school: "The Ottoman lands will be the free and progressive America of the East." Just as New Englanders or Texans thought of themselves as Americans, so Turks and Arabs, Greeks and Armenians, should think of themselves as Ottomans.

Groups preaching such noble ideals proliferated throughout the empire. The group which contrived the revolution of 1908 and which, as a result, controlled Ottoman misfortunes for a decade, were "The Committee for Union and Progress," formed in Salonika, the most westerly and Westernized Ottoman city.

The Ottoman predicament was nowhere clearer than in this busy port. As in the time of St. Paul, Salonika had a large colony of Jews; they had settled there after Spain had expelled them along with the Moors. These Jews still spoke Castilian and were called Sephardim (the Hebrew for Spanish) to distinguish them from the Yiddish-speaking Ashkenazim of Eastern Europe. The Sephardi Jews had benefited from the tolerance of the great sixteenth-century sultans and felt themselves concerned for the welfare of the empire in its decline. Salonika with a Jewish and Muslim majority was the gateway to a mountainous region where Albanians, Serbs and Macedonians fought an expanding guerrilla war against Ottoman control. Salonika was thus a place where Ottomans, whether Turk or Jew, felt themselves menaced. It was a place where reform was urgent.

In 1908 the committee, suspecting that the Sultan was about to crush them, started a revolt which, thanks to Abdul Hamid's telegraph service, had swift reverberations throughout the empire. Branches of the committee were established in all large cities. The demand for change was so clamant that Abdul Hamid immediately granted the committee's prime demand: the restoration of Midhat's constitution. The Sultan convinced himself, if no one else, that he had planned to restore the constitution all the time. He personally welcomed the committee's members to the parliament building, though his suggestion that he should add "President of the Committee for Union and Progress" to his many titles was allowed to drop.

From one end of the empire to another public joy linked Muslim *hoja* to Christian priest, Armenian to Kurd. Turks and Arabs felt as one. An "Ottoman Arab Fraternity" echoed the committee's views in the Arab lands. Two events in one month signified this brotherly spirit. The Hejaz railway linking Damascus to Medina was formally inaugurated and an ambitious, intelligent sherif (a descendant of the Prophet through his grandson Hassan) was appointed Amir of Mecca. These events were hopeful. The railway was useful and generally popular; it enabled Ottoman soldiers and civilians to reach western Arabia without passing through the British-controlled Canal; it made pilgrimage safer and less expensive. The appointment of the new Amir was an act of restitution. For fifteen years Sherif Hussein had been a prisoner-guest of Abdul Hamid. He had lived quietly and piously in Constantinople, supervising the education of his three eldest sons, Ali, Abdullah and Feisal. Abdullah was elected to represent Mecca in the new Ottoman parliament; he was further elected as the parliament's vice-chairman. Feisal was elected to represent Jeddah.

Euphoria swiftly turned to tears. The revolution had taken place on July 24, 1908. Within three months official Europe showed how little it welcomed Ottoman regeneration. On October 5 Bulgaria, till then a nominal dependency, declared its total independence. Two days later Austria-Hungary formally annexed Bosnia and Herzegovina. Five days later Crete, for whose loyalty the Ottomans had doggedly fought, voted for *Enosis,* or union, with Greece.

Such setbacks, coming so soon after the revolution, damaged the committee's prestige. Traditionalists were encouraged, in April 1909, to launch a counterrevolution. This succeeded in Constantinople, whose garrison and people remained faithful to Abdul Hamid. The counterrevolution was only suppressed by the army of Salonika, which, under its Arab commander, moved on the capital and deposed Abdul Hamid in favor of an unimpressive half brother who reigned as Mehemet V.

The physical Sultan was now an old man abjectly concerned to arrange as comfortable an exile as he could; he and his harem were put on the train to Salonika, the revolution's stronghold.

The spiritual Sultan had remained to the end a symbol of persistent power among the empire's Muslims. As Turkey's new democratic coachmen ran into typhoons at home and abroad they were thrown off balance. Their course was increasingly intolerant or neurotic. Since Arab Muslims outnumbered Turks in a ratio of roughly three to two, the Young Turks ordered the immediate disbanding of societies such as the Ottoman Arab Fraternity founded by non-Turk groups. Islam seemed less a bond than a source of dissidence.

Accelerating events increased the committee's collective frenzy. In 1911 the Italians invaded Libya, the last Ottoman possession in North Africa; in 1912 the Balkan states stopped squabbling among themselves and moved in for what they hoped would be the kill. These onslaughts were backed by continuing European coldness towards the committee's modernizing dreams. Many Young Turks had been educated to believe that the secret of Western progress was liberal capitalism with its offspring, free enterprise. They had hoped that Europe would help the new regime in Constantinople; if direct aid was too much to ask for, they hoped for an easing of the terms under which Ottoman finances were milked to repay the piled-up loans of the past. Such hopes were disappointed. Neither assistance nor easement was forthcoming; and on the political level the British refused to allow the Turks to use Egypt as a base for helping Libya.

In 1913 a defeated and bruised committee transformed itself into a dictatorship. The brilliant but ill-judging Enver Pasha headed a triumvirate whose other two members were the ruthless Jemal and the industrious Talaat. Union was the new watchword; and union based on the primacy of the Turkish race.

Turkism, no less than *Deutschtum,* had developed on the periphery. Just as *Deutschtum* flourished in Vienna, where German clashed with Slav, Turkism derived from Central Asia, where Turkish-speaking peoples clashed with an expanding Russia, and from Salonika on the Greek Aegean;

just as Houston Stewart Chamberlain, an English convert, wrote the text-book of German racialism,[1] so the first apostles of Turkism were non-Turks. Three important advocates of Turkism were, ironically, Jews. Arthur Lumley Davids was the first.[2] His *Grammar of the Turkish Language* contained an introduction in which the young scholar argued that the Turks—not Tartars, as they were incorrectly known—formed part of the Caucasian race. The second was Arminius Vambéry, a friend not only of Theodor Herzl but of a wide range of Ottoman exiles. An indefatigable traveler in the Turkish-speaking regions of Central Asia, Vambéry wrote accounts which aroused keen interest in Constantinople and Salonika. Leon Cahun, the third, was a novelist with a bizarre admiration for Jenghiz Khan. Cahun advanced the theory that a proto-Turanian (or Finno-Japanese) race had antedated such relative newcomers as Celts, Greeks and Latins. Cahun, like Vambéry, was a passionate liberal.

Ideas stressing race and language were strange to the Turks of the Ottoman Empire. They traditionally saw themselves simply as Muslims; their language was a mixture of Turkish, Arabic and Persian rather in the way that modern English is a mixture of Anglo-Saxon, Latin and French. But these racial ideas seeped into the collective mind to form a water table on which other more Turkish thinkers would draw. *More* Turkish: Ahmed Vefik Pasha was the grandson of a Greek convert to Islam while Mustafa Jelaleddin Pasha was a Polish convert. The first started a vogue for writing in plain, current Turkish, instead of flowery Ottoman; to mark the distinction he published a Turkish-Ottoman dictionary. The second, revising the theory of Cahun, argued that the Turks were the basic race from which all Europeans derived. He described this race as "Turo-Aryan." To him a policy of Westernization would represent a natural return to their own by a people who had become entangled, to their disadvantage, in the Semitic culture of the Middle East.

These doctrines—which gave an easy excuse for Turkish failings—spread with ominous speed. Ziya Gökalp no longer envisaged an America of the Middle East. He now saw the Turks as a separate and separable people, stifled by an alien culture which the upper-class effendi kept as his preserve. A gap between an upper and lower class was not of course peculiar to Turkey; Disraeli had written of "two nations," in England. But Turkish disparities were more radical, since the culture of the elite was far more alien. The Turks had borrowed "the institutions of foreign peoples and produced an artificial civilization out of them, instead of creating their own by developing their own institutions." Gökalp was referring to two foreign peoples: the Arabs and Persians. In becoming Muslims, the Turks had tied themselves to the elaborate apparatus of Islam; they had been deeply impressed on their journey west through Persia by the powerful cul-

[1] *The Foundations of the Nineteenth Century.*
[2] 1811–32.

ture of the Iranian plateau. From both Arabs and Persians they had taken much of their grammar and vocabulary. Gökalp argued for a rejection of alien accretions and a return to pure Turkish sources.

"We must look for the sources of our literature on the stone engravings or deer skins, on the one hand, and in the folk poems, folk tales, and epics, on the other. Our national language must be based on Turkish grammar. Our national literature must take its themes, its symbols, from Turkish social life, from Turkish social organization, and from Turkish mythology and epics. We must discard foreign rules from our grammar, foreign metre from our poetry, foreign symbolism from our literature."

Gökalp was a humanist. He asserted Turkism because he felt that an important group, his own, were culturally deprived. So far from having a contempt for Islam, he advocated the close study of Islamic institutions and their history, so that Turkish civilization as it developed could incorporate what was beneficial.

But less subtle minds pushed to more brutal conclusions. Instead of foreign grammar and foreign meters, they wanted to suppress foreign peoples, seen as inferior or destructive. The Turkism espoused by the Young Turk dictatorship showed a regression common to many forms of nationalism. Starting out as a generous effort to serve and preserve what is good in a particular group, it ends up by affirming that group's superiority. The attitude of many Ottoman officials began to change. Instead of treating Arabs and Kurds as brother Muslims, some behaved like a *Herrenvolk* mastering inferiors. Of course, many Turks remained good Muslims while most Arabs still looked on the Turks as fellow members of an Islamic empire. But enough friction was engendered for the Ottoman Empire to face its final struggle with vertical rifts in its national unity—rifts that had been studied by those who would destroy it.

Chapter 2

By the summer of 1914 most Ottoman citizens inhabited a gloomy flatland between two extremes: while the dictator Enver dreamed of recreating a vast Turkish empire straddling Anatolia and Central Asia, some Arabs, for reasons of idealism or self-interest, plotted to break away. Turkish extremists could use the resources of the Ottoman state, which meant the police and Army; Arab separatists formed secret societies, civilian and military, in Beirut and Damascus.

The men and women in the middle—and the general stress assisted women to emerge from the harem—felt humiliated by the loss of all but a toehold in Europe, by the Italian conquest of the Libyan coast. Their feelings were patriotic. They acted, or reacted, as though recovery were possible, as though, by reading recent lessons rightly, they might still reverse decay.

The war in North Africa had taught one vital lesson. Thanks to their small but efficient navy, the Italians had captured, and kept supplied, the coastal towns of Tobruk, Derna and Benghazi. In the interior, helped by reinforcements from Turkey, the Senussi Arabs had maintained, were indeed still maintaining, a stout resistance. If Turkey had only had a navy with some punch, the Italians could have been cut off from their bases in Italy and the province saved.

The need for modern warships became a national obsession. Mustachioed men dug into their baggy trousers, veiled women took off their gold pectorals and rings, and the piled-up money went to pay for two modern cruisers. They were ordered from England. Despite the presence in Turkey of a military mission under Marshal Liman von Sanders, a fifty-nine-year-old Prussian, it was Ottoman policy to prevent any one foreign influence from becoming dominant. Britain at this time had the world's largest fleet and the longest experience in building warships. There were still memories of British support at the time of the Crimean War, and after.

By the summer of 1914 the two ships were paid for and ready to leave Britain.

But by the same summer the indigestible provinces of Bosnia and Herzegovina had produced a methane of discontent. The spark flared on June 28, when the Habsburg heir and his wife were assassinated at Sarajevo. One month later Austria-Hungary declared war on Serbia, alleged nurse of the assassin. Russia, protector of the Serbs, mobilized against Austria-Hungary. The Austrians' allies, the Germans, declared war on Russia, then on August 4 invaded Belgium, their aim to strike at France, committed ally of the Russians. At midnight on the same day Britain declared war on Germany. The following day, in Cairo, the British compelled Egypt, despite its status as part of the still neutral Ottoman Empire, and despite the neutralist feelings of its people, to declare itself at war with Britain's enemies.

Britain entered the war as anxious about her Navy as the Ottoman Empire about hers. Public opinion had become increasingly alarmed by the growth of the Kaiser's fleet. Britain's new armored dreadnoughts had not made her as impregnable as she had hoped, since German shipyards had been building similar ships with disturbing efficiency and speed. For the first time in many centuries Britain had reason to doubt her island security.

Against this background the Admiralty, whose First Lord was Winston Churchill, decided to commandeer the two Turkish warships.

However justified in strategic terms, the British decision was a political blunder. The news angered even those traditionalist Turks who had been pro-British; it gave new arguments to the Young Turk radicals who had been urging an alliance with the one European Power which had never stolen an Ottoman province. These pleas were soon given visual reinforcement. The German battle cruiser *Goeben* and light cruiser *Breslau* made a concerted dash from the territorial waters of Italy (which had not yet decided which side to support) and evading a British Navy slow off the mark reached the Turkish narrows between Europe and Asia. All Constantinople could see and applaud the spick, lethal ships lying at anchor off the Golden Horn. The Kaiser's next move was even more dramatic: he placed the cruisers and their crews (who changed caps for fezes) at this disposal of his friend the Sultan. Pro-German sympathies were as hot as summer among ordinary Turks.

Two extraordinary Turks reacted differently: one of whom we mention for the last time, the other for the first.

The deposed Abdul Hamid had been shunted back to Turkey proper after the Greeks took Salonika in the Balkan Wars. He now inhabited a palace on the Asiatic shore of the Bosphorus, but never looked back across the water to the capital he had lost. Although he had regarded the Kaiser as a friend, the old man had always hated bloodshed and now argued in private against Turkish involvement in the war. Mustafa Kemal, a Salonika-born officer and Libyan comrade-in-arms of Enver, hated everything which Abdul Hamid represented. But in a memorandum to his friends in the government he, too, argued against Turkish participation in the Kaiser's struggle.

But Turkey was at the mercy of Enver Pasha's flair. It was the flair of a vain egocentric who had been military attaché in Berlin for most of the time between 1908, when he made the revolution, and 1913, when he made himself the chief triumvir. Energetic, fast-moving, brave, Enver had left Berlin twice, first to help suppress the counterrevolution of 1909 and then to take part in the struggle over Libya. Female admirers in Berlin had force-fed his vanity. He hated the Russians and was convinced that the Kaiser and his allies would win the war quickly. If Turkey wished to get back lost provinces, to win new glory at Russian expense in Central Asia, she must join this alliance.

The Turks made no formal declaration of war. The *Goeben* (commanded by a German admiral) did this for them. Accompanied by three Turkish destroyers, she slipped past the coasts of Bulgaria and Rumania to bombard, on October 29, a number of Russian ports. A week later, first Russia, then Britain and France, declared war on the Ottoman Empire.

For the Kaiser of Europe's newest empire, brotherhood in arms with

Europe's oldest empire was his greatest triumph: his greatest triumph in a war he had not intended. For the Allies it was an expensive complication. From the first month of the war British and French strategists recognized that czarist Russia was the major strength and the major weakness of the Allied cause. Her reserves of manpower were vast; she produced the food which would be vital in a protracted struggle; her cruel climate and wide spaces had overwhelmed Napoleon, the last man to try for hegemony in Europe. But there were things to offset these advantages. The Russian autocracy was hardly a good advertisement for Allied war aims; the country's political stability was as much in doubt as the ability of its factories to equip the Czar's armies.

Turkey's entry into the war sharpened Russia's problems. The Bosphorus and the Dardanelles were her warm jugular; their closure stopped Russian grain ships from coming out and Western armaments from going in. A new front was opened on Russia's southern borders.

At the same time a final crunch with Turkey offered the British compensations. Some tiresome ambiguities could be tidied up. Cyprus could be annexed as a pure and simple colony; more important, Ottoman sovereignty over Egypt could at last be abolished. At least for the war, Egypt became a straightforward British protectorate.

The title "Khedive" passed into history. In August 1914 its last holder, Abbas II, had been on his usual summer vacation in Constantinople. When Turkey entered the war he was deposed on the pretext that he had sided with the King of England's enemies. The poor man had hardly been in a state to return to Egypt. In late July he had been paying a visit to the Turkish Prime Minister when an attempt was made on his life. The would-be assassin (an Egyptian youth) was promptly hacked in pieces by the Khedive's Turkish guard, but the Khedive was confined to bed with facial wounds.

Hussein Kamil, the second of Ismail's sons to reign, but not the last, now reluctantly sat on the Egyptian throne. This respectable and agriculturally minded uncle of the deposed Khedive was a man without ambition. As if to mock the Ottoman ruler, he, too, was given the title of "Sultan." His powers were even less than those of Abdul Hamid's ailing half brother, Mehemet V. To sympathetic visitors he described himself as a "prisoner of war" in a palace. He was not to outlast the war.

In their first bellicose zest the Turks undertook two military initiatives, each inspired by Enver. An attack on Russia through the Caucasus ended in disaster and a Russian counterinvasion of eastern Anatolia. A spectacular raid across Sinai got some Turkish soldiers across the Suez Canal at El Kantara and Ismailia. The move had no sequel: the Turks retreated back to Palestine; and the British were on guard.

In 1915 it was the Allies' turn.

Menaced by Enver's designs on the Caucasus, hard-pressed in Poland, the Czar cabled London for a diversionary attack. The request went to Kitchener. The victor of Omdurman had filled Lord Cromer's post of British agent and consul-general in Egypt from 1911 to the summer of 1914. Then on his way back to Cairo he had been recalled from his Channel crossing to take over the War Office. Finding that there was virtually no British Army with which to fight the war, Kitchener started, in the midst of hostilities, on creating a force of seventy divisions; to its recruitment he lent the stern visage of a man who had been noted in the Sudan for his penny-pinching economy, his generosity in floggings and hangings. Kitchener's response to the Russian appeal was to suggest a purely naval demonstration against the Dardanelles; he could not spare any troops for the project. On Kitchener's bare fabric Winston Churchill now wove a gambler's vision of how with one blow the Turks might be knocked out of the war into which he, as much as anyone, had dragged them.

Against its background of sedentary trench-massacre in Flanders, Churchill's scheme still stands out for its dash and brilliance. In 1915 his eloquence convinced most, but not all, of his Cabinet colleagues. A naval expedition was in any case authorized—"with Constantinople as its objective"—whose preliminary purpose was the seizure of the Gallipoli Peninsula: a territory shaped on the maps like the dangling head of a strangled goose, but which on the ground was to prove a hilly, ravine-split, prickly terrain of ferocious drought. Churchill envisaged great modern guns silencing the Ottoman forts as neatly as Admiral Seymour's guns had silenced those of Alexandria; the appearance of an Anglo-French fleet off Constantinople would produce a defeatist revolution.

The Gallipoli campaign was thus closely linked, in its inspiration and in its failure, to Winston Churchill. Throughout his life Churchill was intermittently involved with the Middle East. As a young Lancer he had fought at the battle of Omdurman, where British machine gunners conquered the Khalifa's Sudan. The victory was not the most chivalrous in British annals. Journalists of repute reported the killing off of wounded Sudanese. The youthful Churchill, joining army chaplains in rebuttal, had produced the argument that the victor had no necessary obligation to give quarter to the vanquished. In his contacts with the Middle East Churchill was to show little sympathy with its indigenous peoples. In this he differed from his father, Lord Randolph, who had been one of Orabi's English defenders. This lack of sympathy, or a positive disdain, may have played some part in the history of the Dardanelles campaign. Churchill underestimated the capacity and will of an Eastern people to resist a Western onslaught. Instead of a balanced force of warships with heavy guns, supported by plentiful minesweepers and co-ordinated spotter planes, an Anglo-French armada of two modern and sixteen obsolescent battleships began operations on February 19. The armada reduced the forts at the wide entrance to the Dardanelles without much difficulty; but the thickly implanted forts at the narrows between Kilid el Bahr on the European side and Chanak on the Asiatic were a harder problem; here the Sultan's gunners, despite barrel-clogging clouds of dust, resisted till their ammunition was almost exhausted. Nature then helped the Turks. The too few minesweepers in the Allied fleet found it hard to advance against the swift flowing current. Drifting mines, released nightly by the Turks, reaped a heavy harvest on March 18: out of eighteen Allied warships six were sunk. Despite an anguished plea from Churchill for a renewed attempt on the narrows, the ships withdrew. During the next month the Allies prepared, in Egypt and on the Aegean island of Lemnos, an army of five divisions with which to conquer where naval power alone had failed. During the same month the forewarned Turks prepared to defend what had now been revealed as the Allied target.

If the Dardanelles current saved the Turks in the first phase of the campaign, in the second phase the landscape of Gallipoli played a lesser role than steadfast morale and brilliant leadership. The morale sprang from "Mehmetchik," or "Little Muhammad," the affectionate nickname for the Ottoman soldier. The leadership sprang from the officer who had advised Turkey not to enter the war. Mehmetchik and Mustafa Kemal between them turned the Gallipoli campaign into a bloody but major Turkish triumph.

Sir Ian Hamilton, product of an Army trained in colonial battles, was the Allied commander. On April 25 he directed, from the sea, a two-pronged landing: near Cape Helles, at the peninsula's southern tip, and at Gaba Tepe, some fifteen miles further up the Aegean coast.

Admittedly Sir Ian's force was inexperienced: the Australian and New Zealand troops who made the second landing knew nothing of the horrors of shrapnel. Admittedly the peninsula's rugged terrain assisted the defense. But for decade on decade Middle Eastern armies had thrown away just such advantages. Mustafa Kemal, at the outset merely commander of one division under the overall direction of Liman von Sanders, at the end commander of the entire Gallipoli front, was no Orabi Pasha. Kemal came to the battle instructed and ice-cold, not buoyed up with verbal gas. He had studied the terrain (a key point in any attack on Constantinople from the West) during the Balkan Wars. Now that it was a battlefield he repeatedly displayed a clairvoyant insight into what the enemy would do. When the sweating, thirsty Tommies reached a commanding summit, Mehmetchik would be waiting with Allah on his lips and his new German rifle in his hands.

At Gallipoli, while the Turks lost as many men as the Allies, the Allies lost the campaign. The sole victory of which the British could boast was a brilliant double retreat: first, from Suvla Bay; second and last, from Cape Helles. Without these skillful withdrawals—the British feigned attacks even as the last men crept into the withdrawing boats—the Allied reverse would have been a disaster.

For the Middle East, and in particular for the Turks, the campaign had two results which even time would not flatten. An army of Turks and Arabs had resisted, and driven back, a Western army. It could be compared on this level to the Japanese defeat of czarist Russia a decade earlier. On a more personal level, in a part of the world where personality counts for much, it marked the emergence of the man who would construct a Turkish national state in Turkish-speaking Anatolia.

But before this could happen Mustafa Kemal had to endure three years in which Ottoman armies fought the losing war of their allies. In a chronicle of defeats, some of them due to what was felt as Arab treachery, the victory of Gallipoli was a fixed star of reassurance.

Chapter 3

DRIFTING mines and Turkish valor having closed the Dardanelles, the Allies had only the Arctic route to western Russia. This seaway was dangerous and uncertain. On June 5, 1916, in cold, turbulent waters off northern Scotland the cruiser *Hampshire,* carrying as its precious freight Field Marshal Earl Kitchener, sank without trace.

No setback in the war caused such consternation in Britain. The doom of her greatest soldier, the man who personified imperial greatness, was the culmination of a process wherein the bright hues of battle had been remorselessly bedrabbed. Stalemate in the Flanders trenches, withdrawal from Gallipoli, a surrender in southern Iraq, casualty lists in London, revolution in Ireland, the sad but unheroic death of Rupert Brooke from a blood infection, grinding patterns, tiny details, all made the war a sunless horror.

On the day Kitchener drowned, more than two thousand miles to the southeast, a ragged Arabian army of around 1,500 men fired ancient rifles into the air at the desert tomb of a legendary hero. A Meccan princeling had just proclaimed that the Arabs were no longer subjects of the Ottoman Sultan. Five days later the Turkish garrison in Mecca were surprised to find themselves under rifle attack in the government buildings. The same day another Arab force attacked Jeddah on the Red Sea coast, while British warships and seaplanes joined in to help.

From sunlit Egypt a group of cheerful Englishmen—the Cairo Bureau —had sponsored a diversion of their own. It was to be more colorful and more successful than the ill-fated Dardanelles campaign. Thanks to an unclouded climate, a picturesque cast and the presence on the British side of a myth-maker of genius, the Arab Revolt was to revive British morale. Thanks to the careful planning of men like Ronald Storrs (Harry Boyle's successor as oriental secretary in Cairo) and Lieutenant-Colonel Clayton, director of Military Intelligence, the revolt also played a useful role in defeating Turkey.

The first architect of the Arab Revolt was the imperial bachelor who drowned the day it started.

In early 1914 Kitchener had been in residence at the British Agency in Cairo. One February afternoon the large gates opened on a visitor wearing the pure silk robes of a prince of Mecca. Abdullah, cleverest son of the Amir Hussein, was passing through Egypt on his way north to his parliamentary duties in Constantinople. While in Cairo he was staying as the guest of a man Kitchener heartily disliked: the Khedive Abbas. Abdullah was now repaying a courtesy call which Kitchener had paid him at the khedivial palace. According to Abdullah's own account, he had called in the afternoon at an hour when he hoped to find the British Field Marshal not at home. Cairo was full of Ottoman spies and he did not wish the Turkish Government to imagine that he was planning to conspire with the British: which was, in fact, the purpose of his visit.

Confidential tea was served for the sixty-four-year-old soldier, burly and plebeian in appearance, and Abdullah, as dapper and smooth a guest as he was likely to receive. Abdullah had profited from his father's long residence in Turkey. He spoke an elegant Stambouli Turkish as well as an Arabic stuffed with poetic echos as a Dundee cake with currants. He knew, too, how bluntness could sometimes confound an Englishman expecting, as he would, all Orientals to be devious and indirect. Abdullah's favorite game was chess.

Kitchener politely raised the question of the Hejaz, Abdullah's homeland, his father's fief. Its mood was known to be uneasy. The Young Turks, as part of their plan to modernize the empire, had decided to extend the railway as far south as Mecca; they planned branch lines from Medina to Yanbo and from Mecca to Jeddah. They had recently appointed a new governor charged with securing the Amir's co-operation. The Amir, Abdullah's father, disliked the governor and opposed the railway since it threatened tighter control over his city. In this he was backed by most of his people. The railway would make the pilgrimage easy and less expensive; they had profited from keeping it difficult and costly.

It was time for Abdullah to be blunt. He was. What, he asked point-blank, would be the British attitude to an Arab revolt?

Abdullah, for all his princely robes, was the second son of a dignitary with more pretensions than power. Horatio Herbert Kitchener, Earl and Field Marshal, was the most important ruler in the Middle East. He could not meet bluntness with bluntness. He contented himself with being correct: Britain's traditional friendship with Turkey made it impossible for her to interfere in Turkey's internal affairs; and trouble in the Hejaz would be internal.

Abdullah was good at scoring points. He rebutted this official answer by reminding Kitchener how the government of British India had established a virtual protectorate over Kuwait. Wasn't that interference in Ottoman affairs? A cautious smile beneath the Englishman's mustache and the interview was over. No guns had been promised.

Yet Kitchener knew the world of Islam. He had started out as a young officer surveying Palestine. Commanding the Egyptian Army under the title of Sirdar, he had conquered the Sudan. He had, more recently, served in India, where some of the best regiments were Muslim. He foresaw that in certain circumstances Arab dissidence might be helpful to Britain. He instructed his oriental secretary, Ronald Storrs, to offer Abdullah the use of a British yacht for his journey to Turkey. Unofficial contacts should be maintained with this outspoken emissary from Mecca.

Mecca had never been the site of the Caliphate. But it retained a unique prestige among Islamic cities. It was, for one thing, the birthplace of the Prophet. Good Muslims prostrated themselves towards it five times daily. Once in his lifetime every Muslim should visit Mecca as a pilgrim and take part in rites older than Islam. For even before the Angel Gabriel brought the Koran to Muhammad Mecca had been important. It had been the paramount city of pagan Arabia, famed for its possession of a holy meteorite surrounded by a pantheon, pivotal for its position at the junction of two caravan routes. Like most prophets, Muhammad had been dishonored in his own city; Islam dated its era from the year (A.D. 622) when he abandoned it for Medina. But Mecca had been won for Islam in the Prophet's lifetime. With his own hand he broke the idols that surrounded the holy place. A revelation then substituted the Kaaba (a cubelike structure embodying the meteorite) for Jerusalem as the focus of Islamic prayer. The Kaaba was now believed to have been built by Abraham, the common father of Jews and Arabs.

Mecca's prestige was religious, not political or cultural. Muhammad and his first three successors had based their expanding state on Medina, more than two hundred miles north. Ali, the fourth Caliph and the Prophet's son-in-law, built a new capital at Kufa in western Iraq. After his murder, Damascus, Baghdad, Cordoba, Cairo, each had been the capital of a Caliphate acknowledged by all Muslims, or some. The last Caliphate, the Ottoman, was based on Constantinople, a city on the edge of Europe. Mecca was a backwater that throbbed to life with the yearly pilgrimage, then subsided into heat. Its leading families could claim (with thousands of others) descent from Hassan, Ali's eldest son; Hassan had renounced his caliphal claims for five million dirhams and a life of much begetting. Some of Hassan's Meccan descendants became feudal leaders whose authority was strong when external control was weak, and vice versa. They were known as Hashemites, from Ali's branch of the tribe of Qoraysh.

Sultan Abdul Hamid had tried to reduce, not flatter, Hashemite importance. But the fifteen years which Hussein spent in Constantinople made a megalomaniac out of a provincial dignitary. The mind behind the flowery tongue was sharp, though one who knew him well compared his sentences to the species of cactus which adds one plate after another to the initial stem; this mind gauged the weakness of the Ottoman Empire as one by one the Balkan nations hived away; it gauged the power of the Britain which had taken over Egypt; it gauged both the prosperity of a British-protected Khedive, and the price in dignity which the Khedive had paid. In his spotless white robes and turban Hussein was a medieval intriguer surveying without stupidity a world ruled from Threadneedle Street and Parliament Square. Having surveyed, having gauged, he asked himself two questions: how could his position be maintained, and then, how could it be improved? Abdul Hamid had not treated him unkindly; his jailer had even shown him respect, giving him an honorary role akin to that of a British privy counsellor. But Abdul Hamid, with his liking for Arabs, was the past. The Young Turks espoused something close to Turkish racialism even before they came to power; from their side the Arabs reacted in a similar way.

Again the paradox: just as Turkish nationalism had been advocated by people from the fringe, so Arab nationalism, unknown in Arabia, was the doctrine of Arabic-speakers from Lebanon and Syria. A disproportionate number were Arab Christians. Lebanese had started the great newspapers and publishing houses of Egypt; other Lebanese had compiled Arabic dictionaries or encyclopedias. Many were admirers of what Lord Cromer had done for Egypt; they wanted to extend the autonomy secured for Lebanon since 1860, even if this meant an alliance with some Western nation against the Turks. The assertion that they were Arabs, not Ottomans, made it easier for them to break from an empire closely linked with Islam.

Vain and ambitious, Hussein hoped to use Arab dissidence and Arab pride to accomplish his dreams. Like Herzl's, they were elastic. They ranged from the modest project of an independent kingdom of the Hejaz, a Red Sea Bulgaria, to fantastic visions in which as an Arab Caliph he taxed all believers throughout the world.

Strong forces worked in favor of Arab nationalism. The idea of territorial patriotism was one ingredient in the Western elixir. Arabs felt proud that Islam had been revealed to an Arabian prophet in an Arabic book, that Arabian horsemen with scant knowledge of navigating seas or besieging cities had halved the Roman Empire in the East and conquered Persia.

Dynasties sprung from Arabian stock (though soon intermarrying with other peoples) had ruled from Damascus and Baghdad over splendid empires. A true Caliph, one tradition demanded, should derive from Muhammad's tribe, the Qoraysh; the commander of the faithful should be a hawk-nosed Arab, not a squat-nosed Turk. That the Arabs had grown degenerate, that one weak ruler after another had imported Turkish slaves as soldiers or lovers, gave a tang of inferiority complex to Arab pride.

Forces as strong worked against the idea of a separate Arab state. Islam was a stronger bond than nationality; an Arab Muslim would allow his daughter to marry a Turk, but not an Arab Christian. The family, the village, the tribe, the world community of Islam, these were precise and accepted ties: Arab nationality was not. Men spoke variants of Arabic from Morocco in the West to the edge of the Persian plateau in the East. But the speakers were Arabized more than Arab. Descendants of Berbers, Egyptians, Phoenicians or Babylonians had adopted the Arabic language with the Arabian religion. Unity was pulled against by centrifugal interests or traditions. To cite only a few: Lebanon's dominant Christian sect, the Maronites, were in communion with Rome and politically linked to France; the Druzes (adherents to a secret religion derived from Islam) relied on British support against the Maronites; the Copts, Egypt's Christians, were attached to Egypt as a separate entity, though they, too, spoke Arabic.

In a sense the dissatisfaction of Arabs with the Ottoman Empire was no different from the dissatisfaction of the Turks themselves; dissatisfaction could unite as well as divide. Both groups felt humbled by their collective backwardness, by their shared inability to withstand the West. Both yearned for a progress often expressed in Western terms. In Arab cities as in Turkish, Western, and in particular American, schools and colleges had molded a generation destined to lead; from Arab cities, as from Turkish, young men had traveled to the schools and universities of Europe. These newly educated young men admired Western achievement even when they fought Western control; they acknowledged the material progress achieved in Egypt under the dynasty of Muhammad Ali with its British and French advisers; they wanted their sons to study at Oxford or the Massachusetts Institute of Technology. They were disinclined to look to Mecca or its picturesque ruler.

For the Mecca of the early twentieth century had little secular to commend it. Its shabby, makeshift architecture crammed a dust bowl; its sixty thousand inhabitants were not renowned for virtuous living. The pilgrims who for a few days more than doubled the population took home religious memories which would hallow the rest of their lives and console their deathbeds. But the religious rites—the circumambulation of the Kaaba, black-garbed in its embroidered covering from Egypt, the stoning of Satan, the sheep sacrifice to commemorate the rescue of Abraham's son—were, like the princess in the fairy tale, hedged with thorns. The thorns were the people of the Hejaz. They robbed the caravans on their way to the holy city; they fleeced them for food and lodging once they had arrived. The Meccans drew water free from an Ottoman aqueduct but sold it for money to the pilgrims. Nor were the Hashemites pious exemplars. They surrounded themselves with handsome slaves; their family record was woven of treachery and violence. Few graduates of the American Protestant College in Beirut or the Sorbonne in Paris would willingly become their subjects. Hashemite princes in sherifian robes, gunfiring horsemen, attracted romantic Europeans, not unromantic Arabs.

But Kitchener and the Cairo Bureau soon had good reasons for espousing Arab dissidence. In November 1914 the religious authorities in Constantinople proclaimed a Jihad. This ancient call to Holy War went back to the days of the Prophet. The male Muslim was obliged to fight for Islam, and also instructed in how to fight, and within what limits. (He was not allowed to fire the first arrow; he must not cut down his enemies' trees; he must respect women and show chivalry to his foe.) The man who died fighting "in the way of God" was promised the instant bliss of the Christian martyr; he was interred in the clothes in which he fought.

The British, who ruled more Muslims than the Sultan, the French, who now ruled Morocco as well as Tunis and Algiers, had long dreaded what might happen if the Ottoman Sultan, who had revived the Caliphate, revived Jihad as well. No one was sure how much or how little the ancient call would affect a world of Maxim guns, motorcars and biplanes. They did not have long to wait. On Egypt's western border the Senussi leader was still confining the Italian invaders to the coast. He enthusiastically endorsed the Sultan's call and captured Sollum on the Egyptian frontier. In Sudanese Darfur there was a similar response.

But more sophisticated Muslims greeted the Jihad with caution. For it was involved with an ironic innovation. For the first time Islam was riding to war with Christian allies. Muslims under British, French or Russian rule were instructed to support, not only the Sultan-Caliph, but his Germanic supporters.

At the same time those who refused Jihad would be aligning themselves with other Christians: the French and British. Britain and France had a worse record of subjecting Muslims to their rule than Germany.

The moral problem posed by the Jihad troubled the sons of Amir Hussein. Hussein himself found it hard to take a moral view, being on at least three payrolls. (In addition to Ottoman douceurs and a British retainer, he was, until the middle of 1915, receiving financial help from Germany.) Ali, the oldest, was too weak, too ill with tuberculosis, to do more than follow the family decision. The youngest, Zeid, was young, and as the son of Hussein's second, Turkish wife, had no great enthusiasm for a revival of Arab greatness. But two of the Amir's sons had independent outlooks. Abdullah, with the clear sight and shallow principles of a fledgling

Machiavelli, argued that the Arabs should seize the moment of Ottoman difficulty to strike the Turks in the back. Feisal, the third son, lacked both Abdullah's brilliance and lack of scruple. As a member of the Ottoman parliament, owing what he knew of the world to Constantinople, he was orally versed in the events of recent decades. Britain and France had already occupied large tracts of Islam; it was very likely that they wanted still more. Feisal argued that the Arabs should swallow their grievances and loyally fight alongside their Turkish fellow Muslims. If they won the war, the grateful Turks would grant reasonable Arab demands, might perhaps transform the empire into a dual monarchy of Turks and Arabs; if they lost, the two Muslim peoples could struggle together against adversity.

An Irish mirror can help to make clear this Arab dilemma.

The Irish, like the Arabs, at this time formed an unwilling part of an imperial system. The Irish, again like the Arabs, were divided as to what to do now that their masters were engaged in a life-and-death struggle. There were, of course, differences. The Irish were not linked to the English by religion as the Arabs were linked to the Turks; to balance this, they were culturally close to an England whose literature they had signally enriched. Many Irishmen argued like Feisal. If in her hour of need they fought loyally for England, they could, when victory was won, present their demands to a grateful ally. Others, like Abdullah, argued that England's difficulty was Ireland's chance. Just as Abdullah had sounded the Cairo British, so Irish patriots had sounded the authorities in Berlin. With similar results. In Ireland, as in the Hejaz, plans for revolt simmered through 1915 and boiled over in 1916. The Irish stormed the Dublin Post Office in Easter Week while Sir Roger Casement landed from a U-boat. The Arabs besieged Mecca and took Jeddah with British help. In both cases brutal reactions by the imperial power drove previous moderates into the separatist camp.

For Feisal and other waverers (including many Arabs in the Ottoman officer corps) conversion to rebellion came in 1915. The Ottoman governor of Syria, Jemal Pasha, had uncovered dissident cells in Lebanon and Syria. Rapid trials were followed by immediate and public executions. The sight of brother Arabs dangling from gallows made the Turkish executioners seem brothers in Islam no longer. What had been an intellectual toy became a cause for which some Arabs would fight and die.

But even when passion fired one side and need the other, much haggling took place between the Arabs, whom Strabo two thousand years earlier had described as a nation of merchants, and the British, more recently characterized as a nation of shopkeepers.

The haggling concerned the area in which the British would recognize Arab independence after the war, and what limits, if any, should be attached to it.

Hussein decided to consult the educated Arabs to the north: members of two secret societies, one civilian, one military, dedicated alike to Arab separation. His emissary to Damascus was his third son, Feisal. The Syrians—the term included those who lived in what would later be Syria, Lebanon, Palestine and Transjordan—insisted that Arab independence must be conceded in the whole area wherein speakers of Arabic comprised the majority. In a protocol they delimited this Arab area. Its northern boundary would roughly follow the southern slopes of the Taurus and the Anatolian plateau from Mersin in the West through Urfa, Mardin and Amadia to the Persian frontier. Its eastern boundary, corresponding with the existing state frontier between the Ottoman Empire and Persia, would follow the edge of the Persian plateau down to the Gulf. Its southern boundary was the Indian Ocean, though at this juncture no one sought to challenge the British occupation of Aden. Its western limit would be the Red Sea and the Mediterranean. No one claimed Egypt for the new Arab state, nor the countries of North Africa under French, Spanish and Italian rule. Nor was much said about the areas of Arabia itself already enjoying some form of independent rule: Yemen had its own Imam and the central plateau was disputed by two rival sheikhs, Ibn Rashid, who had sided with the Turks, and his enemy, Ibn Saud, who was guardedly leagued with British India.

The Arab nationalists conceded two limitations to their independence: a defensive alliance should link the new Arab state to Britain; Britain would be granted economic preference within it.

Britain's representative in Cairo was no longer a strong man swathed in the belittling veil of "consul-general"; a weak man, Sir Henry McMahon, was High Commissioner in charge of a protectorate. He represented a British generation to whom the notion of the black, brown or yellow being able to rule themselves was still preposterous. Cromer had considered the white-skinned Turco-Circassians (whom he heartily disliked) as being the only people capable of ruling the Egyptians. McMahon felt reluctant to concede the far-reaching and revolutionary aims of the Arab nationalists; only Britain's acute predicament made possible what came to be known as the "McMahon Correspondence" between Cairo and Mecca. It was a correspondence whose publication the British were to suppress for decades. In his embarrassment McMahon took refuge in dressing up—not in fancy dress, as Harry Boyle had done and as a member of his staff, T. E. Lawrence, was preparing to do—but in fancy words. As an example of these, George Antonius, who wrote the Hashemite version of the revolt,[1] quotes the opening of the High Commissioner's first letter to Hussein. A very English Arabic was served up in a sauce of "Turco-Persian toadyisms, which someone on McMahon's staff had thought appropriate":

> *To the excellent and well-born Sayyed, the descendant of*
> *Sherifs, the Crown of the Proud, Scion of Muhammad's Tree*

[1] George Antonius, *The Arab Awakening* (London: Hamish Hamilton, 1938), p. 167.

*and Branch of the Qorayshite Trunk, him of the Exalted Presence
and of the Lofty Rank, Sayyed son of Sayyed, Sherif son of
Sherif, the Venerable, Honoured Sayyed, his Excellency the
Sherif Hussein, Lord of the Many, Amir of Mecca the Blessed,
the lodestar of the Faithful and the cynosure of all devout Believers, may his Blessing descend upon the people in their
multitudes!*

Hussein was enough of a carpet dealer to see the evasions behind the
verbiage. McMahon had concentrated on the Caliphal dream to avoid the
frontier realities. Hussein rebuked him. "For our aim, O respected Minister, is to ensure that the conditions which are essential to our future can
be secured on a foundation of reality, and not on highly-decorated phrases
and titles."

On October 24, 1915, McMahon sent the note which was to define
for the Arabs the terms under which, at an opportune moment, they should
start their revolt.

The High Commissioner first explained that his apparent reluctance to
discuss the question of frontiers (in a previous letter he had referred to
these as "details") had only been due to a feeling that such discussion was
not yet timely; but since Hussein regarded the issue as fundamental, he
had the authority of the British Government to give the Arabs certain
assurances.

Britain, the note continued, pledged herself both to recognize and defend Arab independence within the areas proposed by the Sherif, subject
to certain reservations. The most important of these related to territories
in Asia Minor and Syria, but others covered places, such as Kuwait, with
which the British Government was already in treaty relationship; there
were additional provisos about the defense of the Holy Places, the recruitment of British advisers and a special form of administration for the provinces of Baghdad and Basra.

The reservations about Asia Minor and Syria were defined in the following all-important sentence:

"The districts of Mersin and Alexandretta, and portions of Syria lying to
the west of the districts of Damascus, Homs, Hama and Aleppo, cannot
be said to be purely Arab and must on that account be excepted from the
proposed delimitation."

In excluding Mersin and Alexandretta (the modern Iskanderun), Sir
Henry was not thinking of Turkey, the country to which both districts
would eventually revert. He was thinking of Britain's ally, France, who
already had designs upon them. By the vaguely defined "portions of Syria
lying to the west of the districts of Damascus, Homs, Hama and Aleppo"
he was taken to refer to the area where France not only had future designs

but past connections dating from the reign of Louis XIV: the Lebanese mountains whose Christian Maronite majority, while speaking Arabic, were not of Arab origin and felt themselves linked by religion to Rome and by history to France. In their "sanjak of Lebanon" the Maronites had enjoyed, thanks to the intervention of Napoleon III, sixty years of autonomy under Christian pashas. (This autonomy had been suppressed on the outbreak of war.) No mention was made of Palestine, in which the Arabs constituted nine tenths of the population. If the High Commissioner had wished to exclude it from the area of Arab independence, he would have referred to it by its traditional name, or by its Ottoman status: the northern half formed part of the vilayet of Beirut, its southern was the sanjak of Jerusalem.

An agreement on these lines was reached early in 1916 and the revolt started in June.

It came late. Arab dissidence might have damaged the Turks more if it had been encouraged earlier and in more sensitive areas than the Hejaz. One such area was Syria, the province immediately to the south of Anatolia. When the war started the Ottoman Fourth Army, based in Damascus, had been largely Arab. Many of its officers belonged to the military secret society working for Arab secession. But by 1915 Jemal Pasha had uncovered the extent to which Arab agitators were undermining the morale of his men; they were promptly transferred to Gallipoli, where they fought well. Their place in Syria was taken by Turkish-speaking troops.

A second area—and one favored by the Cairo Bureau—was Iraq, another province more vital to the Turks than the Hejaz. The opportunity had been missed. Iraq had been invaded by an army from British India; the largely empty valley was thought of as a possible place for the surplus population of India; the Indian Army commanders were in no mood to make rash offers of independence to the natives. An invasion through Basra was expected to be a walkover. In fact, a long, sullen war resulted in which the Iraqis watched, or needled, from the sidelines.

For the Arabs, the revolt was paid for dearly, in the long term as in the short. The price was paid by all Arabs, though probably less than 10 per cent took part in what was widely considered an act of betrayal. Even in the Hejaz opinion was by no means wholeheartedly behind Hussein. But Hussein's defection, followed by the desertion of officers of Arab or in some cases Kurdish origin, destroyed what was left of the Ottoman ideal. The way was open for a Turkish Turkey. This was in the long term. In the short, Jemal Pasha inflicted brutal sentences on people for whom he felt the same contempt as the British for the Catholic Irish. In Palestine, Arabs were tortured and hanged for their supposed adherence to the Allied cause; in Lebanon, whose Western sympathies were not in doubt, the Turks engineered a famine in which between a quarter and a third of the population (according to statistics collected by American missionaries) perished.

But to the Allies the Arab Revolt was of considerable value. The rejection of the Jihad by the Amir of the holiest Islamic city helped to prevent a mutinous movement in the Indian Army. The capture of Jeddah and then Mecca (Medina was to hold out till after the Armistice) compelled the Turks and their German allies to transfer men and material to the south; more important, it forced them to abandon any further schemes against the Suez Canal. To Ronald Storrs the Hejazi Arabs had seemed a "cowardly and undisciplined rabble": much what they must have seemed at first to the Turks. They certainly differed from European armies; they knew nothing of Western drill or Western tactics. Their experience of fighting had been limited to the raids traditional in nomadic Arabia: pantomimes of violence in which noise exceeded killing. Riven by tribal rivalries, they were hard to unite; having been united, they were hard to keep in one place under one command. But their fierce individualism, their masculine braggadocio, made them excel at a kind of warfare in which dash and ingenuity, not team spirit or discipline, played the major role. The Hejazi tribesmen were the first shadow of the century's later hero: the commando or guerrilla.

But the Arab Revolt had a value to the Allies, and in particular to Britain, which outvalued the opening of a new front on an obscure sea. It came as a tonic when public morale was low. That the gallant sons of the desert had risen in support of Britain compensated for the monotonous slaughter on the Western Front. War was suddenly glamorous again. And in the midst of the glamour was a young Englishman who captivated the imagination of his contemporaries as no one else. T. E. Lawrence, a British Intelligence captain still in his twenties, became to newspaper readers "Al Aruns," the uncrowned King of Arabia, the kingmaker of a new dynasty of Arab kings. Legend had him hero-worshiped from one end of the desert to another. "They did not ask who I was," "Al Aruns" was to write, "for my clothes and appearance were peculiar in the desert. It was notoriety to be the only cleanshaven one, and I doubled it by wearing always the suspect pure silk, of the whitest (at least outside), with a gold and crimson Meccan head-rope, and gold dagger."

Since 1914 a heroic role had been seeking a player; in Lawrence it found an actor trained and ready to perform, first for an almost private audience of the elite, then to the gallery of Britain and the world. The son of a puritanical governess cohabiting with an Anglo-Irish landowner who for her changed his name and deserted his wife and four daughters, Lawrence had that muddled social background which, more than anything in a Brahmin society, predisposes to ambition. Like many men with a ferocious power drive, he was a masochist, punishing his body for his indulgences of soul; like most men whose sexual life is achieved in fantasy, he was, in the words of his only close woman friend, "an infernal liar."[2] But none of this was known to the small but growing band of cognoscenti who saw in the diminutive large-jawed captain the hero they had been craving as much as victory. Winston Churchill, John Buchan, E. M. Forster, Robert Graves, Bernard Shaw, these were only a few of the distinguished Edwardians who found in the unobtrusively self-dramatizing young man the hero the war had so far lacked. He had a chilly, austere remoteness, a glorification of nihilistic violence curiously moving to stiff-collared intellectuals and politicians.

Since Lawrence had a good mind and much charm, since he had mastered his stage in a series of half-archaeological, half-Intelligence "digs" before the war, since he found it as easy to believe his own lies as to tell them, he played his role to the total conviction of his Western admirers. As a silhouette on a moonlit camel, or to his English and American friends, he could pass as an Arab; he claimed, but knew the claim was false, he could similarly convince the Arabs. His knowledge of Arabic was fair; enough, in any case, for him to have seen the obstacle which confronts every Westerner who would converse with Arabs: he must either speak the classical language, which would make him a professor in a poolroom, or must master a local variant, which would link him so closely to a region that he would need an encyclopedia of local knowledge to make the link convincing. To Arabs the fair, blue-eyed Englishman dressed in spotless silk was as convincing as an American in a kimono.

Nor did Lawrence win the Arabs to revolt by his inspiration. Some Arabs, as we have already seen, had planned revolt for their own reasons. Nor did he lead them to victory through his knowledge of strategy. The Bedouin sharpshooters had their own instinctive feeling for the ambush. In the Arab officers who had deserted the Turkish Army Feisal had men trained in the latest German methods. To cite the example of one such officer, destined to play a significant role in Arab history: Nuri Said had left his home in Baghdad at the age of fourteen and joined the Military College in Constantinople. He was commissioned as a junior officer at the age of eighteen and spent the years between 1908 and 1916, when he joined Feisal, studying the military art in practice, in the Balkan Wars, and in theory, at the Staff College.

Lawrence owed his influence to a plentiful supply of gold sovereigns stamped with the emblem of St George on horseback. Sherif Hussein depended on the pilgrimage and foreign subsidies for survival. The tribes would not have rallied to his cause, or stayed rallied, without financial encouragement. An Englishman who saw Lawrence in fancy dress on camel-back, who heard him acclaimed by ecstatic nomads, was puzzled by their greeting: "Hail Abu Khayyal!" The Englishmen knew enough Arabic

[2] Charlotte Shaw, wife of George Bernard Shaw.

to know that *khayyal* meant horseman and *abu,* in this context, meant "father of." Mystified, he asked an Arab bystander why Lawrence was saluted as "father of a horseman?" The answer was a question. "Have you not seen the English gold sovereigns with their picture of a horseman?" Britannia's coin, more than Britain's cause, led the sons of the desert north from Mecca.[3]

The final thing which Lawrence was not, despite the legends, was pro-Arab. Emotionally anti-Turk and anti-French in equal measure, he directed all his actions towards what he saw to be the interests of the British Empire. His policy was first to evict the Turks and then to exclude the French. He went to the Hejaz, a year after the revolt had started, more to control the Arab movement than to inspire it. Lawrence naturally described his visit differently. His first visit to the Hejaz seems, in his own account, half holiday, half pursuit of an inner vision. "My visit was mainly to find the yet unknown master-spirit of the affair, and measure his capacity to carry the revolt to the goal I had conceived for it." The revolt had become bogged down, according to Lawrence; it needed "a prophet, especially the armed prophet who, if history be true, succeeded in revolutions."

Hussein, who was, of course, the revolt's master-spirit, had too strong a will of his own for the British purpose.

Lawrence claims to have assessed Hussein's four sons one by one; since three of them were to play roles in Middle Eastern history it is worth seeing them first through his report.

Lawrence approved the eldest, Ali, as a man, but not as a leader. "He was of middle height, thin and looking already more than his thirty-seven years. He stooped a little. His skin was sallow, his eyes large and deep and brown, his nose thin and hooked, his mouth sad and drooping. He had a sparse black beard and very delicate hands. His manner was dignified and admirable, but direct; and he struck me as a pleasant gentleman, conscientious, without great force of character, nervous and rather tired. His physical weakness (he was consumptive) made him subject to quick fits of shaking passion, preceded and followed by long moods of infirm obstinacy. He was bookish, learned in law and religion, and pious almost to fanaticism. He was too conscious of his high heritage to be ambitious, and his nature was too clean to see or suspect interested motives in those about him."

Having ruled out Ali, Lawrence then disposed of Zeid, the youngest. "Zeid was a shy, white, beardless lad of perhaps nineteen, calm and flippant, no zealot for the revolt. Indeed, his mother was Turkish; and he had been brought up in the harem, so that he could hardly feel great sympathy with an Arab revival . . ." Zeid was nevertheless to play some part in military operations; in later life he worked as a diplomat, married to a Turkish abstract painter; he had the calmest destiny of Hussein's children.

[3] Told to the author by Sir Herbert Todd, Baghdad, 1955.

The obvious choice for leader was the second son, Abdullah, the dapper parliamentarian who had raised the question of a revolt so bluntly to Kitchener. Abdullah was also the only son of Hussein to have impressed the Arabs. "The Arabs thought Abdullah a far-seeing statesman and an astute politician. Astute he certainly was, but not greatly enough to convince us always of his sincerity. His ambition was patent. Rumor made him the brain of his father and of the Arab revolt—but he seemed too easy for that. His object was, of course, the winning of Arab independence and the building up of Arab nations, but he meant to keep the direction of the new states in the family . . ."

Lawrence claimed that he instantaneously recognized the man he was seeking in Hussein's third son, Feisal.

Like Ali, Feisal looked older than his years: at thirty-one he was three years older than his British assessor. "His dark, appealing eyes, set a little sloping in his face, were bloodshot, and his hollow cheeks deeply lined and puckered with reflection." He was no intellectual: which was a welcome relief after the inquisitive, lively Abdullah. "His nature grudged thinking, for it crippled his speed in action: the labour of it shrivelled his features into swift lines of pain." But he was physically impressive: "tall, graceful and vigorous, with the most beautiful gait, and a royal dignity of head and shoulders. Of course he knew it, and a great part of his public expression was by sign and gesture." It must have long puzzled Lawrence's literal readers why Feisal should have been preferred to Abdullah, since the developing portrait reveals a weakling. "He showed himself hot-tempered and sensitive, even unreasonable, and he ran off soon on tangents. Appetite and physical weakness were mated in him, with the spur of courage. His personal charm, his imprudence, the pathetic hint of frailty as the sole reserve of this proud character made him the idol of his followers."

When it is known what Lawrence's purposes were, his choice of Feisal makes sense: just as a man's choice of secretary becomes understandable when it is clear if companionship or shorthand is the main requirement. Lawrence was not looking for a strong man to inspire the Bedouin in their drive north to Syria; he was looking for a weak man with an imposing presence whom he could influence; the Arab Revolt could then be dressed out in desert raiment; its destination would be Damascus; but its purpose would be different from what the Arabs, shouting for freedom, may have imagined.

Lawrence had coldly defined his true attitude to the Arab Revolt in a confidential document written in January 1916 and seen only by a few officials.[4] Hussein's revolt in the Hejaz would be helpful to Britain "be-

---

[4] Headed *The Politics of Mecca*, the document (PRO,FO,414/461) was partially reprinted in Philip Knightley and Colin Simpson, *The Secret Lives of Lawrence of Arabia* (London: Nelson, 1969).

cause it marches with our immediate aims, the break up of the Islamic 'bloc' and the defeat and disruption of the Ottoman Empire, and because the states he would set up to succeed the Turks would be as harmless to ourselves as Turkey was before she became a tool in German hands. The Arabs are even less stable than the Turks. If properly handled they would remain in a state of political mosaic, a tissue of small jealous principalities incapable of cohesion . . ."

If properly handled . . .

After serving with Feisal for almost a year, Lawrence was to compile his equivalent of Dale Carnegie's *How to Win Friends and Influence People*. But Lawrence was concerned with creating puppets and influencing Arabs. His manual was to suggest to a generation of British "advisers" how to rule from behind the curtain.

This was to give the true meaning to Lawrence's rapturous summing up of Feisal: "a prophet who, if veiled, would give cogent form to the idea behind the activity of the Arab revolt."

Poor Feisal was to learn, too late, the idea propelling the desert whirl-wind at whose center, dignified and frail, he rode so sadly.

Chapter 4

THE Arab Revolt, like a desert storm, fed short-lived flowers; like all guerrilla operations it took time to have effects. It had boosted morale; it had not won the war. The winter of 1916–17 was the first season since the summer of 1914 in which Allied leaders seriously envisaged a stalemate, if not defeat. Gloomy predictions were hardly exaggerated. 1917 was to see two revolutions in Russia, Kerensky's overthrow of the Czar in March and Lenin's defeat of Kerensky in November. The Italians were to be routed at Caporetto while the French Army mutinied after sustaining losses twice as heavy as those of Great Britain. Yet even these lesser losses were to be described by the Conservative leader in the House of Lords as "surely but slowly killing off the best of the male population of these islands." These same islands were threatened with starvation by U-boat blockade. To so much gloom a sweeping German advance into Rumania hardly added a shade.

Britain met the crisis with the ruthlessness of instinct. Early in December 1916 the scholarly Asquith, a gentleman before he was a politician, was dumped in favor of Lloyd George, a politician before he was anything else. Lloyd George was buoyed with the distinctive self-intoxication of the Celts, underpinned by the certainty that his cause, unfettered by scruple, would triumph, and in triumphing would be right. In contrast to Asquith and his Foreign Secretary, Sir Edward Grey, Lord Milner and Leopold Amery now trumpeted a New Imperialism. Their motives were not those of complacent confidence. They demanded a greater empire, not as a reward for victory, but as a counterweight to a post-war Europe under probable German control. Lord Milner now sat in the War Cabinet; Amery, the senior but smaller boy whom Winston Churchill had impudently pushed into the Harrow school swimming pool, was in the Cabinet Secretariat. Amery submitted a memorandum in January 1917 which argued that Britain should do all in her power to obtain "a continuity of territory or of control both in East Africa and between Egypt and India."

Then to bleak February an Ottoman reverse brought a whiff of Eastern spring. The Turks were defeated at Kut al-Amara in southern Iraq and withdrew on Baghdad. Next month they surrendered Baghdad, that most resonant of Arab capitals: though the Baghdad of 1917 was an Ottoman provincial town offering mud-brick walls to a mud-brown Tigris.

In a situation where neither the Allies nor the Central Powers seemed able to achieve a decisive victory, where progress on the Western Front was measured in hundreds of yards and thousands of corpses, the balance of factors was tilted neatly. This was the moment which Theodor Herzl had died thirteen years too soon to see: the moment when the Jews were the serious factor he had claimed them to be. In a war wherein factors counted more than principles, both sides in the struggle had an interest in securing Jewish support. The Jewish communities which mattered most were those in Russia and in the United States.

"World Jewry"—the entity which Herzl had posited against the facts— had entered the war as united as World Catholicism. Just as Bavarians rushed to fight their French coreligionists, so Jews had volunteered in all the combatant countries. This included Russia, whose treatment of the Jews had markedly improved during the years immediately preceding 1914. If the Jews of the world were disunited, World Zionism opted, like the Pope, for a wary neutrality; but as the Zionists had no Vatican, they transferred their headquarters from Berlin to Copenhagen, while Dr. Max Bodenheimer, president of the Jewish National Fund, transferred its cash to the safety of The Hague.

If the Zionists were officially neutral, most of their leaders were emotionally bound to Germany. Their organization's official language was still German; its leaders mostly lived in one or other of the German-speaking Powers. Many German Jews not only enlisted in the Wehrmacht—a service for which they were to be churlishly rewarded twenty years later—but pleaded, on the lines of Thomas Mann, that German *Kultur* was superior to the false democracy and superficial *Zivilisation* of Britain and France. (One energetic young Zionist to support Bodenheimer in this attitude was Nahum Goldmann.) Such German-oriented Zionists had set up a "Committee for the Liberation of Russian Jews," and this received the moral support of the World Zionist Organization's Central Committee.

The victory of Tannenberg opened the western provinces of the Russian Empire to the Germans. As the troops in field gray entered the Pale of Settlement—the area where the Czar's Jews were allowed to reside—the border ghettos welcomed them as liberators. The Wehrmacht were delighted to find a quasi-German people among so many Slavs; Yiddish was hardly more remote from German than other fringe dialects in the Low Countries and Switzerland. A secret report to the German Chancellor in the first month of the war described the Zionist Committee as an "invaluable instrument of intelligence and subversion, especially in Russia."

The committee had solid reasons for supporting Germany. Russia had witnessed, and tolerated, the worst anti-Jewish outbreaks; in contrast, Germany had opened its doors to Jews of talent; if anti-Semitism agitated some of the Kaiser's subjects, these were the cranks and the undereducated, not the influential. The president of the World Zionist Organization (Herzl's successor) confided to Bodenheimer his opinion that a German victory would be of great benefit to the world as a whole.

There were, as in all human relationships, snags. Germany's alliance with the Ottoman Empire made it inopportune for the Jews to mention Palestine, at least while the war was in progress. German good offices at Constantinople did, however, help in securing better treatment for many Jewish settlers in Palestine than that to which their Russian passports might have strictly entitled them. Keeping quiet about Palestine, the committee advocated the establishment of autonomous Jewish communities in the liberated border areas. They saw these as stepping stones to Palestine, not as substitutes, rather in the way that Herzl had thought of Cyprus or Uganda. When Germany won the war, she could put pressure on Turkey to concede Jewish rights of settlement in Palestine.

Halfway through October 1914, Bodenheimer and a colleague were invited to meet Ludendorff and Hindenburg, the two German war lords, at their Eastern Front HQ. Both Jews were charmed by the old-fashioned courtesy with which they were received by these representatives of Prussian militarism.

But the establishment of Jewish autonomous areas depended on German victory. This was slow in coming. The German impetus was weakened by the ineffectiveness of Austria further south and by the needs of the Western Front. The Wehrmacht had to evacuate its forward positions in southern Poland. But before doing so the Germans had discovered obstacles to the Zionist plan. The Poles, who naturally outnumbered the Jews, were violently nationalistic; they would tolerate only one form of Zionism—the radical kind that would remove the Jews from Europe. Neither for the first nor for the last time, Zionists and anti-Semites were de facto allies.

Martin Buber, one of the greatest human beings of the century and a Jew whose spiritual influence was to transcend religious barriers, had incautiously written in 1912: "Only in Asia can we truly find ourselves again. Here in Europe we are like a wedge which Asia drove into Europe's structure, a thing of ferment and disturbance. We should return to Asia's bosom, and we will, at the same time, return to the true meaning of our mission, destiny and existence."[1]

These words were to be reprinted in at least a dozen major anti-Semitic publications in the years to come. The Poles were among the first to endorse them. They wanted Jews (whom they saw as business competitors) to emigrate from Poland, not establish self-rule in autonomous communities on Polish soil.

The Zionist Committee's stand had a result which may have helped their long-term objective, but only at the cost of immense Jewish suffering in the First World War. For their pamphlets came to the notice of Russian Intelligence. To the Russians (always prone to suspect the loyalty of their Jewish minority), the committee's writings hinted that there were six and a half million potential traitors on their frontier. In a move of panicky brutality at least a million Jews were deported. This did much to turn public opinion in the neutral countries, and particularly America, against at least one of the Allies. For the Germans were quick to capitalize on the deportations. When the tide of battle turned once more in their favor, they invited American journalists into Eastern Europe to see for themselves the evidence of Russian anti-Semitism.

The men responsible for Allied propaganda were seriously perturbed by the conduct of their Russian ally. The best rejoinder they could think of was a *tu quoque:* if Russian ill-treatment of Jews besmirched the Allied cause, then Turkish ill-treatment of Armenians besmirched German *Kultur.* As an exercise in propaganda this was not effective. Not that public opinion accepted the Turkish argument, that the Armenians were conspiring with the Russians. Public opinion was hazy as to who or what the Armenians were. In contrast to the Jews, the Armenians were a little-known Christian sect with slender resources for bringing their grievances to public attention.

Against this background—of a largely successful German bid to win Jewish support or at least neutrality—America entered the war. She did so as a fellow combatant, rather than an Ally. Her entry posed new problems for the New Imperialists. The administration of President Woodrow Wilson was known for its anti-imperialistic bias, and above all, for its repudiation

[1] *Die Welt,* March 29, 1912; reprinted in *Juedische Bewegung* (Berlin: Juedesche Verlag, 1916), p. 195.

of secret agreements. Britain and America had been making a number of these; their disclosure might upset President Wilson as much as Hussein of Mecca.

The awkward moment produced its fixer: a man of genius able to convince those shaping British policy that if Jewish support were won for the Allied struggle, the interests of the British Empire would be served and the bad effects of Russian atrocities would be countered.

Chaim Weizmann, the man who did this, was living proof of at least part of Herzl's thesis: regimes such as that of czarist Russia were blighting, through their anti-Semitic bias, some outstanding talents. Potential Newtons, perhaps Miltons, must remain inglorious or mute unless they exerted efforts of will unimagined by the children of the Christian majority.

Weizmann's father had been a successful timber merchant in the region of White Russia centered on Minsk. The Weizmann family breathed an atmosphere entirely different from Herzl's Budapest. The Russian Pale of Settlement simmered spiritual truths, folklore and collective neurosis into a rich stock that was more like the nutriment of a nation than a church: the imagination of a Chagall, the revolutionary rage of a Trotsky or the patient determination of a Weizmann were exaggerated but not untypical products of this system of segregation and contempt enforced in the name of the Christ-Loving Autocrat of all the Russias and accepted by a minority disgusted with and afraid of its gentile oppressors. As a boy Weizmann had no social contacts with non-Jews. Although he wrote Russian well—he claimed even that the Jews had a better knowledge of the language and its literature than most Russians—"we were rooted heart and soul in our own culture, and it did not occur to us to give it up in deference to another." Significantly, Chaim used Hebrew in preference to Yiddish. Since the Zionists believed that "assimilation is common treason against the banner and ideals of the Jewish people,"[2] Yiddish, the half-German language of exile was increasingly rejected in favor of Hebrew, a Semitic language cognate with Arabic but even as long ago as the lifetime of Christ used only liturgically.

Chaim's mother, resilient, pious, not much of a manager, presided over a hospitable, eccentric household. Her son has described it vividly: "The bookcases contained probably as strange an assortment of literature as was ever assembled in a private home; the Talmud and the works of Maimonides cheek by jowl with Gorki and Tolstoi; textbooks on chemistry, dentistry, engineering and medicine jostling the modern Hebrew romances of Mapu and the nationalist periodicals of the new Zionism. On the walls were pictures of Maimonides and Baron de Hirsch, of the Wailing Wall in Jerusalem and of Anton Chekhov. The disputes were carried on in three

[2] Simon Dubnow, *Die Grundlagen des Nationalen Judentums* (Berlin: 1906), pp. 44–46.

languages, Russian, Yiddish and Hebrew, and what they lacked in formality or logic they definitely made up in vehemence."

On one subject the disputatious family agreed: the intolerable situation of the Jews in czarist Russia, forced to reside in certain areas and excluded on a quota system from more than a minority of places in Russian universities. While many Russian Jews took refuge in America, two other, more revolutionary courses of action were embodied in the outlooks of Chaim and his brother Shemuel. While Chaim wanted all Jews to leave Russia for The Promised Land, Shemuel wanted them to stay and through revolutionary action make Russia itself into a Promised Land for men of all faiths, or none.

"Whatever happens," the boys' mother retorted, "I shall be well off. If Shemuel is right, we shall be happy in Russia; and if Chaim is right, then I shall go to live in Palestine."

The problem of being a Jew in Russia posed itself for Chaim when he graduated from the Real-Gymnasium in Pinsk. "That I was to continue my studies was taken for granted. But where? In Russia? Was I to try to break through the narrow gate of the *numerus clausus,* and enroll in the University of Kieff—as my two brothers did some years later—or of Petrograd? I would no doubt have succeeded. But the road was one of ceaseless chicanery, deception and humiliation."

The young man decided to move West. His first stepping stone on the road which would eventually lead him to rainy Manchester, England's cotton metropolis, was a small town in Germany. Engaged to teach Hebrew there in a Jewish school, Weizmann evaded the necessity of obtaining a Russian passport by pretending to be a river worker and then skipping ship.

Pfungstadt at the height of Wilhelm II's middle-class empire was neat, orderly, honest, coldly unlike the warm chaos of the Pale of Settlement. It was the difference between cold consommé and borscht. Weizmann was non-plused by the German gentiles, so politely different from the near savages of home; he was even more astonished by the German Jews. The headmaster of the school combined meticulous adherence to the Jewish religious code with wholehearted German allegiance. "Dr. Barness was completely assimilated," Weizmann recorded later with some scorn, "and described himself as a 'German of the Mosaic persuasion.' He took his Judaism to mean that in all respects save that of a religious ritual he was as German, in culture, background and personality as any descendant of the Cerusci . . . If some Germans were anti-Semitically inclined, it was because they did not know the sterling qualities of the Jews, as exemplified in Dr. Barness and his like. They had to be told—that was all. A little enlightenment, judiciously applied, and anti-Semitism would simply vanish."

Like the post-Dreyfus Herzl, Weizmann believed that anti-Semitism was a virus carried by every gentile.

When Dr. Barness was expatiating on the virtues of enlightenment, Weizmann exclaimed:

"Herr Doktor, if a man has a piece of something in his eye, he doesn't want to know whether it's a piece of mud or a piece of gold. He just wants to get it out."

The Herr Doktor—Weizmann himself is the source—was non-plused by what seemed a half acceptance of anti-Semitic postulates.

But this readiness to accept that Jews were an irritant facilitated Weizmann's role as a Zionist apologist in the England where he established himself as a chemist shortly before the outbreak of war and where, in 1917, he was to place Zionism firmly on the stage of history. For the politicians whom he was to influence and convince were men to whom Jews were a mixture of gold and mud and a mixture which they often, in their secret hearts, wanted out.

Lloyd George, the new Prime Minister, had been reared on the Old Testament, as had his Foreign Secretary, Arthur Balfour. The ancient Hebrews represented the gold. Of modern Jews Lloyd George had a poor opinion. On one occasion, after an argument with a most distinguished Jew in his Cabinet, he turned to a friend and exclaimed: "Dirty coward! Men of that race always are."[3] The fastidious Balfour would have found it impossible to utter so coarse a generalization. He admired many qualities which he thought distinctively Jewish but (as he told Weizmann) he had once had a long discussion at Bayreuth, the shrine of German racialism, with Cosima Wagner (she had been the wife of Von Bülow before marrying the musician) and "shared many of her anti-Semitic postulates." Weizmann was never disturbed by such avowals. Indeed, he so much believed in the universality of anti-Semitism that he felt more at ease with gentiles who confessed this bias than with those who denied it. Weizmann could even agree with anti-Semites, he told Balfour, that "Germans of the Mosaic persuasion were an undesirable and demoralising phenomenon."[4]

For politicians like Lloyd George, genuinely patriotic, obsessed with the needs of the Front, or Balfour, dreaming of an alliance of superior races, Weizmann offered a formula as enticing as his chemical substitute for acetone had been useful. Two ingredients in the Zionist formula attracted Lloyd George and Balfour: the resurgence of the Old Testament Hebrews and the reduction of the number of Jews in Britain. But a third ingredient clinched the deal: by offering the Zionists something of what they wanted, Britain might get hold of Palestine. A Palestine under British control would safeguard the approaches to the Suez Canal and give access to that new target of the imperialists, Iraq. More immediately, British support for Jewish aspirations would, in Weizmann's words at the time, "enable us to

[3] W. J. Braithwaite, *Lloyd George's Ambulance Wagon; the Memoirs of W. J. Braithwaite* (London: 1957).
[4] Kenneth Young; *Arthur James Balfour* (London: 1963) pp. 257–58.

counteract the demoralizing influence which the enemy press is endeavouring to exercise by holding out vague promises to the Jews."

For the Jews to throw their support behind the Allies, the promises must, therefore, be more than vague. But they must be less than precise if they were not to weaken the Allied cause on the Arab front. The Arabs had already been assured of independence in an area which included Palestine.[5] President Wilson's Fourteen Points (January 8, 1917) had included in point number twelve the assurance that "the other nationalities which are now under Turkish rule should be assured an undoubted security of life and an absolutely unmolested opportunity of autonomous development." If self-determination meant anything (and it was an Allied watchword), it meant that the Arab majority in Palestine should have the inalienable right to determine the future of their country.

The promise which was given to Lord Rothschild on November 2, 1917, seemed the quintessence of vagueness:

> *My dear Lord Rothschild,*
>
> *I have much pleasure in conveying to you, on behalf of His Majesty's Government, the following declaration of sympathy with Jewish Zionist aspirations which has been submitted to, and approved by, the Cabinet.*
>
> *His Majesty's Government view with favour the establishment in Palestine of a national home for the Jewish people, and will use their best endeavours to facilitate the achievement of this object, it being clearly understood that nothing shall be done which may prejudice the civil and religious rights of existing non-Jewish communities in Palestine, or the rights and political status enjoyed by Jews in any other country.*
>
> *I should be grateful if you would bring this declaration to the knowledge of the Zionist Federation.*
>
> *Yours sincerely,*
ARTHUR JAMES BALFOUR

The vagueness owed nothing to careless, or bureaucratic writing. No handful of words in history had been more worked over. They were not the words of Balfour. The Zionists had in effect written their own declaration, and this gives some piquancy to its last sentence. The text had crossed the Atlantic several times; Mr. Louis Brandeis, Wilson's closest adviser, had been, since 1913, an active Zionist and since 1916 a Supreme Court

---

[5] Interested parties were later to argue that the area of Arab independence had not included Palestine; but two weeks after the 1918 Armistice Lord Curzon, who had been a member of the War Cabinet and who succeeded Balfour as Foreign Secretary, was to state categorically: "The Palestine situation is this. If we deal with our commitments, there is first the general pledge to Hussein in October, 1915, under which Palestine was included in the areas to which Britain pledged itself that they should be Arab and independent in the future." (Public Record Office document CAB 27/24.)

Judge. The first draft, after approval by Wilson and Brandeis, had been submitted to Balfour by Lord Rothschild on July 18. This draft made no allusion to the indigenous population. It recognized Palestine as "the," not "a" National Home of the Jewish People and would have granted "internal autonomy to the Jewish nationality in Palestine, freedom of immigration for Jews, and the establishment of a Jewish National Colonizing Corporation for the resettlement and economic development of the country." It was due to the protests of certain Jews—Lucien Wolf, Claud Montefiore, Sir Matthew Nathan—not to any pro-Arab lobby that this draft was rewritten.

A rewritten draft was again approved in America. In this His Majesty's Government accepted the principle that Palestine should be reconstituted as the national home of the Jewish people and would use its best endeavors to secure the achievement of this object and would discuss the necessary methods and means with the Zionist organization. This draft was strongly fought by Sir Edwin Montagu, then Minister of Munitions.

Instead of seeing the projected declaration as proof of British friendship for the Jews, Montagu composed a memorandum startlingly entitled "The Anti-Semitism of the Present Government." He was a considerable stylist and deliberately chose the title for its paradoxical effect. But he was in deadly earnest: the effect of accepting the Zionist postulate that Jews were a nation, not a religious group, would in the long run harm, not help, the Jewish community. "Zionism," he wrote, "has always seemed to me to be a mischievous political creed, untenable by any patriotic citizen of the United Kingdom. If a Jewish Englishman sets his eyes on the Mount of Olives and longs for the day when he will shake British soil from his shoes and go back to agricultural pursuits in Palestine, he has always seemed to me to have acknowledged aims inconsistent with British citizenship and to have admitted that he is unfit for a share in public life in Great Britain, or to be treated as an Englishman." Montagu then asserted four basic principles.

He first asserted that there was no Jewish nation. "The members of my family, for instance, who have been in this country for generations, have no sort or kind of community of view or desire with any Jewish family in any other country beyond the fact that they profess to a greater or less degree the same religion." Jews in England and Jews in Morocco no more formed one people than Christians in England and Christians in France.

Zionism would cause suffering, first by encouraging anti-Semitic countries to expel their Jews, and then by putting the Jews in a position where they would expel the present inhabitants from Palestine and take all the best land.

Montagu thirdly denied that Palestine, in the twentieth century, was associated with the Jews. "The Ten Commandments were delivered to the Jews on Sinai. It is quite true that Palestine plays a large part in Jewish history, but so it does in modern Mahommedan history, and, after the time of the Jews, surely it plays a larger part than any other country in Christian history. The Temple may have been in Palestine, but so was the Sermon on the Mount and the Crucifixion."

His fourth and final argument was that the acceptance of Zionism's postulates would reverse the tendency, which Montagu welcomed, whereby Jews were becoming absorbed into the structure of British life in the way that such minorities as the Huguenots had been absorbed before them. "More and more we are educated in public schools and at the Universities and take our part in the politics, in the Army, in the Civil Service, of our country. And I am glad to think that the prejudices against inter-marriage are breaking down. But when the Jew has a national home, surely it follows that the impetus to deprive us of the rights of British citizenship must be enormously increased."[6]

In deference to such opinions, yet another draft produced a new prescription: "a National Home for the Jewish People in Palestine." Though the words "a" and "in" made a lawyer's difference, non-Zionist Jews would have still preferred to substitute "religious" or "social" for National.

At this point the Cabinet itself began to have second thoughts. They had been surprised when Montagu's view was formally supported by the signatures of forty-seven prominent Jews;[7] Montagu could justly claim that his list included "every Jew who is prominent in public life, with the exception of the present Lord Rothschild, Mr. Herbert Samuel, and a few others." Curzon, who knew the East as well as any living Englishman, had also warned his colleagues of the harm any new undertaking over Palestine might work, if it were discovered by the Arabs.

In this crisis chance helped the Zionists. On October 14, 1917 Sir Edwin Montagu sailed for the East; as Secretary for India he was to initiate important reforms. His departure removed the most dedicated opponent of the Zionist argument. At the same time American pressure steadied British nerve. The final version approved by President Wilson and Judge Brandeis was issued in the form already quoted. There was one last-minute repair. Somewhere along the line the phrase "the Jewish race" had slipped in; this was hurriedly changed back to "the Jewish people."

The practical results of the Balfour Declaration were less helpful than had been hoped. A major consideration in the minds of those promoting it had been the need to keep the Russian Jews (with their supposed control over the grain trade of the steppes) on the side of the war and the Allies. The publication of the declaration coincided with the Bolshevik Revolution and this (except during the short-lived New Economic Policy of some years later) was to outlaw private commerce. Most Russian Jews supported Lenin's call to end the war. As far as American public opinion

[6] Document dated August 23, 1917, CAB 24/24, marked SECRET, *Circulated by the Secretary of State for India.*
[7] Document dated October 9, 1917, CAB 24/28.

was concerned, the U-boat campaign had already turned Americans anti-German. A young man named David Green (of whom we shall hear much more as Ben-Gurion) found that the declaration vastly encouraged enlistment by New York Jews in a Jewish Legion; this force, while accustoming Jews to the feel of arms, was to play little part in the military struggle.

In the Middle East the declaration had embarrassing results for Britain. Her agents tried to keep news of it from Sherif Hussein and his sons. When the Germans in Damascus brought it to their attention through secret emissaries, British officials were involved in time-wasting attempts to prove that the declaration meant even less than it said: that Jews would only be allowed to settle in marginal, unused land and that political rights were included in the "civil and religious rights" which the declaration safeguarded. The phrase, "the non-Jewish communities in Palestine" was the most unfortunate; as offensive to the Arabs as it would have been offensive to British Protestants to be dismissed as "the non-Roman Catholic communities in England."

Arab trust in British explanations was dynamited when the new Soviet Government published more startling evidence of Allied duplicity. The czarist archives, now laid naked to the world, contained the text of the Sykes-Picot Agreement (named after its initiators Sir Mark Sykes and M. Georges Picot), a project drawn up earlier in the war for the disposal of Ottoman territory between Britain, France and Russia. Under this secret agreement czarist Russia was to have inherited Constantinople, the Straits and a slice of Anatolia. The rest of the Ottoman Empire was to have been shared out in the old-fashioned imperial manner. As her reward for entering the war, Italy was to have received an area in southwest Anatolia as well as the Dodecanese Islands she had already seized. Britain and France were to share out what were considered the potentially wealthy parts of "Turkey in Asia": France would get a swath of territory running from Cilicia in southern Anatolia as far east as Mosul; Britain, a block of territory from the Mediterranean south of Lebanon running east to Iraq. Hussein was left with the stony kingdom of Hejaz.

From the publication of the Balfour Declaration and the Sykes-Picot Agreement in November 1917, official Britain was to have no Arab friends, only Arab clients. The family of King Hussein were too committed to the support of Britain to draw back, though Feisal briefly considered accepting Turkish terms for an honorable peace. But everywhere else the Arabs and Muslims who had warned against accepting the occupiers of Algeria and Egypt as liberators were in a position to mutter the Arabic equivalent of "I told you so." As such skeptics comprised the overwhelming majority in the Middle East, these mutterings would give imperial Britain her final migraine. For the grandchildren of Hussein and his supporters they were to spell out a doom as lurid as that of the House of Atreus in Aeschylean drama.

But the Balfour Declaration achieved part of its aim: at least until British interpretation of its limits clashed with Zionist policy, the followers of Herzl were enthused for Britain, the country the first Zionist had seen as the most logical sponsor of his dream. "The news of the British Declaration," Jon Kimche has written in a short but perceptive account of how *Der Judenstaat*'s title deeds were composed, "spread through the Jewish world even before the Zionist leaders launched their campaign in support of the Allies. It reached Jews living on the eve of the Bolshevik revolution in Petrograd and Kiev, in Warsaw and Odessa; it reached and even delighted the German Zionists, shaken for the first time in their faith in the Kaiser; it travelled to the Americas and the Balkans, to neutral Switzerland and to trembling Palestine. Some heard it sooner, some later; but wherever the tidings reached a Jewish home, Allied or enemy, neutral or friendly to Britain, a toast was drunk to the Balfour whose declaration read like the first sign of the coming of Messiah."[8]

Chapter 5

ON October 30, 1918, off Mudros on the island of Lemnos, a British admiral[1] and the Turkish Minister of Marine[2] signed an armistice on board the *Agamemnon,* the temporary British flagship. The atmosphere had been friendly throughout thirty-six hours of wardroom negotiations. "By signing this armistice," the British admiral piously hoped, "we shall put an end to this bloodshed which has been going on for so many years." The two plenipotentiaries shook hands on the Ottoman Empire's dissolution: for centuries a European dream, and a Turkish dread.

Turkish, soon to be followed by German, acceptance of defeat had been signaled on September 29, when Bulgaria signed an armistice with an Allied force pushing inland from Salonika. Bulgaria's collapse followed the failure of Ludendorff's last great offensive on the Western Front. For the Germans the loss of Bulgaria meant the loss of the Balkans, her bridge to the East; for the Turks the loss of Bulgaria was more decisive than her loss of Syria to Allenby's British Army and Feisal's irregulars. She was now cut off from her only source of arms.

---

[8] Kimche, *The Unromantics.*
[1] Later Admiral of the Fleet Sir Somerset Gough-Calthorpe, G.C.B., G.C.M.G.
[2] Hussein Rauf.

The victorious Allies did not long maintain the cordial manners of the British admiral. As winter grew chill in defeated Constantinople, the representatives of Britain and France showed a puzzling mixture of arrogance and indecision. Ignoble but contrary ambitions were masked by noble platitudes. The two Allies had a dangerous sense of having all power and all time in which to use it. This dangerous illusion was aided by the man with whom they had to deal. A second brother of Abdul Hamid had inherited the wobbly Ottoman throne from Mehemet V in the war's last summer. In Mehemet VI, harem weakness and petulant self-importance rolled themselves into a timid ball. He was a Sultan-Caliph designed by fate to surrender awe and power alike. His one concern was his thronelet and capital. He would have welcomed a solution which left him the Doge of Constantinople with his name mentioned in the Friday prayers. From Mehemet VI the Allies had nothing to fear.

Yet most Allied plans were to be aborted. One reason lay in the nature of Allied victory. After four years of struggle against the numerically weaker but more centrally directed Central Powers, Britain and France were like cancer victims briefly triumphant in a brawl with consumptives. A victory of attrition had weakened the victors as much as the vanquished. The one exception to global exhaustion was the United States of America.

If America could have been involved, or entangled, in a Middle East settlement, something positive might have been worked out, despite the pulling apart of the two European Allies. But the Americans had one overwhelming purpose: to get back to their own continent. On May 6, 1919, the U.S. would categorically refuse to send troops to help occupy Turkey; a tentative acceptance by President Wilson of a U.S. responsibility for Constantinople and an independent Armenia was doomed by the President's illness and his country's unwillingness to accept such a mandate. In an important sense America had felt herself a wartime associate, not an ally, of the two imperial powers.

Without America, the Allies could not agree on how to cut, or cook, the Ottoman carcass. They could hardly be blamed for their bewilderment, but their mutual betrayal dishonored their dead. It was an unprecedented situation. No less than four empires had collapsed as a result of the war. While the defeat of Germany and Austria-Hungary had served the Allied cause, the collapse of czarist Russia had not. The area to the east of Turkey—the Caucasian bridge between Russia and the Middle East— was a patchwork of tiny successor states clamoring for recognition. Of these peoples the most persecuted and the most vocal were the Armenians. Although they were hardly more than a substantial minority in any one region (around 40 per cent in a few districts of eastern Anatolia), one of their delegates demanded a state stretching from the Black Sea in the north to Alexandretta on the Mediterranean.

And what of Turkey in Europe? Now that Russia was out of the Alliance (Allied armies would be contesting Lenin's revolution for some time), Constantinople might as well remain the Sultan's capital; but the Straits must come under the control either of the Allies or the newly formed League of Nations.

Elsewhere rivalries invisible during the drought of war sprang like luxuriant beanstalks in the rain of triumph. The chief arena for Anglo-French rivalry was Syria, the province which then seemed the war's most rewarding prize. The secret Sykes-Picot Agreement had awarded it to France. In other secret discussions British spokesmen had promised Syria to the Arabs; an Arab force under Feisal had entered Damascus as the forerunners of Allenby; Lawrence had hoped that in this way the French might lose what Sykes had promised them. At this time Syria prompted a bitterer dissension than the Palestine in which the Arabs comprised nine tenths of the population and which had been promised as a national home (whatever that meant) to the Jewish people. Most of the Cairo British shared to some degree Lawrence's suspicions of the French. On the French side suspicion of the British was informed and fervent. The way in which Britain had taken over Egypt and the Suez Canal was a bitter memory. Having suffered twice as many casualties as Britain in the war, France was determined to control Syria, a country which had lingered in the French mind since the time of the Crusades; to France, Syria meant Lebanon and Cilicia as well as the region centered on Damascus and Aleppo.

Having taken so long to win the war, and having contradictory ideas about what to do with its spoils, the Allies delayed in making peace. A treaty with Turkey was not to be signed (at Sèvres) until August 1920. The jockeying for position, the underhand bargains, made it not only one of the harshest treaties in history, but one of the most absurd. For between 1918 and 1920 the situation throughout the Middle East underwent seismic changes. President Wilson's idealistic slogans and their echoes in the official statements of Britain and France, were taken seriously in the Arab countries, in British-protected Egypt and finally in what had become, through the amputation of all else, Anatolian Turkey.

The Allies, and particularly the British, were to have trouble in all three regions.

In the Arab countries awareness of the Balfour Declaration and the secret terms of the Sykes-Picot Agreement spread among an effervescent people ruled in name by members of King Hussein's family (though not yet in Iraq) but in fact under the control (except in the Hejaz) of British armies. The Hashemites, irrevocably committed to the Allies, could only appeal, through Colonel Lawrence and other British officers, for a fulfillment of the wartime pledges. Feisal received humiliation after humiliation, first from the French, who refused to recognize him as an official delegate to the Peace Conference; then from the British, who decided that his kingship in Syria was not worth the oil fields of northern Iraq, which France was prepared to swap for Damascus; and finally from the Syrians. Arab exasperation with Feisal was not due to treachery or fickle-mindedness: it was due to his desperate attempt to oblige the Allies, even by agreeing to help the Allied requirements for a Jewish National Home in Palestine. Feisal met Weizmann first in Aqaba and then in Europe, where Lawrence acted as dishonest broker. The Jews should "finance the whole East, I hope, Syria and Mesopotamia alike. High Jews are unwilling to put much cash into Palestine only, since that country offers nothing but a sentimental return. They want 6%." And to those Arabs who feared that the Jews might be able to dominate as well as finance the region, the same letter[3] added that "the Arab Govt. is not afraid of them (can cut all their throats, or better pull their teeth out, when it wishes)." To Feisal and other Arabs, Weizmann insisted that a national home in no sense meant an independent state; on their side the Hashemites said they would welcome Jewish help in rebuilding Semitic civilization. Feisal had the wit to add a postscript in Arabic: his readiness to welcome Jewish settlement in Palestine was conditional on British fulfillment of other pledges to his family.

The Hashemites were trapped by their ironical situation of having revolted against the Caliph in the interests of the powers which had occupied Algeria and Egypt. Ordinary Arabs were not so trapped. But they were increasingly aware of a truth which no one stated better than Balfour when, in August 1919, he wrote in candor, not envisaging for publication: "So far as Palestine is concerned, the Powers have made no statement of fact which is not admittedly wrong, and no declaration of policy which, at least in the letter, they have not always intended to violate." In Damascus, which Feisal had entered to the joy cries of women and the rifle-fire of men, a Syrian Congress explicitly repudiated Feisal's agreement with Weizmann. Meanwhile the French coldly prepared to get rid of Feisal altogether and establish their own mandate over Lebanon and Syria.

In Iraq discontent with the British occupation was so violent that by the early 1920s Britain found herself forced to use 100,000 men to garrison a country which the Ottomans had controlled with a mere 16,000. A secret inquiry,[4] of February 19, 1920, was addressed by the office of the Secretary of State for War and Air, Winston Churchill, to Sir Hugh Trenchard: would the pioneer of air warfare, and Lawrence's hero, be able to take over control of Iraq? "It would . . . entail the provision of some kind of asphyxiating bombs calculated to cause disablement of some kind but not death . . . for use in preliminary operations against turbulent tribes." The need to control Iraq cheaply was made urgent by the steady

---

[3] Letter in Bodleian Library; quoted in Knightley and Simpson, op. cit., p. 120.
[4] From the Trenchard Papers; quoted in Knightley and Simpson, op. cit., p. 139.

drain on Britain's resources. Ireland was in revolt and British soldiers wanted to get home to their wives.

If the Arabs were thus turning sour, the situation in Egypt was explosive.

The war had postponed the overflow of long simmering Egyptian national feeling. When Herzl had visited Cairo, the nationalism of the young Mustafa Kamil (not to be confused with Turkey's Mustafa Kemal) was already arousing the educated, though these were comparatively few. In 1906 a dramatic and terrible incident showed that the apparent amity between the British occupiers and the people who had shouted for Orabi was that of stupor, not heartfelt acceptance. Mustafa Kamil described what happened for readers of *Le Figaro*.

"On the 13 June last, some British officers left their camps and passed close to Dinshwai, in Menufiyah Province, to shoot pigeons on private land. An old fellah warned their interpreter that only the year before the local inhabitants had been angered when British officers shot their pigeons and that it would only enrage them more if this were repeated." Part of the trouble was probably due to the officers not knowing that the fellahin looked on their pigeons, housed in white castlelike towers, more as poultry than game; they represented one of the rare sources of protein in the peasant diet.

"Despite this warning, the shoot begins. Shots are fired; a woman is injured, a barn catches fire. From all sides the villagers rush to the scene; in the ensuing brawl three Egyptians are injured by the British and three officers are injured by the Egyptians. One of those hurt, Captain Bull, escapes from the melee and, running as fast as he can for three miles in a heat of 42 degrees, dies of sunstroke. Learning what has happened to their officers, British soldiers invade another village nearby and kill a peasant by breaking his skull."

If the British had been more relaxed, they might have seen the need to soothe a misunderstanding. But the British were on edge. For some time relations between them and the Egyptians had been getting worse. Lord Cromer was in part to blame: as he grew older he grew more testily convinced that only the mischievous attacked the permanence of British rule or the wisdom of its decisions. Cromer had on occasions recommended flogging as a penalty for peasant insolence. But in the inflammable situation of 1906 he might have cautioned calmer remedies than his imperceptive deputy, who in the absence of the Lord on leave, saw the incident as a challenge to imperial authority, a fuse which if left burning might ignite an Egyptian Mutiny. The elements who supported British rule in Egypt—foreign merchants, Levantines, the minorities—pressed for severity, fearing that unless the villagers were severely punished, Muslim fanaticism might be given its head. Typical of these was the editor of *al-Mokattam*, the newspaper which habitually spoke for the British Agency. Nimr Fares (later made a pasha) was a Christian from the Levant who had taught at the Syrian Protestant College (later to become the American University of Beirut) and come to Egypt because of his hostility to the Ottoman Empire. He was, in a sense, an Arab nationalist; his son-in-law, George Antonius, later wrote the definitive Hashemite account of the Arab Revolt. Yet for the fellahin Fares felt little compassion. Even before the villagers of Dinshwai were sentenced, his newspaper would announce that sets of gallows had been sent to the village.

The British mounted a minatory spectacle. The special tribunal which judged the fifty-two accused villagers was a strange one. Of five judges, only two understood Arabic, only one was a Muslim Egyptian. Three judges were English and a fifth was a Copt. The tribunal was empowered to inflict capital sentences and these would not be subject to appeal; the tribunal operated under a special law giving protection to British military personnel and designed "to administer justice more promptly and inflict punishments of greater severity than is possible if the Egyptian Criminal Code continues to be applied in its integrity."

The tribunal was both prompt and severe. It allotted an average of thirty-four seconds to each of the accused: time for the clerk to write down his name and age. In three days of angry wrangle—for the peasants were defended by an Egyptian of determination[5]—it became clear that the officers had, even if unintentionally, provoked the incident: in particular by wounding the Egyptian woman. The Egyptians—hot-tempered fellahin, but no calculating killers—had reacted against poachers, not against Englishmen. The British physician attached to the Egyptian courts testified that Captain Bull had died from heat exhaustion, and not from his injuries. A police officer who wished to testify that the officers had fired first was not heard and on June 27 judgment was given. Four villagers were sentenced to be hanged; two to forced labor for life; one to forced labor for fifteen years; six to forced labor for seven years; three to a year's imprisonment and public flogging; five to flogging without imprisonment.

If judgment was swift, its execution was swifter. Next afternoon the prisoners were brought to the mud-brick village at exactly one-thirty, the precise time of the brawl two weeks before. Inside a roped-off square gallows and whipping posts stood within clear view of the village's crowded roofs. British dragoons and Egyptian cavalry guarded the scene. Cromer's deputy was present with a group of officers. The son of the first condemned man begged for permission to bid his father farewell. Permission was withheld. Soldiers mounted and drew their swords. The first strangulation was accompanied by ululations from the watching women. Two men were then lashed with the cat (of nine tails) in presence of the dangling corpse. The same sequence was thrice repeated: a hanging, then flog-

---

[5] Ahmad Lutfi al-Sayyid, a well-known writer.

gings. The villagers, immemorially subjected to injustice, muttered "Cursed be all tyrants!" When night fell, they dug up their dead lest they rest forever in British grave-clothes.

The atrocity was small compared with the larger ones the century was to offer. In Britain itself, as Mustafa Kamil conceded, "Dinshwai" was attacked by Bernard Shaw and members of Parliament. But the effect inside Egypt was to be important and permanent, in large part thanks to the very qualities which the British had hitherto exhibited. Such judicial brutality would have caused less surprise from a Turkish governor. This savage reversal of normal British methods converted millions of Egyptians to Mustafa Kamil's thesis: whether of gold or steel, fetters were fetters and the British occupation was an unendurable outrage.

For the Egyptians who had been associated with the tribunal, Dinshwai was fatal. Butros Ghali, the brilliant Copt who had been acting Minister of Justice at the time, protested to his family that he only sat on the tribunal to prevent even harsher sentences from being passed. His protestations remained within the family circle. After becoming the first Egyptian Prime Minister in 1908, he was murdered three years later. His assassin gave as one pretext his connection with Dinshwai.

For the British the results of Dinshwai were equally serious. Many Egyptians had sincerely felt that the British could teach Egypt much of value. Many had admired the work of Cromer and his subordinates. This state of mind was not to recur. Cromer, a sensitive man behind his ice, developed a digestive ailment and resigned the year after Dinshwai. From 1907 to the outbreak of the Great War tension between British and Egyptians constantly sharpened. The death of Mustafa Kamil in 1908 was the occasion of a mammoth funeral.

On the outbreak of war Egyptian public opinion had been warily neutral or sympathetic to Turkey. No one in Egypt had wanted to get involved in the fighting, and Britain, when declaring Egypt at war with the Central Powers, promised that she alone would be responsible for Egypt's defense; Egyptians would not be called upon to contribute to the war or fight their brother Muslims. These undertakings were soon broken. A million and a half Egyptians were conscripted into battalions which gave support to the British in the Hejaz, Palestine or Gallipoli. The war benefited the rich Egyptians, since cotton, which had sold for fourteen dollars a kantar in 1914, had boomed more than tenfold by the spring of 1920. But the fellahin and poor townsmen (whose foodstuffs had to be imported now that so much land was under cotton) became poorer.

On the day after the Armistice the man who as Egypt's Prime Minister in 1914 had reluctantly declared war put the case for Egyptian independence to a Belgian judge. The Prime Minister, Rushdy Pasha, was a portly Turk whose sensual eyes glinted maliciously from behind his glasses; the scene was Cairo's Muhammad Ali Club, the focus of establishment politics:

"We have been good boys during the war and we now demand our promised reward. Egypt gave the Allies loyal, disciplined and effective help. She accepted the British Protectorate as an unavoidable necessity and condition that, when victory was won, independence would be her fee. I received such undertakings in person. The time has now come for the undertakings to be honoured. Besides, there are President Wilson's famous 'Points'."[6]

Rushdy's French—"*Nous avons été sages!*"—carried an unimpassioned note. Rushdy represented the upper-class Egyptians of Turkish origin who were to dominate Egyptian politics for another generation. They were the only people most foreigners met. Rushdy's companion at the Muhammad Ali Club was later to reflect that, in his twenty Egyptian years, all the politicians he had known—with one striking exception—were Turks. These Turco-Egyptians were often nationalistic, either from a residual feeling of difference from the Christian West, or from a wish to take over the positions still held by Europeans. But they were remote from the Egypt of piled-up mud village and crowded, narrow street. "Not that these men do not love the country, or are not devoted to it. But lacking native links to the soil which they rule, they sometimes give the impression of having been superimposed on the country's life and of managing the interests of Egypt with the somewhat dry activity of a company director."[7]

The one exception to this rule was Saad Zaghlul, a Muslim Egyptian whom Cromer had promoted and in his farewell speech at Cairo's Opera had singled out for praise. Zaghlul was to add the note of passion to the Egyptian demand for independence; he was to make the coming decade painful for Britain.

He did not confine his agitation to the quiet purlieus of the Muhammad Ali Club. On a winter's day in 1918 he headed a deputation (in Arabic, *wafd*) which asked the British High Commissioner for leave to proceed to London to discuss Egyptian independence. (The Wafd would become Egypt's major political party.) London at this moment was preoccupied with the aftermath of war and problems which seemed more urgent; the British had long divided Egyptians into cynical aristocrats like Rushdy, who could be fobbed off, or ignorant natives, incapable of action. Zaghlul's request was refused. Uproar started.

"These infernal Egyptians," an Englishman in charge of the Cairo police wrote home on November 24, "are starting to give us a lot of work again. Self-determination of nations may be all very well for the Sandwich Isles or Montenegro, but it doesn't do in a country that is incapable of

---

[6] Baron Firmin van den Bosch: *Vingt Années d'Egypte* (Paris: 1932).
[7] Ibid.

governing itself, where commercial stability depends on our occupation, and where there is an important little canal called the Suez Canal."[8]

Early in 1919 the British reacted to the uproar by deciding to send Zaghlul into Maltese exile. The uproar now turned into violent insurrection against British authority.

But the country where resistance became most radical and most successful was neither Hashemite Arabia nor protected Egypt, but Turkey itself, the defeated enemy. By the end of 1919 Lord Curzon, in charge of British foreign affairs, was beginning to fear that "the weakest and most abject of our foes would end by achieving the greatest triumph." Allied rivalries, Allied delays, had laid a bed of coals for an astonishing phoenix. But the charcoal that set the coals aflame was an act of insolent pride colliding with a hero. The hero was a Turk, but the hybris, as the ancient Hellenes had termed such fatal pride, was Greek.

Twice in three millennia Greece had been the major Power in the Middle East. The first occasion was when Alexander the Great spread Hellenic civilization through Anatolia and Mesopotamia and as far east as India, leaving as heirs such dynasties as the Ptolemies in North Africa and the Seleucids in Syria. The second occasion was when Greek-speaking Byzantium ruled the eastern half of the Mediterranean in the name of Christ.

Since the first Byronic revolt against Ottoman rule, modern Greece had been an expanding state. An extreme wing of the Greek national movement was activated by what it called "The Great Idea." Like Herzl's vision, The Great Idea used nostalgia as its fuel. Lay-minded proponents of The Great Idea were nostalgic for the Hellas of Pericles and Alexander; the religious yearned for the Christian empire of Constantine the Great; but, however proposed, The Great Idea was expansionist; it implied a reversal of everything symbolized by the day in 1453 when the Turkish conqueror rode a white charger into Constantinople. In November 1918 a French general entered the same city riding a white steed without reins and the Greeks cheered themselves hoarse while the Turks wept. The Greeks had been prepared for the symbolic gesture a few days earlier when a procession of Allied warships filled the waters outside the Golden Horn.

But Greek believers in The Great Idea sought no victory by proxy. They wanted to achieve their dream themselves. In the delirium of a victory to which they had contributed little (their pro-German king had prevented the pro-Allied Venizelos from bringing Greece into the war until mid-1917) they began to see few limits to what Greece might, as they saw it, regain. The British had more or less promised the "return" of Cyprus, though on condition that Greece took part in the war. The ancient Greeks

---

[8] Russell Pasha, commandant of the Cairo Police, 1917 to 1948; in a letter quoted by Ronald Seth in *Russell Pasha* (London: 1966), p. 132.

had founded Alexandria and were back there in strength. More immediate demands were a "state of Pontus" based on the Black Sea port of Samsun and the western region of Anatolia based on Smyrna. Reports that the local Turks were ill-treating Greeks in both areas gave emotional urgency to such demands.

Unluckily for Greece, the British Prime Minister was still the Lloyd George whose political astuteness was neatly balanced by ignorance of the world. He considered Venizelos the greatest Greek statesman since Pericles; he was undisturbed by the fact that the Greeks were a minority both in Pontus and western Anatolia. The Greeks, Lloyd George was certain, were the coming people in the eastern Mediterranean; the Turks it was needless to take into account.

Since the Mudros Armistice two British warships had lain at anchor in Smyrna harbor. Under the protection of their guns, on May 15, 1919, Greek troops disembarked in the first stage of turning The Great Idea into a fact. The local Turks wished to fight but orders from the Sultan's government were telegraphed from Constantinople forbidding resistance. The disarmed Turkish troops were frog-marched to the harbor to the jeers of the Greeks. In a massacre powered by bitter memories of the past, hundreds of Turkish civilians were slaughtered and their bodies thrown into the sea which had seen the birth of Hellenic culture.

This was the act of hybris.

Mustafa Kemal, the hero with whom the Greeks were to collide, heard of the invasion in Constantinople. While the great square near the Blue Mosque surged with demonstrators hoping that even at this late hour their Sultan would rally to lead them, the man who would defeat The Great Idea of the Greeks and the lesser ideas of the Allies prepared calmly for a slow boat trip. His destination, like that of his enemies, was Anatolia.

BOOK SIX

Father in a Top Hat

"A civilized, international dress is worthy and appropriate for our nation, and we will wear it. Boots or shoes on our feet, trousers on our legs, shirt and tie, jacket and waistcoat—and of course, to complete these, a cover with a brim on our heads. I want to make this clear. This head-covering is called 'Hat'."

MUSTAFA KEMAL *in a speech extolling the virtues of Western dress*

Chapter 1

FOUR days after the Greek landing in Smyrna, in a less conspicuous port, an avalanche slipped its first silent stone. With gathering momentum and increasing mass succeeding boulders would change the history of the Middle East, making of its strongest Power a convert to the West.

Towards Samsun, the one harbor of importance between the Bosphorus and Trabzon to the east, had chugged, in rough weather, a small British-built cargo ship, the *Bandirma;* she now sidled to anchor some distance from the beach; lighters came out to land passengers on a long wooden jetty, as rickety and weed-grown as the defeated empire whose flag the *Bandirma* flew. On to the jetty stepped Mustafa Kemal, officially appointed inspector-general of the Ottoman Ninth Army, based at Samsun. In the manner of the Zionists writing their own declaration, Kemal had edited the terms of his appointment: his precise charge was left deliberately vague so that it would read as inspector of Anatolia as a whole. But something much greater than an inspector, with however ample powers, strode with stolid dignity towards the shore, taking care not to trip on the creaking woodwork. The first great individual was emerging from the murk of war into the Middle East.

The war, like an altar, had not only claimed victims, but made them anonymous. Names blared from newspaper headlines, but they were faceless names. Wax statues were made for museums, stone statues for squares, but they would captivate few. Joffre and Foch, Jellicoe and Hague, Ludendorff and Samsonov, Allenby and Liman von Sanders, these uniformed figures rose from a Vimy Ridge of corpses, similarly garbed. In the war too much had moved at once; each event had meshed like one bloodstained cogwheel in a Piranesi prison of torturing machines; no individual could believe that his quirks of character controlled or even influenced events. No one dared name one single cause for Allied victory, or German defeat. No one victor could be acclaimed. Lord Kitchener, whose stern finger and huge mustache had summoned English civilians to the front by the hundred thousand, had been an individual of pop art dimensions, reassuring as some ancient god. Thanks to a reputation won in Sudan and South Africa he had been summoned to lead an empire in arms. But the awesome individual had sunk beneath the waves of 1916 and a bereft Britain had mourned him with an un-Saxon despair. The two Englishmen who came nearest to being heroes had been men involved in side shows. One was Rupert Brooke, handsome minor poet; on April 23, 1919, he had died of blood poisoning on the way to Gallipoli. He had left a poem, *The Soldier,* which gave to millions the hope that war was noble still. Lawrence of Arabia, forger of his own exciting myth, persuaded millions more that battle in the desert was faster and more human than the slow killing in the Flanders mud. Other countries similarly discarded their generals. Lenin, who stopped the war, would be canonized by Russians, while in Italy a half-mad poet of cruelty, Gabriele D'Annunzio, would win fame for seizing Fiume when the war was over. Only in Germany did the figure of Hindenburg lower as a tribal totem in the rancor of defeat.

Mustafa Kemal had played an important role in the anonymous war. He was the one Ottoman commander who had not been defeated, who had resisted to the end. The chief figure in the heroic Gallipoli defense, he himself gave the praise to Mehmetchik, the ordinary Turkish soldier. On the Syrian front Kemal had prevented the Turkish defeat at the hands of Allenby from becoming a rout.

But only now, as he stood surveying post-war Samsun, exchanging greetings with welcoming officers, debating which Greek house to commandeer, was a man beginning to emerge who would will precise and idiosyncratic ends; not only will them, but set them in train. First he must secure the allegiance of the Anatolian notables; then control of the all-important telegraph system. Pretending to defend a legitimate government unable to defend itself, he must establish Turkish nationalism as a rallying force in order to rout the Greeks. More and more a dictator, he would control his country while he lived, and he had nearly twenty years to run. Less like a dictator of the usual cut, he would accept the need for an opposition and would leave an enduring prestige. From his tomb he would command, as a kind of honorary president, the succeeding generation.

Kemal had spent sixteen arduous years preparing, as a soldier, for an epic which would begin from this seedy port: an epic of resistance against the victors in the war, against the Greeks, latecomers in that war, against the last Sultan and the last Caliph, and above all, against the past.

Kemal's military years had stamped him physically, coarsening and hardening alike. His physique was unremarkable: a short, slight frame had grown sturdier with middle age. His head and his hands were what no one who saw him forgot: they were emblems of a genius at once intense and shallow. The shape of his skull, being eminently unclassical, was itself a rebuttal of the Greek pretension to his land. Hard features—a great outward jutting nose, high Asian cheekbones, merciless and disdainful lips— were subdued by eyes that held every emotion, every knowledge, save warmth or love. Neither God, man nor woman had held these eyes in dependent sway. Arctic, the eyes flashed when he spoke, as he often did, of the Turks. His sentence—"There is nothing better than to be a Turk"—

would be inscribed on monuments. But the same eyes could look on the deaths of countless Turks with the calm of a Napoleon, but without, behind the eyes, the least flame of personal bravado, only an icy dedication to a national goal fused so completely with his ego that no join marks showed: he worshiped Turkey, and Turkey was himself. His hands were a counterpoint, being long, slim and womanlike. They had held greedily to him, they would hold, women and boys in momentary possession, objects to be subjected or enjoyed, not loved or respected. Kemal's complexion hinted what the neat uniform and clean underwear concealed: a liver slowly hardened by the one appeasement of too taut a nature, and a fancied palliative to chronic constipation. Sultan-Caliph, Allied statesman, Greek general, frenzied bigot, would not kill this man, but alcohol would.

The townscape backing from the sea consorted with the man.

Samsun in no way echoed the mosque-swirling skyline of Stamboul, or the elegant Pera hotels frequented by those Ottomans who spoke French and by the Levantines and Europeans who made money from the sickness of the state. Even in defeat the Bosphorus was as bustling as Venice's Grand Canal; its palaces, some marble, some wood, were built like Venice's from the proceeds of foreign ventures. Low-lying Samsun served the dour plateau, and served it ill. It reflected the Ottoman neglect of basic Turkey. It had no proper harbor facilities; only wooden jetties such as the one from which Kemal had disembarked. Yet the town had a past. As Amisus, it had been founded by Greeks from Miletus and replenished in the fifth century B.C. with settlers from Athens. It was the gateway to the Euxine region which the Greeks knew as Pontus, from one of their words for "sea"; a region of umbrageous coastal plains backed by harsh mountains enclosing fertile valleys. In Samsun and its neighborhood lived a substantial Greek minority; a few middle-class Samsun Greeks owned solid houses with such luxuries as bathtubs and mosquito nets. Kemal chose one of these as his temporary home. In so doing he condemned it to a museum future.

Behind Samsun rose Anatolia proper, named from a Greek word meaning "East." To the Greeks the great earth mass climbing from their sunlit islands and Aegean promontories was the source, in Persia and inner Asia, of their most dangerous foes, in the times of Xerxes as in the times of the Turks. The Ottomans, adapting the Greek name, called the plateau Anadolu; for an empire whose wealth was built on conquest more than husbandry or trade, it was a reservoir of soldiers. Once the Ottomans had crossed into the Balkans, the sultans abandoned their Anatolian capital of Bursa to rule, first, from Adrianople, and then with greater pleasure from Constantinople. They had come to despise the men of the plateau as village bumpkins; they gave them no share in the running of their state. The powerful Janissary corps had been recruited from Christian boys given as a levy to the Sultan and raised for the service of Islam. None were Turks. The later rulers of the empire, from Sultan to functionary, were Ottomans; their blood derived largely from the Balkans and their language was overlaid with foreign loans.

Anatolia was hardly better known to Kemal than to other Ottoman leaders. He had traveled through it on his way to Syria; he had withdrawn towards its southern borders as the Allies and the Arabs advanced northwards to Aleppo. As geography it was all but unknowable, being a vast upland terrain of some forty thousand villages, each isolated from the rest by mountain and capricious river, by plains burnt up in summer or snow-deep in winter. In other Middle Eastern countries the mountains followed some identifiable pattern. The Lebanon and Anti-Lebanon ran like two high mounds with the trench of the Bekaa Valley in between; in Egypt the Nile had forced its way to the sea through eroded cliffs, only a few hundred feet high, and in so doing had given Egypt a highway, not only water. But the Anatolian mountains rolled and rumbled in a tangled mass through which the scant roads had to twist and turn, climb and sink, in a pattern which could be called drunken were alcohol not taboo to their dour inhabitants. Some features stood out. The Taurus Mountains formed a high wall to the south. In central Anatolia a desolate plain was a sump with large lakes; this centered on Ankara, the Galatian capital in which the Emperor Augustus had built a temple to himself, and to whose people St. Paul had written an epistle. In the West the valleys tended to run towards the Aegean and the setting sun; some, like the Menderes, were apt for agriculture, while others were unusable ravines with bosky sides. But even in the West, piled up, haphazard mountains could cut off whole provinces from easy access except by sea. To the east the country's only pattern was repeating strangeness. The weird fairy chimneys of Göreme had been whirled from crumbling tufa by fierce upland gales, then carved into churches by Cappadocian hermits. In another vast area sulphur made a lunar bleakness. In yet another, excessive calcium in flowing water made a landscape of meringue-white stalactites. These were the places that stood out, the places to intrigue the traveler or tourist. Most of the villages in the great quadrilateral bounded by the Greek sea in the west, the Black Sea in the north, Persia in the east and the beginnings of the Arab deserts to the dusty south, were marked only by poverty. The common building material was mud brick, which in summer gave better insulation than stone, while it sweated less in winter; but mud roofs had to be flattened with huge rollers, and they leaked. The diet was rigorously austere, related to the grain culture of the valleys, reaped by hand-sickle as in Hittite times. Tough, tenacious, loyal, the villagers were also superstitious, suspicious of authority, out of touch with the world and conservatively sure that men outranked women as Muslims outranked members of other faiths. The Anatolians lacked national sense. Asked what he was, a *köylü,* or villager, would give a one-word answer: "Muslim." Islam, with its colorful sects, including the skirted dervishes who wheeled in mystic dance, was the chief emotional force in their slow-moving minds; and next to Islam, their extended family groups whose all-male deliberations gave some approximation of democracy to their village decisions.

Kemal was no villager and in no clear sense a Turk. His biographer, Lord Kinross, has called him a Macedonian, a term which bound "Moslem or Christian or Jew, Turk, Greek, Slav, Vlach or Albanian" in a hardened vigor. (The term could also describe the stock of Egypt's then ruling dynasty.) But in Kemal's youth the term had to be bisected by an all-important divide: on one side stood those who felt themselves linked to the Ottoman Empire, on the other those who felt fettered by it. Kemal's parents were loyal Ottomans; his father, a failed minor official, was hampered in his efforts to start a timber business by the activities of anti-Ottoman guerrillas. Kemal's mother, Zübeyde, came from the lake country to the west of Salonika, on the fringes of Albania; but her ancestors, she claimed, had migrated from Anatolia after the first Ottoman conquests. Her son liked to believe that he was related to the Yuruks, Turkish-speaking nomads still wandering the pine-clad slopes of the Taurus range; the Yuruks had the same fair coloring, often the same gray-blue eyes which he had inherited from Zübeyde. Like the Anatolians, and unlike her anti-clerical husband, Zübeyde was a pious Muslim and wanted her son to become a man of religion, either a reciter of the Koran, or a *hoja,* doubling as clergyman and teacher.

However slight Kemal's links with Anatolia, he was the first Ottoman to base his policy on the peasants and their rough Asian homeland.

"As long as the peasant is not master of the country, there can be no real progress in Turkey."

Kemal had framed this sentiment when, six years earlier, he had been military attaché in Bulgaria, King Ferdinand's kingdom.

"One day in Sofia he was sitting in a fashionable cafe at the hour of the *thé dansant,* listening to the orchestra, when a Bulgarian, wearing peasant clothes, came in and sat down at the next table. He called several times for the waiter, who first disregarded him and then refused to serve him. Finally the proprietor told him to leave. The peasant refused, saying, 'How dare you throw me out of this place? Bulgaria lives by my labour. Bulgaria is defended by my rifle.' A policeman was called, who took his side, and the peasant was served with tea and cakes, for which he was well able to pay."[1]

The incident, occurring as it did in a country recently an Ottoman province, inspired Kemal. Bulgaria was a country of the fringe. At the railway station of Sofia, its Ruritanian capital, Herzl had seen the waiting Jews, eyes alight for the Promised Land. Its best-known gift to the West was a

---

[1] Lord Kinross, *Atatürk* (London: 1964), p. 63.

slang word for sodomite, derived from the medieval belief that the Bulgarians, under the influence of a gnostic heresy, practiced unusual sins. Dividing Turk from Slav, the Bulgaria of 1913 was also on the fringe of Europe's *belle époque.*

Enraptured with independence, the Bulgarians had rushed to make things new. They had torn down the Ottoman city with its tortuous, intestinal lanes and had created as Herzl had dreamed of doing for the Jews, a Western-style capital, complete with broad avenues, an opera, cafés, concerts, and a Royal Guard in splendid uniforms whose officers kissed the hands of elegant women in drawing rooms where politics and the tango mixed.

It would be easy to sneer at Kemal for falling in love with Western civilization seen in a distorting mirror. It would also be idle. Genius often glimpses what it needs to see through broken glass. Keats knew more of Homer, through Chapman's rough translation, than many a pedant who knew everything about Greek verbs and the digamma. From Sofia Kemal inferred what Western civilization had to offer, and he liked it. In setting Bulgaria as a model he was being more practical than Abdul Hamid, who had half loved Prussia, or Khedive Ismail, who had wholly loved France. In admiring the way in which a despised province of his own empire had changed course, he was taking the first psychic step to a radical change, and a change which Bulgaria's example proved to be practicable.

In exalting the peasant in the abstract, the ambitious and self-willed Kemal never thought of giving power to peasants in the unwashed flesh. (He had joined the Army as much for the opportunities it gave to climb as to serve.) His affirmation of the peasant was symbolic. Needing something to set against the effendi minority—the suave, often crooked gentleman of Constantinople—he affirmed the majority. By devaluing and belittling the ruling minority he could raise himself on peasant shoulders to a position of power for himself and his vision. This Westernizing vision was, in truth, exactly the opposite of what the Anatolian peasants wanted. To them, Islam was all-important, the Sultan-Caliph a symbol as precious as the Pope to many Catholics. Kemal, on the contrary, saw the Sultan-Caliph as a degenerate traitor and Islam itself as the net which had enmeshed the Turkish people on their journey West and dragged them, to their detriment, into the cause of the Semitic East. Like Rousseau, who taught that men must be forced to be free, Kemal believed that the Anatolians would find their true fulfillment in being deprived of all that they held most dear. He would use prison and the gallows to make his peasants what he wanted them to be: sturdy, independent and dressed in Western clothes. But first he needed them, their minds unfazed by religious doubt, to fight his battles. In asking a Turk to fight, few had ever asked in vain. In asking the Anatolians to fight the Greeks, Kemal evoked a dogged force that was to astound the world.

Chapter 2

KEMAL's fight was not only against Greeks and their "Great Idea." There were other fronts: against a sultan prepared to sacrifice anything so as to keep Constantinople; against the British and French Allies who had fought the Ottoman Empire to defeat and who had sanctioned the Greek invasion; against Italians installed in Antalya as well as Rhodes; against Armenians seeking to carve a state from eastern Anatolia under the shadowy patronage of the United States; not least against those Turks who either failed to understand Kemal's intentions, or, understanding, rejected them.

But he had soon discovered what he had hoped to find—an Anatolia seething with resentment against the infidels, and in particular against the Greeks, who had been insubordinate subjects for a century and were now threatening to be masters. Tales of insult and atrocity in occupied Smyrna helped stoke the fires.

On July 23 the first of two Nationalist congresses was held at Erzerum in the grim east of Anatolia, not far from the mountain on which Noah's Ark had come to land. Ararat's elephantine hulk, shrouded in clouds, marked the frontier with a Russia as war-torn and menaced as Turkey herself.

The congress entitled itself "The Association for the Defense of the Rights of Eastern Anatolia"; Kemal, dominating it from the first, was elected its chairman. A more important congress, and a further manifestation of popular resistance, was held on September 4 at Sivas, three hundred miles further west. In once again electing Kemal to be its chairman, the congress showed its only unanimity. Otherwise various ideas swirled amidst the sometimes panicky tobacco fumes of the assembled notables. The idea was even canvassed of asking the U.S. to assume a mandate for Anatolia. President Wilson had captivated public opinion with the idealism of his Fourteen Points, and his country had not yet retired into its two decades of isolation. But for all its incoherence the congress helped to crystallize opinion towards the regime in Constantinople. Anatolia remained loyal to the Sultan, not for any qualities in himself, but for the resonance of his title. A distinction was made between the Sultan and his government. On September 10 Kemal denounced, in a telegram, the government for treason; on the next day the Anatolian representatives issued a collective denunciation of every member of the government, excepting the Sultan himself. To the Sultan the Army in Anatolia cabled its loyalty.

Mehemet VI might have thought it expedient to rally to the Nationalists even now; he was indeed to claim in later years that he had shared the secret of Kemal's departure for Samsun, having instructed him to save the heart of Turkey. But he was too weak for an athletic leap of faith; Anatolia was an area of barbarism and Constantinople held his palace. But as a result of Nationalist protestations, relations between Constantinople and Anatolia for a while improved. On October 1 the Sultan changed Grand Vizirs, substituting for his despised brother-in-law, Damad Ferid Pasha, a man with some sympathies for Kemal.[1] As a result of negotiations between the two sides at Amasya, new elections were held. These returned a parliament to Constantinople dominated by supporters of Kemal. They at once voted to promulgate the "National Pact." Fruit of the Erzerum and Sivas congresses, this affirmed that Turkey should be free and independent while the non-Turkish areas of the empire should be given the right to self-determination.

The Allied Control Commission, established in Constantinople, now blundered. Either underestimating the extent to which the new parliament represented Turkish opinion, or regarding Turkish opinion as of little import, they forced the Sultan to dismiss his new Vizir in favor of his Minister of the Navy, a man who could be relied upon for compliance. On March 16, 1920, in a policy echoing what had been practiced in Egypt the previous year, the British occupied the purely Turkish quarters of Constantinople and arrested 150 nationalists for deportation. The Turkish Nationalists, like Saad Zaghlul, were exiled to Malta.

The Turkish parliament reacted with spirit. On March 18 it first passed a unanimous motion condemning the arrest of some of its members, and then prorogued itself *sine die*. Its death day was fixed by the Sultan: on April 11 he dissolved what proved to be the last parliament to sit in Constantinople—or Istanbul, the colloquial name by which the demoted city would in future be known.

For Ankara, in the heart of Anatolia, was now the de facto capital of independent Turkey. Kemal had chosen it for its convenient position on the railway linking Constantinople with the South. He had stayed there when the parliament had met in Constantinople; he and his entourage had taken over an agricultural school. Outside, the view was idyllic, since the school stood in a thick cluster of acacias and old beeches. But inside, one of the patriots who had joined Kemal wrote, "it was the dirtiest place I have ever been in. It evidently had not been cleaned for a very long time, for the school had been closed down on account of the revolution, and it

[1] Ali Riza Pasha.

smelt of every possible accumulation of dust and dirt." Typical of the new situation in Turkey, the follower who wrote these words was a woman, Halidé Edib; she was to become a corporal in the Turkish Army.

Kemal had been waiting for just such an Allied blunder. Immediately after the parliament prorogued itself, he announced elections to a new National Assembly to meet in Ankara, a Turkish city under Turkish control.

The elected delegates, the Grand National Assembly, met on April 23 in a most ungrand and makeshift chamber. But they saw themselves as representing a people still loyal to its Sultan; they attributed his moves against the elected parliament as being made against his will, under Allied duress. But Mehemet VI lacked the wisdom to behave ambiguously. He, not Kemal, took the clear measures which forced a break: a break which few Anatolians would have made of themselves.

In his first move he brought back his brother-in-law as Vizir. In his next move, he instructed the religious authorities to issue, the week before the Grand Assembly convened, a *fetva* declaring the Nationalists to be rebels whom it was permissible to kill. This *fetva* was no mumbled prayer. "Disciplinary forces" were recruited hastily to give it effect and hunt down the rebels. On May 11 Kemal and the other Nationalist leaders were solemnly sentenced to death as traitors.

In the summer of 1920 the people of Anatolia were on an emotional seesaw. In ten years their certainties had crashed in undeniable defeat. They approved of Kemal's record as a leader in war and they agreed with his policy of liberating the country from its foreign invaders. The Nationalists in Ankara appointed their own Council of Ministers and on May 19 the Assembly denounced the Grand Vizir as a traitor, just as he had denounced Kemal. The Mufti of Ankara issued a counter-*fetva* to the one from Constantinople: it declared that no decree issued under infidel duress was valid.

But at the same time Mehemet VI still carried authority with the conservative. For six centuries a sultan from the Ottoman house had been their Padishah, protecting them against the infidels and upholding in his person the sacred law revealed to the Prophet Muhammad. The Constantinople *fetva* carried weight. In many parts of Anatolia there were demonstrations against the Nationalists; whole regions were either loyal to Constantinople or affiliated to some local war lord.

Again the Allies helped unwittingly, the Nationalist cause. By June 1920, after tortuous sessions of bargaining and as many sessions of heavy eating and drinking in delectable resorts, the representatives of Britain and France had formulated terms of peace, which they now presented to the Sultan's government. The Sultan's men had a month to consider them; a brief glance was enough to show how draconian these terms were. The only possession the Sultan could retain in Europe was the imperial city with a minuscule hinterland—and this only because the Allies disapproved of the Bolshevik Russians even more than they disapproved of the Turks. The Straits were to be under international control. The Sultan lost all his Arab possessions, but not to the Arabs. Old King Hussein was to be conceded the Kingdom of the Hejaz, but Syria and Lebanon were to be mandates of France, Iraq and Palestine to be mandates of Britain. Britain thus gained control of the land bridge to India as well as the approaches to the Suez Canal, while France wrested Syria from Hussein's son Feisal. Greece would administer Smyrna and its hinterland, until, after five years, there would be a plebescite. Italy would get Rhodes and the Dodecanese. An independent Armenia, comprising four eastern Anatolian governorates, would have its final frontiers fixed by the U. S. President.

Even the feeble Sultan could see that these terms were savage. He protested.

But the Allied severity sprang from a mixture of vainglory and weakness. Britain and France were in a difficult position. To enforce the treaty against Turkish opposition would require Western troops on an enormous scale; and while Britain and France were exhausted from the war, the U.S. was in no mood for a prolonged overseas adventure. Lloyd George believed he had a cheap remedy if the Turks tried procrastination: the Greeks should be encouraged to advance inland from Smyrna. This they did with some verve. On July 9 they captured Bursa; built at the foot of Bithynian Mount Olympus, the beautiful first capital of the Ottomans controlled the northern ledge of Anatolia. On July 25 they captured Adrianople; this second Ottoman capital controlled the last piece of Thrace in Turkish hands. On August 10, in the third and last Ottoman capital, the Constantinople government caved in and put its Arabic signature to the terms of the Treaty of Sèvres.

In rejecting the terms out of hand, the Nationalists not only had the moral support of all Turks (including in their hearts most members of the Sultan's government); they had the practical and moral support of a significant new ally, the Soviet Union. As early as 1917 the Soviet regime had shown its repudiation of the past when it published the secret wartime agreements under which the Allies (including czarist Russia) had undertaken to carve up the Middle East on old-fashioned imperial lines. Since then the Czar's allies had intervened all over the place in attempts to reverse the Revolution. The Russian leaders now condemned the terms of the Treaty of Sèvres and on August 14 diplomatic relations were established between Kemal's government in Ankara and Lenin's in Moscow. Russian supplies, shipped through the Black Sea port of Trabzon, began arriving in September and would play a vital role in the coming two years of struggle. Russian diplomatic support was equally useful to Kemal, particularly because it helped to close a dangerous second front in the East. An Armenian republic under American auspices did not suit the Soviets. After some delays and several misunderstandings a deal between

Kemal and the most realistic Bolshevik—a young Georgian named Joseph Stalin—fixed the frontiers between the U.S.S.R. and Turkey on the same line as the old borders between Sultan and Czar. An area of the Caucasus would become the Armenian Soviet Socialist Republic with its capital at Yerevan.

As a gesture of good will to the Russians, Kemal for some years allowed an authorized Communist Party to function in Turkey; at the same time, unallowed, a genuine party existed underground. Neither the authorized or unauthorized Turkish Communist Party won much support from the Anatolians, who found even Kemal's reforms impiously radical. Kemal's authoritarian temperament never long tolerated other people's opinions, and the Marxist view of history conflicted with his own. When the Communists had served their turn, they would be ruthlessly outlawed.

The struggle between Greeks and Turks became increasingly tinged with a religious dye. This not only militated against Communist ideas but ran counter to the policy of the Greek liberal who had initiated the invasion and the Turk who resisted it. Venizelos was a Hellenist who looked back to the secular glories of fourth-century Athens and their missionary, Alexander of Macedon. But in a reversal typical of modern Greek history Venizelos had been swept from power in 1920. The liberal young King Alexander had been bitten by a pet monkey and despite the transit of the miraculous ikon of Tenos, died. Confident of his popularity with the Greek masses, Venizelos decided to use a plebescite to get rid of the German royal family whose head, the deposed King Constantine, had pressed for his pro-German neutrality throughout the war. But in the ensuing vote, the Greeks rejected Venizelos and Constantine returned from exile with a new version of The Great Idea. The Church, with the Army, the monarchy's chief bulwark, had no liking for the Hellas of paganism. The "Greece of Christian Greeks" had risen on the embers of the Olympian pantheon and through Constantine the Great had dominated the Byzantine Empire. This Christian Empire had included Anatolia and had had its capital at Constantinople; Greece itself, the peninsula and islands, had been comparatively unimportant. The Greeks now invading western Anatolia saw themselves not as the heirs of the skeptical philosophers of the Aegean but as the champions of the monks who had carved the Cappadocian rock churches and the brocaded priests who had said the Eucharist in St. Sophia until cut down by the victorious Turks.

As usually happens when religion involves itself in war, both sides grew crueller. Turkish villages were sacked, Turks of both sexes were murdered, simply for belonging to Islam, the religion which had laid Byzantium low. On the Turkish side defenders of Islam developed a fighting fervor which Kemal, himself a non-believer, was to exploit.

And Kemal needed to exploit everything and everyone. For the initial advantage lay with the Greeks, whose soldiers were better armed and trained than Kemal's hastily mustered volunteers. Minor Turkish successes were offset by major Greek breakthroughs. In the spring of 1921 a Greek offensive captured Eskişehir, lost it to Kemal's wartime comrade, Ismet, later surnamed Inönü from a battle in the campaign, and then took it back in July along with two other key junctions in the railway system. Their guns pushed ahead and were audible in Ankara.

Up till now Kemal had ruled as the dominant personality in a new, rather amateur democracy. Though his temperament was always that of a soldier who prefers to give orders rather than to discuss them, he had had to rule through a National Assembly. The closeness of the Greeks to Ankara gave him the excuse to demand absolute powers for ninety days. In one form or another he was to keep these powers for the rest of his life. He used them to astonishing effect in the crisis of 1922. All Anatolia was mobilized in a "people's war." For the first time women entered the struggle, not so much as soldiers, though there were a few Amazons like Halidé Edib, but as the drivers of the oxcarts which brought food and shells at a creaking rate of three miles an hour through the labyrinthine routes of the mountainous upland.

The shells were used in a decisive battle on the Sakkariya River, the one natural barrier between the Greeks, with their Aegean bases, and Ankara. The Greeks did not plan to rule permanently so un-Mediterranean a landscape, so far inland. But the Greek King and his advisers believed that if the Turks were compelled to move their rebel government to Sivas or Erzerum in the East, two purposes would be served: the Nationalists would be discredited to the advantage of the weakling government in Constantinople; the Turks would be driven into the regions with which the Greeks felt they should be identified, the impoverished plains and valleys of the plateau; the coastlines which they had long ago taken from the Greeks would be Greek again.

Sakkariya was arguably the longest pitched battle in recorded history. From August 23 to September 13 exhausted bodies and tortured spirits fought through a pitiless geography where the grass and flowers of spring had been scorched to a drought-pale cover. Thousands of men on both sides perished in a struggle which sputtered minute by minute, hillock by hillock, until at last Greek élan collapsed against the tenacity which was the speciality of the Turkish soldier. The battle was not, in a formal sense, a victory for the Turks, nor a rout for the Greeks. Both sides claimed that divine help had aided them. While Athenian churches chanted Te Deums, the National Assembly in Ankara conferred the ancient title of Gazi—or Conqueror of Infidels—on Kemal.

But the drawn fight was decisive for Turkey. Anything less than a breakthrough to Ankara was a strategic defeat for the Greeks, while anything less than a defeat was a victory for the Turks. The Turks had gained time and prestige to prepare their real victory in the coming year.

Kemal's last and greatest battle—the first successful Turkish offensive in twelve years of grueling defensive actions—was fought through fifteen days of summer, 1922. The year after the Greeks had been held on the Sakkariya had been spent in consolidation. The Italians had already made terms which left them with Rhodes and the Dodecanese but denied them any claims to Anatolia. Persia had recognized the Nationalists, which not only strengthened the eastern frontier but weakened the position of the now frightened Sultan. The borders with Georgia and Azerbaijan, as well as those with Armenia, had now been fixed. And as a good omen in early August, Enver, Pasha of so many disasters, was killed in Turkistan by Soviet troops; he had made one last mad gesture symbolic of the difference between his firebrand pan-Turkish and Kemal's cautious acceptance of limited goals.

Kemal's objective was now expressed in the simple battle order with which he opened the battle of Dumlupinar: "Soldiers! Your goal is the Mediterranean."

The preparations for reaching the coast were complex and cunning. They showed that one of Kemal's consistent talents was his ability to learn from his enemies as well as from experience. Just as he had inferred a whole concept of Western civilization from Bulgaria, so he inferred a whole strategy of victory from General Allenby, his wartime adversary on the Arab front. In Palestine the British general had undertaken complicated ruses to make the Turks expect an attack from west to east across the Jordan; false orders, false signs, all convinced the Turks that they had nothing to fear from the coastal plain, the real zone of Allenby's attack.

Kemal applied the lesson against the army of King Constantine, spread as it was over a three-hundred-mile front from the Sea of Marmara in the north to the Menderes Valley in the south. Kemal's aim was to advance as quickly as possible by the shortest possible route, from Afyon to Smyrna. He disguised his intentions with Allenbyesque deceit: movements towards Bursa, dust raised towards Eskişehir, while under cover of night the mass of his forces crept towards a complacent Afyon. Greek officers were dancing to within minutes of the Turkish attack. Neither foolish nor cowardly, the Greeks had reason to trust in triple lines of defense based on the rugged geological outcrops typical of eccentric Anatolia. Only total disregard of casualties, a holocaust of Mehmetchiks willingly pouring their blood on the thirsty earth of summer, enabled all the positions to be seized. The Greeks broke. With greater speed than the Turks, who were tied to oxcarts and camels, they panicked towards the sea, using spare hours to burn and massacre as they fled.

By September 11 Smyrna and Bursa were in Turkish hands, Kemal, who had not touched liquor since the offensive began, was on the Aegean waterfront soberly confronting the battleships which first in Constantinople and now here in Smyrna symbolized the real power behind the enemy. But those who controlled the guns of Lloyd George did not fire them; they prudently recognized an accomplished fact, that Anatolia was in Turkish hands. The Greeks sailed back to Greece, whence the King had once more fled and where a revolutionary tribunal would sentence a number of his generals and ministers to death by shooting.

Chapter 3

BY the end of 1923 Turkish ability to reject the humiliation of Sèvres was attested, after much effort, in a new treaty signed at Lausanne. The treaty's gestation and delivery were those of an awkward child. At the start of the nine months of negotiation the Allies had been represented by Lord Curzon, who had been Viceroy of India at the early age of thirty-nine and now treated the Turks as if they were unruly sepoys. The Turks were led by Ismet, who fought patiently and stubbornly for Kemal's limited goals. Kemal was adamant that the Capitulations—the privileged positions held by foreign economic interests in Turkey—should be abolished forever. At the same time, in accord with his conception of a Turkish nation-state based on Anatolia, he conceded the loss of the Arab provinces. For some time Ismet struggled to regain the city of Mosul in northern Iraq, arguing that it was Kurdish and therefore Turkish. This argument was refuted by Curzon, who knew the East better than Ismet; the British Foreign Secretary pointed out that Mosul was an Arab town surrounded by territory in which Turkish-speakers were a small minority; the more numerous Kurds, though certainly not Arabs, were equally certainly not Turks. Turkey regained the two Aegean islands, Tenedos and Imbros, which guarded the entrance to the Dardanelles. Otherwise the islands of the eastern Mediterranean went to Greece, with the exception of Cyprus, which stayed with Britain, and the Dodecanese, which were to remain Italian until the end of World War II. The problem of the Greek minority in Anatolia (the ostensible reason for Kemal's original landing in Samsun) was solved with a brutality which optimists defended as surgical. The Turks still living in Greece and the Greek islands would be exchanged for the Greeks in Anatolia. The exchange was almost total, though some Turks remained in northern Greece and some Greeks remained in Constantinople. But the Treaty of Lausanne finally ended what had been the glory as well as the weakness of the Ottoman Empire: the coexistence of different nations under one rooftree. The talents of the Greeks were lost to the new Turkish state. They were not to prove easy to replace.

Unthreatened by Allied guns or Greek invaders, Kemal was now free to initiate a series of radical reforms such as no individual in history had accomplished before. In unrivaled paradox the victor over the West was preparing to lift his people from one cultural track on to another, a track leading West, the very track of his defeated enemies. The crane which lifted the engine, or oxcart, was Kemal's egoistic will.

Since the will is the central mystery of Mustafa Kemal, it is worth examining it, in so far as mysteries may be examined, through the eyes of the most sensitive person in his entourage, and the most literate: the woman-corporal Halidé Edib. She had been with him at the time the Turks took over Smyrna. In an unguarded moment he had said that anyone who opposed him would now be lynched. "When the struggle ends, it will be dull; we must find some other excitement, Hanim Effendi." Halidé had then reflected: "These words are the key to his temperament. There must be something doing; he must be on the stage, a unique actor perpetually astonishing the world—a dangerous kind of actor, but dangerous for others and safe for himself. He must be exacting all that the spectators can give —fear, wonder, adoration."[1] He had been yet more explicit as to the content of his activism in a lonely Anatolian farm, before the battle of the Sakkariya. In table talk with a group which included Halidé he had revealed his life motive without concealment.[2]

" 'What I mean is this: I want every one to do as I wish and command.'

" 'Have they not done so already in everything that is fundamental and for the good of the Turkish cause?' "

"He swept my question aside and continued in the same brutally frank manner.

" 'I don't want any consideration, criticism, or advice. I will have only my own way. All shall do as I command.' "

The first person who must bow to this violent and now triumphant will was the last of the Sultans.

After defeating the Greeks, Kemal abolished, on November 1, the Sultanate. The situation was now a neat reversal of what had happened four decades earlier in Orabi's Alexandria. Then British warships had reimposed Towfik on Egypt; now, on November 17, another British warship took Mehemet VI, the last Ottoman Sultan, away from Turkey. His cousin, Abdul Mejid, was installed as Caliph only.

To Kemal the separation of mosque and state was a brief, tactical step; he hated the word Caliph no less than Sultan, since both stank of the East.

---

[1] *The Turkish Ordeal, Being the further memoirs of Halidé Edib* (London: John Murray, 1928), p. 355.
[2] Ibid., p. 188.

But millions of Muslims saw the separation as prompted by a genuine concern for religion; Kemal seemed a reformer substituting an Arch-bishop of Canterbury for a Caesar-Pope. Indian Muslims, deeply influenced by the Christian West through British rule, particularly welcomed the change; their spiritual attachment to Turkey was increased, they proclaimed, now that its Caliph was untrammeled by worldly power. In fact, a purely spiritual Caliph was alien to tradition, which posited a Caliphate combining religious and secular power. But Kemal was indifferent to theological concepts. On political grounds he had already decided to abolish the Caliphate at the opportune moment. He could not tolerate a rival focus of power, which is what the brief-lived Caliphate came to be. Despite the proclamation of a new Turkish Republic with Ankara as its capital and Kemal as its President, Anatolian loyalties were still in doubt. Some of Kemal's closest associates (the word "friend" hardly enters the Kemalist vocabulary) looked on the mild new Caliph with affection and respect; they saw in him a check on their autocratic leader.

Rupture with political Islam came in 1924. On March 3 the Caliphate was decreed to have ceased; Abdul Mejid and all members of the Ottoman royal family were banished from Turkish soil. Kemal attacked more than symbols; he worked to destroy the institutions which gave Islam life. The link between mosque and school—most Turks started their education in a *kuttab*, or Koranic school, being taught by a *hoja*, cleric as well as teacher —was formally severed. A new, all-Kemalist generation would be molded in secular schools; an *okol* (suspiciously like a French *école*) replaced the Arabic-named *medrese* of the past. Two other moves broke the economic power of Islam and its privileged position in the country's legal life. The Ministry of Religious Endowments (the Evkaf) was closed down and the large estates which it controlled were taken over by the state. A European civil code replaced the intricate corpus of law derived from the Koran and Islamic tradition.

Kemal had acted alone in these assaults on the Caliphate and Islam. His immense prestige carried his immediate entourage as well as those whose ears had heard the Greek guns thunder, and then withdraw. But in impoverished eastern Anatolia such actions were greeted with horror. Kemal seemed the Islamic equivalent of Antichrist. A Kurdish revolt was suppressed with carnage.

Yet true to his obsessive vision Kemal quickened the pace in 1925. Religious orders were disbanded; the monasteries (*tekkes*) which housed them were closed and the tombs (*turbes*) which often provided their focus were no longer to be honored as shrines. Kemal was now deliberately excising what gave the deepest meaning, often the only warmth, to the bare existences of the Anatolian peasants. In the miracles of their saints, in the feasts associated with their tombs, in the rhythmic movements of the dervish dances, a people who lived grimly and poorly amidst mud and cold had found moments of ecstasy. These were now denied them.

Kemal's moves against religion were deeply unpopular with the peasants, who persuaded themselves that Kemal himself was not responsible. Indeed, Kemal was careful not to avow the doctrinaire atheism of the Communist leaders of Russia. In front of his people he claimed that he believed in the essence of Islam and wished to extricate it from damaging accretions; to his intimates he admitted to being no more than an agnostic. But his dislike of religion was one of his strongest emotions. Even ten years later, when his reforms had been widely if not warmly accepted, the passion stayed with him. One midnight he and the Shah of Persia, in Turkey on a visit, arrived by train at a small town in western Anatolia. The platform was crowded with admirers hoping to greet the Father of the Turks on his brief stop. Kemal "opened the window, and scores of people tried to seize his hand, the Gazi looking quite pleased by this mark of his popularity. Then suddenly, his face became flushed with anger and snatching back his hand, he shouted in a terrible voice: 'How dare this so and so damned fellow try to touch my hand! He is, like all his kind, the enemy of the people, take him and destroy him.' " The eyewitness[3] saw a *hoja* throw his offending turban to the crowd—rather as a matador uses his cloak with an angry bull—and so escape a lynching, disappearing into the dark edges of the scene. The incident inspired yet another move against religion: from that day all *hojas,* as well as Jewish rabbis and Christian priests, were forbidden to wear religious garments outside mosque, synagogue or church. The dating system based on Muhammad's *hijra* from Mecca to Medina was abolished in favor of the European, or Christian, calendar, in the middle twenties. Sunday was also substituted for Friday as the weekly day of rest.

Having changed the dates by which they lived, Kemal determined to deluge every aspect of Turkish life with what he saw as a life-giving Western flood. No Ararat of the East must rise above a manscape cleansed of all that linked Turkey to Arabs or Indians. In his role as Westernizer Kemal far outdid such predecessors as Khedive Ismail. Ismail had carved boulevards through Cairo slums, had completed a Canal to link East with West, had invited a European Empress, had opened an Opera with *Rigoletto.* He had expected his people to gape and admire. He had not expected them to change their personal lives, any more than he had intended to change his own eating habits in the privacy of the harem. Kemal wished to leave no detail in his people's lives unchanged, even the most intimate. His burning vision scorched away humor. In a public speech he announced a dress reform to include the garment that more than any other had separated the believer from the infidel: the hat. "A civilized, interna-

[3] General Hassan Arfa, *Under Five Shahs* (London: John Murray, 1964), p. 250.

tional dress is worthy and appropriate for our nation, and we will wear it. Boots or shoes on our feet, trousers on our legs, shirt and tie, jacket and waistcoat—and of course, to complete these, a cover with a brim on our heads. I want to make this clear. This head-covering is called 'Hat'."

Kemal's nationalism differed strikingly from that of his contemporary, Mahatma Gandhi, who explicitly exalted traditional Indian dress along with many Indian attitudes found strange in the West. Kemal's nationalism was not prompted by love of what was. He loved the Turkish nation that he imagined and was disgusted by the nation that he saw. Eyes formed in Salonika and refocused in Sofia saw the Turks as backward. The plumage of backwardness were the garments identified with Turks: the baggy mountain trousers (useful for sitting on in damp houses, good for padding out in freezing weather) and the scarlet fez, a North African headdress introduced in another mood of modernization a century before.

Kemal knew that the brimmed European hat was unsuitable for prayer, since the believer's forehead should touch the ground in his prostrations. No matter. His people would wear the peaked cloth cap of the industrial workers of the West; if they wanted to pray they could turn the peak round backwards. Kemal himself sported a wide range of hats, ranging from top hat for opera to wide-brimmed panama against the sun.

In forcing his people into what was the uniform of the Depression—and Anatolians would wear it deep into the 1960s—Kemal showed how little he understood the essence of Western dress, which is not one particular style, but constant change.

The fez, or its supplanter the hat, partly covered the head; Kemal was to attack what went on inside the head with the same fervor. As Ottoman as the baggy trousers and the fez was the graceful right-to-left script seen from one end of Turkey to another, on public fountains, over mosques and shops, and on the documents of everyday life. In deciding to attack the Arabic script Kemal was on less flimsy ground than in attacking the fez. The Arabic alphabet had been developed for the language of the Koran, and it fitted Arabic well. It had letters for the distinctive Arabic consonants and the three heavy vowels; since the lighter vowels were not written, the script could be written with the speed of shorthand. But the same letters fitted Turkish less well. Some Arabic consonants did not exist in Turkish, while several important Turkish sounds had no Arabic equivalent. The Arabic script also had disadvantages when it came to printing. Most of its letters had an initial, medial and terminal form, which made typewriters large and costly. The learning of the Arabic script, research had shown, posed considerable difficulties to Turkish students; it was a factor in the overwhelming illiteracy of Anatolians. Armed with a blackboard, dressed in Western clothes, Kemal began to fulfill his mother's dream that he should become a teacher. But his lesson was a startling innovation: a Latin script which within a brief space would become obligatory.

Kemal was by no means satisfied with changing the letters in which Turkish was dressed; he determined to change its content, the living language, too. Under the sultans, Ottoman had developed into a strange convoluted bastard of a tongue—the word bastard is used with no pejorative sense, since it applies equally to all-embracing English; Ottoman grammar sometimes followed Arabic modes and sometimes Persian; nearly all its concept words were borrowed from Arabic or Persian. During his last years Kemal pushed more and more for a purified Turkish, drawing its vocabulary from the vigorous nomads who had arrived on their little horses from Central Asia.

The reform of the script and the language did indeed facilitate literacy; this rose from 10 to 40 per cent in the coming thirty years. It was also part of the Kemalist program of cutting the liana-like coils which linked Turkey to the East and which drew their strength from the Arabic Koran.

But it also proved a traumatic blow to a nation's consciousness, a blow without precedent or rival in the history of any other modern state. A generation was to grow up, reared on the Latin script and the new Turkish, to whom anything published before the 1920s was unintelligible without specialist study; it was as though first editions of Walt Whitman's poetry were literally unreadable to first-year Harvard students. Of course, the classics of Turkish literature could be, and were, transliterated into the new script, so that defenders of the change could argue that the incomprehensibility barrier applied only to inscriptions, such as are still found on the graceful fountains of the Ottoman period, or to manuscripts in learned institutions. But a more formidable barrier was involved. Through the deliberate avoidance of Ottoman terminology, through the replacement of Arabic and Persian words by words of Turanian root, the very language of the pre-Kemalist period, in whatever script it was written, soon became as obscure to a modern Turk as the language of Chaucer, or even *Beowulf*, to a modern American. This exclusion might have been no great tragedy if it put out of use the religious treatises and sophomoric political texts of the nineteenth-century reformers. But it excluded much better writings, and most ironically of all, those of Kemal himself. So rapid and progressive was the Turkification of the language that speeches made by Kemal in the 1920s required careful elucidation by students of the 1960s. It was as if, to cite an American parallel, Hemingway's *A Farewell to Arms* (1929) needed a detailed glossary to be understood by a student of the 1970s.

This rejection of the past was justified as a healthy shock for the Turkish mind, forcing it to reach towards science and sociology, not literature and theology as in the past. For the Turkish soul it represented the cutting of its deepest tap roots.

As a culmination to the process of modernization and divorce from the East (a process which included the prohibition of Eastern music, the trans-

lation of the Call to Prayer into Turkish and the substitution of an old Turkish word for Allah)[4] it was decided in 1934 to introduce the use of sur-
names. In the traditional East a man had been called by his given name
followed by that of his father; so that the new ruler of Egypt, the son of
Khedive Ismail, could be called Fuad Ismail. Sometimes, after the two
given names, an attributive designating a place would be added; thus the
revolutionary Jamal al-Din had been called al-Afghani, or "The Afghan."
Kemal now decreed that every Turkish family must adopt a surname. His
closest adviser, Ismet, took, as we have seen, Inönü, the name of a victory
in the war against the Greeks. On Kemal himself the National Assembly
solemnly bestowed a unique surname: Atatürk, or Father-Turk. If Kemal
had read Freud, he might have hesitated in adopting so plainly the awe of
a Nobodaddy; or on the other hand, he might not.

For whether he liked it or not, Atatürk was the successor to Abdul
Hamid and needed a new charisma, a new title, since he had destroyed
the old. Just as Lord Cromer and Harry Boyle formed a diptych of successful imperialism, Atatürk and Abdul Hamid form a diptych of resistance to foreign control.

Abdul Hamid had been the dogged if enfeebled upholder of the Ottoman ideal: an ideal generous in its acceptance of human plurality but
botched by its inability to translate intentions into acts. Atatürk fought vic-
toriously so that the Turkish people could survive in a Turkish homeland,
under their own rule. At the same time he surrendered most of what had
made the Turks distinctive in the past. "Father-Turk" exalted his people
but despised what they had so far achieved. "The Ottoman Empire,
whose heirs we were, had no value, no merit,"[5] he stated with a certainty
few historians would nowadays share. He had little use for the values
which Eastern society had traditionally honored, such as mercy, piety and,
above all, friendship. His associates perished on the scaffold from his anger
or jealousy, or in bitter exile. In the immediate aftermath of victory he
married Latife Hanim, a well-educated and gentle girl of better family
than his own. His treatment of her during the two and a half years before
they were separated was a mixture of modernity and coarseness. He insisted
that she appear unveiled when this was still by no means general; he displayed her to his friends, getting her to recite poetry by Victor Hugo or
Byron. She was shown little respect or consideration. Her presence did
not inhibit the wild fits of drinking which were to shorten his life.

He had exploited one Turkish talent, a traditional skill at war, to save

[4] All these reforms were to be tacitly abandoned after Atatürk's death. Allah would
remain the common word for God on Turkish lips; the Call to Prayer would be
chanted in accented Arabic; despite widespread study of Western music and the creation of a ballet and opera, the popular songs on Ankara Radio would still be in a
recognizably Eastern mode.

[5] Kinross, *Atatürk*, p. 366.

Anatolia, as a nation-state, from the fate of the rest of the Middle East. This salvation was purchased at a price. When imperial peoples lose their empires, they can become trivial and inward-looking. Turks detached themselves from the Middle East, which had been their arena for centuries. The great faith which Turks had traditionally championed could still have linked them to the outside world. Atatürk wanted no such links. When the Indians of 1923 began to revere a powerless Caliph as a source of spiritual authority, Kemal had responded by abolishing the Caliphate. Though he defended Islam from mosque pulpits as the last and most rational of the three great monotheistic faiths, Atatürk had little use for religion in his heart and excluded it from his private as from his public life.

But religion did not die; nor did it develop as it had done, and was to do, in Abduh's Egypt. It formed one pole in a mental schism.

At one extreme, men and women in the Turkish cities and towns adopted a mishmash of Western ideas with no roots in their past. The descendants of the Janissaries danced the fox trot in cafés-concerts; at Kavaklidere wine was manufactured by the grandchildren of Abdul Hamid's officials, and manufactured well. A shallow modernism and a Western orientation were as easy to assume as trousers and a hat. But in the hour of death or crisis they satisfied few.

The villages, where most Turks lived, were the other extreme. They discovered a pride of an order unforeseen by Atatürk. The villagers had once been despised by the scholars and effendis of the town as uncouth and undoctored in Islam. Now they in their turn could despise the townsfolk for their lack of religion. The villagers were hardly logical. With their contempt for the cities went a near-worship of Atatürk, whom they believed to have been a pious and abstemious warrior for their faith. Though it remained superstitious and fossilized, Turkish Islam gave the Turks a courageous solidarity which was vividly exemplified in the Korean War. Captured Turks did not betray their comrades; they tended their wounded with a tender sense of brotherhood that contrasted with the individualistic egoism of the West.

On November 10, 1938, Atatürk was to die of cirrhosis of the liver with no prayer on his lips. His last days had been passed in the ornate palace on the Bosphorus built by Abdul Hamid's father. After lying in state he was taken from Dolmabahçe to the tune of Chopin's Funeral March and borne on a black-draped train to Ankara, rebuilt in the style of the newer quarters of Berlin.

Nationalism, not the mysteries of Islam, was to comfort the mourning land: "There is nothing better than to be a Turk."

Yet this assurance did not, could not, answer the question facing those faithful to all such creeds:

What do you do with Nationalism—when you have stopped admiring yourselves?

BOOK SEVEN

The Anglo-Arab Twenties

But you may rely upon one thing—I'll never engage in creating kings again; it's too great a strain.

GERTRUDE BELL, *in a letter from Baghdad, July 8, 1921*

Chapter 1

In 1921 an altered Harry Boyle returned to an altered Cairo. With a German wife and a gray mustache Cromer's oriental secretary was now in Egypt as part of a gigantic apparatus with which Britain was probing her restive brown dominions, the swath of Arab states from Egypt in the West to Iraq in the East which, linked by Palestine and Trans-Jordan, she now controlled.

Britain had won the war but been weakened by it. Men formed under Queen Victoria—Lord Curzon, since 1919 the Foreign Secretary, and Lord Allenby, victor of Palestine and now High Commissioner in Cairo—were fumbling to shore up the empire in a world undermined by Soviet Communism in the East and Wilsonian idealism in the West. Men like Boyle were the empire's antennae. But the situation was one in which Boyle felt ill at ease, a ghost.

Britain was still obsessed by the Suez Canal, the lifeline of an empire on which the sun still did not set. To protect the approaches to the Canal, Britain had worked hard to get Palestine under her control. As the country astride the Canal, Egypt could not be given up. At the same time, the postwar world no longer took colonial rule for granted. The term "mandate" had been coined for territories acquired by Britain and France in the war; a tactful euphemism for colony, it also carried a sense of being temporary and open to scrutiny by the League of Nations. Egypt was neither a colony nor a mandate. She had been exploding against another status—that of a protectorate—since 1918. The men whom Boyle had known as personal friends were leading the clamor for independence. Was it madness, or was it betrayal?

His sadness was from the heart. For "Boyle of Cairo" was what Lawrence of Arabia only claimed to be: an Englishman who knew his particular manor to its last inch, its last nuance of dialect, and also loved it. Boyle never pretended that he could pass as a *beledi* Egyptian; but his fluent Turkish, learnt at his first consular post in Turkey, had enabled him to visit in disguise the back streets of khedivial Cairo. Uninterested in money or luxurious living, concerned deeply for Britain's abstract power, unvainglorious, possessed of a sense of humor, Boyle was a total contrast to the inward-looking Lawrence, the mirror-ascetic now employed, boastfully modest and icily erotic, at the Colonial Office in advising Winston Churchill, one of his admirers, on Arab affairs.

The sane, prosaic Boyle still put his thoughts on paper as he had done when he had been Enoch to Cromer's Lord.

"The immense majority of the Egyptian unofficial population—all those who possess a stake, no matter how small, in the continued peace and prosperity of the country—are sincerely in favour of the maintenance of British control."

This dogma could not be questioned. Like other Englishmen in similar situations it was an urgent psychological need to find proof that even if the educated Arabs opposed British rule—the city slickers, the ambitious lawyers, the venal pashas, the glib intellectuals—the ordinary Arab, whether blue-shirted fellah or nomad in agal and keffia, liked being governed by men like Boyle. The little people with whom he had rubbed shoulders on his nocturnal prowls, the wall-eyed proprietor of the tiny coffeeshop, the gigantic owner of the Turkish bath, these must share Boyle's regrets for Cromer, olympian paragon.

Like a journalist searching for a cabdriver to echo his judgments, Boyle sought for proof. People he no longer knew filled the Lloyd Loom chairs on Shepheard's verandah; they no longer recognized in the shabby Englishman an *éminence grise*. Of a sudden an old impulse surged back: to roam the dark lanes, to absorb again what he had named to his wife as "the smells and colours of the East"; the conventional phrase carried connotations he was too Victorian to discuss with women.

The fringe-land of Ezbekieh was the place for slumming. A public garden with canna lilies and caged birds replaced the dry-in-summer lake on whose floor Napoleon had long ago reviewed his troops. Shepheard's Hotel stood on the respectable side of the garden, as did Khedive Ismail's wooden Opera and the equestrian statue of Ibrahim Pasha. On the shady side to the east tangled a labyrinth of half-lit streets. Buildings in the Italianate style had slumped in fifty years of overuse. From peeling doorways of stuccoed stone stairwells climbed to the mysterious abodes of drug peddlars and magicians, agents for importing foreign goods or clinics for every imaginable disease. One pillared thoroughfare, Rue Clot Bey, ironically recalled the Frenchman who a century before had inaugurated the medical services of the Egyptian Army. Planned to facilitate the movement of troops from the station to the Citadel, Clot Bey had become the city's venereal artery. It was out of bounds to British troops; on those who defied the ban it conferred varieties of pox. The brothels were off the thoroughfare, mere hovels in alleys which staggered over what was left of the rubbish dumps which had fringed the Mameluke city. A jangle of cymbals, a plaintive flute, swirled with hashish fumes between close, hot walls. Rough doorways were stenciled with hands of Fatima, the good luck sign of the East, but here an indication of the piasters a customer would have to pay. In its hurly-burly the area also harbored respectable coffeeshops and cheap hotels which the fellahin patronized on their visits to town.

The patterns of the past—when he and Guiro had walked these lanes in Turkish dress—steered Boyle's steps past a strange half-world; a complex of Greek cafés; here Christian and Muslim, *frangi* and *beledi*, were joined by *zebeeb*, the Egyptian arak whose violence and milky appearance made it comparable to tiger's milk. Arguments were common. They would rise to the shrill crescendo of the Egyptian *dowshah*, the pantomime of battle which suddenly dies down to placation and forgiveness.

Boyle was roused from his reveries by a harsh cry. It came from a cul-de-sac. He strode towards it with the brisk steps of an Englishman—since Egyptians saunter, the commonest giveaway for those who would disguise themselves as natives. Boyle came upon a man in *gallabya* being beaten up by a gang in similar garb.

"Police! Police!" shouted the victim. "O 'Kroumer'! I am oppressed. Help me, O 'Kroumer'!"

At his mention of Cromer, one of the men struck the wretch harder. "Say: Help me, O Saad! You son of a dog—'Kroumer' is dead and Saad is in his seat."

Boyle had found his proof that the myth of Cromer was strong still, and golden.

Lord Cromer had survived for ten years after leaving Egypt. His departure had been hastened by psychosomatic disturbance. In the spring of 1907 he had, in Boyle's words at that time, developed "a nervous breakdown of the digestive organs which, though happily he had no organic complaint or hidden fiendishness of any sort (this is beyond doubt) has caused and does cause him daily attacks of such pain as to entirely prostrate him." Prospero felt physically sick when an inferior race showed a will of its own. The Patriotic Party, led by Mustafa Kamil, had launched a post-Dinshwai attack whose "insolence and vehemence exceed all bounds of reason and decency. You would not believe the language they use, even now, about the Lord in their papers." So Boyle at the time.

Cromer, back in England, used his formidable powers of will and mind to the end. He played a leading role in the fight against votes for women; in two masterly volumes he recorded his Egyptian stewardship;[1] and patriotic to his coffin, he had conducted the official inquiry into the Gallipoli fiasco, its strain hastening his death in 1917.

It was ironic that in his last Cairo speech he had praised the "Saad" now allegedly in his seat.

Allegedly: for the night-dressed bullies overstated. In the summer of 1921 Saad Zaghlul was between two exiles. Deported to Malta in 1919, he had soon been allowed to move to France, for he was an old man and the

[1] The Earl of Cromer, *Modern Egypt* (London: Macmillan, 1908).

Maltese water was notoriously hard to drink. In April 1921 (just after a Cairo Conference of which we shall hear more) he had returned to a delirious Egyptian welcome. But later in 1921, after the execution of sixteen "Zaghlulist" rioters by order of a British military court, he would be exiled on a Grand Tour of minor British dependencies—Aden, the Seychelles and Gibraltar, in that order—before being transferred, in 1923, again on the grounds of ill health, to a French spa.

Though he never possessed Cromer's unhampered power, Zaghlul embodied the aspirations and frustrations of the Egyptians as no one had done since Orabi. His hold on their loyalty and imagination was even stronger than that of the soldier who had flashed from his barracks like a meteor to fizzle out in bad generalship at Tel el-Kebir. Unbacked by bayonets, Zaghlul could inspire what Orabi had disappointed and what Cromer had disdained to consider: the love of the Egyptians. That the love was mixed with self-love made it no weaker. The Egyptians saw in Zaghlul one of themselves, and one who had spectacularly made good.

No impressive soldier like Orabi and no youthful dandy like Mustafa Kamil, Zaghlul was a gaunt elderly pasha, ganglingly dressed, whose most memorable features were a breadth of yellowish-brown face and narrow, almost Mongol eyes. Zaghlul was a civilian from the tassel of his large tarboosh (worn tipped to the back of his head in the manner of a peasant turban) to his café-polished shoes. He had the Egyptian townsman's love for earthy jokes, good food, gambling and sensual pleasures.

Yet behind the townsman who had learnt to speak French and to appreciate the good things of France was a man from an Egyptian village. To the rulers of Egypt, and to the ruled, Zaghlul would always remain a fellah. The Turco-Circassians saw few gradations in the men beneath them; a fellah pasha was a fellah still. The fellahin saw Zaghlul as a member of their rural squirearchy. His father had been *omdah,* or headman, of a delta village. His family enjoyed a considerable income from two hundred acres of fertile soil, sunlit and perennially watered. The Zaghlul house of earth brick and roughly painted woodwork had a reception room in which a hundred villagers could seat themselves on rough wooden settles and calico-covered chairs. The village children called the omdah's son a duffer, since he paid little attention to their games and songs. This was not because he was an intellectual. His apartness derived from an exceptional ambition and an acute awareness of possibility.

For Egypt was a layer cake in which each layer envied the one above it. The icing was the Khedive, or "Sultan" as the British had named him since the war; the Sultan wanted to be a genuine king, if not like George V of England, then perhaps like Alfonso XIII of Spain. The British "advisers" dreamed of knighthoods and New Year honors. Turco-Circassian pashas dreamed of getting rid of the British and taking their positions. Educated Egyptians dreamed of becoming pashas; Levantine lawyers, of becoming beys. The fellahin with land dreamed of becoming omdahs; sharecroppers dreamed of owning an acre.

By the time Zaghlul and his brother were children, clever omdahs had seen that social movement began with schooling. After the usual rudiments of education, Zaghlul enrolled at al-Azhar in the same year that Afghani arrived in Cairo. The young Zaghlul had the fleshly good looks, at once sensual and sensitive, which dry out early and later become hard to imagine as having existed. In his teens he was an inner member of the Abduh circle, one of the young men who asked Afghani and Abduh how to revitalise Islam. Abduh's answers impressed him: through the reform of justice and education, through the adaptation of tradition to modern needs. In 1880, still in his early twenties, he was appointed as Abduh's assistant on the Official Gazette. His salary was £8 a month. Like Abduh's other disciples, Zaghlul supported the Orabi revolution; with its collapse he was briefly jailed, and dismissed from his post.

For a young man whose major impetus was ambition the bump was traumatic. Ideals had burnt his fingers. He now turned his talents to making money. He learned French and practiced the law. He was soon earning £5,000 a year. Then, late for an Egyptian, at the age of forty, he turned his thoughts to marriage. Thoughts more than feelings. The woman he chose was the Prime Minister's daughter. Mustafa Pasha Fahmi, the Prime Minister, was one of the elegant, suave nonentities whom the British deferred to in public and in private derided. On Egypt he left, as was intended, little or no impress, though one penchant—"for fine shirts which he sent to England to be washed and ironed"[2]—is remembered. Rumor connected him with only one action of state. The tip of his little finger was missing. People said that it had been bitten off in his death agony by Khedive Ismail's inspector of finances, whom the loyal young Mustafa had undertaken to murder.[3]

Marriage to the Prime Minister's daughter represented an unprecedented triumph for the son of a village headman. Zaghlul had been counsellor at the native court of appeals since 1892; but aristocrats usually gave their daughters to other Turco-Circassians, not to fellahin, however meritorious.

The marriage probably germinated in the salon of a princess who loved surprises. Princess Nazli, the daughter of Khedive Ismail's younger brother,[4] invited le tout Caire—or everyone from Lord Cromer and Harry Boyle downwards—to her drawing room. Witty, beautiful, heterodox, irresponsible, we have already seen the Princess praising Orabi, though despising his lack of generalship, to Wilfrid Blunt. Such anarchic sentiments

[2] Afaf Lutfi al-Sayyid, *Egypt and Cromer, A Study in Anglo-Egyptian Relations* (London: John Murray, 1968).
[3] Ibid., p. 80.
[4] Mustafa Fazil.

annoyed her relations; they saw in Orabi the would-be feller of their family mustard tree. But Nazli did not care. She had a grudge against the family: her father had been done out of the lucrative succession when Ismail had bribed the Sultan to alter the law governing the Egyptian succession. Nazli discerned in the handsome, pushing lawyer with his command of French a potential leader; if also a troublemaker, so much the better! Later, when Cromer looked for "moderates" to promote against the extremer Nationalists, Nazli again pushed Zaghlul forward. Another member of the Abduh circle and Egypt's first male feminist[5] seconded Nazli in furthering the marriage. It was destined to be outstandingly successful. Safiya Zaghlul, twenty years younger than her husband, soon abandoned the role of daughter to the sophisticated lawyer for that of consoling mother. To the Egyptians, too, who identified themselves with her fellah husband, she was known simply as *Umm al-Misriyyin,* or Mother of the Egyptians. The couple were childless.

Zaghlul's prime coincided with the period when British power seemed as solid as the pyramid which a medieval Caliph had tried to dismember but left hardly marked. It seemed idle to challenge the empire that ruled a quarter of the planet; it was more sensible to cultivate the plants which could grow in the protection of such a windbreak: in particular, Law and Education. As a judge, Zaghlul showed himself incorruptible and eager to get to the nub of justice. Cromer approved such civilian virtues as the only ones appropriate to Egyptians. In 1906, the year of Dinshwai, the year before he retired, Cromer recommended Zaghlul to be Minister of Education. The job was frustrating since the Egyptian could not change an educational system under the effective control of his "adviser," a dour Scot named Dunlop convinced that Egyptians only required education to the level of clerkdom and that the medium of their instruction should be English. But one story illustrates how Zaghlul applied his shrewd integrity. Since Egypt still lacked a secular university, young men were sent to study abroad. Students intended for such missions were personally vetted by the Minister, who knew that many would-be scholars were more attracted by the Place Pigalle than the Sorbonne. One applicant with the right family connections seemed distinctly mature.

"Have you got married?"

"Yes, Pasha."

"What will you do about your wife, while you're absent in Europe?"

Big smile. "I've already taken care of that—I have divorced her."

The man had acted in accord with the letter, if not the spirit, of his religion. Nevertheless Zaghlul scratched his name from the list.

[5] Qasim Amin's *The Liberation of Women* argued that Muhammad had raised the position of women and that polygamy, necessary in the Prophet's lifetime in order to make up for Muslim husbands killed in battle, was in modern life unnecessary and bad. Amin still believed that the sexes were unequal, while vehemently defending the necessity of primary education for all Muslim women.

"Such a person cannot be entrusted with education."[6]

In 1913 Zaghlul resigned his post as Minister of Education to stand for election to a National Assembly authorized, after some deliberation, by the British, and intended as a safety valve; he was duly elected and then chosen as vice-president. The Assembly did not last long. It was closed— to the protests of a new generation of Egyptian Nationalists—under martial law.

The Great War revealed to the now elderly Zaghlul the extent to which nationalism was again a force among young Egyptians. Orabi's contemporaries had been stunned by his defeat; a new generation stirred by Mustafa Kamil were coming into their own. The Turkish victory at Gallipoli showed that the empire which had seemed all-powerful could be defeated. As the war drew to its end, as President Wilson proclaimed his Fourteen Points, as these were echoed in statements issued by Britain and France, Zaghlul reverted to the politics of his youth to head the delegation which demanded independence. British refusal even to discuss these demands and Zaghlul's exile to Malta ignited what Egyptians would remember as the "Revolution of 1919."[7] Students swirled through the streets of Cairo demanding independence and denouncing the British; women still half veiled in yashmaks semaphored the green Egyptian flag with its crescent and three stars. Egyptians were shot and wounded by British soldiers, who in turn were beaten up or killed by Egyptians. This spluttering of squibs, some lethal, many verbal, revealed the passion which belched lavalike below the surface.

In the Egypt of the 1920s Zaghlul was more widely popular than Atatürk in Turkey. He was supported by Copts as well as by Muslims, by rich and poor, by town and country. But he was not to control Egypt in the positive manner in which Atatürk controlled Anatolia. The total political independence which he sought eluded him; lacking the freedom of action which Atatürk had secured by deposing the Sultan and then the Caliph and by expelling the Greek invaders, he could not attend to profounder problems; he could enforce no constructive vision of social change upon his people. The Egyptians themselves overlooked their basic problems: how to feed a growing population, how to bridge the abysses dividing the different sections of Egyptian society. Egyptian devotion was focused on the man Zaghlul; for to his followers the fellah at their head was a talisman. When he was fighting Adly Pasha, a Turco-Circassian rival working more cautiously for similar goals, the Zaghlulists would chant: Rather occupation at the hands of Zaghlul than independence at the hands of Adly! Their leader did not rebuke them.

[6] The source for this anecdote, as for much of the material relating to Zaghlul, is the standard life of Zaghlul by Abbas al-Aqad, in Arabic; the translation is by the present author.

[7] The Arabic word for revolution, *thowra,* does not carry the connotation of success, or accomplished fact, which seems inherent in the European term. It can refer to a prolonged period of violent unrest.

Egyptian independence of a kind arrived sooner than was expected. It was handed down in 1922 as the gift of the British acting on the advice of their High Commissioner. Allenby saw the inevitability of deadlock if negotiations continued and of murder and outrage if the situation stayed as it was. A unilateral British announcement ended the protectorate and recognized Egypt as an independent and sovereign kingdom.

The donor's advantage is that he can wrap his gift as he chooses. The gift of Egyptian independence came as swaddled in conditions as a pharaonic mummy in its bandages.

First condition: Britain assumed the defense and control of the Suez Canal. This enabled her to prolong her partial occupation indefinitely, since to defend the waterway she needed an army on Egyptian soil; the presence of such an army meant the continued possibility of interference in Egyptian affairs.

Second condition: Britain undertook the defense of Egypt; Egyptian soldiers were thus reduced to being support battalions for a foreign army.

Third condition: Britain made herself responsible for the protection of minorities; besides casting doubts on Egypt's good intentions towards her Christian and other minority groups, this gave further pretexts for intervention.

Britain's fourth and last condition seemed the most menacing: she reserved to herself control of the Sudan, the gigantic geographical area controlling the headwaters of the Nile, without which Egypt must parch.

Zaghlul fought these limitations on Egyptian sovereignty during the five years left to him. But the fervent backing of the Egyptian people was not enough to secure him victory. Passionate and volatile enthusiasm could be diverted by apparent yet unreal concessions, or could be misdirected through misinformation. The petrol of violence would flare to Zaghlul's peril. He narrowly escaped the attempt of one assassin; his one brief period as Prime Minister was brought to an end by the act of seven others.

Though Zaghlul's party, the Wafd, won every election it fought, the British had constructed a system of checks and balances designed to thwart him.

Zaghlul was never to be defeated in the National Assembly. Indeed, in thirty years of parliamentary life from 1922 onwards, no Egyptian Prime Minister would fall through an adverse vote. Political decisions were taken through the combination of two out of three points in a political triangle. The weakest point, the apex, was the electorate and its representatives. The two strong points at base were the Palace and the British embassy. The King or the British ambassador decided on the fate of one Prime Minister after another. Sometimes a telephone call sufficed, or a whisper. Often a weary pasha felt disposed for a Riviera holiday. On one desperate occasion British tanks would crash through the portals of Abdin and a bearlike ambassador charge rudely into the King's apartments to nominate his choice.

But in the 1920s the palace had a realistic tenant. Fuad, the sixth and youngest son of Khedive Ismail, had been born the year before Ismail opened the Canal. Fuad accompanied his father into exile and was educated in Turin alongside the future Victor Emmanuel III of Italy; he later served in the Italian artillery with the rank of captain. Fuad had reigned over Egypt since the death of his brother, Sultan Hussein Kamil, in 1917. A burly man of fifty with large upturned mustaches, he had taken as his second wife Nazly Sabry, descendant of a Frenchman who had embraced Islam and worked for Muhammad Ali.[8] In the early spring of 1920 Nazly had presented Fuad with a sturdy male child. Fuad had a fixation on the letter F; he was to give his one son and his many daughters names with this initial. The boy was named Farouk, he who distinguishes between good and evil. Just as the British heir apparent was known as the Prince of Wales, the Egyptian princeling would be known as the Prince of Said, or Upper Egypt. The men of Said (or the Nile Valley south of Cairo) constituted the tougher, more conservative third of Egypt's people. Their lands were still watered in the immemorial way, by summer flooding; as a result they were free from bilharziasis, the debilitating illness caught when a fellah's bare feet entered the mud of stagnant canals. If healthy, Said was poor and its sons migrated North to Cairo and the delta. One such migrant, Abdul Nasser Hussein, had moved in the first year of the war to Alexandria; armed with a certificate of primary education, he found a job in the Post Office and rented a modest house in the Bacos quarter. Abdul Nasser had fathered a son two years sooner than his sovereign. In those days it was considered tactful to name children after members of the dynasty founded by Muhammad Ali: hence a plethora of Ibrahims, Ismails and Towfiks. But Abdul Nasser named his son Gamal. By 1918, the year of Gamal's birth, the year when Zaghlul demanded independence, nationalist feeling had percolated far below the world of Princess Nazly's salon or the Muhammad Ali Club. The memory of Afghani, whose first name had been, in the Egyptian pronunciation, Gamal al-Din, was respected in the coffeeshops, the clubs of the poor.

The violence associated with nationalism worried the conservative; many of them found in Fuad a figure of reassurance. "Throughout these great events," a courtier wrote after the disturbances of the early 1920s, "all Egyptians feel the effective action of their Sovereign and love him very sincerely, as they love their little Heir-Apparent, His Royal Highness Prince Farouk."[9] Though only a courtier could claim that Fuad was as popular as

---

[8] Colonel Sèves, or Suliman Pasha; his statue in fez and baggy trousers dominated one of Cairo's main squares until the 1960s, when it was replaced by that of Talaat Harb, founder of Bank Misr and a pioneer of industrialization.

[9] Foulad Yeghen, *L'Egypte sous le règne de Fouad Ier* (Cairo: 1929).

Zaghlul, the king was a skillful politician. He read widely and worked long hours; he showed an active interest in Egyptology, the arts and desert reclamation. He gave his powerful support to the creation of Cairo's first modern university, an institution which would bear his name for a generation.[10] Described as "having the soul of the East and the mind of the West," he was as Egyptian as Zaghlul in his love of carnal pleasures. He knew Egypt backwards and the role he could play.

The Egyptian triangle seemed harmoniously balanced on March 15, 1924, when King Fuad and Prime Minister Zaghlul joined in a stirring ceremony smiled on by the British. Gunfire from the beige hills to the east of Cairo released a cavalry procession from the same Citadel where Muhammad Ali had butchered the Mamelukes; the horses trotted through a city verdant with Egyptian flags. (The Egyptian flag until after the Revolution of 1952 was green with a white crescent and three stars.) Behind the slim glass windows of a state coach the King could be seen, dressed as a general, his face radiant but wax-pale; beside him was the tortured profile of Zaghlul, decked in a frock coat with gilt frogging and a broad ribbon. Lord Allenby awaited them at the parliament building; as a field marshal he was dressed one better than Fuad. Inside, Zaghlul and his ministers assembled to the King's left, the princes of the dynasty to the King's right. To an Assembly dominated by his supporters, the fellah Prime Minister read his speech of policy. It was studiedly restrained, combining a calm affirmation of independence with a polite call for negotiations with Great Britain.

For Zaghlul planned to embellish the status of Egypt by a visit to London. A new era seemed promised with the coming to power of Ramsay MacDonald, a Scot who enjoyed uniforms and the company of kings no less than Zaghlul, but also a socialist whose pacifist opinions had led him to oppose the war.

Fuad, listening impassively to Zaghlul's Arabic, had plans to embellish the status of his throne. Three weeks earlier, by Law 341 of the Turkish Revolution, Atatürk had abolished the Ottoman Caliphate. His move left vacant the most prestigious position in Islam. Hussein, now King of the Hejaz, had been quick to make a bid for it. A week later in the dusty township of Amman, the capital of a new princedom of Trans-Jordan under his son Abdullah, Hussein had had himself proclaimed as the new Arab Caliph. But despite his impeccable descent, Hussein, as Caliph, was a nonstarter. His control over the Hejaz was precarious, since in the Arabian uplands a new man of power, Ibn Saud, was consolidating a forceful and expanding kingdom. Hussein's hold over Muslim sentiment was no stronger; few non-Arabs trusted the man who had sided with Britain and France against the Ottoman Sultan.

[10] Fuad I University became known as Cairo University after the Revolution of 1952.

The creation of a new Caliphate would depend in great part on Britain. Having previously feared caliphal authority over Indian Muslims, the British now toyed with reviving the office for their own purposes. The best, but the least possible, solution would have been an Englishman arrayed as God's shadow on earth; second best to a "Caliph Lawrence" would be a willing client. To caliphy the King of a British-dominated Egypt (the younger brother of Towfik, that most satisfactory of puppets) could be helpful.

The plans of both King and Prime Minister were to be thwarted.

A pamphlet punctured Fuad's dream of becoming Caliph. Entitled "Islam and the Principles of Government" and the work of a young sheikh from al-Azhar, the pamphlet was quietly lethal.[11] In arguing that the Caliphate formed no essential part of Islamic doctrine, the young sheikh seemed to be defying immemorial doctrine; he was in fact reverting to the teachings of several earlier and respected theologians. His argument was expressed in cogent simplicity. Islam should be seen as a religion, not a political system; Muhammad had been sent as a Messenger, not a dynast. Neither the holy book nor the recorded sayings of Muhammad recommended any particular form of government. The third pillar of Islamic authority—the consensus of believers—was equally feeble for those who would support the necessity of a Caliph. Except for the first three Caliphs[12]—friends of the Prophet who had been chosen by a rudimentary form of election—all succeeding rulers had depended on the sword.

The pamphlet raised a dust storm. Sycophants rushed into print with counterassertions. The press, with one honorable exception, assailed the sheikh; after a heresy trial at al-Azhar the culprit-author was forbidden to teach religion or receive his stipend as a religious judge. Doffing his turban (the symbol of an Azhar graduate) the sheikh reverted to lay dress.

But the pamphlet crystallized new attitudes. A conference held at al-Azhar in May 1925 reluctantly concluded that the political divisions in the modern world, as well as the spread of nationalism, made a Caliphate impossible.

A force stronger than a pamphlet frustrated Zaghlul's plans for Egypt. He journeyed to London and visited Britain's first Socialist Prime Minister. But power had made the idealist depressingly pragmatic. "No British Government," Ramsay MacDonald told the Egyptian Prime Minister, "can divest itself wholly, even in favour of an ally, of its interest in guarding such a vital link in British communications as the Suez Canal."

Disappointed in London, Zaghlul returned to a bitterer shock in Cairo.

[11] Sheikh Ali Abdul Razik.
[12] Abu Bakr, Omar and Othman were all connected to the Prophet by marriage. The fourth Caliph, Ali, was the Prophet's cousin and also son-in-law; but Ali's caliphal claims were contested by Moawiya, founder of the Omayyad dynasty, whose claim rested on the swords of his Syrian Army. Ali was assassinated.

Sir Lee Stack, a British general, was the Sirdar, or commander-in-chief, of the Egyptian Army. Nationalists found it as irksome to have their camel corps and artillery commanded by an Englishman in a tarboosh as Americans would have found it to have their marines under a Japanese general dressed up like Uncle Sam. One November afternoon Egyptian anger flared in murder. The Sirdar was driving home for tiffin, the Indian Empire word for the midday meal, when seven gunmen assaulted his car, leaving him dying. The Sirdar died from his wounds.

The act shocked Zaghlul for its violence and alarmed him for its predictable results. He at once expressed his personal regrets to the British. This was not enough. Allenby issued an ultimatum: Egypt must offer an official apology; she must pay a fine of half a million sterling; she must withdraw her troops from the Sudan; she must formally recognize the right of the British controllers of the Sudan to draw off as much water for Sudanese use as they saw fit. Furthermore, despite his four-to-one majority in the National Assembly, Zaghlul must resign. On the King's advice, his place was taken by Ziwar Pasha, a portly Turco-Circassian delighted by the turn of events: "These rogues have got what they deserve with their insane policy! They had better clear out fast unless they want something worse for themselves and Egypt." When the National Assembly elected Zaghlul as its president, this pasha's remedy was simple: he dissolved the Assembly. Ziwar next advised Fuad to change the electoral law, since "its strength was believed to be with the ignorant and the humble, and the Prime Minister thought by confining the vote to the educated and propertied class, he would destroy Zaghlul's following."

Fuad was shrewd enough to see that democracy had advanced a step too far for such open gerrymandering to work. Instead, he would use his royal prerogative to choose and to dismiss.

But Ziwar was right in his assessment of the "educated and propertied class" which filled the ground area inside the Egyptian triangle. Ziwar, as a Jesuit-educated Turk, was typical of one of the strangest ruling castes ever assembled. Its chief bond was its foreignness to the country it ruled. It spoke Turkish, French, Greek, English or Italian, not the language of the country. It comprised the near and distant relations of the royal family, then Turco-Circassians who began to proclaim themselves Egyptian Nationalists now that Constantinople had been demoted to a purely Turkish Istanbul; behind them, beneath them, serving as their financial advisers, dentists, doctors, moneylenders or pimps, bowed the sons and grandsons of the Europeans who had come penniless to Egypt from Italy, Greece, Malta, France or England. They had grown rich on Egyptian soil. They no longer saw themselves as pioneers; they lived in luxurious villas in Cairo or Alexandria.

Just as Atatürk could picture Europe from the mirror of Bulgaria, we may picture this vanished caste from our own glass fragment. The year that saw Zaghlul as Prime Minister from March to November—1924—saw also the constitution of the Royal Automobile Club d'Egypte. Since car ownership was still confined to the very rich, the club's membership hints who possessed the economic power. Even by 1927, the year of Zaghlul's death, the club only had around 250 members in Cairo and district. Its *Annuaire* survives like the coprolite of a strange social dinosaur. Less than a quarter of its Cairo members had recognizably Egyptian names. Each name is followed by its owner's profession. The commonest is *rentier* (or person of independent means); the second commonest, *commerçant*. The club's committee comprises three princes of the royal house, three pashas, six beys and a litany whose exotic names evoke a recent but eradicated past: E. Homan Mulock, Parissi Belleni, Gaston Ades, Arnold S. Parker, E. Constantinidis, A. Armstrong, C. Pilavacchi, Pericles Demetrious, Robert Rolo, Charles Brehler, René Cohen, M. C. Comanos, Edward Malatesta, Felix Green, Jack Goar, Charles Rofe, W. Iversen, Ralph S. Green, and, at the very end, a Muslim: Abdelhamid Chawarbi.

These holders of non-Egyptian names (they usually held foreign passports also) possessed property which felt itself menaced by whoever represented the 99 per cent of the population, whether Muslim or Copt, who were true Egyptians. Their nervous power backed the King and the British. The courtier who had testified to the popularity of the King and the little Prince rejoiced when the Wafd was out of power: "Today, Egypt, wisely directed, goes towards a better future. After the happy intervention of the Sovereign, who put the extremists where they could no longer inflict a dangerous policy on the nation, she enters a new era."

The era's upholder, and beneficiary in chief, was the British Empire. The rulers remained British generals, ambassadors and chiefs of police. When Zaghlul was arrested in March 1919, an Englishman had done the arresting. When Sir Lee Stack was shot in 1924, this same Englishman did the detective work which, along with bribes to those prepared to turn King of England's evidence, convicted the assassins.

Russell Pasha, commandant of the Cairo Police from 1917 to 1948, was a Crusoe with patrician connections. His father, a parson who preferred riding to hounds to preaching, derived from a Whig family which had produced not only peers and statesman, but such brilliant sports as Bertrand Russell, the philosopher and mathematician, and the Duke of Bedford, who with cranky courage opposed the Second World War. Russell Pasha was no intellectual, was a total conformist. He had abandoned the pursuit of an honors degree for a career in the Egyptian Police since this promised advancement unlikely in England. Russell had the Englishman's love of animals and the aristocrat's toughness. When he was being trained as a sub-inspector in 1902, he was put through the goose step under the shouts, in his own words, of "a black man yelling at me in Arabic, or rather Turkish, as all the words of command are in Turkish."[13]

When he had arrested Zaghlul, he had done so with consideration; knowing that the old man was a diabetic, he arranged for bedding and special food. This led to a lasting friendship between the Russells (for this particular Crusoe was married) and the Zaghluls. Russell was not only kind to the influential. He cared for his policemen like a father, fighting spectacular battles on their behalf against Levantine grafters; on one occasion he took on, and defeated, no less a person than the Greek in charge of the secret police.

Kind to animals, courteous to women, fatherly to his men, Russell reserved his venom for the elements he despised: drug peddlers, Nationalists and the disorderly lower classes. He attended the hangings which the British struggle against the Nationalists (or terrorists, as they were known) made fairly frequent. He did not enjoy these occasions; nor did they spoil his appetite for breakfast as his sometimes jocular descriptions of them (in letters to his clergyman father) testify. At Haileybury, the old East India college, he had been reared in a tradition of wholesome violence.[14] Like Cromer he approved the floggings normally handed down to those who took part in unruly demonstrations. In the troubles of 1919 he wrote home in typical vein: "We are now arresting various of the most seditious preachers in the mosques and at meetings. This week we are going to take various of the roughest quarters of Cairo, surround bits of them and carry out a house-to-house search for arms, etc. I don't expect to find much but it's a great thing stirring up these rough quarters and submitting them to a bit of rough handling."[15]

Gentlemanly manners backed by rough handling held the triangle of Egyptian power together for a generation. The Palace (Fuad was to be succeeded by the schoolboy Farouk in 1936) and the British embassy balanced the Wafd (in the broad sense in which it continued to be a manifestation of Egyptian nationalism) for exactly thirty years.[16] The triangle safeguarded the caste symbolized by the Royal Automobile Club d'Egypte; in the short term the triangle served the needs of those who erected it. But in the longer term it worked against the monarchy, made Britain detested and undermined the parliamentary system.

The monarchy had always been foreign to Egypt. But on occasions—during Muhammad Ali's victories, when Ismail had joined Egypt to Europe, even when the young Abbas had supported the Nationalists and stood up to Kitchener—it had been identified with Egyptian pride. After

[13] Seth, Ronald; *Russell Pasha;* William Kimber, London, 1966.
[14] This tradition persisted at least into the early 1940s, when the author of this present volume was at the same school.
[15] Seth, op. cit., p. 147.
[16] From 1922, year of Egyptian independence, to 1952, year of Nasser's Revolution.

1922 the monarchy's role in the Egyptian triangle was that of frustrator. The King could dismiss ministers or dissolve the Assembly; he could, and did, prevent any Egyptian individual or party from doing for Egypt something of what Atatürk had done for Turkey. And this against a background of problems mounting with the population.

The British, as architects and beneficiaries of the system, would exploit Egypt so long as they could hold the country down. Once Egypt struggled free it was inevitable that she would show herself an implacable enemy of imperial rule.

Monarchy and embassy were forces whose loss or reduction we need not weep. Genuinely sad for Egypt was the loss of repute inflicted on a partially democratic system unable to challenge the King or the British ambassador.

Zaghlul, dying of scarlet fever in 1927, perished before the impotence of party politics was fully discerned. From plinths which became rallying grounds for student demonstrations his giant statues, realistically carved in Western suit and tarboosh, would confront the Mediterranean in Alexandria and the Mokattam Hills in Cairo. There is a gaunt, sad twist to the old Nationalist's once sensual mouth, an inward look to the almost Mongol eyes. The disappointment was personal: after November 1924, the British would never allow him to be Prime Minister again, despite his parliamentary majority. His disappointment was also patriotic: he foresaw that his followers would inherit his impotence, but not his magic. The gangrene which affects an unused limb would assail his party, the Wafd. Since a triangular situation encouraged two points to align themselves against the third, his wall-eyed successor Nahas would align himself with the British embassy against the King during the Second World War; Nahas even allowed himself to be imposed as Prime Minister by the force of British tanks. This second Abdin incident would dynamite all three points of power and lead to the destruction of the caste which the triangle had protected.

When the Egyptians next took their destiny into their hands, they would disregard the parliamentarians of the 1920s and look back to the soldier who in the first Abdin incident had stood up to the Khedive. A second Orabi, not a second Zaghlul, would win Egypt its independence and destroy the foreign caste which had ruled it for so long. He would do so at the cost of a generation's democratic experience and, like Orabi, at the peril of war.

Chapter 2

SOME seven hundred miles east of Egypt, British officials were constructing another political triangle by the banks of the Tigris.

The Baghdad of the Arabian Nights had been devastated by the Mongols. A two-story provincial town now straddled its dun river. When one of its dust storms blew up from the desert, Baghdad seemed congealed from an all-pervading mud. Only in Kadhimain, a few miles north of the town, did golden domes in a forest of metallic palms suggest a caliphal city; but these and a few scattered fragments only stressed the abyss between the glorious past and the dingy present. Otherwise the dust-brown capital of Mesopotamia boasted but a single imposing piece of architecture: the monumental Ottoman serai, a fortress of governmental buildings dating from the rule of Midhat Pasha.

In late August 1921, this serai witnessed an unusual pageant. For week after nervous week the temperatures had scorched in the lower 120s. For the Tigris, unlike the helpful Nile, flooded in spring when its waters were unwanted and slumped low in summer; then islets surfaced from the brown water to be briefly green with Indian corn and melons. The ceremony in progress was to induct a Hashemite king. The kingdom of Iraq, seen against a scale going back to Ur and Sumer, Babylon and Assyria, would be as brief-lived as one of these summer islands. The kingdom's summer was the forty years of British supremacy in the Middle East.

Fifteen hundred spectators were arranged round a modest dais, which rose only knee high in their midst. The front seats were occupied by the British: Sir Percy Cox, tall, silent Prospero of this brown dominion; officers, officials, experts in everything from dams to police work, and one tall woman, Miss Gertrude Bell, oriental secretary to Sir Percy. Behind were Arab officials, many of them deserters from the Ottoman Army and still wearing the fez. Behind these stood massed delegations representing the layers of Mesopotamian society: rich merchants, townsmen, the Islamic, Christian and Jewish clergy, and beyond these the sharp-nosed tribal sheikhs in their robes of black, their checkered keffias snaked with dark agals; the shaved, flat-backed heads of Kurds were shaded by large fringed turbans while strangely gaudy on such stolid waists, pink flowered sashes divided a costume of long-sleeve blouse and baggy pantaloons.

On the dais, dignified and shy, stood Hussein of Mecca's third and most attractive son, the sensitive if none too clever Feisal whom Colonel Lawrence had selected as the most suitable leader for a British-prompted side show. Five years of struggle, doubt, exhilaration, dejection, exile, culminated in this late moment of precarious triumph. Trembling in his eminence among a people with a reputation for being two-faced and violent, a people he had only lived among for the last two months, Feisal caught the eye of the doughty Englishwoman in her early fifties who, as much as anyone, had made him King. Miss Bell gave him an encouraging smile, a hardly perceptible salute. He half smiled in return: but only half. The moment had its dangers, its ironies. Feisal was descended from the Prophet, and this same people of Iraq had summoned the Prophet's grandson from the Hejaz, only to murder him and his family. An Iraqi was now shouting a proclamation from Sir Percy Cox, the British High Commissioner: No less than 96 per cent of the people had chosen Feisal to be King of Iraq! After the announcement of this astounding figure— people were not yet used to such sweeping plebiscites—a new flag was flown and an army band, in the absence of an Iraqi anthem, struck up: "God Save The King!" Nothing had gone amiss.

The pageant had been arranged by the dour Sir Percy and his bluestocking assistant. But the decision to stage it had been taken in March when Mr. Winston Churchill, the British Colonial Secretary, had summoned a galaxy of imperial servants to meet him in Cairo. The subject: the future of the British Middle East. This was only part of the former Ottoman Empire. Anatolia was in dispute between Greeks and Turks. The French had snatched Syria and Lebanon as their spoils of war, invoking the secret agreement between Sir Mark Sykes and M. Georges Picot. Arabia, under its vigorous warrior king, Abdul Aziz ibn Saud, was beyond Britain's grasp, though not her influence; with no discovered assets, the king was in grateful receipt of an annual subsidy of £100,000. The little ports of the Gulf, dependent on pearl diving and dhows, were too poor to matter and their hereditary rulers could continue under paternal British guidance; so could the steaming southern coastline between Muscat in the east and the colony of Aden to the west. After Egypt, the three zones whose future must be decided were Iraq itself, and then, to its west, the expanse of desert from the palm-fringed Euphrates to the Jordan Valley, and, finally, the hills and coastal plain of Palestine.

Winston Churchill, the man primarily responsible for the colonial decisions, was one of the most fervent admirers of Lawrence of Arabia. Haunted by the casualties on the bleak Western Front and his Dardanelles failure, Churchill was as ideally equipped to swallow the Lawrence legend as Lawrence himself was "ideally equipped to play the hero of a national compensation neurosis. He was a man of mystery. Scarcely anyone had met him; little was known about him. Ignorance encouraged the growth of a legend. He posed for innumerable photographs against palm trees, black tents and coffee pots; it was natural to identify him with the Sheikh of Araby. And then, as more facts became available, another image became imposed upon the first, of a Nordic giant, or as some averred, a Nordic pygmy, but at all accounts handsome and energetic; with penetrating eyes, muscles like cord, vast powers of endurance; disinterested, dedicated, indifferent to discomfort, content with little food and no bed; a stranger to sexual desire, and yet manly. Dauntless, humorous and just; it was Ivanhoe, the Sheikh of Araby and Bulldog Drummond all rolled into one."[1] Churchill was an innocent where complex characters were involved. He had grabbed this young celebrity for his adviser on Arab affairs. He did not know that Lawrence was an inaccurate guide; he could not intuit that in 1921 Lawrence was clasped by a psychological octopus which was to leave its traces throughout his long prose account of the revolt, the epic which Churchill was to rank "with the greatest books ever written in the English language." When in a few months' time Lawrence would resign his official post, he would seek spiritual degradation in the punishing discipline of a peacetime soldier; he would puzzle service doctors by displaying buttocks and thighs scarred from flagellation; Lawrence's explanation for these wounds was a Turkish flogging at Deraa in Syria, but it is more probable that they were the recent handiwork of the young Scots soldier, retained to administer periodical birchings throughout the remaining years of the hero's life.

The truths about this man of mystery would take decades to unravel. Churchill was in his dotage when Richard Aldington, in an assailed but essentially accurate study, revealed the author of *The Seven Pillars of Wisdom* to be a pathological romancer;[2] Churchill and Aldington were alike in their graves when two London journalists revealed that masochism was the core to Lawrence's enigma.[3] The legend that Lawrence had been prompted by sympathy for Arab freedom was also durable. In fact, Lawrence had seen himself in the role of a servant of empire; while posing as an aspirant archaeologist, he had been used for espionage by Commander Hogarth in the years immediately preceding the war; his two extracurricular emotions were hatred for the Turks, Britain's enemy, and for the French, Britain's ally. He had little respect for the Arabs in general, though one particular donkey boy, Salim Ahmed, had been the "Mr. W.H." of his twisted life. His emotions were not involved in the coming conflict between Jews and Arabs. His rueful admission that "had I been an honest adviser of the Arabs I would have advised them to go home and not risk their

---

[1] Alan Neame's essay, "T. E. Lawrence—Security Risk," in *The European*, July 1954.

[2] Aldington, Richard, *Lawrence of Arabia* (London: Collins, 1955).

[3] Philip Knightley and Colin Simpson, *The Secret Lives of Lawrence of Arabia* (London: Nelson, 1969).

lives fighting for such stuff . . ."[4] was as much an instance of self-punishment as honesty. But for Feisal Lawrence felt a proprietary concern. He had chosen him as figurehead for the Arab Revolt; on his prompting Feisal had ridden with him ahead of Allenby's army to possess Damascus before the French. Lawrence's plans had been miscarried. On behalf of the Arabs but against French opposition, Feisal had reached the corridors of Versailles and, for one speech, the conference chamber. An outsider robed in desert abba and honor, he had been baffled by hard-faced victors contriving, albeit unconsciously, a yet worse war for the coming generation. From Versailles Feisal had returned, disappointed, to the East. Early in 1920 his followers proclaimed him King of Syria while simultaneously naming his older brother Abdullah as candidate king of Iraq. But the Syrians themselves had cooled towards Feisal: in part because of apparent concessions to Dr. Weizmann, in part because his character did not live up to his looks. The French, who had by now imported the requisite military forces, exploited the Syrians' lukewarm feelings to evict him from Syria. Feisal traveled wanly through Palestine to England, there to sit heavy on the British conscience. To those under the spell of Lawrence—and they had become a multitude since Mr. Lowell Thomas, an American publicist of genius, had started retailing his exploits to huge wrapt audiences—Feisal seemed the Hamlet of their imperial play. If amends to Feisal could be linked with their advantage, the British were ready to make them. There were two small obstacles to his Iraqi coronation.

There was already a candidate for the throne and some Iraquis had petitioned King Hussein to send Abdullah to Baghdad. Indeed, if the Iraqis had to be ruled by one of Hussein's sons, a majority might have preferred Abdullah. Arabs were always susceptible to eloquence; they could discern under traditional courtesy the reefs of a political talent; Abdullah seemed a man who could sell and be sold, but also a man who could maneuver for a profitable deal. But the British, never fond of clever natives, preferred the slow Feisal to his nimble brother; Abdullah could be given an alternative, less prestigious kingdom somewhere else.

This left the second obstacle: the sentiments of Iraq's three million people.

From turbulent Cairo this hurdle had seemed easy. On the ground, in Iraq, it was more formidable. The territory did not enfold a homogeneous society whom one argument could convince. Apart from the Yezidis, who worshiped the devil in the guise of a peacock-angel, apart from Jews and various kinds of Christian, the population of Iraq was divided into three substantial fractions. In the North, the Kurds inhabited beautiful mountain valleys on the fringes of Anatolia and Persia. While professing the Sunni form of Islam upheld by the Ottomans, they spoke a language first

---

[4] *The Seven Pillars of Wisdom* (Penguin Modern Classics), p. 24.

cousin to that of the Shiite Persians. Claiming to be the descendants of the ancient Medes, the hardy mountaineers were as poor as medieval Scots and were compared by the Arabs, on whom they often preyed, to the rat or the locust. They were stubborn fighters and if won over could constitute an effective third of the population. The South and West were Semitic, Arab townsmen, farmers and nomads occupying the dust-shimmering valley of Euphrates and Tigris. Yet they too were divided. The Arabs of the North were mostly Sunnis; they had co-operated with the Ottomans; they had close links with Sunni Syria. The South, including such towns as Najaf, Kerbela and Basra, as well as the impoverished Amara swamps, adhered to the Shia. Because of the many shrines devoted to the imams of the house of Ali, Iraq was thronged by Persian pilgrims; there was, indeed, a lively traffic in the coffins of dead Shiites from the East, since it was thought good to be buried as near as possible to an imam. Having suffered for centuries under Sunni rule, the Shia had a revolutionary tradition. When the British mandate had first been mooted in 1920, the Shiite tribes of the South had risen in rebellion; pacification had cost the British £30 million.

At the best of times—and 1921 was a bad time—it would have been hard to persuade these groups to agree on a ruler. Each of them had objections to the British-sponsored King. The Kurds would have preferred independence to an Arab ruler. Many Sunnis despised the Hashemites for their alliance with the British; some would have preferred to remain with Turkey. Since the Hashemites were Sunnis, many Shiites would have chosen a republic.

Gertrude Bell and Sir Percy Cox—her superior knowledge of the country entitles her to priority—opposed the continuance of overt occupation. Armed collisions with popular forces would lead to more savage repression, or, worse, to British disengagement from this new brown dominion. They proposed to create an outwardly Arab administration. It would have the authority to coerce the Iraqis but would be directed at every level by British advisers. The lynchpin of this system would be an Arab king of the noblest lineage. No one was nobler than the docile and gentlemanly Feisal.

The woman who labored to have him crowned had been born, like Fuad of Egypt, the year before the opening of the Suez Canal. For an English-woman to be born in 1868 was to be born on the boundary between suppression and emancipation. Her father, Sir Lothian Bell, was rich; he belonged to the caste which had both served the empire and benefited from it; this caste had been accustomed to deferring to unemancipated females; it deferred the more when one of its daughters took a First in modern history at Oxford and then learnt Arabic and Persian on courageous travels in the Persian plateau and the Arab deserts. As a girl she had excelled at every subject except music and scripture. Her genius was prosaic, her ironic temperament was opaque to religion. "I have called on all the missionaries," she was to exclaim in pre-war Palestine. "Heaven preserve us, what a set of scarecrows! It seems a pity that the Christian religion should be exclusively represented by ladies with wispy hair and spectacles." Along with scholarship and archaeological exertions—her published plans of Arab palaces in the desert remain unrivaled—she indulged an interest in clothes. Hardly unpacked from the Cairo Conference she wrote home from Baghdad: "Will you send me some thick woollen tricotine of a blue as near as may be to the enclosed colour, enough for Marie to make me a winter everyday gown, jumper and skirt. Also some soft blue silk on which to mount the skirt, the same colour. Further will you give a pattern of the blue to my hat maker, Anne Marie in Sloane Street, and tell her to send me by parcel post a blue felt hat—she knows the kind of shape like the green felt she made for me last year trimmed with reddish brown wings, pheasant would do or a red brown feather trimming of some kind. No ostrich feathers, that's too dear."

Economical, cultivated, cool, Miss Bell assumed that she sprang from superior stock and felt no need to argue the self-evident. "Dearest Mother," she wrote on the same pre-war visit to Palestine, "I now take my meals with a black. He's my fellow lodger in this hotel. He's a very pleasant black, and since he talks Arabic to me his colour leaves me quite indifferent; still, it's comic. He wears a dark brown kid glove on one hand, and except for the buttons I can't tell which is the ungloved hand. We solemnly discuss the Koran, and he assures me that the sum of all human knowledge is to be found in it. To which I politely agree."

As a woman in a male empire, Miss Bell received the deference of her superiors as well as her peers. Ordinary Englishmen probably smiled at her much as she had smiled at the black man. As for the Arabs, they regarded the unveiled, commanding mem-sahib (this Indian term was introduced for a colony of British wives of whom she was the precursor) as a sexless creature somehow intermediate between men and what they considered women. She did not care. She was the loved daughter of an affectionate family. She had known the great. She cared deeply for beautiful or ancient things. She had a Boyle-like enthusiasm for the city of her adoption and would leave a more permanent mark on Baghdad than Harry Boyle on Cairo. When few Iraqis yet bothered about their Sumerian or Babylonian antiquities, she labored through hot summers in her winged hats and long dresses at assembling the nucleus of an Iraqi museum. She died on the job. In recognition of what she had done for their archaeology, the Iraqis placed her modest bust in the museum entrance; then, in the 1960s, a grander edifice with air conditioning but no momento of Gertrude Bell was built with money from the trust of an Armenian, Calouste Gulbenkian, who had wangled five per cent on the oil exploited in Iraq. (He had arranged the contract with the Ottoman authorities.) Miss Bell had not thought of fame for herself or oil for Iraq. She had dreamed instead of reviving the greatness which had made Baghdad the Paris of the ninth-century world; she had thought that the right first step was to crown an Arab king. She hero-worshiped Feisal as some mothers hero-worship a dependent child. He turned to her for advice on soft furnishings and Western etiquette. She was an active, but probably innocent, participant in the campaign to coerce the Iraqis into accepting him, accomplished as it was by a whirlwind of bribery, pageants and, where necessary, the ruthless use of force. One notable[5] who opposed Feisal was invited to tea with Sir Percy and Lady Cox and Gertrude Bell. As he left, he was bundled into an armored car and shipped to Ceylon. Gertrude Bell knew that resentment against British control, whether direct or indirect, smoldered still. "We get reports," she wrote at the end of June 1921, "about the lower Euphrates tribes preparing monstrous petitions in favour of a republic; and of Shiah Alim Mujtahids being all against Feisal." Pro-British businessmen, on the other hand, urged her to dispense with the democratic facade: "we must finish the business, we couldn't wait for elections. Somehow or other Feisal must be proclaimed King."

Two weeks later, July 16: "The heat is terrific, day after day over 121 and the nights hot too . . . On the other hand, politics are running on wheels greased with extremely well melted grease and Sir Percy and Feisal are scoring great triumphs. On Monday the 11th the Council, at the instance of the Naqib . . .[6] unanimously declared Feisal King, and charged the Ministry of the Interior with the necessary arrangements. I was dining alone that night and feeling anxious; the heat makes one not quite normal, I think. You may fancy what it was like to get to the office next morning and hear this news from Sir Percy, the moment I arrived. He added that he felt, good as this was, that it wasn't enough and that we must have an election by Referendum to be able to prove that Feisal really had the voice of the people."

The campaign to sell Feisal to Iraq was masterminded by officers with a British feeling for the picturesque; Miss Bell responded to their efforts. "I never saw him look so splendid," she wrote of Feisal on the occasion of one jamboree. "He wore his usual white robes with a fine black abba over them, flowing white headdress and silver bound Aqal." The scene was a large tent by the Euphrates with improvised walls of fresh green boughs and roof of goat cloth. Outside, the camel riders of the Dulaim were mustered round their standard, borne by a Negro on a giant white camel. Two tribal leaders stood on either side of Feisal to proclaim: "We swear allegiance to you because you are acceptable to the British Government." This was a little too near the bone for Feisal, who raised his eyebrows at Miss Bell. "No one can doubt what my relations are to the British, but we must settle our affairs ourselves." She quickly responded by clasping her

[5] Sayid Talib.
[6] This particular omission comes in the published text of Gertrude Bell's letters.

two hands together—a symbol, as she wrote, of the union of the Arab and British governments.

The tribal leaders had, of course, recognized realities: Feisal was the British choice which people were required to endorse. There was no balloting, open or secret. Printed forms were sent in large numbers to all the districts that would receive them. An agent of the British, usually one of the ex-Ottoman Arab officers who had escaped from Syria with Feisal and had no wish to travel further, would retail the praises of Feisal to a hastily summoned mob. Did not such a man, with such a record of service to the Arabs, deserve a reward? Agreed! Agreed! Then let the reward be the Crown of Iraq! Again, Agreed! And that was that. The officials then wrote down, at leisure, a long list of names. (Sulaimaniya, the Kurdish capital, had nothing to do with the Referendum.) But apart from Sulaimaniya, the people of Kirkuk, future center of the oil industry, voted against Feisal en masse, asking instead for a son of the Ottoman Sultan; Erbil and Mosul stipulated that minorities should be given self-rule; Basra added a curious rider—perhaps sponsored by British Indians who had not abandoned southern Iraq as a place for surplus Indians to be settled—that they should pay no taxes to the government in Baghdad.

Nevertheless, on August 26, 1921, Miss Bell could write home: "We have had a terrific week but we've got our King crowned." She had rejected a last-minute cable from the Colonial Office suggesting that "Feisal in his Coronation speech must announce that the ultimate authority in the land is the High Commissioner." Feisal's authority must appear less trammeled if he were to control his extremists.

But words apart, Britain retained authority in Iraq; her novel instrument for enforcing it was air power. The cheapness of airplanes for controlling large areas of desert and farmland turned the balance in favor of maintaining this large, unruly country under British influence. Two summers before she died, Gertrude Bell described how this worked: "The most interesting thing which has happened during this week was a performance by the RAF, a bombing demonstration. It was even more remarkable than the one we saw last year at the Air Force show because it was much more real. They had made an imaginary village about a quarter of a mile from where we sat on the Diala dyke and the two first bombs dropped from 3000 feet, went straight into the middle of it and set it alight. It was wonderful and horrible. Then they dropped bombs all round it, as if to catch the fugitives and finally fire bombs which even in the brightest sunlight made flares of bright flame in the desert. They burn through metal and water won't extinguish them. At the end the armoured cars went out to round up the fugitives with machine guns. I was tremendously impressed."

The demonstration was intended, of course, to impress the Iraqis. Not the support of the people, but an air base at Habbaniya, a lake west of Baghdad, supported the system.

The monarchy was never to seem indigenous to Iraq. Unlike the dynasty in Egypt, it created no nobility, no proliferating roots to uphold its trunk. Although British theoreticians advocated the enlargement of a sheikhly class, the tribal leaders retained the qualities of a desert hierarchy. The monarchy stood alone. Showing no interest in things of the mind and little in culture, it patronized horse racing. In a curious parody of Ascot, one of Queen Victoria's state coaches, bought discreetly from Buckingham Palace, would trundle round the Mansur racecourse with the King and some male visitor at his side. The use of the old-fashioned coach puzzled Iraqis, who would have been more impressed by a Cadillac or a tank. Another importation was the Royal Harithiya Hunt. With an English MFH and hounds flown in from Britain, Feisal's nephew, Abdul Ilah, the gown of an honorary Canadian degree cut down to fashion the traditional "pink," would hunt jackals through palm groves on the outskirts of Baghdad. The monarchy's serious work was conducted in the Royal Bilat, a one-story structure of brick and adobe; a gigantic wooden crown lit up by electric jewels was its sole adornment. Only after the expansion of the oil industry in the 1950s was money set aside to build a palace as grandiose as Cairo's Abdin. But no Hashemite slept there. Completed too late, it was to house the military dictator who ended the dynasty.[7]

The founder of the dynasty, Feisal I, deserved neither hatred nor great respect. Well intentioned, he lent a symbolic hand at teaching in a primary school; a higher level of instruction was beyond him. He lacked his brother Abdullah's machiavellian instincts, and flair. His greatest assets had been his looks and these withered early and consorted less well with the Western clothes which he soon assumed. But his innocence seemed rewarded by a twelve-year reign and an apparently natural death in Switzerland in 1933. Other members of his dynasty suffered fates worthy of an Elizabethan drama. King Hussein of the Hejaz, driven from Mecca like an angry Lear, lived out his days in Cypriot exile. Feisal's eldest brother, the religious, consumptive Ali, ruled the crumbling kingdom for an inglorious year; expelled by Ibn Saud, who incorporated the Hejaz in Saudi Arabia, he died as Feisal's pensioner in a rambling palace by the Tigris. Ali's son, Abdul Ilah, patron of the hunt and for many years Regent, would be dragged round Baghdad with a palm stave *in recto* before slivers of his thigh were cut as butcher's meat for an angry rabble. Feisal's son Ghazi died in a motor crash, the result of his own bad driving, though some alleged a plot between his cousin, Abdul Ilah, and his sister, Ghazi's wife, who in turn died prematurely of an agonizing cancer. As distressing as murder to a clan steeped in Arabian tradition was the apostasy of one of its princesses and her marriage in a church to a Greek Orthodox waiter.

[7] Abdul Salaam Arif, not Abdul Karim Kassem; the former is believed to have ordered the execution of the Royal Family; the latter made the Ministry of Defense into his residence.

Ghazi's son, named Feisal after his grandfather, was shot down before concluding his marriage to an Ottoman princess. Abdullah inherited no better fate by losing Iraq. He was assassinated on his way to prayer in Jerusalem, suspected of colluding with the Jews of Palestine. His son Tallal was certified mad after a brief reign; his grandson Hussein, named after the Sherif who launched the Arab Revolt, would surrender Jerusalem, the third holy city of Islam, to non-Muslim hands.

Gertrude Bell and Sir Percy Cox had built in sand. Their legacy to Iraq was curiously similar to Allenby's legacy to Egypt. Perhaps if Sir Percy had listened to the Baghdad businessmen and dispensed with a democratic facade, things would have been more honest, and in the long run better. Democracy would not have been half tried and in the trying discredited. Instead, Iraq, like Egypt, had a parliament of sorts; even less than the Egyptian was it allowed to represent the people; had it tried to express their will it would have been more swiftly frustrated. The British ambassador, whose embassy was on the west bank of the Tigris, was known to Baghdad as *"mukhtar thak-as-sob"*, or "the mayor of that side." He was believed to be the supreme authority in the country, to make or unmake, not only ministers, but directors-general. The Hashemites who deferred to this *mukhtar* were never linked to Iraq as the dynasty of Muhammad Ali, were linked, at times, to Egypt. When they fell they would do so amidst greater hate and greater derision. The proliferation of these two unpleasant qualities were the Hashemites' revenge on the people they had come to rule and stayed to lose. For Britain Iraq had been short-term gain.

Chapter 3

THE Cairo Conference which promoted Feisal to Iraq had received disturbing news about his brother. A telegram from Amman announced Abdullah's sudden arrival in the British-controlled wilderness to the east of the Jordan. He planned, it was rumored, to lead his tribesmen north into Syria in an attempt to restore Feisal to his throne; there had already been a clash between Hashemite soldiers and the French forces on the Syrian border.

If Abdullah had seemed likely, in a phrase of T. E. Lawrence's, to "biff the French out of Syria," the British might not have minded. But they had a clear picture of Abdullah's scant resources and no opinion of his military skill. An abortive invasion of Syria might prompt a French counterattack to the south. Though unimportant in itself, Trans-Jordan mattered to the British as the geographical link between Iraq and Palestine. Abdullah's militant pose was calculated to remind the all-powerful British that he, no less than Feisal, had royal claims. But the situation had its perils.

As soon, therefore, as the conference was over, and while Sir Percy Cox and Gertrude Bell returned to Baghdad, Winston Churchill, in spats and a soft hat, left Cairo for Jerusalem by way of Gaza. Government House had been established in a large German building on the Mount of Olives; the British had chosen a distinguished Jew, Sir Herbert Samuel, to be High Commissioner. Churchill sent Lawrence across the Jordan to bring Abdullah to Jerusalem. With him Lawrence took a summary of Churchill's terms: Feisal could not return to Syria but he could have Iraq; if Abdullah behaved, he could have Trans-Jordan. A British sergeant then drove the two short little men, kingmaker and future King, back to Jerusalem by way of Jericho. Palestinians lined the road to show their desire for an Arab ruler, but a dispatch rider intercepted the convoy and told them to drive fast. At Government House there were the trappings of respect, a guard of honor and a band. "At the door was Sir Herbert Samuel, the High Commissioner," Abdullah later remembered, "who received me in a very friendly way and I had tea with his family." Taking tea with High Commissioners could be dangerous, as the Iraqi notable discovered when he took tea with Sir Percy and Lady Cox in Baghdad. But no strong measures were needed with Abdullah. He listened politely to what he could expect, and what he could not. He must not annoy the French, but in return for collaboration with the British he would, like his father in the Hejaz or Ibn Saud in Arabia, be put on the list of British clients; as Trans-Jordan was lacking in developed resources, he would need a subsidy. Abdullah toyed with the killing-bottle whose imprisoned genie would be tiresome to the British and lethal to himself. "The people of Palestine," he claims to have told Sir Herbert and Mr. Churchill, "refuse the Balfour Declaration and insist on the retention of the Arab character of Palestine. We shall not agree to the annihilation of the Arabs for the sake of the Jews." Abdullah's memory could be creative and this statement was written down many years later for an Arab audience.[1] Churchill gave a polite, evasive answer while Sir Herbert insisted that a Jewish National Home by no means meant a Jewish state. Reassured, Abdullah returned to Amman. He was not again to trouble the British, nor they him. His Arab Legion would employ a considerable number of Bedouin and provide Britain with a valuable auxiliary force. Trouble from his own people was to dog, but not depress, Abdullah for the rest of his days. Amused by chess, Arabic poetry and handsome young men, he was to combine

[1] *Memoirs of King Abdullah* (London: Jonathan Cape, 1950), p. 204.

ebullience with dignity under the spotless turban which crowned his tricky and complex head. He was to have doubts about the wisdom of the Arab Revolt, to feel that while the Turks "at least remained Turks in everything," the Arabs of his generation had "turned blindly towards the West," abandoning their Eastern, Islamic culture. But when, late in his life, a film about the Arab Revolt was projected, Abdullah offered to play his original role himself. "But, Your Majesty," the embarrassed producer demurred, "you were then a young man of thirty . . ." In a moving tribute to Western technological magic the septuagenarian Abdullah replied: "But surely with your make-up techniques I could regain my youth?"[2]

That Sir Herbert Samuel spoke as Abdullah says he did is almost certain. For he said the same thing in a public speech delivered in Jerusalem that summer. The occasion was the official birthday of King George V.

"Let me in the first instance refer to the unhappy misunderstanding that has existed with reference to the phrase in the Balfour Declaration 'the establishment in Palestine of a National Home for the Jewish people.' I hear it said in many quarters, that the Arab people will not agree to their country, their Holy Places, their lands, being taken from them and given to strangers; that they will never agree to a Jewish Government being set up to rule the Moslem and Christian majority. People say that they cannot understand how it is that the British Government, which is famous throughout the world for its justice, could ever have consented to such a policy. I answer that the British Government, which does indeed care for justice above all things, has never consented and never will consent to such a policy. That is not the meaning of the Balfour Declaration. It may be that the translation of the English words into Arabic does not convey their real sense. They mean that the Jews, a people that are scattered throughout the world but whose hearts are always turned to Palestine, should be enabled to found here their home, and that some among them, within the limits that are fixed by the numbers and interests of the present population, should come to Palestine in order to help by their resources and efforts to develop the country, to the advantage of all the inhabitants." Sir Herbert was speaking as a British official and few have ever impugned his integrity. His words were in line with other official statements. When the Balfour Declaration had first been bruited in the Middle East—not by the British, who tried to keep it quiet, but by the Germans in Ottoman Damascus—King Hussein had demanded an explanation for what seemed a flat contradiction of the promises already made to him and the Arabs. Commander Hogarth, who had acted as father and spymaster to T. E. Lawrence, took an answer to Jeddah in early January 1918. Hogarth was authorized to state, he then told Hussein that "Jewish settlement in Palestine would only be allowed in so far as would be consistent with the

---

[2] This hitherto unpublished story was told to the author by the son of Rikabi Pasha, Abdullah's first Prime Minister; the film in question was never made.

political and economic freedom of the Arab population." The pledge had the effect of redefining the vague, second part of the declaration. Mr. Churchill gave a similar reassurance to an Arab delegation which called on him while he was in Jerusalem. Refusing to recommend the rescinding of the declaration, he stressed that the second part was as important as the first. "If one promise stands, so does the other. We shall faithfully fulfil both. Examine Mr. Balfour's careful words, Palestine to be 'a national home,' not 'the national home,' a great difference in meaning. The establishment of a national home does not mean a Jewish Government to dominate the Arabs." On the face of it, there was little surprising in the assurances of Commander Hogarth, Sir Herbert Samuel or Mr. Winston Churchill. They were in accord with the published war aims of the Allies. Only a month after Hogarth's visit to Hussein, President Wilson had put part of these succinctly: "People are not to be handed about from one sovereignty to another by an international conference or an understanding between rivals and antagonists." Nor were the committed Zionists any less reassuring. Nahum Sokolov had been Weizmann's closest collaborator in negotiating the Balfour Declaration. A year after the declaration was issued Sokolov wrote with apparent indignation: "It has been said and is still being obstinately repeated by anti-Zionists again and again, that Zionism aims at the creation of an independent 'Jewish State.' But this is wholly fallacious. The 'Jewish State' was never a part of the Zionist programme."

The term "national home," in place of "Jewish state," had been coined by Max Nordau, Herzl's writer friend, at the First Zionist Congress in Basel. Although Herzl's book was called *Judenstaat,* Nordau advised against using this term. "I did my best," he wrote, "to persuade the claimants of the Jewish state in Palestine that we might find a circumlocution that would express all we meant, but would say it in a way so as to avoid provoking the Turkish rulers of the coveted land. I suggested 'Heimstätte' as a synonym for 'State' . . . It was equivocal, but we all understood what it meant. To us it signified *'Judenstaat'* then and it signifies the same now."[3]

There is no need for us to picture the highest British authorities as blinded by a Zionist smoke screen. The issue was frankly discussed at a meeting held in Balfour's London house on July 22, 1921. Weizmann, Churchill and Lloyd George were among Balfour's guests. Weizmann had been upset by Sir Herbert Samuel's speech in Jerusalem. It meant, to him, a "virtual negation of the Balfour Declaration." Churchill, who had had no hand in the declaration but who sympathized with its general aims, asked him to explain. Weizmann thereupon read the published version of the speech sentence by sentence to argue that it clashed with the declaration, which, according to him, "meant an ultimate Jewish majority—and this speech would never permit such a majority to eventuate." Churchill shook

[3] Sykes, op. cit., p. 24.

his head at this interpretation of Sir Herbert's words, which only echoed his own to the Arabs. Whereupon Lloyd George and Balfour "both said that by the Declaration they always meant an eventual Jewish state."[4]

If British or Zionist intentions were ambiguous, the feelings of Palestinian Arabs were clear. In 1919 President Wilson had sent two emissaries to assess them. Dr. Henry Churchill King and Mr. Charles Crane were both in their early sixties and both had good qualifications for their task. King, who had worked with the YMCA attached to the American Expeditionary Force in Europe, was the author of several biblical studies, so knew the scriptural background well; he had been president of Oberlin College since 1902. Crane was a Chicago businessman who had frequently visited the Middle East and was on the Board of Trustees of Robert College in Istanbul. The two men's arrival in the Levant had coincided with the Greek invasion of Anatolia. In a cable from Palestine, dated June 12, they informed Wilson of the general exacerbation of clan feelings provoked by this action. As to the Holy Land: "Here the older inhabitants, both Moslem and Christian, take a united and most hostile attitude towards any extensive Jewish immigration or toward any effort to establish Jewish sovereignty over them. We doubt if any British or American official here believes that it is possible to carry out the Zionist program except through the support of a large army." A major problem, the professor and the businessman agreed, was religious. Palestine possessed shrines sacred to Muslim and Christian Arabs alike. "With the best possible intentions, it may be doubted whether the Jews could possibly seem to either Christians or Moslems proper guardians of the holy places, or custodians of the Holy Land as a whole. The reason is this: the places which are most sacred to Christians—those having to do with Jesus—and which are also sacred to Moslems, are not only not sacred to Jews, but abhorrent to them. It is simply impossible, under these circumstances, for Moslems and Christians to feel satisfied to have these places in Jewish hands, or under the custody of Jews. There are still other places about which Moslems must have the same feeling. In fact, from this point of view, the Moslems, just because the sacred places of all three religions are sacred to them, have made very naturally much more satisfactory custodians of the holy places than the Jews could be."[5]

While politicians equivocated and experts argued, on the Palestinian

[4] The account of this important discussion is based on the document first published in Richard Meinertzhagen's *Middle East Diary: 1917–1956* (London: 1959). It is reprinted in Sykes, p. 78. Of Weizmann's record, now in the Israel State Archives, Sykes comments that it is, even if allowance is made for some unconscious misreporting in his favor, telling evidence of an extraordinary unseriousness in the approach to this matter of the leading British ministers (Winston Churchill possibly to be excepted).

[5] U. S. Department of State, Papers Relating to the Foreign Relations of the U.S. The Paris Peace Conference 1919. (Washington: U. S. Government Printing Office, 1947.) Available in Harry N. Howard's "The King-Grane Commission" (Beirut: Khayats, 1963).

ground there was an increasing, and changing, Jewish fact. The first Jewish settlers of the 1880s had followed the practice of the Germans and Swedes already installed there by employing Arab labor to run their farms. These Jewish seigneurs contributed to the budgets of the Arabs, who in return taught them the basic facts of Palestinian agriculture, in which the planting of citrus already played an important role.

But a second wave of immigrants had come to Palestine in the wake of the First Zionist Congress and the pogroms in czarist Russia. A new type of colonist introduced a new philosophy—"the way of manual labor."[6] At its grandest the way was trodden by the man who used this phrase, Aaron David Gordon, a native of Vilna. Gordon, a weakling child, had been sent to a farm to regain his strength. Later, for twenty-three years, he managed an estate belonging to a distant relation, Baron Horace Günzburg. In both experiences he felt on the land, but not of it. He was nearly fifty and in failing health when he decided to go and work in Palestine. He arrived there in the spring of 1904 and sought employment as a laborer. With difficulty he got taken on in an orange grove. He was as much exalted by the toil as disciples of William Morris by handicrafts or Tolstoy (whom Gordon admired) by the wearing of a moujik's blouse. Martin Buber, a later Zionist of Gordon's spiritual stamp, believed that Gordon's heart was wounded by the sense that the Jews had fallen "not from political self-determination but from the Cosmos. No merely receptive behaviour will enable them to find their place in it again. Man can participate in the Cosmos only when he *does* something in the cosmic context that is his particular sphere, just as the stars revolve in their courses and the trees grow towards the sun. To work on the land entrusted to his care is what befits man. The men sent by a newly arising Israel to work on the soil of its land represent its reunion, not merely with the earth but with the Cosmos."[7] Gordon himself repeated one basic message: "The Jewish people has been completely cut off from nature and imprisoned within city walls these two thousand years. We have become accustomed to every form of life, except to a life of labor—of labor done at our own behest and for its own sake. It will require the greatest effort of will for such a people to become normal again."[8]

Gordon's notion of a return to normality clashed with the philosophy of those Zionists who wanted Jews "to become normal again" by imitating other nationalists. Such a nationalism would lack the qualities of a specifically Jewish spiritual renaissance which Gordon saw as the justification of Zionism. "He saw the crucial test," Samuel Hugo Bergman has written, "in the attitude of the Jews towards the Arabs. He never tired of stressing that

[6] Arthur Hertzberg, ed., *The Zionist Idea* (New York: 1959), p. 376.

[7] Martin Buber, *Israel and Palestine: The History of an Idea* (New York: Farrar, Straus and Young, 1952), pp. xi–xii.

[8] Hertzberg, op. cit., p. 372.

the land belonged to both peoples and that that nation had the greater claim upon the land which suffered more for its sake."

These early pioneers suffered everything from calluses to malaria. They hardly knew, with their urban background, the difference between spade and mattock; they had crop failures and poor harvests; yet they were, in the kibbutz, to create an agricultural innovation of unpredictable importance. The resources of the Jewish spirit long denied outlet in physical labor turned the pockets of Palestine which they purchased into smiling oases of scientific agriculture. The communities which slowly transformed marshes or barren hillsides into orange groves or vineyards marked a new experiment in human living. Whether religious, secular or socialist (and there were various kinds of kibbutz), all were activated by a collective ideal for which the only previous parallels would be the religious communities of the Middle Ages; the transformation wrought by the kibbutzim was indeed comparable to the way in which Cistercian monasteries had turned the empty dales of Yorkshire into rich farmland.

Not all the Jews who took up manual labor did so in Gordon's Tolstoyan spirit. Ben-Gurion was another settler from Eastern Europe who worked, though not for so long, as an agricultural laborer. While Ben-Gurion's grandfather had been a deeply religious Orthodox Jew, his father had been merely observant. "I myself had an orthodox spell when I was about seven," he tells us, "but not thereafter. My father did not seem to mind. I think he knew I would be what he called a "good Jew" because of my interest in Hebrew, Jewish history and Zionism." Such a conception of a "good Jew" was very different from that of Gordon or Martin Buber. More than a "good Jew," Ben-Gurion was an instinctive politician who had begun contributing articles to a newspaper called *Ahdut* (or *Unity*). "What set me writing were some incidents in Petach Tikvah which made me very angry—Jewish workers being turned down by Jewish farmers in favour of Arab laborers at a lower wage."[9] Ben-Gurion was an activist and a socialist. He worked not only for the employment of Jewish labor at whatever its cost, but for the organization of this labor in pursuit of socialist ideals—but socialist ideals for the benefit of the Jewish nation, not the Arab. He played a leading role in organizing an association of armed Jewish workmen. This was the germ from which sprang the Haganah and, later, the Israeli armed forces.

For with the growth of Jewish settlements employing only Jewish labor a colonial situation had arisen in which the colonists needed to protect themselves from the natives. This had existed even before the 1914 war; it was to become more acute after the Balfour Declaration. While Ben-Gurion, the pragmatist, was forming his armed bands to protect Jewish settlements against attack from Circassians, Druzes or Arabs, theoreticians from the

[9] These quotations come from Moshe Pearlman, *Ben-Gurion looks back in talks with . . .* (London: Weidenfeld & Nicolson, 1965).

settlements saw their own situation in colonial terms. On April 24, 1909 —the year when the deposition of Sultan Abdul Hamid accelerated the development of divisive nationalism inside the Ottoman Empire—a Zionist settler of this second philosophy, Aaronsohn by name, addressed an audience of French settlers in Tunisia on *La Colonisation Juive en Palestine*. He described Zionism as a "movement of colonization, little known, ill judged, and which, being a work of private enterprise, is inevitably small-scale, but has much in common, nevertheless, with French colonialism in Tunisia." Aaronsohn even found significance in the fact that the Jewish settlement of Palestine had started in the same year—1882 —as the French occupation of Tunisia. There were deeper similarities. "One of the proofs that our Jewish colonization in Palestine has been fruitful is the jealousy which it arouses. You know that this is an infallible human criterion. People begin to complain that the Jewish element will soon replace the native. Your own experience in Algeria and Tunisia will have taught you how absurd such suggestions are. The Jewish colon in Palestine, like his French opposite number in Tunisia, wins his land from the bush. So far from turning the natives out, the Jewish colon encourages them to come in, giving a livelihood to scores who profit from the benefit of land which they were too lazy, or too ignorant, or too impotent to work themselves . . . The Jew in Palestine, just like the Frenchman here, does not put himself in the place of the native, but alongside him. It is a question of juxtaposition, and not substitution, to use a Tunisian formula." Aaronsohn concluded his address with an invitation to the French colons to visit Palestine. *"Vous vous croirez en une colonie française."*[10]

Juxtaposition or substitution? This basic question haunted the Englishmen who administered the mandate for Palestine, linked as it was with the implementation of the Balfour Declaration. They tried to be fair. Some favored the Arabs, some the Jews, but the majority endeavored, while preserving British control over Palestine, to balance the declaration's two undertakings. They found themselves in a position hardly less agonizing than that of Pilate.

On one side clamored the "Arabs," in fact the descendants of the Canaanites who had lived in Palestine before the Hebrews and who had stayed on to intermarry with Phoenicians, Greeks and Arabs. Numbering 90 per cent of the population, they claimed a natural right, not only to the country they regarded as their own, but to democratic institutions. The British knew that once such institutions were permitted, the Arab majority would use them to prevent further Jewish immigration. For while the Arabs had got on well with the religious Jews of the past, they were deeply suspicious of the intentions of the post-war immigrants from Europe. They did not understand, or could not tolerate, messianic dreams which derived

10 A. Aaronsohn, *La Colonisation Juive en Palestine*. Bulletin de la Societé Botanique de France, 1909. Allocution prononcé le 24 Avril 1909 à Tunis.

from a religion which they regarded as at the best having only partial truth, and which involved their own subordination to the role of a minority. To the Arabs, arguments that the Jews were "returning" to the land of Israel had a disturbing echo: the two Catholic colonizers in North Africa, France and Italy, often stressed that North Africa had been Latin once and was becoming Latin again. In this mood Algeria had been declared part of metropolitan France and the use of Arabic forbidden in the schools; in Libya the Italians used ruthless measures to subdue the Arabs into second-class citizens. It is unlikely that the Arabs would ever have welcomed large-scale immigration; in the context of their recent experience they viewed with apprehension, at its mildest, with terror at its worst, the steady increase of a minority which claimed a vaguely defined Palestine as its inalienable home. They felt towards the Jews as nestlings to a cuckoo child. Once the Jews had become a majority in Palestine—or felt themselves sufficiently strong—they would either evict the Arabs by force or reduce them to the status of an impotent minority.

On the other side were the Jews, who could clamor with the Arabs but also speak the languages of Western culture. The immigrants of the 1920s had been educated in Europe; they were ahead of the Arabs in technology; they were often highly idealistic. But no less than the Arabs they had suffered wounds in their recent and distant past. Great suffering can induce a state akin to what philosophers call solipsism: the sense that only oneself exists, for in Schiller's words, "The Solipsist thinks that *he is the one!*" The ordinary Jewish settlers—which excepts such extraordinary men as Gordon or Buber—were at first not so much hostile as indifferent to the Arabs. But Arabs were an inconvenience in Eretz Israel; they made questionable a Zionist slogan of wide dispersion: "A Land without a People for a People without a Land." And then, as the Arabs reacted with growing hostility to growing immigration, they were felt as bothersome, like mosquitoes, and like mosquitoes, sometimes lethal. Then, as the Arab leadership brought pressure on the British to prevent the sale of land, they became a baffling obstacle; in the thirty-one years from the Balfour Declaration to establishment of the state of Israel in 1948, the Jews were only able to increase the proportion of Palestine they owned through purchase from around 2 to around 7 per cent of the total. Just as the Arabs showed an inability to understand the Jewish nostalgia for Bronze Age Palestine, the Jews showed an equal inability to understand the Palestinian attachment to the land where their parents and grandparents were buried. Since the Jews were a people with humane traditions, they found the Arabs a moral embarrassment; since they also excelled at talmudic argument, they tried to overcome the embarrassment with debating points. The Palestinians were not a nation; they did not feel attachment to the soil; they could be moved elsewhere, to other soil; they were not as numerous as they claimed to be. Levi Eshkol belonged to the same generation of immigrants from Eastern

Europe as David Ben-Gurion, whom he was to succeed as Prime Minister of the Jewish state. In the last interview of his life, in February 1969 with *Newsweek,* he was to ask: "What are Palestinians? When I came here there were 250,000 non-Jews, mainly Arabs and Bedouins." The Encyclopaedia Britannica for the period gives the population of Palestine as around 650,000, not more than 10 per cent of these being Jews.

Faced with this collision of claims and the violence which was its concomitant, the British hoped that somehow the problem would go away, or at least subside. The early 1920s saw large migrations because of xenophobic new governments in some countries of Eastern Europe. As Europe recovered from the war, as prosperity returned, the pressure on Jews decreased. In 1927 the British had reason to rejoice. For the first time since the war more Jews left Palestine than came in. With the recovery of world trade and the growth of tolerance in Europe the land of miracles might become a country where the word impossible could put on living flesh. The British in Pilate's seat crossed their fingers; the time when they would wash them had not yet come.

BOOK EIGHT

Europa Furens

Know that the Fascist, and in particular the soldier, must not believe in perpetual peace.
First principle of the Fascist Decalogue, 1934 version

In this world what is not Race is dross.
ADOLF HITLER, *Reichs-chancellor, 1933–45*

Chapter 1

THE hopes of a flimsy decade burst on October 29, 1929, with Wall Street's bubble. The shock waves were the more destructive for starting in America. American prosperity and American loans had underpinned the Europe of the victorious wartime Alliance and since the United States had not joined the League of Nations, Europe was still the political fulcrum of the world.

The first effects of the Depression were economic. America no longer pumped her helpful dollars to the rest of the world. The chief sufferers were the countries, already poor, who produced the world's basic products; as American companies ceased to buy their raw materials, these countries became yet poorer. But since these producers of raw materials could not afford to import manufactured goods, the industrialized countries who owned the factories and the shipping lines were hit as well. Unemployment in Europe rose from plateau to plateau.

Blows to the pocket involved more dangerous blows to heart and head. The financial disaster which had begun on Wall Street left no country in Europe unscathed; not even the Soviet Union could isolate itself from the effects of what was fundamentally a capitalist crisis, since the moods in the capitalist countries of Europe affected Russian security. The society to be most radically affected was the Weimar Republic, shallow-rooted successor to the German Empire of the Kaiser. As a result of military defeat in the war, the humiliation of prolonged occupation and the collapse of its currency, the largest and best-educated nation in the Old World was to reject the Christian civilization which it had upheld since the age of Charlemagne. Christian Italy was to puff an obscure local dictatorship known as Fascism into a system openly dreaming of the restoration of the pagan Roman Empire. After ruthlessly subduing the Senussi tribesmen in Cyrenaica (practices such as dropping the recalcitrant from airplanes were to set a pattern for coming decades) the Italians would turn the daydreams of the 1870s into a reality and conquer Coptic Abyssinia with the blessing of a Latin Pope. England and France, weakened victors, would resist the violent creeds of Rome and Berlin; but no less than Germany and Italy they would suffer from the general shaking of the foundations. Before two decades of violence were over, Britain would have exhausted her energies in a global struggle while France would have experienced at the hands of the Germans the military occupation she had inflicted on Arabs in North Africa and Syria. The Europe which had seemed united in its civilization when Ismail had opened the Canal would split apart; warring factions would not merely pound each other with arms, as had been the case in 1914–18, but tear at each other's entrails in ideological rage. Europeans by the million would perish in an eruption of violence which would leave the old continent almost without power; the United States and the Soviet Union would become the twin poles of attraction in the decades to come. The olympian Europe of the Victorian era would fade like a dream.

To this dream the Middle East had been reacting as membrane to drumstick since the time of Napoleon. A Europe torn by a dionysian fury still sent waves of vibration amongst the natives and newcomers in the Middle East.

One country was curiously immune. Turkish-speaking Anatolia, all that survived of the Ottoman Empire, had paid Europe the supreme compliment of adopting its alphabet, its system of law, its weekly day of rest and its style of dress. After Atatürk's death in 1938 Turkey continued to cut its dated stencil of European civilization. Its leaders—men like Ismet İnönü, who had experienced to the full the ruin of war—would do their best to save Turkey from adventures. In 1938 Turkey regained the sanjak of Alexandretta (renamed Iskanderun) from the French, who still administered Syria and Lebanon; after the war Turkish governments would show some interest in the fate of the Turkish minority in Cyprus; otherwise the Turks would be conspicuous by their absence in the arena they had so long commanded; when in the 1950s a religious-minded Prime Minister, Adnan Menderes, showed signs of involving Turkey in the affairs of her Arab neighbors, he would be overthrown by a military coup and in the name of Atatürk's principles be hanged until death from a tripod gallows. It was as if by abolishing the Caliphate the Turks had opted out of history.

The opposite was the case in the Arabic-speaking lands which the Ottomans had ruled. The new time of troubles would show how illusory were the achievements of the Hashemites and the followers of Zaghlul.

In Egypt the confused violence of the early 1920s had won the country only nominal gains. Instead of leaving an Egypt seriously engaged in fashioning a juster society, Zaghlul had bequeathed to his impoverished valley and delta a parliamentary system; in this his party, the Wafd, was one among several alliances feuding for place. Against an inhibiting background of British occupation and royal autocracy a fever of intestinal dispute, some trivial, some profound, gave evidence that Egypt was mortally sick.

"No one but God," wrote an Egyptian student then in his early twenties and perhaps the most significant disputant, "knows how many nights we spent discussing the state of the nation . . . its present sickness and the possible remedies. How to treat, how to halt the disease!"[1]

Like many of those who have affected modern Egyptian history, Hassan al-Banna was the son of a prosperous villager. His father doubled the trade of watch repairer with devoted immersion in traditional Islam. But characteristically his son claimed that his true paternity was popular Islam. The first influence on his life was the Koran, which he knew by heart. The second was one of the Sufi brotherhoods which brought fervor and warmth to the impoverished lives of the fellahin: chanting the name of Allah! in time to bodily movements of rhythmic repetition participants in a *zikr* achieved much the same state of ecstasy as the whirling dervishes of Turkey. Al-Banna had been born in 1906, the year when the Dinshwai executions exploded the myth of a happy coexistence between British and Egyptians; adolescent in 1919, he had demonstrated with the noisiest; in 1929 he formally challenged the westernizing tradition in which so many of the characters in this book had stood: Ismail and Atatürk *par excellence*, but also Orabi and Zaghlul. By a significant accident al-Banna issued his challenge—an action which would involve many violent deaths, his own included—in Ismailia, the city which symbolized the nineteenth-century dream, the city where Ismail the complacent had offered his myriad guests *Poisson à la Réunion des Deux Mers* washed down with château-bottled wines. He was appointed, newly graduated, to teach Arabic and religion in a government school which continued the Europeanizing program which Ismail had favored. The young man found nothing to admire in the sixty-year-old city, swollen as it had from the November days when Eugénie had cantered to the villa of De Lesseps. Ismailia in the late 1920s was thronged with the polyglot foreigners who from the headquarters of the Suez Canal Company and a plethora of offices exploited Egypt's geographical position and most of her trade. Nearby stretched the neat encampments of the British Army, their edges marked by whitewashed stones. The chasm between the European city with its shady boulevards, yacht club and churches and the slum town of the natives had become yet more marked. The English or French street names—"in the tongues of the economic occupation," as al-Banna put it—symbolized thralldom.

In this unpromising soil the twenty-year-old teacher planted the first seeds of a movement which would grow with beanstalk speed to shadow the next twenty years of Egyptian public life. His "Association of the Muslim Brothers" consciously trod on the heels of a "Young Men's Muslim Association" founded a year earlier in innocuous competition with the Egyptian YMCA. Al-Banna was not concerned with the provision of uplifting leisure activities; his aims were political, and revolutionary, from

[1] Quoted from *"Min Kutab Hasan al-Banna"* in Ishak Musa Husaini, *The Moslem Brethren* (Beirut: Khayat's, 1956).

the beginning; the Brotherhood's sports clubs had a militant aim; after 1940 they sponsored terror.

Al-Banna used the railway timetable like a businessman, addressing audiences of thousands in mosques or coffeeshops in a perpetual tour of Egypt. His listeners shared a sense of humiliation and despair; he reached those who felt alienated from Egyptian society—the fellahin whom no political party had touched and the students for whom there were no jobs. They reacted passionately to his evocation of a golden past and his angry disdain for a pewter present. Al-Banna represented a recurrent phenomenon in Islamic history: a preacher demanding a return to the fundamentals of Muhammad. He had had two precursors in particular. In the eighteenth century an Arabian visionary had founded the Wahhabi movement in protest against the cult of tombs and saints; the last offspring of this movement in the 1920s was King Ibn Saud of Arabia, the desert warrior who had chased the Hashemites from the Hejaz. The Sudanese Mahdi, who had expelled the Khedive's administration from Khartoum, had been another such militant protester. Al-Banna had things in common with both these men. He wanted to remodel Egyptian society on purified Islamic lines; he also wished Egypt to resist, not embrace, the culture of the West. If the imitation of Europe seemed to him treachery, the gentle reformism of Abduh and his disciples, the balanced duel between rationalism and faith, embodied a subtlety alien to him. Though no untutored boor, he was still less an intellectual in the tradition which derives from the questioning Socrates. His mental capital was a memory prodigiously stocked: before his final examinations he is said to have memorized 18,000 lines of poetry or gnomic utterance; he could produce sayings like a conjuror—always the right rabbit for the right occasion. His emotional force involved will and charm in a hypnotic mixture. He was physically wiry, short and tough.

His appeal was simple: "We call you to Islam, the teachings of Islam, the rules of Islam, and the guidance of Islam. If this means politics to you, then this is our politics."[2] Muslims, he argued, had constituted a great people when they had been totally faithful to Islam, which besides being the last and most perfect of the monotheist religions, also offered the blueprint for an ideal society. Muslim disobedience had created a situation in which "the norms of morality have been smashed and the standards of virtue have crumbled away."[3] The tacit divorce between the law of religion and the law of the state was practical blasphemy. Although he praised Atatürk for abolishing political parties, al-Banna believed that Islam should have a political head and towards the end of his life he was accused of plotting to seize power in Egypt and to make himself Caliph. He would have been a Caliph in the sternest sense, remodeling Egypt, and any other country which accepted his ideas, through the literal application of koranic

[2] Husaini, op. cit., p. 62.
[3] Ibid., p. 45.

rules. If the holy book decreed that a thief's hand should be cut, then the state should restore this penalty. (It remained, in fact, the standard practice in Saudi Arabia.) If women were required to cover all but their hands and face, then dress should be redesigned accordingly. If Christians and Jews were to be treated kindly, but as second-class citizens, then the Brotherhood would not have shied away from creating a theocratic hierarchy. Since tradition accepted that Jihad was a pillar of faith, the Brotherhood not merely accepted Holy War as a theoretical possibility (rather as Catholics accepted the possibility of a "just war"), but trained its adepts to fight. Al-Banna did not reject the machinery of a Western state: "there is much good and much evil in Western civilization and it is indispensable to our modern renaissance to adopt what is beneficial from its industry and science."[4] The Brotherhood succeeded in a worldly sense; it owned factories, shops and printing presses. More somberly, the practice of selective assassination which had marked Islamic society from its apostolic age (only one of the first four Caliphs had died un-murdered) was adopted as part of the Brotherhood's strategy.

The Brotherhood's militancy and its later use of terrorism reminded some people of National Socialism, different though a religious movement led by men in *gallabya* and turban was from a pagan movement led by jack-booted politicians. Like Hitler (whose use of the radio "to enlighten his people" he praised), al-Banna was a great simplifier. But the simplicities of the Brotherhood owed nothing to Europe. A more ironic, and perhaps truer, comparison would be with its major opponent, the Zionism which would increasingly attract the Jews of Eastern Europe. A return to Islam resounded as plangently as a return to Zion. In a season of insecurity and humiliation, when the British occupation seemed eternal and a fall in cotton prices engendered unemployment, such a return was pleasing to those who had reached nowhere pleasant. Those who had attained a certain level of security or sophistication were less susceptible; and just as Zionism failed to lure many immigrants from England or America, so the Brotherhood convinced few of the prosperous. But most Egyptians were neither secure nor sophisticated; the Brotherhood would expand year by year until from a population still numbering less than twenty million it claimed, without too much exaggeration, two and a half million adherents. In its heyday it controlled the universities of Egypt, holding the loyalty of teachers and taught alike; it became a movement dangerous to offend, striking at police chiefs or prime ministers with equal ferocity. There were other parallels with Zionism too. Tough and well organized, it seemed of use to those outside its magic circle. Just as first the British, and then the French and the Americans, would find uses for a Jewish state, so many who could not share the Brotherhood's philosophy found it a useful barrier to

[4] Ibid., p. 79; I have modified Husaini's translation.

socialist ideas. A good tactician, al-Banna preached the superiority of Islam to communism in much the same way that Herzl had stressed, in his conversation with Von Bülow, the anti-socialist nature of Zionism. Both movements knew how to be elastic. The Brotherhood did not initiate kibbutzim, but it preached and practiced a form of socialism for its members. Idealistic and energetic, both movements kept their charity to themselves. Just as Arab Palestinians felt themselves excluded from the Israel of the future, so non-Muslims foresaw their exclusion from a society reconstructed by the Brotherhood. Almost certainly the Brotherhood's triumph would have robbed them of all they had gained since the nineteenth century. Thanks to the dynasty of Muhammad Ali, they had reached the highest positions in society; British favor had secured them a preponderant position in the bureaucracy and the professions. Not only the Copts were alarmed by the Brotherhood's advance. For all those who did not believe in orthodox Islam, including Jews who did not wish to emigrate to Palestine and Christians from Europe or the Levant, the progress of the Brotherhood throughout the Middle East was as alarming as the Nazi Party to non-Aryans—or the Zionist movement to Palestinians.

Those immune to al-Banna's message were often more highly educated than the Muslim majority; they included (besides the Copts of Egypt, the Christians of Lebanon, Syria, Palestine and Iraq and the Jews) an undisclosed number of Muslims who no longer accepted all the doctrines of their faith. These together formed an intellectual elite. They had profited from the Western schooling—in French, American or British institutions—which had been one by-product of the imperial age. To this elite, seeking an alternative to fundamentalist Islam, the neurotic Europe of the 1930s offered disturbing counsel in various forms.

The politicians in their polished shoes and well-ironed tarbooshes were untempted by extremes. The members of the Royal Automobile Club d'Egypte wanted to consolidate their wealth, either by investing it in land (the safest investment in Egypt) or depositing it abroad. Although a largely desert and overpopulated country needed industry, the rich feared the risks of investing in factories; their local investments were usually in apartment blocks, shops or cinemas; Egyptian studios had begun to fabricate a synthetic and cheap hashish, the musical daydream. The capitalist Egypt of the 1930s produced imitations of France's Pierre Laval or Britain's Sir Samuel Hoare. Thanks to King Fuad's upbringing, the court was italianate, thronged with Italian courtiers, hairdressers, gunmen or pimps; a vague sympathy with Mussolini was in fashion; some, like Fuad's son, Farouk, even supposed that their semi-Aryan blood would exonerate them from the Nazi downgrading of the Egyptians as a miscegenated *Untermensch*.

So much for the elite. To the man in the Beirut street or the Baghdad bazaar Communism and Fascism hawked their opposite wares. Both these philosophies had some success, in particular with the minorities.

The first dictatorship of the proletariat had been established, in Russia, by the end of 1917, and it is hardly surprising that this event evoked little response in the Middle East. Russia was identified in the popular mind with the Orthodox Church and the czarist empire; Russians were the traditional enemies of the Ottoman Empire, and therefore Islam. To the religious, the atheism of the Communist leaders was unpopular. To the Bedouin of the deserts or the villagers of Anatolia and Egypt, the very notion of a proletariat lacked not only meaning but the words in which the notion could be expressed. The two most widely felt bonds were the inter-related ones of resistance to the West and Islam. Atatürk's nationalism was unchallenged by either of the two Turkish Communist Parties, while in Egypt the Muslim Brotherhood outnumbered the Communist Party by at least a thousand to one.

Even so, a brave start had been made when the first Egyptian Communist Party was recognized by the Comintern in 1922. It had been founded as a socialist party two years earlier. Its birthplace was not the Cairo over-shadowed by al-Azhar but cosmopolitan Alexandria. Its three founders—a jeweler named Joseph Rosenthal, Antun Marun, a lawyer, and Husni al-Arabi, the first party delegate to the Comintern—rejected the three old faiths of Judaism, Christianity and Islam to propound the "scientific socialism" in whose name Lenin had ended the war between Russia and Germany and started on the construction of the Soviet Union. Throughout the 1920s and 1930s the party never mustered more than two thousand members and of these less than one in five was Egyptian, the membership being dominated by Greeks and Jews. The party's predictable difficulties were compounded by its leaders' errors of judgment. Their dogmas made them approach the workers and peasants, rather than the intellectuals, among whom they might have had more success. They failed to see that the national struggle for liberation meant more to the peoples of the Middle East than the class struggle. Communism was little more than an alien-sounding word until the imposing Soviet victories in the Second World War.

The intellectuals and the minorities were more aware of the revolution-ary new movements in Italy and Germany than of Soviet Communism. The Middle East had always felt closer to the Italians and the Germans than to the Russians. Giuseppe Donizetti had taught music in the Constantinople of the 1830s and the Germans had been the allies of Turkey in the First World War; large numbers of Italians lived in Cairo and Alexandria and a far larger number of Arabs and Muslims lived under Italian rule in Libya and Eritrea. The Arabs in particular could understand the inferiority complex which played so significant a role in Fascism but taken neat, neither the Italian nor the German doctrine could attract them greatly. Fascism stood for a revival of the Roman Empire at Arab, as well as Greek, Albanian or Abyssinian expense; the Egypt of the 1930s was to find Italy as menacing as the traditional foe, Great Britain. Although the Germans had never subdued a Muslim people, a race doctrine exalting the purity of Nordic blood meant nothing to the descendants of Pharoahs, Phoenicians and Babylonians.

But the trappings of the two exciting movements—the cult of youth, military music, torchlight processions, devotion to an infallible leader— these were adaptable for authoritarian movements committed to their own brand of irrationality.

One man came near to implanting a successful fascist movement in part of the Middle East. Antun Saada fully obeys the rule that nationalists spring from the fringe. His father, Dr. Khalil Saada, was one of the many educated Lebanese Christians who left their beautiful but impoverished mountain home for the relatively prosperous flatland of Lord Cromer. They quickly dominated the intellectual and commercial life of Cairo; Lebanese founded such famous newspapers as *al-Ahram* and such publishing houses as Dar al-Hillal. Dr. Saada's contribution was an English-Arabic dictionary. Instead of staying in Egypt, he migrated to South America to start a magazine for a growing community of Syrians, most of them Christians, who were making their fortunes in polychrome Brazil. There Antun was born in 1904 and there, amidst a medley of Amerindians and Negroes speaking Portuguese, he began to pose the fundamental question of his life. "Who are we?" was a question of identity sharpened by his plural environment. The answer he gave had been foreshadowed by his father, who as a young man had discussed the problem of replacing the Ottoman system so insufferable to many Christians. A common alternative was Arab Nationalism, since the bond of Arabic could link Christians with Muslims, and for that matter with Arabic-speaking Jews. Dr. Saada's friends and contemporaries had toyed with another notion: that of a Syrian nation underlying the eastern regions of the Mediterranean. In the late 1920s he returned to a Syria (he never differentiated begween Syria and Lebanon) under French rule. Antun honed his father's vague ideas into a philosophy which disposed of both Arabic and Islam: "We are Syrians and we constitute a distinct national entity." He and his followers were never to regard Islam as more than an accident which had influenced the development of this Syrian nation for a mere thirteen centuries; nor did he think of language as an important bond; he looked down on such dark-skinned speakers of Arabic as the Egyptians and Sudanese. To him the two realities were a submerged Syrian nation and the geographical homeland of Syria. This homeland was defined twice: in the first version, made in the 1930s, it extended "from the Taurus mountains in the north to the Suez Canal in the south, embracing the Sinai peninsula and the Gulf of Aqaba; and from the Syrian Sea in the west to the desert in the east until it meets the Tigris." (As a polymath, Saada could be vague on his facts—the desert met the

Euphrates, not the Tigris; but facts mean little to nationalists.) In a post-war definition the island of Cyprus was included as the star to a Fertile Crescent which arched east to include Iraq. Saada could rival Hitler at verbose pseudo-science: "The common stocks, Canaanite, Chaldaean, Aramaean, Assyrian, Ammorite, Mitanni, and Akkadian, whose reality and blending are an indisputable historical and scientific fact, constitute the ethnic-psychological-historical-cultural-basis, whereas the regions of nat-ural Syria (the Fertile Crescent) constitute the geographic-agricultural-economic-strategic-basis of Syria's unity."

A political organization to propel Saada's ideology into battle was secretly founded in the early 1930s; it became known as the PPS (Parti Populaire Syrien) from a French mistranslation of its name in Arabic. The PPS offended every conceivable interest. Its secular trend made it unpopu-lar with mosque and church; its concept of a Syrian homeland including Palestine ensured that it clashed with Zionism; its belief that capital and labor should be united under a paternalistic government made it anathema to socialists; but its opposition to organized state power led to its leader's exile and final martyrdom. In 1936 the French brought Saada to trial for conspiracy against the state; two years later he retreated from Lebanon to South America, where he sat out the war. In 1947, returning to the arena of his love, he challenged the Lebanese successor state to the French mandate. Underrating the extent to which an independent Lebanon cor-responded with the wishes of the Lebanese Christians, and in particular the Maronites, he launched an abortive coup, fled to Syria and was traded back to Beirut by a Syrian dictator. He was shot after a hasty and secret trial.

Though, like the Muslim Brotherhood, the PPS was not to gain power in any Middle Eastern state, its blend of extreme nationalism, military organization and violence showed in the Levant, as the Brotherhood had shown in Egypt, the shock waves sent by Europe to the weaker shores of the "White Middle Sea." Many of the men who would influence the eastern Arab world after the Second World War, under whatever political labels of later adoption, had spent their political adolescence in the PPS.

Chapter 2

WHILE psychotic Europe gave Arab adolescents poles of attraction and repulsion, it gave those Jews it did not kill an unprecedented wound. Middle Eastern society would remain substantially unaltered between 1929 and 1948. The neurotic years for the Arabs would come when Europe's masters had massacred part of the Jews and scarred the rest. Arab society would only be shaken from an apparently eternal stability by the presence in its midst of an exacerbated Jewish community.

Until the early 1930s few people outside Germany had taken seriously the movement known as National Socialism. A revival of tribalism had been the party's published program since February 24, 1920, when its Fourth Point had proclaimed: "None but members of the nation may be citizens of the State. None but those of German blood, whatever their creed, may be members of the nation. No Jew, therefore, may be considered a member of the nation." The party had two basic scriptures. Its leader, a failed Austrian artist with wartime service as a corporal in the German Army, had composed his frank testament, *Mein Kampf*, while imprisoned for attempting an abortive coup d'état. Alfred Rosenberg's *The Myth of the Twentieth Century* ranked second in the canon of the new faith. Rosenberg argued that the class war was illusory; history could only be understood in racial terms and the real struggle was between "values of soul." *The Myth* rejected even the sanities of ecclesiastical intolerance: the Church had always accepted that baptism incorporated Jews into the Christian body. Conversion made not a scrap of difference to Hitler and Rosenberg: blood, not belief, was "that mysterium which has replaced and conquered the old sacraments."

Indifference to these ideas became impossible in the winter of 1932–33, when Adolf Hitler, the author of *Mein Kampf* and the Fuehrer of the Nazi Party, was elected Chancellor of what was still the largest state in Western Europe. The Nazis quickly showed that they intended to practice their philosophy. A *Law for the Protection of German Blood and Honor*[1] prohibited marriage or any form of sexual relationship between Jews and Germans; it became illegal for Jews to employ pre-menopausal German housemaids; while Jews were allowed to display "Jewish colors," they were

[1] September 15, 1935.

forbidden to fly the German flag. Pseudo-scientific objectivity was used to define a Jew or person of mixed Jewish blood as "one who had one or two grandparents who were racially full Jews; Jewish grandparents shall be considered full-blooded Jews if they belonged to the Jewish religious community." As part of this folk-weave fanaticism: a peasant had to prove that he had no Jewish or colored blood since January 1, 1800. A final provision added a grotesquely arbitrary touch: "The Fuehrer and Chancellor of the Reich is empowered to release anyone from the provisions of these administrative decrees."[2]

It would hardly surprise if the adoption of such legislation by a storm-trooping state stirred something akin to mass psychosis among the Jews of Europe. The fuel which Herzl had envisaged as powering his engine was spouting from a well of unsuspected purity. Jews who had toyed with Zionism now had two serious grounds for migrating to Palestine. The obvious reason was that it was a place of refuge; and faced with expulsion or worse, few would bother to question the title deeds of Zion. A deeper, perhaps stronger reason was the cataclysmic deterioration of the position of Jews in gentile society. If a country with Germany's high culture could revert to tribalism, what other country was immune? It is a remarkable tribute to the long-term optimism of German Jews that the great majority chose England and America, not Palestine, as their new homes. Their contributions to the arts and sciences of their countries of adoption were to be incalculable.

But enough Jews chose Palestine to produce a resonant effect on that sensitive country.

They did not join an entirely balanced or irenic community. There had been a zealot, or chauvinistic, current of opinion among the Jewish settlers in Palestine even before the First World War. When Ben-Gurion wore the Ottoman fez and Palestine was still administered by Turks, an attitude of racial exclusiveness had disgusted Moshe Menuhin, later the father of a famous violinist but then a student. Moshe attended a school named in Herzl's honor. "All through the years of our studies at the Gymnasia, we daily imbibed an endless harangue about our sacred obligations toward *Amaynooh, Artzaynooh, Moladtaynooh* (our nation, our country, our fatherland). It was drummed into our young hearts that the fatherland must be ours, "goyim rein" (clear of Gentiles—Arabs); that we must dedicate our lives to serving the fatherland and fighting for it."[3] Moshe Menuhin found this attitude so pervasive and so repugnant that he left Palestine and settled in California.

The summer of 1929—the last season before the Depression—shows the dry grass on which the sparks of anti-Semitic Europe would shortly fall.

[2] Article 7, Decree Law of November 14, 1935.
[3] Moshe Menuhin, *The Decadence of Judaism in our Time* (New York: Exposition Press, 1965), p. 52.

The Sixteenth Zionist Congress had just met in Zurich. Though the moderates, under the leadership of Chaim Weizmann and Nahum Sokolov, maintained control, the speech which had attracted most attention on the first day was given by Vladimir Jabotinsky, leader of an extremist faction known as the Revisionists. Jabotinsky joined in the fashionable game of definitions to clarify what he meant by Palestine: "Palestine is a territory whose chief geographical feature is this: that the River Jordan does not delineate its frontier but flows through its centre." In the same speech[4] he demanded that the British mandatories should "organise the necessary administrative machinery to open up territory on either side of the Jordan for the reception of great colonising masses." As Christopher Sykes has commented, "It is not altogether surprising that utterances of this kind, followed by a demonstration of all Jews of all parties in favour of the national home policy gave Arabs the idea that the Jews of the world were massing for an attack on them." At no time in history had Trans-Jordan been Jewish; only two Jewish individuals had lived in it in 1918.

That tinder-dry summer of 1929 saw the arrival in Palestine of a young American writer. Vincent Sheean was a gentile who, when at Chicago University, had joined a Jewish fraternity. He was fond of Jewish traditions, Jewish food, the Jewish theater and the society of Jewish friends. He describes himself as sharing Romain Rolland's opinion, as expressed in his novel *Jean-Christophe,* that "the Jews of western Europe constituted the one international layer of culture, through which everything good in literature, music and art spread from nation to nation and slowly tended to give the Western world a closer relationship between its parts. I was, in short, as thoroughgoing a pro-Semite (if there is such a word) as you could have found anywhere." After a decade spent in traveling as far afield as the Soviet Union and China, Sheean had accepted a commission from a New York paper, *The New Palestine,* to give his impressions of the Jewish experiment in colonization.

Palestine at once impressed the young American as forming an essential part of the surrounding Arab world. Jerusalem, where he stayed, "was as Arab as Cairo or Baghdad, and the Zionist Jews (that is, the modern Jews) were as foreign to it as I was myself." He had expected this in theory. He knew from what he had read that the old city had not been changed, that the large Zionist population of Jerusalem (an actual majority) lived in new quarters outside the walls, and that Palestine was still predominantly a country of Arabs. "But a fact on paper has not the same effect as its physical configuration."

On July 9 Sheean learned that an Arab newspaper had announced that he had come to Palestine in the pay of the Jews. Initial indignation gave way to self-questioning. "Was I in the pay of the Jews or was I not? If not,

4 Quotation taken from Sykes, op. cit., p. 135.

why did the statement make me angry? And if I was, what then? It took me about half an hour to see that I must either make up my mind to be, as the Arabic newspaper said, 'in the pay of the Jews,' and to accept any comment that might be made on the subject, or else break my connection with the Zionists altogether and go my own way." His diary narrates his decision: "Tuesday was distinguished for me by a thing I have never done before. I gave away fifteen hundred dollars."

Sheean could now survey Palestine as a free observer. He swiftly arrived at two conclusions: "that the difficulty of Zionism is essentially one thing only, its attempt to settle a country that is already settled; and second, that the Balfour Declaration is a document that really guarantees only one thing, the permanence of the British occupation of Palestine."[5]

In 1929 the British Empire still seemed Gibraltar-solid. Sheean regarded Palestine "as the most flagrant example of the British betrayal of Arab interests after the war. These Arabs had no political rights of any kind, no parliament or council or legislature, and were governed by ukase. The law was whatever the High Commissioner wanted it to be." Sir John Chancellor, an inept choice for a worsening situation, was completing his first year as High Commissioner; his previous experience had been in Trinidad and Africa.

Yet the first problem—of settling an already settled country—was what perplexed the Zionist leadership, recently consolidated in a Jewish Agency. The Arabs owned nearly all the land and thanks to the services provided by the mandate authorities, they were increasing in numbers, education and wealth; and thanks again to Jewish contributions of capital and skill, Palestine was becoming a more, not less, valuable country. Between 1920–1935 at least £80 million of Jewish capital came into the country—or forty times the annual budget in the early years of the mandate. The Zionists must either persuade the Arabs to sell; or they must secure legislation compelling them to sell; or they must somehow, some time, evict the Arabs by force. Otherwise the Jews would be confined to a small portion of what they regarded, on the basis of Old Testament verses, as their eternal home.

With a journalist's luck (though luck that brought him anguish) Sheean had arrived in a year of violence; but more than by murderous riots Sheean was chilled by one particular conversation. The violence and the conversation must be seen in context.

Mid-August marked the annual commemoration of the destruction of the Temple foretold by Christ and accomplished by the Emperor Titus. Since the coming of Islam the site of the Temple mound and its chief relic, the West Wall, had formed the Haram al-Sharif, or Noble Precinct, supporting two Islamic shrines of ancient beauty: the rotunda dome marking

[5] Vincent Sheean, *In Search of History* (London: Hamish Hamilton, 1935), p. 381.

the rock from which Muhammad ascended on his night journey into heaven and the Aqsa Mosque. Throughout the centuries Muslims, who regarded the Jews as fellow Scriptuaries, allowed the Jews to pray at the Wall, while insisting that it formed part of an Islamic *waqf,* or pious endowment. That this was the legal position Chaim Weizmann had conceded, he relates in his memoirs,[6] in a conversation in the early 1920s with the King of Italy. "There were no Holy Places in Palestine to which the Jews laid actual physical claim—except, perhaps, Rachel's tomb, which was at no time a matter of controversy. The Wailing Wall we did not own, and never had owned since the destruction of the Temple."

But by 1929 extremist Jews were laying a claim to physical possession of the Wall. The Wall, Sheean found, had begun to obsess Jewish opinion. "Jews who frankly confessed themselves to be without religious belief could not discuss the subject without getting excited. They did not themselves want to go there and pray or lament; they did not think they could put petitions into crevices of the Wall (as Orthodox Jews did) and get them received by the holy spirit of the Temple; they did not want the Wall for themselves at all. But they felt that the Jewish nation in Palestine (as they conceived these minority settlements to be) ought to have possession of one holy place, the relic of the Temple (the only relic, as they somewhat loosely believed), and that the genuinely religious Jews, for the most part not Zionists, should have Zionism to thank for it. The Arabs, for whom they had contempt as an "uncivilized race," to whom some of them referred as "Red Indians" and other as "savages," were in possession of a place that signified a great deal to the Jewish world in general."

That particular mid-August Sheean ran into an American woman whom he had already met in Zionist circles. In his book *In Search of History,* Sheean referred to her as Miss X, though he cited her real name when giving evidence before one of the innumerable and ineffectual royal commissions with which the British punctuated their mandate. Miss X had come up to Jerusalem from Tel-Aviv to report for the New York *Times.* She had got wind of an exciting story: hundreds of Haluzim, or young pioneers of Jabotinsky's temper and party, were coming, armed, three quarters of them, to the Wall, after sundown, to cause trouble with the Arabs. "It would be a good thing if there was a row at the Wall, to 'show that we are here.' I didn't believe a damn word of it; too fantastic; but I told her I'd be ready to go along at five o'clock if she would come back. She said there wouldn't be any trouble until sundown, and five o'clock would do. I went along with her when she came back. She was inconceivably cynical and flippant about the whole thing; said a row would be a very good thing for the Zionist cause, arouse world Jews and increase contributions to the new Agency."

In fact, the only people disturbed were a number of oriental Jews genuinely engaged in prayer; the Arabs on this occasion stayed indoors.

[6] Weizmann, op. cit., p. 286.

Later that evening Sheean dined with Miss X in an open-air restaurant. It was evident that she, who had probably never seen a street fight, regarded Sheean (who from Chicago had voyaged widely in the realms of violence) as a milksop. "It won't do a bit of harm if a couple of people get hurt." In vain Sheean tried to persuade her, as they sat in the idyllic summer night, where this rationale of violence was bound to lead. "She only laughed. I think she thought I was crazy to take it so hard. According to her, it can't do any harm and will only bring in the shekels. I told her she had definitely killed any remnant of sympathy I had for the Zionist movement."

A week later Sheean was proved an unhappy prophet. In riots in the Holy City twenty-nine Jews and thirty-eight Arabs were killed and a large number of each community wounded. "I was bitterly indignant with the Zionists for having, as I believed, brought on this disaster; I was shocked into hysteria by the ferocity of the Arab anger; and I was aghast at the inadequacy of the British government."

Arab anger was ferocious because few could distinguish between Miss X and the Haluzim on the one hand and idealists like Gordon on the other. The Arabs increasingly assumed that all Jews were the same and that differences between them were merely tactical. This injected a note of tragedy into the violence. For as late as 1930 the Gordon tradition was still powerful. No one upheld it more nobly than Judah Magnes, an aristocratic Jew from San Francisco whose whole career showed a noble willingness to "do different." In defiance of family tradition he had identified with the Jewish refugees on the Lower East Side when, trained in Germany, he became rabbi to Temple Israel, the leading Reform synagogue in Brooklyn. From 1905 to 1908 he was secretary of the American Zionist Federation, an organization whose appeal was largely to the poor and the newly arrived. In 1915 he broke with official Zionism with an abruptness equal to that with which he had embraced it. The patient, careful colonization that he sought must, to be of value, link itself with a spiritual rebirth; political activism could only involve the Jews in compromises. Magnes was an uncompromising idealist. During the war he adopted a pacifist position similar to that which landed Bertrand Russell in an English jail. When peace came, he migrated to Jerusalem and made the Hebrew University his chief concern. He was elected its first chancellor in 1925 and ten years later its president. Magnes disagreed with the Zionist leaders who, while denying that a Jewish state was their aim, in private conceded no other destination. He doubted that a Jewish state could ever be established in Palestine, or if it were, at any price but unending violence. He started a "League of Peace," to work for a binational state shared by Jews and Arabs. In 1930 he composed an eloquent if lonely reply to those Zionists who wished to create a Jewish state as self-worshiping as other nation-states. "The desire for power and conquest seems to be normal to many human beings and groups, and we, being the ruled everywhere, must here rule; being the minority everywhere, we must be here in the majority. There is the *Wille zur Macht,* the state, the army, the frontiers. We have been in exile; now we are to be masters in our own Home. We are to have a Fatherland, and we are to encourage the feelings of pride, honour, glory that are part of the paraphernalia of the ordinary nationalistic patriotism. . . . We are told that when we become the majority we shall then show how just and generous a people in power can be. That is like the man who says that he will do anything and everything to get rich, so that he may do good with the money thus accumulated. Sometimes he never grows rich—he fails. And if he does grow rich under these circumstances, his power of doing good has been atrophied from long lack of use."[7]

Although the issues were to be blurred by the pressure of events and the half-truths of propagandists, Magnes defined, with a precision that deserves remembrance, the two opposed policies confronting those rebuilding Zion.

"The one maintains that we can establish a Jewish Home here through the suppression of the political aspirations of the Arabs, and therefore a Home necessarily established on bayonets over a long period—a policy which I think bound to fail because of the violence against us it would occasion, and because good opinion in Britain and the conscience of the Jewish people itself would revolt against it. The other policy holds that we can establish a Home here only if we are true to ourselves as democrats and internationalists, thus being just and helpful to others, and that we ask for the protection of life and property the while we are eagerly and intelligently and sincerely at work to find a *modus vivendi et operandi* with our neighbours."

By the Arabs who knew him Magnes was loved; but they knew that his policy was regarded as impracticable by most of his own people.

On the Jewish side, "after 1929 the Jabotinsky spirit became an integral part of Zionism in action."[8] Vladimir Jabotinsky was in every respect the opposite of Judah Magnes. While Magnes came from the Pacific, Jabotinsky came from an Odessa set between the wild Black Sea and the persecuting steppe. The ghetto-sharpened activist in the secular, nationalistic tradition of Herzl appealed to the Jews in flight from Europe. Like Saada from Syria, he spent most of his life exiled from Palestine. An extremist viewpoint can give a sharp, as well as a distorted vision. Unlike many of the moderates, Jabotinsky did notice that there were Arabs in Palestine and he spoke about the implications of Jewish settlement with less hypocrisy than was usual. "What I did not deny is that in the process, the Arabs of Palestine will necessarily become a minority in the country of Palestine. What I do deny is that *that* is a hardship." To back Jewish settlement Jabotinsky demanded a Jewish Army. He did so when, exiled in England,

[7] Judah Magnes, "Like All The Nations?", 1930, in Hertzberg, op. cit.
[8] Sykes, op. cit., p. 152.

he gave evidence before a House of Lords commission. To the peers he spoke as a would-be colonist to experts: "A nation with your colossal colonizing experience surely knows that colonization never went without certain conflicts with the population on the spot, so that the country had to be protected." He squarely compared the Jews in Palestine to the British settlers then occupying Kenya's White Highlands. "Legalize our self-defense, as you are doing in Kenya. In Kenya until recently every European was obliged to train for the Settlers Defense Force." Jabotinsky wanted to dispense with the veils of prevarication which Zionist moderates often pulled over their intentions: it was Britain's duty to reveal the full implications of Zionism to the Arabs and to give the Jews the right to create a military instrument for dealing with Arab resentment. He may also have convinced himself that this resentment might evaporate if the Arabs were confronted with a force overwhelmingly stronger than their own.

As Jabotinsky, not Magnes, became the pole of attraction to Hitler-harassed Jews, as the immigration rate soared like a fever chart, the Arabs became more and more persuaded that they were being tranquillized until such time as the Jews had the strength to take what they wanted for themselves.

Arab alarm increased when in 1936 the British seemed about to abandon the stance of Pilate for that of Solomon. A new commission under Lord Peel found the mandate unworkable and proposed to partition Palestine into a Jewish and an Arab state while reserving an enclave in the middle, including Jerusalem, for Britain. In the biblical story Solomon's threat to bisect a disputed baby discovered the true mother from the false. The ruse did not work in Palestine, where two peoples, Jew and Arab, disputed one and the same land with clamorous sincerity. Each people confronted the British Solomon with its own revolt. The Arabs were in armed resistance during the three years preceding the Second World War, the Jews during the four years after it. Both revolts testified to the perspicacity of Dr. King and Mr. Crane when they had predicted in 1919 that only a large army could enforce the Zionist program.

The Arab revolt flared from a summer of strikes held to protest continued and mounting Jewish immigration. The Arabs had chosen a bad moment for their challenge. By 1936 Britain was rearming in preparation for war against the German-Italian Axis. A large body of soldiers and police fought the Arabs with the same pointless efficiency the British were to show after the war in Cyprus, Kenya and Aden, and with the same paradoxical result: that having fought, flogged and hanged the Arabs to a standstill, they conceded their viewpoint. Anxious to secure Arab quiescence in the coming war, which the Jews would willy-nilly have to support, the British produced a White Paper which met the majority of Arab demands. The British Government promised that only 75,000 more Jews would be admitted over the next five years; thereafter Jewish immigration would stop "unless the Arabs of Palestine are prepared to acquiesce in it." The British argued in effect that a Jewish national home, in their understanding of the term, would by then have been achieved. Palestine would have retained an Arab majority over the Jews of around two to one.

Despite this apparent victory, their revolt was a disaster for the Arabs. Their leadership was decimated; as a community they were left exhausted. Their trust in the White Paper took from them any stimulus to further action. Lulled into the desired quiescence, they had a quietly profitable war, cultivating their orange groves or working for the British. The Arab Legion, on the other side of the Jordan, would play an important role in suppressing a pro-Axis revolt against the Hashemites of Iraq. But the Arabs of Palestine acquired no further experience of fighting.

For Jews such as Ben-Gurion, who now made no secret of aiming at statehood, the White Paper was more tonic than catastrophe: it focused energies, it gave strychnine to energies, exacerbated by the plight of Europe's Jews. The White Paper marked for Zionism the end of its special relationship with official Britain. The new policy was summed up in a slogan: to fight the White Paper as though there was no war and to fight the war as though there were no White Paper.

It was a policy of consummate, if cynical, realism. A clandestine Jewish Army, the Haganah, had existed since the 1920s; thousands of its members now saw service with the British throughout the Middle East, acquiring valuable experience and training. Moshe Dayan, to quote only one example, participated in a British invasion of Syria after the collapse of France.

Ben-Gurion, the politician, sensed that the source of power would now be America, for, whatever its outcome, the war could only leave Britain exhausted. "During the Second World War," he has said, "I spent a good deal of time in the United States on several visits trying to mobilize the support of the American Government for the creation of a Jewish Army and for our general aims in Palestine. I also worked among the various Zionist bodies preparing them for our major political demand of statehood when war would end."[9]

He spent, he tried, he mobilized, he worked, he prepared, with as much effect as Weizmann in England a quarter of a century before. Part of his achievement was to reverse Weizmann's policy of delicate gradualism and alliance with England. To the end, Weizmann disdained to be a demagogue and exalted moderation. Ben-Gurion disdained nothing that could achieve his ends. His victory over the older man was symbolized at a conference held in May 1942, at the Biltmore Hotel, New York. Zionist leaders as well as prominent Jews from all over America demanded the total rejection of official British policy and the declaration of Palestine as an independent Jewish state with its own control over immigration. Germany should also

[9] Pearlman, *Ben Gurion looks back,* p. 108.

pay reparations to this Jewish state and for a start, all German property in Palestine should be forfeit.

As the amplitude of Hitler's Final Solution became known, Ben-Gurion's demands were given emotional support tinged with guilt: a potent mixture. The Labour Party was a junior partner in Britain's wartime coalition. Its annual conference in 1944 went almost as far as Jabotinsky (who had died in New York in 1940) in asking for a population transfer: "Let the Arabs be encouraged to move out as the Jews move in." The Fabian intellectuals and hymn-singing miners' leaders who dominated the Labour Party envisaged financial compensation and accommodation in some other Arab country as adequate encouragement for the Arabs to abandon their homes.

Though Jabotinsky was dead, a disciple, Menachem Begin, had other ideas—ideas deriving from psychotic Europe—for how to push the British aside and the Arabs out. Begin reached Trans-Jordan in 1942 wearing the uniform of a Polish soldier, having trekked to the Middle East by way of Russia and Iran. Deserting his unit, he slipped into Palestine resolved to apply methods of terror in order to implement the full Jabotinsky program. Side by side with the Haganah, which though clandestine was "respectable," Begin's Irgun Tsva'i Leumi and another group founded by Abraham Stern, were to introduce, directly, and unequivocally, the methods of direct, selective violence into the Holy Land. They were to be even more murderous, and far more successful, than the Muslim Brotherhood of Egypt.

In deciding to fight the British—whose interests in the Middle East were more solid than their word—the Jews risked a suppression as ruthless as that of the Arab revolt before the war. But they had weighed their moment with shrewder eyes than the Arabs could yet focus on world realities. Although a nominal victor in the war, Britain was overextended and weak. Threats of a boycott of British goods in New York could daunt a war-weakened economy; British recovery would be dependent on American support, and American disapproval of the White Paper's restrictions on immigration might diminish this. The Zionist leadership also knew something which the Arab leaders had not learnt: how to pursue an objective on several levels at once. While the Arabs seemed united in extremism, the Jews could address different audiences in different tones. Abroad, Weizmann manifested the moderation of an elder statesman; in Palestine, Ben-Gurion exhibited the studied immoderation of a superb tactician. The Haganah worked respectably with the Jewish Agency, and for the most part in responsible self-defense. The Stern Gang and the Irgun attacked targets which moderate opinion approved with a violence which, at least for the record, it could condemn.

It is difficult to write of the period of troubles which began towards the end of the war without taking sides. Few have tried. A pro-Jewish writer would show the British, interested only in Arab oil, combining with Arab fanatics, interested in murder and loot, to rob the victims of a Nazi holocaust of a safe asylum. In such a context the chain of killings which began with Lord Moyne, the British Minister of State, in Cairo in 1944, and ended with that of Count Bernadotte, a UN mediator, were nationalist excesses made inevitable by a refusal to recognize the Jewish claim to Palestine. If the writer were pro-Arab, he would show the Arabs being prized from land their ancestors had owned for centuries by a combination of British treachery and Zionist violence. British journalists and statesmen at the time were bitter at what seemed to them Jewish ingratitude. Lord Moyne's death made Winston Churchill meditate in the House of Commons on the possibility of revising his lifelong support for the Zionist cause; the murder of two British sergeants led to outbursts of anti-Semitism back home in Britain and among the soldiery in Palestine itself. There is probably some truth in all three arguments; there is no pleasure in retelling the day-to-day violence committed by all three parties to the dispute. If a puma and a bear are caged together, they will maul their keeper and fight each other. To accuse the Jews and Arabs of violence and the British of hesitation would be like blaming a mousetrap or scolding an electric chair.

The roots of guilt lay in the past. Theodor Herzl had seen a vision without counting its cost in human suffering. Far worse, the British Government had promised what was not in its gift to two different parties, one the actual possessors, another those who had possessed it in the past. A mandate to enforce so crooked a bargain was an Alice in Wonderland commission from the start. By 1947 its unworkability was apparent to the world, its unprofitability to the British. Resuming the role of Pilate, they washed their hands of the responsibility they had once demanded. The mandate was returned to the United Nations, as legal successor to the League of Nations.

In 1947 the United Nations was in its infancy; its small membership was as overweighted against the Arabs as it would later become weighted for them. While nearly all Africa and much of Asia was still not independent, all the states of Latin America belonged as founder members. The influence of the United States on the new organization was therefore overwhelming. The General Assembly appointed a special committee to visit Palestine and report. The result was a majority plan recommending partition and a minority plan recommending a federal state. The majority plan awarded the Jews just over half the total area; it included the fertile coastal plain of ancient Philistia as well as eastern Galilee. The Arabs were awarded the rest, while Jerusalem was to be an international zone under UN administration.

The partition plan was opposed by the five Arab states who were then members of the UN, on the grounds that it denied the rights of the Arab majority in Palestine to determine their own future. The plan was accepted by even the extremists among the Jews, since it marked a concrete first step towards the Jabotinsky dream. The voting on the plan was repeatedly delayed while the required two-thirds majority for the recommendation was mustered. "By direct order of the White House," Undersecretary of State Sumner Welles recorded, "every form of pressure, direct or indirect, was brought to bear by American officials upon those countries outside the Moslem world that were known to be either uncertain or opposed to partition. Representatives or intermediaries were employed by the White House to make sure that the necessary majority would at least be secured."[10] The decisive, last-minute votes were those of three countries remote from the Middle East and ignorant of its complexities: the Philippines, Liberia and Haiti. Harvey Firestone, owner of gigantic rubber plantations in Liberia, convinced Monrovia; Adolf Berle, adviser to the Haitian President, convinced Port-au-Prince.

If the plan was unacceptable to the Arabs, it was unworkable by anyone except angels or Swiss. The United Nations General Assembly made no suggestion how the intricate geometry of interlocking Jewish and Arab states should be greased into place. The British, who had abstained on the vote, announced that they would surrender their mandate on May 15, 1948. Far from making plans for an orderly transfer, they forbade either community to set up a nucleus of state administration in advance. This gave an advantage to the Jews, whose Agency and Haganah were far in advance of anything at the disposal of the Arabs.

The General Assembly had adopted the partition plan on November 29 by a vote of thirty-three in favor, thirteen against and ten abstentions. In the following five and a half months a British administration continued to function against a background of communal violence. It may have been that the British had come to the desperate conclusion that only violence could settle the issues. If so, they may have been thinking in terms of their Indian experience. There they had announced a deadline for departure, thus forcing the Hindus and Muslims either to arrange a solution, or come to one after a period of slaughter. The Russians seem to have imagined at the time that Britain, with machiavellian skill, was going out of the Mediterranean door in order to return with the victorious Arabs by way of Trans-Jordan. If so, the Russians had a very foggy picture of the rival forces. Arab military action lacked strategic vision. Jewish military action fitted in with a long prepared contingency plan. The Haganah fought a defensive war of consolidation in the areas awarded to the Jewish State, while the terrorists used their particular methods to induce the Arabs who would have formed almost 50 per cent of the population of the Jewish state to move out. It would be unfair to associate the majority of the Jewish leaders with terrorism, even though their general policy—"to encourage the Arabs

[10] Sumner Welles, *We Need not Fail* (Boston: Houghton Mifflin, 1948), p. 63.

to quit their homes"[11]—profited from it. Men like Ben-Gurion, who had been in Palestine since the Ottoman period, were often contemptuous of the Arabs, but they knew them as human beings; they would not willingly, or at least unprovokedly, treat them as inanimate things; atrocity was alien to their philosophy. But Europa Furens, the old continent in psychotic seizure, had sent newer recruits and to these the natives of Palestine were as alien, as abstract, as the Algerians to the Foreign Legionnaires (many of them former Nazis) now embarked on the first stages of a long colonial struggle in North Africa. Menachem Begin, leader and apologist of the Irgun, had only been in Palestine for six years when his troops accomplished an action denounced by the Jewish author Jon Kimche as "the darkest stain on the Jewish record"[12] but defended by Begin as a "victory" without which the Jewish state could not have been achieved.[13]

On April 10, 1948, Jacques de Reynier, the Red Cross representative in Jerusalem visited the small Arab village of Dir Yassin not far from the Holy City. It was an unremarkable village but for the unusual fact that its people had enjoyed better relations with the Jews than most. To his horror De Reynier discovered on this and three succeeding visits spread over the next two days the corpses of two hundred and fifty-four non-combatant men, women and children, either thrown down the village wells or scattered nearby. Among the survivors were forty orphaned children whom a kindly Jewish woman, not a Zionist, took to the Anna Spafford Children's Home in Jerusalem, of which she was in charge. "When she approached one little boy he screamed 'She is one of them,' and fell down with a heart attack from which he died soon after."[14] Ben-Gurion, much to the indignation of Menachem Begin, sent a telegram of regrets to King Abdullah of Jordan. Begin believed in the logic of violence, a logic shared with those from whom he had fled in Eastern Europe. A Lidice or Hiroshima in little, Dir Yassin undoubtedly aided the fulfillment of the first stages of the Jabotinsky program. "The Arabs began to flee," a gratified Begin stated in his account of the struggle, "shouting 'Dir Yassin!' "[15] Defying orders from their own Arab Higher Command and requests from such liberal Jews as the mayor of Haifa that they should stay put, unarmed Arabs with no effective leadership jammed the roads leading away from the war zone. By the middle of May, before any Arab state moved one soldier in their defense, 400,000 had already fled. The presence of an Arab majority in Palestine had always been the baffling obstacle to the creation of a Jewish state. Chaim Weizmann, chosen to be the first President of Israel, described the *fait accompli* as a "miraculous cleaning of the land; the miraculous simpli-

[11] Edgar O'Ballance, *The Arab-Israeli War, 1948* (London: 1956), p. 64.

[12] Jon Kimche, *The Seven Fallen Pillars* (London: 1950).

[13] Menachem Begin, *The Revolt: Story of the Irgun* (London: Henry Schuman, 1951), pp. 162 ff.

[14] Sykes, op. cit., p. 417.

[15] Begin, op. cit., p. 162.

fication of Israel's task." Weizmann was old and almost blind. In his younger days he would have seen the miracle for the all too prosaic, all too colonial action it really was. As for the Arabs who moved into neighboring Arab countries, who had put up hardly more resistance than the Jews to their Nazi butchers in Europe, they were to prove a stunned generation. In their tents in Jordan, their mud and tin can huts in Lebanon, they would endlessly rehearse how they had come to lose their homes. The children who had stumbled with them, or been carried on father's back or at mother's breast, would sift from their elders' lamentations one lesson only, a lesson derived from wartime Europe but outliving its lectors: force, including terror, had dispossessed them. As the years passed, as one resolution was passed after another by the General Assembly, affirming and reaffirming their right to repatriation or compensation, as they lived on doles, as their lands were confiscated in their absence and made over to new farmers born far from Palestine, the generation born after 1944 would become the unloving disciples of Menachem Begin, as he, in the Eastern Europe of 1940, had been the unloving disciple of Nazi Europe.

BOOK NINE

The Temple of Janus

We should form part of a wall of defense for Europe in Asia, an outpost of civilization against barbarism.

THEODOR HERZL,
Der Judenstaat

We cannot ignore that we live at the center of an Arab circle which blends with us as we with it. Can we ignore either that fate has placed us on the continent of Africa? Or that we are bound to the world of Islam by the facts of history as well as faith?

GAMAL ABDEL NASSER,
The Philosophy of the Revolution

Chapter 1

THE ancient temple of Janus, an arched gateway in form, stood at the northeast end of the Roman marketplace. The god it sheltered had two antipodal profiles, one facing east, the other west. His temple was closed to worshipers only in times of peace. Only four times in the seven and a half centuries before the birth of Christ was the temple of Janus shut.

In mid-May 1948, in what had been the Eastern Roman Empire and what the West had christened the Middle East, the gates were wedged firmly open. But the spirit of the region still looked in two directions.

On May 14, the last British High Commissioner had embarked at Haifa: a day earlier than planned. That afternoon David Ben-Gurion addressed a gathering of men and women in the Museum of Modern Art, Tel Aviv. Mustered beneath a photograph of Theodor Herzl, born for the most part in Eastern Europe, and looking back to a cloudy but better past, they heard him announce the independence of a Jewish state in Palestine to be known henceforth as Israel.

Ben-Gurion did not specify this state's new borders. Herzl had suggested the Anatolian plateau in the north and the Suez Canal in the south as desirable limits; the 1947 Partition Plan had been less expansive, awarding the Jews just over half of mandated Palestine. At the moment when Ben-Gurion spoke the Jewish authorities had cleared the Palestinians from several important areas awarded to the Arab state. In the candor of old age, nineteen years later,[1] Ben-Gurion would claim that his reticence on borders had been deliberate. He had had in mind the infant United States comprising its handful of territories on the Atlantic seaboard but destined to expand across the continent within a century.

The British, who had made no preparations for an orderly transfer of authority, watched from the sidelines. Arab villagers and townsmen panicked across the fighting lines to Lebanon and Jordan, making plans to come back next week, next month, when things were quieter. Crowds in Baghdad and Cairo, in Christian Mount Lebanon and the Muslim Hejaz, gathered round café radios. News vendors hawked incandescent headlines. Preachers in mosques, student leaders in classrooms, demanded support

[1] David Ben Gurion, "Hollow Words and No Action", *Ha-Aretz,* October 20, 1967.

for the Palestinians. Salesmen of surplus war material got out their order lists.

The same day, by telephone from Abdin Palace, King Farouk of Egypt ordered his army across the Canal which his grandfather had opened. The Muslim Brotherhood's Supreme Guide, the second man in Egypt, some said the first, had already sent volunteers to help the Palestinians. They had been doing for the Arabs what the Irgun and Stern Gang had been doing for the Jews. They had received rudimentary training from sympathetic officers. In suburban Cairo one such officer, a tall, serious major of four days' promotion, said good-by to his dark plump wife Tahia and two baby daughters; Gamal Abdul Nasser then joined his battalion, the Sixth, in the hurly-burly of Cairo Station. It was the night of May 16 as the train packed with soldiers rumbled on its journey East to the one swing bridge across the Canal. The bridge and the Canal were guarded by smiling British soldiers, neutral in this struggle and, unlike the tarbooshed Egyptians, well equipped. In early morning the trainload of now hungry soldiers reached Rafa, the frontier town. No food, no transport had been arranged. General Muhammad Naguib of the Frontier Force had to hire lorries from local Arabs. The Egyptians had no air support and for weapons little more lethal, at this time, than ancient rifles. But Gaza was taken with ease and some of the 4,000-strong force moved by way of Beersheba to link up with the Jordanians in the Hebron region. In Cairo scarlet headlines bombasted the Egyptian advance as though the chariots of Ramses were on the roll.

In the cool gloom of Abdin, Farouk's military thoughts brooded, not on Ramses, but on Ibrahim Pasha, the family soldier and his own great-grandfather. Ibrahim had led an Egyptian army across a desert then unbroken by any canal to liberate Palestine and Syria from Ottoman control. In ordering his army to follow the same route, Farouk had overruled the hesitations of his Prime Minister, Nokrashy Pasha, who was well aware of the inadequacies of an Egyptian Army whose ten thousand men had taken no active part in the recent war. A satirical British officer had stated, with some verisimilitude, that promotion in the Faroukian army went by waistline. If this were so, the King's figure qualified him for supreme command. Only twenty-eight years old, he weighed well over 250 pounds on his bathroom scales. Nothing else spoke of the soldier. A large hirsute body the color of candle wax entombed the handsome schoolboy who had inherited the throne in 1936. Farouk had then returned from studies in England to an unprecedented exchange of affection with his people. In fluent Arabic he had expressed a concern for his people's welfare as touching as that expressed around the same time by Edward VIII of England; the new Egyptian King enhanced his popularity by marrying an attractive young Egyptian, Ferida Zulficar. Ten years had sufficed to bury the schoolboy in tumescent flesh. Eager hands had helped the entombment. One such helper was his mother, King Fuad's second wife. Queen Nazli was a hedonistic businesswoman whose shrewd investments in oil-bearing American real estate would stand her in good stead. When her husband died, her long-distance shriek vibrated to England: *"Chéri,* you're King! Come home and enjoy it."

Royal favorites, many of them Italians, helped in the good corrupting work. The young king was encouraged to indulge most sensual whims. (The public consumption of alcohol was an exception.) Those who purveyed women and gigantic meals won his trust and kept his attention from their business. Farouk fattened fast. He was congenitally underendowed for his role of Casanova and as his belly grew outwards, the sexual act became harder and harder to achieve. He became a Tantalus of the bedroom, forever panting for a pleasure just out of reach. His eventual fathering of four children proves his persistence.

A third royal appetite—for sleep—inconvenienced his ministers. After hours spent gambling or watching the swirl of stomachs at the Auberge des Pyramides the King would stagger to his rococo bed as the muezzin called the decent to morning prayer. The hour when Majesty might be disturbed for the trivia of state moved steadily later into the day, and then the afternoon.

Yet more than debauch had ruined this hopeful prince. A quick, sometimes witty mind flickered behind the bedroom eyes; his mouth was sensitive as well as sensual; his cousins found him a considerate playmate; he could be a gentle tease as when to a stewardess on the ship bringing him home he pretended to be a mere Mr. Farouk Fuad, too poor to afford the Egyptian cloth whose merits she praised. Farouk was as much punctured in spirit as inflated in flesh. During the Second World War, as during the First, Egypt had been at the disposal of Britain. But on different terms. She was now a member of the League of Nations and an ally, not a protectorate. Farouk was thus incensed when to please the British his Prime Minister broke relations with Vichy France—something which the United States had not done. In revenge, and against the background of Rommel's advances in the western desert, he decided to appoint a friend, Aly Maher, to the post. On February 3, 1942, the British ambassador, the arrogant Sir Miles Lampson, called at Abdin and told Farouk to appoint instead the head of the Wafd Party, Nahas Pasha, as his next Prime Minister. The choice was surprising. The Wafd had a record of anti-British agitation dating from its foundation by Zaghlul in 1918. Its attitude to the war was equivocal. While the Wafd had denounced the Italians for the invasion of Abyssinia, they opposed much British policy in Egypt and demanded that Cairo be proclaimed an "open city." Lampson calculated that the Wafd might have enough prestige to swing the Egyptians into support of the Allies. Indifferent to such arguments but furious at this naked British pressure, Farouk, then only twenty-two, had hesitated. The next morning the embassy delivered an ultimatum: let the King appoint Nahas by 6 P.M., or the responsibility would be his. Again Farouk made no move. At nine that evening Lampson, a great bearlike man with a bulbous nose, drove up to the state entrance at Abdin with three light tanks. The commander-in-chief of British troops in Egypt, as well as two South African officers carrying pistols, dismounted with him.

Farouk had given his guards orders not to resist.

"Fayn al-walad?" Lampson demanded in kitchen Arabic. "Where's the boy?"

A chamberlain who offered to conduct him to His Majesty was pushed aside. "I know the way."

In his pocket Lampson carried two documents, one of which Farouk must choose: a deed of abdication and a decree appointing Nahas. Impotently angry Farouk signed the second paper. With it he signed the delayed death warrant of his dynasty, of British influence in Egypt and of constitutional rule.

The Egyptians could no longer regard their monarchy as a symbol of independence. The British were plainly occupiers, not allies. Only Zaghlul's heir had a momentary triumph. But Nahas' compromise in receiving power at the hands of Lampson would eventually lead to the end of parliament and his own career.

But the immediate effect was on Farouk. If he had abdicated or resisted, he would have become a hero, or perhaps a martyr. As it was, he stayed on as a British employee. He kept a pair of palaces in Cairo, two more in Alexandria, a country house at Inchas, a rest house at the pyramids, erotica, postage stamps, scores of thousands of fertile acres. But he had lost his own respect as well as that of his people. He was a geometrical blot in the triangle of Palace, Embassy and Parliament.

By 1948 Farouk could see that this triangle was falling apart. If pressed, not one of its points would hold. As to his own prestige he had few illusions. He coined a joke: "Soon there will be only five Kings left: the King of England and the four card Kings."

But the King of England, or his heir Princess Elizabeth, headed a dissolving empire. Its brightest jewel, the Indian raj, had been lost in 1947. Its reserves had been spent in the war. Its treasury was more indebted than the Khedive Ismail's. Its citizens still queued for rationed food. The British had not put down the Jewish revolt as they had put down the Arab revolt before the war. Either they could not, or they no longer cared about the approaches to the Canal, now that it led to an independent India and Pakistan. (Britain's abdication in Palestine had signaled the shrinking of her Middle Eastern ambitions.) Britain's discomfiture pleased Farouk the man; it worried the King who might be overthrown. If things got bad, the British bases in the Canal Zone represented at the very least a way of escape. But if things got bad, if there was a revolution, it would not come from the politicians. Parliament was as much devalued as Embassy and Palace. In a gap-toothed jaw, the Wafd was still the strongest molar, but a molar crumbling with decay. The molar had bitten Farouk and Farouk longed to break it in revenge. He was also a gambler, and beneath the gambler's dream of winning nestles a need to lose. It was a gambler's situation. Each point in the triangle was on its own. The British would strike for their bases, the politicians for their private gains. The King of Egypt would strike for glory and, later in the summer, would seek an heir (Ferida had borne nothing but daughters) from a new buxom queen.

The odds were against such a gamble succeeding, but Farouk was desperate. In supporting the Palestinian cause he could gain new allies. Not from the old clubs. The old caste, the members of the Royal Automobile Club, the Gezira, or the Muhammad Ali, dreaded adventures; many were themselves Jews; more were Greeks or Italians, unconcerned. A new force was claiming the middle ground: the Muslim Brotherhood. One man still had some credit with the Egyptian masses: Hasan al-Banna, its Supreme Guide.

On the surface it was ironic for Fanatic and King to make common cause. An abyss divided the ascetic Guide in his turban and scarlet robe from the pseudo-European King with his passion for gastrophily, fornication and chemin de fer. But there were bridges. Both men wanted to resist the British. Neither had denied the other's myth. Farouk practiced the duties of a Muslim. He was photographed at weekly prayer; he did not drink; and even old Nahas in a moment of aberration had said that, after Mecca, the second prayer focus had become Abdin. This may have reminded Farouk of his father's caliphal daydream. The League of Arab States, born in 1945 on the suggestion of Mr. Anthony Eden, the British Foreign Secretary, offered Farouk wider scope for influence than Fuad had known. If the King conformed to Islam, the Brotherhood conformed to the throne. Before the war, when the court had moved to Alexandria for the summer, the Brotherhood's Rover Scouts had lined the wayside platforms as Farouk's train passed. In their first conference after the war, the Brotherhood prefaced a list of political demands (including armed resistance to the British) with allegiance to Farouk. Having compounded with terror, the Brotherhood could compound with a corrupted King.

In backing the Palestinians both King and Fanatic were responding to powerful feelings throughout the Arab world. What neither knew were the weakness of the army and the strength of the Jews—or the "Israelis," as the press now described them, in ironic quotes.

Chapter 2

F AROUK's gamble had failed on the battlefield and in the bedroom.

Skillfully exploiting a midsummer truce, scouring Europe for arms, fighting with the consciousness that they had no Cairo or Baghdad on which to retreat, the Israelis in October pushed into the Negev, splitting the Egyptians from the Transjordanians. Behind them in the north, the Israelis had by now conquered almost the whole of Galilee; King Abdullah was planning to add the major part of what was left of Arab Palestine to his kingdom. The Egyptians in the south put up a stubborn resistance; their retention of the key point of Falluja and its outpost, Irak al-Manshia, prevented the Israelis from capturing Gaza. On December 28 Major Gamal Abdul Nasser launched a decisive counterattack from Irak al-Manshia which enabled the Egyptians to sustain the siege until the war ended with the armistice of February 24, 1949. But this small defensive success was a thousand miles from the triumph needed to put Farouk in the same league with Ibrahim Pasha. Things were no better at home. His divorce, designed to remove a censorious and daughter-prolix wife, had also misfired. Ex-queen Ferida was applauded when she appeared in public; the royal portrait was booed when it was flashed on the cinema screens. Farouk could no longer drive his sports car through Gezira, his dark glasses goggling for a pretty girl. Now when he was moved from one part of the capital to another, black-serge policemen lined the streets, their guns towards the sidewalks.

Egyptian society was collapsing with creaks as sharp as gunshots. Russell Pasha's Egyptian successor as Cairo police chief was shot dead outside the university. Nahas Pasha narrowly escaped from a number of similar attempts. In the last week of December Nokrashy Pasha persuaded a frightened Farouk that the Brotherhood must be suppressed. Three days later—just as Major Nasser was leading his counterattack in the Negev—Nokrashy was murdered in the Council of Ministers. His Muslim Brother assassin was disguised as a policeman. A new Prime Minister[1] used the suppression of terrorism as an excuse for imposing virtual dictatorship. A few weeks later, in a quiet Cairo street, the Supreme Guide was gunned down by policemen disguised as civilians.

[1] Ibrahim Abdul Hadi.

Egypt was as bleak as the Turkey of 1918. But the Turks were grim-faced realists who recognized a disaster when they saw one. Not so the Egyptians —Merry Andrews with a genius for self-deception. Faced with setbacks, they decked them with myths as pleasing as the flimsy tents of scarlet and green arabesque they put up for funerals. The Victory of Falluja disguised the Israeli seizure of much of the Arab portion of Palestine; it disguised Egyptian failure to solve a problem which, in the years to come, would loom large and expensive. But it brightened the winter. Banners lauding the Victorious Heroes draped front pages and back streets. Gamal Abdel Nasser, knowing the truth, feeling himself unsullied in the general defeat, frowned through the celebrations.

The tough Prime Minister knew from history the perils presented by defeated armies. There were prodding reminders. In Damascus, a Syrian general of Kurdish origin and American sympathies arrested the President lying sick in the hospital, seized buildings, broadcast military marches from the captured radio station and set the pattern for a generation of coups.[2] The Syrian Army was hardly more serious than its grievance: the soldiers' *samnah,* or cooking fat, had been made from evil-smelling bone waste. Civilians mocked officers in the streets by holding their noses. In Egypt the gossip in Groppi's garden café, at cocktail parties under sparkling chandeliers, fed on leaflets pushed into letter boxes, slipped under doors. They were signed by "The Free Officers"; their grievances were with faulty arms, inept leadership and general corruption. Rumor linked them with the banned, still active Brotherhood. Rumor as usual was right. The link between the two organizations was one Mahmoud Labib, the Supreme Guide's adviser on military affairs. As well as enlisting officers to train his volunteers for Palestine, Labib had penetrated the Army itself. He devised an impressive ceremonial for officer recruits. In the depths of night they would be conducted through the labyrinthine lanes of the sleeping city, past mameluke doorways fuming of hashish, to where in a ruined, dim-lit palace a Koran and a revolver lay waiting on a table. The candidate put one hand on the revolver, the other on the illuminated Book, and repeated a chilling oath.

An indignant Army plus a mass movement added up to danger. The Prime Minister made inquiries about the so-called Free Officers. One name cited more than others was that of Major Nasser. The Prime Minister summoned the Hero of Falluja to his office. "I know about your group; I want to know who else belongs. Do you know Mahmoud Labib?"

"Of course. We worked together for the Palestinians."

"Who introduced you?"

The major named a captain. The Prime Minister pounced:

"And where may this captain be found?"

---

[2] Husni Zaim. Miles Copeland in *The Game of Nations* (New York: 1970) claims that Zaim was prompted by the infant CIA (Central Intelligence Agency).

"With God—he died in the war."

The chief organizer of the Free Officers could smile at the Prime Minister's angry threats of calling in police. In implicating a man who could no longer speak, in protecting his still living contact with the Muslim Brothers, Major Nasser lied like a trooper. He was also practicing a talent for subterfuge that deserved an Alpha Plus. In a talkative society where wives shared their husbands' secrets with their friends, where Don Juans in uniform tattled secrets to whores, he had kept a conspiracy on the boil for year after patient year without one blabbermouth or traitor giving it away. He observed the canons of conspiratorial routine; the Free Officers, eventually numbering close to a thousand, were formed in cells, each linked to the next by a single contact. Major Nasser's disarming smile concealed a nature forever on guard, congenitally suspicious. But he owed his lasting success as plotter to the degree in which he dominated, beyond question, his entourage, men of the same profession and age group as himself. Nasser did not do this by the exhibition of an original or eccentric mind. His hold, first over half a dozen, then many more, was due to the intensity with which he felt what they felt, the profundity of his private response to events shared by all. He seemed consensus embodied.

That one young man could stand for all, though in heightened degree, is characteristic of the Islamic East. As a religion and as a culture Islam had developed on other lines than Christendom, despite common links. Its monotheism had a different stress, its cultural borrowings from ancient Greece a different slant. Islam, as a faith, stressed the remoteness and autocracy of God; as a culture it preserved and developed the sciences of Hellas, rather than the philosophic ideas which influenced the West. Men, the result of faith and culture, become what their biographers want them to be, and biographers are formed by tradition. Since Plutarch, Western biographers have sought out the distinctive, the unusual, attempting to reach the kernel in each man through his quirks, his warts, the incidents which show his difference from everyone else. Christianity did not change this. The Lives of the Saints show an astonishing range of temperament and talent. St. Paul with his misogyny balances the happily married Thomas Moore; St. Francis preaching to the birds balances St. Margaret Mary abasing herself before the bedpans of the sick. The Islamic biographer stressed, not the various proliferations of grace, but uniform submission to a pattern of perfection. What constituted perfection had been ordained in detail; sanctity consisted in conforming to a stencil already cut, not in cutting a new one for yourself. Autobiography was the same. No Islamic Boswell had confessed to gonorrhea. The stencil is so strong that public opinion will push the non-conformist into it, once he is dead. The ordinary Turk of 1970 is assured that Atatürk was a sober Muslim who kept the rules. Islamic biographies make dull reading.

Gamal Abdul Nasser was normal, in many senses humdrum. His only vices were tobacco, coffee and the pursuit of power; and these were shared by his friends. The particular circumstances and events of his life had merely heightened this significant normality.

His birthplace was different from any other Egyptian city; Alexandria can claim to be the longest, thinnest city in the world, stretched east to west on a limestone ridge cut off from Egypt by a lake. A commercial sea linked this reborn city of the Ptolemies with southern Europe. Spiritually it looked to the Mediterranean, which washed its long corniche, as much as to Egypt at its back. It was, *par excellence,* a Janus city. It was also a city where Egyptians felt themselves outsiders, and were seen as such. Lawrence Durrell's crowded *Alexandria Quartet* has in its caste of Levantines one Muslim Arab: appropriately a servant, "one-eyed Hamid." On the fringes of this cosmopolitan society Gamal Abdel Nasser's father rented a one-story, flat-roofed house in the Bacos quarter. It was a modest advance on the unhygienic mud dwellings of Beni-Morr, his village of origin near Assiout. Yet to his derivation from Upper Egyptian fellahin—his mother, too, came from south of Cairo—Gamal owed his sturdy physique, imposing height and dark complexion. To his father's profession—which kept him on the move from one place to another—he owed an intimate knowledge of Egypt. When Gamal was three, the family moved to Assiout. They next lived in Khatatba, a township on the edge of the desert to the west of Cairo. Gamal was a reflective child. It puzzled him that the shepherds who tended the sheep near Khatatba could not afford mutton, while the governmental employees, who had no sheep, could. His father's only answer to this puzzle was to say that the world was constituted so. When the boy was ready for primary education, he was boarded with an uncle who lived in Cairo. He was homesick and lived for his mother's letters. These suddenly ceased in his eighth year. His father wrote evasively: she was busy with her two younger sons, she was visiting relations in Alexandria. The postmaster had a respect for examinations typical of the new competitive Middle East; he wanted his son to do better than he had. Only when Gamal had passed his examinations and come home for the holidays was he told that his mother had suddenly died. The shock marked him for life. He became introspective and inclined to brood.

Children mature early in Egypt and by the time he was twelve, Nasser (to keep henceforward to the name by which he would be known in the West) was a student demonstrator. Nahas Pasha, the leader of the Wafd, demanded, with the backing of parliament, an end to the British occupation. King Fuad intervened, dissolved parliament once again and installed as Prime Minister a politician backed only by the police. Schoolboy riots swept the streets of Egyptian cities. For Nasser it was the beginning of an obsession with politics entirely typical of his generation.

When not shouting "Down with the English!", Nasser was weaving an inner tapestry which would give his life its guiding myths. Since the East is personal it was populated by heroes and villains. The Victorian British had also liked heroes, and their advisers to the Egyptian school system gave Nasser one of his earliest heroes: Admiral Horatio Nelson, glimpsed in a potted biography adapted for schoolboys. Nasser admired the young Norfolk sailor for risking his life for a companion.[3] He was pleased that Nelson had destroyed the French fleet at Aboukir, a tram ride from Alexandria; he already resented Napoleon's occupation of his country. But the British soon loomed as the prime enemies of Egyptian freedom. At the age of sixteen, while a secondary school student, Nasser started on a novel, *For the Sake of Freedom*. The six chapters he completed show the remote influence of Sir Walter Scott; but their theme was an Egyptian success against the British at Rosetta in 1807.

The two great heroes of Nasser's boyhood, the Prophet Muhammad and Mahatma Gandhi, were not Europeans. But it was through European eyes that a generation of Arabs began to see the revealer of Islam as a great man of action. In his *On Heroes and Hero-Worship* Thomas Carlyle had selected Muhammad as an example of the hero as prophet; his book represented a change in the West's approach to a man whom Dante had put in Hell and whom Gibbon had treated as a sexual prodigy. In the East, where the essay was translated and widely read, Muslims were heartened to find the historian of the French Revolution holding their Prophet in so high esteem. Carlyle delivered Muhammad from hagiography and offered him to young Arabs as a maker of history. Carlyle, the Scotsman, admired Muhammad for his sincerity; Nasser, the Egyptian, admired him for his patience. For many years the Prophet's only disciples were his wife and son-in-law; but though scorned, he continued to believe in his mission.

Nasser's second hero, the "half-naked fakir" of Winston Churchill's phrase, was the most spectacular opponent of European colonial rule in the 1930s. At a time when Egyptian politicians in their lounge suits and spats were ineffectually mimetic, Gandhi defiantly exalted the very things which Europeans saw as symbols of Indian backwardness: the dhoti and the spinning wheel. More important, Gandhi had invented a technique whereby the weak could resist the strong. Gandhi believed that evil should not be resisted by evil weapons. His answer was *satyagraha,* or soul force. Instead of firing bullets into flesh, the non-violent warrior accepted pain himself and so shot arrows of remorse into his opponent's heart, thus rendering him a friend. To Egyptians aware of British firepower, Gandhi's technique was impressive for its effects. He was taken seriously. In sandals and dhoti he was invited to Buckingham Palace. Though Nasser admired Ghandi as a resister rather than as a pacifist, a dislike of bloodshed encased an ambition as palpable in himself as it had been in the young Zaghlul.

[3] This information on Nasser's childhood heroes, etc., came from discussion with Nasser himself.

But in forming an attitude to history and the world Nasser in the 1930s drew on a richer intellectual compost than had been available to Zaghlul. As well as journalists, serious writers had begun to show the results of cross-fertilization with the West. Nasser's favorite, on the strength of a novel exalting the hidden resources in the Egyptian character, was Towfik al-Hakim, the most Europeanized of Egyptian novelists. Nasser was well placed for reading; in 1933, the year that Hitler came to power, his father was transferred to a small Cairo post office standing between a Jewish shop and a synagogue. The family lodgings round the corner were within easy distance of *Dar al-Kuttub,* the National Library. From the back numbers of the Cairo press he imbibed the political education that no school could give. He read with avidity every word that Mustafa Kamil, coiner of striking phrases and striker of extremist poses, had published.

In the fire of debates that flared through classrooms like fire through stubble, in the flashlight of books read under covers when his family slept, Nasser the adolescent saw in bold relief the characters that had dominated the previous century. He never lost a certain sympathy for the Khedive Ismail. The Khedive's expansion of an Egyptian empire south into Africa, his zeal to modernize Cairo, struck resonant notes in a young man picturing foreigners as contemptuous of Egypt for being weak or out of date. He despised Ismail's son who had bartered Egyptian independence for his throne. Orabi might have succeeded but for a lack of stamina in himself as well as of any outside force to help him. Towards Abdul Hamid, the Sultan who might have helped Orabi but was too weak, Nasser felt disdain compounded with the dark-skinned Egyptian's resentment of the pale-skinned Turk. Nasser felt neither admiration nor gratitude for Lord Cromer, Britain's proconsul; Cromer had worked for Britain's interests, and not for Egypt's. In a dislike for Cromer, Nasser shared common ground with Theodor Herzl. It was a small bond. Nasser's first moves towards the Arab Nationalism that would become his passion were made when he took part in the annual demonstrations on November 2 against the Balfour Declaration. Egyptian students protested more against the British and the Jewish settlers to whom they had opened Palestine than for the Arabs. The bond between Egyptians and Palestinians was one of predicament. Egypt at this time did not stress its Arab links. In the tradition of Khedive Ismail, most fashionable writers stressed Egypt's links, as a Mediterranean country, to Europe. Many Egyptians were still unsure of themselves; they feared to be identified with the Arabs, whom they saw through the eyes of Europeans as backward or picturesque. An Egyptian effendi with his collection of French novels and memories of a stay in Paris saw little that linked him and the uncouth citizens of Baghdad or Amman; what he saw, he disliked. But the development of Jewish settlement in Palestine and the British suppression of Arab resistance to it made the Palestine issue seem a flagrant instance of imperial disdain for native wishes.

The eighteen-year-old Nasser was an opinionated young man with intense beliefs on every subject affecting his country. But they did not earn him money. His father had remarried and Nasser was one of eleven children; a family budget never higher than fifty dollars a month made the choice of a career an urgent one. For three reasons a military career tempted Nasser as it had tempted Atatürk: the reasons did not include any particular bellicosity. Since the early nineteenth century the military academies of Turkey and Egypt had offered the best higher education available; their prestige survived the growth of better, or more liberal, institutions. The second appeal was social. To become an officer implied the advancement so overwhelmingly desirable in a hierarchical society; for the son of a minor official to become an officer, with the possibility of ending up a pasha, or general, was a beguiling prospect. The third and deepest appeal was political. As a schoolboy Nasser acted in only one play, an adaptation of Shakespeare's *Julius Caesar*. He played the title role. He enlarged his understanding of a part for which Shakespeare felt little sympathy by background reading. He came to the conclusion that Caesar was a democrat who had used his Gaulish legions to defeat an aristocracy. When faced with the choice of a career, he thought not so much of arms as of the armory. Only military weapons could topple a hated but entrenched regime.

The threshold of the Military Academy was the more tempting for being hard to cross. The monarchy had nearly foundered in 1882 thanks to the "native officers" so imprudently recruited by Said Pasha. Since the restoration of Towfik the officer corps had been restricted to the caste whose interests it protected. It required boldness on the part of the youthful Nasser to approach this aristocratic preserve. Dressed in his one tidy suit he presented himself to a selection committee seated round a table. He was not made less nervous by the sight of his dossier, inevitably including reports of his political activities at school, open before them.

"Your name?"

"Gamal Abdul Nasser."

"Your father's profession."

"He works in the post office."

"As a senior official?"

"No, a simple employee."

"Where are you from?"

"Beni-Morr, in the province of Assiout."

"So you are fellahin?"

"We are."

"You have had no army officers in your family before?"

"No."

"Then why do you wish to be one?"

"To serve my country."

"Have you any property?"

"None; I am an ordinary citizen."

"Have you a sponsor?"

"If you mean, do I have any influence? No, I have none."

"Did you take part in the 1935 demonstrations?"

"Yes."

"Good. You may go."

So Nasser remembered the interview of rejection. The lack of *wasta*—the Arabic term for a powerful mediator or influence—was as lethal as his student record. Rebuffed, he made his second choice: the law. Things were no longer as easy as when Zaghlul, his fingers burnt in the Orabi revolt, had taken to law and raised his earnings to £5,000 a year. Then all that was needed was a knowledge of French and a ready tongue; the field had been empty. The Cairo Faculty of Law, where Nasser enrolled in October 1936, was a road crowded as a Cairo tram; but it still could jog towards a political career.

At the same time as starting on freshman law, he applied to join the Police College. Here again he was rebuffed. The Cairo Police would remain under Russell Pasha's control for another ten years.

Nasser's law studies lasted a mere six months. Their termination was due in part to accident, in part to his persistent will. The year he had first applied for acceptance at the Military Academy the Wafdist government had signed a treaty with Britain. Although the treaty recognized Egypt as entirely independent with the right to join the League of Nations, it allowed British troops to defend the Canal and so tied Egypt to Britain for the foreseeable future. It meant that Egypt would be involved *de facto* on the British side in any future war. Young hotheads discounted the Wafdist argument that Italy's invasion of Abyssinia had shown that Egypt was in greater danger from Fascism than liberal democracy. They denounced the Wafd for reneging on Zaghlul's policy of total independence and asserted corrupt motives for the deal. Whatever the rights of the dispute, Egypt as a future ally of Great Britain was encouraged to enlarge its army. This meant, if not the democratization of the officer corps, at least the attempt to make it a little more serious. This policy alone might not have got Nasser through the forbidden doors. In an impetuous gesture typical of his character, he presented himself at the house of the new Secretary of State at the Ministry of War.[4] Shown into the Pasha's study, Nasser—tall, serious, intense—put his question with embarrassing bluntness: was entry to the Military Academy dependent on *wasta,* or merit? Nasser was lucky. The Secretary of State was one of those rare Egyptians to respond to an un-byzantine approach. Nasser had found his *wasta*—though its protection would be short-lived. The Secretary of State was genuinely concerned to improve the quality of the Army and to substitute professional-minded officers for the polo-

[4] Ibrahim Khairy Pasha.

playing aristocrats of recent tradition. His implicit challenge to the ruling caste was to be taken up and he would be dismissed in 1939 in favor of successors who helped Farouk impose his control on the Army, which became, in the popular mind, devoted to the throne. But in the few years at his disposal the single-minded official, himself a pasha, was the unconscious gardener of revolution. Besides Gamal Abdul Nasser, he admitted a considerable number of other young men from a similar background; though the Pasha did not know it, the plebian names of his protegees were destined to replace the princes, pashas and beys who dominated Egypt in the 1930s: Anwar al-Sadat, Abdul Hakim Amer, Ali Sabri, Abdul Latif al-Baghdadi, Kemaleddin Hussein, Zakaria Mohiaddin made a list in striking contrast with the polyphonic litany of the Royal Automobile Club. Another innovation was as important. If these young men were the seedlings of revolution, he prepared their seedbed. To entice young officers away from the temptations of Cairo, he inaugurated an officers' club and endowed it with prestige. In the club the officers got to know each other and each other's ideas; a consensus of opinion developed; and in the elections for office in the club significant expressions of this consensus would be made.

The fertilization of the seeds took place at Mankabad, in an army camp as dusty as the desert in which it stood, halfway between Cairo and Aswan. One sub-lieutenant who in 1938 "spent all day on manoeuvres, returning dog-tired in the evening to our tents"[5] has told how these recent graduates of the Military Academy sat round their evening camp fire almost till next day's bugle. "We were young men full of hope. We were brothers-in-arms, united in friendship and in a common detestation of the existing order of things. Egypt was a sick country. The social and political unrest in Egypt was the theme of our debates." These debates made up for the dull routine of the day. From the start they were dominated by the tall, withdrawn young officer whose basic message to his brother officers was as cogent as, in another country, Aaron Gordon's exaltation of physical toil: "We must fight imperialism, monarchy and feudalism, because we are opposed to injustice, oppression and slavery. Every patriot wants to establish a strong and free democracy. This aim will be achieved, by force of arms if need be. The task is urgent because the country has fallen into chaos. Freedom is our natural right. The way lies before us—revolution."

Nasser's closest friend was the tall, slight Abdul Hakim Amer, a fellow Upper Egyptian but compared with Nasser impulsive and volatile. Anwar al-Sadat was the enthusiast as well as the historian of the group: adventurous, emotional, a good-humored fanatic for Egyptian freedom.

The world war which began over Poland in September 1939 seemed as peripheral to the aspirant revolutionaries of Mankabad as Arab aspira-

[5] Anwar al-Sadat (or El Sadat), *Revolt on the Nile* (London: Wingate, 1957).

tions did to the statesmen of the competing blocs. The British would try to hush the Middle East while the Axis Powers would try to rouse it. Neither Allies nor Axis cared profoundly for the peoples involved and these returned the compliment. The young officers looked on the war as a major event to be studied with wary opportunism. A world war, whatever its cause or result, constituted a political earthquake; what was seemingly fixed would move, what was fluid might congeal. The officers wanted to ensure that when the map resettled, it would not be to the advantage of "Imperialism." Imperialism meant different things to different Arabs. To Egyptians, Iraqis and Palestinians, it meant the direct or indirect control of their affairs by Britain. To Syrians and North Africans it meant France. To Libyans it meant Italy. There was a good chance that imperialism, in all of its forms, would be weakened by what seemed from the Middle East a European civil war. Such a weakening would be the Arabs' chance to regain their freedom.

Lieutenant Nasser, as he had now become, spent a peaceful war. Wishing to remove himself from supervision, he volunteered with Amer for service in the Sudan and spent the first three years of the war remote from Cairo; he passed what was virtual exile reading up on military history and strategy. He was away at the time of the British insult to Farouk. The ordinary Egyptians had been kept unaware of what had happened. An English-language newspaper in Cairo claimed that Sir Miles Lampson had been greeted by a friendly crowd chanting "Long Live Britain!" and that the ambassador had replied with "Long Live Egypt!" But the Army knew the true story. A half-Sudanese brigadier, Muhammad Naguib, offered his resignation: the Army had not been given the chance of defending their King. "Dear Hassan," Nasser wrote to the friend whose letter gave him the details, "I have received your letter and its story makes me flame with anger. But what can we do against accomplished facts? We took it lying down. But I am convinced the English held only a single card. They were bluffing. If they had felt that even a few Egyptians existed who would meet force with force, they would have withdrawn—like whores!"

Thanks to a growing reputation for intelligence as well as popularity, Nasser was promoted to the Staff College in late 1942. He was now that much nearer to the armory keys. But he had still had no experience of war.

Sadat was the only member of Nasser's group to have an adventurous war. It won him a prison sentence, not a decoration. Sadat's blend of courage, opportunism and bad luck illustrates an aspect of his generation.

Sadat had decided from the start to make England's danger Egypt's opportunity. A similar decision in the First World War had ranged some Arabs on the side of Britain and some Irish on the side of Germany. In deciding to collaborate with the German-Italian Axis, Sadat can have had few illusions as to the basic motives in Rome and Berlin. In the early stages of the war the Germans gave their Italian partners priority in deciding policy with regard to the Mediterranean and the Arabs. After the Italian collapse in North Africa, the Germans overrode their partners. Neither state backed Arab aspirations explicitly, though Hitler was to receive the chief Mufti of Palestine and use him to some effect among Balkan Muslims. Fascist Italy treated the Arabs of Libya as little more than helots and Rome stubbornly opposed any declaration of support for Arab aims which might be construed as questioning Italian control over Libya— a control which Mussolini wished to extend to Tunisia as well. With regard to Egypt, Rome valued the pro-Italian sympathies of the court but resented the Wafd for its hostile attitude to the conquest of Abyssinia. The Germans had no Arab subjects and no Arab commitments. They were only fettered by their ideology. In *Mein Kampf* Hitler had classified Egyptian nationalists with those "Asiatic mountebanks" who thought they could get the British out of India. The only Middle Easterners for whom Nazi theoreticians could feel kinship were those like the Egyptian royal family with some distant claim to Aryan blood. Farouk's cousin, the deposed Khedive Abbas, was their warmest friend; exiled in Europe he was on good terms with German industrialists while keeping close ties with Turkey. The Germans might have substituted Abbas for Farouk in the event of their victory. Abbas regarded Arab Nationalism as a joke. Hitler had said of the Hebrew branch of the Semitic race: "They lack those qualities which characterize those creative races that are the founders of civilization." A snob and a millionaire, Abbas felt the same about his former subjects; he denied their aptitude for state formation and diplomacy.[6] To Nazis and Nazi sympathizers Sadat with his dark skin was the antithesis of the Nordic ideal. Yet despite such reservations, the Germans were prepared to make trouble for the British if such trouble did not embarrass their Axis partner.

One elderly Egyptian, General Aziz al-Misri, was genuinely respected by those Germans who knew the Middle East. The general had fought bravely against the Italians before the First World War, as a brother officer with Atatürk in the Ottoman Army. General Misri opposed the anglophile Arab Nationalism of the rulers of Jordan and Iraq. In the First World War he had held it the duty of Muslims to support the Sultan and his German allies; at the beginning of the Second, British influence had led to his removal from his post as Chief of Staff of the Egyptian Army. In March 1941 an emissary of the Wehrmacht, then preparing the Afrika Korps for a major offensive, was sent to Cairo to contact General Misri and propose collaboration. The seasoned nationalist was willing to visit German headquarters if only he could get out of Egypt. The young Sadat was involved. He tried two ways to evade the British, who were in entire control of the country's ports and airports. The first idea was for the Ger-

---

[6] See Lukasz Hirsczowicz, *The Third Reich and the Arab East,* tr. from Polish (London: Routledge & Kegan Paul, 1966), *passim.*

mans to send a U-boat into Lake Barollos at the northern end of the Suez Canal, to the west of Port Said. But Lake Barollos was a shallow stretch of water too reedy and too near British encampments for a self-respecting submarine. The second plan was to smuggle the general out on a German plane. This came to nothing when the car in which the general was racing to a secret desert rendezvous developed engine trouble. Despairing of the Luftwaffe the gallant old general and a companion with some knowledge of flying took off in a stolen Egyptian plane but crashed into a post on take-off. General Misri spent time in a prison infirmary. A second flamboyant and inefficient venture would land Sadat himself behind barbed wire.

In June 1942 the name of Rommel resounded in Cairo like a tocsin. While the exiled Greek Army burnt its papers, the British made contingency plans for withdrawal to Palestine, or even South Africa. In an atmosphere of bubbling excitement—Egyptians, with nothing to lose, enjoyed sensation for its own sake—two unusual guests were led to Sadat's house by an officer friend. They were German spies dressed in the casual uniform of British officers: ankle-high suede bootees known as brothel-creepers and khaki bush shirts. They had reached Cairo despite disregarding the professional spy's most elementary precautions. For one of the two, Hans Appler, prewar Egypt had been home, since his mother had taken an Egyptian for her second husband and Hans had changed his name to Hussein. "Hussein" had become a Cairo night bird, the despair of his stepfather. Just before the outbreak of war "Hussein" had returned to the Third Reich and military service as Hans. The Wehrmacht decided to use his intimate knowledge of Egypt. Hans-Hussein was too much of an Egyptian to prove a Teutonic T. E. Lawrence, and despite a copious supply of forged British bank notes and radio equipment, his trip ended on a note of farce. The Egyptian Jew with whom the spies changed £40,000 took a 33⅓ commission. Their base was one of the moldering houseboats which, moored in a branch of the Nile, served as love nests for Cairo's bohemians; this particular houseboat belonged to a distinguished belly dancer. Above her boat's flat roof, their transmitter flaunted its antenna like a cock's comb. When the machine broke down, they called Sadat (who had taken a course in signals) to put it right. "I began to be worried," he relates. Not a moment too soon; but, as things proved, too late. When he reached the houseboat he found an extraordinary chaos of perfume, female underwear and whiskey. The unserious pair had opted out of the war. As Sadat checked the transmitter, hidden inside an ornate gramaphone, he realized that the young men had damaged it on purpose. They hoped in this way to prolong their Cairo vacation. A few nights later they brought home a pair of Jewish prostitutes, who doubled their earnings by denouncing their young friends to the British military police. It was fortunate for the Free Officers and Nasser that the spies were discovered in this way, and not by the British secret service, who might have investigated further. The spies were interrogated, Sadat tells us, by Winston Churchill in person, who was passing through Cairo on his way to Moscow. Promised a reprieve if they would denounce their local contacts, they denounced the only two they had had time to make: Sadat and his officer friend. A British military judge sentenced Sadat to be cashiered from the Egyptian Army and detained at a concentration camp near Minia, south of Cairo.

Sadat's escapade, as well as the total British control over Egypt, gave Nasser another six years of reading and reflection before, in 1948, he found himself for the first time on active service. In a dugout in the Negev he found a parable for the predicament of Egypt. " 'Our country,' I would say to myself, 'is a second, but larger Falluja. Egypt too is faced with problems and besieged by enemies. It too has been duped, pushed into battle unprepared, while ambitions, plots and lusts make a plaything of its destiny. Egypt too is under fire, unarmed.' " When an Israeli officer met him to discuss the burial of Jewish war dead, Nasser wanted to discuss another topic: the techniques by which the Israelis had defeated the British and secured their independence.

Chapter 3

WHILE thinking of Egypt from besieged Falluja, Nasser had not ignored the refugees blown like starlings round the outpost's wire. A small girl scrounged for crusts amidst the pot shots of the armies. "I said to myself, this might happen to my own daughter. I was sure what had happened in Palestine must happen, and would happen again, to any country in this region which let itself be dominated by the present power-system." For in 1948 Israel seemed only one facet of the colonial system. Morocco and Tunisia would still pass several years as French protectorates; Algeria was still considered an integral part of France; Libya's future was still debated by the victorious Allies; the British maintained an army of 80,000 along the Canal; British influence over the Hashemite kingdoms of Iraq and Jordan was still firm—Jordan's Arab Legion was officered by Englishmen, while Iraq was tied to Britain by a treaty. The deeper message of the Palestine War was summed up in the words of a popular officer who died in the Negev: "Listen . . . the supreme struggle is in Egypt." There was more irony in the valediction than appeared. The officers who quoted it to each other meant: the struggle against Farouk, the British and the pashas. Those who knew that the officer had been shot in error by one of his own men might have added: the struggle against incompetence as well.

The battle of Falluja, trivial compared with the exploits of Atatürk, was Nasser's Gallipoli in little. He had already decided on the need for revolution; he now felt himself confirmed as its pilot; after an incident when he was struck by a bullet on the chest, but saved by a pocket Koran, his sense of dedication was made yet stronger. During the coming years of mounting national despair he sent his thoughts on a reconnaissance patrol towards the future. The result was a personal manifesto, *The Philosophy of the Revolution*. The title was grandiloquent for a booklet of some sixty short pages. Its "philosophy" would seem vague and woolly to a positivist professor, though its opening sentence would be familiar to anyone who had corrected a student essay:

> *Before going any further in this essay, I should like to pause for a moment at the word "philosophy." It is a big word. It is gigantic. Indeed when I stand before it I feel I am facing a world without limits, an infinity.*

The struggle after profundity, with its inevitably portentous results, punctures the pages: "I am one of those who believe that nothing can exist in a vacuum. Even truth cannot exist in a vacuum . . ." Perhaps even at this early stage he was advised by Muhammad Hassanain Haikal, the fledgling journalist who would become the editor of *al-Ahram* and Nasser's spokesman. Haikal more than Nasser is likely to have inserted the reference to Luigi Pirandello's *Six Characters in Search of an Author:* "I do not know why I always imagine that in this region where we live there is a role wandering aimlessly in search of an actor to play it." The debased Arabic rhetoric which would give fatal openings to his enemies in the years to come is here in germ, unedited by the author or any friend. "I have all my life been a believer in *'askariyyah."* (An official Cairo version[1] translates this as "soldiery"; in fairness to Nasser, it means something more like "the qualities of being a soldier.") "It is the fundamental principle of *'askariyyah* that the army's sole duty is to die on the frontiers of the motherland." The affirmation seems curiously passive from an instructor at the Staff College: more like a woman poet's threnody on those who have laid down their lives than the words of a commander planning for the enemy's men to die on the frontier, not his own.

But for all these faults, compounded with evidence that Nasser's teachers never taught him to practice compression or avoid repetition,

[1] Gamal Abdul Nasser, *The Philosophy of the Revolution*, introduction by Dorothy Thompson (Cairo: 1954).
NB: I have made my own translation of the original on further occasions.

The Philosophy marks a development in the Janus profile. Out of thematic periods lengthy as an Arabic song jag perceptions of truth: "Every people on earth passes through two revolutions: first, a political revolution which frees them from an imposed despot or an occupying army; and second, a social revolution—a conflict of classes whose resolution brings justice to the people as a whole." Truth, however veiled, had been perceived in Egypt and Turkey before. What is new is the candor, the self-revelation, including, as we shall see, some surprising admissions. The Khedive Ismail would have shrunk from disclosing his thoughts to his subjects; if he had been compelled to do so, he would have clothed them in phrases voluminous as crinolines. Sultan Abdul Hamid communicated through secretaries and whispers, Atatürk through pithy sentences or speeches droning through summer afternoons. King Feisal of Iraq left it to T. E. Lawrence to tell his story. Compared with Western statesmen, who collect their detritus as it accumulates, who negotiate the publication of their memoirs before they resign, Eastern statesmen gave few clues to their inner lives and often, therefore, seemed to lack them. *The Philosophy of the Revolution* gives a key with which to unlock the heart of Nasser, the pilot in the 1950s of Arab Nationalism and in the 1960s of its further evolution, Arab Socialism.

Since irony is a feature of the Janus face, it is appropriate that Nasser's manifesto has one forerunner, the *Judenstaat* of Theodor Herzl.

As a composition Herzl's booklet belongs to the literary tradition which starts with the Greeks and never willingly abandons a sense of control, of construction, of climax. But half Eastern, wholly amateur though the essay of the Egyptian soldier seems, compared with that of the Viennese intellectual, the two men share assumptions. Nasser defines his intentions in terms which Herzl might have used. "They are an attempt to scrutinize our aims and determine the forces we can mobilize to achieve them. They are an exploration of the surrounding territory to realize that we do not live on a lonely island, cut off from the rest of the world." His aims—to find a basis of power for his people, a possibility for a total national renaissance—link him to his effective antagonist more than to his Middle East predecessors. He bears the traces of Europe, as Herzl bore them, not in his clothing, but in his soul.

Judah Magnes, the pacific Jew who had repudiated Herzl, diagnosed the Will to Power as the stamp of "the other nations," of modern Europe. The problem of power beat at Nasser's head as it had beaten at Herzl's. Herzl fashioned an engine to carry the Jews from exile among the gentiles to a land of their own. Nasser's problem was related but different: not to get the Arabs away from the Europeans, but to get the Europeans away from the Arabs. As a staff officer he had brooded on Egyptian defeats, had fumbled for means to prevent them in the future. He had come up with a revelatory intuition: Egypt should turn its weakness—that strategic centrality which made Napoleon describe it as "the most important country"[2] —against its tormentors. Such a vision of political jujitsu exactly echoes Herzl's prescription for the fuel to power his engine: "I say that this force" —Herzl was referring to anti-Semitism and the Jewish reaction to it—"if properly handled, is powerful enough to propel a large engine and to move passengers and goods, let the engine have whatever form it may."[3]

Nasser saw Egypt—hitherto dominated for its strategic position—as the bull's-eye of three concentric circles of influence: the Arab, the African and the Islamic. Egyptians spoke Arabic, lived in Africa and were nine-tenths Muslim. Each of these circles could see in Egypt an outpost of its interests and therefore aid in its defense. Herzl had made an entirely opposite but entirely related argument: "We should form part of a wall of defense for Europe in Asia, an outpost of civilization against barbarism."[4] Herzl had seen in Jewish finance a weapon against an indifferent world. "If his Majesty the Sultan were to give us Palestine, we could in return undertake the complete management of the finances of Turkey."[5] Arab finance was no such weapon when Nasser was writing. What Arab capital existed was the horded gold of Baghdad merchants, the cotton estates of Egyptian pashas, the pearls brought up from the waters of the Persian Gulf. But Nasser had discerned—and he quotes a report published by Chicago University—a lever as potent as the Jewish money Herzl invoked. "Oil is the backbone of material civilization; without it, factories, the means of communication, weapons of war, would become immobile blocks of steel . . . The cost needed to extract a barrel of oil in the United States is 78 cents; in South America it is 48 cents; in the Arab countries it is 10 cents only. The center of the world's oil production has shifted from the United States, where the oil wells are nearing exhaustion and where land prices and wages have soared, to the Arab world, whose wells are still untapped, whose lands go for a song and whose labor is unbelievably cheap. Half the world's known reserves are buried under Arab soil." He wrote when Kuwait had only just begun producing, when Algerian and Libyan oil was still undiscovered.

The Palestine affair had an effect on Nasser akin to the effect of the Dreyfus affair on Herzl. The inability of the independent Arab states to preserve more than a fraction of Arab Palestine balanced the inability of an emancipated Jewish officer to obtain justice in the Third Republic. *The Philosophy* is more autobiographical than *Der Judenstaat*. It throws a lurid torchlight on Nasser himself and the seething situation in an assassin's Egypt. In the gloom of the Palestine defeat the man who

---

[2] Cromer quotes J. H. Rose, *Life of Napoleon*, on the title page of his *Modern Egypt:* "In his first interview with the Governor of St Helena, Napoleon said emphatically: 'Egypt is the most important country in the world.'"
[3] Preface to *Judenstaat;* vide Hertzberg, op. cit., p. 205.
[4] Hertzberg, op. cit., p. 222.
[5] Ibid.

admired Gandhi and disliked violence accepted for a season the thesis of selective killing already espoused by the Muslim Brotherhood and the Irgun. Nasser and the Free Officers held General Sirri Amer responsible for providing the faulty arms—hand grenades that blew up in the thrower's face, as Sadat, in jail for a second time during the Palestine War, described them from hearsay. Nasser admits with the candor of a Rousseau that he participated in an attempted assassination. He reacts like a prodigal son, or if we want to compare him to a writer, to no one born further West than Dostoevsky:

"I was in a state of perplexing conflicts: patriotism warring with religion, skepticism with belief, cruelty with compassion, ignorance with knowledge. But gradually the dream of political assassination lost its hold on me. The climax came the night we had set aside for the removal of one particular individual. After studying his every habit, we had planned to shoot him dead on his way home. One group would attack, another cover the attackers, a third cover the general retreat. I was one of these. All went to plan. The street was empty, as we had forseen. The groups took up their prepared positions and the man arrived. Shots rang out. The three groups beat a retreat. I started my engine and drove off at a terrific speed. But not before I heard the screams of women, appeals for help, the cry of a frightened child . . . The cries echoed in my ears as I lay feverish in my bed. I lit cigarette after cigarette, while I gave my thoughts free rein. Question and answer clashed on the rocks of those remembered sounds. "Did I do right?" . . . "My motives were love of country . . ." "But was there no other way?" My arguments no longer convinced me. Could the death of one individual solve Egypt's problems? Our dream of national glory . . . did it depend on the disappearance of individuals . . . or on the appearance of new men? As I tossed and turned in my smoke-filled room, the certainty came to me: political assassination was the wrong road. Daybreak found me praying that the man I had planned to kill might live. I rushed out to buy the morning papers and was overjoyed to find that our intended victim would recover."

Nasser watched Farouk's decaying kingdom with the fixed stare of a cat at a mousehole. Not one Egyptian retained prestige. The murdered Hassan al-Banna could not reign from the tomb, since the Supreme Guide had lost his aura for responsible Egyptians when he espoused assassination. Farouk was upping the stakes for popularity, but in vain. He had himself proclaimed as King of Sudan as well as Egypt. It was a paper title. British troops remained stubbornly in charge of the vast country to Egypt's south. He married Narriman Sadek, a maiden as lusciously plump as Turkish delight, but nobody cared. He backed a guerrilla campaign against the British along the Canal, but it fared no better than the Palestine campaign. Yet it added momentum to his fate. On January 25, 1952, the British commander in the Canal Zone ordered a strategically located

Egyptian police station to surrender. On telephoned instructions from Cairo, from the Wafdist Minister of the Interior, the police resisted with futile heroism. At the close of day around seventy lay dead. Next day, the twenty-sixth, the Cairo police stood with folded arms as mobs armed with petrol put Cairo's modern quarter to the flames. Disciplined agitators in jeeps ensured that the mobs destroyed, but did not loot. The planners of the conflagration were never indicted but the targets were such as the Brotherhood would have picked: cabarets, drink shops, cinemas, the Turf Club, expensive stores, above all, Shepheard's Hotel, where generations of imperial servants had clapped for their sundowners in the sudden violet of a Cairo dusk. The dun, sullen city now flickered in smoke and scarlet as the downtrodden East rejected all that symbolized the disdainful West. In Abdin Palace, like some lesser Nero, Farouk giggled through the afternoon at the discomfiture of the hated Wafd. His first male child had just been born. At nightfall the Army was summoned to cool the ash.

Another half dozen governments succeeded each other till on July 10 Nasser listened to Rimsky-Korsakov's "Scheherezade" with two officer friends, then, lifting the needle from its groove, declared: "We shall strike at the beginning of next month." But the King had got wind of the plot and planned to appoint his brother-in-law War Minister and arrest the leaders. The date was advanced to the night of July 22–23.

The coup d'état was as facile as shooting an old hippopotamus. In one act of token resistance two soldiers died. Otherwise there was no bloodshed. An excited Sadat announced the coup d'état over the national radio while the King, on his annual holiday in Alexandria, appealed to the British on the Canal. But this time in vain. An American ambassador with a partiality for "my boys," as he called the young officers, advised the British not to move. Farouk owed his life not only to American pressure but to Nasser's character. "I saw that if we began with violence and blood, like the French revolutionaries, we should never stop; I preferred Voltaire." Every other member of the junta wanted Farouk done to death: only the King's execution would show that the revolution had teeth as well as good intentions. Nasser argued that if the King were done to death without a trial, it would be murder; a trial, on the other hand, would sully precious time with the rehearsal of the past. Nasser's total dominance over his followers was now shown. By hinting that he might take some drastic, suicidal step if the junta insisted on Farouk's death, he swung them behind him.[6] On July 26, 1952, the grandson of the Khedive who had opened the Canal embarked himself and 204 pieces of baggage on the royal yacht and sailed away to the night clubs of Europe.

[6] These details from Anwar al-Sadat, now UAR President. Naguib, of course, was not a member of the junta. He admired Nasser's decision to spare Farouk.

Chapter 4

THE revolution hastened to delete the past. Statues and street names connected with Farouk's family were removed or replaced. The fashionable Cairo street named after his father Fuad was renamed 26 July Street after the day of Farouk's abdication; Suliman Pasha in his baggy trousers and soft fez, his mother's forebear, would yield to an industrialist of the 1930s in ugly square-cut suit. But the founder of the family fortunes, a turbaned figure on a dusty horse, would still command the largest square in Nasser's birthplace; and though the metal letters on his plinth were gouged out, their ghost remained. Muhammad Ali Pasha deserved to survive. His feat in relinking Alexandria to the Nile had transformed the fishing village where Napoleon landed into a great sea harbor and the second capital. His open space between the pillared Bourse, where fortunes were made or lost in cotton, and the squalid beginnings of the port, had been the focus of Alexandrian life for a hundred years. Here in good times the cotton brokers and their wives sauntered to St. Mark's Anglican Church on the side towards the sea; on the seamy side, in upstairs rooms the verb "to love" was declined in exotic moods. Here in the bad times after the Orabi revolt, summary naval tribunals had executed Egyptians accused of looting or resistance; here in two world wars soldiers from the ends of the earth bought fly-whisks or leather poufs for home. Muhammad Ali's square would yet witness, at an interval of two years, two great events. Each took place at night in the open air; in both Nasser played the actor's role.

On the first occasion, October 26, 1954, Nasser stood to address the docile organization he had substituted for Egypt's warring parties. Neither he nor the National Liberation Rally had roots in popular affection. Attendance at the meeting was a duty. There was an atmosphere of yawns, of kicking off of shoes, of wandering thoughts. As Nasser addressed the crowd in earnest Arabic his young, anguished profile was lit by an over-hanging lamp; the platform was mounted below the pillars of the Bourse. Suddenly three shots shivered the dark. One smashed the lamp. None touched the speaker. "Let them kill Nasser!" Nasser shouted amid the sudden excitement. "What is Nasser but one among many?"

The rhetoric suddenly seemed true. The attempt evoked sympathy and horror. It marked the beginning of an upward surge which would spiral him away from the nagging sense that he was acting without support, to unprecedented heights of popularity and applause.

The Philosophy of the Revolution had been published that same year. It would not, perhaps, have been publishable in any other. Earlier, its publication would have laid him open to critics, to whom he was still vulnerable. Later his authority would be too canonized for such revealing candor. One striking passage evoked the disappointment which, according to Nasser, had clouded his enjoyment of the bright morning when he had overthrown Farouk.

"I had imagined ourselves as an advance force of commandos. Within a few hours the whole nation, marching in step and in serried ranks, would have caught up with us. I had heard in imagination the triumphal roar as these great masses moved in unison towards the supreme goal. But the event was surprisingly different. In fulfillment of their mission, the leaders had stormed the citadel of tyranny and dethroned the despot. Now they waited to be joined by a marching nation. They continued to wait. My dream picture turned to a sour reality. The masses came, but in dribs and drabs. Instead of accomplishing our mission, I realized bitterly, we had only started. We needed discipline but found chaos. We needed unity but found division. We needed hard work but found passivity and indolence." Nasser's account goes on to show him politely consulting leaders of opinion and finding, not constructive counsellors, but egoists eager to settle scores or advertise their merits.

The American journalist, Dorothy Thompson, in an introduction to an English version of *The Philosophy*,[1] claimed that it revealed "a patriotic idealist animated initially by too naive a faith in his own people." Miss Thompson may have been animated by too naïve a faith in her author. Without the shrewdest sensitivity to his own people, Nasser could not have piloted his conspiracy to success. He was always litmus-sensitive to Egypt. From the start he must have expected opposition from the politicians of the Muhammad Ali Club and only fair-weather cheers from the crowded sidewalks. Yet an effective machinery for popular control could only be fashioned from such politicians or from the people, and Nasser distrusted both. He rationalized his distrust. In a poor country, he would often repeat, outside money, outside influence, could always play havoc. But the decision not to share power was rooted in inner complexities that were revealed, not in what he said, but the imagery through which he said it. The conception of a "whole nation, marching in step and in serried ranks" had become flesh in the murals of Mexican artists: nowhere else. Yet as an idea it appealed to a man accustomed to giving orders and being answered with an obedient Yes Sir! or, in Egypt, *Effendim!* In his one highbrow reference he had written of a role awaiting an actor. The use of the singular was

[1] The edition already cited.

not accidental. His first decisive intervention—against the majority eager to kill Farouk—had been humane. It had been no less autocratic.

Nasser had probably known quite well that his revolution would be greeted with the mixed emotions of an unserried people who had often been deceived. What distressed him was the slowness with which this people granted him its love.

The people were hardly to blame.

By 1952 Farouk and his succession of feeble governments were generally despised. The crowd would cheer anything new. There was brief dancing in the streets.

But a stronger emotion, in drawing room or mosque, classroom or coffeeshop, was curiosity. Not one member of the junta was known to the public.

A darker feeling accompanied excitement and curiosity—apprehension. A barracks was replacing Abdin as the pivot of Egyptian life and the Army was not a popular institution. The fellahin had a tradition of evading military service: not too difficult in a country without family names where one province might contain a hundred thousand Muhammad Alis of military age. Fellahin who became Army officers joined a largely alien caste. The Army's lack of success in Palestine had become widely known. Yet weapons which had not defeated the Haganah and Irgun could easily deal with Egyptians. Hence a prudent reticence.

Individuals showed unease in different ways. A prince with no home but Egypt telephoned the Turkish embassy: would descendants of Muhammad Ali be welcomed "back" by the Turkish Republic? A Greek grocer lowered his steel shutters. A Coptic bank clerk noted that not one of the new rulers had a Christian name. Noting the same fact, a Muslim Brother lawyer rejoiced—only to pause: would a military dictatorship tolerate rivals? A university professor with no religious beliefs concealed his *Works of Lenin* when he heard Sadat, the wartime ally of the Germans, read the pronunciamento on the radio, when he learnt of the resignation of the junta's only leftist, Khalid Mohiaddin. A belly dancer at the Auberge sewed gold in her bolero and bought a seat for Beirut. A ten-year-old Nubian schoolboy pulled the blankets over his head, fearing chaos. It occurred to only one person—a journalist—to start a frank discussion with Colonel Nasser. The Cairo editors, as ignorant as their readers about the officer-plotters, appointed a journalist to tail each member of the junta. Muhammad Hassanain Haikal had covered the Palestinian and later the Korean War; he had met some of the Free Officers before the coup; but he had a flair for politics and in attaching himself to Nasser was picking the winner.

Nasser had himself picked a winner when he chose General Muhammad Naguib to be the figurehead for the revolution: though a winner to whom there would be objections later. Naguib had won the respect of Nasser and his close friend Amer for his attitude to the British action in 1942. After carefully vetting Naguib, Nasser allowed him, a few months before the coup, to take over his own position as president of the Free Officers. Naguib's seniority kept him away from day-to-day plotting; at the time of the coup he had met only five of the junta. The avuncular family man in his early fifties was a good replacement for Farouk. He made the revolution attractive and respectable. In other Arab countries his kindly, pipe-smoking face helped to refute suggestions of American collusion in the coup d'état; at home he showed a baby-kissing talent new to Egyptians.

But like some Roman emperor slowly persuaded of his own divinity, Naguib began to believe that he was what he was acclaimed: Egypt's liberator and revolutionary hero. The general in him resented junior officers giving him orders; the conservative suspected their long-term goals. He complained to foreign diplomats and local politicians; he looked around for allies.

The politicians, the Muslim Brotherhood, the Left—all had much to lose. But in enlisting their help against Nasser, Naguib was challenging his superior at intrigue. A summary of the steps by which Nasser seized total, personal power reveals a steely side to his nature not to be inferred from the avowals of his *Philosophy*.

The parliamentary system had survived the coup. The Wafd was still Egypt's largest political organization, possessed of a network of support in villages voting as their landlords told them. The Wafd's secretary-general, Fuad Seragaddin, as obese and corrupt as Farouk, symbolized this political dinosaur more than the now elderly Nahas. Naguib's charm, exploited on a triumphal tour through the delta, helped to eclipse the Wafd. More lethal, a law published in September restricted individual landowner-ship to a ceiling of two hundred acres. The law affected only a tenth of the country's arable land and of itself did little to enrich the hungry fellahin. But it effectively broke the big landlords' political power. The next step was the publication of an innocuous decree requiring political parties to register their programs, personnel and finances with the Minister of the Interior. In the early winter, military trials involved the leaders of the Wafd, including Madame Zuzu Nahas and her intimate friend the secretary-general, in the scandal of faulty arms. So much for the first six months. It took a further six months to destroy what remained of the Constitution. Political parties were dissolved in January and the National Liberation Rally substituted for them. The monarchy, still surviving in the form of a Regency Council acting for Farouk's baby son, was formally abolished in June. Naguib was declared President and Prime Minister; Nasser served as Naguib's deputy in the first post but as his own master in the Ministry of the Interior.

Having disposed of the Constitution, Nasser confronted three remain-ing obstacles: Naguib, the Muslim Brotherhood and the Egyptian Left.

All three sensed a common danger; their attempts to combine hastened their common doom.

Nasser made the first move in the long, final contest by dismissing a senior army officer close to Naguib and critical of the junta. In February 1954 student demonstrations gave him a pretext to suppress the Brotherhood, which had organized them; he did this without consulting President Naguib. Against such evident encroachments on his powers, Naguib tried a tactic difficult for all but the most skilled: that of calculated retreat. Sure of his own popularity, he offered his resignation to the junta on February 23, 1954, as long ago he had done to Farouk. The junta accepted it. Naguib was not dispirited. From dignified house arrest he sanctioned a move on his behalf from the Left. Egypt's Communists distrusted Nasser as much as did the Muslim Brothers; in Khalid Mohiaddin they had a leader who had been a friend of Nasser's and an early member of the conspiracy. The day after Naguib's resignation Mohiaddin staged a protest meeting at the cavalry barracks. It was now Nasser's turn to give a master's lesson in the tactic of retreat. The streets were allowed to show their love for the Naguib of myth and welcome him back to his presidential powers. But his wish to have Mohiaddin as his Prime Minister was vetoed by the Army, largely hostile to the Left. Outside Abdin Palace, in the same square where Orabi had defied Towfik, Naguib and Nasser joined in a rally of reconciliation. Egyptians were once more soothed with a myth. Instead of indulging in mutual carnage, their military leaders planned to restore a democratic system, suitably overhauled. At this juncture Nasser showed a rare but characteristic ability to move at once in two opposite directions. Secretly he filled the jails with Communists and Muslim Brothers, at the same time purging the Army and police. Openly he threw himself into preparations for free elections. On March 9 he resigned his posts as Prime Minister and president of the Revolutionary Command Council, as the junta was officially known, to Naguib. The army censors carried their brief cases from the newspapers they had bored. Fatigued from two tongue-tied years, happy journalists shouted for a return to normal political life. Most educated Egyptians probably wished for this, too.

But Nasser knew what he was doing. In seizing the keys to the armory, he had planned to seize the Egyptian future and reshape it as his ideals and opportunity allowed. The same armory keys had opened doors on more tangible objectives for his essential partners. The thousand officers in the plot, the many others who applauded its success, constituted with their families a bulky new caste. Their expectations of material welfare had increased spectacularly. Empress Fowzia's emeralds—for a brief time Farouk's beautiful sister had been married to the Shah—attracted one member of the junta, whose wife was discovered selling them to a Swiss jeweler; the property and belongings of a cosmopolitan plutocracy sparkled before the eyes of middle-class majors and captains to whom previously a washing machine or a secondhand car had been the limit of desire. A return to the dusty barrack square would mean a retreat from this Aladdin's Cave. Yet just such a retreat seemed the program of the man they had accused of being autocratic. On March 25 Nasser proposed to the junta that they set July 25 as the date for a complete restoration of political parties and the electoral free-for-all. The fixed date, only four months ahead, halted the stampeding caste: their natural anarchism was reined in by the steel of self-interest. The National Liberation Rally and the trade unions mounted demonstrations against such a betrayal of the revolution. The country was paralyzed and Naguib surrendered. In hoping to fight Nasser by restoring the party system Naguib had threatened the caste to which both men owed their power. Both men would have a bill to pay. Naguib paid now. Nasser was returned as Prime Minister; the military censors returned to the newspapers; in a matter of months Naguib was retired to house arrest without a murmur on his behalf.

Against this recent background of events the assassin's shots justified Nasser the policeman in dismantling the remaining obstacle to Nasser the revolutionary. The Brotherhood's new Supreme Guide was jailed for life; six of its leaders were hanged; its rank and file were dealt with by the police.

Nasser's power was complete if unostentatious. He continued to occupy the villa near Abbasia Barracks he had rented before 1952. A high wall concealed its modest enlargement; from its plain study a battery of telephones linked his voice with every power point in the state. This meant his detailed control over the revolution. It also meant, since even he had only two eyes, two ears, inordinate delays in accomplishing simple matters; men in whom he confided could contrive great muddles or amass great fortunes before he had time to intervene. The inert bureaucracy had new duties but less responsibility than in the past. Nasser's congenital distrust led to the fashioning of several separate secret services in his nearest approach to a system of balances and checks. All this would have been onerous to the Egyptians if Nasser the revolutionary policeman had not spent the next two years turning into something else: the living embodiment of Egyptian and Arab hopes. He made this remarkable transition rather as a sleepwalker gets from his bed to the icebox, by allowing the feel of obstacles to redirect him on his way. "I don't act," he tried to explain it, "but react." In seizing popularity he showed something less conscious and more mysterious than his cold talent for intrigue: a genius for allowing a people's emotional priorities to guide his actions. He read them as a soothsayer reads his client's secret wishes: sometimes with mistakes, often with hesitations, but getting to the mainspring at last. It was a process divorced from ratiocination; it led him at times against his own conscious beliefs.

In settling two of the foreign disputes which had bothered the monarchy he had secured a predictable increase of popularity. One agreement got the British out of Egypt (though leaving them the right to return in the event of a major war); another got both British and Egyptians out of the Sudan, which would become an independent republic in 1956. His own conscious preferences might have led to a smooth solution of the Palestine problem. "At the start of the revolution," Nasser was to say,[2] "I was against having a big Army. I was pacific, even in regard to Israel. The officers, not I, insisted on the danger of Israel. I wanted to concentrate on rebuilding Egypt. All this changed on the night when the Israelis raided Gaza. I saw we had to have arms."

A raid on Gaza at the end of the Jewish state's sixth year of independence killed forty-two Egyptian soldiers and wounded thirty;[3] it also showed that the Palestine problem was not going to be soothed away by the United Nations. Israel had been refused admission to the international body on its first application in December 1948, since it then occupied more Arab territory than it had been assigned under the partition plan. After signing armistices with each of its Arab neighbors in the spring of 1949, Israel was admitted to membership on the understanding that it would adhere to the partition resolution and allow the refugees to return. The right of refugees to receive back their property, or compensation for it, reflected the norms of international law; the Jews themselves were to receive massive compensation for the property they had been forced to leave behind in Nazi Europe.

But it is to be doubted if the Israeli leadership ever entertained the notion of allowing the bulk of the refugees to return. The pretext most often advanced for refusing to comply with the General Assembly demand was that it would mean the incorporation into Israel of a potential fifth column. Another reason may have weighed more. The Zionists had been unable, under the British mandate, to secure by purchase more than 7 per cent of Palestine. The Israelis had followed the "miraculous cleaning of the land" —the flight, for whatever motive, of around a million Arabs—with legislation designed to keep the land clean in perpetuity. Under a system described by one Jewish writer as "extraordinary, even in modern times,"[4] the land of absentees could be immediately confiscated, without compensation, for the benefit of Israel and its new citizens. To the credit of the Jews, the most cogent attacks on such legislation have been made by Jews who have maintained the ideals, if not the hopes, of Aaron Gordon or Judah Magnes. "Every Arab in Palestine who had left his town or village after November 19, 1947," writes Don Peretz, in a study of how Israel has treated her Arab minority, "was liable to be classified as an absentee under the regulations." Peretz goes on to show how this system worked in the case of Acre, a town originally awarded to the Arabs in the partition plan but seized by the Jews in the fighting that preceded the British withdrawal

[2] In an interview with the present author.
[3] The figure given in Glubb Pasha's *A Soldier with the Arabs* (London: 1957).
[4] Derek Tozer, "How Israel Treats Her Arabs"; *American Mercury,* August 1957.

and the arrival of Arab armies. As was common in Palestine, a modern suburb, largely Jewish but including many prosperous Arabs, had grown up round an old city exclusively Arab. "All Arabs who held property in the New City of Acre, regardless of the fact that they may never have travelled farther than the few meters to the Old City, were classified as absentees. The 30,000 Arabs who fled from one place to another within Israel, but who never left the country, were also liable to have their property declared absentee."[5] Worse injustice, from the Arab point of view, was the right of a military governor to declare a certain Arab zone a prohibited area; the Arabs who owned the land would be debarred from entering it; whereupon their property would become liable to confiscation.[6]

What seemed abstract injustice to humane Jews based in America was felt as burning outrages by the Palestinians, a quarter of a million of whom were bottled up under Egyptian administration in the Gaza strip. From their barbed wire they could see fields once their own grow green for others; or hardly less galling, they could see where Israeli zeal backed by vast foreign aid had turned desert to clover. As an Arab leader Nasser could not afford to deny the hopes of these refugees for a return, when these hopes were backed each year by the General Assembly. But while he could not ask less for the Palestinians than the UN, he could do nothing practical to get them back. In allowing the refugees to make raids into what they still considered their own land, he may have argued that such desperate acts might remind the Powers which had created the Palestine problem that it was still not solved.

To the Israelis the Gaza raid was part of a habit of response to what they saw as Arab provocation. It had been preceded by two such raids: one on Qibya in October 1953, in which seventy-five people perished and the village was destroyed; the second at Nahhalin on March 29, 1954, in which 14 people died and the village was similarly smashed. It would be followed by many more and in each case Israel would be censured by international opinion. But the Gaza raid was the first against revolutionary Egypt and as the leader of a coup which accused the previous regime of having weakened the Army, Nasser was obliged, as a condition of political survival, to obtain the means of defense. Immediately after the raid he hinted that if he could not get arms from Egypt's traditional suppliers in the West, he would turn East. The threat was perhaps regarded as empty blackmail.

In April Nasser still hoped that the West might give him the arms demanded by his Army. The same month his wife packed his bags for what seemed an interlude of lotus-eating in Indonesia, the chain of islands which marked the last penetration of Islam towards the East. Bandung was welcoming the first gathering of Afro-Asian leaders. The voyage proved one

[5] Don Peretz, *Israel and the Palestine Arabs* (Washington: Middle East Institute, 1958), p. 152.

[6] Tozer; op. cit.

of double discovery. The Arabs, not only the Egyptians, took pride in a youthful spokesman who moved at ease among statesmen as distinguished or famous as India's Nehru and China's Chou En-lai. Nasser's somnambulistic instincts discovered a new circle of strength in what might be called "the silenced majority," men of brown, black or yellow skins with a shared experience of Western domination. Their strongest common sentiment was a wish to escape from the rivalry of the Powers.

The recognition of the passion behind "non-alignment" came at a critical moment in the Middle East's relationship with the West. Turkey, with its traditional fears of Russian expansion, had allied itself with America, and derived some benefit from the alliance. In the rest of the Middle East the situation was different. Israel was increasingly dependent on American diplomatic and financial support, but was not a formal member of any Western alliance; a France involved with Arab Nationalism in Algeria looked with sympathy on a state irrevocably committed to an anti-Arab stance. The rest of the Middle East, in the last bitter chapters of the saga that had started with the Arab Revolt, had either just escaped from British influence or were still trying to escape. Interest in Soviet Russia was declining among Israelis and minimal among Arabs.

But the United States of the first Eisenhower administration had in John Foster Dulles a Secretary of State as obsessed with Communism as Elizabeth Tudor with the Jesuits. The break-up of the traditional empires might give the Soviet Union an opening to the south. Dulles and his British counterparts were anxious to recorral the Arabs in a secure network of alliances and bases.

The Nasser of 1954–55 had less inherent objection to American friendship than many Arabs. He had enjoyed American diplomatic support and some financial aid. As late as 1955 he was strongly anti-Communist, and for rather American reasons, as is proved by the preface he wrote to an anti-Communist booklet published that year under the title *The Reality of Communism*.[7] His preface attacked Marxism from a liberal standpoint as the negation of freedom, the individual and religion. He also distrusted the Egyptian Communists, regarding them as more loyal to the interests of the Soviet Union than those of their native land.

If the West had imposed a Palestine settlement which brought a measure of justice to the refugees . . . if the West had provided arms sufficient for Egyptian defense . . . if Western statesmen had acted with more tact . . . Nasser might have blundered into a Western alliance and forfeited his popularity at the price of material gains. What came to be known as the Baghdad Pact might have been the Cairo Pact instead. But Western policy in the Middle East was as sibylline as the Balfour Declaration and largely framed in the same capital. But while the British of 1917 had been weary

[7] Peter Mansfield, *Nasser* (London: Methuen, 1969), p. 98.

world-rulers, the British of 1954 were weary and irritable world-resigners. Their policy was incoherent. On the one hand they stressed a Soviet danger which required the countries to the south of the Caucasus to co-operate in strengthening their military power; on the other, they met Arab requests for arms with the argument that the Arab armies combined must not out-weigh the strength of an Israel with a population then numbering around one million. Illogic was coupled with psychological crassness. Nuri Said, one of the survivors from the Arab Revolt, had been since the 1920s the abiding strong man of Iraq. He was perhaps the only statesman ever pro-duced by that factious new state to know how to rule it. But he did not know how to win the trust of the younger generation. Nuri, like the feline and vengeful Prince-Regent Abdul Ilah, was a committed ally of the British. In 1954 Nuri was allowed to jump the gun and become the first Arab sponsor of the projected anti-Communist pact. A treaty was signed in Baghdad between Nuri's Iraq and the Turkey of Adnan Menderes round which Britain, Persia, Pakistan and the U.S.A. would cluster. In giving Nuri this prestige—as insubstantial as the plywood crown on the Royal Bilat—the British were hastening the destruction of what they had labored to create since the days of Gertrude Bell. For this assertion of Hashemite leadership was too dangerous for Egypt to ignore. Egypt was the largest and most de-veloped Arab state; her dominant position was recognized in the constitu-tion of the Arab League (a regional association originally suggested by Britain's Foreign Secretary Anthony Eden), which stipulated that its secretary-general should be an Egyptian and its headquarters in Cairo. If the challenge had come from minuscule Lebanon, it would have been less irksome, since Lebanon would not rival Egypt except in education. But Iraq possessed enormous potential wealth; in the Middle Ages Baghdad, not Cairo, had been the chief Arab city. If its oil and sulphur were de-veloped, if its vast acres of salt-encrusted land were restored to even medieval fertility, modern Iraq would in time be richer and stronger than Egypt. Nasser's government had reacted to the challenge to its *amour-propre* by damning the Baghdad Pact. Bandung and its aftermath showed how popular this position was with Iraqis as much as with other Arabs.

Nasser had returned from Indonesia to a Cairo where a new Soviet diplomat, Daniel Solod, was smiling in a new un-Stalinist interpretation of Soviet policy. Solod argued that, despite their different social systems, the Arabs and the Russians shared certain objectives. Russia feared the ex-pansion of a Western defense system to her south; the Arabs, who had just got rid of Western rulers, did not want their return under a new guise. In September Nasser again reacted—this time to renewed Western refusal to supply his arms. An agreement was announced whereby Russia, acting through Czechoslovakia, would supply Egypt with an amplitude of modern arms. Professional gratification among the military caste was echoed emo-tionally by the Arab public. They saw this, not as Communist penetration

of their area, but as an act of defiance. For the first time in more than a
century there was a focus of power outside the Middle East to which defiant
Arabs could appeal.

The lesson was construed with panicky haste in the West. The spiral
mounted. The more Nasser was denounced, the more popular he became.
In December 1955 the British paid an unconscious tribute to his growing
prestige by sending the chief of their Imperial General Staff to Amman,
the second capital in the area which they regarded as safely theirs. By this
time Abdullah was dead, believed by his assassin to have entered into secret
negotiations with the Israelis; Abdullah's heir, Tallal, had been certified
insane by competent physicians. On the junior Hashemite throne sat a
volatile but courageous youth named after his great-grandfather, the Sherif
Hussein who had launched the Arab Revolt. Everything in King Hussein's
upbringing, including education at Harrow and Sandhurst, had conditioned
him to rely on Britain. But street-swirling demonstrations powered by the
Palestinians who comprised two thirds of his subjects decided him and his
advisers that it would be imprudent for Jordan to join the pact whose
nominal head was his young cousin, Feisal II of Iraq. In March 1956 he
took a more dramatic step in the Nationalist direction. On his own initiative
he suddenly dismissed the Englishman who commanded his Arab Legion.
For Glubb Pasha this sudden, unexplained dismissal was a bitter, Falstaffian
tragedy. He had been a soldier with the Arabs for thirty-six years; for sixteen years he had commanded the Arab Legion, making it into a disciplined force with a gallant esprit de corps. In his own terms Glubb was
devotedly pro-Arab; they were terms which saw no contradiction between
what was good for Britain and what was good for the Arabs; he idealized
his country of origin no less than the country of his adoption. Glubb's account[8] of how he returned earlier than usual from his office to his wife's
smiles, then sorrow, as she learnt of his dismissal, is an epitaph on a
thousand relationships between Arabs and English which perished in a
context too large for individuals to alter, or in some cases to understand.

" 'My dear,' I said, 'the King has dismissed me. We leave Jordan at
seven o'clock tomorrow morning—and we shall never come back.'

"She looked at me for a moment with wide eyes. She turned away from
me and looked out of the window. On the dusty hill opposite to us, on
the other side of the valley, I could see the little cemetery where our second
son was buried. It was nine years now since I had stood there, with only
five Arab companions and had lowered that tiny body into the soil of
Jordan. I remembered how I had thought that perhaps I should be buried
there too, amongst the simple folk of Jordan whom I loved.

[8] Glubb Pasha (Lieutenant-General Sir John Bagot Glubb, K.C.B., etc.), op. cit.,
p. 424. Note that Glubb says, "The King was the originator of the order . . . My dismissal was perfectly legal. I was ordered to leave by the King and the Cabinet in office.
I was a servant of the Jordan, not of the British, government." p. 427.

"My wife turned and looked at me.

" 'We'll have some tea now,' she said . . ."

Hussein's motives in getting rid of his faithful servant were patriotic: it was not the first time that patriotism included opportunism and lack of heart.

But Britain's conservative Foreign Secretary, Selwyn Lloyd, then on a visit to Cairo, took the news as a spiteful display by Nasser of his potency for mischief. Britain decided to use economics to do what gunboats had done in the past. Two economic broadsides, one negative, the other positive, were mounted. First, Britain cut down her purchases of Egyptian cotton. Second, she mooted withdrawal of Anglo-American support for Nasser's largest internal project, the High Dam at Aswan.

Egypt meanwhile increased her sales of cotton to the Eastern bloc and in May 1956 announced her recognition of Communist China.

The High Dam broadside was directed towards a project as basic to Egyptian pride as cotton to her former economic structure. Some kind of large-scale planning was required to improve on Britain's own efforts on the Nile half a century before. Much water was still wasted; Egypt south of Assiout still practiced basin irrigation, whereby the Nile's waters were spilled out over the fields once a year only; the vast power of Africa's largest river had not yet been utilized to generate electricity. Some engineers advocated a stepladder of smaller dams mounting the Nile from Cairo to Aswan; others had advocated one enormous structure in the granite hills south of the existing British dam near Aswan. The second project—which required the dumping into the Nile of seventeen times more rock than had made the Great Pyramid—appealed for its very gigantism to the men of the revolution. It is probable that neither Britain nor the United States had seriously intended to help with its construction, since the vast expense would hardly appeal to a public opinion formed by a generally pro-Israeli and anti-Egyptian press. In any event, Mr. Dulles had the icy pleasure, in July 1956, of informing the Egyptian ambassador in Washington that, in view of Egypt's economic instability, the offer to help build the High Dam at Aswan was withdrawn. Britain, who had probably put Dulles up to the move, announced her withdrawal at the same time. The British were confident that the Soviet Union would look on the financing of the Dam with as jaundiced eyes as her own: after all, the Communist Party was proscribed in Egypt and many of its members were in jail. Nasser had been put in the position of a man who asks his bank manager for a loan and is refused, not in the manager's office, but in front of his friends and enemies alike. It was hoped that in this situation Nasser would either break or bend.

About one thing Britain was right. The days were gone when ultimatums or rebuffs could be kept to quiet, overfurnished rooms where men in tarbooshes clicked their prayer beads in gloomy but secret despair. The advent of the cheap transistor radio made the Arabic-speaking millions a lively audience. They followed each move in the political game with the informed attention Americans gave to baseball or Englishmen to soccer. They had noted the insult to Nasser for what it was intended to be: an attempt to reduce him to size.

In a tense, world-final atmosphere Nasser came for the second time to Muhammad Ali's square by the Alexandrine sea. It was July 26, the fourth anniversary of Farouk's abdication. The meeting was again nocturnal, again against the backcloth of the pillared Bourse. But the interaction between Nasser and his audience was now as crackling as a summer storm. He was no longer "one among many": he was the one figure on whom the Middle East was focused. Even Nuri Said, in London on a state visit with King Feisal, cocked one ear to the Mediterranean square during a London dinner.

Nasser's earlier speeches had bored his listeners. Now he confided to them in the caressing, spoken Arabic of the coffeeshop or home, as different from classical as the wisecracks of a Brooklyn cabdriver from the teutonic sentences of a Harvard sociologist. His speech seemed impromptu, a re-hearsal of what had gone before, one small point in common with the Hitler whom he otherwise resembled only in British cartoons. But it was not unprepared. It contained a password. At several places in Egypt men whom he could trust held sealed envelopes. As he mentioned "De Lesseps" —the man under whom 120,000 Egyptians had died to build the Canal, the man who had promised Orabi that not one English soldier should set foot by "his" Canal—the envelopes were ripped open. They contained de-tailed instructions on taking over the administrative offices and property of the Suez Canal Company. By the time Nasser announced to rising cheers that the nationalized Canal would pay for the High Dam, the act was ac-complished. Far away in London a pale Nuri Said, handed the news agency telex, turned to Sir Anthony Eden, his host. "You must strike hard, and strike soon!"

Chapter 5

FIVE months after Nasser's challenge the last British invaders had pulled out of Port Said and the northern reaches of the Canal. Sir Anthony Eden had listened to half of Nuri Said's advice. He had struck, but not soon. Nor had he struck alone as Nuri intended. A French force sailed back to Cyprus with the British, while some weeks later, under heavy pressure from the United States, Israel evacuated Gaza and the parts of Sinai which she, too, had seized. A United Nations Emergency Force moved in behind the departing invaders. Since Israel refused to have these soldiers stationed on her side of the 1949 armistice lines, they were the guests of Egypt alone, staying on her soil only so long as she allowed them.

"Thus," a British correspondent in the Middle East has argued, "it happened that Egypt lost the battle and won the war."[1] To an Arab world in *delirium clamans*—Cairo radio produced an almost Elizabethan spate of new songs—even the loss of a battle seemed in doubt. Schools from sophisticated Beirut to mud-walled Omdurman were blazoned with ikons of heroic Egyptian soldiers picking off descending parachutists by the hundred; in a popular poster an Egyptian army boot crushed a tiny hook-nosed figure with a Star of David. December 23 was set aside in the official Egyptian calendar of holidays as *Yom al-Nasr,* The Day of Victory. When Nasser came to Port Said on its first anniversary, Amer, now a field marshal, had to use his baton to beat off the enthusiastic crowd which mobbed the Victor's car.

But in the Temple of Janus all is irony. Nothing is as it seems, though myths, like mosaics or mummies, last long in a dry, preserving air.

There were three parties to the "Suez incident" of 1956. It is important to assess the aims of each and then the extent to which these aims were achieved, or missed.

The first party was what the Arabs, in indignant shorthand, called *ista'mar,* or imperialism. Britain and France, the possessors of the two largest Victorian empires, were rapidly becoming ex-colonial powers. Having, since 1945, granted independence to a horde of peoples in Africa and Asia, Britain retained as Middle Eastern colonies only Cyprus and Aden; a resistance movement was already at work among the Greek majority on Cyprus; Aden, too, would have one in good time. Britain retained as loose-bolted fiefs the two Hashemite monarchies of Iraq and Jordan; she still enjoyed a paramount position in the Sheikhdom of Kuwait and a chain of statelets on the western shores of the Persian Gulf. France had taken a theoretical lead in freeing colonies ever since General de Gaulle's Brazzaville declaration in 1943. Her two Middle Eastern tributaries, Lebanon and Syria, she had lost thanks to British pressure in 1945; this had gained Britain a short-lived popularity in Beirut and Damascus at the cost of a long-smoldering resentment in Paris. But further west, in Algeria, the France of 1956 was engaged in a colonial war whose fury would not be matched until American involvement, a decade later, in the former French possession of Vietnam. A French army of half a million, backed by around a million settlers of French allegiance, was fighting nine million Algerian

---

[1] Mansfield, op. cit., p. 107.

fellahin. Egypt gave the Algerian rebels much more moral than material support; Algeria belonged to all three of the circles which Nasser had defined as surrounding Egypt, since she was Arabic-speaking,[2] African and Islamic all at once. Paris took the same angry comfort from the myth that Nasser was responsible for Algerian dissension as London from the myth that Nasser had dismissed Glubb Pasha.

The Suez Canal was an emotive symbol to both countries, though hardly of alliance. The French had largely paid for it and wholly planned it, while Frenchmen (and women) held a majority of the privately owned shares in the Suez Canal Company. The manner in which Disraeli had won the Canal for Britain was for the French a rankling irritation; to Britain it had proved a wondrous speculation which had paid for itself again and again. More important than its profitability had been its utility as a connecting link between the British Isles and the empire East of Suez. Although its importance had diminished with the loss of empire, the Canal had been as sensitive an attack point for two generations of Englishmen as a lion's neck vein.

But the serious minds who planned imperial strategy recognized that the Canal was a symbol. What was involved was Egypt's strategic relationship to great bodies of water—the Mediterranean as an extension of the Atlantic and the Red Sea as an extension of the Indian Ocean—and a surrounding subterranean sea of oil.

The decision to strike was made soon after the nationalization of the Canal; but the strike itself was slowed down by the smoke screen of verbiage under which it was mounted and which had its own dismomentum. The aim of the Suez invasion was clear. It would be an attempt to re-establish Anglo-French hegemony, not merely to seize one particular ditch. The operation would be justified by the extent to which it fortified the Middle Eastern positions of Britain and France. For Britain, this meant the tightening of the loose bolts in her system of indirect control over Iraq and Jordan, and possibly the extension of such a system to a quiescent Egypt. Ideally, the refurbishment of British power would silence Archbishop Makarios in Cyprus and scotch any nascent trouble in southern Arabia. France would be rewarded if Nasser's defeat punctured the Algerian movement for independence.

But in a sense less mythical than the simplifications of Egyptian propaganda, Britain and France represented a force larger than themselves. The British Prime Minister showed awareness of this in his eagerness to recruit support from other "Canal users," and his later claims that large caches of Soviet blankets in Sinai revealed plans for a Communist takeover. The force was, in a sense, "the West"; in a sense, the white races; in a sense, the developed as opposed to the developing countries; in a sense, the capitalist

[2] To a large extent; other dialects and languages were also spoken.

system. Other Western countries had material and strategic interests in the Middle East. An American monopoly produced and sold the oil in Saudi Arabia while the Dutch had a substantial interest in the Iraq Petroleum Company. Strategically, the Arab world was the southern flank of the North Atlantic alliance.

The Anglo-French venture had therefore to justify itself as a prudent way of securing, not only the immediate interests of Britain and France, but the much more complex interests of Western Europe and North America.

The second party to the invasion was Israel. Ben-Gurion, as it would be suspected at the time and established years later, flew secretly to France to discuss a tripartite attack in which Israel's role would be that of cat's paw. An Israeli invasion of Egyptian Sinai would give Britain and France, two of the five permament members of the Security Council, the excuse to intervene, ostensibly to prevent damage to an international waterway, in reality to reimpose their control on the Middle East.

Israel's motives for associating itself with Britain and France involved no particular loyalty to the Herzlian formula of providing an outpost for Europe. They sprang from a mood of anguishing bafflement following the achievement of independence. Despite grandiose success in developing confiscated land and populating it with Jews from abroad, the state which was planned to destroy the ghetto had become a larger ghetto more implacably enclosed. Israelis shared a national mood of claustrophobia. They had no land communications in any direction and were particularly dependent on the sea lanes to the outside world. Those through the Mediterranean were not endangered; but those to the east were blocked. The small Arab village of Um Rashrash at the head of the Gulf of Aqaba had been seized two weeks after the armistice agreement of 1949 and renamed "Elath." But Elath was cut off from the high seas, since the only entrance to the Aqaba Gulf lay through Egyptian territorial waters at the narrows of Tiran, and Egypt, under the republic as under the monarchy, had kept these closed. The Egyptians had also barred the Suez Canal to Israeli ships and cargoes. (The British had similarly closed it to the Germans in two world wars.) To UN demands that she should open the Canal to Israeli shipping, Egypt had in effect replied: not unless and until Israel had complied with the UN resolutions relating to the partition plan and the return of the refugees. Israel had adopted her policy of reprisals in part to clobber the refugees: but in part to break out of this ghetto isolation. The policy had not prevented the infiltration of desperate Palestinians or soothed the enmity of Israel's Arab neighbors.

On November 29, 1956, Israeli armor surged into Sinai. Tel Aviv gave two explanations for this major violation of the UN Charter.[3] One represented the invasion of Sinai as simply a retaliatory raid on an increased

[3] For text of communiqué see *U.S. Policy in the Middle East Documents* (U. S. Dept. of State, 1957), pp. 135–36.

scale; another represented it as a preventive war intended to destroy Egypt's new Russian weapons before their use was mastered. Since the UN Charter sanctioned neither retaliatory raids nor pre-emptive strikes, the Israeli explanations convinced few members of the United Nations. They failed to convince the United States, which a fortnight earlier had joined the rest of the Security Council in condemning a raid on Sammu in Jordan which had caused around a hundred and fifty casualties and destroyed over a hundred buildings.

Israel's Arab policies fanned out from a central consensus contested by no one: the need to ensure the survival of the Jewish community in Palestine. The heirs of Gordon and Magnes argued that the only final basis for Israeli survival would be acceptance of the Jewish state by its Arab neighbors. Domestic laws which reduced Israeli Arabs to second-class citizens or foreign adventures which increased Arab hatred would be counterproductive, as well as immoral. The other extreme, a spectrum which included Ben-Gurion and Menachem Begin, wanted to increase the population of the Jewish state and expand its frontiers. In announcing the invasion Ben-Gurion claimed that "the army did not make an effort to occupy enemy territory in Egypt proper and limited its operations to *free* the area from northern Sinai to the tip of the Red Sea." The Israeli Prime Minister described the Egyptian island of Tiran "as the island of Yotvat, south of the Gulf of Elath, which was *liberated* by the Israeli army."[4] There is no reason to believe that Ben-Gurion used the italicized verbs in the ironic World War II sense as a synonym for stealing.

Thus, from opposed points of view—the pacific on the one hand, the expansionist on the other—the operation would be a success for Israel either if it won Arab acceptance or established something approaching an Israeli empire, based on secure force.

The Egyptian aims in 1956 were, in the narrowest sense, to retain control of the Canal and, in the broadest, to defeat any attempt by "imperialism" to restore its domination. The first aim would be achieved if British and French were thwarted in their attempts to seize back the waterway; the second, more difficult aim would only be achieved if Israel ceased to exist as "a wall of defense for Europe in Asia, an outpost of civilization against barbarism." As in the case of Israel, extremes in Egypt fanned out from an irreducible consensus, in this case, that Israel must expand no further. One extreme advocated, with more damage to Arab reputation than Israeli security, that the Jews be driven into the sea; another hoped, in a silence that did little credit to Arab freedom of speech, for a peace to be negotiated with future Jewish leaders with less aggressive policies than those of Ben-Gurion or Begin.

[4] New York *Times,* November 8, 1956.

Having defined the objectives of the various parties, we can assess the results of what was arguably the gravest international crisis since the end of the Second World War.

Britain and France were doomed by their allies from the start. Other Western countries saw early that if they condoned a revival of gunboat politics, they would alienate the growing numbers of ex-colonial states. The United States (in a sense the first country to have been decolonized) was angered by two circumstances in particular. The operation had been timed to coincide with U.S. presidential elections, in which the Jewish vote would play no inconsiderable part; and though Eisenhower was returned with an increased majority, despite his disapproval of the Israeli action, his nostrils had scented the whiff of blackmail. The U.S. Government was also aggrieved at having been kept in the dark by states which it trusted as allies, or in the case of Israel, as a friend. Liberal public opinion was shocked by the deed of force, and still more by the changing but obvious lies with which it was masked. Collusion between Britain and France on the one hand, and Israel on the other, was suspected ten years before it was proved. Dag Hammarskjold, the UN Secretary-General, spoke for such liberal opinion. Not content with Buddhist-style affirmations of virtue, he threatened to resign from his post if the Security Council did not compel the three aggressors to withdraw.

The loss of the battle may have been as stimulating to Britain and France as certain illnesses to certain patients. The long, irritating process of decolonization may have needed some trauma wherein each power could confront the changed realities and act upon them. King Lear's problem, it has been said, was not renunciation of power, but incomplete renunciation. After 1956 Britain and France found it easier to renounce their colonial empires. France's concession of total Algerian freedom would lead to far better relations with Algeria and the other Arab states than might have been predicted.

The Western interests inside, behind and around Britain and France had been resolved that one blunder should not mean the loss of the war. How to protect their interests in the Middle East became a new obsession, attended with new blunders.

The events of 1956 were construed in different ways by the two wings of Israeli opinion.

The heirs of Gordon and Magnes had had the anguish of seeing Jews lauded by the fascist-minded while condemned by nearly everyone else as aggressors. Far from having gained acceptance from their Arab neighbors, Israelis had involved themselves as accomplices in an attempt to revive the colonial past. One terrible incident far from the battlefront showed that what Magnes had dreaded had happened. Israel had become so like other nations that it had produced its own pogrom: "This pogrom," Hal Draper writes,[5] "was directed against an Arab village in Israel named Kfar Kassem. On the day that Israel attacked Egypt in 1956, the Israeli government declared a new curfew for its Arab citizens (who, remember, were under military control anyway, even without a war). The new decree advanced the curfew from 11 p.m. to 5 p.m. Israeli officers showed up in Kfar Kassem, as well as other places, to make known the change on that day. They were told that the men had already gone out to the fields; the officers' reply was, roughly speaking, 'Don't bother us with details.' In the evening, when the men of the village returned from working in the fields after the new curfew hour, they were shot down in cold blood by the Israeli soldiers —for violating a curfew that had never been told them. The government admitted that 46 men were thus killed; the number wounded was not made public. The government admission applied only to Kfar Kassem but it was reliably reported that the same thing happened that day at other Arab villages. Even this much was admitted by the government only after a week had passed and the reports could no longer be hushed up. All of Israel was appalled. Some underlings were made the scapegoats."

The activists had not managed to retain Gaza, let alone Sinai. In return for much effort and much unpopularity they had made one small gain. American pressure, which had forced the Israelis to withdraw, had in return ensured that a UN force should guard Sharm al-Shaikh at the top of Sinai and thus spike the guns which had closed the Aqaba Gulf. Elath could now be used for the export of goods to Africa and the Far East and the import of oil from Persia.

In the long term, activist Israel wrung a larger compensation for the reverse: the Zionist leaders read the results with a clarity unfogged by sentiment. Invoking no pleasing myths, they recognized the loss of a campaign in a prolonged war. It had been lost because they had been linked with overt allies less determined than themselves. The withdrawal of Britain and France had made it impossible for Israel not to follow suit. Israel had needed allies in her attack on Egypt because of the need to protect Tel Aviv and Haifa from aerial attacks; this protection had been provided by French airplanes. The lesson was stark. In the next campaign Israel must allow no overt allies to share the credit of victory or to compel retreat. To dispense with such overt allies, Israel would have to build, at great cost and without advertisement, an overpowering air force. Covert allies would of course be welcome.

Their mythopoeic genius prevented the Egyptians from analyzing the events of 1956 as coldly as Europeans or Israelis educated in European modes.

[5] Walter Laqueur reprints this essay from *New Politics,* Winter 1967, in his *The Israel-Arab Reader* (London: Weidenfeld and Nicolson, 1969). See p. 299. The essay was entitled *The Origins of the Middle East Crisis* and arose from a talk given at Berkeley shortly after the Arab-Israeli war of 1967.

Egypt had won no military battle. In strictly military terms this first Sinai campaign, for in due course it would be followed by a second, was a fiasco for the Egyptian Army. After four years of military rule, Amer's officers had fought with less distinction than Farouk's. Many had exchanged their uniforms for *gallabyas* and hid up in Port Said apartments while at the street corners of the "hero city" teenage snipers put up the only real resistance. Nor had Egypt won the war. This would be won only when a peace favorable to Arab interests had been signed.

What Egypt had won was a battle of will power and diplomacy. The people of Egypt and Nasser himself had at no moment contemplated surrender, and in the context of Egyptian history this was remarkable. Nasser had conducted his campaign in the UN as faultlessly as his campaign against Naguib. As a result, Egypt was still in the field.

But a victory of the spirit was presented to public opinion as a victory due to arms. One incident may stand for many. A Syrian volunteer—his name, Jules Jamal, showed him to be a Christian—was acclaimed for having sunk, single-handed, at the cost of his life, the French battleship *Jean Bart*. The warship sailed serene and unscathed through the eastern Mediterranean in the weeks and months to come, but no more serenely than the unchallenged myth of "Gool Gamal," as the Egyptians pronounced the hero's name.

The myth aborted any popular demand, such as any other tax-paying country would have raised, that the Army be reofficered, reorganized and retrained. Instead, the power of the officer corps, and its social prestige, grew vastly between December 1956 and the occasion, ten and a half years later, when it would be given its next chance to shine.

The Victory he was to celebrate each December till 1966 had an insidious effect on Nasser. While paying lip service to the myth, he conceded in private conversations the impossibility of an Arab army defeating Israel in the foreseeable future and his own miscalculations in predicting that Eden would not attack Egypt. But such minor admissions were drowned in a major satisfaction at his diplomatic miracle. Diplomacy, he felt, could solve any future problem too. Diplomacy had been the peculiar skill of Byzantium, long dead but ghost-present in the Middle East. Against force of arms, the Byzantine rulers used intrigue, sometimes poison, always the gentle art of playing one foe against another. Byzantium had, of course, finally succumbed; but it had taken many centuries finally to become *finis*. Nasser knew, but chose not to know, that he had been saved by a concatenation of circumstances which might not recur: the old-fashioned principles of men like Hugh Gaitskell, leader of the British opposition, President Eisenhower and John Foster Dulles; the incisive virtue of Dag Hammarskjold; a cold war phase in which America and the Soviet Union competed for the favors of smaller states; above all, a liberal opinion which had not become inured to the use of aerial attack in everyday relations between societies not officially at war. He overlooked these lessons, or misread them. His strengthened confidence in his own powers to do two things at once, in other words, to bluff, would contrive his great defeat in a second campaign in ten years' time. The extraordinary quality of the man would then be shown, not in his hybristic march to defeat, but in his emergence from it.

But as in Greek tragedy, where the cannibal dinner produces its cosmic indigestion after half a generation, these effects of mythopoeia were to be delayed. The immediate aftermath of Victory exalted Nasser Caliph-high in other regions of the Arabian Nights.

The first and most dramatic was Syria, the turntable of the Arab East, a land of flat red deserts, upland steppe and emerald oases sparsely divided between individualistic, talkative townsmen and dour fellahin. The Syrians had rejected the provincial nationalism of Antun Saada; instead they saw themselves as the aggressive vanguard of a wider Arab Nationalism reborn through struggle. Syrians were febrile and unstable in their convictions. In the first days of 1958 their leaders felt threatened by a Communist current and flew *en bloc* to Cairo—this newly radiant focus—to offer their collective submission to Nasser and to ask to be gathered into his charismatic state. Nasser was trapped. His own mythology as well as a deep-seated yearning for the grandiose made it impossible for him to refuse or impose conditions. The result was the fusion of Egypt and Syria in one "United Arab Republic" after a vote more overwhelming than that which had elected Feisal as King of Iraq. The two regions of this first and only Afro-Asian state were separated by Israel and the sea. In an attempt to overcome these obstacles by denying their existence, in a further attempt to blend two very different peoples, local or regional associations were condemned; it became an offense for a journalist to write of "Egypt" or "Syria." This supposedly indissoluble union was between unequal partners. Syria had had no social revolution whatsoever and was ruled by a middle-class elite based on trade, small industry and highly successful but entrepreneurial farming. The differences between the Syrian and the Egyptian fellah were no greater than the effects of two contrasted climates, western Asia being ruder and harsher than Egyptian Africa. A union between two peasantries might have been feasible. But the bourgeoisie of Damascus and Aleppo was anarchic, outspoken, libertarian; they regarded the right to change money in Beirut in much the same light as Americans regarded the right to own firearms. The Syrian currency was stronger than the Egyptian. Egypt by contrast had replaced its cosmopolitan elite (the Greeks and Italians who had left after 1952 had resemblances to the Syrian bourgeoisie) with a class of educated but unindependent functionaries overawed by the Army. In the euphoric spring of 1958 Nasserism could seem a self-generating fountain of hope. "I am Syrian and you are Egyptian," clamored a popular Cairo ditty. Gaudy dreams of union and glory infected the suppressed majority of Muslim Lebanese, but alarmed that small republic's Christian elite. The Maronites had traditionally sought a strong Christian power to back them against the surrounding Islamic sea. In 1958 the United States seemed willing to follow France and Britain in this role. Although Mr. Dulles had done as much as anyone to rescue Nasser, he had deplored the opening to Russian influence given by the Suez campaign; in order to protect any traditionalist regimes which felt threatened by the new leftist wave he had formulated the "Eisenhower Doctrine." Camille Chamoun, now in his seventh and last year as President of Lebanon, had made two disastrous decisions: to have the constitution altered to allow him to run for a second term (and this necessitated rigged elections) and to accept the doctrine. The Muslims accused Chamoun of breaking the country's "National Pact"—an unwritten agreement whereby the two major communities agreed not to drag the other too far in its own direction: thus the pro-Western Christians, richer if less numerous than the Muslims, would not involve Lebanon in alliances with Europe or America, while the Muslims would recognize Christian fears of being engulfed if the country joined an Arab union.

Civil war fizzled malevolently throughout the summer, with the Lebanese Army (under General Chehab, the next President) remaining neutral. Chamoun's party had the support not only of the United States but of conservatives throughout the Middle East; the Nasserist opposition was not entirely Muslim: one notable opponent of Chamoun was the Maronite patriarch, the country's senior churchman.

The war was watched attentively by outside Arab states. Egypt and Syria provided arms and applause to the rebels; Saudi Arabia and Iraq assisted Chamoun.

Nuri Said had been alarmed by the increase of Nasser's prestige which had followed the rapturous union between Egypt and Syria. He had concluded his own federation with Jordan, to no acclaim. Nuri was perhaps too old (he had been Prime Minister thirteen times) to see how Eden's attack on Egypt with Israel as ally had doomed the Iraqi monarchy. It was now difficult for any Arab statesman to uphold the Gertrude Bell thesis that what was good for Britain was good for the Arabs. Since 1956 only police oppression had silenced Iraqi opposition. In the summer of 1958 Nuri recognized that if Lebanon was won for Nasser, Iraq would be isolated. The old man made two tentative plans for counterattack. Having given Chamoun moral and monetary support in May and June, he decided in July to transfer a trusted army division to Jordan for possible use against Syria. At the same time he planned to leave with the young king for Ankara: a routine meeting of the Baghdad Pact would enable him to discuss how to meet the threat of Nasserism. Adnan Menderes, the Turkish Prime Minister, shared Nuri's fear of Communism to the full.

But early on the morning of July 14, as the King was shaving, the soldiers

of Abdul Salaam Arif and Abdul Karim Kassem defied orders to by-pass
the capital on their way to Jordan and moved into Baghdad. As usual, the
radio station was the first target and from it Arif broadcast a bloodthirsty
call to revolution. His army had meanwhile invested the modest palace
where the King still lived pending the completion of the new one by the
Tigris. The Army had secretly hoarded ammunition from maneuvers. They
now used it to compel the royal bodyguard to surrender. As the royal party
filed out into the courtyard, men, women and servants were shot down
without warning. Only the young wife of Abdul Ilah, the former Regent,
escaped in the melee; seeing that she was still alive, a kindly officer whispered to her not to move. The King's body was buried later that day in a
secret place. Abdul Ilah's corpse was dragged through the streets; Nuri
lived a further day but was shot dead when his man's shoes were seen peep-
ing beneath a woman's abba; he was dug up from his hasty grave and
municipal buses were run over his cadaver until, in the words of a horror-
struck eyewitness, it resembled *bastourma,* an Iraqi sausage meat.

An important street in Baghdad which had been named after Feisal was
now renamed after the apparent victor: Gamal Abdel Nasser. Though
U.S. marines landed on the beaches south of Beirut, Chamoun was replaced by a President whose major aim was good relations with the United
Arab Republic.

Chapter 6

EGYPT's myth factories were more potent than its regiments. Along
with television studios diffusing more programs than Britain, radio antennae inciting Africa in a dozen languages, newspapers cozening whatever
Arab countries allowed them in, presses publishing a new book every six
hours, Cairo's Hollywood on the Nile, Studio Misr, produced on midget
budgets the visual myths of the revolution. One such told the story of a
gardener's son who became an officer, was loved by a feudalist's daughter
and after 1952 had the pleasure of expropriating the feudalist's land. This
colored melodrama had audiences in Westernized Beirut standing on their
chairs to applaud as the officer's hands joined on a Koran to swear the
Liberation Oath. The most ambitious of such sagas, allocated three times
more capital than usual, was *Al-Nasser Salahuddin—The Victorious*

Saladin. The title played on the meaning of Nasser's name; it showed the mythic flower to which Nasser was now the stamen.

Saladin was the warrior who, in a corrupt, unidealistic age united Egypt and Syria by his virtue, and by his courage defeated the Crusaders. Nasser's identification with the greatest hero of medieval Islam, the resemblance of Israel to the Crusader state, had helped to sell the Egyptian revolution to the Syrians, to the Arab party in Lebanon and to those Iraqis who echoed Abdul Salaam Arif's interpretation of the July 14 Revolution.

A myth need not be a lie. It may be an illuminating or inspiriting way of confronting complexities which would otherwise need a mountain of textbooks to be understood. The great Jewish thinker Martin Buber declared that "Each living man is rooted in living myth"; in Buber's approach to the Old Testament, Adam, Noah and Moses were mythical archetypes which had luckily survived the demythologizing handiwork of the later priests.

But myths could also resemble the whitewashed walls that hide slums from state visitors.

The myth of Victory had straightened Egyptian spines; it heartened individuals at work on land reform, education and an industrial renaissance of ambitious scope. But it also helped to conceal certain major defects in Egyptian society. It saved from criticism an Army which, while bad at its job, remained the ruling caste; under the myth's protection this caste grew more arrogant and more greedy for power and its perquisites. More immediately, it masked the inefficiency of an ever expanding bureaucracy and the tyrannical power of the secret service.

The bureaucracy expanded in response to the many new ways in which the state intervened in the lives of ordinary Egyptians, sometimes beneficially. But a policy of guaranteeing employment to the increasing numbers of university graduates was another reason. If such redundant graduates had been put to work on the roads, or located in some enclosed, self-serving silo, writing idle papers on the top floor and burning them on the bottom, things might have been better. Instead, seven employees filled an office where one or two could have done the work; and since every employee needed, to satisfy his proper pride, some responsibility other than flipping through the pages of *al-Ahram* or ordering a coffee, the citizen requiring documentation would run a slow gauntlet of yawning bureaucrats, to be told triumphantly at the penultimate station of his via dolorosa: "you must come back tomorrow—the Happiness of the Bey is in Alexandria." The bureaucrats were underpaid and in revenge combined the titles of the old regime with a parody of lordly manners. Attempts to ginger up this system were periodically heralded with trumpets; small beachheads were made; major enterprises like the Suez Canal were well run; but all too often, a feather pillow punched by a fist, inefficiency would sag back again.

If the bureaucracy was a negative blight, the secret services of the state were a positive cancer. They, too, overemployed. The word *mukhabarat* acquired the sinister tones of Gestapo or Ogpu. One seed for this byzantine hedge was the conspiratorial streak in Nasser's nature; another was the undoubted existence of external enemies. The Israeli secret service was believed to be as formidable as the CIA. Its agents had detonated bombs in the Alexandria branch of the USIS. If the perpetrators had not been caught red-handed (causing secondary detonations inside Israel with what came to be known as "the Lavon Affair"), American relations with Egypt might have become embittered earlier. The reactionaries were also persistent plotters. King Saud of Saudi Arabia was believed to have signed an astronomical check on a Riad bank in favor of a Syrian official pledged to murder Nasser.

Bureaucracy and counterespionage would have inconvenienced the Egyptians only if the Saladin myth had not exported the Egyptian system to Syria. The junior partner in the UAR had a smaller, more intimate bureaucracy, since Damascus interfered less than Cairo in the lives of citizens. The Syrians lacked a tradition of police informers even though they had experienced tyrants; no one was accustomed to looking over his shoulder before inveighing against the government in his local coffeeshop. Like the Iraqis, the Syrians retained the nomadic tradition that the important should be accessible. A barefooted fellah could wander into a minister's bureau and address him by his name.

The Syrian middle class had fallen in love with the myth of Nasser; they fell out of love with a reality which took the form of Egyptian bosses and Egyptian regulations. The one outlet for their feelings was a monolithic successor to the National Liberation Rally, the "National Union." But this substitute for a parliament exercised no check, let alone veto, on government decisions. It was not consulted in the summer of 1961 when a new series of socialist laws were decreed for both provinces of the UAR. Amer, Nasser's viceroy in Damascus, was in his pajamas, allegedly hung over from a night of hashish, when a group of officers, acting for the class most hit by the new laws, seized him and the city to announce secession. Nasser's first reaction was the same as that of Lincoln in America or Gowon in Nigeria: to maintain the union by force. Egyptian soldiers were already over Syria, some of them even jumping with parachutes, when orders reached them to return, or surrender to the Syrians. Nasser declared himself aghast at the prospect of Arab shedding Arab blood. He was probably also influenced by threats to his best friend's life.

Not for the last time Nasser seemed finished, as publicly humiliated as a man divorced for impotence. His rejoicing enemies included not only Kings Hussein of Jordan and Saud of Saudi Arabia but Kassem, now the "Unique Leader" of Iraq. For the Nasserist movement had failed earlier in Iraq than in Syria. The advocates of union with Egypt had pressed too hard on a country where major factions were suspicious of Sunni Arab domination. Kassem was an eccentric, ill-read but captivating man who understood as well as Nuri Said the Iraqi complexities; under his leadership Baghdad had shied away from Cairo's embrace.

But as in the tussle with Naguib, Nasser showed his exceptional talent for turning retreat into counterattack. He read the lessons of the Syrian rebuff severely, inflexibly and in public. He pondered, spoke and acted in equal measure.

Intellectually he recognized that Arab Nationalism was barren if left without social content. When the Syrian merchants had seen a conflict between their interests and Arab unity, they had not hesitated to betray the second. The Syrian branch of the National Union (a hand-picked sampler of the ruling class) had seceded with the secessionists. In Cairo, members of the Gezira Club toasted the Syrians—which warned that what had happened in the northern province might be repeated in the southern. Nasser decided that the only way to preserve his revolution was to break the financial power of its enemies and have it defended by a people conscious of real, as opposed to mythical, gains.

The names which had figured in the yearbook of the Royal Automobile Club now appeared for the last time, in the lists of those whose property was put under sequestration. At the same time, in verbose but sincere discussions with two hundred and fifty members of a Preparatory Committee for Popular Powers, Nasser worked towards a National Charter whose paragraphs would contain both a critique and a program. The committee included university professors, fellahin, cabinet ministers, workers, women. Initially some doubted if the discussion would be free. But as contradictory opinions were expressed in Nasser's presence, skepticism disappeared. One youngish writer, Khaled Muhammad Khaled, defended the right of the "reactionaries" to participate in the new society, arguing that no one should be penalized for acts which were not offenses when they were committed. He quoted a 1952 statement by Nasser that the Army would be purged. "If the army needed to be purged, but not abolished, why should not the parliamentary system be purged, but not abolished?" This was in such flat contradiction to Nasser's known views that some toadies rose to object. The Speaker, Anwar al-Sadat, silenced such objectors and insisted that Khaled should have the right to say exactly what he wanted. Nasser then gave his own view, that the social revolution could only be accomplished by the sections of society in whose interest it was; he claimed that he had himself overruled the censor who had tried to ban one of Khaled's books on the grounds that it was Communist. But the head of the Lawyers' Syndicate would not allow that such interventions sufficed to create a climate of freedom. "Freedom does not exist at the moment. There may, in fact, be no governmental obstacle, but people sense that there is. We must now make them feel free to say whatever they think."

Arab Nationalism was transformed in the course of a year into Arab Socialism. No intellectual paradigm had directed Nasser. In his youth he had been as little interested in economic theories as his hero Mustafa Kamil; as ruler he had consistently put leftists in jail. Two practical reasons helped direct his steps. A form of socialism could help to bridge the abyss between the ruled and the rulers; in the assembly of the new Arab Socialist Union, Nasser's third attempt at a constitutional vehicle for his state, at least 50 per cent of the members were required to be either fellahin or workers. Nasser also believed that socialism could provide the means whereby the unpublicized millions of ordinary Egyptians—fellahin dying prematurely of bilharziasis, townsmen subdividing the once proud tenements of Ismail's uncrowded era—could slowly but surely swell the national product so that the share of each would suffice to sustain dignity and health. In a country with very limited private capital, only the state could amass, through taxation or loans, the capital needed for industrial developments that could turn Egypt's surplus population to advantage. Here, too, would be a way of using manpower more effectively than in government offices.

Once again Nasser had chosen a popular course like a sleepwalker. The new socialist dimension to Nasser's revolution turned his defeat to victory: though once again at a cost.

The victory was signaled by sudden changes in the Arab world. In 1961 Nasser had seemed isolated and vulnerable; within two years he had isolated his enemies. Algeria, independent from France, followed policies closely resembling those of Egypt. The Syrian secessionists were overthrown by socialists from a pan-Arab party known as the Baath; though rivals to Nasser, they shared most of his fundamental assumptions. In Iraq Kassem was murdered and replaced by Arif. But Nasser's far-ranging penetration was shown most dramatically in the furthest, obscurest and poorest Arab country, the backward mountain kingdom of Yemen.

In the distant past this southwestern corner of Arabia had been in the Arab vanguard; a freak rainfall and its proximity to Africa made it rich; it was the fecund nursery for Arab migrations to the north. In the period preceding Islam, Yemen produced statuary influenced by Greece and dams rivaling the engineering achievements of the Romans. By the twentieth century it had dwindled to a mountain slum, a member of the Arab League to make other members blush. Its ruler, the Imam Ahmad, was as vengeful and diseased as Henry VIII of England; his one innovation (for he lacked Henry's Renaissance culture) was a military band; its barefoot minstrels played merry airs as a swordsman beheaded the Imam's enemies before the watching public. In gratitude to a woman dentist from Europe who repaired his fangs, the old tyrant suggested that she might like, as a treat, to watch some of his soldiers being flogged. His heir, Prince Badr, had incurred the Imam's disapproval for his Nasserist ideas. But Badr, who succeeded his father in the late summer of 1962, had no time to put his ideas to the test. Abdullah Sallal, a much imprisoned officer of the guard, mounted an immediate coup and called for Egyptian support.

The call came a year after the Syrian secession. The implied compliment was too welcome to be refused and Nasser decided to risk the spilling of Arab blood by Arab.

A weakness of the Egyptians, turned like sunflowers to the West, was their ignorance of the Arab East. British imperialists with first-class degrees would spend twenty years in the Sudan or Kurdistan compiling anthologies of folklore by hurricane lamp. Neither Nasser nor the Egyptians he sent to help Sallal had a precise idea of the ant hill they were disturbing. Yemen was a clan society as riddled with mutual distrust as seventeenth-century Scotland, as divided religiously as modern Ulster.

A Janus war puttered in the mountain valleys until 1967. It spilt ironies as freely as Arab blood. In this struggle between the old and the new, the British supported the old from their modern base at Aden; they refused to recognize the Republic; with British and Saudi help, as well as a motley collection of mercenaries and eccentrics, the royalists fought back in the hard-to-subdue mountain valleys. Egyptians, on the contrary, were playing the same modernizing, and often resented role that the French had played with them at the time of Napoleon. Despite much suffering and devastation, Egyptian hands dragged Yemen within hailing distance of modern ideas and gadgets.

This was done at double cost to Egypt. The Yemeni war marked the beginning of what Nasser's journalist friend Haikal (now editor of *al-Ahram*) was later[1] to describe as a "silent coup d'état." The Army made Yemen its private fief; it fought and it bombed; it also enriched itself; not only officers, but sergeants and enlisted men took, by Egyptian standards, enormous wages. The cost of the war was as heavy to Egypt as Vietnam to America. No military genius, Field Marshal Amer was a political boss who earned his men's devotion by his attention to their interests. As a closed corporation privately convinced that it would never have to fight a serious war, the Army rewarded pilots or staff officers, trained in the Soviet Union, with comfortable jobs, if they were reliable, or anesthetized them with similar comfortable jobs, if they were not. Nearly every state enterprise was headed by an officer; officers sat thick in embassies abroad. The Army was unchallengeable; it could neither be investigated nor assessed. Even Nasser could not call it to account. Whereas before 1962 corruption had been covert, it was now overt to anyone with eyes to see or ears to hear. At a time when hard currency was in short supply, officers and their wives would arrive in Paris or London with bulging handbags and empty suitcases to jet

[1] *Al-Ahram,* June 21, 1968; tr. *Egyptian Gazette,* June 22, 1968: "a silent coup had disturbed the political leadership's control of the armed forces, causing a kind of secession. . . ." etc.

back to Cairo with the situation reversed. The Army protected itself from criticism by ruthless use of the security services.

Egypt thus approached the middle sixties with its own private version of the Janus face. To the world at large, Nasser seemed, if not a dictator, then a popular ruler whose power was untrammeled by the need for elections. In fact he was paying the price for having come to power through a military coup. He and the Army were as closely linked as Siamese twins. The idealistic profile of Arab Socialism was conjoined at the back of the skull with the cynical mask of a corrupted Bellona. Nasser put up with the Army because if he moved against it he was doomed. The people applauded the Army because they thought it would defend them.

Chapter 7

OTHER Arab rulers were alarmed by the persistent power of Nassar's myth. Cairo's idealistic profile addressed the deepest longings of the Arabized, whether they lived in Iraq or Libya, Sudan or Yemen; the appeal was to what was shared and this outweighed what was particular. Most of those who spoke Arabic, however different their cultural or genetic past, had experienced to greater or less degree the humiliation of foreign occupation. The Saudi Arabians and the Yemenis knew it least, having existed on the fringes of the Ottoman Empire, and then of the British. In Lebanon, the Muslims had resented the French presence more than the Maronites, who had sometimes welcomed it as a protection. But Algerians and Libyans, Tunisians and Syrians, Iraquis and Sudanese had known as much as the Egyptians what it was to be commanded by Europeans. Those Palestinians who had not been evicted from the four fifths of their country which had become Israel were second-class citizens.

The humiliated dream of power, and although the Egyptian Army had done nothing powerful in 1956 and little thereafter, the myth had enough rationalizing gas to float it above mundane considerations. No one could deny that Nasser had retained the Canal in defiance of Britain and France; he was less bogged down in Yemen than the Americans in Vietnam; and behind the Yemeni royalists Britain and other mysterious forces could be blamed.

Almost as attractive as military power were the shiny mills of modern technology. Arabs had suffered acutely from the sense of being picturesque: avid cinema-goers, they had seen themselves stereotyped as gallant sons of the desert or less gallant touts. They now took more pride in a new factory than an old temple.

A third longing—for social justice—was felt strongly by those whose rulers were particularly profligate. The egalitarian aspect of Egyptian society had a strong appeal.

The power of the myth gave conservatives nightmares. To Nasser's machinations they attributed all the upheavals, all the violence, in the area. The spectacle of Crown Prince Abdul Ilah posthumously impaled, of Prime Minister Nuri Said flattened to sausage meat, haunted King Feisal of Saudi Arabia (Nuri's contemporary) and King Hussein of Jordan (Abdul Ilah's kinsman). Radicals, too, had grounds for disquiet. Abdul Salaam Arif, the representative of the myth in Iraq, had contrived for Abdul Karim Kassem a fate hardly pleasanter than that of Nuri. Nasser's enemies and rivals were indignant that he could purvey his myth so successfully. They were more aware than their transistor-cradling peoples of the other profile to the Egyptian Janus. They not unnaturally launched a counter war of words. They attacked Nasser and his regime through secret radio stations, through the newspapers they controlled at home or subsidized in Beirut, and through the rumors that crisscross the Arab world as fast as greetings telegrams in the West.

Three lines of attack had varying degrees of success. Nasser's adoption of socialism and his friendship with the Soviet Union were denounced as a betrayal of Islam. This was a soft punch. Most Arabs wanted arms, from whatever source; most Muslims were tired of ineffective, turbaned leaders. There was a consensus that Islam needed restating in terms of the modern world. Traditional Islam frequently masked hypocrisy. Though the Saudi Government punished the drinking of alcohol severely, more than one Saudi prince kept a bar in his palace. A harder punch was the argument that a free economy brought the individual (and Arabs were individualists) more profit than bureaucratic socialism; King Hussein, in particular, could claim that the economy of Jordan, expanding proportionately even faster than that of Israel, gave the citizens of Jerusalem and Amman a higher standard of expectancy than Nasser's socialism had yet brought Egyptians. The surreptitious wealth of some Egyptian leaders was also stressed. But the punch that hurt Nasser most was the allegation that, for all his incendiary speeches, he was soft on Israel. Further allegations that the Americans had sponsored him in his earlier years precisely because of his "realism" over Palestine were strengthened by some of the more talkative CIA men in the region.[1] As evidence of this supposed

---

[1] Of which no better example than Mr. Miles Copeland, author of *The Game of Nations* (New York: 1970).

two-facedness Nasser's rivals, and in particular Hussein, cited his willingness to allow the United Nations Emergency Force to patrol his frontier with Israel. U Thant's skirts had protected Egypt from the kind of reprisal raids suffered intermittently by Jordan; they also prevented Palestinians from raiding into Israel. Another point for attack was Sharm al-Shaikh. The UN presence at the southern tip of Sinai had, as we have seen, been Israel's one gain from the 1956 war, enabling her to import Persian oil through Egyptian territorial waters and up a gulf bordered by Arab states.

In the winter of 1966–67 Nasser was as much concerned by economic problems as by verbal brickbats. The Egyptian economy had reached the grievous trough which often precedes takeoff in newly industrializing countries. The goods being manufactured were still shoddy, though they would improve; the industrial workers were still virtual apprentices, though they would become skilled workers; the High Dam was consuming vast quantities of cash and concrete, though it would eventually more than repay its cost. At the moment so much had been spent that there was no cash left for vital spare parts. Many factories, such as the automobile plant, had shut down.

In a situation where he must snatch at any gains, Nasser snatched dangerously.

Syria, whose unstable support had already brought him his gravest setback, put him in jeopardy again by proposing a military alliance. Nasser's doctrine of Arab union, as well as recent Israeli raids on Jordan, forced him to welcome an offer which amounted to taxation without representation. A defense agreement signed in November 1966 obliged him to defend Syria if she were seriously threatened but gave him no control over Syrian policy and no use of Syrian airfields.

This alliance was but a mild puff to a flagging sail; in early 1967 stronger winds began to blow. Not on Egypt alone, but the Middle East as a whole. But egocentric like all nationalists, the Egyptians were unaware how closely their predicament was paralleled across the barbed wire in Israel. There unemployment was soaring to unacceptable heights; the country felt trapped in a cul-de-sac. Israelis felt that the time might soon be opportune to seize security (if this could be seized) by force. Both opponents needed a success. Nasser needed a puff to his prestige, and therefore his economic credit; the leaders of Israel, realistic since the days of the British mandate, saw success in more tangible terms.

Volatile Syria posed opportunity to both parties. The disputed border between northern Israel and southwest Syria had provided, in the absence of any UN presence, an area of friction. In early 1967 a series of incidents hinted that worse was to come. Israeli tractors working a demilitarized border zone were strafed by Syrian planes; the Israelis then shot down, with ominous efficiency, six Syrian Migs; the Syrians reported an alarming

Israeli build-up on their frontier. Syrian reports alone would not have created a crisis. But the Russians, according to Nasser, told a parliamentary delegation to Moscow that they considered an Israeli invasion of Syria to be imminent.

Nasser now embarked on the most fatal bluff of his career while Israel prepared its most fatal success.

Although Egypt's population was fifteen times larger than that of Israel, the Egyptian Army was considerably smaller than the citizen army which Israel could mobilize in a day. The Israelis enjoyed a similar superiority to that of the British in 1882 over the Egyptians. In the spring of 1967 a large proportion of the Egyptian Army was still controlling the towns and main roads of Yemen. Nasser and Field Marshal Amer both knew how unprepared their forces were to take on those of Israel. But after pointed Israeli threats in mid-May to retaliate heavily against Syria if Syrian raids continued, Nasser decided on a series of grandiose gestures designed to give support to his ally, to rebut his critics and to distract attention from economic problems. Egypt first asked the UN Secretary-General to withdraw the UN soldiers who patrolled the border with Israel, though not those in Gaza or at Sharm al-Shaikh. The UN Secretary-General, probably on a hint from the U.S., took this as an all-or-nothing request and withdrew all. In bombastic pageantry tanks rumbled through Cairo on their way to Sinai; each issue of the Cairo press carried some new harangue or threat. To an Arab world subdued by the Egyptian myth the public moves, the martial songs, were as exciting as a movie car chase. Behind the scenes, an Egypt denuded of her UN protection was warned by the U.S. and implored by the U.S.S.R. not to strike the first blow. Nasser had never contemplated doing any such thing. He had instead decided, as the next move in the scenario, to send Zakaria Muhiaddin, his most conservative lieutenant and the one best liked by Americans, to New York, there to make, in the interests of world peace, a spectacular accommodation with the UN over navigation through the straits of Tiran; in return, the long ignored problem of the Palestinians—the problem which made it most difficult for any settlement to be reached with Israel—might at last get serious attention; and as a reward for moderation, Egypt would surely receive more foreign aid.

Pageantry and harangues convinced those who knew the Middle East that the last thing in Nasser's mind was an invasion of Israel; if he had been serious he would surely have recalled his men and tanks from Yemen while employing a minimum of discretion in their deployment. The same pageantry and harangues provided the Israelis with the first of a chain of circumstances favorable for a pre-emptive war. A former CIA man who knew Nasser well has written,[2] "When I left Cairo for London

[2] Copeland, op. cit.

at about this time, I told my Egyptian friends that I would bet my last dollar that Nasser had let himself in for a Pearl Harbor, although Zakaria's mission to Washington had received the Israelis' assurance that they would not attack until the world saw what he had to say in New York." Cairo's bellicose words and music, backed by quantitatively impressive supplies of Soviet arms, inspired sympathy for an Israel seen, at least in the West, as a trussed lamb before approaching butchers; while in strict contrast to the Yemen-bound Egyptians, Israeli reservists hurried to the front from as far afield as London and New York. Another favorable circumstance was the mood in Washington: exasperation over Vietnam spilled over onto other irritatingly alien countries such as Egypt. Perhaps no Great Power in modern times has had an administration as parochial in outlook and as indisposed to make allowances for cultures of a different order from its own than the United States presided over by Lyndon Johnson. The Israeli Government had studied this administration well; they knew that, for all its warnings to Israel, as to Egypt, not to initiate hostilities, if Israel brought things to a head, she would find an understanding ally at the United Nations in the U.S. representative, Arthur Goldberg, a sympathetic gallery in Washington if the war went well, and in the Sixth Fleet a last-resort protector if it did not.

In their gravest crises nations echo their past. The first days of June 1967 will, at least to readers of this book, bring to mind the summer of 1882, when Egyptians and Englishmen were poised in imminent hostility. Orabi's eloquent threats were now echoed by Nasser; so was that refusal to fire the first shot which might have given a chance, if not of winning, then of inflicting heavy damage; and just as Orabi had failed to close the Canal, so elementary precautions seem now to have been overlooked. The reluctance to strike first reflected Nasser's character quite as much as the Islamic taboo on striking the first blow in war. Nasser genuinely hated bloodshed and had written much of his biography (one remembers his account of the attempted assassination and then his reaction to the Syrian secession of 1961) in the "I could if I would but I would not" mood.

Nasser claimed later that he had not only informed his military chiefs that war was a virtual certainty, but had predicted that Monday, June 5, would be the most likely date for an Israeli attack. Certainly Nasser's closest confidant, the editor of *al-Ahram,* had written on May 26, after a lengthy analysis of the situation: "Israel must resort to arms. An armed clash between the UAR and the Israeli enemy is unavoidable."

The night before the decisive battle of Tel el-Kebir in 1882 had been frivolously spent; the night of June 4, 1967, it was later whispered, kept many Egyptian pilots busy as wedding guests. They woke, on June 5, with hangovers.

Early that predicted morning the wire services of the world rattled out the first communiqué of what came to be known, for a while at least, as the Six-Day War. It came from Tel Aviv. An Egyptian armored force, it stated, was invading southern Israel and the Israeli defense force was fighting back. In later statements the same day Prime Minister Levi Eshkol, Foreign Minister Abba Eban and War Minister Moshe Dayan declared, in similar terms, that Israel was fighting a war of defense and had no intention of acquiring a single inch of land. Egyptian communiqués claiming aerial successes wilted as fast as wild flowers picked in the desert —or as the first Israeli protestations.

In a matter of hours the well-rehearsed Israeli air force had virtually annihilated the Egyptian air force, whose planes had been drawn up like skittles on the glaring airfields of cloudless June. The airfields of Syria and Jordan (whose King Hussein had signed a last-minute defense agreement with Nasser) were similarly dealt with. Without defense against bombs and napalm, the Arab armies were doomed. First Egypt, then Jordan and lastly Syria were defeated.

On June 9 a gaunt, exhausted Nasser addressed his people: "I tell you truthfully and despite any factors on which I might have based my attitude during the crisis that I am ready to bear the whole responsibility. I have taken a decision in which I want you all to help me. I have decided to give up completely and finally every official post and every political role and return to the ranks of the masses and to do my duty with them like every other citizen. The forces of imperialism imagine that Gamal Abdul Nasser is their enemy. I want it to be clear to them that their enemy is the entire Arab nation, not just Gamal Abdul Nasser. The forces hostile to the Arab national movement try to portray this movement as an empire of Abdul Nasser. This is not true, because the aspiration for Arab unity began before Abdul Nasser and will remain after Abdul Nasser. I have always told you that the nation remains, and that the individual—whatever his role and however great his contribution to the causes of his homeland—is only a tool of the popular will, and not its creator. In accordance with Article 110 of the Provisional Constitution promulgated in March 1964 I have entrusted my colleague, friend and brother Zakaria Muhiaddin with taking over the post of President."[3]

The defeat seemed as total as the morning when Orabi Pasha handed his sword to the polite British officers at Abbasia Barracks. The British radio, for long hostile to Nasser, now politely broadcast a reverent obituary.

But if human motivations and actions recalled those of 1882, the

[3] For the text of Nasser's resignation broadcast I have followed Laqueur (*The Israel-Arab Reader*) except in three points. I have omitted the paragraphing after *every other citizen* and *not its creator*. I have not described the Egyptian president as "Jamal Abd al-Nasser" since Nasser pronounces his name with a hard G. I have also written "post of President," as Laqueur has "the point of President," which sounds absurd.

theater's scenery and rules had changed. After Tel el-Kebir General Wolseley had pressed on to Cairo, knowing that victory in war, as opposed to victory in a battle, is signified by the power to impose one's peace terms on the enemy. In 1967 the Security Council had imposed a cease-fire on the contestants; to the Arabs, it was a bad cease-fire, since, on U.S. insistence, it did not require the Israelis to withdraw to the borders from which they had launched their attack; but it left Israel in occupation of no Arab capital. Again, Nasser was far more resourceful, far more resilient than Orabi. The very terms of his resignation speech concealed an intention to resist. But two decisive differences lay at home in Egypt and abroad in the North. In 1882 Orabi's popular support had melted overnight and Towfik had received all Egypt's abject submission; only Orabi's black servant, his English lawyer had remarked, maintained a tattered loyalty to a defeated chief.

A great open space lays bare the heart of modern Cairo, providing lawns and fountains which attract great crowds on hot summer nights. On the Nile side, the headquarters of the Arab League and the Hilton Hotel stand on the former site of Kasr el-Nil Palace, from whose barrack wing Orabi and his officers had entrained for exile. To the north, the Pharaonic Museum, built under Abbas II, houses the evidence of Egypt's former glory; to the south, a monolithic edifice worthy of Stalin Allee in East Berlin hordes bureaucratic offices. A watcher on the roof of a high building to the east saw, the night Nasser spoke, a most curious spectacle. A multitude of Egyptians, men in *gallabya* or trousers and shirts, girl students and black-garbed women holding babies, silently watched a giant TV screen flickering with the President's elephant-gray features. As the broadcast ended, as the announcer was seen breaking down in tears, so the multitude moved from the screen like some huge animate creature, not listlessly, but with collective purpose, to demand and join others demanding that the man who led them into defeat should get them out of it.

The outside world differed as much as the Egyptian stage. In the summer of 1881 Orabi had looked north to the Prince of Believers, the Shadow of God on Earth, reigning from the secret enclosure of Yildiz Kiosk. But Abdul Hamid had been unable to move a finger to support the Egyptians. In 1967 Nasser turned north to the Soviet Union, preparing to celebrate its fiftieth anniversary. In obeying his own and his people's instincts to resist, Nasser had the backing of the second most powerful state on earth and of its allies. Within days of the cease-fire, giant-bellied Antonovs were ferrying in the arms which would make it possible to resist.

At a conference in Khartoum later that summer the Arab states (with the exception of Syria) agreed to seek a peaceful solution, if one were possible, but not to negotiate with an Israel whose occupation of four times more territory than before June gave her powerful leverage. This was a logical consequence of the recognition that a battle, not a war, had been lost. The Arab states together formed a gigantic and lumpy feather bolster, impossible to galvanize into efficiency, but equally difficult to bludgeon into acceptance of defeat. The sport in which the Arabs do best is long-distance swimming.

Chapter 8

RESOLVING nothing, the hostilities of 1967 marked a six-day crisis in a protracted and dangerous struggle. Its results were very different from what those indirectly or directly involved had foreseen or wished.

The Suez Canal, as one consequence, was closed for its hundredth birthday; in November 1969 Ismailia and Suez were ghost towns, their mosques, churches and houses battered by Israeli shells. But the loss of the Canal had proved less damaging, at least to the influential nations, than had been feared. Giant tankers transported Persian Gulf oil round South Africa, which was an unintended beneficiary of what had happened; new oil fields west of Suez, particularly in Algeria and Libya, helped lessen the Canal's importance. To the countries bordering the Indian Ocean, however, the longer sea route to Europe proved an irksome expense.

Three republics and one monarchy were the twentieth century equivalents of the crowned heads who had preoccupied Khedive Ismail. The balance of power had moved from Western Europe. Now the United States of America, officially absent from the opening of the Canal but unofficially concerned with its closure, was the world's strongest state. American public opinion had generally supported Israel in the war and American arms, including Phantom bombers, were to help Israel retain the occupied territories pending a settlement. In the immediate aftermath of the June war, American diplomacy backed Israel at the UN, not only by opposing any demand that the cease-fire should be linked to an Israeli withdrawal, but by mustering support against a Soviet attempt to have Israel's actions condemned by the General Assembly. Arabs ascribed American support for Israel to the powerful Jewish pressure group in the United States. But there were other reasons. Americans, like many Europeans, felt guilty for not having acted earlier to prevent Jewish sufferings in Europe; they also had a traditional admiration for the efficient, whose obverse was a distaste for losers; they found it easier to identify with Israelis—who came from Europe or in some cases America—than with Arabs. An Israeli victory would produce, Americans hoped, a number of desirable changes. The discrediting of radical Arab regimes would quiet an area rich in resources and of strategic importance. Above all, the Arab refusal to recognize Israel—in itself no more illogical than American non-recognition of Communist China—would finally crumble.

America gained a satisfying spectacle of split-second military timing but little else. Her identification with Israel damaged her interests and eroded her prestige in the whole Islamic world. Even in Turkey American servicemen were increasingly harassed by student demonstrators. But in the Arab countries public opinion was clamant against America, its bitterness reflecting a previous admiration. In May 1969, as a first delayed reaction, a Sudanese Government not unfriendly to America was overthrown by pro-Nasser revolutionaries. For a while, U.S. officials visiting the area dismissed such surges of public opinion as of little moment. "We can afford," ran one cynical argument, "to hand the populated Arab countries to the Soviets; we'll settle for the underpopulated deserts and the oil." But in September 1969 the desert Kingdom of Libya was taken over by Arab Nationalists whose watchword was "Jerusalem." The new regime immediately demanded U.S. evacuation of Wheelus, the largest American airbase outside North America. The continuance of the struggle would probably involve similar reversals elsewhere.

During the six-day campaign the apparent passivity of the Soviet Union had disappointed the Arabs. They had persuaded themselves that in Russia they had a committed ally. Russian prudence during the fighting was prompted by reasons they little understood: a resolve to avoid an armed collision with the U.S. and a clear-sighted recognition that the initial Arab defeat was too complete for any amount of indirect aid to change the situation. To their Arab friends, Soviet diplomats cited the precedent of Lenin, who in 1917 accepted the Treaty of Brest-Litovsk and the temporary loss to Germany of much of western Russia. But most Arabs recognized that if they wished to resist, the only power which could and would provide them with the means to do so was the Soviet Union. Although arms were supplied cheaply, Russia received in return substantial quantities of Egyptian and Syrian consumer goods. But Russia's strategic earnings were immense. Syria, Egypt, Libya and Algeria controlled between them a major portion of the Mediterranean littoral; thanks to their friendship, Russia could, for the first time in her history, play the role of a Mediterranean power. There was every likelihood of more countries in the Middle East following Libya's example and producing governments of a revolutionary stamp. This meant the possibility, if the conflict between Israel and the Arabs continued, of Russia winning the whole Middle

East as its area of influence, while America retained an enlarged Israeli Formosa.

Britain and France—the two dominant Powers of 1869—had become secondary Great Powers by 1967. Nevertheless France gained much as the result of her policy in June and afterwards. President de Gaulle had warned, immediately before the outbreak of war, that he would oppose whichever side turned the state of provocation into active hostilities. Since Israel had, unquestionably, fired the first shot, De Gaulle had refused to supply her with further arms; the ban was made more rigorous after an Israeli raid in 1969 on Beirut's civil airport. De Gaulle justified his stand on moral grounds, arguing that the principle of the pre-emptive war (which could be applied to other disputes than that in the Middle East) was unacceptable in a world of nuclear arms; his anger over Beirut owed much to France's traditional role as the patron of the Maronites. De Gaulle's attitude, inherited by his successor Georges Pompidou, made France as pleasing to the ordinary Arab as the France of Napoleon III and Eugénie had been to Khedive Ismail. French popularity was increased by the desire of most Arabs to have other friends besides the Soviet Union. It was a psychological relief to find a Western country which seemed to understand their case.

Britain, the victor in the nineteenth-century wrangles with France, was now a pallid second to the United States: suffering similar disadvantages, but in a minor key.

Yet it was Britain, famed for her diplomacy, which produced a formula designed to bring peace to the Middle East. In November 1967 the Security Council unanimously approved a resolution phrased by Britain's Foreign Secretary, George Brown. After a preamble affirming the inadmissibility, in terms of the UN Charter, of territorial gains made through conquest, the resolution upheld two principles in delphic balance: the evacuation by Israel of territories she had taken in the June War against her de facto recognition by the Arabs. A UN envoy, Dr. Gunnar Jarring, was to discuss the implementation of these principles with the parties concerned. After some hesitation Egypt and Jordan accepted the resolution, while stressing that they understood it to mean that Israeli withdrawal must be complete and that the resolution's reference to justice for the Palestinians should mean a choice of repatriation or compensation. Israel quibbled, one moment proclaiming that the integration of Arab Jerusalem into the state of Israel was non-negotiable, then that everything was negotiable if only the Arabs would enter direct negotiations, something which the Arabs had already declared they would not do and something which the resolution did not require of them. Syria and a number of other Arab states rejected the resolution since they refused to accept the principle of a Jewish state in Arab Palestine.

Dr. Jarring spent much of 1968 flying between Tel Aviv and the Arab capitals. The Israelis refused to commit themselves to a timetable for withdrawal or a clear statement that they would withdraw at all; the Arabs refused to commit themselves further until such a timetable had been agreed or such a commitment made. In 1969, under French propulsion, the Powers proceeded to bilateral and quadrilateral discussions in an effort to prevent another outburst of major fighting and possibly to contrive a lasting peace. In these discussions America came to be recognized as the spokesman for Israel and the Soviet Union for the Arabs. The long failure of such attempts to produce results can be understood after an analysis of how the Six-Day War had affected the main parties directly involved.

Egypt's losses in the campaign were at first sight crippling: the bulk of her Soviet weaponry, around fifteen thousand officers and men (the great bulk of them in the retreat across Sinai), Sinai itself, and above all, the radiance of her myth. The losses in military personnel, though only a quarter of what Britain had sacrificed in one day on the altar of the Somme, were nevertheless severe, since Egypt lacked military reserves. Sinai was important for two reasons. It was rich in minerals, including oil; strategically, it acted as a buffer between the delta and Palestine; from advanced positions in Sinai the Israelis could shell the three cities of the Canal Zone and bomb the delta. As to the myth: few attributed infallibility to Nasser or Spartan qualities to his Army any more.

Each of these losses soon had a compensatory side. The weaponry was more than replaced by the Soviet Union; several thousand Soviet experts gave the Egyptians better military training than before. The loss of the oil wells in Sinai was made up by the discovery of important new wells on the Red Sea coast and in the Western Desert. The Canal's revenues were replaced by subventions from the three oil-rich states of Saudi Arabia, Kuwait and Libya. Since the revenues from the functioning Canal had been offset by expenses on its upkeep, these Arab contributions gave Egypt a larger income than before. The Canal's cities were not replaceable while the war continued; their evacuated population gave Egypt a refugee problem of its own. The collapse of the myth was painful. In the first months after the defeat, officers were ashamed to appear in uniform; Egyptians abroad felt humiliated; other Arabs did not spare their feelings. But the pain was therapeutic. The mood in Egypt grew noticeably more sober. In the last three years of his life, Nasser was simply regarded as the only leader who could unite the country till peace was achieved. Egyptians hoped that he might, like a Phoenix, rise from the ashes of his disgrace. As for Nasser himself, he at last had an opportunity to put the Army in its place: on the front line, away from influence and power in Cairo. This gain was secured through the loss, by suicide, of Field Marshal Amer, his closest friend.

Israel's gains and losses were no less paradoxical. Prestige (the elusive element which Nasser had sought and lost) was her chief new asset. But prestige had not been her war aim. The motives for her pre-emptive strike were as complex as her small, compact but diverse population. They were not those proclaimed on the morning of June 5—that is, a riposte to an Egyptian invasion. Nor was concern over Elath more than symbolic, though to Israel lines of communication were important symbols. Israeli moderates had hoped, by destroying weapons which might at some future time become a danger, to force their maddeningly unrealistic neighbors to accept the Jewish state. Whatever the dimensions of this state might be, they wanted security for it. A complicating difficulty was the wide spectrum of opinion as to the frontiers of the Jewish state. Some, including the now retired Ben-Gurion, seemed disposed to accept the Israel of 1967 as the reality they wished to secure; but more and more Israeli politicians spoke of retaining now this, now that portion of conquered land.

But though Israel had won land, as well as prestige, from her six days of effort, settlements were established in the Syrian Golan Heights, in Jordan's West Bank, and even in Sinai and Gaza. Neither the temporary possession of territory nor prestige could produce security. Before 1967 Israeli losses from border incursions had been irregular and small; they were certainly far less than the toll she had periodically inflicted on the Arabs in reprisal raids; the losses might have ceased altogether if the problem of the Palestinians had been considered as important a priority as defense. After 1967 the numbers of Israelis killed or wounded were to mount with steady momentum, reaching in some months of 1969–70 around one hundred; this monthly figure expressed in American Vietnam terms (taking into account America's hundredfold larger population) would be around 10,000. By 1970 Israel was spending, in money, more than three million dollars a day on defense. For such an expenditure in blood and cash the territories under her temporary control offered a bleak return.

Many Israelis recognized that strategic rivers, deserts or heights could never make the Jewish state secure. Security could only come with Arab acceptance. Some generous move, some reversion to her prophetic tradition, might, in the aftermath of June 1967, have melted Arab hostility to Israel and Arab susceptibility to extremists. No such move was made. The strongest army in the Middle East was controlled by a weak coalition. Its moderates were unable to make a clear bid for peace while its extremists continually expanded the list of territories whose return was considered as "non-negotiable."

The severities involved in military occupation brought victorious Israel into closer, bitterer contact with the last and most important party to the Middle Eastern conflict—the Palestinians. After the June War every single member of a people numbering approximately two and a half millions—or about the same as the Jewish population of Israel—lived either in unwilling exile or under Israeli rule.

Before the June War most Palestinians had existed on the Arab side of the armistice lines. Three hundred thousand were enclosed in the narrow Gaza Strip unable to visit Egypt without a pass. The larger number on the West Bank of the Jordan were oppressed by a Bedouin army loyal to the Hashemite throne. Those who had migrated to other Arab countries fared little better. Lebanon had the highest standard of living in the Arab East and more millionaires than Britain; yet she treated the Palestinians with cynical discrimination; Christians were welcomed as counterweights to the country's Muslims, while the Muslims, mostly dispossessed fellahin, rotted in sordid camps.

The first generation of the Palestinian diaspora were impotent because stunned. In losing their land fellahin had lost their reason for existence; they slouched in their wretched camps, collecting a UN dole and begetting children. But townsmen had taken with them into exile considerable talents; traditional Palestinian aptitudes had been sharpened by an admirable British educational system. Many Palestinians went on to higher study in Europe or America. Others made fortunes as the new oil wells gushed by the Persian Gulf. Others acquired experience in Arab military academies. But even more acquired experience of Arab jails when they showed signs of wanting a say in their own future. For, with the solitary exception of Syria, all Arab governments had tried, while exploiting the plight of the refugees, to prevent them provoking major clashes with Israel.

The second generation of Palestinians—those who had been led or carried into exile by their fleeing parents—were to produce a different mood. Their elders had hoped for some justice from the United Nations or some miraculous deliverance from the Arab states. The new generation had no such hopes. They felt they had nothing to lose but their tents.

An autonomous Palestinian guerrilla movement had started in a small, unremarked incident in January 1965, two years before the June War. After a minor incursion into Israel, a group calling itself Al-Asifa, or "The Storm," published the following communiqué:

> We declare to the world at large our attachment to the soil of Palestine and our claim over the generous bounties of our land. Our resort to armed struggle is motivated by our belief that it is the only path towards the rescue of our cause from the state of isolation and forgetfulness in which it has been dormant for the last twenty years. We appeal to the Palestinian people, in particular, and to the Arab nation and freedom-loving peoples, in general, to lend their support to our revolutionary struggle. To the Palestinian people, we vow to keep our oath to liberate the land, and not to relinquish our arms until such time as Palestine is reinstituted in its natural place in the Arab homeland.

At the time, neither Israel, inured to occasional incursions, nor most of the Arab states, opposed as they were to activities unsanctioned by themselves, regarded this as more than rhetoric.

Paradoxically, the defeat of the Arab armies in 1967 gave a huge new impetus to the movement represented by Al-Asifa. For one thing, the Palestinians now had a cause which they could compare to that of occupied Europe in the Second World War. For the first time the Arab struggle against Israel began to get some sympathy in the West. Photographs of Arab houses blown up by the Israelis in reprisal for acts of resistance (or terror, as they were naturally termed by the occupation authorities) aroused sympathy in countries which remembered Nazi occupation. Violence also begot violence. The more frequent the attacks by the fedayyin—"self-sacrificers" as they were known to the Arabs—the more ruthless the reprisals. The chain reaction was depressingly similar to what had happened in other countries occupied by other invaders, British as well as German, French as well as Italian. The fedayyin were venerated by an Arab world which had lost its heroes. And though they were split into many groups (for the Arabs were as hard to unite as the Celts), though their treeless terrain offered little protection, they had behind them a vast Arab hinterland, suddenly rich in the cash produced by oil and linked to friendly powers. The fedayyin lacked neither money nor weapons.

The first resistance group, Fatah,[1] stated that their aim was to make of Israel, Gaza and the West Bank—in other words, what had been Palestine —a unitary secular state in which Jewish, Muslim and Christian Palestinians would exist as equals. They were totally opposed to an Israel, in Weizmann's phrase, "as Jewish as England is English and France is French." But they discarded the vitriolic extremism of Arab propaganda machines and proposed their willingness to treat as fellow Palestinians all Israelis who would co-exist with them.

The fedayyin spoke of the "Palestinian Revolution," more than of the struggle for liberation. Their revolution was not only against the tradition of Herzl and Weizmann: they opposed their feudal leaders, who, under the British mandate, had misled them to disaster; their challenge to the other Arab states was fundamental. Their demand for a new Arab seriousness, their guerrilla challenge to Israel involved all other Arabs. Fedayyin attacks would certainly encourage Israel to raid more deeply into Jordan, Egypt, Syria and Lebanon. This many guerrilla theoreticians welcomed, since only the enlargement of the fighting zone could overextend the Israelis in the Middle East as the French had been overextended in Algeria.

For the first time in the modern history of the Middle East spontaneous

[1] As a noun, Fatah means Conquest; but its consonants, F T H, form, when read from right to left, as Arabic, like Hebrew is to be read, the initials of the *haraka tahrir falastin:* Palestine Liberation Movement. If the letters are read from left to right, in the European way, they form a concept of more somber meaning: *hataf,* a place of burial, a grave.

public opinion—not the public opinion sponsored by ministers of national guidance—had spokesmen who, being armed, could not easily be suppressed. This gave the Palestinian movement the right to call itself a revolution. No revolution is, of course, popular with those whose interests it menaces or whose prestige it undermines. Israelis who had hoped consciously or unconsciously that the Palestinians would fade into the deserts saw in this second-generation rebirth a danger; they gave the guerrillas the same epithet of "terrorist" which the British had given to the Zionist activists a generation earlier. The Arab governments publicly extolled the guerrillas and publicized their operations. But they, almost as much as the Israelis, felt this autonomous armed movement to be a threat. Most obviously, the guerrilla attacks mounted from Jordan or Lebanon prompted Israeli reprisals, usually in the ratio of ten eyes for one, which scorched the east bank of the Jordan valley and threatened to turn southern Lebanon into a no-man's land. More insidiously, the glamour of the young men and women in camouflage suits and sneakers threw into relief the failure of the expensive Arab armies. Fatah, the largest guerrilla organization, strove to reduce tensions between the various guerrilla bodies and their hosts, arguing that all Arabs, of whatever ideological tendency or tradition, must unite. But an important radical wing of the movement, the Popular Front for the Liberation of Palestine, had in its leader Dr. George Habbash, a harsher physician. Habbash, who had in fact forsaken his medical clinic for the battle tent, argued that Israel had been able to implant itself in the Arab world, and then progressively expand, because of the corrupt nature of Arab society. It was useless to fight imperialism and Zionism, the two enemy abstractions, under the banner of men whose quarrels and frailties had caused the defeat. Social revolution was the precondition of liberation.

The prestige of the guerrillas, the bite of their arguments, posed a challenge even to the leadership of Nasser, for long the undisputed symbol of the Arab revolutionary movement. Nettled by this challenge as well as by the failure of the Jarring mission, Nasser sanctioned a "war of attrition" against Israel which would end only, he proclaimed, when the Israelis made it clear that they were ready to evacuate all occupied territory. In response to heavy Egyptian shelling across the Canal, the Israelis used their latest American airplanes in raids which penetrated more and more deeply into Egypt. The aim of these raids was probably to discredit Nasser and achieve his downfall; a new Egyptian government might be more ready to meet Israeli terms. But it was impossible to raid as thickly populated a country as the Egyptian delta without involving civilians. A devastating attack on an Egyptian steelworks was followed by the deaths of dozens of children in an infants' school. As in the Europe of the Second World War, or more recently in Vietnam, such tragic incidents had the effect of uniting the Egyptian people around Nasser's leadership. It also became politically impossible for the Soviet Union to remain inactive while the industrial basis of Nasser's revolution was progressively destroyed. The most direct result of the Israeli raids was to accelerate the involvement of the Soviet Union in the defense of Egypt.

If American Phantoms were thus juxtaposed to Soviet missiles, it was not hard to envisage as a next step the direct confrontation of American with Soviet power. The evident danger that the Middle East problem might provide the trigger for a nuclear war was a prospect to charm few.

The lowering summer of 1970 was punctuated by an American initiative, the Rogers Plan, designed to settle the problem of Palestine once and for all. To the surprise of nearly everyone Nasser returned from a long visit to Moscow and announced, on July 23, that he was prepared to accept the proposals communicated to him by Secretary of State William Rogers. These called for a three months' cease-fire along the Suez Canal, during which time the mission of Dr. Gunnar Jarring could be reactivated.

Israel, which had not expected Nasser to accept the proposals, accepted them, too, but with considerable reluctance; she speedily used the excuse that Egyptians had moved ground-to-air missiles nearer the Canal to boycott the talks; at the same time she strengthened her own chain of defensive positions on the east bank of the Canal.

The Egyptian acceptance of the Rogers Plan had been immediately assailed by all but a minute section of the guerrilla movement. The November 22 Resolution on which the Plan was based amounted to a de facto recognition by the Arabs of the Israel of June 4, 1967: that is, an Israel embodying four fifths of mandated Palestine. True, there was talk of justice for the Palestinian refugees, but few believed that Israel would ever willingly return the lands she had taken over or allow back their original owners. Living in a region which kept no secrets, the Palestinians learned that the Americans had privately informed both Nasser and Hussein that the United States would only use its influence to obtain an Israeli withdrawal if the Arab governments concerned controlled the guerrillas. In a suspicious environment, they suspected that the Central Intelligence Agency was active in Amman. Against a background of millennial deception, they disbelieved official denials that Hussein had been in direct, personal contact with Israeli leaders. What seemed realism in the West seemed treachery nearer home.

Nasser used the intemperate Palestinian attack on his acceptance of the Rogers Plan to suppress the only manifestation of guerrilla power in Egypt, the Palestinian broadcasting stations. He argued, in public at least, that there was no contradiction between Egyptian acceptance of the Rogers Plan and the Palestinian right to continue fighting. Since there was no autonomous body of armed Palestinians in Egypt, he had to take no further steps.

Hussein of Jordan was in a different situation. Until the 1967 war he had been able to suppress any manifestation of independence among the

Palestinian majority in his kingdom. His instrument for rule was the army which the British had founded as the Arab Legion and used for their own ends. This army reflected the cleavage in Jordanian society. The armored regiments and artillery were largely recruited from the Bedouin, tribesmen who even in the time of the Prophet Muhammad had been noted for cynical indifference to anything save the pleasures and profits of the raid. The infantry contained a substantial proportion of Palestinians, more educated and politically aware than their Bedouin brothers. Hussein, owing as much to his demented father Tallal as to his wily grandfather Abdullah, was a Janus kinglet. One side of his character was responsive to the arguments of Arab nationalism. In this mood he would say, "We are all guerrillas now." Another side of his character reflected his dynasty's traditional dependence on foreign powers and willingness to accept their bidding. Under such influences he listened to the urging of relatives and foreign well-wishers that he should assert his authority against the Palestinians.

In October guerrillas working for the Popular Front hijacked a number of planes in a gesture designed to do two things: first, to obtain the release of guerrillas held in Britain, Germany, Switzerland and Israel; and, secondly, to dramatize the existence of the Palestinian problem. One giant plane was deliberately taken to Cairo and burned on the runway as impotent officials watched. Three other planes were flown with their passengers, to "Revolutionary Airport" in North Jordan. Both actions were vivid acts of defiance to the two states involved. For Hussein, the much publicized event provided a perfect pretext for suppressing the guerrilla movement.

Nasser must have known that the King of Jordan was going to control the more unruly guerrillas; to a military man of Nasser's autocratic temper the existence of such a state within a state was something he would never have tolerated in Egypt; in the present situation the guerrillas also made it difficult for him and his Jordanian partner to pursue the peaceful solution which they considered in the best interests of the Arabs. But neither man can have foreseen that the royalist operation would take so long or involve a massacre. Hussein could not, however, rely on his infantry, which would have been the normal instrument for searching the guerrillas who lived in the pitiful refugee camps around Amman. Instead, he used artillery to shell them to pieces. Cairo was, for the first two days of the Jordanian civil war, uneasily silent. As the horrendous details of the fighting became known he was forced, as the leader of the Arab revolutionary movement, to take a stand against what the King was doing. At the same time he exerted all his efforts, used all his charisma, to reconcile the guerrillas and the regime which they had been comparing to that of Nero.

The Nasser of October 1970 was outwardly robust, his smile still as attractive as in the propaganda photographs displayed throughout the Middle East. But the previous winter a heart attack, played down as "influenza," had given its dire warning. An invalid commanded by his physicians to rest, he had become not less but more pertinacious in his grasp of power. Although Anwar al-Sadat was now his vice-president, Nasser kept effective power in his own hands, filling the roles of Prime Minister and head of the Arab Socialist Union as well as President. He was now facing the most lethal crisis in his career. That was the reality of Syrian intervention on the side of the guerrillas[2] and the threat of intervention by Israel and possibly America on the side of Hussein. There was a grave threat to his own leadership if the struggle should proceed to the point where he must choose between Hussein—whom in an earlier mood of disapproval he had once described as "the whore of Jordan"—and the guerrillas whom he has described in his July 23 speech as the noblest force to have emerged in the Arab world since the 1967 defeat. At the cost of a supreme effort he achieved a supremely incredible tableau: himself smiling and linking hands with Hussein and Yassir Arafat, the Fatah leader. After saying good-by to one of the emissaries to the conference which had framed the tableau, he returned to his home and collapsed. Anwar al-Sadat, perhaps the one true revolutionary in the original junta, announced his death over television to a stunned and incredulous people. So great was his legend that he not only received a funeral which dwarfed that of his hero Mustafa Kamil but was mourned hysterically in every major city of the Arab world. The foreign dignitaries who attended his funeral—including the prime ministers of the Soviet Union and France, the aristocratic foreign minister of Britain and the prime minister of Turkey—showed the extent to which the overthrower of the Egyptian monarchy had raised the prestige of Egypt. This man, for all his miscalculations the greatest Arab statesman since the Middle Ages, was the latest victim of the Palestinian killing-bottle. It was unlikely that the lethal vapors would long spare the two other partners in Nasser's last tableau: Hussein, surely marked out for death by some Palestinian, and Arafat, marked out for something hardly better, in the eyes of the extremists at least, when he shook hands with Hussein.

In 1869, when Ismail had welcomed his Western visitors to Ismailia, pessimists discounting the chance of reconciliation between East and West might have predicted a conflagration based on the Bosphorus, the narrows between Asia and Europe. Instead, the Canaan of the Old Testament and the *falastin,* or Palestine, of the Arabs was the arena of harshest conflict. Where Herzl had proposed to build his *Judenstaat* and Balfour had imposed the contradictions of his sibylline declaration, the Temple of

[2] Western statesmen attempting to draft a resolution against the Syrian intervention had a problem of phraseology. One of them was surprised when he found that Dr. al-Zayat, the United Arab Republic ambassador to the UN, eagerly accepted the idea of a resolution calling on "the withdrawal of all foreign troops in Jordan." Slowly it dawned on the Western statesman that such a resolution must include the troops of Israel, on Jordanian territory since June 1967.

Janus stood with open gates. It could become, in a land of miracles, a gateway leading wayfarers East and West; but if discussions failed, if violence continued in mounting spiral, it could become a grave of unpredictable depth: the site not of New Jerusalem, but Armageddon.

Bibliography

Abdullah, King of Transjordan. *Memoirs,* ed., Philip P. Graves. London: 1950.
Ahmed, Jamal Muhammad. *The Intellectual Origins of Arab Nationalism.* Oxford: 1960.
Aldington, Richard. *Lawrence of Arabia.* London: 1955.
Ali Haydar Midhat Bey. *The Life of Midhat Pasha.* London: 1903.
Anderson, M. S. *The Eastern Question; 1774–1923.* London: 1966.
Annual Register: London.
Antonius, George. *The Arab Awakening.* London: 1938.
Anwar Abdel Malek. *Egypte, Société Militaire.* Paris: 1961.
Arfa, General Hassan. *Under Five Shahs.* London: 1964.

Barbour, Nevill. *Nisi Dominus, A Survey of the Palestine Controversy.* London: 1946.
Batbedat, Th. *De Lesseps Intime.* Paris: 1894.
Bein, Alex. *Theodor Herzl, A Biography,* tr. London: 1957.
Bell. *The Letters of Gertrude,* ed., Lady Bell. London: 1947.
Bemmelen, van. *L'Egypte et l'Europe par un ancien Juge Mixte.* Leiden: 1884.
Bennett, Ernest N. "After Omdurman," *The Contemporary Review,* January 1899.
Berger, Elmer. *The Jewish Dilemma.* New York: 1956.
Bergman, Samuel Hugo. *Faith and Reason; An Introduction to Modern Jewish Thought.* New York: 1963.
Berkes, Niyazi. *The Development of Secularism in Turkey.* McGill: 1964.
Bioves, Achile. *Francais et Anglais en Egypte 1881–1882.* Paris: 1910.
Birdwood, Lord. *Nuri as-Said, a Study in Arab Leadership.* London: 1959.
Blunt, Wilfrid Scawen. *Secret History of the Occupation of Egypt.* London: 1907.
——. *My Diaries, being a personal narrative of events, 1888–1914,* 2 vols. London: 1919.
Borde, Paul. *L'Isthme de Suez.* Paris: 1870.
Bosch, Baron Firmin van den, *Vingt Années d'Egypte.* Paris: 1932.
Bourdon, M. Cl. "Le Miracle de l'Eau; histoire de l'eau dans l'Isthme de Suez," *Roy. Geog. Soc. of Egypt Bulletin,* xviii, pp. 311–31.
Boyle, Clara. *A Servant of the Empire; a Memoir of Harry Boyle.* London: 1938.
——. *Boyle of Cairo.* England: 1965.
Braithwaite, W. J. *Lloyd George's Ambulance Wagon; the Memoirs of W.J.B.;* London: 1957.
Broadley, A. M. *How We Defended Arabi.* London: 1884.

Buber, Martin. *The Writings of,* ed., Will Herberg. New York: 1956.

Burgogne, Elizabeth. *Gertrude Bell, From her Personal Papers.* London: Vol. I., 1889–1914, 1938; Vol. II., 1914–26, 1961.

Burns, Lt. Gen. E. L. M. *Between Arab and Israeli.* London: 1962.

Caractacus (pseud.). *Revolution in Iraq.* London: 1959.

Cameron, D. A. *Egypt in the Nineteenth Century.* London: 1898.

Carré, J.-M. *Voyageurs et Ecrivains Francais en Egypte.* Cairo: 1932.

Charmes, Gabriel. "L'Insurrection militaire en Egypte," *Revue des deux Mondes,* August 15, 1883.

——. *Voyage en Palestine, Impressions et Souvenirs.* Paris: 1891.

Chennels, E. *An Egyptian Princess by her English Governess.* London: 1893.

Childers, Erskine B. *The Road to Suez.* London: 1962.

Colvin, Sir Auckland. *The Making of Modern Egypt.* London: 1906.

Cohn, Norman. *Warrant for Genocide, the myth of the Jewish world-conspiracy and the Protocols of the Elders of Zion.* London: 1967.

Crabitès, Pierre. *Ismail, The Maligned Khedive.* London: 1933.

Cromer, Earl of. *Modern Egypt,* 2 vols. London: 1908.

Crouchley, A. E. *The Economic Development of Modern Egypt.* London: 1938.

Eaton, F. A. "The Suez Canal," *Macmillans Mag.,* Vol. xxi.

Edelman, Maurice. *Ben Gurion, a Political Biography.* London: 1964.

Edib, Halidé. *The Turkish Ordeal.* London: 1928.

Elgood, P. G. *The Transit of Egypt.* London: 1928.

Encyclopaedia Britannica, 13th ed.

Finch, Edith. *Wilfrid Scawen Blunt: 1840–1922.* London: 1938.

Fitzmaurice, Lord Edmond. *The Life of the Second Earl Granville.* London: 1905.

Fontane, Marius. *A Travers l'Isthme de Suez.* Paris: 1869.

Freeman, Edward A. *The Ottoman Power in Europe: Its Nature, Its Growth, and Its Decline.* London: 1877.

Fromentin, Eugène. *Voyage en Egypte 1869,* ed., F. Aubier. Paris.

Furlonge, Geoffrey. *Palestine is my country; the story of Musa Alami.* London: 1969.

Gibbe, Sir H. A. R. *Modern Trends in Islam.* Chicago: 1947.

Gide, André. *The Journals of,* tr., Justin O'Brien, Vol. II, p. 7. London: 1948.

Giffard, Pierre. *Les Français en Egypte;* Paris: 1883.

Glatzer, Nahum N., ed. *A Jewish Reader.* New York: 1964.

Glubb Pasha. *A Soldier with the Arabs.* London: 1957.

Gökalp, Ziya. *Turkish Nationalism and Western Civilization,* tr. & ed., Niyazi Berkes. London: 1959.

Hadawi, Sami. *Palestine in Focus.* Beirut: 1968.

Herold, J. Christopher. *Bonaparte in Egypt.* London: 1962.

Hertzberg, Arthur. *The Zionist Idea; A historical Analysis and Reader*. New York: 1959.
Herzl. *The Diaries of Theodor*, ed. & tr., Marvin Lowenthal. London: 1958.
Hirsczowicz, Lukasz. *The Third Reich and the Arab East*, tr., London: 1966.
Hourani, Albert. *Arabic Thought in the Liberal Age; 1798–1939*. Oxford: 1962.
Howard, Harry N. *The King-Crane Commission; An American Inquiry in the Middle East*. Beirut: 1963.
Husaini, Ishak Musa. *The Moslem Brethren*. Beirut: 1956.
Hutchinson, E. H. *Violent Truce*. New York: 1956.

Ionides, M. *Divide and Lose: the Arab Revolt 1955–1958*. London: 1960.
Issawi, Charles. *Egypt in Revolution*. Oxford: 1963.

Jeffries, J. M. N. *Palestine: the Reality*. London: 1939.
Jerrold, Blanchard. *Egypt under Ismail Pacha*. London: 1879.
Jiryis, Sabri. *The Arabs in Israel*. Beirut: 1968.

Kamil, Mustafa. *Egyptiens et Anglais*, preface, Madame Juliette Adam. Paris: 1906.
Khadduri, Majid. *Independent Iraq; 1932–1958, 2nd ed.* London: 1960.
Kimche, Jon. *Seven Fallen Pillars*. London: 1950.
——. *The Unromantics; The Great Powers and the Balfour Declaration*. London: 1968.
Kinross, Lord. *Atatürk, the Rebirth of a Nation*. London: 1964.
Kipling's Mind & Art, ed., Andrew Rutherford. Edinburgh: 1964.
Kirk, George E. *A Short History of the Middle East*. London: 1948.
——. *The Middle East 1945–1950*. Oxford: 1954.
Knightley, Philip and Colin Simpson. *The Secret Lives of Lawrence of Arabia*. London: 1969.
Kusel, Baron de (Bey). *An Englishman's Recollections of Egypt, 1863 to 1887*. London: 1915.
Kurtz, Harold. *The Empress Eugénie*. London: 1964.

Lacouture, Jean & Simone. *Egypt in Transition*. London: 1958.
Landes, David S. *Bankers and Pashas*. London: 1958.
Lane-Poole, Stanley. *Cairo, Sketches of its History, Monuments and Social Life*. London: 1893.
Laqueur, Walter Z. *Communism and Nationalism in the Middle East*. London: 1956.
——. *The Israel-Arab Reader; A documentary history of the Middle East conflict*. London: 1969.
Lav-Lavie, Naphtali. *Moshe Dayan*. London: 1968.
Lawrence, T. E. *The Seven Pillars of Wisdom*. London: Cape, 1935; reprinted Penguin, 1962.
Leconte, Casimir. *Promenade dans l'Isthme de Suez*. Paris: 1864.
Lewis, Bernard. *The Emergence of Modern Turkey*. Oxford: 1961.

Little, Tom. *Egypt*. London: 1958.

Longrigg, S. *Iraq: 1900–1950*. London: 1953.

Lorenzo, Francesco de. *Memoria circa la posizione attuale della colonia italiana in Egitto*. Naples: 1876.

Lutfi al-Sayyid, Afaf. *Egypt and Cromer, A Study in Anglo-Egyptian Relations*. London: 1968.

Lynch, W. F., U.S.N. *Narrative of the United States' Expedition to the River Jordan and the Dead Sea*. Philadelphia: 1856.

Magnus, Philip. *Kitchener—Portrait of an Imperialist*. London: 1958.

Mannoni, O. *Prospero and Caliban, the Psychology of Colonization*. London: 1956.

Mansfield, Peter. *Nasser*. London: 1969.

Marlowe, J. *The Seat of Pilate*. London: 1959.

Meinertzhagen, R. M. *Middle East Diary: 1917–1956*. London: 1959.

Menuhin, Moshe. *The Decadence of Judaism in our Time*. New York: 1965.

Minnaert. *Le Caire*. Paris: 1891.

Monroe, Elizabeth. *Britain's Moment in the Middle East; 1914–1956*. London: 1963.

Morris, James. *Pax Britannica, The Climax of an Empire*. London: 1968.

Nasser, Gamal Abdul. *The Philosophy of the Revolution*, introduction by Dorothy Thompson. Cairo: 1954.

Neame, Alan. *The Happening at Lourdes*. London: 1968.

Nicole, G. *Inauguration du Canal de Suez, Voyage des Souverains; aquarelles d'après nature et potraits, Riou*. Paris: 1870.

Nicolson, Harold. *Peacemaking 1919*. London: 1933.

Nutting, Anthony. *No End of a Lesson*. London: 1967.

O'Ballance, Edgar. *The Arab-Israeli War, 1948*. London: 1956.

Observer, The, of the 19th Century. Sel., Marion Miliband; intro., Asa Briggs. London: 1966.

Oliver, Roy. *The Wanderer and the Way; The Hebrew Tradition in the Writings of Martin Buber*. London: 1968.

Orwell, George. *Critical Essays*. London: 1946.

Pannikar, K. M. *Asia and Western Domination*. New York: 1954.

Pearlman, Moshe. *Ben Gurion looks back in talks with . . .* London: 1965.

Pears, Sir Edwin. *Forty Years in Constantinople, 1873–1915*. London: 1916.

Peretz, Don. *Israel and the Palestine Arabs*. Washington: Middle East Institute (1958). p. 152.

Philby, H. St John. *Arabian Jubilee*. London: 1952.

Polk, William R. *The Opening of South Lebanon, 1788–1840*. Harvard: 1963.

(Rashid Ridha. *History of Imam Abduh*. [Arabic] Cairo.)

Ravaisse, Paul. *Ismail Pacha 1830–1895; Revue de l'Egypte*. Cairo: 1896.

Roberts, David. *The Holy Land from Drawings Made on the Spot with His-*

torical Descriptions by the Rev. George Croly, 2 vols. London: 1842 and 1843.
Robinson, Richard D. *The First Turkish Republic*. Harvard: 1963.
Royal Automobile Club d'Egypte. *Annuaire 1927*. Cairo.

Sadat, Anwar al-. *Revolt on the Nile*. London: 1957.
Safran, Nadav. *Egypt in search of Political Community*. Harvard: 1961.
Saleh, Zaki. *Mesopotamia (Iraq) 1600–1914; A Study in British Foreign Affairs*. Baghdad: 1957.
Sammarco, Angelo. *Histoire de l'Egypte Moderne*. Vol. III. Cairo: 1937.
Seale, Patrick. *The Struggle for Syria*. Oxford: 1965.
Seth, Ronald. *Russell Pasha*. London: 1966.
Sheean, Vincent. *In Search of History*. London: 1935.
Stein, Leonard. *The Balfour Declaration*. London: 1961.
Stewart, Desmond. *New Babylon, A Portrait of Iraq* (with John Haylock). London: 1956.
——. *Young Egypt*. London. 1958.
Storrs, Ronald. *Orientations*. London: 1937.
Sykes, Christopher. *Cross Roads to Israel; Palestine from Balfour to Bevin*. London: 1965.

Thomas, Hugh. *The Suez Affair*. London: 1967.

Vambéry, Arminius. "Personal Recollections of Abdul Hamid II and his Court," *The Nineteenth Century*, June 1909.
Van Horn, Maj. Gen. Carl. *Soldiering for Peace*. New York: 1967.
Vaucher, Georges. *Gamal Abdel Nasser et son Equipe*. Paris: 1959.

Warriner, Doreen. *Land Reform and Development in the Middle East*. London: 1962.
Weizmann, Chaim. *Trial and Error*. London: 1949.
Welles, Sumner. *We Need not Fail*. Boston: 1948.
Wittlin, Alma. *Abdul Hamid, The Shadow of God*, tr. London: 1940.

Yeghen, Foulad. *L'Egypte sous le règne de Fouad Ier*. Cairo: 1929.
Young, Kenneth. *Arthur James Balfour*. London: 1963.
Youssef, Amine. *Independent Egypt*. London: 1940.

Zeine, Z. N. *The Struggle for Arab Independence*. Beirut: 1960.
Zetland, the Marquess of. *Lord Cromer, being the authorized life of Evelyn Baring, first Earl of Cromer*. London: 1932.

THE DYNASTY OF MUHAMMAD ALI: 1805–1953

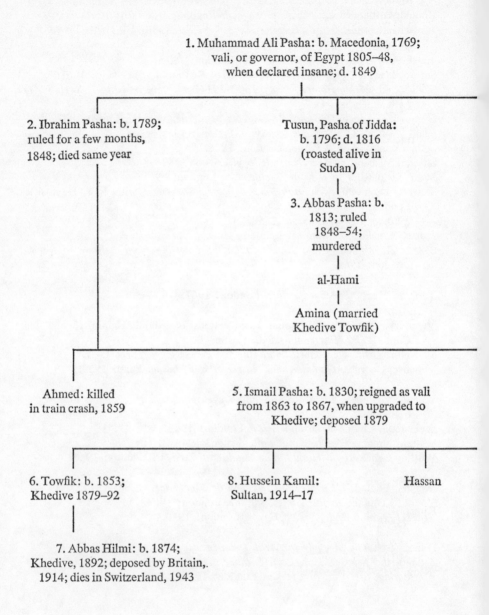

1. Muhammad Ali Pasha: b. Macedonia, 1769;
vali, or governor, of Egypt 1805–48,
when declared insane; d. 1849

2. Ibrahim Pasha: b. 1789;
ruled for a few months,
1848; died same year

Tusun, Pasha of Jidda:
b. 1796; d. 1816
(roasted alive in
Sudan)

3. Abbas Pasha: b.
1813; ruled
1848–54;
murdered

al-Hami

Amina (married
Khedive Towfik)

Ahmed: killed
in train crash, 1859

5. Ismail Pasha: b. 1830; reigned as vali
from 1863 to 1867, when upgraded to
Khedive; deposed 1879

6. Towfik: b. 1853;
Khedive 1879–92

8. Hussein Kamil:
Sultan, 1914–17

Hassan

7. Abbas Hilmi: b. 1874;
Khedive, 1892; deposed by Britain,.
1914; dies in Switzerland, 1943

This family tree, pruned of members unmentioned in this book, serves to show the regnal dates and titles of the dynasty founded by Muhammad Ali Pasha. Asterisks mark those whose interests were adversely affected when, in 1866, Ismail persuaded the Ottoman Sultan to change the law of succession in Egypt to the European pattern. Ottoman rulers were succeeded by the eldest male of the family, not necessarily by the eldest son.

4. Said Pasha: b. 1823; ruled 1854–63

*Abdul Halim: b. 1831; survived train crash, 1858; d. 1894

*Muhammad Ali, The Younger

*Mustafa Fazil: b. 1830; d. 1875; Ottoman reformer

Princess Nazli: salon revolutionary

9. Fuad: b. 1868; Sultan, 1917–22; King of Egypt, 1922–36

10. Farouk: b. 1920; King, 1936–52, when abdicates

11. Ahmed Fuad: b. 1951; nominal king, 1952–53, when monarchy formally abolished

THE HASHEMITES

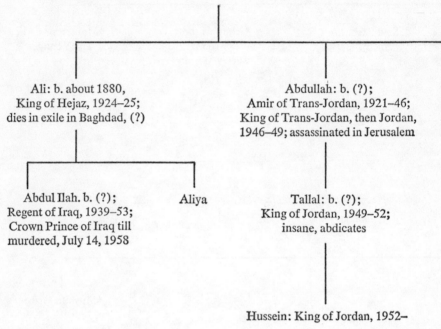

Sherif Hussein: b. about 1854; Amir of Mecca under the Ottomans, 1908–16; self-styled 'King of the Arabs,' British-recognized King of Hejaz, 1916; unsuccessfully proclaimed 'Caliph,' 1924; abdicates, 1924; dies in exile, (?)

Ali: b. about 1880, King of Hejaz, 1924–25; dies in exile in Baghdad, (?)

Abdullah: b. (?); Amir of Trans-Jordan, 1921–46; King of Trans-Jordan, then Jordan, 1946–49; assassinated in Jerusalem

Abdul Ilah. b. (?); Regent of Iraq, 1939–53; Crown Prince of Iraq till murdered, July 14, 1958

Aliya

Tallal: b. (?); King of Jordan, 1949–52; insane, abdicates

Hussein: King of Jordan, 1952–

A leading Meccan family who trace their descent directly from Hassan, grandson of the Prophet Muhammad through his daughter Fatima

Feisal I: b. 1885;
King of Syria, 1918–20;
King of Iraq, 1921–33

Amir Zeid: b. (?);
Iraq's ambassador
in London in years
preceding 1958
Revolution

Ghazi, King of Iraq: 1933–39;
marries his cousin, Aliya;
dies in car crash

Feisal II: b. (?);
King of Iraq, 1939;
crowned, 1953;
head of Hashemite Federation with Jordan, 1958;
murdered, July 14, 1958

1. Mahmud II: 1808–39.
   (Muhammad Ali's nominal sovereign and de facto pupil; the first sultan to wear European dress, he massacred the Janissaries in 1826 as Muhammad Ali had massacred the Mamelukes fifteen years earlier.)

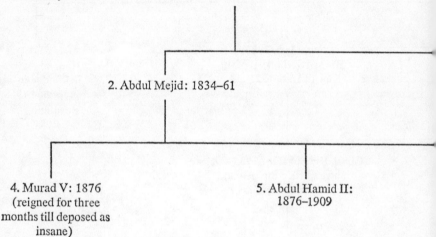

2. Abdul Mejid: 1834–61

4. Murad V: 1876
(reigned for three
months till deposed as
insane)

5. Abdul Hamid II:
1876–1909

3. Abdul Aziz: 1861–76
(deposed; then found dead)

6. Mehemet V:
1909–18

7. Mehemet VI:
1918–22;
(last Sultan)

Abdul Mejid:
Caliph from 1922
to March 3, 1924,
when Caliphate
abolished

Index

M